WEST ACADEMIC PUBLISHING'S LAW SCHOOL ADVISORY BOARD

JESSE H. CHOPER
Professor of Law and Dean Emeritus,
University of California, Berkeley

JOSHUA DRESSLER
Distinguished University Professor, Frank R. Strong Chair in Law
Michael E. Moritz College of Law, The Ohio State University

YALE KAMISAR
Professor of Law Emeritus, University of San Diego
Professor of Law Emeritus, University of Michigan

MARY KAY KANE
Professor of Law, Chancellor and Dean Emeritus,
University of California, Hastings College of the Law

LARRY D. KRAMER
President, William and Flora Hewlett Foundation

JONATHAN R. MACEY
Professor of Law, Yale Law School

ARTHUR R. MILLER
University Professor, New York University
Formerly Bruce Bromley Professor of Law, Harvard University

GRANT S. NELSON
Professor of Law, Pepperdine University
Professor of Law Emeritus, University of California, Los Angeles

A. BENJAMIN SPENCER
Earle K. Shawe Professor of Law,
University of Virginia School of Law

JAMES J. WHITE
Robert A. Sullivan Professor of Law Emeritus,
University of Michigan

CIVIL PROCEDURE
CASES, PROBLEMS, AND EXERCISES

Fourth Edition

■ ■ ■

John T. Cross
Grosscurth Professor of Law
University of Louisville, Louis D. Brandeis School of Law

Leslie W. Abramson
Frost Brown Todd Professor of Law
University of Louisville, Louis D. Brandeis School of Law

Ellen E. Deason
Joanne Wharton Murphy/Classes of 1965 and 1973 Professor of Law
The Ohio State University, Michael E. Moritz College of Law

AMERICAN CASEBOOK SERIES®

The publisher is not engaged in rendering legal or other professional advice, and this publication is not a substitute for the advice of an attorney. If you require legal or other expert advice, you should seek the services of a competent attorney or other professional.

American Casebook Series is a trademark registered in the U.S. Patent and Trademark Office.

© West, a Thomson business, 2006, 2008
© 2011 Thomson Reuters
© 2016 LEG, Inc. d/b/a West Academic
    444 Cedar Street, Suite 700
    St. Paul, MN 55101
    1-877-888-1330

West, West Academic Publishing, and West Academic are trademarks of West Publishing Corporation, used under license.

Printed in the United States of America

ISBN: 978-1-63460-017-0

To my parents, who never let me think for a moment that there was anything I could not do, provided I tried hard enough.

JTC

For Sam, Shel, and Will.

LWA

To my mother, Elizabeth McGregor Deason, and my grandmother, Gertrude Ellen McGregor, from whom I received my names and so much more.

EED

PREFACE

Teaching (and learning) Civil Procedure. Civil Procedure can be one of the most difficult courses in law school, not only for the student, but also for the professor. And yet, it also can prove to be among the most rewarding. This book is designed to help both the student and the professor overcome the challenges and reap the rewards. We have tapped into our many years of combined experience teaching Civil Procedure to produce a book that we hope is highly "teachable," while also providing a solid foundation in the subject matter.

What makes Civil Procedure difficult? The problem is really not the subject matter. Although Procedure is not easy, the rules and doctrines are by and large no more difficult than in most of the other courses in law school. Instead, the real problem in learning—and teaching—Procedure is one of perspective. Most students dealing with the subject for the first time have one of two vastly different preconceptions of the course. Some students think Procedure will be one of their practical or "hands on" courses. Those in this camp are surprised to learn that Procedure, no less than their other courses, is laden with difficult policy concerns. While they readily adapt to making policy-based arguments in their other courses, such arguments may seem somehow out of place in a rules-dominated course like Procedure.

The second group of students has quite a different preconception. To those in this camp, Civil Procedure's apparent complexity is intimidating. Overwhelmed by the arcane nature of the subject, students in this group tend to want to approach the subject as a Herculean task of remembering hundreds of individual and isolated rules.

Both of these views represent a problem of perspective. It is an inescapable fact that Procedure may seem like a foreign language to most students. Everyone has a rough idea of what a tort, contract, or property interest is. More importantly, most students have their own basic notions as to how the law ought to treat those matters. Although those ideas may not be correct, it is much easier to learn a legal rule when you have a preconceived notion of what that rule ought to be. Students rarely have such preconceived notions for rules of Civil Procedure. Indeed, students often think the rules of Procedure are mainly arbitrary choices about time limits, wording, and motions. Nothing could be further from the truth. Although it may be difficult for the newcomer to spot, Civil Procedure is a system in which choices as to individual rules are generally made with a certain model of litigation in mind.

This book provides students a more accurate perspective on Civil Procedure. For those intimidated by the subject, it focuses on the basics: how to commence and prosecute (or defend) a simple civil case. On the other hand, the book pays considerable attention to the underlying policy concerns, both to deal with students who think of Procedure as merely practical, and to foster a greater appreciation of the subject in all students. Moreover, the book presents Procedure as a system, something that is much greater than the sum of its seemingly unrelated parts. This approach provides a better long-term understanding of the subject. After all, although the actual *rules* of Procedure may change with some regularity, the basic system has remained remarkably stable. Studying Procedure as a system will help the student throughout a career that may span forty or more years.

This book differs from other Civil Procedure casebooks in five main ways. The first is its "modular" approach. This aspect will be most apparent to students enrolled in a course of three to five credit hours. Some of the chapters that professors are likely to omit in a three- to five-hour course are set out in electronic form only (although they are still included in the Table of Contents). In addition, the authors have provided professors with condensed alternative versions, in electronic format, of several of the chapters. A professor who lacks the classroom time to cover all parts of the course in depth may elect to substitute some of these condensed overview chapters for materials in the book. Taken together, the "paper" and electronic materials allow this book to be used in Procedure courses ranging from three to six hours.

Second, the book makes extensive use of problems and exercises. Most sections include both an Introductory Problem, which encourages students to think about the issues, and review problems at the end of the section. These problems serve two primary purposes. On the one hand, they help the students become comfortable in *applying* the rules they have learned. Such application aids immensely in overcoming any fear of Procedure and gaining a deeper understanding of the underlying rule. In addition, Civil Procedure is the most "statutory" of the traditional first-year courses. Problems give the students the incentive to look closely at the language of the statute or Federal Rule itself, rather than simply relying on how that language is paraphrased in a judicial opinion. The exercises go one step further, typically asking the students to use their recently acquired skills to research local law, which may differ from the Federal Rule being discussed.

The third main feature of this book is its extensive notes. Although some notes explain the preceding case, most provide additional information that provides a fuller understanding of the doctrine in question. While this book cannot completely replace a good secondary source, the extensive notes should greatly reduce the frequency with which students need to refer to outside sources to understand what is being discussed.

Fourth, the book whenever possible uses newer cases. Most of the cases in the book were decided during the last twenty years. In some cases, we elected to forego an old Supreme Court case that established a rule in lieu of a lower court decision that applies that rule to a new situation. The newer decisions often do an excellent job explaining the earlier cases, providing the students a good exposition of the rules and policies. Moreover, using newer cases reinforces in the reader's mind that Civil Procedure remains a vibrant, changing field of the law.

Fifth, we present dispute resolution methods like mediation, not as a recent curiosity at the book's end, but throughout the book as part of the overall procedural context. Despite media depictions that all cases go to trial, settlement and dispute resolution are essential elements for keeping the American litigation system moving.

PREFACE TO THE FOURTH EDITION

This Fourth Edition of the casebook represents a radical departure from the prior three. The past two decades have witnessed a trend to reduce the number of hours allocated to the first year Civil Procedure course from the traditional two-semester, six hour course to a single course of three to five hours. (Civil Procedure is admittedly not alone in this regard, as coverage of other traditional first year subjects has likewise been reduced). Many schools have tried to offset this reduction with an upper-level elective such as Complex Litigation, Advanced Procedure, or the like. Professors teaching one of the "condensed" first-year courses simply do not have time to cover in depth all the topics that previously comprised the standard Civil Procedure course. Most have responded by adopting an all-inclusive book, but "cutting" various topics of their choosing in the hope students will be exposed to those topics later in their law school career.

But cutting materials sometimes creates problems. First, some students may not take upper-level courses in Civil Procedure (including Conflicts and Federal Jurisdiction). For these students, the first-year course will be their only exposure to the subject area. This consideration is especially relevant given the recent addition of Civil Procedure to the multistate bar examination. Therefore, even if there is not time to explore every part of the course in depth, students will benefit from at least some exposure to most of the major issues included in the traditional year-long Civil Procedure course. Second, many topics in Civil Procedure are logically interconnected. As just one example, a student who has had no exposure to jurisdiction and venue will have a hard time understanding the purpose of the Federal Rule 12(b) motions to dismiss.

The obvious solution would be for all Civil Professors to agree on what should be covered in depth in the first year, and what warrants only a brief mention. Were that to occur, it would be possible to prepare a condensed Civil Procedure book specifically designed for a 3- to 5- hour course. But of course no such consensus exists. In fact, we have seen just the opposite: different schools (and sometimes even different professors at the same school) making very different decisions as to what the condensed course needs to address. In this environment, it would be futile to try to prepare a "one size fits all" book for a 3- to 5- hour course.

This Fourth Edition takes a different approach. We have tried to prepare a book that can be taught in a condensed Civil Procedure course, but still leaves it to the individual professor to decide what to emphasize in that course. The solution is what we call a "modular" approach.

Basically, this paper book you hold in your hands is only part—admittedly the main part—of the whole. These materials are also complemented by two distinct groups of electronic materials. (For professors, the electronic materials are also available in the Teachers Manual).

Electronic-only chapters. First, certain topics are covered in electronic format only. However, to avoid a piecemeal approach, these topics still appear in the Table of Contents. The electronic-only materials include:

Chap. (Section)	Coverage
8	Advanced joinder (impleader, intervention, necessary parties, interpleader, and class actions)
9	Alternate dispute resolution
12(A)	Seventh Amendment right to a jury in federal court
13(A)	Enforcing judgments
13(E)	Parties affected by claim and issue preclusion (privity and mutuality)
13(F)	Full faith and credit
13(G)	Law of the case and judicial estoppel
14(B)	Final judgment rule for federal appeals
14(D)	U.S. Supreme Court review

We chose these materials for electronic-only format because they tend to be the most likely choices to omit from a 3- to 5- hour Procedure course. However, because they do appear in the Table of Contents, a professor who wishes to cover one or more can include them in relatively seamless fashion.

Electronic condensed alternative chapters. The second aspect of the modular approach allows for even greater flexibility. For many of the main topics, we offer *both a full version and a condensed* (often mainly textual) version. The full version is set out in this book. The condensed version is available in electronic format. A professor may elect to assign some of the condensed chapters in lieu of some chapters in the book, or allow the students access to the condensed version to review the material (possibly freeing them of the compulsion to purchase a study aid). The following materials are available in both full and condensed form:

Full coverage (in book)	Alternative condensed version
Jurisdiction and Venue (Chaps 3 & 4)	A single chapter entitled "Considerations in Choosing a Forum" deals with Jurisdiction, venue, Choice of Law, and the *Erie* Doctrine
Erie and Choice of Law (Chap 5)	See above
Pleading (Chaps 6 & 7)	A single condensed chapter covering all pleading
Trial (Chap 12)	A condensed chapter setting out the basic principles
Preclusion and Full faith and credit (Chap 13)	A condensed chapter setting out the basic principles

Any professor adopting this book may freely use either or both sets of the electronic chapters in their courses. Professors may distribute the electronic files in pdf form, print out the files for distribution to students, or direct students to www.crosscivilprocedure.com.

Again, our goal in this modular approach is to ensure students learn the system of Civil Procedure as a unified whole (not a hodgepodge of parts), while giving each individual adopter the ability to choose what to emphasize. Those with the luxury of a full six-hour course can cover the entire book (including the electronic-only chapters). Those teaching a reduced course can chose a number of topics to cover in the traditional depth, with the assurance students will still have at least some exposure to the other important components of the system.

These features make for what we feel is a highly teachable book, as well as an excellent desk reference for the students. Of course, we would also welcome any input that you might offer as to how the book could be improved. Although everyone teaches Civil Procedure in his or her own unique way, we hope this book proves useful to many of you.

Finally, we would be ungrateful if we failed to acknowledge that several student research assistants helped us in the production of this book. We are especially grateful to Katherine Vesely for her keen eyes, hard work, and encouragement. We likewise appreciate the unflagging support of Reva Campbell, Amanda Hartley, Caitlin McQueen, Barbara Kehoe, Karen Paulin, Peyton Sands, and Elizabeth Worthing.

JOHN T. CROSS
LESLIE W. ABRAMSON
ELLEN E. DEASON

October 2015

ACKNOWLEDGMENTS

We gratefully acknowledge permission to reprint the following:

Marc Galanter, "The Vanishing Trial: An Examination of Trials and Related Matters in Federal and State Courts," 1 *Empirical Legal Studies* 459 (2004), reprinted with permission from Marc Galanter.

" 'The Vanishing Trial' Report: An Alternative View of the Data" by John Lande, published in *Dispute Resolution Magazine*, Volume 10, No. 4, Summer 2004. © 2004 by the American Bar Association. Reprinted with permission from John Lande.

Joseph B. Stulberg, "The Theory and Practice of Mediation: A Reply to Professor Susskind," 6 *Vermont Law Review* 85 (1981), reprinted with the permission of Joseph B. Stulberg and the *Vermont Law Review*.

"The Senate Table: An Introductory Adjudication/Mediation Exercise," is used by permission of Gary A. Weissman. The teaching materials are adapted with permission from those authored by Barbara McAdoo.

Summary of Contents

Preface V
Preface to the Fourth Edition IX
Acknowledgments XIII
Table of Cases XXXI

Chapter 1. An Overview of Civil Procedure 1
A. The Role of Procedure 1
B. Dealing with Civil Procedure 4
C. The Federal Rules of Civil Procedure 6
D. Dealing with Disputes 8
E. A Civil Procedure Timeline 19

Chapter 2. Joinder of Claims and Parties 27
A. Counterclaims 28
B. Additional Plaintiffs and Defendants 35
C. Cross-Claims 42
D. Additional Claims by Existing Parties 46

Chapter 3. Personal Jurisdiction and Venue 53
A. Exercising Jurisdiction over Defendants 53
B. Venue 144

Chapter 4. Federal Subject Matter Jurisdiction 173
A. The Concept of Subject Matter Jurisdiction 173
B. Federal Question Jurisdiction 176
C. Diversity Jurisdiction 186
D. Supplemental Jurisdiction 218
E. Removal 241

Chapter 5. Determining the Applicable Law 263
A. Choice of Law 264
B. The *Erie* Doctrine 272

Chapter 6. Pleading Claims 323
A. Philosophy and History of Pleading 323
B. Pleading a Claim Under the Federal Rules 333
C. Notifying Opposing Parties: Service of Process 373
D. Veracity Standards for Pleadings and Other Filed Documents 396
E. Amended and Supplemental Pleadings 415

Chapter 7. Responding to Claims 431
A. Dismissals 431
B. Objecting to the Complaint by Motion 448
C. Responding to the Complaint: The Answer 459
D. Failure to Respond: Default Judgment 477
E. Judgment on the Pleadings 486

Chapter 8. Advanced Joinder (available at
www.crosscivilprocedure.com) 489

Chapter 9. Alternative Dispute Resolution and Settlement
(available at www.crosscivilprocedure.com) 491

Chapter 10. Discovery 493
A. The Scope of Discovery 494
B. Discovery Devices 521
C. Discovery Sanctions 552

Chapter 11. Taking the Case from the Jury 561
A. Summary Judgment 562
B. Judgment as a Matter of Law 583

Chapter 12. Jury Trial 595
A. The Constitutional Right to a Jury Trial in Federal Civil Cases
(available at www.crosscivilprocedure.com) 596
B. Demanding a Jury Trial 596
C. Selecting a Group of Prospective Jurors 599
D. Challenging Individual Prospective Jurors 604
E. Jury Instructions and Jury Verdicts 623
F. New Trial 635
G. Relief from Judgment 647

Chapter 13. The Effect of a Judgment 657
A. Enforcing a Judgment (available at www.crosscivilprocedure.com) 657
B. Preclusive Effect of a Judgment: An Overview 657
C. Claim Preclusion 659
D. Issue Preclusion 671
E. Parties Affected by Claim and Issue Preclusion (available at
www.crosscivilprocedure.com) 690
F. Applying Preclusion Across State Lines (available at
www.crosscivilprocedure.com) 690
G. Doctrines Similar to Preclusion (available at
www.crosscivilprocedure.com) 690

Chapter 14. Appeals 691
A. Who May Appeal 691
B. The Timing of an Appeal—The "Final Decision" Rule (available at
www.crosscivilprocedure.com) 696

C.	Scope of Appellate Review 696
D.	United States Supreme Court Review (available at www.crosscivilprocedure.com) 703

INDEX 705

TABLE OF CONTENTS

PREFACE	V
PREFACE TO THE FOURTH EDITION	IX
ACKNOWLEDGMENTS	XIII
TABLE OF CASES	XXXI

Chapter 1. An Overview of Civil Procedure 1
A. The Role of Procedure 1
    Beeck v. Aquaslide 'N' Dive Corp. 1
    Notes and Questions 4
B. Dealing with Civil Procedure 4
C. The Federal Rules of Civil Procedure 6
D. Dealing with Disputes 8
    Marc Galanter, The Vanishing Trial: An Examination of Trials and Related Matters in Federal and State Courts 9
    John Lande, 'The Vanishing Trial' Report: An Alternative View of the Data 12
    Notes and Questions 14
    Notes and Questions 17
    Problem 18
E. A Civil Procedure Timeline 19
    1. Pre-litigation Phase 20
    2. Plaintiff Commences Its Case 20
    3. Defendant's Initial Response 21
    4. Refining the Case 21
    5. Case Management 22
    6. Discovery 22
    7. Resolution of the Case by the Judge 23
    8. Jury Trials 23
    9. Appeals 24
    10. Effect of a Judgment 25

Chapter 2. Joinder of Claims and Parties 27
A. Counterclaims 28
    Introductory Problem 28
    Nasalok Coating Corp. v. Nylok Corp. 29
    Notes and Questions 32
B. Additional Plaintiffs and Defendants 35
    Introductory Problem 35
    Liberty Media Holdings, LLC v. Bittorrent Swarm 36
    Notes and Questions 40

C. Cross-Claims 42
　Introductory Problem 42
　Rainbow Management Group, Ltd. v. Atlantis Submarines Hawaii,
　　L.P. 43
　Notes and Questions 45
D. Additional Claims by Existing Parties 46
　Introductory Problem 46
　McCoy v. Like 47
　Notes and Questions 48
　Problems 50
　Exercise 51

Chapter 3. Personal Jurisdiction and Venue 53
A. Exercising Jurisdiction over Defendants 53
　Introductory Problem 1 53
　Introductory Problem 2 54
　1. Jurisdiction over Defendants: The Early Decisions 55
　　Notes and Questions 58
　　Problems 59
　　International Shoe Co. v. Washington 61
　　Notes and Questions 65
　2. Jurisdiction over Nonresident Defendants 67
　　a. Specific Jurisdiction 68
　　b. General Jurisdiction 70
　　　Exercise 71
　　　Problems 72
　3. Emerging Personal Jurisdiction Principles 74
　　Shaffer v. Heitner 76
　　Notes and Questions 83
　　World-Wide Volkswagen Corp. v. Woodson 84
　　Notes and Questions 90
　　Problems 92
　　Burger King v. Rudzewicz 93
　　Notes and Questions 102
　　Burnham v. Superior Court 104
　　Notes and Questions 110
　　J. McIntyre Machinery, Ltd. v. Nicastro 113
　　Note and Question 123
　　Walden v. Fiore 124
　　Notes and Questions 127
　　Daimler AG v. Bauman 129
　　Notes and Questions 137
　4. To the Internet—and Beyond! 139
　　Advanced Tactical Ordnance Systems, LLC v. Real Action
　　　Paintball, Inc. 139
　　Exercise 143

B.	Venue		144
	Introductory Problem		145
	1.	Federal Venue Standards	145
		Astro-Med, Inc. v. Nihon Kohden America, Inc.	146
		Notes and Questions	149
		Problems	150
	2.	Transferring the Lawsuit	151
		a. By Statute	151
		Meteoro Amusement Corp. v. Six Flags	152
		Notes and Questions	156
		b. By Forum Non Conveniens	158
		Piper Aircraft Co. v. Reyno	159
		Notes and Questions	164
		Problems	166
		c. By Forum Selection Clause	168
		Atlantic Marine Constr., Co., Inc. v. U.S. Dist. Ct. for the Western District of Texas	168

Chapter 4. Federal Subject Matter Jurisdiction 173

A.	The Concept of Subject Matter Jurisdiction		173
B.	Federal Question Jurisdiction		176
	Introductory Problem		176
	1.	How Does a Party Invoke Federal Question Jurisdiction?	178
		Louisville & Nashville Railroad v. Mottley	178
		Notes and Questions	180
	2.	What Types of Claims Present a "Federal Question?"	183
		a. United States Constitution	183
		b. Treaties	184
		c. International Law	184
		d. Federal Common Law	184
		e. Special Federal Statutes	184
		f. State Law	185
		Problems	185
C.	Diversity Jurisdiction		186
	Introductory Problem		186
	1.	The Policy Underlying Diversity Jurisdiction	187
	2.	Determining Diversity	189
		a. Individuals	189
		Lundquist v. Precision Valley Aviation, Inc.	189
		Notes and Questions	193
		b. Corporations and Other "Legal Persons"	194
		Hertz Corp. v. Friend	194
		Notes and Questions	201
		Zambelli Fireworks Mfg. Co., Inc. v. Wood	202
		Notes and Questions	204
	3.	The Amount in Controversy	206

	4.	Additional Issues in Diversity Jurisdiction	209
		a. Alienage Jurisdiction	209
		b. Time for Determining Diversity	210
		c. Manipulating § 1332	211
		d. States	214
		e. Exceptions to Diversity Jurisdiction	214
		f. Other Diversity Statutes	215
		Problems	216
		Exercise	217
D.	Supplemental Jurisdiction		218
	Introductory Problem		218
	1.	The Theoretical Basis for Supplemental Jurisdiction	219
		United Mine Workers v. Gibbs	219
		Notes and Questions	223
	2.	The Supplemental Jurisdiction Statute	225
		Problems	226
	3.	Supplemental Jurisdiction and Joinder of Parties	228
		Exxon Mobil Corp. v. Allapattah Services, Inc.	229
		Notes and Questions	236
		Problems	240
E.	Removal		241
	Introductory Problem		241
	1.	General Rules Governing Removal	242
		Caterpillar Inc. v. Williams	242
		Notes and Questions	244
	2.	Removal in Diversity Cases	246
	3.	More Complex Cases	248
		a. State Law Claims with an Essential Federal Element	248
		Grable & Sons Metal Products, Inc. v. Darue Engineering & Mfg.	248
		Notes and Questions	252
		b. Complete Preemption	253
		Beneficial National Bank v. Anderson	253
		Notes and Questions	258
		Problems	259
	4.	Procedure for Removal	259
		Problems	261

Chapter 5. Determining the Applicable Law 263
A. Choice of Law 264
   Introductory Problem 264
   Paul v. National Life 265
   Notes and Questions 270
B. The *Erie* Doctrine 272
   Introductory Problem 272
   1. Genesis of the *Erie* Doctrine 274
      Notes and Questions 276

   Erie R. Co. v. Tompkins 278
   Notes and Questions 282
   Guaranty Trust Co. of New York v. York 286
   Notes and Questions 292
   Notes and Questions 295
   Hanna v. Plumer 295
   Notes and Questions 301
  2. Post-*Hanna* Cases Applying the *Erie* Doctrine 303
   a. Rules Promulgated Under the Rules Enabling Act 304
   b. Other Federal Judge-Made Law 307
   c. Federal Statutes 310
    Stewart Organization v. Ricoh Corporation 310
    Notes and Questions 313
  3. Federal Common Law 314
   Texas Industries, Inc. v. Radcliff Materials, Inc. 314
   Notes and Questions 318
   Problems 320

Chapter 6. Pleading Claims 323
A. Philosophy and History of Pleading 323
 1. Historical English Pleading 324
  Charles E. Clark, Handbook of the Law of Code Pleading 326
  Notes 328
 2. Code Pleading 330
  Charles E. Clark, Handbook of the Law of Code Pleading 331
  Notes and Questions 332
B. Pleading a Claim Under the Federal Rules 333
 1. The Form of the Complaint 333
  Notes and Questions 337
 2. The Basic Pleading Standard of Federal Rule 8(a) 339
 3. Applying the Rule 8(a) Standard 340
  Swierkiewicz v. Sorema, N. A. 340
  Bell Atlantic Corp. v. Twombly 343
  Ashcroft v. Iqbal 349
  Notes and Questions 359
 4. Heightened Pleading Standards 362
  Wallace v. Tesoro Corp. 362
  Notes and Questions 366
  Browning v. Clinton 368
  Notes and Questions 370
 5. The Prayer for Relief 371
  Problems 372
  Exercise 373
C. Notifying Opposing Parties: Service of Process 373
 Introductory Problem 374
 1. Constitutional Standards 374
  Mullane v. Central Hanover Bank & Trust Co. 374

		Notes and Questions 378

      2. Procedural Standards for Service of Process 380
          Larsen v. Mayo Medical Center 381
          Notes and Questions 384
          Cox v. Quigley 385
          Notes and Questions 389
          Problems 394
          Exercise 395

D. Veracity Standards for Pleadings and Other Filed Documents 396
      Ruszala v. Walt Disney World Co. 398
      Notes and Questions 402
      Exercise 403
      Christian v. Mattel, Inc. 404
      Notes and Questions 410
      Problems 414

E. Amended and Supplemental Pleadings 415
      Introductory Problem 416
      1. Amending Pleadings with (or Without) the Court's Permission ... 416
          Beeck v. Aquaslide 'N' Dive Corp. 416
          Notes and Questions 416
      2. Amendments to Add Issues at Trial 418
          Otness v. United States 418
          Notes and Questions 420
          Problems 421
      3. Amendments Filed After the Limitations Period Has Expired 421
          Erwin v. McDermott 421
          Notes and Questions 425
      4. Supplemental Pleadings 427
          Stewart v. Shelby Tissue, Inc. 427
          Notes and Questions 429
          Exercise 430

Chapter 7. Responding to Claims 431

A. Dismissals 431
      Introductory Problem 431
      1. Voluntary Dismissals 432
          Marques v. Federal Reserve Bank of Chicago 432
          Notes and Questions 434
          Hinfin Realty Corp. v. Pittston Co. 435
          Notes and Questions 439
      2. Involuntary Dismissals 440
          Aura Lamp & Lighting Inc. v. International Trading Corp. 441
          Notes and Questions 445
          Problems 447
          Exercise 447

B.	Objecting to the Complaint by Motion			448
	1.	Timing Rules Governing Rule 12 Motions		449
		a.	Defenses Other than Subject-Matter Jurisdiction	449
			Introductory Problem	449
			Problems	451
		b.	Subject-Matter Jurisdiction	452
			Notes and Questions	453
	2.	Challenging the Substantive Allegations of a Claim		454
		Introductory Problem		454
		a.	When a Pleading "Fails to State a Claim"	456
		b.	Procedural Aspects of the Rule 12(b)(6) Motion	456
		c.	Motion for a More Definite Statement and Motion to Strike	457
		d.	Objecting to the Statement of a Claim and Settlement	458
			Problems	458
C.	Responding to the Complaint: The Answer			459
	Introductory Problem			459
	1.	Menu of Responses		460
		King Vision Pay Per View, Ltd. v. J.C. Dimitri's Restaurant, Inc.		463
		Problems		465
		Exercise		465
	2.	Affirmative Defenses		467
		Red Deer v. Cherokee County, Iowa		467
		Notes and Questions		471
	3.	Responding to the Answer		473
		Reyes v. Sazan		473
		Notes and Questions		475
		Exercise		476
D.	Failure to Respond: Default Judgment			477
	Introductory Problem			477
	KPS & Associates, Inc. v. Designs by FMC, Inc.			477
	Notes and Questions			483
	Problems			485
	Exercise			486
E.	Judgment on the Pleadings			486
	Introductory Problem			486

Chapter 8. Advanced Joinder (available at www.crosscivilprocedure.com) 489

Chapter 9. Alternative Dispute Resolution and Settlement (available at www.crosscivilprocedure.com) 491

Chapter 10. Discovery ... 493
A. The Scope of Discovery ... 494
  1. Mandatory Disclosure ... 494
     Introductory Problem ... 494
  2. Discovery of Relevant and Non-Privileged Information ... 496
     Introductory Problem 1 ... 496
     Introductory Problem 2 ... 496
     Thompson v. Department of Housing and Urban Devel. ... 497
     Notes and Questions ... 500
     Problems ... 503
  3. Discovery of Attorney Work Product ... 504
     Introductory Problem ... 504
     Hickman v. Taylor ... 504
     Spirit Master Funding, LLC v. Pike Nurseries Acquisition, LLC ... 508
     Notes and Questions ... 511
     Gutshall v. New Prime, Inc. ... 513
     Problems ... 515
  4. Discovery About Experts ... 516
     Introductory Problem ... 516
     Spirit Master Funding, LLC v. Pike Nurseries Acquisition, LLC ... 517
     Notes and Questions ... 519
     Problems ... 520
     Exercise ... 521
B. Discovery Devices ... 521
  1. Depositions ... 521
     Alexander v. F.B.I. ... 522
     Notes and Questions ... 527
  2. Interrogatories ... 529
     O'Connor v. Boeing North American, Inc. ... 529
     Notes and Questions ... 535
     Exercise ... 537
  3. Request for Production of Documents ... 537
     Notes and Questions ... 540
     Exercise ... 542
  4. Request for Admissions ... 543
     Asea, Inc. v. Southern Pac. Transp. Co. ... 543
     Notes and Questions ... 546
     Exercise ... 547
  5. Physical and Mental Examinations ... 548
     Ali v. Wang Laboratories, Inc. ... 548
     Notes and Questions ... 551
C. Discovery Sanctions ... 552
  Lee v. Walters ... 552
  Notes and Questions ... 558

Chapter 11. Taking the Case from the Jury 561
A. Summary Judgment 562
  1. The Rule 56 Standard 562
     Introductory Problem 562
     Celotex Corp. v. Catrett 563
     Notes and Questions 569
  2. Using Inferences 574
     Jorgensen v. Epic/Sony Records 574
     Notes and Questions 580
     Problems 582
B. Judgment as a Matter of Law 583
   Introductory Problem 1 583
   Introductory Problem 2 584
   Kinserlow v. CMI Corp., Bid-Well Div. 585
   Notes and Questions 590
   Problems 593

Chapter 12. Jury Trial 595
A. The Constitutional Right to a Jury Trial in Federal Civil Cases
   (available at www.crosscivilprocedure.com) 596
B. Demanding a Jury Trial 596
   Marseilles Hydro Power, LLC v. Marseilles Land and Water
       Company 596
   Notes and Questions 597
   Problems 599
C. Selecting a Group of Prospective Jurors 599
   Floyd v. Garrison 601
   Notes and Questions 602
   Exercise 604
D. Challenging Individual Prospective Jurors 604
   Introductory Problem 604
   Thompson v. Altheimer & Gray 606
   Notes and Questions 609
   Exercise 611
   Alverio v. Sam's Warehouse Club, Inc. 616
   Notes and Questions 620
   Problems 621
   Exercise 622
E. Jury Instructions and Jury Verdicts 623
  1. Requesting and Objecting to Jury Instructions 623
     Jarvis v. Ford Motor Co. 624
     Notes and Questions 628
  2. Jury Verdicts 628
     Lavoie v. Pacific Press & Shear Co. 629
     Notes and Questions 632
     Problems 634
     Exercise 635

F.	New Trial	635
	Introductory Problem	635
	Piesco v. Koch	637
	Notes and Questions	642
	Problems	646
	Exercise	646
G.	Relief from Judgment	647
	Tate v. Riverboat Services, Inc.	648
	Notes and Questions	653
	Exercise	656

Chapter 13. The Effect of a Judgment ... 657
A. Enforcing a Judgment (available at www.crosscivilprocedure.com) 657
B. Preclusive Effect of a Judgment: An Overview 657
C. Claim Preclusion 659
    Introductory Problem 659
    1. The Basics of Claim Preclusion 659
        Rodgers v. St. Mary's Hospital 659
        Notes and Questions 662
    2. Precluding Counterclaims, Cross-Claims, and Defenses 666
    3. Final Judgment on the Merits 668
    4. Exceptions to Claim Preclusion 669
        Problems 670
D. Issue Preclusion 671
    Introductory Problem 671
    1. Same Issue 673
        Williams v. City of Jacksonville Police Dept. 673
        Notes and Questions 678
    2. Actually Litigated 679
    3. Actually Decided 680
    4. Necessary to the Judgment 681
        Stemler v. Florence 681
        Notes and Questions 686
    5. Exceptions 687
        Problems 688
E. Parties Affected by Claim and Issue Preclusion (available at www.crosscivilprocedure.com) 690
F. Applying Preclusion Across State Lines (available at www.crosscivilprocedure.com) 690
G. Doctrines Similar to Preclusion (available at www.crosscivilprocedure.com) 690

Chapter 14. Appeals 691
A. Who May Appeal 691
    Introductory Problem 691
    In re DES Litigation 692
    Notes and Questions 695

B.	The Timing of an Appeal—The "Final Decision" Rule (available at www.crosscivilprocedure.com)	696
C.	Scope of Appellate Review	696
	1. Need to Raise the Issue Below	696
	2. The Standard of Review	698
	Notes and Questions	701
D.	United States Supreme Court Review (available at www.crosscivilprocedure.com)	703

INDEX 705

TABLE OF CASES

The principal cases are in bold type.

A.F. Dormeyer Co. v. M.J. Sales & Distrib. Co. 648
A.H. Fischer Lumber Co., United States v. 425
Acridge v. The Evangelical Lutheran Good Samaritan Society 194
Adams v. City of Montgomery 509, 510
Adley Express Co. v. Highway Truck Drivers & Helpers, Local No. 107 545
Adlman, United States v. 510
Advanced Tactical Ordnance Systems, LLC v. Real Action Paintball, Inc. **139**
Aetna Cas. and Sur. Co. v. Leahey Const. Co., Inc. 700
Aetna Ins. Co. v. Meeker 403
Alexander v. FBI **522**, 538
Alexander v. Fulton Cnty., Ga. 37, 38
Ali v. Wang Laboratories, Inc. **548**
Allen v. Admin. Review Bd. ... 363, 364
Allen v. R & H Oil and Gas Co. 208
Alternative System Concepts, Inc. v. Synopsys, Inc. 366
Alverio v. Sam's Warehouse Club, Inc. **616**
American Cyanamid Co. v. McGhee 434
American Elec. Power Co., Inc. v. Connecticut 319
American National Red Cross v. S.G. 253
American Rwy Express Co., United States v. 697
American Soccer Co., Inc. v. Score First Enterprises 434
American States Insurance Company v. Dastar Corp. 417
Ampex Corp. v. Mitsubishi Elec. Corp. 532
Anderson v. Liberty Lobby, Inc. 571, 587
Anderson v. Smithfield Foods, Inc. 411

Andover, Inc. v. American Bar Ass'n 664
Ankenbrandt v. Richards 214
Apache County v. Superior Court 32
Appelbaum v. Milwaukee Metro. Sewerage Dist. 591
Aristech Chemical Intern. Ltd. v. Acrylic Fabricators Ltd. 72
Art Metal-U.S.A., Inc. v. United States 369
Art Press, Ltd. v. Western Printing Mach. Co. 613
Asahi Metal Industry Co. v. Superior Court of Cal., Solano Cty. 113, 116, 123
Asea, Inc. v. Southern Pac. Transp. Co. **543**
Ashcroft v. Iqbal **349**
Astro-Med, Inc. v. Nihon Kohden America, Inc. **146**
Atlantic Marine Constr., Co., Inc. v. U.S. Dist. Ct. for the Western District of Texas **168**
Aura Lamp & Lighting Inc. v. International Trading Corp. **441**
Avco Corp. v. Machinists 255
Ayres v. Jacobs & Crumplar 380
Babcock v. Jackson 268
Baidoo v. Blood-Dzraku 379
Baird & Warner Inc. v. Addison Industrial Park, Inc. 661
Baker v. Gold Seal Liquors 33
Ball v. City of Chicago 443, 444
Baltimore & Ohio R.R. Co. v. Baugh 280
Baltimore S.S. Co. v. Phillips 221
Banco Nacional de Cuba v. Sabbatino 316
Bank of Credit and Commerce International Ltd. v. State Bank of Pakistan 165
Bank of United States v. Deveaux 195
Barnet v. National Bank 257
Batson v. Kentucky 617
Be2 LLC v. Ivanov 142
Beatty v. Dunn 699

xxxi

Beckstrom v. Coastwise Line 475
Beeck v. Aquaslide 'N' Dive Corp. **1**, **416**
Bell Atlantic Corp. v. Twombly **343**, 351
Belleville Catering Co. v. Champaign Market Place, L.L.C. 411
Benchmark Elecs., Inc. v. J.M. Huber Corp. 365
Beneficial National Bank v. Anderson **253**
Bevevino v. Saydjari 641
Bills v. Aseltine 633
Bivens v. Six Unknown Fed. Narcotics Agents 124, 183
Black and White Taxicab & Transfer Co. v. Brown and Yellow Taxicab & Transfer Co. 196, 287
Bleecker v. Standard Fire Ins. Co. 541
Blonder-Tongue Lab. v. University of Illinois Found. 469
Bockweg v. Anderson 674
Boggs v. West 697
Boisson v. Banian, Ltd. 577
Bond Leather Co. v. Q.T. Shoe Mfg. Co. 479
Borden v. CSX Transportation, Inc. 581
Bowen v. Parking Authority of City of Camden 551
Boyce, United States v. 502
Brandt v. Schal Assocs., Inc. 407
Bridgeport Music, Inc. v. Still N The Water Publishing 70
Brockmeyer v. May 393
Brooke Group Ltd. v. Brown & Williamson Tobacco Corp. 345
Brown v. Webster 207
Browning v. Clinton **368**
Buffalo Courier-Express, Inc. v. Buffalo Evening News, Inc. 702
Burford v. Sun Oil Co. 215
Burger King Corp. v. MacShara 96
Burger King Corp. v. Rudzewicz **93**, 125, 133
Burlington Northern Railroad v. Woods 306
Burnham v. Superior Court **104**
Business Guides, Inc. v. Chromatic Communications, Enters., Inc. 403
Byrd v. Blue Ridge Rural Electric Co-operative, Inc. 293, 309
Caldarera v. Eastern Airlines, Inc. 643
Calder v. Jones 124, 126, 127
Campania Management Co. v. Rooks, Pitts & Poust 418
Capron v. Van Noorden 453

Carden v. Arkoma Assocs. 204
Cardtoons, L.C. v. Major League Baseball Players Ass'n 182
Carlsbad Technology, Inc. v. HIF Bio, Inc. 246
Carnival Cruise Lines v. Shute 66
Castaneda v. Partida 602
Caterpillar Inc. v. Lewis 206, 210
Caterpillar Inc. v. Williams **242**
Cauley v. Ingram Micro, Inc. 551
Celotex Corp. v. Catrett **563**
Chambers v. NASCO 396
Chicot County Drainage Dist. v. Baxter State Bank 454
Christian v. Mattel, Inc. **404**
Cincinnati Ins. Co. v. Reybitz 41
Citizens for Open Access to Sand and Tide, Inc. v. Seadrift Ass'n 663
Clark v. Clark 269
Clark v. Paul Gray, Inc. 231, 235
Claude G. Dern Electric, Inc. v. Bernstein 698
Clifford, United States v. 601, 602
Colgrove v. Battin 604
Colombrito v. Kelly 438
Columbia Gas Transmission Corp. v. Drain 252
Commercial Space Management Co., Inc. v. The Boeing Co., Inc. 434
Computer Access Tech. Corp. v. Catalyst Enters., Inc. 591
Confederate Acres Sanitary Sewage & Drainage Sys., United States v. 44
Conklin v. Horner 268, 269
Conley v. Gibson 342, 346, 359
Convergent Technologies Securities Litigation, In re 535
Cooper Stevedoring Co. v. Fritz Kopke, Inc. 316
Cooter & Gell v. Hartmarx Corp. 408, 410
Copperweld Corp. v. Independence Tube Corp. 345
Cox v. Quigley **385**
Crawford v. State Highway Board 699
D'Alto v. Dahon Cal., Inc. 438
Daimler AG v. Bauman 71, **129**
Dandridge v. Williams 697
Daniels v. USS Agri-Chemicals 361
Davey v. Lockheed Martin Corp. 621
Davis v. HSBC Bank Nev., N. A. 199
Day & Zimmermann, Inc. v. Challoner 308
Delno v. Market St. Ry. 702
Dennis v. Dillard Dept. Stores, Inc. 417
DES Litigation, In re **692**

Dickerson v. Board of Educ. of Ford Heights, Ill. 444
Dillard v. Security Pacific Brokers, Inc. 34
Dimick v. Schiedt 644
Dimmie v. Carey 577
Doe v. Del Rio 338
Dunlap-McCuller v. Riese Organization 640, 641, 642
Duren v. Missouri 601, 602
Durfee v. Duke 454
Eagle Assocs. v. Bank of Montreal 479
Earle M. Jorgenson Co. v. T.I. United States, Ltd. 44
Eastman Kodak Co. v. Kavlin 165
Edmonson v. Leesville Concrete Co. 617
EEOC v. Kohler Co. 591
Eiland v. Westinghouse Elec. Corp. 643
Electrical Fittings Corp. v. Thomas & Betts Co. 694, 695
Employees Committed for Justice v. Eastman Kodak 520
Enron Oil Corp. v. Diakuhara 479
Erie R. Co. v. Tompkins **278**, 297, 316
Erwin v. McDermott **421**
ESI, Inc. v. Coastal Power Prod. Co. 581
Essex Builders Group, Inc. v. Amerisure Ins. Co. 509
Evans v. National Bank of Savannah 257
Evans, United States v. 617, 618
Exxon Mobil Corp. v. Allapattah Services, Inc. **229**
Falchetti v. Pennsylvania R. Co. 281
Fanselow v. Rice 158
Faulkner v. Caledonia County Fair Ass'n 659
FDIC v. Francisco Inv. Corp. 481
Federated Department Stores v. Moitie 487, 669
Feed Management Systems, Inc. v. Brill 33
Ferens v. John Deere Company 157, 171
Finley v. United States 236
First National Bank of Pulaski v. Curry 260
Florence, City of v. Chipman 682, 683, 684, 685
Floyd v. Garrison **601**
Fogarty v. Near N. Ins. Brokerage, Inc. 627
Foman v. Davis 2

Fought v. Hayes Wheels Int'l, Inc. 588
Fowler v. Curtis Publ'g Co. 369
Franklin America, Inc. v. Franklin Cast Products 390
Freeman, United States v. 601
Frew v. Hawkins 654
Gambelli v. United States 194
Garcia, United States v. 609
Garrett v. Fleming 427
Gasperini v. Center for Humanities, Inc. 308
Gaste v. Kaiserman 577
General Contracting & Trading Co. v. Interpole, Inc. 479
Getter v. Wal-Mart Stores, Inc. 613
Global NAPs, Inc. v. Verizon New England, Inc. 239
Golden Eagle Distrib. Corp. v. Burroughs Corp. 408
Gomez v. Toledo 472
Gonzalez, United States v. 609
Goodyear Dunlop Tires Operations, S.A. v. Brown 71, 130, 131, 133
Gould Paper Corp. v. Madisen Corp. 495
Grable & Sons Metal Products, Inc. v. Darue Engineering & Mfg. **248**
Grace v. MacArthur 59
Graham v. Connor 643
Grannis v. Ordean 375
Graziose v. American Home Prods. Corp. 41
Greene v. Lindsey 379
Griffin v. McCoach 285
Griffin, United States v. 617, 618
Grubb v. KMS Patriots, L.P. 409
Grupo Dataflux v. Atlas Global Group, L.P. 211
Guaranty Trust Co. of New York v. York **286**, 294, 297, 299
Gulf Oil Corp. v. Gilbert 159
Gully v. First National Bank in Meridian 178
Gunn v. Minton 253
Gutshall v. New Prime, Inc. **513**
Hadges v. Yonkers Racing Corp. 411
Hallett Constr. Co. v. Iowa State Highway Comm'n 483
Hamling v. United States 603
Hanna v. Plumer **295**, 305, 311
Hanson v. Denckla 75, 113, 115
Hanson v. Hunt Oil Co. 3
Hard Drive Prods., Inc. v. Does 1–188 .... 38, 39
Harries v. Air King Products Co. ... 695
Hart v. Terminex Int'l 204

Table of Cases

Haseltine v. Central Bank of Springfield 257
Hawkins v. Kiely 367
Hazel-Atlas Glass Co. v. Hartford-Empire Co. 653
Headwaters Forest Defense v. County of Humboldt 593
Helicopteros Nacionales de Colombia, S.A. v. Hall 130, 131
Hernandez v. New York 620
Hertz Corp. v. Friend **194**
Herzog v. Castle Rock Entm't 577
Hess v. Pawloski 60, 67
Hickman v. Taylor **504**
Higgins v. E.I. DuPont de Nemours & Co. 247
Hinderlider v. La Plata River & Cherry Creek Ditch Co. 318
Hinfin Realty Corp. v. Pittston Co. **435**
Hishon v. King & Spalding 342
Hoffman v. Blaski 157
Holland v. Illinois 600
Holston Investments, Inc. B.V.I. v. LanLogistics Corp. 201
Honda Motor Co., Ltd. v. Oberg 701
Horne v. Flores 655
House v. Combined Ins. Co. of America 510
Howard Johnson International, Inc. v. Wang 391
Howard Motor Co. v. Swint 40
Hurd v. American Hoist and Derrick Co. 591
Hurn v. Oursler 221, 222
Hutchinson v. Chase & Gilbert 63
Illinois v. City of Milwaukee 184, 320
Indianapolis v. Chase Nat'l Bank 212
Insurance Corp. of Ireland v. Compagnie des Bauxites de Guinee 120
International Controls Corp. v. Vesco 385
International Shoe Co. v. Washington **61**, 115, 125, 130, 141
Irvin v. Dowd 611
J. McIntyre Machinery, Ltd. v. Nicastro **113**
J.E.B. v. Alabama ex rel. T.B. 617, 619, 620
Jacobs v. Felix Bloch Erben Verlag fur Buhne Film 166
Jaffe and Asher v. Van Brunt 389
Jakobsen v. Massachusetts Port Auth. 470, 471
Jarvis v. Ford Motor Co. **624**, 628

Jinks v. Richland County 238
Jones v. Ford Motor Credit Co. 239
Jones v. Lincoln Elec. Co. 653
Jones, United States v. 618
Jorgensen v. Careers BMG Music Publ'g 578
Jorgensen v. Epic/Sony Records **574**
Josephson, In re 702
Junk v. Terminix Intern. Co. 212
Kadic v. Karadzic 184
Kagan v. Caterpillar Tractor Co. 651
Kasap v. Folger Nolan Fleming & Douglas, Inc. 185
Keal v. Monarch Life Ins. Co. 433
Keeton v. Hustler Magazine, Inc. 128
Kell v. Henderson 268
Key Bank of Me. v. Tablecloth Textile Co. 479
King Vision Pay Per View, Ltd. v. J.C. Dimitri's Restaurant, Inc. **463**
Kinserlow v. CMI Corp., Bid-Well Div. **585**
Klaxon Co. v. Stentor Electric Mfg. Co. 285
Kolb v. Scherer Bros. Financial Services Co. 45
Kowal v. MCI Communications Corp. 368
KPS & Associates, Inc. v. Designs by FMC, Inc. **477**
Kramer v. Caribbean Mills, Inc. 213
Krupski v. Costa Crociere S. p. A. 424
Kuhn v. Fairmont Coal Co. 281
Kwoczak, United States v. 591
LaFace Records, LLC v. Does 1–38 39
LAK, Inc. v. Deer Creek Enterprises 103
Lambert v. Kysar 148
Larsen v. Mayo Medical Center **381**
Larson v. Domestic & Foreign Commerce Corp. 183
Lavoie v. Pacific Press & Shear Co. **629**, 698
Leatherman v. Tarrant County Narcotics Intelligence and Coordination Unit 343, 367
Lee v. Walters **552**
LeSane v. Hall's Security Analyst 440
Levin v. Ruby Trading Corporation 394
Liberty Media Holdings, LLC v. Bittorrent Swarm **36**

Table of Cases

Liljeberg v. Health Services Acquisition Corp. 655
Limon-Hernandez v. Lumbreras ... 391
Lincoln Property Co. v. Roche........ 247
Link v. Wabash Railroad Company 445, 446
LinkAmerica v. Co.......................... 141
Local Union No. 11, IBEW v. G.P. Thompson Electric, Inc. 34
Louisiana Power and Light Co. v. City of Thibodaux............................... 215
Louisville & Nashville R. Co. v. Mottley....................... **178**, 181, 254
Louisville, C. & C.R. Co. v. Letson... 196
Lundquist v. Precision Valley Aviation, Inc. **189**
M.K. v. Tenet 40
MacPhail, United States v. 226
Mann v. Lewis 446
Marine Equip. Management Co. v. United States 453
Marques v. Federal Reserve Bank of Chicago **432**
Marseilles Hydro Power, LLC v. Marseilles Land and Water Company..................................... **596**
Marshall v. Marshall....................... 215
Martinez-Salazar, United States v................................ 606, 609
Mason v. United States 279
Matrixx Initiatives, Inc. v. Siracusano................................... 366
McCallum v. N.C. Coop. Extension Serv.................................... 675, 676
McCoo v. Denny's Inc. 501
McCormick v. City of Chicago........ 648
McCoy v. Like................................ **47**
McCulloch v. Maryland 257
McDonald v. Mabee 63, 378
McDonough Power Equip., Inc. v. Greenwood................................. 611
McGee v. International Life Insurance Co.. 74
McHenry v. Ford Motor Co. 428
McKennon v. Nashville Banner Pub. Co.........................468, 469, 470, 471
McKinnon v. Kwong Wah Restaurant 479
McMillan v. McMillan 269
McPherson v. Coombe 576
Melkaz International Inc. v. Flavor Innovation Inc............................ 392
Memphis Cotton Oil Co., United States v....................................... 221
Merrell Dow Pharmaceuticals Inc. v. Thompson.............249, 250, 251, 252
Mesa v. California 181

Meteoro Amusement Corp. v. Six Flags..**152**
Metropolitan Life Ins. Co. v. Taylor... 255
Milkovich v. Saari 269
Miller v. LHKM................................. 44
Miller v. Miller 269
Miller-El v. Dretke.......................... 620
Milliken v. Meyer................ 63, 67, 115
Mobile, In re City of 245
Mohr v. Chicago Sch. Reform Bd. of Trs. of the Bd. of Educ................ 591
Mohr v. State Bank of Stanley 44
Mollan v. Torrance......................... 210
Montgomery v. City of Ardmore..... 697
Moore v. N.Y. Cotton Exch. 30, 31
Morris v. Lindau 577
Morse v. Hanks 617
Moses H. Cone Mem. Hosp. v. Mercury Constr. Corp. 185
Mosley v. General Motors Corp. 40
Mudd v. Busse.................................. 41
Mullane v. Central Hanover Bank & Trust Co. **374**
Murphy v. Florida 611
Mutual Federal Savings & Loan Ass'n v. Richards & Assoc..................... 559
Mutuelles Unies v. Kroll & Linstrom 210
Myrick v. Cooley............................. 677
Nasalok Coating Corp. v. Nylok Corp. **29**
National Development Co. v. Triad Holding Corp. 390
National Hockey League v. Metropolitan Hockey Club, Inc. 556, 559
National Mutual Insurance Co. v. Tidewater Transfer Co. 214
National Society of Professional Engineers v. United States 317
Nelson v. Adams USA, Inc.............. 426
Nippon Credit Bank, Ltd. v. Matthews.......................................33
North Am. Watch Corp. v. Princess Ermine Jewels 553, 555
North Central F.S., Inc. v. Brown... 452
Northwest Airlines, Inc. v. Transport Workers................................ 316, 318
Norwood v. Kirkpatrick 166
O'Connor v. Boeing North American, Inc............................**529**
O'Keefe, United States v................. 542
O'Toole v. Arlington Trust Co........ 189, 192
Oliver v. Haas 209
Oneida Indian Nation v. County of Oneida.. 258

Table of Cases

Oregon Trail Elec. Consumers Coop., Inc. v. Co-Gen Co. 699
Otness v. United States **418**
Pahuta v. Massey-Ferguson, Inc. 626, 627
Palmer v. City of Decatur 652
Palmer v. Fox Software, Inc. 701
Palmer v. Hoffman 627
Paul v. National Life **265**
Pavelic & LeFlore v. Marvel Entertainment Group 403
Pearson v. Dennison 702
Pennoyer v. Neff 55, 62, 76
Peralta v. Heights Medical Center 483, 656
Perkins v. Benguet, Consol. Mining Co. 131
Personnel Administrator of Mass. v. Feeney 351, 353
Pfeiffer v. William Wrigley Jr. Co. 661
Phillips Petroleum Co. v. Shutts 264
Pickett v. IBP, Inc. 510
Piedra v. Mentor Graphics Corp. 440
Pierce v. Underwood 552
Piesco v. Koch **637**
Pioneer Inv. Services Co. v. Brunswick Associates Ltd. P'ship 648, 649, 655
Piper Aircraft Co. v. Reyno **159**
Portage II v. Bryant Petroleum Corp. 633
Poynter v. Ratcliff 610
Primus Auto. Fin. Serv., Inc. v. Batarse 410
Prior v. Pruett 677, 678
Procter & Gamble Company, United States v. 493
Pryer v. C.O. 3 Slavic 644
PSEG Power New York, Inc. v. Alberici Inc. 541
Ptaszynki v. Ferrell 158
Purkett v. Elem 617, 618
Race Tires America v. Hoosier Racing Tire Corp. 538
Railroad Commission v. Pullman Co. 215
Rainbow Management Group, Ltd. v. Atlantis Submarines Hawaii, L.P. **43**
Rainbow Pioneer No. 44–18–04A v. Hawaii-Nevada Investment Corp. 531
Red Deer v. Cherokee County, Iowa **467**
Reed v. United Transp. Union 293
Reeves v. Sanderson Plumbing Prods., Inc. 588
Religious Tech. Ctr. v. Gerbode 413

Repp v. Webber 577
Reyes v. Sazan **473**
Rio Properties, Inc. v. Rio International Interlink 394
Rockefeller Center Properties, Inc. Securities Litigation, In re 367
Rodgers v. St. Mary's Hospital **659**
Rodgers, United States v. 250
Rodriguez-Diaz v. Sierra-Martinez 193
Rosario Ortega v. Star-Kist Foods, Inc. 207, 235
Rose v. Beaumont School District 338
Rose v. Giamatti 212
Roth v. District of Columbia Courts 185
Roy v. Inhabitants of City of Lewiston 581
Rufo v. Inmates of Suffolk County Jail 654
Rush v. Sawchuk 124
Ruszala v. Walt Disney World Co. **398**
Ruvalcaba v. City of Los Angeles ... 642
Safeco Ins. Co. v. City of White House 212
Sayre v. Musicland Group, Inc. 469
Scheuer v. Rhodes 342, 343
Schlagenhauf v. Holder 548, 549, 551
Schnabel v. Abramson 591
Schultea v. Wood 474, 475
Scott v. Paramount Pictures Corp. 577
Sedley v. City of West Buechel 684
Semtek International Inc. v. Lockheed Martin Corp. 305
Shady Grove Orthopedic Associates v. Allstate Insurance Co. 307
Shaffer v. Heitner **76**, 107
Sharpe v. United States 581
Shovah v. Roman Catholic Diocese of Albany, New York, Inc. 138
Sibbach v. Wilson & Co. 297
Simeon v. T. Smith & Son, Inc. 644
Simmons v. Simmons 34
Sims v. Great American Life Insurance Co. 302
Sindell v. Abbott Laboratories 692, 693
Singletary v. Continental Illinois National Bank 194
Sinochem International Co., Ltd. v. Malaysia International Shipping Corp. 166
Skipper v. French 697

TABLE OF CASES

Smith Kline & French Laboratories Ltd. v. Bloch 165
Smith v. Diamond Offshore Drilling, Inc. 514
Smith v. Kansas City Title & Trust Co. 249
Smith v. Lightning Bolt Productions 640
Smith v. World Ins. Co. 587, 588
Snead v. American Export-Isbrandtsen Lines, Inc. 514
Societe Internationale Pour Participations Industrielles Et Commerciales, S.A. v. Rogers, Attorney General 558
Southern Construction v. Pickard ... 34
Spectacor Mgmt. Group v. Brown 208
Spencer ex rel. Spencer v. Heckler 550
Spirit Master Funding, LLC v. Pike Nurseries Acquisition, LLC **508, 517**
St. Paul Mercury Indem. Co. v. Red Cab Co. 207
State Farm Mutual Auto Ins. Co. v. Narvaez 207
Stemler v. Florence..... **681**, 682, 683
Steward v. Up North Plastics, Inc. 157
Stewart Organization v. Ricoh Corporation **310**
Stewart v. Ramsay 112
Stewart v. Shelby Tissue, Inc. **427**
Strawbridge v. Curtiss 205, 234
Summers v. Copeland 48
Sweeney v. Westvaco Co. 189
Swierkiewicz v. Sorema, N. A. **340**, 348
Swift v. Tyson 274, 278
Tahfs v. Proctor 412
Tate v. Riverboat Services, Inc. **648**
Telluride Mgmt. Solutions, Inc. v. Telluride Inv. Group 552
Ten Taxpayer Citizens Group v. Cape Wind Associates, LLC 185
Tennessee v. Union & Planters' Bank 179
Texas Industries, Inc. v. Radcliff Materials, Inc. **314**
Textile Workers v. Lincoln Mills... 317, 319
The Bremen v. Zapata Off-Shore Co. 171
Thillens, Inc. v. Community Currency Exch. Assoc. of Ill., Inc. 41

Thompson v. Altheimer & Gray **606**, 610
Thompson v. Department of Housing and Urban Devel. **497**
Tiffany v. National Bank of Mo. 257
Towler v. Sayles 578
Travelers Health Assn. v. Virginia 97
Troy Bank v. G.A. Whitehead & Co. 234
Tulip Computers Intern., B.V. v. Dell Computer Corp. 547
Turpeau v. Fidelity Financial Services, Inc. 40, 41
Uffner v. La Reunion Francaise, S.A. 148
Ugarriza v. Schmieder 581
Union Carbide Corp. Gas Plant Disaster at Bhopal, India, In re 165
United Mine Workers v. Gibbs 37, **219**
Unitherm Food Systems, Inc. v. Swift-Eckrich, Inc. 593, 702
Upjohn Co. v. United States 501
Vaden v. Discover Bank 185
Valedon Martinez v. Hospital Presbiteriano de la Comunidad, Inc. 189
Van Dusen v. Barrack.... 157, 169, 170, 171, 311
Verizon Communications Inc. v. Law Offices of Curtis v. Trinko, LLP 343
Vermont Teddy Bear Co., Inc. v. 1-800 BEARGRAM Co. 569
Vitamins Antitrust Litigation, In re 528
Von Dunser v. Aronoff 210
Walden v. Fiore **124**, 142
Walker v. Armco Steel Corp. 304, 311, 382, 383
Wallace v. Tesoro Corp. **362**
Walther v. Walther 34
Wanderer v. Johnston 559
Werbungs v. Collectors' Guild, Ltd. 628
Wheaton v. Peters 276
Wheeldin v. Wheeler 316
Whitacre P'ship v. Biosignia, Inc. 675
Whitaker v. Ameritech Corp. 662
White v. Nix 453
Williams v. City of Jacksonville Police Dept. **673**
Windauer v. O'Connor 34
Wolf v. Reliance Standard Life Ins. Co. 470, 471

World-Wide Volkswagen Corp. v. Woodson 84
Wyman v. Newhouse 111
Young, Ex parte 183
Zagano v. Fordham Univ. 435
Zahn v. International Paper Co. ... 206, 231
Zambelli Fireworks Mfg. Co., Inc. v. Wood **202**
Zervos v. Verizon New York, Inc. ... 702
Zubulake v. UBS Warburg LLC 541
Zuk v. Eastern Pa. Psychiatric Inst. of the Med. College of Pa. 411

CIVIL PROCEDURE
CASES, PROBLEMS, AND EXERCISES

Fourth Edition

CHAPTER 1

AN OVERVIEW OF CIVIL PROCEDURE

■ ■ ■

A. THE ROLE OF PROCEDURE

BEECK V. AQUASLIDE 'N' DIVE CORP.
562 F.2d 537 (8th Cir. 1977)

BENSON, DISTRICT JUDGE.

This case is an appeal from the trial court's exercise of discretion on procedural matters in a diversity personal injury action.

Jerry A. Beeck was severely injured on July 15, 1972, while using a water slide. He and his wife, Judy A. Beeck, sued Aquaslide 'N' Dive Corporation (Aquaslide), a Texas corporation, alleging it manufactured the slide involved in the accident, and sought to recover substantial damages on theories of negligence, strict liability and breach of implied warranty.

Aquaslide initially admitted manufacture of the slide, but later moved to amend its answer to deny manufacture; the motion was resisted. The district court granted leave to amend. On motion of the defendant, a separate trial was held on the issue of "whether the defendant designed, manufactured or sold the slide in question." This motion was also resisted by the plaintiffs. The issue was tried to a jury, which returned a verdict for the defendant, after which the trial court entered summary judgment of dismissal of the case. Plaintiffs took this appeal, [arguing that the trial court abused its discretion in permitting an amendment that denied manufacture after the statute of limitations had run].

I. Facts.

... In 1971 Kimberly Village Home Association of Davenport, Iowa, ordered an Aquaslide product from one George Boldt, who was a local distributor handling defendant's products. The order was forwarded by Boldt to Sentry Pool and Chemical Supply Co. in Rock Island, Illinois, and Sentry forwarded the order to Purity Swimming Pool Supply in Hammond, Indiana. A slide was delivered from a Purity warehouse to Kimberly Village, and was installed by Kimberly employees. On July 15, 1972, Jerry A. Beeck was injured while using the slide at a social gathering sponsored at Kimberly Village by his employer, Harker

Wholesale Meats, Inc. Soon after the accident investigations were undertaken by representatives of the separate insurers of Harker and Kimberly Village. On October 31, 1972, Aquaslide first learned of the accident through a letter sent by a representative of Kimberly's insurer to Aquaslide, advising that "one of your Queen Model #Q-3D slides" was involved in the accident. Aquaslide forwarded this notification to its insurer. Aquaslide's insurance adjuster made an on-site investigation of the slide in May, 1973, and also interviewed persons connected with the ordering and assembly of the slide. An inter-office memo dated September 23, 1973, indicates that Aquaslide's insurer was of the opinion the "Aquaslide in question was definitely manufactured by our insured." The complaint was filed October 15, 1973. Investigators for three different insurance companies, representing Harker, Kimberly and the defendant, had concluded that the slide had been manufactured by Aquaslide, and the defendant, with no information to the contrary, answered the complaint on December 12, 1973, and admitted that it "designed, manufactured, assembled and sold" the slide in question.

The statute of limitations on plaintiff's personal injury claim expired on July 15, 1974. About six and one-half months later Carl Meyer, president and owner of Aquaslide, visited the site of the accident prior to the taking of his deposition by the plaintiff. From his on-site inspection of the slide, he determined it was not a product of the defendant. Thereafter, Aquaslide moved the court for leave to amend its answer to deny manufacture of the slide.

II. Leave to Amend.

Amendment of pleadings in civil actions is governed by Rule 15(a), F.R.Civ.P., which provides in part that once issue is joined in a lawsuit, a party may amend his pleading "only by leave of court or by written consent of the adverse party; and leave shall be freely given when justice so requires."

In *Foman v. Davis*, 371 U.S. 178 (1962), the Supreme Court had occasion to construe that portion of Rule 15(a) set out above:

> Rule 15(a) declares that leave to amend "shall be freely given when justice so requires," this mandate is to be heeded. . . . If the underlying facts or circumstances relied upon by a plaintiff may be a proper subject of relief, he ought to be afforded an opportunity to test his claim on the merits. In the absence of any apparent or declared reason such as undue delay, bad faith or dilatory motive on the part of the movant, repeated failure to cure deficiencies by amendments previously allowed, undue prejudice to the opposing party by virtue of allowance of the amendment, futility of amendment, etc. the leave sought should, as the rules require, be "freely given." Of course, the grant or

denial of an opportunity to amend is within the discretion of the District Court....

This Court in *Hanson v. Hunt Oil Co.*, 398 F.2d 578, 582 (8th Cir. 1968), held that "(p)rejudice must be shown." The burden is on the party opposing the amendment to show such prejudice. In ruling on a motion for leave to amend, the trial court must inquire into the issue of prejudice to the opposing party, in light of the particular facts of the case....

It is evident from the order of the district court that in the exercise of its discretion in ruling on defendant's motion for leave to amend, it searched the record for evidence of bad faith, prejudice and undue delay which might be sufficient to overbalance the mandate of Rule 15(a), F.R.Civ.P., and *Foman v. Davis*, that leave to amend should be "freely given." Plaintiffs had not at any time conceded that the slide in question had not been manufactured by the defendant, and at the time the motion for leave to amend was at issue, the court had to decide whether the defendant should be permitted to litigate a material factual issue on its merits.

[The Defendant's] reliance upon investigations of three insurance companies, and the fact that "no contention has been made by anyone that the defendant influenced this possibly erroneous conclusion," persuaded the court that "defendant has not acted in such bad faith as to be precluded from contesting the issue of manufacture at trial." The court further found "(t)o the extent that 'blame' is to be spread regarding the original identification, the record indicates that it should be shared equally."

In considering the issue of prejudice that might result to the plaintiffs from the granting of the motion for leave to amend, the trial court held that the facts presented to it did not support plaintiffs' assertion that, because of the running of the two year Iowa statute of limitations on personal injury claims, the allowance of the amendment would sound the "death knell" of the litigation. In order to accept plaintiffs' argument, the court would have had to assume that the defendant would prevail at trial on the factual issue of manufacture of the slide, and further that plaintiffs would be foreclosed, should the amendment be allowed, from proceeding against other parties if they were unsuccessful in pressing their claim against Aquaslide. On the state of the record before it, the trial court was unwilling to make such assumptions, and concluded "[u]nder these circumstances, the Court deems that the possible prejudice to the plaintiffs is an insufficient basis on which to deny the proposed amendment." The court reasoned that the amendment would merely allow the defendant to contest a disputed factual issue at trial, and further that it would be prejudicial to the defendant to deny the amendment.

The court also held that defendant and its insurance carrier, in investigating the circumstances surrounding the accident, had not been so lacking in diligence as to dictate a denial of the right to litigate the factual issue of manufacture of the slide.

On this record we hold that the trial court did not abuse its discretion in allowing the defendant to amend its answer. . . .

NOTES AND QUESTIONS

1. In the United States, cases are decided in two court systems: federal and state. *Beeck* was litigated in the federal system. In the first sentence of the opinion, the court indicates the dispute is a "diversity personal injury action." This is a reference to diversity jurisdiction, one of the two main ways a party may take its dispute to federal court. You will study diversity jurisdiction in Chapter 4.

2. Every jurisdiction has a "statute of limitations": a period of time, established by law, in which a claim must be brought. Claims not brought within the required time are lost. You will encounter statute of limitations issues not only in Civil Procedure, but also in your other courses.

The problem in *Beeck* is that if the court allows defendant to amend and deny liability, plaintiff will probably be left without a remedy. Because of the statute of limitations, plaintiff cannot recover against the actual manufacturer of the slide.

3. Review Federal Rule 15(a)(1) in your Supplement. This rule is the current version of the rule at issue in *Beeck*. If defendant had realized sooner that it was not the proper defendant, it would not have needed the court's permission. At what point did defendant need the court's permission?

4. Do you agree with the court's ruling in this case? Are either Beeck or Aquaslide more "at fault" for the mistake in the complaint? If neither side is at fault, who should suffer from the mistake?

5. You will encounter Rule 15(c) again in Chapter 6, pt. E which deals with amending a pleading. The discussion here is meant merely to provide an introduction to Civil Procedure.

B. DEALING WITH CIVIL PROCEDURE

Beeck deals with what at first glance may appear to be a fairly narrow and technical issue of court procedure. However, the real impact of the case goes far beyond merely construing the language of Federal Rule 15. The case is, after all, an actual dispute between living people, under a legal system that proudly calls itself a system of justice. The issue of whether Aquaslide may amend its answer ultimately determines whether Beeck has any chance of receiving a judgment compensating him for his injuries.

Never lose sight of these broader concerns. Students often claim Civil Procedure is one of the most difficult courses in law school. However, although the subject is by no means easy, the rules of Procedure are no more numerous or complex than those in other required courses. The problem in learning Procedure is that the subject matter is almost completely foreign to most law students. Courses such as Contracts, Torts, Criminal Law, and Constitutional Law present issues of the sort often reported in the news. Because they usually understand the underlying issue, students typically have a "gut" feeling as to what the rule of law ought to be. Although these hunches are not always correct, it is easier to learn a rule with which you strongly agree or disagree.

The rules of Civil Procedure may seem cold and mechanical in comparison. The outcome of a dispute concerning whether a party should be given permission to amend a pleading has no immediately obvious effect on the greater social good. Civil Procedure students therefore often find they have no hunch as to how most issues should be resolved. This can lead to the perception that Civil Procedure comprises a mass of arbitrary rules that must be memorized. Like many non-lawyers, some students view Procedure as a "bag of tricks" that a crafty litigator can use to win an otherwise weak case.

That view misses the essence of Procedure. Civil Procedure is much more than a collection of rules setting standards for mundane minutia such as filing deadlines and paper size. It is instead a coordinated system that sets out a particular way in which disputes are to be resolved. As with other types of systems, an individual component cannot be fully understood or appreciated until you see how it fits into the overall system.

As just one example, consider pleading, the topic of Chapters 6 and 7 of the casebook. Pleadings are the papers that a litigant serves on the other side to inform it of the claims and defenses being asserted. One basic issue in pleading is how detailed a pleading should have to be. The system could require simply a bare-bones notice of what the suit is about—"I'm suing you because you breached our contract last Wednesday"—or could instead require a detailed exposition of the facts and the legal theories on which the claimant relies. The choice between the two extremes may at first glance seem arbitrary. Realize, however, that pleading is merely one stage in a lawsuit. Once the other stages, especially the processes of discovery and summary judgment, are considered, it becomes clear that the choice of a standard for pleading has implications throughout the remainder of the lawsuit.

Throughout this course, then, you may find it useful to ask yourself how a given rule fits into the overall system of dispute resolution. In so doing, you will soon come to realize that the *system* of Civil Procedure does have basic underlying principles that guide the content of the rules.

Another factor to consider is that the system of Procedure exists not for its own sake, but in order to resolve disputes that for whatever reason were not resolved by society's informal methods of dispute resolution. Any system of dispute resolution must balance two basic concerns. The first is *efficiency*. The court system should operate as smoothly and quickly as possible, so that it is cost-effective to have disputes resolved by the official mechanism.

The second concern is *fairness*. Society will continue to submit its disputes to the legal system only as long as it produces outcomes that in most cases comport with people's expectations of how disputes should be resolved. Part of this, of course, involves the substantive law, the legal rules that you learn in other law school courses. Courts must select the proper rule to apply in a given case, and apply it correctly. However, disputes that find their way to the courts rarely involve only a disagreement as to the rule of law. In most cases, the parties also disagree on exactly what happened. The role of the court is to ferret out the "truth" of what happened, an often arduous and time-consuming process. Reaching a fair result in a given case, then, involves both determining what happened, and applying the proper rule of law to govern the rights and liabilities of the parties.

The rules of Civil Procedure attempt to strike a balance between efficiency and fairness. It would be tremendously costly in all cases—and probably impossible in most—to reach the "perfect" result. Procedural rules place limits on litigation in order to ensure that the system works efficiently, while still reaching a result that comports with society's expectations in most cases. Maintaining this balance is often difficult.

When you review a particular procedural rule, ask yourself whether it strikes an optimal balance between efficiency and fairness. Does the rule sacrifice the ultimate truth in an effort to speed up the process? Or does the result drag out the process of litigation, perhaps helping courts reach a "better" result in some cases, but at a cost of making the process more burdensome for *all* litigants? There are no right or wrong answers to these questions. Nevertheless, by reminding yourself from the outset that there are underlying normative goals in Civil Procedure, you will better understand both the overall process and the constituent rules.

C. THE FEDERAL RULES OF CIVIL PROCEDURE

The *Beeck* case that led off this chapter turned on an interpretation of Federal Rule of Civil Procedure 15. The Supplement to this book contains the entire body of the Federal Rules of Civil Procedure, along with other rules and statutes that deal with procedure. The laws set out in the Supplement are there for a very important reason. In fact, the Federal Rules of Civil Procedure will dominate your study in this course.

While a few of the topics you will study evolved primarily through case law, many more are controlled by the explicit terms of the Federal Rules.

In late 2007, a completely revised set of Federal Rules came into force, replacing the previous set. The revised rules are in most respects little more than a rewrite. The Rule numbers are unchanged. Moreover, with a few exceptions, the basic rule remains the same, but is cast in a more readable manner. Given that many cases in this book involve the pre-2007 version of the Federal Rules, you should be sure to read the current text of every Federal Rule in the Supplement.

While the Federal Rules of Civil Procedure technically govern only litigation in the federal district courts, their actual impact reaches far beyond the federal system. The Federal Rules, originally enacted in 1938, have had a tremendous impact on both the federal and state court systems. The Federal Rules fundamentally altered a number of traditional concepts in civil litigation. Because the system offered many advantages, a number of states adopted the language of the Federal Rules virtually wholesale (although many alter the numbering scheme to some extent). Other states, while not copying the language of the Federal Rules, have borrowed many of the underlying concepts. As a result, there is a noticeable similarity among many United States courts in the basic issues of Civil Procedure.

However, do not assume that all states follow the federal approach. Some of the largest states, including California, Illinois, and New York, have their own systems of procedure, systems that differ in many important ways from the federal. Other states, although structuring their systems on the federal model, have tinkered with one or more of the rules in significant ways. In fact, the differences between state and federal procedure have tended to increase over the past few years. Recent amendments to some of the Federal Rules of Civil Procedure have proven controversial. Many states have adopted a "wait and see" approach to these changes, refusing to amend their rules until the wisdom of those changes is borne out by experience.

The Federal Rules of Civil Procedure are not the only example of "positive law" (that is, rules created in advance, rather than made in the context of a particular case) you will encounter in this course. Several issues of Civil Procedure are controlled by federal statutes. These statutes are typically codified in title 28 of the United States Code, which is commonly referred to as the "Judicial Code." The Supplement includes some provisions of the Judicial Code. Finally, you will also occasionally encounter other bodies of federal rules, including the Federal Rules of Appellate Procedure and the Federal Rules of Evidence.

D. DEALING WITH DISPUTES

Much of the focus in law school curricula is on published appellate cases like the *Beeck* case. This can give the false impression that most cases are pursued to a decision in a trial court and then appealed. In popular culture, television shows and movies re-enforce this image of the trial as the central event in legal disputes. In fact, civil trials and, to an even greater extent, appeals are exceptional events that occur only in a small minority of cases. Moreover, court cases occur only in a small proportion of disputes.

The Civil Procedure system applied in court cases—both federal and state—is part of a larger landscape in which individuals and businesses attempt to deal with disputes. It is important not to lose sight of the fact that many disputes never reach court, and that many of those that do enter the court system are resolved, not by a judge or jury, but by the parties themselves. Just as questions of efficiency and fairness are central to the study of Civil Procedure, they also affect the extent to which disputants involve the litigation system in the resolution methods they choose.

Disputes are problems that go through several stages. Depending on how a problem is handled at each stage, it may or may not reach the Civil Procedure system. A dispute begins as a grievance, which can be thought of as a feeling that a circumstance is unjust or that an individual (or organization) is entitled to something. Sometimes a grievance is abandoned without any action; a person decides to avoid confrontation or potential conflict. Other times a person makes a claim based on that grievance. If the claim is satisfied—for example, if the insurance company pays the damages, or the retailer replaces the defective goods—that is the end of the matter. But if the claim remains unsatisfied, it becomes a dispute. The parties may be able to resolve the dispute on their own, but sometimes a dispute escalates until one or more of the disputants involves a lawyer. Even then, it may be resolved by negotiation or using another non-court process such as mediation or arbitration. If the dispute involves legal rights, then the claimant might decide to become a plaintiff, file a complaint in court, and formally convert the dispute into a court case. A major study of a wide variety of different types of grievances conducted several decades ago found that, on average, only about 5% actually become filed cases. The others are resolved, or abandoned, before entering the Civil Procedure system.

Once a case is filed in court, it may exit the system at many points prior to trial. For example, the judge may dismiss it early in the process because the complaint fails to state a claim upon which relief may be granted, the parties may reach a settlement, or the judge may decide the case without trial after a motion for summary judgment. Relatively few cases are actually tried before a judge or jury and this number is becoming smaller. Consider the findings of the following study.

MARC GALANTER, THE VANISHING TRIAL: AN EXAMINATION OF TRIALS AND RELATED MATTERS IN FEDERAL AND STATE COURTS

1 J. Empirical Legal Stud. 459, 460–61, 464–65, 477–78, 481–83 (2004)

I. THE NUMBER OF CIVIL TRIALS

This project reflects the growing awareness of a phenomenon that runs counter to the prevailing image of litigation in the United States. Over the past generation or more, the legal world has been growing vigorously. On almost any measure—the number of lawyers, the amount spent on law, the amount of authoritative legal material, the size of the legal literature, the prominence of law in public consciousness—law has flourished and grown. It seems curious, then, to find a contrary pattern in one central legal phenomenon, indeed one that lies at the very heart of our image of our system—trials. The number of trials has not increased in proportion to these other measures. In some, perhaps most, forums, the absolute number of trials has undergone a sharp decline. . . .

[Between 1962 and 2002] dispositions [of civil cases in the federal courts per year] increased by a factor of five—from 50,000 to 258,000 cases. But [as indicated in Figure 1] the number of civil trials in 2002 was more than 20 percent lower than the number in 1962—some 4,569 now to 5,802 then. So [as shown in Figure 2] the portion of dispositions that were by trial was less than one-sixth of what it was in 1962—1.8 percent now as opposed to 11.5 percent in 1962.

Figure 1 Number of Civil Trials, U.S. District Courts, by Bench or Jury, 1962–2002

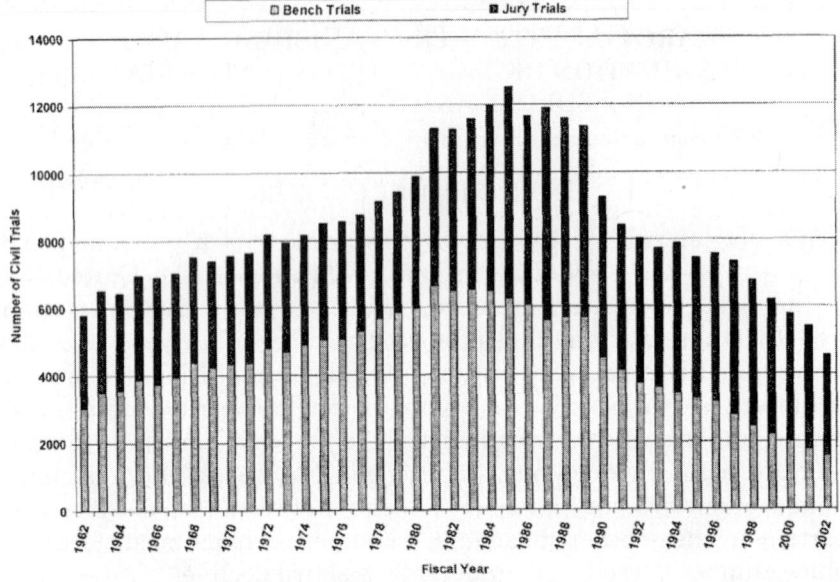

Source: Administrative Office of the United States Courts, Annual Report of the Director, Table C-4 (1962-2002)

Figure 2 Percentage of Civil Terminations During/After Trial in U.S. District Courts, 1962–2002

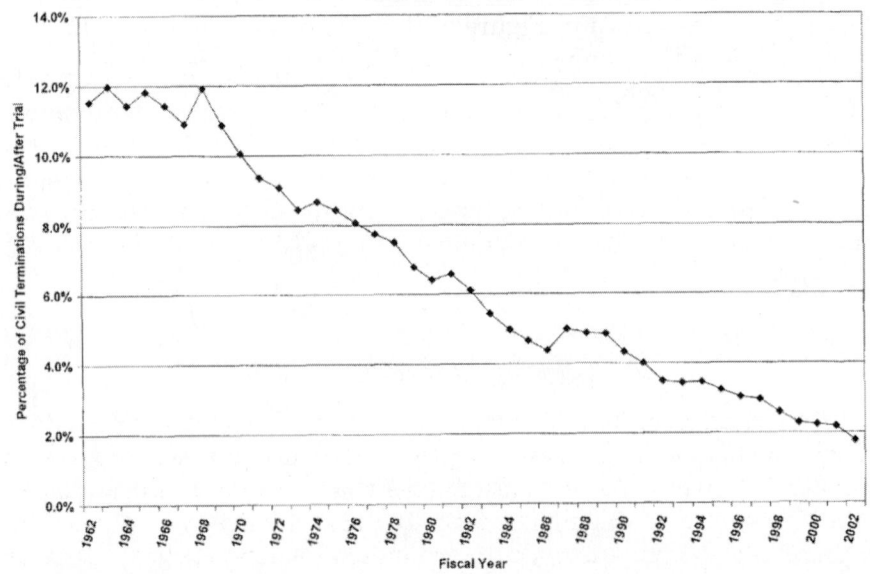

Source: Administrative Office of the United States Courts, Annual Report of the Director, Table C-4 (1962-2002)

The drop in civil trials has not been constant over the 40-year-period; it has been recent and steep. As Figure 1 shows, in the early part of our period, there was an increase in trials, peaking in 1985, when there were 12,529. From then to now, the number of trials in federal court has dropped by more than 60 percent and the portion of cases disposed of by trial has fallen from 4.7 percent to 1.8 percent.

. . .

II. THE CHANGING CHARACTER OF TRIALS: TIME AND COMPLEXITY

As we busy ourselves counting trials, we should not overlook the possibility that what constitutes a trial may have changed over the years.... [I]n earlier eras trials were often brief and perfunctory. The elaboration of procedure, the enlargement of evidentiary possibilities, and the increased participation of lawyers have made the trial more complex and refined than its remote ancestors. It is widely believed that within the period covered here, the cases that are tried have become more complex and consume larger investments of resources.... Studies of [state] courts suggest that complexity, investment, and length of trial are connected. In their study of Los Angeles Superior Court, Selvin and Ebener note that from their earlier (1915–1949) to their later (1950–1979) period, the number of events in filed cases increased as did the portion of cases with discovery and that the length of trials "dramatically increased." "In the earlier sample of civil filings, 60 percent of the trials lasted no longer than one day. Since 1950, only 20 percent of all trials took one day or less."

. . .

Few measures of complexity are available for cases in federal courts. There is data on the length of trials in federal courts. A larger portion of trials takes longer. Civil trials that lasted four days or more were 15 percent of trials in 1965 and 29 percent of trials in 2002; trials of three days or more rose from 27 percent to 42 percent over the same amount of time.... [T]his shift to longer trials is produced by an increase in the number of the longest trials combined with a shrinking of the number of short trials.

. . .

III. FROM FILING TO TRIAL

Interestingly, although the number and rate of trials has fallen, judicial involvement in case activity—at least on some level—has increased. Although the portion of cases that terminate "during or after pretrial" has fallen only slightly from 15 percent in 1963 to 11 percent in 2002, the number of cases that terminated "before pretrial" (but with some type of court action) rose from 20 percent in 1963 to 68 percent in 2002. Clearly, courts are more involved in the early resolution of cases than they used to be.

Figure 15 shows the portion of cases that terminated at each stage of the process. In 1963, more than half (55 percent) terminated before the occurrence of any "court action." By 2002, only 19 percent terminated at this stage. The big change came in the late 1980s, when the number of cases moving into the "before pretrial" stage began a dramatic increase, so that today nearly 70 percent of cases terminate at this stage as opposed to some 20 percent in 1962.

Figure 15 Percentage of Civil Cases Terminating at Each Stage, U.S. District Courts, 1963–2002

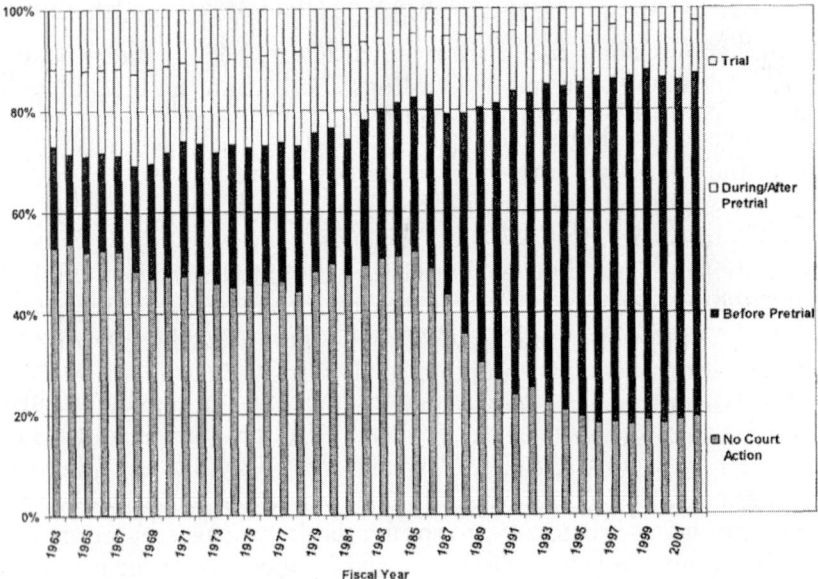

Source: Administrative Office of the United States Courts, Annual Report of the Director, Table C-4 (1962-2002)

JOHN LANDE, 'THE VANISHING TRIAL' REPORT: AN ALTERNATIVE VIEW OF THE DATA
Disp. Resol. Mag., Summer 2004, at 19–21

The title of the report and emphasis on [the data showing a decline in the civil trial rate] imply that something has gone wrong with the legal system. Like Mark Twain's reported death, however, accounts of the demise of the trial may be exaggerated.

... Galanter's report could just as well have been titled, "The Amazing Success of Judicial Case Management." Relying primarily on data cited in his report, this article shows that (a) there are many trials in the state courts, which have substantially higher trial rates than federal courts, (b) the expansion of pretrial activity and the increased complexity of cases have added reasons for litigants to settle, (c) courts have shifted some of their efforts from trials to pretrial work, and (d) declining trial rates have not reduced the production of case law. ...

CHANGES IN LITIGATION PATTERNS

Comparing trial rates in state courts. Although trial rates in state courts have declined in recent decades, state courts still resolve a substantial number of cases by trial. Galanter's report focuses primarily on federal courts, though it also presents data on trials in the state courts, where the vast majority of litigation occurs. A recent analysis by the National Center for State Courts (NCSC) shows that in 1999, for example, "state courts of general jurisdiction resolved nearly 28 times as many civil cases . . . as federal district courts."

The NCSC study analyzes data from 22 states between 1976 and 2002 and shows that the civil trial rate dropped by more than half, primarily because the number of filings more than doubled during that period. . . . [T]he trial rate dropped from 36.1 percent to 15.8 percent. Even so, the lowest state court civil trial rate is substantially higher than the highest federal court civil trial rate since 1962, which is 11.5 percent. Similarly, the number of state court trials dwarfs the largest number of federal civil trials shown in Galanter's report. . . .

Increasing size and complexity of cases. Cases are bigger and more complex than they used to be. Before litigants can get to trial, they often have to deal with the increased use of discovery, expert testimony, legal research and pretrial conferences and hearings. . . . Galanter presents data indicating that, on average, court files are fatter and trials are longer than they used to be. As a result, there is an apples-and-oranges phenomenon when comparing 1960s-era trials with their modern counterparts. Thus, contrasting trial statistics from different eras can be misleading.

Some cases settle these days because each side knows more about the case before trial than it would have known in earlier eras. Moreover, litigation costs are higher, which increases incentive to settle. Thus, it should not be surprising—or particularly disturbing—if litigants use litigation to help resolve disputes short of trial.

Judges doing more pretrial work. Galanter's report indicates that federal judges continue to work hard and have shifted some of their efforts from trials to pretrial work. The workload of federal district court judges has grown substantially as the caseload of district judges "more than doubled, from 196 in 1962 to 443 in 2002." . . . A recent major study found that federal judges are actively involved in holding pretrial conferences, setting pretrial schedules and trial dates, setting limits on discovery and ruling on motions. In more than half the cases, the judges described their level of pretrial management as moderate or intensive. . . .

Increasing case law. Although Galanter argues that trials have been vanishing, he does not find a problem of vanishing case law. He reports that the number of pages of federal opinions published yearly has more than doubled since 1962. If there is too little precedent to guide lawyers and judges, presumably it would be more appropriate to increase the publication rate of appellate decisions than to increase the number of trials.

Smaller numbers of trials do, however, reduce the number of trial judgments that provide legal "signals" for lawyers or judges to use in settling and adjudicating future cases. But it is not clear that lawyers or judges suffer from a lack of such signals in most cases or that additional trial judgments would help them. Indeed, further proliferation of legal signals could aggravate problems of legal complexity and information overload.

VILLAINS OR HEROES?

Rhetoric of "vanishing trials" feeds the fears of "litigation romanticists" who lament the passing of an era when it was easier to get to trial, and a judge's primary role was to try cases with little thought of "managing" cases. Such critics argue that by settling cases without court adjudication, ADR impedes the development of public norms and vindication of public values.

. . .

All the changes in the litigation environment in recent decades that reduced the trial rate probably also increased ADR use. Given the increases in many aspects of the legal system, such as judicial caseloads and the complexity of litigation, courts are quite prudent to devote more resources to pretrial case management and ADR.

Telling this story as a success would cast ADR as one of the heroes rather than a possible villain. Similarly, judges would be applauded as wise managers of public institutions rather than suspected of shirking their duty and letting trials vanish.

NOTES AND QUESTIONS

1. Professor Galanter's study provoked some strong reactions: " 'What's documented here,' William G. Young, the chief judge of the Federal District Court in Boston, said in an interview, 'is nothing less than the passing of the common law adversarial system that is uniquely American.' . . . 'This is a cultural shift of enormous significance,' said Arthur Miller, a law professor at Harvard." Adam Lipak, *U.S. Suits Multiply, but Fewer Ever Get to Trial, Study Says*, N.Y. Times, Dec. 14, 2003. Based on the data in the articles, do you agree that the changes are this dramatic?

2. The percentage of cases that reach trial depends on both the number of case filings and the number of trials. Over the time period of Galanter's study, the number of cases filed in federal district courts increased about fivefold. For years, the number of federal civil trials also increased (as shown in Figure 1) but not as fast, so there was a decline in the percentage of

cases that went to trial (as shown in Figure 2). But since the mid-1980s the pattern has changed: the actual number of trials is falling as well as the percentage. The trend continued following the publication of this study, although the decline appears to have leveled off starting in 2009. According to data from the Administrative Office of the U.S. Courts, in 2013, there were only 3,219 civil trials in the federal court system. Since 2009, 1.1% to 1.2% of federal civil cases have ended in trial, with juries deciding about two-thirds of them. All the rest settled or were terminated as a result of a pre-trial motion. Is this cause for concern? Do you think a minimum number or proportion of cases should be decided by trial each year? How should we decide the appropriate level of adjudication?

3. One of the concerns with a shift away from trials is the worry that it will reduce the important judicial function of producing precedent. Legal precedent not only guides future court decisions; it also guides social behavior by indicating the line between legal and illegal courses of action. Court judgments are also important for settlement in that they signal what the outcome of a dispute would be in court. Professor Lande argues that if the development of precedent is inadequate, the courts could publish more of their opinions. Studies have shown that, depending on the jurisdiction, 60 to 90 percent of appellate decisions are unpublished.

4. The numerical trends are important for judicial creation of precedent, but so are the characteristics of the cases that courts decide. What would be the consequences if parties were routinely encouraged to settle cases raising issues of privacy and First Amendment rights on the Internet? Would you have the same reaction to settlement if you learned that parties typically settle contract cases about sales of goods between merchants when the disputes do not raise novel issues? Although Professor Galanter observed trials declining in all categories of cases, he reported a shift from a predominance of trials of tort cases to trials of civil rights cases.

5. Other concerns are also raised by the trend toward fewer trials. The following describes a settlement in which the parties agreed to keep the documents they shared in discovery confidential. What are the consequences of the private dispute resolution settlement in this case?

> As Wall Street sex discrimination suits go, last week's $54 million deal between Morgan Stanley and the Equal Employment Opportunity Commission wasn't a bad one for women. Allison Schieffelin, the 43-year-old former saleswoman whose problems led to the E.E.O.C. suit in 2001, gets $12 million. As many as 340 current and former Morgan Stanley women share $40 million. And women who continue to work at Morgan Stanley—which denies having presided over any discrimination—get the benefit of a brand-new $2 million diversity program.
>
> So what's not to like?
>
> An honest lawyer might say it's always good to avoid the risk of losing a trial. Government lawyers up against Morgan Stanley's

deep pockets and blue-chip legal army got the investment bank to agree to write a big, fat check just minutes before opening arguments.

But Morgan Stanley, and all of Wall Street, scored an even bigger win: the statistics remain under wraps. No matter how generous a dollar settlement the Commission garnered, it is still an important step short. Wall Street will make changes only when its culture, and the hard numbers of compensation and promotion, are exposed in open court. But don't hold your breath.

Susan Antilla, *Money Talks, Women Don't*, N.Y. Times, July 21, 2004.

You might wonder why it is necessary to study Civil Procedure when federal courts try such a small percentage of civil cases. One answer is that Civil Procedure governs the initiation of law suits and pre-trial litigation. As you will see, many cases that do not proceed to trial are decided by the courts as a matter of law during the pre-trial process, either on a motion to dismiss the case or a motion for summary judgment.

A second answer is that even when the parties resolve a case on their own, litigation is often intertwined with the process of reaching a settlement. Based on earlier studies, Professor Galanter coined the term "litigotiation" to describe cases in which litigation is combined with negotiation in a "strategic pursuit of a settlement through mobilizing the court process." Galanter, *World of Deals: Using Negotiation to Teach about Legal Process,* 34 J. Legal Educ. 268, 268 (1984). In fact, many argue that the term "alternative" in "alternative dispute resolution" is misleading, for litigation, negotiation, mediation, and arbitration are all common methods of resolving disputes that may be deployed separately or in combination.

A third answer is that even in private settlements that do not involve court cases, most settlement takes place "in the shadow of the law." This means, first, that potential settlements are often compared with legal counsel's prediction of the outcome that would be obtained in court, taking into account the cost to achieve it. That prediction is based on both the application of substantive law and the operation of the Civil Procedure system. The Civil Procedure system also provides a backdrop, or shadow, in a second sense. Settlements are consensual and depend on the agreement of all the parties to a dispute. When that cannot be achieved, parties must rely on the Civil Procedure system for resolution.

The rate of trials in civil cases is part of a complex, dynamic dispute resolution system and many factors have contributed to the decline. A quest for efficiency is a large part of the equation: litigation is extremely costly and time consuming. Clients and lawyers have responded with strategic decisions about how to resolve disputes that are designed to minimize costs. More contracts contain dispute resolution clauses that direct disputes to mediation or arbitration and more clients see litigation as only one of several possible ways to resolve conflict.

Attempts to increase efficiency have also stimulated institutional reforms that have changed the role of judges and expanded the services offered by courts. Judges now actively manage cases to move them along more expeditiously. Courts routinely offer alternative dispute resolution programs with processes such as mediation, early neutral evaluation, non-binding arbitration, or judicial settlement conferences. Some courts even require parties to participate in these processes.

In addition to seeking efficiency, clients and lawyers now tend to consider both alternatives and traditional court processes in the context of the overall interests at stake. For some disputes, it may not be necessary to obtain a decision on legal rights. In some relationships, it may be desirable to avoid the adversary process at the heart of the Civil Procedure system. For some problems, the best outcome may not be the money damages that are usually available as a remedy in court. The most appropriate choice of a dispute resolution procedure will depend on the broader interests of the client and the circumstances of the problem.

Considering the ways that the individual procedural rules balance efficiency and fairness will help you understand the way they fit together into a system of Civil Procedure. Considering how that overall system responds to disputants' underlying interests and needs for efficiency will help you understand Civil Procedure in the broader context of resolving disputes in the United States.

NOTES AND QUESTIONS

1. Can you think of some benefits of proceeding with litigation as part of the process of attempting to settle a case?

2. Many cases settle just before trial "on the courthouse steps." Why do you think that might be? Are there detriments to delaying settlement until this late stage of the case?

3. Often a key procedural step or outcome can influence a party's decision to consider settlement during the course of litigation. What considerations would you discuss with your client in the following situations?

   a. You represent Dan Defendant in a tort suit brought by Priscilla Plaintiff. She claims an amount that exceeds Dan's insurance coverage. You had a theory that even if Priscilla could prove the facts she alleges, the claim is not justified under current interpretations of tort law. As permitted by the rules of procedure, you made this argument before filing an answer to the plaintiff's complaint in a motion to dismiss the case. The judge denied the motion and now the next step will be to file an answer and proceed with discovery in the case.

b. You represent Pablo Plaintiff in a product liability suit. He is besieged with medical bills he has no way to pay. The judge has granted extension of time after extension of time at the request of the defendants and you anticipate that trial is about a year away at the earliest.

c. You represent Polly Plaintiff in an antitrust suit. She will be entitled to treble damages if she prevails, but antitrust suits are often extremely expensive with extensive discovery and heavy use of expert witnesses on economic issues. Early discovery yielded an incriminating document that will embarrass the defendants if it is made public.

d. You represent Donald's Detailing, Inc., which is the defendant in an employment discrimination suit filed by Paul Plaintiff, a former employee. Based on discovery in the case you think Paul's claim is frivolous. You filed a motion for summary judgment to have the case decided without a trial, but the judge has not yet issued a decision. The plaintiff's attorney has suggested mediation.

PROBLEM

Your new client, Ms. Patsy Parker, is employed in the transportation industry as a local truck driver for Rising Sun Delivery, an international express service headquartered in Japan that specializes in delivering fragile shipments for the electronics and computer industries. Ms. Parker has worked for the company for five years, advancing from a part-time substitute to a full-time driver with seniority. She has been attending night school to earn a degree in business and her dream is to advance to a management position within the company. She has been encouraged by Rising Sun Delivery's policy of promoting workers from within its ranks, which it believes will foster employee loyalty and productivity.

Six months ago, Mr. Dan DuPont began work as the new dispatcher and supervisor for the delivery district. There was immediate friction. According to Ms. Parker, DuPont attempted to fondle her and she rebuffed him. Since then, he has ignored her seniority in assigning routes, insulted and taunted her constantly and given her an unfavorable evaluation. She complained to Mr. DuPont about this treatment, but he merely laughed at her. She also wrote a letter to DuPont's immediate superior, the division delivery director, but never received a response to her complaint. Parker says she doesn't know what else to do; the company is hierarchical and she doesn't know of any other complaint procedure. She can no longer tolerate the stress caused by DuPont's retaliation and decided to consult you about filing some sort of claim against him. She is extremely angry with him and thinks he should be made to "pay for his conduct." When you asked what she meant, Parker said she would like to see him fired or demoted. At a minimum, she doesn't want him to continue as her supervisor.

You could recommend suing Rising Sun for maintaining a hostile workplace environment, but Ms. Parker seems very hesitant to think about suing her employer. Her experience at the company was entirely positive until Mr. DuPont became her supervisor. She is frustrated with the company's seeming lack of concern for her situation, but the top executives in the U.S. division of the company are of Japanese descent and she fears they do not approve of what they probably see as a penchant for lawsuits in the United States. She is afraid of ruining her prospects for advancement or that she might even lose her job. As the sole supporter of two sons, she needs a good job. Moreover, after two more years at Rising Sun, she would be vested in an excellent pension plan.

In terms of suing Mr. DuPont, your legal research reveals that most courts have held that supervisors are not subject to individual liability under Title VII and the other federal employment civil rights statutes. Some courts, however, have found supervisors liable for monetary damages under state employment discrimination statutes. This would be an issue of first impression in your jurisdiction. The senior partner in the firm is enthusiastic about the prospect of a ground-breaking case and has authorized you to offer to represent Ms. Parker in a suit against DuPont at half your normal litigation rates.

If Ms. Parker decides to proceed against either Rising Sun or Mr. DuPont (or both) under the state statute, the first step would be to file a claim with the state civil rights agency to exhaust administrative remedies. That agency has a voluntary mediation program that could be used to try to settle the dispute without filing suit.

You have an upcoming meeting with Ms. Parker to discuss her litigation and mediation options. What factors weigh in favor of obtaining a judicial decision? What other factors weigh in favor of initiating settlement discussions, either through the mediation program or privately?

E. A CIVIL PROCEDURE TIMELINE

Throughout this book, you will encounter a host of separate issues that affect the resolution of disputes. At times, it can be difficult to figure out exactly how and when these issues arise in an actual civil case. While the book organizes these materials in roughly the same order as they usually arise in litigation, it can be difficult for someone who has never sat through a case to understand where in the case each step "fits."

The following discussion provides a *very rough timeline* setting out the order in which Civil Procedure cases progress, and when the various issues discussed in this book typically arise. Of course, every case has its unique aspects, and any given dispute may diverge from the given order. You may nevertheless find it useful to refer back to this timeline whenever you begin discussion of a certain issue, so that you can see where and how that issue fits into the overall picture. Note that terms set out in **bold** (or, in some headings, ***bold italics***) are terms of art, which you will find in the Index.

1. PRE-LITIGATION PHASE

A party who learns he has a claim against another does not go straight to court. Instead, the party will ordinarily first try to resolve the dispute amicably by **settlement** (Ch. 9 pts. C & D). In some situations, the parties may call in third parties by submitting the dispute to **mediation**, or perhaps even more formal **arbitration** (Ch. 9 pt. B).

If no resolution is forthcoming, the party will then prepare its case, especially by conducting an investigation to marshal its facts for the upcoming dispute. In very limited circumstances, the potential plaintiff may be able to use **discovery** to help it preserve facts for trial (Ch. 10).

2. PLAINTIFF COMMENCES ITS CASE

Plaintiff commences its case by preparing, filing, and serving its complaint. Plaintiff must often make a number of threshold choices in this process. These include (in rough order):

A. *Selecting what claim(s) to bring*. This determination turns largely on the substantive law, but may also be guided by procedural considerations.

B. *Selecting the forum in which to sue*. Depending on the nature of the case, plaintiff may be able to sue in either state or federal court (or both). The choice of court is governed by the rules dealing with **subject-matter jurisdiction** (Ch. 4). In addition, plaintiff must select the courts in a state with **personal jurisdiction**: the authority to issue a judgment that binds defendant (Ch. 3). Finally, the selected court must be a proper **venue** for the action (Ch. 3). Depending on the number of hours allocated to Civil Procedure at your school, your professor may elect to defer detailed discussion of these topics to an upper-level procedure course, or make use of the condensed alternative chapter outlining these issues.

C. *Selecting who will sue and be sued*.

    1. **Joinder of plaintiffs**. Multiple plaintiffs with related claims may voluntarily join in a single suit (Ch. 2 pt. B).

    2. **Joinder of defendants**. Plaintiff(s) may also sue more than one defendant (Ch. 2 pt. B).

D. *Drafting and filing the complaint*. Plaintiff then drafts and files its "complaint", the pleading that commences the case.

    1. Various **pleading rules** dictate the form of, and how much information must be provided by, the complaint (Ch. 6, pt. B).

SEC. E   A CIVIL PROCEDURE TIMELINE   21

   2. Plaintiff may **join** all claims it may have against defendant, regardless of whether they are related (Ch. 2 pt. D).

E. *Serving the complaint.* Plaintiff must **serve** the complaint on all defendants (Ch.6 pt. C).

3. DEFENDANT'S INITIAL RESPONSE

Defendant(s) must respond to the allegations in the complaint. Defendant has several options.

A. ***Pre-answer motion.*** Certain defenses, including challenges to the form or content of the complaint, or to jurisdiction, venue, or service, may be raised by a **motion** filed prior to the answer (Ch. 7 pt. B).

B. ***Answer.*** Unlike a motion, which deals with one or a few issues, defendant's **answer** is its comprehensive response to plaintiff's complaint. Specific rules govern the answer (Ch. 7 pt. C).

   1. If the defendant fails to answer, the court may enter a **default judgment** in favor of plaintiff (Ch. 7 pt. D).

C. *Joinder of claims and parties by defendant.* Defendant may bring claims of its own against existing parties. (Defendant may also bring new parties into the suit through the process of **impleader**, a concept your professor may choose to defer to an advanced procedure course).

   1. **Counterclaims.** Defendant may file any claims it may have against one or more plaintiffs (Ch. 2 pt. A). Some counterclaims must be brought, or they are lost.

   2. **Cross-claims.** Defendant may also file claims against other defendants (Ch. 2 pt. C). (Plaintiffs may also cross-claim against other plaintiffs).

   3. **Additional joinder by defendant.** Like a plaintiff, a defendant may join additional claims to a proper counterclaim, cross-claim, or impleader.

4. REFINING THE CASE

A. *Responding to claims.* All parties who are subject to claims in the case must respond to the claims against them. In most situations, this involves an answer, as well as possible challenges by motion (Ch. 7 pts. B & C).

B. *Amendments.* The parties may be able to amend their pleadings, perhaps following a successful challenge by an opposing party (Ch. 6, pt. E).

C. *Resolving the case based on the pleadings.* Once the pleadings are complete, one or more parties may make a **motion for judgment on the pleadings** (Ch. 7 pt. E). If the court determines that the pleadings make it clear that one party will win on a particular claim (or the entire case), it will issue a judgment in favor of that party.

5. CASE MANAGEMENT

A. *Meeting with the parties.* Depending on the jurisdiction, the court may use case management techniques to organize the case, including the **discovery conference** (Ch. 10) or a **pre-trial conference**.

B. *Alternate dispute resolution.* Even after the case is underway, the parties may choose to resolve the dispute by other means, including **settlement**, **mediation**, or **arbitration** (Ch. 9).

   1. Some court systems require the parties to meet—or in some cases submit the case to mediation—as a condition to continuing in court (Ch. 9 pt. B).

6. DISCOVERY

Once the case is underway, the parties will continue to investigate, interview witnesses, examine property, and otherwise marshal their facts for trial. Unlike the situation before the case is filed, however, the parties may now force others to provide information. In larger cases, this process of "discovery" will consume most of the hours the attorneys spend in the case, often continuing for months or years. In small cases, by contrast, little or no discovery takes place.

A. *Mandatory disclosure.* In federal court, the parties may be required to disclose certain information to other parties, even without a request. This mandatory disclosure occurs in separate stages, one at the beginning of the case, and another on the eve of trial (Ch. 10 pt. A).

B. *Discovery methods.* A party has a variety of means to discover information from others, including (Ch. 10 pt. B):

- **depositions** (oral questions and answers, under oath)
- **interrogatories** (written questions, answered by the other party and its attorney)
- **depositions by written questions** (written questions, but posed orally to the witness)
- **inspection of documents, land, and other tangible things**
- **physical and/or mental examinations**
- **requests for admission**

If the information is held by a non-party, the party may discover it only by a deposition or an order to make documents, land, or other property available for inspection.

C. *Trial preparation materials*. While the rules generally allow for free-ranging discovery, special rules limit the discovery of **privileged** information, **work product** information, and the opinions held by **testifying and non-testifying experts** retained by a party (Ch. 10 pt. A).

7. RESOLUTION OF THE CASE BY THE JUDGE

Even when the parties have demanded a jury trial in the case (see pt. 8 below), there are a number of circumstances in which the judge, rather than the jury, will decide one or more of the key issues. The **default judgment**, which occurs when a party fails to file an answer to a claim, is discussed above in Section 3 (Ch. 7 pt. D). Similarly, Section 4 discusses the **judgment on the pleadings** (Ch. 7 pt. E).

A. *Dismissals*. If plaintiff fails to prosecute its case diligently, or if either party violates certain procedural rules, the case can be dismissed by the judge (Ch. 7 pt. A). Plaintiff may also be able to dismiss the case voluntarily, possibly to refile in a different forum.

B. *Summary judgment*. In summary judgment, the judge decides the case *before it even gets to trial*. Because summary judgment considers the evidence, it usually occurs after discovery is complete, or nearly complete (Ch. 11 pt. A).

C. *Judgment as a matter of law*. Once trial has commenced, summary judgment is no longer an option. However, either party may move, based on the evidence presented at trial, for **judgment as a matter of law**. This motion may occur before the jury goes out to decide the case, or after the jury has come back with its verdict. (Ch. 11 pt. B).

D. *New trial*. Rather than decide the case himself, the judge may order a new trial, which means that some later jury is likely to decide the case. New trials may be granted either for procedural errors, or because the judge is convinced the jury has rendered a clearly incorrect verdict (Ch. 12 pts. F & G).

8. JURY TRIALS

When a case is to be decided by a jury, rather than by a professional such as a judge or arbitrator, several additional wrinkles arise.

A. *Right to a jury*. In federal court, and in many states, a party may have a right to a jury, either because of the national or state constitution, or by statute (Ch. 12 pt. A).

B. *Demand*. Even when a party has a right to a jury, a timely **demand** for a jury must be filed with the court (Ch. 12 pt. B).

C. *Selecting the jury.* The rules governing who may serve on a jury, both in general and in a particular dispute, are designed to ensure an unbiased jury, as well as a broad cross-representation of society.

    1. The court system itself calls people to "jury duty", using rules designed to include a wide array of jurors (Ch. 12 pt. C).

    2. The parties have considerable control over the actual jurors who will decide the case. The parties engage in ***voir dire***, in which the jurors are asked questions to determine bias. Based in part on the responses to this *voir dire*, the parties may strike individual jurors pursuant to a **challenge for cause** or a **peremptory challenge** (Ch. 12 pt. D).

D. *Jury instructions.* When the case is about to be submitted to the jury for decision, the court instructs the jury in the governing law using **jury instructions** (Ch. 12 pt. E).

E. *Form of verdict.* Most cases are decided using the **general verdict**, in which the jury simply declares who wins (and if a claimant wins, how much). However, on some occasions the court may use a **general verdict with interrogatories** or a **special verdict** (Ch. 12 pt. E).

F. *Challenges to verdicts.* Jury verdicts may be overturned by the court rendering a **judgment as a matter of law** or by ordering a **new trial**, both of which are discussed in Part 7 above.

9. APPEALS

A party who loses at trial court may ordinarily appeal.

A. *Federal appeals.* Not all trial court decisions may be appealed immediately to the federal appellate courts. In most cases, only ***final decisions*** may be appealed (Ch. 14 pt. B).

B. *Role of the appellate court.* The appellate court may review both the procedure in the court below, as well as the outcome (Ch. 14 pt. C).

    1. *Review of procedure.* If the trial court made an error that may have affected the outcome of the case, the appellate court will typically nullify the judgment and **remand** the case to the trial court for a new trial.

    2. *Review of merits.* The appellate court does not overturn simply because it thinks the trial court or jury erred. Instead, the appellate court will give the trial factfinder considerable deference on its findings of fact and issues committed to the trial court's discretion. However the appellate court gives no deference on findings of law.

SEC. E — A CIVIL PROCEDURE TIMELINE

    a. If the appellate court does reverse, it may either remand for a new trial, or if the correct outcome is clear, may enter judgment in favor of the victor on appeal.

C. *Higher courts*. Depending on the case and the system in which it is heard, further appeals may be available, possibly even to the United States Supreme Court (Ch. 14 pt. D).

10. EFFECT OF A JUDGMENT

A. *Enforcing judgments*. A judgment allows a victorious claimant to enlist the aid of government in enforcement. Depending on the relief awarded, the victor may be able to have the loser held in contempt, or have the loser's assets seized and sold to satisfy the judgment (Ch. 13 pt. A).

B. *Effect of judgment in later litigation*. A judgment may also limit parties in later litigation. Several doctrines combine to have this effect.

    1. **Claim preclusion** prevents the same parties from litigating not only the actual claims presented to the court in the first case, but also related claims that were not raised (Ch. 13 pt. C).

    2. **Issue preclusion** prevents a party from relitigating an issue that she actually litigated and that was actually decided by the first court, even if that issue arises in a different claim (Ch. 13 pt. D).

    3. Other doctrines, especially **judicial estoppel** and **law of the case**, may also prevent the relitigation of issues (Ch. 13 pt. G).

    4. Because of the constitutional requirement of **full faith and credit to judgments**, courts in one state may have to apply claim and issue preclusion to judgments issued by courts in other states (Ch. 13 pt. F).

GENERAL RULES DEALING WITH CANDOR AND GOOD FAITH

In addition to these particular issues, the rules of Civil Procedure also require litigants and their attorneys to meet certain standards of candor and good faith. These issues can arise at virtually any point in the case.

A. *Pleadings and motions*. Federal Rule 11 requires that all pleadings, motions, and other representations to the court be warranted by existing law, set forth facts believed in good faith to be true, and be presented to the court for a proper purpose (Ch. 6 pt. D).

B. *Discovery*. Federal Rule 26(g) sets out a similar rule for discovery requests (which are usually made directly to the other party, not to the court) (Ch. 10 pt. C).

C. *Sanctions*. Violation of these rules of candor can result in sanctions.

Chapter 2

Joinder of Claims and Parties

■ ■ ■

Much of the analysis in law school assumes a case involving one plaintiff, one defendant, and a single claim. The discussion focuses on how these parties have interacted prior to the case and whether defendant ought to be liable to plaintiff. Distilling the case to a two-party dispute is undoubtedly the easiest way to learn the legal rules in courses such as Torts, Contracts, and Property. But this pedagogical tool is somewhat unrealistic when compared to most real civil cases. Lawsuits involving only one claim, one plaintiff and one defendant are rare. Instead, many lawsuits today involve several plaintiffs, a bevy of defendants, and perhaps even other parties bearing names such as "third-party defendant" and "intervenor". Once all these parties are in the case, they tend to file claims against each other. As a result, courts are increasingly called upon to resolve complex cases involving myriad joined claims and parties.

Several different factors may underlie this trend toward increasingly complex lawsuits. A major cause is the increased prevalence of large corporations in the national and international economy. A large corporation can injure many different people in similar ways. In addition, the substantive law itself is partly to blame for the growing trend toward complex lawsuits. For reasons you will discuss in your other courses, the law increasingly holds multiple parties responsible for a single injury.

Not everyone agrees that this trend toward larger and more complex cases is desirable. Allowing joinder of everyone who is in any way connected with a dispute certainly has some benefits. The primary benefit is the potential for efficiency. A great deal of judicial time can be saved if one court can wrap up all of the disputes that may arise from, for example, a complex commercial transaction. But these benefits are not without cost. A larger lawsuit is not always more efficient. At some point, allowing uncontrolled joinder of claims and parties will result in a case so unwieldy that justice cannot be properly administered. The court rules governing joinder, then, are an attempt to balance the benefits of consolidated litigation with the detrimental effects on fair litigation.

A. COUNTERCLAIMS

INTRODUCTORY PROBLEM

Midway Motors, Inc. ["Midway"], operates a large car dealership. To be competitive, all car dealers must keep a large inventory on the lot at all times. Maintaining that inventory is extremely expensive. To help it meet these costs, in August of last year Midway borrowed money from Financial Bank ["Financial"], pursuant to a rolling line of credit agreement.

Midway decided to expand its showroom a few months later. Because the line of credit agreement did not allow funds to be used for this sort of expense, Midway entered into a second loan agreement, called a building loan, with Financial in March of this year. Midway owes large sums of money to Financial under both loan agreements.

When rising fuel prices dampen demand for cars, Midway cannot make the required payments under either loan. Financial therefore sues Midway ["Case #1"]. However, because it is still negotiating with Midway on a way to pay the building loan, Financial sues only for the outstanding balance on the line of credit. Midway files an answer which both denies liability and asserts a counterclaim. In this counterclaim, Midway claims that Financial failed to make certain disbursements to the plumber and electrician who worked on the showroom expansion, as called for by the explicit terms of the building loan agreement. Midway paid these parties itself, and now seeks reimbursement. Before filing a responsive pleading, Financial moves to dismiss the counterclaim, arguing that the rules of procedure do not allow Midway to file a counterclaim that involves a different transaction than that which gave rise to the complaint.

Midway then files a new case against Financial ["Case #2"]. In this action, Midway seeks damages from Financial for failure to make the disclosures required by federal law in connection with the line of credit. Even though it has not yet responded to Midway's counterclaim in Case #1, Financial files an answer in Case #2. Financial's answer asks the court to dismiss this new action, arguing that Midway was required to bring the disclosure claim as a counterclaim in the action involving the line of credit.

Financial's next step is to file its answer to Midway's counterclaim in Case #1. Financial denies liability. Financial then files a new action against Midway ["Case #3"], in which it seeks to recover the outstanding balance on the building loan. Midway moves to dismiss this new action, arguing that Financial was required to bring this claim in its answer to Midway's counterclaim in Case #1.

How should the court resolve the challenges that Financial and Midway have raised in these three separate actions?

Governing Rule: Federal Rules of Civil Procedure 13(a) and (b).

The basic notion of a counterclaim is simple. If plaintiff sues defendant for breach of contract, it seems only fair that defendant should be able to ask that court to resolve defendant's claim that plaintiff breached that contract. But what about claims that have nothing to do with the contract? And what if, when afforded the opportunity to bring its contract claim against plaintiff into the case, defendant instead chooses to sue in a different court, perhaps one it considers more convenient?

Nasalok Coating Corp. v. Nylok Corp.
522 F.3d 1320 (Fed. Cir. 2008)

Dyk, Circuit Judge.

Appellant Nasalok Coating Corporation ("Nasalok") appeals from a decision of the Trademark Trial and Appeal Board ("Board"). The Board granted summary judgment in favor of appellee Nylok Corporation ("Nylok") in a cancellation proceeding brought by Nasalok. . . .

BACKGROUND

Both parties in this case are engaged in business related to self-locking fasteners using nylon locking elements. A nylon element, such as a patch or strip of nylon, is applied to the threads of such a fastener, and prevents the fastener from loosening when exposed to vibration, stress, or temperature extremes. Appellant Nasalok, a Korean corporation, applies nylon coatings to self-locking fasteners for use in industrial applications. Although Nasalok does business primarily in Korea and other parts of Asia, its products are purchased by many companies based in the United States, or whose product end users are located in the United States. Appellee Nylok, a U.S. corporation, manufactures and sells a variety of fasteners, including self-locking fasteners. Nylok is the owner of federal trademark Registration No. 2,398,840 ("'840 Registration"). The registered mark consists of "a patch of the color blue on a selected number of threads of an externally threaded fastener. . . ."

On November 18, 2003, Nylok filed a complaint against Nasalok (and four other companies that are not parties in the present case) in the United States District Court for the Northern District of Illinois, alleging infringement of several trademarks, including the '840 Registration. . . . [T]he district court entered . . . [a default judgment] in favor of Nylok on May 12, 2005. . . . The district court's order also stated that Nylok is the proper owner of the '840 Registration and that the trademark is valid and enforceable. Nasalok did not appeal the district court's order.

In October 2005, five months after the default judgment, Nasalok filed a petition to cancel the '840 Registration with the Board. The petition alleged that the registered mark is invalid because it is functional, a phantom mark, descriptive, generic, not distinctive, and ornamental; that Nylok's use has not been substantially exclusive; and that Nylok fraudulently obtained the '840 Registration....

On March 28, 2007, the Board granted summary judgment in favor of Nylok....

DISCUSSION

...

II

Nylok urges that Nasalok was required to raise the invalidity issue as a counterclaim in the district court action. We first consider whether trademark invalidity, the basis of Nasalok's petition to cancel the '840 Registration, was a compulsory counterclaim in the trademark infringement action brought by Nylok. Federal Rule of Civil Procedure 13(a)(1) provides:

> A pleading must state as a counterclaim any claim that—at the time of its service—the pleader has against the opposing party if the claim: (A) arises out of the transaction or occurrence that is the subject matter of the opposing party's claim; and (B) does not require adding another party over whom the court cannot acquire jurisdiction....

In response to an action for infringement, a defendant may assert a counterclaim of invalidity. District courts have the authority, in any action involving a registered trademark, to "determine the right to registration" and "order the cancellation of registrations, in whole or in part." 15 U.S.C. § 1119. This statute allows a trademark infringement defendant to assert a counterclaim to cancel the registration, but the question remains whether such a counterclaim is compulsory or permissive. Surprisingly, we have been unable to locate any court of appeals decisions, in our circuit or any other circuit, directly addressing the question of whether a claim of trademark invalidity is a compulsory counterclaim to a claim of trademark infringement. For several reasons we conclude that it is not.

The subject matter of the plaintiff's infringement claim in the first proceeding and the subject matter of the invalidity claim in the cancellation proceeding do not arise out of the same "transaction or occurrence." Fed.R.Civ.P. 13(a)(1)(A). The Supreme Court has explained the "transaction or occurrence" test in ... *Moore v. N.Y. Cotton Exch.*, 270 U.S. 593, 46 S.Ct. 367, 70 L.Ed. 750 (1926). The plaintiff in *Moore* had sought permission to receive quotations of cotton prices from the defendant's exchange, and its application had been refused. The plaintiff then brought an antitrust claim against the exchange based on this refusal, and the exchange counterclaimed, asserting that the plaintiff was stealing the quotations and seeking an injunction against continued misappropriation. The district court dismissed the plaintiff's claim, and entered the injunction sought by the defendant. The Supreme Court affirmed the judgment, holding that because the counterclaim was compulsory the district court retained jurisdiction to rule on the counterclaim after the plaintiff's claim was dismissed. The Court noted that the basis of the counterclaim was "one of the links in the chain which constitutes the transaction upon which appellant here bases its cause of action," that the common ground between the claim and counterclaim was "the one circumstance without which neither party would have found it necessary to seek relief," and that "[e]ssential facts alleged by appellant enter into and constitute in part the cause of action set forth in the counterclaim." *Moore*, 270 U.S. at 610, 46 S.Ct. 367.

Following the *Moore* decision, our court has utilized three tests to determine whether the "transaction or occurrence" test of Rule 13(a) is met: (1) whether the legal and factual issues raised by the claim and counterclaim are largely the same; (2) whether substantially the same evidence supports or refutes both the claim and the counterclaim; and (3) whether there is a logical relationship between the claim and the counterclaim. In each of the three tests for what constitutes the same "transaction or occurrence," the question is the extent of factual overlap between what the plaintiff must establish to prove its claim and what the defendant must establish to prove its counterclaim. The mere possibility that, as a result of affirmative defenses, the first suit might involve additional issues does not obligate the defendant to assert those affirmative defenses as a counterclaim.

In this case, Nylok's trademark infringement claim was based on Nylok's alleged ownership of a registered mark, Nasalok's alleged use of the color blue in nylon patches on the external threads of self-locking fasteners, its promotion of those fasteners in advertisements in publications distributed in the United States, and the likelihood of confusion of the consuming public as a result of Nasalok's activities. Invalidity of the mark was an affirmative defense that could have been raised, not part of the plaintiff's cause of action. Nasalok's cancellation petition, by contrast, was based on alleged attributes of Nylok's registered mark that rendered it subject to cancellation, including allegations that the mark was functional and was a phantom mark, and on Nylok's allegedly fraudulent actions in obtaining registration of the mark. In this case, therefore, the "essential facts" alleged by Nylok in its infringement action—related to Nylok's ownership of the mark and Nasalok's allegedly infringing behavior—do not form the basis of the cancellation claim now asserted by Nasalok, which is based on attributes of Nylok's mark and on Nylok's actions in obtaining registration of that mark. The two claims raise different legal and factual issues, will not be supported or refuted by substantially the same evidence, and are not "logically related" in the sense described by the Supreme Court in *Moore*. Therefore, the claims do not arise out of the same "transaction or occurrence," and the petition to cancel was not a compulsory counterclaim in the infringement action.

. . . At the time of an infringement suit, it will be difficult to anticipate the new products and future disputes that may later arise between the two parties. A plaintiff who brings an infringement suit as to one allegedly infringing use of a mark would not be precluded from later bringing a second infringement suit as to another use; similarly, a defendant in the first infringement suit should not be precluded from raising invalidity of the mark in the second action simply because it was not raised as a counterclaim in the first action. . . .

III

[The court then found that the claim was barred under the common-law doctrine of claim preclusion, because it would effectively undermine the relief granted by the court in the first action. This concept is explored in Ch. 13 pt. B.]

CONCLUSION

Because Nasalok's claim of trademark invalidity . . . amounted to a collateral attack on the district court's judgment in the earlier infringement suit, the rules of defendant preclusion are properly applied to bar Nasalok from asserting that claim. Therefore we affirm the Board's grant of summary judgment in favor of Nylok.

[JUDGE NEWMAN's concurrence is omitted]

NOTES AND QUESTIONS

1. *Compulsory and permissive counterclaims.* Rule 13(b) places no restrictions on the claims a defendant may file as a counterclaim. As a result, there is relatively little case law dealing with permissive counterclaims. The vast majority of case law under Rule 13 deals instead with compulsory counterclaims under Rule 13(a).

Rule 13(a) is somewhat unusual. Aside from Rule 19, a complex provision that does not apply in that many cases, joinder of claims and parties is usually optional, not mandatory. Why should counterclaims be any different? Are "compulsory" counterclaims logically necessary to the main case in the sense that the court must determine the merits of the counterclaim before it can rule on plaintiff's claim?

2. The court uses three tests to determine whether the counterclaim arises from the same transaction or occurrence as plaintiff's claim. Be prepared to explain the differences between the three. Is a counterclaim compulsory if it satisfies any of the three tests, or must all three be met?

3. A number of older cases do not use the logical relationship test, but apply only the same evidence and same factual/legal issue test. *See, e.g., Apache County v. Superior Court*, 785 P.2d 1242 (Ariz. App. 1989) (applying

Arizona rules, which are essentially identical to the Federal Rules). Other cases used *only* the logical relationship test, not the others. Thus, for a period of time there was a distinct split between those courts as to what test to use to determine "same transaction or occurrence." Today, however, virtually all courts use an approach similar to that in *Nasalok*, where all three tests are considered.

4. The "logical relationship" test does not limit itself to considering the evidence, but instead considers all factors that may exist in a particular case. Because of this flexibility, one influential treatise on federal civil procedure commends the logical relationship test as the best approach. 7 Wright, Miller, and Kane, Federal Practice and Procedure: Civil 2d § 1653 (3d ed. 2001). Many state courts also use this test.

5. How can the court in *Nasalok* find no logical relationship between the claim in the earlier infringement action and the claim Naslok now seeks to bring? If Nylok's trademark is invalid, then it would have had no right to recover against Nasalok in the earlier case. Just as in the *Moore* case cited in the opinion, isn't the issue of validity "one of the links in the chain" giving rise to plaintiff's claim?

6. There are relatively few reported cases dealing with the question of what happens when a party fails to file a "compulsory" counterclaim. The reason is practical: once litigation is commenced, attorneys tend to file all available claims. In cases where a compulsory counterclaim is omitted, the court must determine the consequences of failing to comply with Rule 13. The Rule itself does not clearly state that a party who fails to file such a counterclaim loses it. Courts seem to assume, however, that this is the only sanction that makes sense. *See Nippon Credit Bank, Ltd. v. Matthews*, 291 F.3d 738, 755 (11th Cir. 2002). The United States Supreme Court appears to agree, although its statement to this effect is *dictum*. *Baker v. Gold Seal Liquors*, 417 U.S. 467, 469 n. 1, 94 S.Ct. 2504, 41 L.Ed.2d 243 (1974). Can you conceive of any possible sanctions for failing to file a compulsory counterclaim other than barring the omitted claim?

7. Note that failure to bring a compulsory counterclaim may prevent a party not only from bringing the claim before a court, but also before other adjudicatory bodies. Nasalok's claim to cancel the trademark registration was brought before the Patent and Trademark Office, a federal agency.

8. Are defendants the only parties required to counterclaim? What if defendant counterclaims against plaintiff, and plaintiff has another claim against defendant that arises from the same transaction as that counterclaim? *See Feed Management Systems, Inc. v. Brill*, 518 F.Supp.2d 1094 (D. Minn. 2007).

9. Nasalok defaulted in the original district court action filed by Nylok. As you will learn in Chapter 7, a party defaults when it fails to file an answer or take any other action to defend itself. Does that fact suggest an easier way to decide the counterclaim was not compulsory? Read Rule 13(a) carefully. At

what point in the case must a party file a compulsory counterclaim? Does a case involving a default judgment reach that point?

10. *Exceptions to Rule 13(a)*. Not all counterclaims that arise from the same transaction as the original claim are compulsory. Rule 13 contains four explicit exceptions. First, because the rule covers only those claims the defendant has on the date it files its answer, *unmatured* claims are not compulsory. *Dillard v. Security Pacific Brokers, Inc.*, 835 F.2d 607 (5th Cir. 1988). Suppose, for example, Tenant sues Landlord for failing to provide heat to Tenant's apartment building. If Tenant had already withheld rent payments, many courts would treat Landlord's claim for the rent as a compulsory counterclaim in Tenant's suit. However, Landlord cannot sue for any rent payments that are not yet due. What if Tenant continues to fail to pay rent while its suit is pending? Rule 13(e) admittedly allows Landlord to ask the court for permission to supplement its answer to add the counterclaim. However, because the claim is not matured on the day the answer was filed, Landlord is not *required* to add the counterclaim by amendment.

The second exception involves situations in which the counterclaim cannot be adjudicated without joining unavailable third parties. In certain cases, especially those involving multiple claimants to a will, a piece of property, or a fund, the rules require that certain parties be joined. Compulsory joinder is covered in Chapter 8 pt. C.

Third, a claim is not a compulsory counterclaim if it is already pending before a court when the original complaint is filed. For example, suppose X and Y both claim the other breached a contract. X sues first, in a jurisdiction that does not have a compulsory counterclaim rule. If Y then sues X for breach of contract in federal court, X does not have to counterclaim for breach because his claim is already being heard by another court.

Fourth, counterclaims are not compulsory in cases where the court acquires jurisdiction by seizing property. This exception will make more sense once you discuss *in rem* jurisdiction in Chapter 3.

11. Courts have also recognized exceptions to the compulsory counterclaim rule that are not set out in Rule 13(a) itself. Several have held that tort claims between spouses are not compulsory counterclaims in a divorce proceeding. *See, e.g., Simmons v. Simmons*, 773 P.2d 602 (Colo. App. 1988); *Walther v. Walther*, 709 P.2d 387 (Utah 1985); and *Windauer v. O'Connor*, 485 P.2d 1157 (Ariz. 1971). In addition to divorce cases, see *Local Union No. 11, IBEW v. G.P. Thompson Electric, Inc.*, 363 F.2d 181 (9th Cir. 1966) (a party that chooses to submit a claim arising under a collective bargaining agreement to arbitration instead of a court does not lose the claim, because of the federal policy encouraging arbitration) and *Southern Construction v. Pickard*, 371 U.S. 57, 83 S.Ct. 108, 9 L.Ed.2d 31 (1962) (where a party is sued in two related cases, and has a claim that arises out of the same transaction as *both* complaints, it can elect to bring its counterclaim in either the first or second suit). To what extent should a court have the

B. ADDITIONAL PLAINTIFFS AND DEFENDANTS

INTRODUCTORY PROBLEM

As you may have noticed already, law school can be quite competitive. Some students will try any technique (other than simply studying, that is) to gain an advantage over their colleagues. In recent years, a number of more competitive law students have even experimented with mind-altering drugs. But these are not the same sorts of drugs that were used in the 1960s and 1970s. Instead, they are over-the-counter medications that are advertised as effective in improving one's memory or analytical skills. In some cases, the drugs cause slight improvement in performance. In other cases, however, students who take the drugs suffer serious detriment.

Five students, who attend five different law schools, bring three separate cases relating to these new performance drugs. The first is a claim by Alice and Brian against Xacto, Inc., the manufacturer of a drug called STEELTRAP. Xacto's ads claim that STEELTRAP will cause significant improvements in retention. Alice and Brian both took the drug for an entire semester as directed, but their memories did not improve at all. Alice and Brian therefore attempt to join as plaintiffs to sue Xacto. Their complaint alleges both breach of warranty and negligence in the manufacturing process for the drug. The pills that Alice took were produced in an Xacto factory in her state, while those that Brian took were produced in a different Xacto facility.

In the second case, Claire sues both Xacto and Yin/Yang Co. Claire bought one bottle of a drug that was touted as effective in improving logical skills. In truth, the drug induced a bout of sheer irrationality during the middle of a Civil Procedure class, causing Claire serious emotional distress. Because she is frugal, Claire did not buy the name-brand drug, but instead purchased the generic equivalent from her local pharmacy. This generic equivalent was produced by either Xacto or Yin/Yang. However, as Claire is not sure which company produced the bottle she took, she plays it safe and decides to sue both manufacturers. Xacto and Yin/Yang object to their joinder as defendants.

The third case is brought by David and Eunice against Xacto and Yin/Yang. David took STEELTRAP, which is produced by Xacto. Eunice took a chemically identical drug called PACHYDERM, produced by Yin/Yang. David and Eunice suffered serious side effects from the drugs they took. Unlike Alice and Brian, however, David and Eunice claim that the problems stem from chemical makeup of the drug itself, not the manufacturing process. They therefore join to bring products liability claims against the respective manufacturers. David alleges a claim only against Xacto; Eunice only against Yin/Yang. Both defendants challenge joinder.

Governing Law: Federal Rule of Civil Procedure 20.

Federal Rule 20 lists three separate criteria that must be satisfied in order to bring a case involving multiple plaintiffs and/or defendants. Although these criteria may overlap to some extent, each deals with a distinct concern.

The first criterion, that the right to recover (in the case of multiple plaintiffs) or the liability (in the case of multiple defendants) be *joint, several, or in the alternative*, may at first glance seem the most complex. Other courses, especially the basic Torts course, discuss the precise meanings of these terms. For our purposes at this point, however, it is enough to note that taken together, joint, several, and in the alternative comprise *all* the possible ways in which liability for a single injury can be imposed or relief granted. Because Rule 20 requires that only one of these be present, this part of the test rarely presents a problem. However, you should always be prepared to identify which of the three is satisfied in a particular case.

Turning to the third part of the test, all claims by or against the joined parties must share a *common question of law or fact*. This criterion illustrates the underlying purpose of Rule 20, which is to encourage judicial efficiency by reducing the extent to which the same issue is litigated in separate lawsuits. Later we will explore the difference between a question of "law" and "fact." The issue of whether a question is one of law or fact—or a "mixed" question involving both—has a number of important consequences; for example, as discussed in Chapter 12 it determines whether the judge or jury will decide the question. But the difference is not that important for purposes of Rule 20. As long as claims by or against joined parties share a common question of law *or* fact, joinder is proper.

It is the second element of the test, the requirement that the claims arise out of the *same transaction, occurrence, or series of transactions or occurrences*, that ordinarily proves the most difficult to satisfy. This language is very similar to what you just encountered in Rule 13(a), dealing with compulsory counterclaims. You will also see that some of the other rules discussed in this Chapter rely on the same concept.

LIBERTY MEDIA HOLDINGS, LLC v. BITTORRENT SWARM
277 F.R.D. 672 (S.D. Fla. 2011)

MICHAEL MOORE, DISTRICT JUDGE.

This cause came before the Court upon a *sua sponte* examination of the record. . . .

I. BACKGROUND

Plaintiff Liberty Media Holdings, LLC is the registered owner of the copyright to the motion picture, "Corbin Fisher Amateur College Men Down on the Farm" ("Motion Picture"). On May 3, 2011, Plaintiff filed a Complaint against John Does 1–38 for allegedly infringing Plaintiff's exclusive rights in the Motion Picture. According to Plaintiff, Defendants were all users of "BitTorrent," a "peer-to-peer file sharing protocol used for distributing and sharing data on the Internet."

Unlike traditional peer-to-peer ("P2P") networks that require a user to download a file from a single source, the BitTorrent protocol decentralizes distribution of a file by allowing users to join a "swarm" of hosts to download and upload from each other simultaneously. The process begins with one user, commonly referred to as a "seed," who makes the file available. The seed then creates a "torrent" file. . . . Other users, referred to as "peers," then download the torrent file, which in turn, allows them to identify and download from other peers who possess portions of the file described by the torrent. As each peer downloads a new piece of the file the peer becomes a source of that piece to other peers. Once a peer has accumulated enough individual pieces of the file, software allows the peer to reassemble the aggregate file.

. . . This Court now takes up the issue of whether Defendants have been properly joined.

II. STANDARD OF REVIEW

"On motion or on its own, the court may at any time, on just terms, add or drop a party. The court may also sever any claim against a party." Fed.R.Civ.P. 21. Federal Rule of Civil Procedure 20(a)(2) provides, in relevant part:

> (2) Defendants.
>
> Persons . . . may be joined in one action as defendants if:
>
> > (A) any right to relief is asserted against them jointly, severally, or in the alternative with respect to or arising out of the same transaction, occurrence, or series of transactions or occurrences; and
> >
> > (B) any question of law or fact common to all defendants will arise in the action.

"[T]he central purpose of Rule 20 is to promote trial convenience and expedite the resolution of disputes, thereby eliminating unnecessary lawsuits." *Alexander v. Fulton Cnty., Ga.*, 207 F.3d 1303, 1323 (11th Cir.2000). "Under the Rules, the impulse is toward entertaining the broadest possible scope of action consistent with fairness to the parties; joinder of claims, parties and remedies is strongly encouraged." *United Mine Workers v. Gibbs*, 383 U.S. 715, 724, 86 S.Ct. 1130, 16 L.Ed.2d 218

(1966). "The Federal Rules, however, also recognize countervailing considerations to judicial economy." *Alexander*, 207 F.3d at 1324. . . .

III. ANALYSIS

A. Joinder

Numerous courts have found that alleged copyright infringement through the use of P2P networks is insufficient to sustain permissive joinder. See *Hard Drive Prods., Inc. v. Does 1–188*, 809 F.Supp.2d 1150, 1156–59 (N.D.Cal. Aug. 23, 2011) (analyzing pre-BitTorrent P2P case law). Courts, however, have struggled to uniformly apply this case law to actions involving the use of BitTorrent technology. Consequently, courts have split as to whether joinder under Rule 20 is appropriate in actions alleging copyright infringement against a BitTorrent swarm.

In *Hard Drive Prods., Inc.*, the court analyzed whether joinder of 188 defendants alleged to be members of the same BitTorrent swarm was appropriate. In support of the court's decision finding misjoinder, the court stated:

> Does 1–188 did not participate in the same transaction or occurrence, or the same series of transactions or occurrences. Under the BitTorrent Protocol, it is not necessary that each of the Does 1–188 participated in or contributed to the downloading of each other's copies of the work at issue—or even participated in or contributed to the downloading by any of the Does 1–188. Any "pieces" of the work copied or uploaded by any individual Doe may have gone to any other Doe or to any of the potentially thousands who participated in a given swarm. The bare fact that a Doe clicked on a command to participate in the BitTorrent Protocol does not mean that they were part of the downloading by unknown hundreds or thousands of individuals across the country or across the world.

Id. at 1163. The court cited an exhibit submitted by the plaintiff that detailed the defendants' BitTorrent activity. The activity of the defendants occurred on "different days and times over a two-week period," and according to the court, this supported the court's finding that though the defendants may have participated in the same swarm, there was "no evidence to suggest that each of the [defendants] 'acted in concert' with all of the others." *Id.*

In the instant case, Plaintiff has voluntarily dismissed all but eighteen Defendants alleged to have used BitTorrent to infringe Plaintiff's copyright in the Motion Picture. Plaintiff provides information regarding BitTorrent usage and activity for the Defendants. A close examination of Defendants' activity reveals that all remaining Defendants used BitTorrent on different days and at different times over a two-month period. Even if Defendants did use BitTorrent at the same time, however, due to the decentralized operation of BitTorrent, this fact alone would not imply that Defendants "participated in or contributed to the downloading of each other's copies of the work at issue." *Id.* Merely participating in a BitTorrent swarm does not equate to participating in the same "transaction, occurrence, or series of transactions or occurrences." Fed.R.Civ.P. 21; see *LaFace Records, LLC v. Does 1–38*, 2008 WL 544992, at *7 (E.D.N.C. Feb. 27, 2008) ("[M]erely committing the same type of violation in the same way does not link defendants together for purposes of joinder."). As a result, this Court concludes that joinder of Defendants in this action does not satisfy Rule 20(a).

B. Severance

Federal Rules of Civil Procedure 20(a)(2) provides that "[m]isjoinder of parties is not a ground for dismissing an action. On motion or on its own, the court may at any time, on just terms, add or drop a party. The court may also sever any claim against a party." . . .

This Court finds it appropriate to exercise its discretion to sever and dismiss all but Defendant John Doe 1, identified by the Internet Protocol address 68.204.43.200, from the current action. Even if joinder were appropriate, severance is necessary to avoid causing prejudice and unfairness to Defendants, and to expedite and economize the litigation. . . . Moreover, "permitting joinder would force the Court to address the unique defenses that are likely to be advanced by each individual Defendant, creating scores of mini-trials involving different evidence and testimony." *Hard Drive Prods., Inc.*, 2011 WL 3740473, at *14. Finally, permissive joinder of Defendants would likely prejudice Defendants due to the numerous logistical burdens that would arise. See *id.* ("[E]ach defendant must serve each other with all pleadings—a significant burden when, as here, many of the defendants will be appearing *pro se* and may not be e-filers. Each defendant would have the right to be at each other defendant's deposition—creating a thoroughly unmanageable situation. The courtroom proceedings would be unworkable—with each of the [Defendants] having the opportunity to be present and address the court at each case management conference or other event. Finally, each defendant's defense would, in effect, require a mini-trial.").

IV. CONCLUSION

For the foregoing reasons, it is ORDERED AND ADJUDGED that all Defendants, with the exception of Defendant John Doe 1, identified by the Internet Protocol address 68.204.43.200, are SEVERED from the current matter.

NOTES AND QUESTIONS

1. The court indicates Rule 20 would have been satisfied if defendants had acted in concert or conspired among themselves. Why would that additional fact matter? For two other cases discussing this concept, compare *Howard Motor Co. v. Swint*, 448 S.E.2d 713 (Ga. App. 1994) (employees of a company alleging sexual harassment by a single individual could not join) with *M.K. v. Tenet*, 216 F.R.D. 133 (D.D.C. 2002) (former employees of CIA could join to sue director and others for constitutional violations).

2. Like Rule 13(a) in the prior section, Rule 20(a) uses the "same transaction or occurrence" test. Most courts interpret the rules the same way, using something akin to the three alternative tests discussed in *Nasalok*. But *should* courts interpret the phrase "same transaction or occurrence" the same way under Rules 13 and 20? After all, the consequences of failing to meet the two rules are quite different. Should a court therefore be more hesitant to conclude that two claims arise from the same transaction under Rule 13, in order to avoid dismissal of possibly meritorious claims on technical procedural grounds? But does it make sense that the same words could have different meanings in the same set of rules?

3. One possible difference between Rules 13 and 20 is that the latter refers not only to the same transaction or occurrence, but also to a *series* of transactions or occurrences. Although this language seems to be broader, in practice courts do not interpret Rule 20 any more broadly than other permissive joinder rules that use the "same transaction" test. 4 Coquilette, Joseph, Schreiber, Solovy, Vairo & Freer, Moore's Federal Practice 20.05[3] at 20–34 (3d ed. 2010).

4. The discussion to this point has focused on multiple plaintiffs *or* multiple defendants. Does Rule 20(a) also allow a situation like that posed in the third case in the Introductory Problem, where multiple plaintiffs combine to join multiple defendants? The answer is a qualified "yes." The key limitation is that the plaintiffs must either all allege a similar claim against all defendants, or demonstrate some sort of link among the defendants that affects plaintiffs in the same way.

To illustrate, consider *Turpeau v. Fidelity Financial Services, Inc.*, 936 F.Supp. 975 (N.D. Ga. 1996). Seven plaintiffs sued eleven defendants, alleging that defendants—automobile lenders and life insurance companies—wrongfully sold "credit life" insurance policies. No single plaintiff had a claim against all defendants. The court held joinder of the plaintiffs and defendants was improper:

> In the instant case, each credit transaction at issue was made by different Plaintiffs with different Defendants. The court, therefore, is persuaded that the transactions are not sufficiently related so as to permit joinder under Rule 20(a). Plaintiffs, however, urge this court to embrace the statement in *Mosley v. General Motors Corp.*, 497 F.2d 1330, 1333 (8th Cir.1974), that joinder is permitted under Rule 20 if the transactions are "reasonably related." In *Mosley*,

however, each plaintiff was asserting a discrimination claim against General Motors and the union for a company-wide policy of discrimination. Each plaintiff, therefore, was allegedly injured by the same actors which is distinguishable from the instant case where each Defendant has not injured each Plaintiff.

... [Generally,] each named plaintiff must have a colorable claim against each defendant.... *Thillens, Inc. v. Community Currency Exch. Assoc. of Ill., Inc.*, 97 F.R.D. 668, 675 (N.D.Ill.1983). The notable exceptions to this rule are cases involving conspiracy, which is not alleged in the instant case, and "juridical links." A juridical link has been defined as a "legal relationship" which sufficiently relates all the defendants so that a single action is preferable. *Thillens*, 97 F.R.D. at 676. Juridical links are most often found in cases involving a defendant class whose members are "officials of a single state [who] are charged with enforcing or uniformly acting in accordance with a state statute, or common rule or practice of a state-wide application, which is alleged to be unconstitutional." *Mudd v. Busse*, 68 F.R.D. 522, 527–28 (N.D.Ind.1975), aff'd, 582 F.2d 1283 (7th Cir.1978), *cert. denied*, 439 U.S. 1078, 99 S.Ct. 858, 59 L.Ed.2d 47 (1979). While violations of a single statute are at issue in the instant case, Defendants are not state officials. Accordingly, this court must find that there is no sufficient juridical link that would permit the maintenance of this action against the named Defendants.

936 F.Supp. at 978–79. *See also Graziose v. American Home Prods. Corp.*, 202 F.R.D. 638 (D. Nev. 2001).

5. Although Rule 20(a) may allow multiple parties to be joined, it does not guarantee that all claims thus joined will be tried as a single unit. Rule 42(b) gives a judge considerable discretion to dissect a case into convenient trial units, and to conduct a separate trial for each unit. Some of the reasons the Rule gives for separate trials—"[f]or convenience" and "to expedite and economize"—are obvious. After all, litigation does not enjoy unlimited economies of scale. A case that involves multiple parties can be both cumbersome and confusing, especially when a jury is involved.

On the other hand, Rule 42(b) also allows severance of claims or parties to avoid "prejudice." How might a party be prejudiced by having claims by or against it heard at the same time as other claims?

6. Rule 42(a) allows a judge to consolidate separate cases for a single trial. The standard for consolidation is much easier to satisfy than Rule 20. Does this offer a back-door way around Rule 20? Can a party achieve joinder of a case that does not satisfy Rule 20 by the simple expedient of filing separate cases and consolidating them? Practically speaking, what is the crucial difference between this option and Rule 20(a)?

7. Even when multiple claims meet the standards of Rule 20, other factors may cause a court to deny joinder. For example, in *Cincinnati Ins. Co.*

v. Reybitz, 421 S.E.2d 767 (Ga. App. 1992), the court refused to allow a plaintiff, who was claiming that he had been struck by a large sports utility vehicle while riding his bicycle, to sue both the driver of the vehicle and the driver's insurance company in the same lawsuit. In most states, a party is precluded from introducing evidence that the defendant has insurance coverage (do you see why?). The court in *Cincinnati Insurance* held that allowing the plaintiff to name the insurance company as a second defendant would effectively evade this strict rule excluding evidence of insurance coverage.

8. *Rule 13(h)*. P and D are involved in an automobile accident. P works for X, and was running an errand for X when the accident happened. P sues D for her injuries. If D also suffered injuries, his claim against P is a compulsory counterclaim. But is there any way D may also file a claim against X in the same case? Federal Rule 13(h) provides a means to do so. Under that rule, a party who files a counterclaim or cross-claim may join additional parties to that claim if the party could have joined both the existing party and the new party as co-defendants under Rule 20. In our example, D could have sued both P and X for his injuries, as joinder of P and X would satisfy Rule 20. However, P filed her lawsuit first. Under these circumstances, it makes sense to allow D to add X as an additional party to the case. The resulting case is the same as the suit that would have occurred had D filed first, suing P and X as codefendants.

Of course, X must formally be made a party to the case. When a plaintiff sues a defendant, he must serve her with the complaint and other court papers. A party joined under Rule 13(h) will likewise be served with a copy of the claim against it. In addition, he receives copies of the other pleadings filed in the case. X may file counterclaims and cross-claims of his own against D and P; possibly resulting in the addition of still other parties under Rule 13(h) or other joinder rules.

C. CROSS-CLAIMS

◆ INTRODUCTORY PROBLEM

Attorney has represented Client in numerous legal matters during the last ten years. One day, the two decide to meet at 7:00 a.m. at Attorney's office to discuss a new matter. While walking down the hallway in Attorney's office building, both slip and fall, suffering serious injuries. An investigation reveals that Janitor, an independent maintenance contractor, had that morning experimented with a new and very slippery silicone-based floor wax. Attorney and Client therefore join to sue Janitor and Sili Co., the company that manufactured the wax. They allege negligence against both defendants.

Janitor files a cross-claim against Sili Co. Several weeks before the accident, Sili Co. approached Janitor to try to persuade him to try out the new silicone wax. Although initially reluctant, Janitor eventually agreed to use the product. However, Janitor insisted that the parties sign a contract in which Sili Co. agreed to indemnify and hold harmless Janitor for any losses Janitor might suffer due to using the wax. Janitor's cross-claim seeks indemnity under this contract.

Sili Co. then files a permissive counterclaim against Client. Eleven months prior to the accident, Client had written a scathing newspaper article detailing Sili Co.'s use of animal testing for one of its other products, a silicone-based hair spray. Because of this article, the market for the product disappeared, causing Sili Co. to suffer significant losses. Sili Co.'s counterclaim seeks recovery for these losses under a theory of defamation.

After being served with the counterclaim, Client files a legal malpractice cross-claim against Attorney. Client had vetted the newspaper article with Attorney before submitting it for publication. Attorney had assured Client that the article was not defamatory. In the cross-claim, Client seeks reimbursement for any damages she must pay Sili Co.

Attorney and Sili Co. move to dismiss the cross-claims filed against them, arguing that they are not proper under the procedural rules governing cross-claims. How should the court rule on these motions?

Governing Law: Federal Rule of Civil Procedure 13(g).

In addition to mastering the rules, the newcomer to joinder must also deal with a technical and sometimes arcane terminology. We have already discussed "counterclaims," which are governed by Rule 13(a) and (b). Rule 13(g) also allows parties to file "cross-claims." What is the difference between a counterclaim and a cross-claim? A careful review of Rule 13 reveals that cross-claims are filed against a "coparty," whereas counterclaims are filed against an "opposing party." However, these terms are nowhere defined in the rules.

Courts themselves often confuse the terminology. There are a number of cases in which courts mislabel a counterclaim as a "cross-claim" or "countersuit." Usually the mistake does not affect the outcome of the case. However, given that counterclaims, unlike cross-claims, can be compulsory, it is important to exercise care in applying the proper label.

RAINBOW MANAGEMENT GROUP, LTD. V. ATLANTIS SUBMARINES HAWAII, L.P.
158 F.R.D. 656 (D. Haw. 1994)

HAROLD M. FONG, DISTRICT JUDGE.

[Atlantis conducted submarine tours off Waikiki Beach. A separate company, Rainbow Management Group ["RMG"] ferried passengers from the shore to the submarine. On January 27, 1992, RMG's vessel, the Elua, collided with the Boston Whaler, a ship owned by Haydu. The Boston

Whaler was destroyed, and several of its passengers injured. The Elua was also damaged in the collision. A Boston Whaler passenger, George Berry, sued RMG and Atlantis [the "Berry case"]. Atlantis filed a cross-claim against RMG, both for indemnity and for breach of contract. The Berry case was eventually resolved.

RMG then filed the instant action against Atlantis and Haydu, seeking compensation for the damage to the Elua.]

Atlantis argues that RMG's claims are compulsory counterclaims, barred by Fed. R. Civ. P. 13(a) because RMG failed to assert them in the Berry case.... Atlantis argues that, after it filed its initial cross-claim against RMG, RMG became an "opposing party" within the meaning of Rule 13(a), and thereafter was required to plead any claims against Atlantis that arose out of the same transaction or occurrence as the initial cross-claims.

In response, RMG argues that its Elua claim is not a compulsory counterclaim, but is instead a permissive cross-claim pursuant to Fed. R. Civ. P. 13(g). Rule 13(g) provides in pertinent part:

> **Cross-Claim Against a Co-Party.** A pleading may state as a cross-claim any claim by one party against a coparty arising out of the transaction or occurrence that is the subject matter either of the original action or of a counterclaim therein....

RMG argues that Atlantis was a co-party in the Berry case, not an opposing party. Thus, RMG could have asserted its Elua claim in the Berry case, but it was not required to do so.

This issue appears to be an open question in the Ninth Circuit, and the case law from other circuits is limited and contradictory. See, e.g., *U.S. v. Confederate Acres Sanitary Sewage & Drainage Sys.*, 935 F.2d 796, 799 (6th Cir. 1991) ("cross-claims against co-defendants are permissive"); *Earle M. Jorgenson Co. v. T.I. United States, Ltd.*, 133 F.R.D. 472, 474 (E.D.Penn. 1991) ("Once a cross-claim has been pleaded, the cross-claimant becomes an opposing party, and 'the party against whom the cross-claim is asserted must plead as a counterclaim any right to relief that party has against the cross-claimant that arise from the same transaction or occurrence.'" (internal citations omitted))

Professor James W. Moore addresses this problem in his treatise, and concludes that co-parties become opposing parties within the meaning of Rule 13(a) after one party pleads a crossclaim against the other.

The Supreme Courts of Kansas and Alaska have also adopted this approach. See *Miller v. LHKM*, 751 P.2d 1356 (Alaska 1988); *Mohr v. State Bank of Stanley*, 241 Kan. 42, 734 P.2d 1071 (Kansas 1987). Furthermore, this approach is consistent with the goal of judicial economy and reducing unnecessary litigation, because it encourages parties to plead all claims arising out of a single incident and to resolve such claims in a single lawsuit.

The court finds Professor Moore's approach to this issue to be persuasive, and, accordingly, adopts the following rule: Co-parties become opposing parties within the meaning of Fed. R. Civ. P. 13(a) after one such party pleads an initial cross-claim against the other. The court holds, however, that this rule should be limited to situations in which the initial cross-claim includes a substantive claim (as opposed to merely a claim for contribution and indemnity). The reason for this modification is that an unlimited rule may actually increase the amount or complexity of litigation. . . .

In the instant case, Atlantis' initial cross-claim included a claim for contribution and indemnity, as well as an additional substantive claim for breach of contract. RMG was therefore on notice that it would have to defend against claims other than its own original claim. Accordingly, under the rule adopted today, the court GRANTS Atlantis' motion for summary judgment. . . .

NOTES AND QUESTIONS

1. Rule 13(g) states that a party "may" bring a cross-claim. Compare Rule 13(a), which requires a party to bring certain counterclaims. Given the clear language, how can the court in *Rainbow* conclude that a party was required to bring a cross-claim in the earlier action? Is the court, like others discussed in the introductory notes to this section, confusing counterclaims and cross-claims, or is something more involved?

2. Parties can be treated as opposing parties even when neither has filed a claim against the other. In *Kolb v. Scherer Bros. Financial Services Co.*, 6 F.3d 542 (8th Cir. 1993), a subcontractor, seeking payment for work it had performed, began foreclosure proceedings on its mechanics lien. (Under the law of most states, anyone who performs work to improve real property has a lien on that property in the amount that the owner agreed to pay for the work. That lien may be foreclosed like a mortgage.) The subcontractor named as defendants all other lienholders, including Kolb and Scherer. Kolb and Scherer filed answers in that case. Once that case was complete, Kolb then commenced a new action challenging Scherer's liens on the property. Although Kolb and Scherer were both defendants in the first case, the court held that Kolb's new action was barred because he failed to bring his claims as cross-claims in the first action:

> Although all parties in a mechanic's lien action, other than the one who originally files the complaint, are designated as codefendants [under Minnesota law], it would be pure fiction to conclude that no adversity in fact exists between the parties merely because they are all designated as defendants. . . . Minnesota law is unambiguous. Any party who files an answer in a mechanic's lien action, though

nominally a defendant, may actually function as a plaintiff with regard to other named defendants.

Because Kolb and Scherer were adverse, the court held that Rule 13(a) required him to bring the claim in the first case.

3. Perhaps the best way to keep track of claims in complicated cases is always to remain focused on exactly who is claiming what against whom. Labels are important only insofar as they help you determine what rule to apply when considering if the claim is properly before the court. Once the claim is part of the suit, the label is no longer relevant. A tort claim, for example, will be resolved much the same way regardless of whether it is filed as an original claim, counterclaim, or cross-claim.

D. ADDITIONAL CLAIMS BY EXISTING PARTIES

INTRODUCTORY PROBLEM

The Springfield Dome is the newest landmark in the City of Springfield. The Dome is a modern marvel, an inflatable dome stadium equipped with the latest in technology and creature comforts. The City hired Contractor to build the dome. However, because inflatable domes are tricky to build, Contractor subcontracted the roof work to Subcontractor.

Disaster struck when Springfield residents packed the Dome on opening day. The City had arranged for a fireworks display to inaugurate the new stadium. One of the fireworks pierced the roof, causing it to collapse on the crowd below.

The City sues Contractor and Subcontractor for $1,000,000 in damages, based on the harm caused by the fallen roof. City also includes two additional claims in the complaint. First, two years ago City hired Contractor to perform minor improvements to City Hall. Because the work was performed in shoddy fashion, City had to have another company repair the problem. City therefore includes a claim for $50,000 to cover the costs of repair.

Second, City files a claim against Subcontractor for $10,000 in unpaid city property taxes on Subcontractor's office building.

May City include these two additional claims in the case?

Governing Rule: Federal Rule 18(a).

The theme of this Chapter thus far has been determining what claims a party to a lawsuit may bring against the other parties. We have assumed all along that each claimant has only one claim against a given party. In many cases, however, there are multiple claims. For example, a plaintiff may have been injured on more than one occasion by a given defendant, resulting in several separate claims. Even where there has been but a single injury, the law may allow recovery under more than one theory. As just one example, a business that discovers that one of its competitors has been engaging in false advertising may be entitled to recover under a federal statute,[1] state statutes,[2] and the common law of unfair competition. Finally, you will see in Chapter 6 that the Rules allow a pleader to plead inconsistent theories of recovery, such as, "Defendant breached a contract; however if this court should find there was no contract, Defendant committed an intentional tort."

In all of these situations, a plaintiff might prefer to bring its claims in a single action. After all, litigation is not free. Parties in the United States are ordinarily required to pay their own attorneys. One suit will generally be cheaper than several. On the other hand, allowing multiple claims to be litigated together can confuse the jury, especially when the claims involve similar but unrelated transactions or inconsistent legal theories.

McCoy v. Like
511 N.E.2d 501 (Ind. App. 1987)

Ratliff, Chief Judge.

The facts as set forth in the plaintiffs' amended complaint reveal that Martha McCoy died in a nursing home at the age of seventy-nine (79) in Knox County on July 11, 1985. The following day, her will, dated February 16, 1984, was probated in the Knox Circuit Court. Dr. Jerry Like was appointed personal representative of the estate pursuant to the terms of the will. Dr. Like exercised Martha McCoy's power of attorney from November 17, 1983 until her death. Also on November 17, 1983, Martha, as seller, entered into a contract for the conditional sale of over 120 acres of real estate with Dr. Like and his wife, Georgialee. Martha McCoy was Georgialee's aunt. Less than one month later, the same parties amended the agreement by lowering substantially the purchase price. Dr. Like and his wife never made any payments to Martha on the contract. . . .

William McCoy, George McCoy, Mildred Robison, and Betty Hayes (hereinafter referred to as the plaintiffs), were Martha McCoy's nephews and nieces who were legatees under the 1984 will. They filed a complaint to contest the will on several grounds, including fraud and undue influence. All other heirs and beneficiaries were named as defendants as well as Dr. Like in his capacity as Martha's personal representative. . . .

After taking Dr. Like's deposition, the plaintiffs filed an amended complaint which was served upon all of the defendants, and added as a defendant Dr. Like as an individual. The amended complaint added several claims to the will contest. In Count I, the original will contest

---

[1] Lanham Act § 43(a), 15 U.S.C. § 1125(a).
[2] See, e.g., the Uniform Deceptive Trade Practices Act.

allegations were restated and a claim was made against Dr. Like for his exertion of undue influence and fraud in the will's execution. Count II sought to set aside the land contract because of Dr. Like's undue influence and fraud and to impose a constructive trust. Finally, Count III alleged Dr. Like's failure to act during Martha McCoy's lifetime in her best interests and other alleged acts of misconduct and breaches of his fiduciary duty. The amended complaint requested compensatory and punitive damages against Dr. Like individually. . . .

The defendants argue that a will contest is not subject to the rules of joinder of claims. They rely upon very old cases. [*Summers v. Copeland*, 125 Ind. 466 (1890)] is cited for the proposition that joinder of claims is improper for will contests. . . . However, *Summers* is predicated upon the civil code predating our current Trial Rules which were enacted into law on January 1, 1970. Trial Rule 18(A) speaks in very broad terms; it does not delineate any exceptions. "An era of past Indiana procedural law will be wiped out by this rule which permits unlimited joinder of claims. . . ." 2 W. Harvey, Indiana Practice 185 (2d ed. 1987), quoting from the Civil Code Study Commission Comments. See also 6 C. Wright and A. Miller Federal Practice and Procedure § 1582 (1971) (no restriction on claims that may be joined under federal counterpart to T.R. 18(A)). . . . Thus, once a person is properly made a party, joinder of claims is unfettered.

In the present case, Dr. Like as an individual was properly joined as a defendant under T.R. 20(A), thus enabling the plaintiffs to assert against him any and all claims they have under T.R. 18(A) as a matter of right. The holding of *Summers* clearly is no longer applicable under our present, liberal joinder provisions. Therefore, since joinder of Dr. Like in his individual capacity was proper, the trial court erred when it dismissed Dr. Like as an individual defendant and the portions of the amended complaint dealing with claims other than the will contest. If all of the plaintiffs' allegations as set forth in their amended complaint are taken as true, the plaintiffs certainly are entitled to the relief they seek.

It must be noted that T.R. 18(A) joinder is an initial matter. For trial convenience or to avoid confusion or prejudice, the trial court has broad discretion in deciding whether certain claims which have been joined with other claims should be tried together or severed into separate trials. Ind. Rules of Procedure, Trial Rule 42(B). . . . Thus, in the present case, the trial court can exercise its discretion in deciding whether to sever the will contest action from any of the other issues under T.R. 42(B).

Judgment reversed and remanded for further proceedings not inconsistent with this opinion.

NOTES AND QUESTIONS

1. Compare Rule 18 (joinder of claims) with Rule 20 (joinder of plaintiffs and defendants). Why the difference? Is there any possible

Sec. D Additional Claims by Existing Parties 49

justification for a joinder rule as liberal as Rule 18? Will there be any real gains in efficiency from allowing the claim against Dr. Like to be joined, or by allowing joinder in the Introductory Problem? Isn't jury confusion likely?

2. Because Rule 18 places no limits on joinder, there are very few cases containing any meaningful discussion of the Rule. Most cases citing the Rule actually involve a party who cites Rule 18 when joining a new *defendant* to the case, which as we saw in Part C of this Chapter is governed by Rule 20.

3. As the foregoing demonstrates, Rule 18 does not stand alone. Instead, whenever Party X wants to file several claims against Party Y, the court must first determine whether X may bring *any* claims against Y. This initial question is governed not by Rule 18, but by some other rule. If any one of the claims is proper under that other rule, Party X can join *all* remaining claims with it under Rule 18, regardless of any transactional relationship.

To illustrate, suppose X and Y are co-defendants who have been sued by a single plaintiff. X has several claims she wants to file against Y. Because X and Y are co-parties, X must first look to the cross-claim rule, Rule 13(g), and determine whether any of the claims arise from the same transaction as the original case. As long as any of the claims satisfies 13(g), Rule 18 also allows her to bring all of the remaining claims, regardless of whether those additional claims are related. However, if none of the claims are related, X cannot bring any of them in the action.

4. In practice, considerations other than Rule 18 also play a role in determining if claims can be joined. One is the issue of *subject-matter jurisdiction*. Until now we have been assuming that a court can hear every possible claim. However, that is often not the case. Every state assigns certain types of claims to specialized courts. For example, cases involving wills or domestic matters may be confined to Probate or Family courts. Joinder of two claims is proper only if the court has jurisdiction over all of the claims.

Subject matter jurisdiction is a special problem when the case is filed in federal court. Federal courts have a very carefully-defined jurisdiction, which is discussed in Chapter 4.

5. *Claim preclusion.* Most of the joinder rules merely address when a party *may* bring a claim or add a party. With the exception of Rule 13(a) (compulsory counterclaims) and Rule 19 (mandatory joinder of parties, discussed in Chapter 8), the Rules do not require parties to add claims or other parties.

However, the joinder rules do not operate in isolation. Other doctrines in the law of Civil Procedure *require* a party with related claims to join them into a single lawsuit. These rules, commonly referred to as claim preclusion, are dealt with in detail in Chapter 13 pt. C. In essence, claim preclusion prevents a party who fails to bring a claim in one case to assert that claim in a later case. While the actual test varies from state to state, claim preclusion typically requires a plaintiff to join all claims arising out of the same core facts, an analysis that is on its face highly similar to the same transaction or occurrence test used under the Federal Rules.

Consider, for example, a plaintiff with multiple claims arising out of a single event. Federal Rule 18 allows, but does not require, the plaintiff to join the claims. However, because of claim preclusion, the plaintiff should ordinarily bring all the claims in its first case, or risk losing the claims it omits.

PROBLEMS

1. P, who leases a house and yard from D1, is upset when D2 practices "offroading" with her large SUV in P's yard. P learns that after D1 leased the property to P, D1 gave D2 a license to drive on the property. P sues D1 and D2. P's claim against D2 is for trespass. His claim against D1 arises under the lease, in which D1 promised that he would do nothing to disturb P's exclusive possession of the house and yard. D1 and D2 object to joinder, arguing that the trespass and contract claims are too dissimilar in nature and origin to be joined. How should the court rule?

2. P, D1, and D2 are involved in a three-way car accident at an intersection. P sues both D1 and D2. D1 was also injured in the accident. Because it is not clear who is responsible, D1 wants to file claims against P and D2. May D1 file either or both claims in this action? Must D1 file either or both claims?

3. Same facts as Problem 2. Assume the court allows D1 to file his claims against P and D2. Once the case is complete, D2 sues D1 for the injuries that D2 suffered in the accident. D1 argues that the claim should have been brought in the first action. How should the court rule?

4. Same facts as Problem 2. D2 wants to file a counterclaim against P for the injuries that D2 suffered in the accident, arguing that P failed to have the brakes on his car maintained. D2 would also like to join P's mechanic to this counterclaim. May D2 join the mechanic?

5. P1 and P2 were both injured when they were struck by city buses. However, although their injuries were caused by the same driver, that driver was operating different buses, at different locations, on different days. P1 and P2 would like to join as plaintiffs in order to sue the driver and the city for their injuries. May they join as plaintiffs to sue both defendants?

6. D is a caterer who obtains produce from X and Y. After several of its employees contract food poisoning at a luncheon catered by D, P sues D, X, and Y for negligence. Under governing law, D is entitled to be reimbursed by its supplier for any damages that D must pay because of food poisoning. However, D is unsure whether the produce in question came from X or Y. Is there any way D may bring claims against both X and Y in D's case?

SEC. D ADDITIONAL CLAIMS BY EXISTING PARTIES

EXERCISE

Because the federal rules permit litigants much flexibility in bringing claims, it is useful to inquire about whether state rules are equally permissive. For the state a) where you intend to practice after graduation, b) where your law school is located, and/or c) your professor assigns, go to that state's annotated statutes and research the procedural rules by which joinder of parties and claims occurs. Based on your research, print the rules and bring them to class for discussion. In addition, answer the following questions.

1. Identify the minimum requirements for:

   a. Joinder of parties.

   b. Joinder of claims.

2. Identify whether the following are compulsory or merely permissive, as well as whether they must arise from the same transaction as the claim brought by the plaintiff:

   a. Counterclaims

   b. Cross-claims

3. Identify whether additional parties may be added for counterclaims and cross-claims.

CHAPTER 3

PERSONAL JURISDICTION AND VENUE

■ ■ ■

A. EXERCISING JURISDICTION OVER DEFENDANTS

INTRODUCTORY PROBLEM 1

Jaye Bizer was a cruise ship passenger who has brought suit in the U.S. District Court for the Western District of Washington against the DizzyWhiz Cruise Lines for damages sustained in a slip and fall case. The defendant cruise line has filed a motion to dismiss based upon improper personal jurisdiction.

DizzyWhiz Cruise Lines is a Colombian corporation with its principal place of business in Miami, Florida. DizzyWhiz is not registered to do business in the state of Washington. It owns no property in Washington, maintains no office or bank account in Washington, and pays no business taxes in Washington. It has never operated ships which have called at Washington ports. It has no exclusive agent in Washington. DizzyWhiz does, however, advertise its cruises in local Washington newspapers. It also provides brochures to travel agents in Washington, which in turn are distributed to potential customers. DizzyWhiz also holds seminars for travel agents in the State of Washington to inform them about, and encourage them to sell DizzyWhiz cruises. DizzyWhiz pays travel agencies a 10% commission on proceeds from tickets sold for DizzyWhiz cruises.

Jaye Bizer is a Washington resident who purchased her ticket through the Jesse Boyer Travel Agency in Tacoma, Washington, for a seven-day cruise on a DizzyWhiz Cruise Lines ship called the SENECA. She was to embark in Los Angeles, California, sailing from there to Puerto Vallarta, Mexico. The tickets were purchased through the travel agent, who forwarded payment to DizzyWhiz in Miami. The tickets were issued in Florida, then forwarded to Jaye Bizer in Washington.

Ms. Bizer suffered injuries when she slipped on a deck mat while on a guided tour of the ship's galley. The incident occurred in international waters off the coast of Mexico. Ms. Bizer alleges that the fall was due to the negligence of DizzyWhiz and its employees, and she requests damages arising out of her personal injuries. Washington's jurisdictional statute has been construed by the Washington Supreme Court to permit the assertion of jurisdiction to the extent permitted by due process.

You are the judge in this case. Write your opinion granting or denying the defendant's motion to dismiss.

INTRODUCTORY PROBLEM 2

Defendant Wendy Baker is a Tennessee attorney who, in 2011, performed legal services for plaintiff, Mrs. Susan James, in connection with her deceased husband's estate. Mrs. James was at that time a resident of Tennessee. As part of her services, Baker set up and supervised a "discretionary investment account" for Mrs. James in a Tennessee bank.

In 2012, Mrs. James moved to California and Baker handled (in Tennessee) the closing on the sale of Mrs. James's Tennessee home. In 2013, Baker recommended that Mrs. James close the investment account in the Tennessee bank and place the funds instead with a newly established investment firm (also in Tennessee). Baker subsequently recommended the investment of these funds in various real estate investment trusts, and Mrs. James followed these recommendations.

At the end of 2013, Mrs. James became concerned about the steady decline in the value of her investment as indicated by the quarterly reports, and asked Baker to take corrective action. Baker did not do this and, allegedly as a result of Baker's negligent inaction, Mrs. James's funds were substantially dissipated. Baker communicated with Mrs. James by telephone and e-mail on most occasions, but in some instances they exchanged letters between Mrs. James's home in California and Baker's office when it became necessary for her to execute investment contracts.

In 2014, Mrs. James commenced a lawsuit against Baker in a federal court in California, which has a "due process" long-arm statute. Can a California federal court exercise personal jurisdiction over Baker in a lawsuit filed by Mrs. James?

One of the important decisions that you will make in deciding to file a lawsuit on behalf of a client is to determine which court(s) would have the authority to bind the defendant to a judgment after your client prevails at trial. By filing a lawsuit, *your* client has consented to the power of the court to issue binding orders and judgments. But usually the defendant has not consented to being sued in a particular state. (As discussed later in this Chapter, it is possible for a defendant to consent to be sued in a particular court.)

Because the defendant has neither invoked the authority of the court nor consented to be sued in a particular court, your goal is to file the lawsuit in a court that can exercise power over the defendant. If a defendant cannot be served within the state where the lawsuit is filed, the court will be unable to adjudicate the plaintiff's claim unless it obtains *in rem* jurisdiction over the defendant's property.

SEC. A EXERCISING JURISDICTION OVER DEFENDANTS   55

When a court has personal jurisdiction over a defendant, its judgment in the case is valid and is enforceable locally, or in another state by virtue of the Full Faith and Credit Clause of the United States Constitution. Conversely, a judgment from a court lacking personal jurisdiction is invalid and cannot be enforced in the place where the issuing court sits, another part of the same state, or another state. However, if the court has jurisdiction and your client prevails at trial and is awarded damages, you can enforce the judgment for damages locally, elsewhere in the state, and/or in another state by identifying property belonging to the defendant that can be used to satisfy the judgment.

1. JURISDICTION OVER DEFENDANTS: THE EARLY DECISIONS

PENNOYER V. NEFF, 95 U.S. (5 Otto) 714, 24 L.Ed. 565 (1877) is the landmark case in personal jurisdiction. Mitchell, an Oregon attorney, sued Neff in an Oregon state court for failing to pay him for his services. Mitchell served Neff by publishing an advertisement containing information about the lawsuit in an Oregon newspaper for six weeks, and Mitchell did not attach Neff's Oregon property. A nonresident, Neff probably never saw the ad and therefore never knew that he had been sued. As a result, when Neff did not answer Mitchell's complaint or otherwise appear to defend, Mitchell obtained a default judgment against Neff, and was able to have Neff's land in Oregon sold at a sheriff's auction to satisfy the judgment. Pennoyer obtained title to Neff's land at the sale. Neff responded to Pennoyer's claim to the land by suing him in an Oregon federal court to reclaim the land. The trial court in *Neff v. Pennoyer* decided in Neff's favor; Pennoyer appealed to the United States Supreme Court, claiming that the prior sheriff's sale from *Mitchell v. Neff* was valid. Neff claimed that the service by publication was ineffective to give the Oregon state court jurisdiction over him. Justice Field first identified

> two well-established principles of public law respecting the jurisdiction of an independent State over persons and property.... [E]xcept as restrained and limited by that instrument, they possess and exercise the authority of independent States, and the principles of public law to which we have referred are applicable to them. One of these principles is, that every State possesses exclusive jurisdiction and sovereignty over persons and property within its territory.... The other principle of public law referred to follows from the one mentioned; that is, that no State can exercise direct jurisdiction and authority over persons or property without its territory.... And so it is laid down by jurists, as an elementary principle, that the laws of one State have no operation outside of its territory, except so far as is allowed by comity; and that no tribunal

established by it can extend its process beyond that territory so as to subject either persons or property to its decisions.

So the State, through its tribunals, may subject property situated within its limits owned by non-residents to the payment of the demand of its own citizens against them; and the exercise of this jurisdiction in no respect infringes upon the sovereignty of the State where the owners are domiciled. Every State owes protection to its own citizens; and, when non-residents deal with them, it is a legitimate and just exercise of authority to hold and appropriate any property owned by such non-residents to satisfy the claims of its citizens. It is in virtue of the State's jurisdiction over the property of the non-resident situated within its limits that its tribunals can inquire into that non-resident's obligations to its own citizens, and the inquiry can then be carried only to the extent necessary to control the disposition of the property. If the non-residents have no property in the State, there is nothing upon which the tribunals can adjudicate.

Substituted service by publication, or in any other authorized form, may be sufficient to inform parties of the object of proceedings taken where property is once brought under the control of the court by seizure or some equivalent act. The law assumes that property is always in the possession of its owner, in person or by agent; and it proceeds upon the theory that its seizure will inform him, not only that it is taken into the custody of the court, but that he must look to any proceedings authorized by law upon such seizure for its condemnation and sale.... In other words, such service may answer in all actions which are substantially proceedings in rem. But where the entire object of the action is to determine the personal rights and obligations of the defendants, that is, where the suit is merely in personam, constructive service in this form upon a non-resident is ineffectual for any purpose.... Process sent to him out of the State, and process published within it, are equally unavailing in proceedings to establish his personal liability....

The force and effect of judgments rendered against non-residents without personal service of process upon them, or their voluntary appearance, have been the subject of frequent consideration in the courts of the United States and of the several States, as attempts have been made to enforce such judgments in States other than those in which they were rendered, under the provision of the Constitution requiring that "full faith and credit shall be given in each State to the public acts, records, and judicial proceedings of every other State;" and the act of

Congress providing for the mode of authenticating such acts, records, and proceedings. . . .

In the earlier cases, it was supposed that the act gave to all judgments the same effect in other States which they had by law in the State where rendered. But this view was afterwards qualified so as to make the act applicable only when the court rendering the judgment had jurisdiction of the parties and of the subject matter, and not to preclude an inquiry into the jurisdiction of the court in which the judgment was rendered, or the right of the State itself to exercise authority over the person or the subject matter. . . .

"The international law," said the court [in *D'Arcy v. Ketchum*], "as it existed among the States in 1790, was that a judgment rendered in one State, assuming to bind the person of a citizen of another, was void within the foreign State, when the defendant had not been served with process or voluntarily made defence, because neither the legislative jurisdiction nor that of courts of justice had binding force."

And the Court held that the act of Congress did not intend to declare a new rule, or to embrace judicial records of this description. . . .

It follows from the views expressed that the personal judgment recovered in the State court of Oregon against the plaintiff herein, then a non-resident of the State, was without any validity, and did not authorize a sale of the property in controversy.

To prevent any misapplication of the views expressed in this opinion, it is proper to observe that we do not mean to assert, by any thing we have said, that a State may not authorize proceedings to determine the status of one of its citizens towards a non-resident, which would be binding within the State, though made without service of process or personal notice to the non-resident. The jurisdiction which every State possesses to determine the civil status and capacities of all its inhabitants involves authority to prescribe the conditions on which proceedings affecting them may be commenced and carried on within its territory. The State, for example, has absolute right to prescribe the conditions upon which the marriage relation between its own citizens shall be created, and the causes for which it may be dissolved. . . .

Neither do we mean to assert that a State may not require a non-resident entering into a partnership or association within its limits, or making contracts enforceable there, to appoint an agent or representative in the State to receive service of process and notice in legal proceedings instituted with respect to such partnership, association, or contracts, or to designate a place where such service may be made and notice given, and provide, upon their failure, to make such appointment or to designate such place that service may be made upon a public officer designated for that purpose, or in some other prescribed way, and that judgments rendered upon such service may not be binding upon the non-residents both within and without the State. . . .

NOTES AND QUESTIONS

1. With *in personam* jurisdiction, a court has the authority to enter a judgment against a defendant that is personally binding and which can be taken to other parts of the same state or to another state to be enforced. With *in rem* jurisdiction, a court has the power to determine the rights of the parties in specific property within the state's boundary. Using *quasi in rem* jurisdiction enables a court to exercise power over a defendant's property by attachment, and use it to satisfy a plaintiff's personal claim against the defendant. However, *quasi in rem* jurisdiction limits the plaintiff to recovering an amount not exceeding the value of the property.

What did *Pennoyer* hold? Which type of jurisdiction (*in rem*, *in personam*, or *quasi in rem*) was being asserted? Why did the assertion of that jurisdiction not succeed?

After *Pennoyer*, states could exercise personal jurisdiction over any defendant served while present in the state where a claim was filed. Courts could not ordinarily serve nonresident defendants who were outside the forum state, because service would assume the sovereign power of the other states. Any judicial decision without the proper use of "power" was void and unenforceable. *Pennoyer* protected a nonresident defendant from being sued in a state where he could not be served and owned no property.

2. Based on the *Pennoyer* dicta, describe the two exceptions to the general rule that are available to invoke the jurisdiction of the court over the non-present defendant.

3. After *Pennoyer*, what type of service of process is necessary for a personal judgment against a defendant? When, if ever, is constructive service of process permitted? In *Mitchell v. Neff*, what could Mitchell have done to protect the validity of any judgment he obtained?

What is the purpose of notice to the defendant? For example under the Court's "principles of public law" as to an *in personam* judgment, even if Neff had learned about the lawsuit when he was outside Oregon, the Oregon court still would have lacked the power to enter a binding judgment against Neff. By contrast, if Mitchell had seized any property owned by Neff (with notice by publication to Neff) at the commencement of the lawsuit, the seizure itself would have been sufficient, because the property's seizure has the effect of informing the owner about the seizure. Does either of these notice concepts make sense?

4. What practical limitations does the *Pennoyer* principle impose on plaintiffs who want to sue nonresident defendants? What options does a plaintiff have to sue a nonresident defendant?

5. In dicta, the Court referred to the Fourteenth Amendment, but that provision was not in effect until 1868, after the sheriff sold Neff's property. However, the Court left no doubt that the Due Process Clause of the Fourteenth Amendment would be important in future decisions about the exercise of jurisdiction over nonresident defendants.

6. When is a nonresident defendant considered to be within a state? Suppose that a nonresident is on a jet going from California to New York. He has recently been sued in a Kansas state court. Can the Kansas sheriff sitting next to the defendant on the flight validly invoke the jurisdiction of the Kansas court by serving him with the court papers when the jet is flying over Kansas? See *Grace v. MacArthur*, 170 F.Supp. 442 (E.D. Ark. 1959), where the court upheld jurisdiction because it had occurred when the defendant was within the "territorial limits" of the forum state. The court noted that "a time may come ... when commercial aircraft will fly at altitudes so high that it would be unrealistic to consider them as being within the territorial limits" of a particular state. Does the jet's altitude matter under *Pennoyer* if the defendant's presence "within" the state can be determined?

7. For an entertaining discussion about the parties in *Pennoyer*, read Wendy Collins Perdue, "Sin, Scandal, and Substantive Due Process: Personal Jurisdiction and *Pennoyer* Reconsidered," 62 Wash. L. Rev. 479 (1987).

PROBLEMS

Based on your reading of *Pennoyer*, check on your understanding of the scope of its holding by thinking about the following problems.

1. If a Florida resident sues a North Carolina resident in a Florida state court, where does the defendant have to be served?

2. Can the North Carolina defendant be served while traveling through Florida?

3. The North Carolina defendant owns property in Florida. What can the Florida plaintiff do to obtain jurisdiction?

4. What if the defendant voluntarily appears in Florida to contest the merits of the plaintiff's claim?

5. If the Florida plaintiff notifies the defendant by publication and obtains a default judgment, can the Florida judgment be enforced against the defendant in North Carolina?

6. The claim in the Florida lawsuit seeks a divorce, and the defendant is served with court papers in North Carolina. Is the defendant's objection to the location of the notice proper?

7. The claim in the Florida lawsuit seeks a divorce, plus maintenance, custody, and child support. The defendant is served with court papers in North Carolina. Is the defendant's objection to the location of the notice proper?

As interstate travel expanded and as litigation involving corporations from other states increased, legislators decided that it was important to exercise state authority over the nonresident person or entity causing harm to their citizens. "Eventually the pressures of a rapidly growing country attenuated the need to reduce the restrictions placed on amenability by the sovereignty theory in *Pennoyer*, and the law of amenability began its complex evolution." Diane Kaplan, "Paddling Up the Wrong Stream: Why the Stream of Commerce Theory Is Not Part of the Minimum Contacts Doctrine," 55 Baylor L.Rev. 503 (2003). There were numerous assertions of jurisdiction over persons who could not be served while physically in the forum state. The enacted statutes authorized courts to assert personal jurisdiction over nonresident defendants in specified circumstances that were limited in scope.

Fifty years after *Pennoyer v. Neff*, the Court extended the explicit, knowing appointment of an agent within a state for business dealings to the implicit appointment of an agent within the state resulting from a nonresident driving in another state. *Hess v. Pawloski*, 274 U.S. 352, 47 S.Ct. 632, 71 L.Ed. 1091 (1927) upheld a Massachusetts nonresident motorist statute that specifically deemed driving within the state as implied consent to being sued there for any claim arising from that driving. Even though the nonresident driver was unlikely to have been present at the time the lawsuit was filed, at least the driver had been present in the state at the time of the relevant conduct.

The Court stressed that because "[m]otor vehicles are dangerous machines, even when skillfully and carefully operated, ... the use of the highway by the nonresident is the equivalent of the appointment of [an agent] on whom process may be served." Despite the policy reasons for implied consent, the consent is a fiction because the defendant probably does not understand that consent has occurred. The Court also noted the statute provides a plaintiff from the forum state "a convenient method" to enforce his rights, i.e., by suing in a state that he may never have left. Many states retain nonresident motorist statutes, even though additional, broader "long-arm" statutes have supplanted the need for the older legislation. A discussion about long-arm statutes occurs in the next section.

SEC. A   EXERCISING JURISDICTION OVER DEFENDANTS   61

The next case, *International Shoe v. Washington,* also addressed the application of a long-arm statute in a specific factual context. The Court announced a test that still governs whether a state's exercise of jurisdiction over a nonresident is consistent with Fourteenth Amendment due process.

INTERNATIONAL SHOE CO. V. WASHINGTON
326 U.S. 310, 66 S.Ct. 154, 90 L.Ed. 95 (1945)

MR. CHIEF JUSTICE STONE delivered the opinion of the Court.

The questions for decision are (1) whether, within the limitations of the due process clause of the Fourteenth Amendment, appellant, a Delaware corporation, has by its activities in the State of Washington rendered itself amenable to proceedings in the courts of that state to recover unpaid contributions to the state unemployment compensation fund exacted by state statutes, and (2) whether the state [has the power to tax the defendant].

The statutes in question set up a comprehensive scheme of unemployment compensation, the costs of which are defrayed by contributions required to be made by employers to a state unemployment compensation fund. Section 14(c) of the Act, Wash.Rev.Stat. 1941 Supp., § 9998—114c, authorizes respondent Commissioner to issue an order and notice of assessment of delinquent contributions upon prescribed personal service of the notice upon the employer if found within the state, or, if not so found, by mailing the notice to the employer by registered mail at his last known address. . . .

In this case notice of assessment for the years in question was personally served upon a sales solicitor employed by appellant in the State of Washington, and a copy of the notice was mailed by registered mail to appellant at its address in St. Louis, Missouri. Appellant appeared specially before the office of unemployment and moved to set aside the order and notice of assessment. . . .

The motion was heard on evidence and a stipulation of facts by the appeal tribunal which denied the motion and ruled that respondent Commissioner was entitled to recover the unpaid contributions. That action was affirmed by the Commissioner; both the Superior Court and the [Washington] Supreme Court affirmed. Appellant in each of these courts assailed the statute as applied, as a violation of the due process clause of the Fourteenth Amendment, and as imposing a constitutionally prohibited burden on interstate commerce. . . .

Appellant is a Delaware corporation, having its principal place of business in St. Louis, Missouri, and is engaged in the manufacture and sale of shoes and other footwear. It maintains places of business in several states, other than Washington, at which its manufacturing is carried on and from which its merchandise is distributed interstate through several sales units or branches located outside the State of Washington.

Appellant has no office in Washington and makes no contracts either for sale or purchase of merchandise there. It maintains no stock of merchandise in that state and makes there no deliveries of goods in intrastate commerce. During the years from 1937 to 1940, now in question, appellant employed eleven to thirteen salesmen under direct supervision and control of sales managers located in St. Louis. These salesmen resided in Washington; their principal activities were confined to that state; and they were compensated by commissions based upon the amount of their sales. The commissions for each year totaled more than $31,000. Appellant supplies its salesmen with a line of samples, each consisting of one shoe of a pair, which they display to prospective purchasers. On occasion they rent permanent sample rooms, for exhibiting samples, in business buildings, or rent rooms in hotels or business buildings temporarily for that purpose. The cost of such rentals is reimbursed by appellant.

The authority of the salesmen is limited to exhibiting their samples and soliciting orders from prospective buyers, at prices and on terms fixed by appellant. The salesmen transmit the orders to appellant's office in St. Louis for acceptance or rejection, and when accepted the merchandise for filling the orders is shipped f.o.b. from points outside Washington to the purchasers within the state. All the merchandise shipped into Washington is invoiced at the place of shipment from which collections are made. No salesman has authority to enter into contracts or to make collections.

. . .

Appellant . . . insists that its activities within the state were not sufficient to manifest its 'presence' there and that in its absence the state courts were without jurisdiction, that consequently it was a denial of due process for the state to subject appellant to suit. It refers to those cases in which it was said that the mere solicitation of orders for the purchase of goods within a state, to be accepted without the state and filled by shipment of the purchased goods interstate, does not render the corporation seller amenable to suit within the state. . . . And appellant further argues that since it was not present within the state, it is a denial of due process to subject it to taxation or other money exaction. It thus denies the power of the state to lay the tax or to subject appellant to a suit for its collection.

Historically the jurisdiction of courts to render judgment in personam is grounded on their de facto power over the defendant's person. Hence his presence within the territorial jurisdiction of court was prerequisite to its rendition of a judgment personally binding him. *Pennoyer v. Neff*, 95

U.S. 714, 733. But now that the *capias ad respondendum* has given way to personal service of summons or other form of notice, due process requires only that in order to subject a defendant to a judgment in personam, if he be not present within the territory of the forum, he have certain minimum contacts with it such that the maintenance of the suit does not offend 'traditional notions of fair play and substantial justice.' *Milliken v. Meyer*, 311 U.S. 457, 463. See Holmes, J., in *McDonald v. Mabee*, 243 U.S. 90, 91.

... To say that the corporation is so far 'present' there as to satisfy due process requirements, for purposes of taxation or the maintenance of suits against it in the courts of the state, is to beg the question to be decided. For the terms 'present' or 'presence' are used merely to symbolize those activities of the corporation's agent within the state which courts will deem to be sufficient to satisfy the demands of due process. L. Hand, J., in *Hutchinson v. Chase & Gilbert*, 2 Cir., 45 F.2d 139, 141. Those demands may be met by such contacts of the corporation with the state of the forum as make it reasonable, in the context of our federal system of government, to require the corporation to defend the particular suit which is brought there. An 'estimate of the inconveniences' which would result to the corporation from a trial away from its 'home' or principal place of business is relevant in this connection.

"Presence" in the state in this sense has never been doubted when the activities of the corporation there have not only been continuous and systematic, but also give rise to the liabilities sued on, even though no consent to be sued or authorization to an agent to accept service of process has been given. Conversely it has been generally recognized that the casual presence of the corporate agent or even his conduct of single or isolated items of activities in a state in the corporation's behalf are not enough to subject it to suit on causes of action unconnected with the activities there. To require the corporation in such circumstances to defend the suit away from its home or other jurisdiction where it carries on more substantial activities has been thought to lay too great and unreasonable a burden on the corporation to comport with due process. ...

Finally, although the commission of some single or occasional acts of the corporate agent in a state sufficient to impose an obligation or liability on the corporation has not been thought to confer upon the state authority to enforce it, other such acts, because of their nature and quality and the circumstances of their commission, may be deemed sufficient to render the corporation liable to suit.

It is evident that the criteria by which we mark the boundary line between those activities which justify the subjection of a corporation to suit, and those which do not, cannot be simply mechanical or quantitative. The test is not merely, as has sometimes been suggested, whether the activity, which the corporation has seen fit to procure through its agents in another state, is a little more or a little less. Whether due process is satisfied must depend rather upon the quality and nature of the activity in relation to the fair and orderly administration of the laws which it was the purpose of the due process clause to insure. That clause does not contemplate that a state may make binding a judgment in personam against an individual or corporate defendant with which the state has no contacts, ties, or relations.

But to the extent that a corporation exercises the privilege of conducting activities within a state, it enjoys the benefits and protection of the laws of that state. The exercise of that privilege may give rise to obligations; and, so far as those obligations arise out of or are connected with the activities within the state, a procedure which requires the corporation to respond to a suit brought to enforce them can, in most instances, hardly be said to be undue.

Applying these standards, the activities carried on in behalf of appellant in the State of Washington were neither irregular nor casual. They were systematic and continuous throughout the years in question. They resulted in a large volume of interstate business, in the course of which appellant received the benefits and protection of the laws of the state, including the right to resort to the courts for the enforcement of its rights. The obligation which is here sued upon arose out of those very activities. It is evident that these operations establish sufficient contacts or ties with the state of the forum to make it reasonable and just according to our traditional conception of fair play and substantial justice to permit the state to enforce the obligations which appellant has incurred there. . . .

Affirmed.

Mr. Justice Black delivered the following opinion.

. . . I believe that the Federal Constitution leaves to each State, without any "ifs" or "buts", a power to tax and to open the doors of its courts for its citizens to sue corporations whose agents do business in those States. Believing that the Constitution gave the States that power, I think it a judicial deprivation to condition its exercise upon this Court's notion of "fair play", however appealing that term may be. Nor can I stretch the meaning of due process so far as to authorize this Court to deprive a State of the right to afford judicial protection to its citizens on the ground that it would be more "convenient" for the corporation to be sued somewhere else.

There is a strong emotional appeal in the words "fair play", "justice", and "reasonableness." But they were not chosen by those who wrote the original Constitution or the Fourteenth Amendment as a measuring rod for this Court to use in invalidating State or Federal laws passed by elected legislative representatives. No one, not even those who most feared a democratic government, ever formally proposed that courts should be given power to invalidate legislation under any such elastic standards. Express prohibitions against certain types of legislation are found in the Constitution, and under the long settled practice, courts invalidate laws found to conflict with them. This requires interpretation, and interpretation, it is true, may result in extension of the Constitution's purpose. But that is no reason for reading the due process clause so as to restrict a State's power to tax and sue those whose activities affect persons and businesses within the State, provided proper service can be had....

NOTES AND QUESTIONS

1. Near the end of the majority opinion Chief Justice Stone stated:

> Whether due process is satisfied must depend rather upon the quality and nature of the activity in relation to the fair and orderly administration of the laws which it was the purpose of the due process clause to insure. That clause does not contemplate that a state may make binding a judgment in personam against an individual or corporate defendant with which the state has no contacts, ties, or relations.

After *International Shoe*, is *Pennoyer*'s holding about power or presence still sound? Is the minimum contacts standard relevant when a nonresident defendant is served in the forum state? *International Shoe* appears to assume that jurisdiction over a defendant could be based on his physical presence alone:

> [D]ue process requires only that in order to subject a defendant to a judgment in personam, *if he be not present within the territory of the forum*, he have certain minimum contacts with it such that the maintenance of the suit does not offend "traditional notions of fair play and substantial justice." [emphasis added]

Did the Court intend the minimum contacts standard to control jurisdiction over nonresident defendants, regardless of whether they are served inside the forum state?

2. What did the Court hold? Was there an implied consent statute in Washington, providing for service of process on a nonresident, similar to the Massachusetts provision in *Hess*? Pursuant to the statute, how was the defendant served with the papers about the lawsuit?

3. How did International Shoe raise its objection to Washington's assertion of jurisdiction over it? What is meant when the Court states that the defendant appeared "specially"?

4. The Court says that a nonresident defendant must have minimum contacts with a state in order to be required to defend itself in that distant place. What is a "contact"? Does a contact have to be a literal contact between

two vehicles? Does "contact" include doing business within a state? Making solicitation phone calls? Publishing a periodical? Does *any* relationship of a defendant with a state or with persons inside the state satisfy the definition of a contact, or is something more required to constitute a contact relevant to personal jurisdiction?

5. Under the facts, was there anything inconvenient for International Shoe about defending itself in Washington State against Washington's attempt to collect its unemployment compensation fund premiums?

6. What was Justice Black's concern in his dissent? Was his concern legitimate? From a practical perspective, what potential problems accompany a vague legal standard? As general counsel for a corporation doing business in a variety of states, how do you advise your client about anticipating its legal obligations in different locales when the legal standard in each state is vague?

7. One method to limit the places a business can be sued is to include a "forum selection" clause in the contract. The clause constitutes consent by the other party to the contract that any claim against the business based on the contract must be brought only in a federal or state court of a particular state. In *Carnival Cruise Lines v. Shute*, 499 U.S. 585, 111 S.Ct. 1522, 113 L.Ed.2d 622 (1991), the Court presumed that in a maritime case any forum selection clause is valid, even a clause in an adhesion contract (a contract where one party has no bargaining power), if it is reasonably communicated to the claimant. In *Shute*, the forum selection clause was printed on a cruise passenger ticket and required the Washington plaintiff to bring suit in Florida. However, the claimant did not have the opportunity to review the clause until after she had paid for the ticket.

The Court cited several reasons justifying a forum selection clause in travel contexts: because passengers are from many places, in case of a mass disaster the business could be sued in many places; the clause clarifies where any claim should be brought, thereby reducing the time and expense of litigation; and any savings to the business by limiting the courts where it could be sued would result in lower passenger fares.

The *Shute* forum selection clause prescribing Florida as the forum for litigation was not overreaching or unreasonably inconvenient to the Washington resident, because in the absence of fraud the plaintiff "presumably retained the option of rejecting the contract with impunity." Do you agree? Does it matter that many of the cruise line's trips departed from Florida? Does the option of rejecting the contract exist when the ticket is non-refundable? In terms of inconvenience, suppose the clause designates a foreign court system as the "agreed" forum? Do the plaintiff's limited resources to pursue a distant claim under a forum selection clause constitute an unreasonable inconvenience to the claimant?

8. An arbitration clause can be thought of as a special type of forum selection clause: one that selects a process rather than merely a location. Rather than specifying that claims must be brought in court in a particular

location, arbitration clauses specify that parties must have their claims decided by an arbitrator rather than in court. The clause may also include a limitation on the location of the arbitration. Like forum selection clauses, arbitration clauses are enforceable against consumers in the United States. In most other countries, arbitration agreements do not bind consumers.

2. JURISDICTION OVER NONRESIDENT DEFENDANTS

The concept of domicile attempts to locate a person's "one true home." A person always has one—and only one—domicile. Chapter 4 discusses how domicile is determined. Domicile is also relevant to personal jurisdiction. When a defendant's domicile is in the forum state, the state has power to decide all claims of whatever nature against the defendant. An individual who lives in the state or a corporation that is incorporated there is domiciled in that state, giving the state the power to adjudicate claims brought against either the individual or corporation. The rationale for exercising this power is that, because the state provides privileges to its citizens and protects them, the citizens have a reciprocal duty to defend lawsuits brought in the courts where they reside. See *Milliken v. Meyer*, 311 U.S. 457, 61 S.Ct. 339, 85 L.Ed. 278 (1940).

A second method of exercising jurisdiction over an individual or a business defendant occurs when either type of defendant consents to be sued in the courts of the state. As noted earlier, the consent may occur prior to the filing of the lawsuit. In *Hess v. Pawloski*, 274 U.S. 352, 47 S.Ct. 632, 71 L.Ed. 1091 (1927), the Court approved the fiction of implied consent to jurisdiction by a nonresident who consents to being sued in a state where he drives.

Explicit consent also provides authority for a trial court to adjudicate disputes. For example, a contract between business entities or even an airline ticket may include a provision that the parties to the contract consent to a particular state's authority, i.e., a forum selection clause. Another method of consent was mentioned in *Pennoyer*: a person or entity seeking to do business in a state must appoint a local agent to accept service of process.

It is also possible for a defendant to consent to the jurisdiction of a court following the filing of a lawsuit. As discussed later in Chapter 6 pt. C, unless defendant challenges personal jurisdiction, waiver of service of process operates as consent to the jurisdiction of the court where the lawsuit was filed. *See* Federal Rule 4(d)(5); 12(h). Frequently, in divorce cases for example, a defendant will enter his appearance in a case and waive service of process in order to reduce the costs of the litigation.

a. Specific Jurisdiction

Courts use specific jurisdiction to exercise authority over a plaintiff's claim that arises out of or relates to a nonresident defendant's activities within a state. The type of conduct by a defendant that can subject him to the jurisdiction of the court is diverse. For example, the plaintiff's claim may be that the defendant has engaged in a tortious act or some illegal business activity, or improper property ownership. In *International Shoe*, the obligation to pay unemployment compensation taxes arose from the activities of International Shoe Co.'s salesmen in the forum state.

The nature of the analysis for specific jurisdiction cases is twofold. The plaintiff must show that 1) her claim arises from the defendant's conduct, which fits the language of the state's "long-arm" statute, and 2) the exercise of jurisdiction by the court over the nonresident does not offend the Due Process Clause of the Fourteenth Amendment.

The Due Process Clause defines the outer boundaries of permissible jurisdictional power. It is left to the legislatures within each state to grant power to its courts to exercise specific personal jurisdiction through long-arm statutes. What is meant by a "long-arm" statute? As to the nature and scope of long-arm statutes, you already have read about two of them. The implied consent nonresident motorist statute in *Hess* was an early example of a long-arm statute that has a precise scope. The unemployment compensation statute in *International Shoe* also permitted a state judiciary to reach beyond its borders to exert its authority over a nonresident defendant based on that defendant's activities in the state. As you will learn in Chapter 6 pt. C, a plaintiff also typically uses a long-arm statute to achieve service of process over a nonresident defendant who may not be physically present in the forum state.

There are two types of modern long-arm statutes. A "laundry list" long-arm simply lists the types of particular activity by the defendant which the legislature has decided justifies subjecting the nonresident defendant to jurisdiction there. With a laundry-list long-arm, the plaintiff's task is to match the legislative language with the defendant's conduct within the state (e.g., the plaintiff's claim arises from a defendant "transacting business" in the forum). If the facts fit at least one of the provisions of the laundry list long-arm statute, the legal analysis can progress to the next step. A plaintiff's inability to convince the court of that fit will end the inquiry as to specific jurisdiction.

In the early 1960s, the National Conference of Commissioners on Uniform State Laws adopted a uniform long-arm statute, which provided:

> (1) A court may exercise personal jurisdiction over a person, who acts directly or by an agent, as to a claim for relief arising from the person's
>
> > (a) transacting any business in this state;

(b) contracting to supply services or things in this state;

(c) causing tortious injury by an act or omission in this state;

(d) causing tortious injury in this state by an act or omission outside this state if he regularly does or solicits business, or engages in any other persistent course of conduct, or derives substantial revenue from goods used or consumed or services rendered, in this state;

(e) having an interest in, using or possessing real property in this state; or

(f) contracting to insure any person, property or risk located within this state at the time of contracting.

While few states adopted the precise language of the uniform act, it served as a model for many early attempts by states to draft a broad, yet constitutional, laundry list long-arm statute.

Consider the scope of the uniform statute. Its language may preclude filing a claim against a nonresident based on a breach of warranty, a common alternative claim for relief to negligence. For example, does the uniform act include a claim against a nonresident arising from injuries to any person in the state by an express or implied breach of warranty made in sale of goods *outside* the state, when the seller knew that the person would use the goods *in* the state? A section of the uniform act deals with tortious injuries, but not injuries from a breach of warranty. It appears that neither the "transacting any business" or "contracting to supply . . . goods" sections would apply to a breach of warranty made outside the state.

==The second type of long-arm statute is known as a "due process" long-arm.== Instead of listing situations when jurisdiction over a nonresident is proper, the statute merely states that the particular state can exercise personal jurisdiction over a nonresident to the extent permitted by due process (the second step of the specific jurisdiction analysis). Two examples of due process long-arm statutes follow. California Code of Civil Procedure § 410.10 states:

A court of this state may exercise jurisdiction on any basis not inconsistent with the Constitution of this state or of the United States.

Rhode Island General Laws Annotated § 9–5–33(a) declares:

Every foreign corporation, every individual not a resident of this state or his executor or administrator, and every partnership or association, composed of any person or persons, not such residents, that shall have the necessary minimum contacts with the state of Rhode Island, shall be subject to the jurisdiction of the state of Rhode Island, and the courts of this state shall hold such foreign corporations and such nonresident individuals or their executors or administrators, and such partnerships or associations amenable to suit in Rhode Island in every case not contrary to the provisions of the constitution or laws of the United States.

The effect of a due process long-arm statute on the judicial analysis is to reduce an otherwise two step procedure into one step. Analysis under the due process long-arm and constitutional due process is identical. See, e.g., *Bridgeport Music, Inc. v. Still N The Water Publishing*, 327 F.3d 472 (6th Cir. 2003). Instead of requiring compliance with both a laundry list long-arm statute and constitutional due process, a court in a state using a due process long-arm only needs to apply the constitutional due process analysis to the case.

Even if the defendant's activities satisfy the long-arm statute, it is still possible that exercising jurisdiction over the nonresident defendant nevertheless will fail because of a due process violation. As you read in *International Shoe*, due process requires that, in order to subject a nonresident defendant to the jurisdiction of the court, the defendant must have minimum contacts with the forum state and entering a judgment against that defendant will not violate "fair play and substantial justice."

Even if the requisite contacts with the forum have been shown by the plaintiff, the defendant still can try to prove that exercising jurisdiction over him is nonetheless constitutionally unreasonable, i.e., it violates fair play and substantial justice to exert authority over the nonresident defendant. Courts have identified at least five factors that are relevant to a fair play analysis: the burden on the defendant, the plaintiff's interest, the forum state's interest, the interstate judicial system's interest in obtaining the most efficient resolution of controversies, and the common interests of the states in promoting substantive social policies.

b. General Jurisdiction

Besides specific jurisdiction, the other focus of jurisdictional case law is general jurisdiction, under which a plaintiff's claim does not have to arise from the activities of the defendant in the forum state. In other words, a court in Ohio can exercise jurisdiction over a defendant even if the plaintiff's claim arose from the defendant's activities outside Ohio, because the defendant has such continuous and systematic contacts with the forum state that it is fair to subject that defendant to suit in Ohio on every possible claim.

The legal analysis for general jurisdiction centers on constitutional due process alone. General jurisdiction may function as a back-up to specific jurisdiction in the event that a nonresident defendant's conduct in the forum state does not satisfy the language of the long-arm statute.

When the defendant's contacts with the jurisdiction are continuous and systematic enough to establish general jurisdiction, the plaintiff can provide notice about the filing of the lawsuit in a federal district court by using service of process under Federal Rule of Civil Procedure 4, without regard to the state's long-arm statute.

For general jurisdiction, the nonresident's contacts with the forum state must be "continuous and systematic," rather than the minimum contacts test used for specific jurisdiction. "For an individual, the paradigm forum for the exercise of general jurisdiction is the individual's domicile." *Goodyear Dunlop Tires Operations, S.A. v. Brown*, 131 S.Ct. 2846, 2851 (2011) stated that "[a] court may assert general jurisdiction over foreign (sister-state or foreign-country) corporations to hear any and all claims against them when their affiliations with the State are so 'continuous and systematic' as to render them essentially at home in the forum State." *Daimler AG v. Bauman*, 134 S.Ct. 746 (2014) clarified that a corporation is "essentially at home" in the states where it is incorporated or where it maintains its principal place of business. Unlike specific jurisdiction, *Daimler AG* noted that the "fair play and substantial justice" concept is inapplicable to general jurisdiction cases.

EXERCISE

For the state a) where you intend to practice after graduation, b) where your law school is located, and/or c) your professor assigns, go to that state's annotated statutes and research the long-arm statute typically used for exercising specific jurisdiction over nonresident defendants. Based on your research, print the statutory portion of the statute and bring it to class for discussion. In addition, answer the following questions.

1. Identify whether the type of long-arm statute in your state is a laundry list or due process long-arm.

2. If it is a due process long-arm statute:

a. Does the legislative history of the statute show that at one time there was a laundry list long-arm used in the state instead of a due process long-arm statute?

b. If the answer to part A) is yes, was the adoption of a due process long-arm made in response to a judicial decision that the former laundry list long-arm should be construed as if it were a due process long-arm statute?

3. If it is a laundry list long-arm statute:

a. Note the types of statutory conduct available for a plaintiff's counsel to try to fit with the nonresident defendant's factual conduct.

b. Note the specificity or generality of some or all of the provisions, e.g., "transacting business," "contracting for services."

c. Note whether the list includes the possibility that jurisdiction can be exercised over a nonresident defendant whose conduct outside the state has caused some harm within the state.

d. Note when it was enacted as well as how many times the legislature has amended the long-arm statute since it was enacted.

e. Note how the federal and/or state courts have interpreted the laundry list long-arm statute, i.e., despite its laundry list specificity, have the courts nevertheless interpreted the long-arm statute as if it were a due process long-arm statute? See, e.g., *Aristech Chemical Intern. Ltd. v. Acrylic Fabricators Ltd.*, 138 F.3d 624 (6th Cir. 1998) (state laundry list long-arm statute extends as far as the federal due process clause).

PROBLEMS

1. An Illinois resident's automobile collides in Georgia with a truck driven by a Georgia resident who has never been outside Georgia. If the Georgia resident sues the Illinois resident in an Illinois state court, can an Illinois court adjudicate the claim under jurisdiction based on:

   a. Domicile?

   b. Specific jurisdiction?

   c. General jurisdiction?

2. In #1, if the Georgia resident sues the Illinois resident in a Georgia state court, can a Georgia court adjudicate the claim under jurisdiction based on:

   a. Domicile?

   b. Specific jurisdiction?

   c. General jurisdiction?

3. In #1, if the Illinois resident sues the Georgia resident in a Georgia state court, can a Georgia court adjudicate the claim under jurisdiction based on:

   a. Domicile?

   b. Specific jurisdiction?

   c. General jurisdiction?

4. In #1, if the Illinois resident sues the Georgia resident in an Illinois state court, can an Illinois court adjudicate the claim under jurisdiction based on:

   a. Domicile?

   b. Specific jurisdiction?

   c. General jurisdiction?

5. Randy was driving on I–65 from his home in Indianapolis, Indiana to his spring break condominium in Mobile, Alabama. At Exit 2 in Franklin, Kentucky, he went to Ben's Franklin full service gas station to have his brakes checked. In a very short time, Ben replaced the brake shoes on Randy's SUV. After Ben wrote down Randy's license plate number when Randy paid him with a credit card, Randy resumed his trip to the Gulf of Mexico. Still traveling on I–65, Randy tried to apply his brakes, swerved and hit the center median. The SUV and Randy were both damaged in the Alabama wreck, which a later investigation revealed was caused by improperly installed brake shoes.

You are Randy's attorney, trying to determine your client's options for where to file a claim for personal injuries and property damage against Ben Brakeman, doing business as Ben's Franklin Gas Station. Assume that Indiana, Kentucky, and Alabama all have long-arm statutes identical to the Uniform Long-arm Act. Without reaching the due process issue, can a court in any of the states assert jurisdiction over Ben under the long-arm statute? Because laundry list long-arm statutes are phrased in the disjunctive, remember that it is necessary to identify only one statutory basis for invoking a long-arm statute.

6. In #5, assume that instead of having his brakes immediately repaired, Randy had to leave his SUV with Ben and take a bus to Alabama for his vacation. Before leaving his SUV with Ben, Randy signed a contract with Ben agreeing to pay for the brake shoes and the labor for installing the brake shoes. When he returned to the gas station a week later, he refused to pay the bill because he thought it was well in excess of Ben's original estimate. This time, you are counsel for Ben. Again, assume that the Uniform Long-arm Act applies in all three states. Can a court in any of the states assert jurisdiction over Randy under a long-arm statute? Using domicile?

7. An Ohio resident read a product advertisement in her local newspaper, and ordered the product from a Pennsylvania manufacturer that advertises every Sunday in all major Ohio Sunday newspapers. The customer offered to pick up the product in Pittsburgh. On the outskirts of Pittsburgh, the Ohio resident collided with the Pennsylvania manufacture's minivan. To make things worse, after returning to Ohio, the product malfunctioned but the manufacturer refused to return the purchase price. In an Ohio state court, the Ohio plaintiff sues the Pennsylvania manufacturer for negligence in connection with the wreck and for breach of contract in connection with the defective product. Can the Ohio court exert jurisdiction over the manufacturer, using domicile, specific jurisdiction, or general jurisdiction?

8. Same facts as #7, except that the plaintiff's claim was for the vehicular collision only. In addition to the Pennsylvania manufacturer, the plaintiff also names the manufacturer's employee who was driving the minivan as a co-defendant. The employee lives in eastern Ohio. Can the Ohio court exert jurisdiction over the defendants, using domicile, specific jurisdiction, or general jurisdiction?

9. Fly-by-Night Insurance Co. operates a large bank of telephones in Michigan to solicit persons throughout the northeastern United States to purchase term life insurance policies. Each evening between 5:00 p.m. and 8:00 p.m., Fly-by-Night's agents interrupt countless families and individuals to sell them life insurance policies. You work for the Attorney General of Massachusetts considering a lawsuit to enjoin such telephone solicitations. Under the Uniform Long-arm Act, can your office file its claim in Massachusetts or in Michigan? If you were a state legislator who wanted to amend the long-arm statute to be more explicit about jurisdiction over telephone solicitors, what language would you propose to amend the statute?

3. EMERGING PERSONAL JURISDICTION PRINCIPLES

Following *International Shoe*, the Court decided several cases which led to confusion about the scope of the due process standard for exercising specific jurisdiction over a nonresident defendant under newly adopted long-arm statutes. In *McGee v. International Life Insurance Co.*, 355 U.S. 220, 78 S.Ct. 199, 2 L.Ed.2d 223 (1957), a Texas insurance company had bought out another company after the other company sold a life insurance policy by mail to an insured living in California. After the death of the insured, his mother attempted to collect the proceeds of the policy by suing the insurer in a California state court and serving the insurance company under the California long-arm statute. When the Texas company did not appear to defend the lawsuit, the California court awarded a default judgment to the insured's mother. However, because the Texas company had no assets in California, the insured's mother had to go to Texas to try to enforce the California judgment against the insurer. The precise issue before the Court was whether a Texas court had to enforce the California default judgment. If the California court had personal jurisdiction, the Texas court was required by the Full Faith and Credit Clause to enforce the California judgment.

The Supreme Court held that the insurer's isolated contact through the continuation of the policy was sufficient contact with California to subject the insurer to the authority of the California courts. Even though the insurer had no office or agent in California, the Court upheld the jurisdiction of the California court, because the insurance contract had a substantial connection with California: the contract was delivered there, the premiums were mailed there, and the insured was a California resident when he died. From a convenience viewpoint, the insured's mother could not bear the cost of going to Texas to litigate the validity of the insurance contract as easily as the Texas company could afford to hire counsel in California to defend the lawsuit. The connection of the nonresident insurance company was the most tenuous of any case in which the Court has upheld jurisdiction.

A year later, *Hanson v. Denckla*, 357 U.S. 235, 78 S.Ct. 1228, 2 L.Ed.2d 1283 (1958) checked the expansion of jurisdiction under *McGee*'s economic rationale, and showed that there are limits beyond which due process cannot be stretched. After a Pennsylvania woman executed a trust in Delaware with a Delaware bank as trustee, she moved to Florida where she exercised her power to appoint the beneficiaries of the trust. Following her death, her children fought over whether her assets should pass to them under her will, or whether her grandchildren should receive her estate through the trust. The children challenged her appointment of trust beneficiaries by suing the Delaware trustee and the grandchildren in Florida, and having them served under the Florida long-arm statute. Several defendants challenged Florida's jurisdiction over the trustee. Before a Florida judgment for the plaintiffs was rendered, a parallel lawsuit was brought by the grandchildren in Delaware. The Florida judgment winners took their judgment to Delaware for enforcement, arguing that the Florida judgment operated as *res judicata* on the Delaware case. However, the Delaware court refused to give it full faith and credit because the Florida court lacked personal jurisdiction over the Delaware trustee.

Were the bank's activities in Florida regarding the trust sufficient for the Florida court to have jurisdiction over the nonresident trustee? The Supreme Court held that the Delaware trustee lacked the necessary minimal contacts with Florida. Therefore, the Delaware court was under no obligation to give full faith and credit to the Florida judgment because it was invalid under the due process clause of the Fourteenth Amendment. The trustee had no office in Florida, no trust assets were administered or held there, and the claim did not arise from any act done or transaction consummated in Florida by the Delaware trustee. It was immaterial to jurisdiction over the trustee that the deceased and most of the beneficiaries lived in Florida, or that she exercised the power of appointment unilaterally in Florida. The *Hanson* opinion noted that

> the unilateral activity of those who claim some relationship with a nonresident defendant cannot satisfy the requirement of contact with the forum State. . . . [I]t is essential in each case that there be some act by which the defendant *purposely avails* itself of the privilege of conducting activities within the forum State, thus invoking the privileges and protections of its laws. [emphasis supplied]

To compare the two cases, *McGee* and *Hanson* each involved an out-of-state corporate defendant that had only one customer in the forum state. However, the relationships in each case began differently. In *McGee*, the insurance company's predecessor had sent an offer to insure a person in California, and the defendant insurance company's purposeful act was to continue to insure. In *Hanson*, the Delaware trustee did not

SHAFFER V. HEITNER
433 U.S. 186, 97 S.Ct. 2569, 53 L.Ed.2d 683 (1977)

Mr. Justice Marshall delivered the opinion of the Court.

[Plaintiff Heitner brought a shareholders' derivative suit in Delaware against 28 present or former nonresident officers and directors of Greyhound Corporation, a Delaware corporation with its national headquarters in Arizona, for damages they had caused the corporation through mismanagement in Oregon. (The Court noted in fn. 37 of its opinion that the case did not raise and it was not considering the issue of "whether the presence of a defendant's property in a State is a sufficient basis for jurisdiction when no other forum is available to the plaintiff.") Delaware law permitted Heitner to ask the trial court for an order sequestering (an equity term for attachment) a defendant's property in the state. Because Heitner was unable to acquire personal jurisdiction over the nonresident defendants, the sequestration allowed him to proceed against any of their property located within Delaware by using quasi in rem jurisdiction.

The trial court ordered that the defendants' Greyhound stock be subject to "stop transfer orders" on Greyhound's records. The orders had an effect similar to a seizure of 82,000 shares of Greyhound stock by the court. Under Delaware law, the location of all Greyhound stock was deemed to be in the state, due to Greyhound being a Delaware corporation, even though the stock certificates were located elsewhere. The controversy in the case concerned the constitutionality of the Delaware sequestration statute. The defendant made a special appearance to quash service and to vacate the trial court's order of sequestration. Delaware state courts all rejected the defendants' due process arguments.]

II

The Delaware courts rejected appellants' jurisdictional challenge by noting that this suit was brought as a *quasi in rem* proceeding. Since *quasi in rem* jurisdiction is traditionally based on attachment or seizure of property present in the jurisdiction, not on contacts between the defendant and the State, the courts considered appellants' claimed lack of contacts with Delaware to be unimportant. This categorical analysis assumes the continued soundness of the conceptual structure founded on the century-old case of *Pennoyer v. Neff*, 95 U.S. 714 (1878)....

From our perspective, the importance of *Pennoyer* is not its result, but the fact that its principles and corollaries derived from them became the basic elements of the constitutional doctrine governing state-court jurisdiction. As we have noted, under *Pennoyer* state authority to adjudicate was based on the jurisdiction's power over either persons or property. This fundamental concept is embodied in the very vocabulary which we use to describe judgments. If a court's jurisdiction is based on its authority over the defendant's person, the action and judgment are denominated "*in personam*" and can impose a personal obligation on the defendant in favor of the plaintiff. If jurisdiction is based on the court's power over property within its territory, the action is called "*in rem*" or "*quasi in rem*." The effect of a judgment in such a case is limited to the property that supports jurisdiction and does not impose a personal liability on the property owner, since he is not before the court. In *Pennoyer*'s terms, the owner is affected only "indirectly" by an *in rem* judgment adverse to his interest in the property subject to the court's disposition.

By concluding that "(t)he authority of every tribunal is necessarily restricted by the territorial limits of the State in which it is established," *Pennoyer* sharply limited the availability of *in personam* jurisdiction over defendants not resident in the forum State. If a nonresident defendant could not be found in a State, he could not be sued there. On the other hand, since the State in which property was located was considered to have exclusive sovereignty over that property, *in rem* actions could proceed regardless of the owner's location. Indeed, since a State's process could not reach beyond its borders, this Court held after *Pennoyer* that due process did not require any effort to give a property owner personal notice that his property was involved in an *in rem* proceeding....

The question in *International Shoe* was whether the corporation was subject to the judicial and taxing jurisdiction of Washington. Mr. Chief Justice Stone's opinion for the Court began its analysis of that question by noting that the historical basis of *in personam* jurisdiction was a court's power over the defendant's person. That power, however, was no longer the central concern:

> But now that the *capias ad respondendum* has given way to personal service of summons or other form of notice, due process requires only that in order to subject a defendant to a judgment in personam, if he be not present within the territory of the forum, he have certain minimum contacts with it such that the maintenance of the suit does not offend "traditional notions of fair play and substantial justice."

Thus, the inquiry into the State's jurisdiction over a foreign corporation appropriately focused not on whether the corporation was "present" but on whether there have been "such contacts of the corporation with the state of the forum as make it reasonable, in the context of our federal system of government, to require the corporation to defend the particular suit which is brought there." Mechanical or quantitative evaluations of the defendant's activities in the forum could not resolve the question of reasonableness:

> Whether due process is satisfied must depend rather upon the quality and nature of the activity in relation to the fair and orderly administration of the laws which it was the purpose of the due process clause to insure. That clause does not contemplate that a state may make binding a judgment in personam against an individual or corporate defendant with which the state has no contacts, ties, or relations.

Thus, the relationship among the defendant, the forum, and the litigation, rather than the mutually exclusive sovereignty of the States on which the rules of *Pennoyer* rest, became the central concern of the inquiry into personal jurisdiction. The immediate effect of this departure from *Pennoyer*'s conceptual apparatus was to increase the ability of the state courts to obtain personal jurisdiction over nonresident defendants.

No equally dramatic change has occurred in the law governing jurisdiction *in rem*. There have, however, been intimations that the collapse of the *in personam* wing of *Pennoyer* has not left that decision unweakened as a foundation for *in rem* jurisdiction. Well-reasoned lower court opinions have questioned the proposition that the presence of property in a State gives that State jurisdiction to adjudicate rights to the property regardless of the relationship of the underlying dispute and the property owner to the forum. The overwhelming majority of commentators have also rejected *Pennoyer*'s premise that a proceeding "against" property is not a proceeding against the owners of that property. . . .

It is clear, therefore, that the law of state-court jurisdiction no longer stands securely on the foundation established in *Pennoyer*. We think that the time is ripe to consider whether the standard of fairness and substantial justice set forth in *International Shoe* should be held to govern actions *in rem* as well as *in personam*.

III

The case for applying to jurisdiction *in rem* the same test of "fair play and substantial justice" as governs assertions of jurisdiction *in personam* is simple and straightforward. It is premised on recognition that "(t)he phrase, 'judicial jurisdiction over a thing', is a customary elliptical way of referring to jurisdiction over the interests of persons in a thing." Restatement (Second) of Conflict of Laws s 56, Introductory Note (1971) (hereafter Restatement). This recognition leads to the conclusion that in order to justify an exercise of jurisdiction *in rem*, the basis for jurisdiction must be sufficient to justify exercising "jurisdiction over the interests of persons in a thing." The standard for determining whether an exercise of jurisdiction over the interests of persons is consistent with the Due

Process Clause is the minimum-contacts standard elucidated in *International Shoe*.

This argument, of course, does not ignore the fact that the presence of property in a State may bear on the existence of jurisdiction by providing contacts among the forum State, the defendant, and the litigation. For example, when claims to the property itself are the source of the underlying controversy between the plaintiff and the defendant, it would be unusual for the State where the property is located not to have jurisdiction. In such cases, the defendant's claim to property located in the State would normally indicate that he expected to benefit from the State's protection of his interest. The State's strong interests in assuring the marketability of property within its borders and in providing a procedure for peaceful resolution of disputes about the possession of that property would also support jurisdiction, as would the likelihood that important records and witnesses will be found in the State. The presence of property may also favor jurisdiction in cases such as suits for injury suffered on the land of an absentee owner, where the defendant's ownership of the property is conceded but the cause of action is otherwise related to rights and duties growing out of that ownership.

It appears, therefore, that jurisdiction over many types of actions which now are or might be brought *in rem* would not be affected by a holding that any assertion of state-court jurisdiction must satisfy the *International Shoe* standard. For the type of *quasi in rem* action typified by . . . the present case, however, accepting the proposed analysis would result in significant change. These are cases where the property which now serves as the basis for state-court jurisdiction is completely unrelated to the plaintiff's cause of action. Thus, although the presence of the defendant's property in a State might suggest the existence of other ties among the defendant, the State, and the litigation, the presence of the property alone would not support the State's jurisdiction. . . .

Since acceptance of the *International Shoe* test would most affect this class of cases, we examine the arguments against adopting that standard as they relate to this category of litigation. Before doing so, however, we note that this type of case also presents the clearest illustration of the argument in favor of assessing assertions of jurisdiction by a single standard. For in cases such as . . . this one, the only role played by the property is to provide the basis for bringing the defendant into court. Indeed, the express purpose of the Delaware sequestration procedure is to compel the defendant to enter a personal appearance. In such cases, if a direct assertion of personal jurisdiction over the defendant would violate the Constitution, it would seem that an indirect assertion of that jurisdiction should be equally impermissible.

The primary rationale for treating the presence of property as a sufficient basis for jurisdiction to adjudicate claims over which the State would not have jurisdiction if International Shoe applied is that a wrongdoer "should not be able to avoid payment of his obligations by the expedient of removing his assets to a place where he is not subject to an *in personam* suit." Restatement § 66, Comment a. This justification, however, does not explain why jurisdiction should be recognized without regard to whether the property is present in the State because of an effort to avoid the owner's obligations. Nor does it support jurisdiction to adjudicate the underlying claim. At most, it suggests that a State in which property is located should have jurisdiction to attach that property, by use of proper procedures, as security for a judgment being sought in a forum where the litigation can be maintained consistently with *International Shoe*. Moreover, we know of nothing to justify the assumption that a debtor can avoid paying his obligations by removing his property to a State in which his creditor cannot obtain personal jurisdiction over him. The Full Faith and Credit Clause, after all, makes the valid *in personam* judgment of one State enforceable in all other States.[36] . . .

We therefore conclude that all assertions of state-court jurisdiction must be evaluated according to the standards set forth in *International Shoe* and its progeny.

IV

. . .

Appellee Heitner did not allege and does not now claim that appellants have ever set foot in Delaware. Nor does he identify any act related to his cause of action as having taken place in Delaware. Nevertheless, he contends that appellants' positions as directors and officers of a corporation chartered in Delaware provide sufficient "contacts, ties, or relations" with that State to give its courts jurisdiction over appellants in this stockholder's derivative action. This argument is based primarily on what Heitner asserts to be the strong interest of Delaware in supervising the management of a Delaware corporation. . . . In order to protect this interest, appellee concludes, Delaware's courts must have jurisdiction over corporate fiduciaries such as appellants.

This argument is undercut by the failure of the Delaware Legislature to assert the state interest appellee finds so compelling. Delaware law bases jurisdiction, not on appellants' status as corporate fiduciaries, but rather on the presence of their property in the State. . . . If Delaware perceived its interest in securing jurisdiction over corporate fiduciaries to be as great as Heitner suggests, we would expect it to have enacted a statute more clearly designed to protect that interest.

---

[36] Once it has been determined by a court of competent jurisdiction that the defendant is a debtor of the plaintiff, there would seem to be no unfairness in allowing an action to realize on that debt in a State where the defendant has property, whether or not that State would have jurisdiction to determine the existence of the debt as an original matter.

Moreover, even if Heitner's assessment of the importance of Delaware's interest is accepted, his argument fails to demonstrate that Delaware is a fair forum for this litigation. The interest appellee has identified may support the application of Delaware law to resolve any controversy over appellants' actions in their capacities as officers and directors. But we have rejected the argument that if a State's law can properly be applied to a dispute, its courts necessarily have jurisdiction over the parties to that dispute.

Appellee suggests that by accepting positions as officers or directors of a Delaware corporation, appellants performed the acts required by *Hanson v. Denckla*. He notes that Delaware law provides substantial benefits to corporate officers and directors, and that these benefits were at least in part the incentive for appellants to assume their positions. It is, he says, "only fair and just" to require appellants, in return for these benefits, to respond in the State of Delaware when they are accused of misusing their power.

But like Heitner's first argument, this line of reasoning establishes only that it is appropriate for Delaware law to govern the obligations of appellants to Greyhound and its stockholders. It does not demonstrate that appellants have "purposefully avail(ed themselves) of the privilege of conducting activities within the forum State," *Hanson v. Denckla*, in a way that would justify bringing them before a Delaware tribunal. Appellants have simply had nothing to do with the State of Delaware. Moreover, appellants had no reason to expect to be haled before a Delaware court. Delaware, unlike some States, has not enacted a statute that treats acceptance of a directorship as consent to jurisdiction in the State. And "[i]t strains reason . . . to suggest that anyone buying securities in a corporation formed in Delaware 'impliedly consents' to subject himself to Delaware's . . . jurisdiction on any cause of action." Appellants, who were not required to acquire interests in Greyhound in order to hold their positions, did not by acquiring those interests surrender their right to be brought to judgment only in States with which they had had "minimum contacts." . . .

Delaware's assertion of jurisdiction over appellants in this case is inconsistent with that constitutional limitation on state power. The judgment of the Delaware Supreme Court must, therefore, be reversed.

MR. JUSTICE POWELL, concurring.

. . . I would explicitly reserve judgment, however, on whether the ownership of some forms of property whose situs is indisputably and permanently located within a State may, without more, provide the contacts necessary to subject a defendant to jurisdiction within the State to the extent of the value of the property. In the case of real property, in particular, preservation of the common-law concept of *quasi in rem* jurisdiction arguably would avoid the uncertainty of the general

International Shoe standard without significant cost to "'traditional notions of fair play and substantial justice.'" Subject to the foregoing reservation, I join the opinion of the Court.

MR. JUSTICE STEVENS, concurring in the judgment.

. . . One who purchases shares of stock on the open market can hardly be expected to know that he has thereby become subject to suit in a forum remote from his residence and unrelated to the transaction. As a practical matter, the Delaware sequestration statute creates an unacceptable risk of judgment without notice. . . . I therefore agree with the Court that on the record before us no adequate basis for jurisdiction exists and that the Delaware statute is unconstitutional on its face.

How the Court's opinion may be applied in other contexts is not entirely clear to me. I agree with Mr. Justice POWELL that it should not be read to invalidate *quasi in rem* jurisdiction where real estate is involved. I would also not read it as invalidating other long-accepted methods of acquiring jurisdiction over persons with adequate notice of both the particular controversy and the fact that their local activities might subject them to suit. My uncertainty as to the reach of the opinion, and my fear that it purports to decide a great deal more than is necessary to dispose of this case, persuade me merely to concur in the judgment.

MR. JUSTICE BRENNAN, concurring in part and dissenting in part.

I join Parts I–III of the Court's opinion. I fully agree that the minimum-contacts analysis developed in *International Shoe Co. v. Washington* represents a far more sensible construct for the exercise of state-court jurisdiction than the patchwork of legal and factual fictions that has been generated from the decision in *Pennoyer v. Neff*. It is precisely because the inquiry into minimum contacts is now of such overriding importance, however, that I must respectfully dissent from Part IV of the Court's opinion.

I

. . . [T]he Court in Part IV reaches the minimum-contacts question and finds such contacts lacking as applied to appellants. Succinctly stated, once having properly and persuasively decided that the quasi in rem statute that Delaware admits to having enacted is invalid, the Court then proceeds to find that a minimum-contacts law that Delaware expressly denies having enacted also could not be constitutionally applied in this case.

In my view, a purer example of an advisory opinion is not to be found.

. . .

II

Nonetheless, because the Court rules on the minimum-contacts question, I feel impelled to express my view.... I am convinced that as a general rule a state forum has jurisdiction to adjudicate a shareholder derivative action centering on the conduct and policies of the directors and officers of a corporation chartered by that State. Unlike the Court, I therefore would not foreclose Delaware from asserting jurisdiction over appellants were it persuaded to do so on the basis of minimum contacts.

... I, therefore, would approach the minimum-contacts analysis differently than does the Court. Crucial to me is the fact that appellants voluntarily associated themselves with the State of Delaware, "invoking the benefits and protections of its laws", *Hanson v. Denckla*. I thus do not believe that it is unfair to insist that appellants make themselves available to suit in a competent forum that Delaware might create for vindication of its important public policies directly pertaining to appellants' fiduciary associations with the State.

NOTES AND QUESTIONS

1. Where does the *Shaffer* decision leave *Pennoyer*'s principles? Justice Marshall stated, "It is clear, therefore, that the law of state-court jurisdiction no longer stands securely on the foundation established in *Pennoyer*." Prior to that statement, he had noted that "the relationship among the defendant, the forum, and the litigation, rather than the mutually exclusive sovereignty of the States on which the rules of *Pennoyer* rest, became the central concern of the inquiry into personal jurisdiction." He then cited language from *International Shoe* that the exercise of jurisdiction over nonresidents required "contacts, ties, or relations" with the forum.

After *Shaffer*, an *in rem* claim is no longer about the property; instead the jurisdictional inquiry addresses whether the court has jurisdiction over the person who *owns* the property. The fact that the defendant owns property in the state may be sufficient proof that the defendant can satisfy a minimum contacts analysis there. Why?

After *Shaffer*, can you argue that there is anything left of *Pennoyer*'s rules about power? Do the principles about power over persons and property in the forum state survive *Shaffer*?

2. The plaintiff argued that the defendants' positions as directors and officers of a Delaware corporation gave the Delaware courts a sufficient tie to a shareholders' derivative suit, thereby rendering jurisdiction constitutional. The Court responded simply that Delaware had no implied consent statute asserting such an interest in the management of a Delaware corporation. Shortly after *Shaffer* was decided, the Delaware legislature passed an implied consent law that formed the basis of Heitner's position. Doesn't Justice Marshall's recognition that acceptance of a directorship is the equivalent of consent to be sued simply perpetuate consent as a legal fiction?

3. Justice Powell's concurrence maintained that when the attached property "is undisputably and permanently located within a State, a court of that State, without more, might constitutionally invoke *quasi in rem* jurisdiction." Did Justice Powell make clear whether he felt that *Pennoyer*'s rationale survived to that extent, or whether the indisputable presence of real property within a state satisfied the *International Shoe* test?

Similarly, Justice Stevens emphasized the connection between the type of property at issue and the expectations of the owner. Someone who acquired realty or opened a bank account might assume the risk that the state would assert jurisdictional power over him. But under *Shaffer*'s facts, did Justice Stevens explain how the expectations of the parties could be identified (e.g., could a purchaser of stock be expected to know that he is subject to suit in a remote forum on an unrelated claim merely because the stock was in a corporation chartered in the forum state)? Are the *Shaffer* defendants' expectations different because they were not merely purchasers of stock on the open market? Do the expectations turn on the existence of a particularly worded statute or on the nature of the defendants' contacts? Even if the former were dispositive, how does a due process long-arm statute satisfy *Shaffer*'s expectation requirement?

4. After *Shaffer*, what if anything remains of a meaningful distinction between *in personam* and *quasi in rem* jurisdiction? Unlike *quasi in rem* jurisdiction, an *in personam* claim would be more attractive because the plaintiff's recovery is not limited to the value of any property that was attached. The plaintiff also can try to recover his damages by going elsewhere in the jurisdiction or to another jurisdiction to enforce the judgment. Nevertheless, one remaining benefit of *quasi in rem* jurisdiction and its accompanying attachment of property is the pressure placed on a defendant to settle that results from "tying up" the attached property.

Shaffer also leaves open the possibility that the presence of defendant's property in the forum would support jurisdiction even if the plaintiff's claim may be unrelated to the defendant's property there. Therefore, jurisdiction in the forum may be proper if no other forum is available to the plaintiff.

WORLD-WIDE VOLKSWAGEN CORP. v. WOODSON
444 U.S. 286, 100 S.Ct. 559, 62 L.Ed.2d 490 (1980)

MR. JUSTICE WHITE delivered the opinion of the Court.

The issue before us is whether, consistently with the Due Process Clause of the Fourteenth Amendment, an Oklahoma court may exercise *in personam* jurisdiction over a nonresident automobile retailer and its wholesale distributor in a products-liability action, when the defendants' only connection with Oklahoma is the fact that an automobile sold in New York to New York residents became involved in an accident in Oklahoma.

I

Respondents Harry and Kay Robinson purchased a new Audi automobile from petitioner Seaway Volkswagen, Inc. (Seaway), in Massena, N. Y., in 1976. The following year the Robinson family, who resided in New York, left that State for a new home in Arizona. As they passed through the State of Oklahoma, another car struck their Audi in the rear, causing a fire which severely burned Kay Robinson and her two children.

The Robinsons subsequently brought a products-liability action in the District Court for Creek County, Okla., claiming that their injuries resulted from defective design and placement of the Audi's gas tank and fuel system. They joined as defendants the automobile's manufacturer, Audi NSU Auto Union Aktiengesellschaft (Audi); its importer Volkswagen of America, Inc. (Volkswagen); its regional distributor, petitioner World-Wide Volkswagen Corp. (World-Wide); and its retail dealer, petitioner Seaway. Seaway and World-Wide entered special appearances, claiming that Oklahoma's exercise of jurisdiction over them would offend the limitations on the State's jurisdiction imposed by the Due Process Clause of the Fourteenth Amendment.

The facts presented to the District Court showed that World-Wide is incorporated and has its business office in New York. It distributes vehicles, parts, and accessories, under contract with Volkswagen, to retail dealers in New York, New Jersey, and Connecticut. Seaway, one of these retail dealers, is incorporated and has its place of business in New York. Insofar as the record reveals, Seaway and World-Wide are fully independent corporations whose relations with each other and with Volkswagen and Audi are contractual only. Respondents adduced no evidence that either World-Wide or Seaway does any business in Oklahoma, ships or sells any products to or in that State, has an agent to receive process there, or purchases advertisements in any media calculated to reach Oklahoma. In fact, as respondents' counsel conceded at oral argument, there was no showing that any automobile sold by World-Wide or Seaway has ever entered Oklahoma with the single exception of the vehicle involved in the present case.

Despite the apparent paucity of contacts between petitioners and Oklahoma, the District Court rejected their constitutional claim and reaffirmed that ruling in denying petitioners' motion for reconsideration. Petitioners then sought a writ of prohibition in the Supreme Court of Oklahoma to restrain the District Judge, respondent Charles S. Woodson, from exercising *in personam* jurisdiction over them. They renewed their contention that, because they had no "minimal contacts," with the State of Oklahoma, the actions of the District Judge were in violation of their rights under the Due Process Clause.

The Supreme Court of Oklahoma denied the writ, holding that personal jurisdiction over petitioners was authorized by Oklahoma's "long-arm" statute. Although the court noted that the proper approach was to test jurisdiction against both statutory and constitutional standards, its analysis did not distinguish these questions, probably because [the long-arm statute] has been interpreted as conferring jurisdiction to the limits permitted by the United States Constitution. The court's rationale was contained in the following paragraph:

> In the case before us, the product being sold and distributed by the petitioners is by its very design and purpose so mobile that petitioners can foresee its possible use in Oklahoma. This is especially true of the distributor, who has the exclusive right to distribute such automobile in New York, New Jersey and Connecticut. The evidence presented below demonstrated that goods sold and distributed by the petitioners were used in the State of Oklahoma, and under the facts we believe it reasonable to infer, given the retail value of the automobile, that the petitioners derive substantial income from automobiles which from time to time are used in the State of Oklahoma. This being the case, we hold that under the facts presented, the trial court was justified in concluding that the petitioners derive substantial revenue from goods used or consumed in this State.

We granted certiorari to consider an important constitutional question with respect to state-court jurisdiction and to resolve a conflict between the Supreme Court of Oklahoma and the highest courts of at least four other States. We reverse.

II

. . .

As has long been settled, and as we reaffirm today, a state court may exercise personal jurisdiction over a nonresident defendant only so long as there exist "minimum contacts" between the defendant and the forum State. *International Shoe Co. v. Washington*. The concept of minimum contacts, in turn, can be seen to perform two related, but distinguishable, functions. It protects the defendant against the burdens of litigating in a distant or inconvenient forum. And it acts to ensure that the States through their courts, do not reach out beyond the limits imposed on them by their status as coequal sovereigns in a federal system.

The protection against inconvenient litigation is typically described in terms of "reasonableness" or "fairness." We have said that the defendant's contacts with the forum State must be such that maintenance of the suit "does not offend 'traditional notions of fair play and substantial justice.'" *International Shoe Co. v. Washington*. The relationship between the defendant and the forum must be such that it is "reasonable . . . to require the corporation to defend the particular suit which is brought there." Implicit in this emphasis on reasonableness is the understanding that the burden on the defendant, while always a primary concern, will in an appropriate case be considered in light of other relevant factors, including the forum State's interest in adjudicating the dispute, see *McGee v. International Life Ins. Co.*, the plaintiff's interest in obtaining convenient and effective relief, at least when that interest is not adequately protected by the plaintiff's power to choose the forum, the interstate judicial system's interest in obtaining the most efficient resolution of controversies, and the shared interest of the several States in furthering fundamental substantive social policies....

Nevertheless, we have never accepted the proposition that state lines are irrelevant for jurisdictional purposes... Even if the defendant would suffer minimal or no inconvenience from being forced to litigate before the tribunals of another State; even if the forum State has a strong interest in applying its law to the controversy; even if the forum State is the most convenient location for litigation, the Due Process Clause, acting as an instrument of interstate federalism, may sometimes act to divest the State of its power to render a valid judgment. *Hanson v. Denckla*.

III

Applying these principles to the case at hand, we find in the record before us a total absence of those affiliating circumstances that are a necessary predicate to any exercise of state-court jurisdiction. Petitioners carry on no activity whatsoever in Oklahoma. They close no sales and perform no services there.... In short, respondents seek to base jurisdiction on ... the fortuitous circumstance that a single Audi automobile, sold in New York to New York residents, happened to suffer an accident while passing through Oklahoma.

It is argued, however, that because an automobile is mobile by its very design and purpose it was "foreseeable" that the Robinsons' Audi would cause injury in Oklahoma. Yet "foreseeability" alone has never been a sufficient benchmark for personal jurisdiction under the Due Process Clause. In *Hanson v. Denckla*, it was no doubt foreseeable that the settlor of a Delaware trust would subsequently move to Florida and seek to exercise a power of appointment there; yet we held that Florida courts could not constitutionally exercise jurisdiction over a Delaware trustee that had no other contacts with the forum State....

This is not to say, of course, that foreseeability is wholly irrelevant. But the foreseeability that is critical to due process analysis is not the mere likelihood that a product will find its way into the forum State. Rather, it is that the defendant's conduct and connection with the forum State are such that he should reasonably anticipate being haled into court there. The Due Process Clause, by ensuring the "orderly administration of the laws," *International Shoe Co. v. Washington* gives a degree of predictability to the legal system that allows potential defendants to structure their primary conduct with some minimum assurance as to where that conduct will and will not render them liable to suit.

When a corporation "purposefully avails itself of the privilege of conducting activities within the forum State," *Hanson v. Denckla*, it has clear notice that it is subject to suit there, and can act to alleviate the risk of burdensome litigation by procuring insurance, passing the expected costs on to customers, or, if the risks are too great, severing its connection with the State. Hence if the sale of a product of a manufacturer or distributor . . . is not simply an isolated occurrence, but arises from the efforts of the manufacturer or distributor to serve directly or indirectly, the market for its product in other States, it is not unreasonable to subject it to suit in one of those States if its allegedly defective merchandise has there been the source of injury to its owner or to others. The forum State does not exceed its powers under the Due Process Clause if it asserts personal jurisdiction over a corporation that delivers its products into the stream of commerce with the expectation that they will be purchased by consumers in the forum State.

. . . In our view, whatever marginal revenues petitioners may receive by virtue of the fact that their products are capable of use in Oklahoma is far too attenuated a contact to justify that State's exercise of in personam jurisdiction over them. . . .

Reversed.

[The dissenting opinions of JUSTICE MARSHALL and JUSTICE BLACKMUN are omitted.]

JUSTICE BRENNAN, dissenting.

. . .

I

The Court's opinions focus tightly on the existence of contacts between the forum and the defendant. In so doing, they accord too little weight to the strength of the forum State's interest in the case and fail to explore whether there would be any actual inconvenience to the defendant.

. . . Because lesser burdens reduce the unfairness to the defendant, jurisdiction may be justified despite less significant contacts. . . . Due process limits on jurisdiction do not protect a defendant from all inconvenience of travel, *McGee*, and it would not be sensible to make the constitutional rule turn solely on the number of miles the defendant must travel to the courtroom. Instead, the constitutionally significant "burden" to be analyzed relates to the mobility of the defendant's defense. For instance, if having to travel to a foreign forum would hamper the defense because witnesses or evidence or the defendant himself were immobile, or if there were a disproportionately large number of witnesses or amount of evidence that would have to be transported at the defendant's expense, or if being away from home for the duration of the trial would work some special hardship on the defendant, then the Constitution would require special consideration for the defendant's interests.

That considerations other than contacts between the forum and the defendant are relevant necessarily means that the Constitution does not require that trial be held in the State which has the "best contacts" with the defendant. The defendant has no constitutional entitlement to the best forum or, for that matter, to any particular forum. Under even the most restrictive view of *International Shoe*, several States could have jurisdiction over a particular cause of action. We need only determine whether the forum States in these cases satisfy the constitutional minimum.

II

... I would find that the forum State has an interest in permitting the litigation to go forward, the litigation is connected to the forum, the defendant is linked to the forum, and the burden of defending is not unreasonable. Accordingly, I would hold that it is neither unfair nor unreasonable to require these defendants to defend in the forum State.

... [T]he interest of the forum State and its connection to the litigation is strong. The automobile accident underlying the litigation occurred in Oklahoma. The plaintiffs were hospitalized in Oklahoma when they brought suit. Essential witnesses and evidence were in Oklahoma. The State has a legitimate interest in enforcing its laws designed to keep its highway system safe, and the trial can proceed at least as efficiently in Oklahoma as anywhere else.

The petitioners are not unconnected with the forum. Although both sell automobiles within limited sales territories, each sold the automobile which in fact was driven to Oklahoma where it was involved in an accident. It may be true, as the Court suggests, that each sincerely intended to limit its commercial impact to the limited territory, and that each intended to accept the benefits and protection of the laws only of those States within the territory. But obviously these were unrealistic hopes that cannot be treated as an automatic constitutional shield.

An automobile simply is not a stationary item or one designed to be used in one place. An automobile is intended to be moved around. . . .

The Court accepts that a State may exercise jurisdiction over a distributor which "serves" that State "indirectly" by "deliver[ing] its products into the stream of commerce with the expectation that they will be purchased by consumers in the forum State." It is difficult to see why the Constitution should distinguish between a case involving goods which reach a distant State through a chain of distribution and a case involving goods which reach the same State because a consumer, using them as the dealer knew the customer would, took them there. In each case the seller purposefully injects the goods into the stream of commerce and those goods predictably are used in the forum State. . . .

III

. . . The plaintiffs . . . brought suit in a forum with which they had significant contacts and which had significant contacts with the litigation. I am not convinced that the defendants would suffer any "heavy and disproportionate burden" in defending the suits. Accordingly, I would hold that the Constitution should not shield the defendants from appearing and defending in the plaintiffs' chosen fora.

NOTES AND QUESTIONS

1. Did the New York distributor and the retailer purposely avail themselves of conducting activities in Oklahoma? Could (or should) they be able to foresee being subject to the jurisdiction of the Oklahoma court?

2. Why does foreseeability matter? Should a defendant be subject to suit anywhere a product malfunctions, even if it had nothing to do with the product's location? What is the relationship between minimum contacts and foreseeability? Why did the manufacturer and the importer not contest jurisdiction in Oklahoma?

3. a. As plaintiffs' counsel, what factual argument supports jurisdiction over the manufacturer and the importer in Oklahoma?

b. As defendants' counsel, what factual argument opposes jurisdiction over the manufacturer and the importer in Oklahoma?

c. As plaintiffs' counsel, what factual argument supports jurisdiction over the New York retailer in Oklahoma?

4. How would you argue that *World-Wide Volkswagen* is not a stream-of-commerce case? Were the defendants present in Oklahoma? Did any of them use a sales or distribution scheme in which their vehicles would reach Oklahoma as products for sale? Was the chain of events leading to the arrival of the Robinson's vehicle in Oklahoma commercial in nature? Was the vehicle's arrival in Oklahoma entirely due to the Robinson's unilateral activity?

5. Is a stream-of-commerce analysis different in the case of a manufacturer of a finished product, as opposed to the manufacturer of a component product? What is the nature of the distinction? Can the manufacturer of a finished product structure its conduct to limit the geographic scope of its liability? Can a component part manufacturer do the same?

6. In *World-Wide Volkswagen*, the Court begins to explain the meaning of "fair play and substantial justice." The Court's relevant balancing criteria for evaluating the "fair play" factors are:

a. "[T]he burden on the defendant" of litigating the claim in a place removed from its principal place of business. Modern transportation tempers this burden, which also is mitigated when a defendant already has ongoing connections in the forum. Even though all defendants attempt to articulate the burden of going to a distant place to litigate, courts seriously consider this factor for a foreign defendant who has to travel a long distance in another nation's legal system. When another forum within the federal court system would not constitute a burden, changing venue to that other forum accommodates the interest.

b. "[T]he forum state's interest in" deciding the case. States have an interest in providing a place for their residents to seek a remedy for injuries caused by nonresident persons. The forum also has an interest if its law will apply to the case. When the interest is satisfied by settlement of the resident's claim, the forum's interest no longer is nearly as strong.

c. "[T]he plaintiff's interest in obtaining convenient and effective relief." This factor is especially important when the plaintiff's chances of recovery would be greatly reduced by forcing her to litigate elsewhere because of the latter forum's laws. It is also promoted when the plaintiff is financially unable to litigate elsewhere.

d. "[T]he interstate judicial system's interest in obtaining the most efficient resolution of controversies." Courts generally consider where the witnesses and evidence are likely to be located, although there is always some inefficiency in having one side travel to the other's forum state. To avoid piecemeal litigation, when numerous defendants are from diverse locations, a court may evaluate whether, as in *World-Wide Volkswagen*, it is better for plaintiffs to maintain the case in Oklahoma against the two defendants and sue the other two in New York, or whether it would be more efficient to dismiss the Oklahoma case and sue all four defendants in a New York court. If much of the evidence is documentary and can easily be sent to the forum, this factor is less important.

e. "[T]he shared interest of the several States in furthering fundamental substantive social policies." This is a positive factor when there is a common interest in dealing with a common problem. Courts have the most difficulty articulating this factor, but it is peculiar to the type of lawsuit, e.g., hazardous waste, bad drivers, bad air, ensuring that valid contracts are not breached. When the subject of the litigation is the conduct of foreign defendants so that foreign law might apply, this factor works against invoking the jurisdiction of the court over the foreign defendant.

See Leslie W. Abramson, "Clarifying 'Fair Play and Substantial Justice': How the Courts Apply the Supreme Court Standard for Personal Jurisdiction," 18 Hastings Const. L.Q. 441 (1991).

In *World-Wide Volkswagen*, why did the majority merely refer to the "fair play" factors, while the dissent discussed their applicability in detail?

7. With the Court's decision, what options remain for the plaintiffs? If you were plaintiffs' counsel, would you continue to pursue damages in Oklahoma against the manufacturer and the importer and file a separate claim in New York against the distributor and the retailer? Or, would it be more efficient to voluntarily dismiss the claims against the remaining Oklahoma parties and file against all four defendants in New York?

PROBLEMS

Evaluate the following problems from the perspective of due process contacts, for specific or general jurisdiction.

1. Tater Computer Chips, Inc. is a Delaware corporation manufacturing its products in Delaware and selling computer and electronic components to Swell Computer Corporation (which is incorporated and has its headquarters in Tennessee). Swell Computer has assembly facilities in Maryland, Delaware, and Pennsylvania. Swell Computer uses the components to manufacture computers that it advertises and sells in every state except Alaska and Hawaii. Because of Swell's nationwide sales, Tater Computer Chips has become a very profitable company. Klausing lives in Delaware and delivers the components to Swell in all three states. On his way to make a delivery in Pennsylvania, his truck collides with Grossman who lives in Pennsylvania but has never ventured outside the Erie, Pennsylvania metropolitan area.

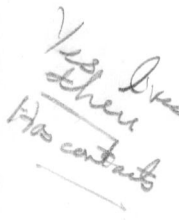

   a. As counsel for Klausing, can Klausing sue Grossman in Delaware? In Pennsylvania?

   b. As counsel for Grossman, can Grossman sue Klausing in Pennsylvania? In Maryland?

2. Loeb lives in Texas and is vacationing in Miami Beach, where he purchased a Swell Computer at a local store. At the time of the purchase, Loeb told the store manager that he was from Dallas and intended to take the computer back to his home. During the transaction, Loeb also tells the manager to call his sister-in-law Fidelow in Colorado who would be very interested in the Swell Computer products.

The computer exploded while Loeb was still in Florida, injuring Loeb seriously. A consumer products safety investigation revealed that the cause of the injuries was a malfunctioning component part made by Tater Computer Chips.

   a. As counsel for Loeb, can Loeb sue Tater Computer Chips, Inc. in Florida? In Texas? In Delaware?

b. As counsel for Loeb, can Loeb sue Swell Computer Corporation in Florida? In Texas?

3. Fidelow, who lives in Colorado, receives a call from the Miami store promoting Swell's new line of laptop computers. Fidelow orders two of the laptops for her children, but neither works as speedily as the store manager claimed. When Fidelow calls the Miami store to complain, the only message is that the phone number has been disconnected. When Fidelow calls the Swell U.S. national service center, the Swell representative denies that Swell ever had a Swell store in Miami Beach.

a. As counsel for Fidelow, can she sue the Miami Beach store for fraud in a Colorado court?

b. As counsel for Fidelow, can she sue Swell Computer Corporation for fraud in a court in Colorado? In Florida?

4. Swell Computer Corporation wants to begin selling computers in Alaska. It buys advertising in Anchorage, Alaska's daily newspaper starting on September 1. Watson lives in Anchorage. In early August of the same year, Watson's cousin e-mails Watson to persuade Watson to buy a Swell desktop computer system. The next day, Watson calls Swell's 800 number, 1-800-COMPUTR (1-800-266-7887), from his home and orders a Swell desktop. After delivery, Watson discovers that Swell has sent him a laptop instead. When Watson calls the Swell U.S. national service center, the Swell representative cannot locate Watson's order and refuses to help him.

a. As counsel for Watson, can he sue Swell Computer Corporation for breach of contract in a court in Alaska?

b. If Watson had written a letter to the national Swell headquarters in August to order a computer instead of calling the 800 number, would it be easier for an Alaska court to exercise personal jurisdiction over Swell?

Until 1984, the Court had referred to "fair play and substantial justice," but it had not indicated 1) the role of the "fair play" factors in the due process analysis, or 2) how a trial court should allocate the burden of proof on that issue. The *Burger King* case addressed these issues.

BURGER KING V. RUDZEWICZ
471 U.S. 462, 105 S.Ct. 2174, 85 L.Ed.2d 528 (1985)

JUSTICE BRENNAN delivered the opinion of the Court.

The State of Florida's long-arm statute extends jurisdiction to "[a]ny person, whether or not a citizen or resident of this state," who, *inter alia*, "[b]reach[es] a contract in this state by failing to perform acts required by the contract to be performed in this state," so long as the cause of action arises from the alleged contractual breach. Fla.Stat. § 48.193(1)(g)

(Supp.1984). The United States District Court for the Southern District of Florida, sitting in diversity, relied on this provision in exercising personal jurisdiction over a Michigan resident who allegedly had breached a franchise agreement with a Florida corporation by failing to make required payments in Florida. The question presented is whether this exercise of long-arm jurisdiction offended "traditional conception[s] of fair play and substantial justice" embodied in the Due Process Clause of the Fourteenth Amendment. *International Shoe Co. v. Washington*. . . .

I

A

Burger King Corporation is a Florida corporation whose principal offices are in Miami. It is one of the world's largest restaurant organizations, with over 3,000 outlets in the 50 States, the Commonwealth of Puerto Rico, and 8 foreign nations. Burger King conducts approximately 80% of its business through a franchise operation that the company styles the "Burger King System"—"a comprehensive restaurant format and operating system for the sale of uniform and quality food products." Burger King licenses its franchisees to use its trademarks and service marks for a period of 20 years and leases standardized restaurant facilities to them for the same term. In addition, franchisees acquire a variety of proprietary information concerning the "standards, specifications, procedures and methods for operating a Burger King Restaurant." They also receive market research and advertising assistance; ongoing training in restaurant management; and accounting, cost-control, and inventory-control guidance. By permitting franchisees to tap into Burger King's established national reputation and to benefit from proven procedures for dispensing standardized fare, this system enables them to go into the restaurant business with significantly lowered barriers to entry. . . .

Rudzewicz and MacShara jointly applied for a franchise to Burger King's Birmingham, Michigan, district office in the autumn of 1978. Their application was forwarded to Burger King's Miami headquarters, which entered into a preliminary agreement with them in February 1979. During the ensuing four months it was agreed that Rudzewicz and MacShara would assume operation of an existing facility in Drayton Plains, Michigan. MacShara attended the prescribed management courses in Miami during this period, and the franchisees purchased $165,000 worth of restaurant equipment from Burger King's Davmor Industries division in Miami. Even before the final agreements were signed, however, the parties began to disagree over site-development fees, building design, computation of monthly rent, and whether the franchisees would be able to assign their liabilities to a corporation they had formed. During these disputes Rudzewicz and MacShara negotiated both with the Birmingham district office and with the Miami headquarters. With some misgivings, Rudzewicz and MacShara finally obtained limited concessions from the Miami headquarters, signed the final agreements, and commenced operations in June 1979. By signing the final agreements, Rudzewicz obligated himself personally to payments exceeding $1 million over the 20-year franchise relationship....

The Drayton Plains facility apparently enjoyed steady business during the summer of 1979, but patronage declined after a recession began later that year. Rudzewicz and MacShara soon fell far behind in their monthly payments to Miami. Headquarters sent notices of default, and an extended period of negotiations began among the franchisees, the Birmingham district office, and the Miami headquarters. After several Burger King officials in Miami had engaged in prolonged but ultimately unsuccessful negotiations with the franchisees by mail and by telephone, headquarters terminated the franchise and ordered Rudzewicz and MacShara to vacate the premises. They refused and continued to occupy and operate the facility as a Burger King restaurant.

B

Burger King commenced the instant action in the United States District Court for the Southern District of Florida in May 1981, invoking that court's diversity jurisdiction pursuant to 28 U.S.C. § 1332(a) and its original jurisdiction over federal trademark disputes pursuant to § 1338(a). Burger King alleged that Rudzewicz and MacShara had breached their franchise obligations "within [the jurisdiction of] this district court" by failing to make the required payments "at plaintiff's place of business in Miami, Dade County, Florida," and also charged that they were tortiously infringing its trademarks and service marks through their continued, unauthorized operation as a Burger King restaurant. Burger King sought damages, injunctive relief, and costs and attorney's fees. Rudzewicz and MacShara entered special appearances and argued, inter alia, that because they were Michigan residents and because Burger King's claim did not "arise" within the Southern District of Florida, the District Court lacked personal jurisdiction over them. The District Court denied their motions after a hearing, holding that, pursuant to Florida's long-arm statute, "a non-resident Burger King franchisee is subject to the personal jurisdiction of this Court in actions arising out of its franchise agreements."...

After a 3-day bench trial, the court again concluded that it had "jurisdiction over the subject matter and the parties to this cause." Finding that Rudzewicz and MacShara had breached their franchise agreements with Burger King and had infringed Burger King's trademarks and service marks, the court entered judgment against them, jointly and severally, for $228,875 in contract damages. The court also ordered them "to immediately close Burger King Restaurant Number 775 from continued operation or to immediately give the keys and possession of said restaurant to Burger King Corporation," found that they had failed to prove any of the required elements of their counterclaim, and awarded costs and attorney's fees to Burger King.

Rudzewicz appealed to the Court of Appeals for the Eleventh Circuit. A divided panel of that Circuit reversed the judgment, concluding that the District Court could not properly exercise personal jurisdiction over Rudzewicz pursuant to Fla.Stat. § 48.193(1)(g) (Supp.1984) because "the circumstances of the Drayton Plains franchise and the negotiations which led to it left Rudzewicz bereft of reasonable notice and financially unprepared for the prospect of franchise litigation in Florida." *Burger King Corp. v. MacShara*, 724 F.2d 1505, 1513 (1984). Accordingly, the panel majority concluded that "[j]urisdiction under these circumstances would offend the fundamental fairness which is the touchstone of due process." *Ibid.*

Treating the jurisdictional statement as a petition for a writ of certiorari, we grant the petition and now reverse.

II

A

The Due Process Clause protects an individual's liberty interest in not being subject to the binding judgments of a forum with which he has established no meaningful "contacts, ties, or relations." *International Shoe Co. v. Washington.* By requiring that individuals have "fair warning that a particular activity may subject [them] to the jurisdiction of a foreign sovereign," the Due Process Clause "gives a degree of predictability to the legal system that allows potential defendants to structure their primary conduct with some minimum assurance as to where that conduct will and will not render them liable to suit," *World-Wide Volkswagen Corp. v. Woodson.*

Where a forum seeks to assert specific jurisdiction over an out-of-state defendant who has not consented to suit there, this "fair warning" requirement is satisfied if the defendant has "purposefully directed" his activities at residents of the forum, and the litigation results from alleged injuries that "arise out of or relate to" those activities, *Helicopteros Nacionales de Colombia, S.A. v. Hall.* Thus "[t]he forum State does not exceed its powers under the Due Process Clause if it asserts personal jurisdiction over a corporation that delivers its products into the stream of commerce with the expectation that they will be purchased by consumers in the forum State" and those products subsequently injure forum consumers. *World-Wide Volkswagen Corp. v. Woodson.* Similarly, a publisher who distributes magazines in a distant State may fairly be held accountable in that forum for damages resulting there from an allegedly defamatory story. *Keeton v. Hustler Magazine, Inc.*, see also *Calder v.*

Jones. And with respect to interstate contractual obligations, we have emphasized that parties who "reach out beyond one state and create continuing relationships and obligations with citizens of another state" are subject to regulation and sanctions in the other State for the consequences of their activities. *Travelers Health Assn. v. Virginia*, 339 U.S. 643, 647 (1950). See also *McGee v. International Life Insurance Co.*

[T]he constitutional touchstone remains whether the defendant purposefully established "minimum contacts" in the forum State. *International Shoe Co. v. Washington*. Although it has been argued that foreseeability of causing injury in another State should be sufficient to establish such contacts there when policy considerations so require, the Court has consistently held that this kind of foreseeability is not a "sufficient benchmark" for exercising personal jurisdiction. *World-Wide Volkswagen Corp. v. Woodson*. Instead, "the foreseeability that is critical to due process analysis . . . is that the defendant's conduct and connection with the forum State are such that he should reasonably anticipate being haled into court there." *Id.*, at 297. In defining when it is that a potential defendant should "reasonably anticipate" out-of-state litigation, the Court frequently has drawn from the reasoning of *Hanson v. Denckla*:

> The unilateral activity of those who claim some relationship with a nonresident defendant cannot satisfy the requirement of contact with the forum State. The application of that rule will vary with the quality and nature of the defendant's activity, but it is essential in each case that there be some act by which the defendant purposefully avails itself of the privilege of conducting activities within the forum State, thus invoking the benefits and protections of its laws.

This "purposeful availment" requirement ensures that a defendant will not be haled into a jurisdiction solely as a result of "random," "fortuitous," or "attenuated" contacts, *World-Wide Volkswagen Corp. v. Woodson*, or of the "unilateral activity of another party or a third person," *Helicopteros Nacionales de Colombia, S.A. v. Hall*. Jurisdiction is proper, however, where the contacts proximately result from actions by the defendant himself that create a "substantial connection" with the forum State. *McGee v. International Life Insurance Co.* Thus where the defendant "deliberately" has engaged in significant activities within a State, *Keeton v. Hustler Magazine, Inc.*, or has created "continuing obligations" between himself and residents of the forum, *Travelers Health Assn. v. Virginia*, he manifestly has availed himself of the privilege of conducting business there, and because his activities are shielded by "the benefits and protections" of the forum's laws it is presumptively not unreasonable to require him to submit to the burdens of litigation in that forum as well.

Jurisdiction in these circumstances may not be avoided merely because the defendant did not *physically* enter the forum State. Although territorial presence frequently will enhance a potential defendant's affiliation with a State and reinforce the reasonable foreseeability of suit there, it is an inescapable fact of modern commercial life that a substantial amount of business is transacted solely by mail and wire communications across state lines, thus obviating the need for physical presence within a State in which business is conducted. So long as a commercial actor's efforts are "purposefully directed" toward residents of another State, we have consistently rejected the notion that an absence of physical contacts can defeat personal jurisdiction there.

Once it has been decided that a defendant purposefully established minimum contacts within the forum State, these contacts may be considered in light of other factors to determine whether the assertion of personal jurisdiction would comport with "fair play and substantial justice." *International Shoe Co. v. Washington.* Thus courts in "appropriate case[s]" may evaluate "the burden on the defendant," "the forum State's interest in adjudicating the dispute," "the plaintiff's interest in obtaining convenient and effective relief," "the interstate judicial system's interest in obtaining the most efficient resolution of controversies," and the "shared interest of the several States in furthering fundamental substantive social policies." *World-Wide Volkswagen Corp. v. Woodson.* These considerations sometimes serve to establish the reasonableness of jurisdiction upon a lesser showing of minimum contacts than would otherwise be required. See, e.g., *McGee v. International Life Insurance Co.* On the other hand, where a defendant who purposefully has directed his activities at forum residents seeks to defeat jurisdiction, he must present a compelling case that the presence of some other considerations would render jurisdiction unreasonable. Most such considerations usually may be accommodated through means short of finding jurisdiction unconstitutional. For example, the potential clash of the forum's law with the "fundamental substantive social policies" of another State may be accommodated through application of the forum's choice-of-law rules. Similarly, a defendant claiming substantial inconvenience may seek a change of venue. . . .

B

(1)

Applying these principles to the case at hand, we believe there is substantial record evidence supporting the District Court's conclusion that the assertion of personal jurisdiction over Rudzewicz in Florida for the alleged breach of his franchise agreement did not offend due process. At the outset, we note a continued division among lower courts respecting whether and to what extent a contract can constitute a "contact" for purposes of due process analysis. If the question is whether an individual's contract with an out-of-state party alone can automatically establish sufficient minimum contacts in the other party's home forum, we believe the answer clearly is that it cannot. The Court long ago rejected the notion that personal jurisdiction might turn on "mechanical" tests, *International Shoe Co. v. Washington*, or on "conceptualistic . . . theories of the place of contracting or of performance." Instead, we have emphasized the need for a "highly realistic" approach that recognizes that a "contract" is "ordinarily but an intermediate step serving to tie up prior business negotiations with future consequences which themselves are the real object of the business transaction." . . .

In this case, no physical ties to Florida can be attributed to Rudzewicz other than MacShara's brief training course in Miami. Rudzewicz did not maintain offices in Florida and, for all that appears from the record, has never even visited there. Yet this franchise dispute grew directly out of "a contract which had a *substantial* connection with that State." *McGee v. International Life Insurance Co.* (emphasis added). Eschewing the option of operating an independent local enterprise, Rudzewicz deliberately "reach[ed] out beyond" Michigan and negotiated with a Florida corporation for the purchase of a long-term franchise and the manifold benefits that would derive from affiliation with a nationwide organization. *Travelers Health Assn. v. Virginia*. Upon approval, he entered into a carefully structured 20-year relationship that envisioned continuing and wide-reaching contacts with Burger King in Florida. In light of Rudzewicz' voluntary acceptance of the long-term and exacting regulation of his business from Burger King's Miami headquarters, the "quality and nature" of his relationship to the company in Florida can in no sense be viewed as "random," "fortuitous," or "attenuated." *Hanson v. Denckla*; *World-Wide Volkswagen Corp. v. Woodson*. Rudzewicz' refusal to make the contractually required payments in Miami, and his continued use of Burger King's trademarks and confidential business information after his termination, caused foreseeable injuries to the corporation in Florida. For these reasons it was, at the very least, presumptively reasonable for Rudzewicz to be called to account there for such injuries.

The Court of Appeals concluded, however, that in light of the supervision emanating from Burger King's district office in Birmingham, Rudzewicz reasonably believed that "the Michigan office was for all intents and purposes the embodiment of Burger King" and that he therefore had no "reason to anticipate a Burger King suit outside of Michigan." This reasoning overlooks substantial record evidence indicating that Rudzewicz most certainly knew that he was affiliating himself with an enterprise based primarily in Florida. The contract documents themselves emphasize that Burger King's operations are conducted and supervised from the Miami headquarters, that all relevant notices and payments must be sent there, and that the agreements were made in and enforced from Miami. Moreover, the parties' actual course of dealing repeatedly confirmed that decisionmaking authority was vested in the Miami headquarters and that the district office served largely as an intermediate link between the headquarters and the franchisees. When problems arose over building design, site-development fees, rent computation, and the defaulted payments, Rudzewicz and MacShara learned that the Michigan office was powerless to resolve their disputes and could only channel their communications to Miami. Throughout these disputes, the Miami headquarters and the Michigan franchisees carried on a continuous course of direct communications by mail and by telephone, and it was the Miami headquarters that made the key negotiating decisions out of which the instant litigation arose.

Moreover, we believe the Court of Appeals gave insufficient weight to provisions in the various franchise documents providing that all disputes would be governed by Florida law.... Nothing in our cases ... suggests that a choice-of-law provision should be ignored in considering whether a defendant has "purposefully invoked the benefits and protections of a State's laws" for jurisdictional purposes. Although such a provision standing alone would be insufficient to confer jurisdiction, we believe that, when combined with the 20-year interdependent relationship Rudzewicz established with Burger King's Miami headquarters, it reinforced his deliberate affiliation with the forum State and the reasonable foreseeability of possible litigation there....

(2)

Nor has Rudzewicz pointed to other factors that can be said persuasively to outweigh the considerations discussed above and to establish the unconstitutionality of Florida's assertion of jurisdiction. We cannot conclude that Florida had no "legitimate interest in holding [Rudzewicz] answerable on a claim related to" the contacts he had established in that State....

The Court of Appeals also concluded, however, that the parties' dealings involved "a characteristic disparity of bargaining power" and "elements of surprise," and that Rudzewicz "lacked fair notice" of the potential for litigation in Florida because the contractual provisions suggesting to the contrary were merely "boilerplate declarations in a lengthy printed contract." ... To the contrary, Rudzewicz was represented by counsel throughout these complex transactions and, as Judge Johnson observed in dissent below, was himself an experienced accountant "who for five months conducted negotiations with Burger King over the terms of the franchise and lease agreements, and who obligated himself personally to contracts requiring over time payments that exceeded $1 million." Rudzewicz was able to secure a modest reduction in rent and other concessions from Miami headquarters; moreover, to the extent that Burger King's terms were inflexible, Rudzewicz presumably

III

Notwithstanding these considerations, the Court of Appeals apparently believed that it was necessary to reject jurisdiction in this case as a prophylactic measure, reasoning that an affirmance of the District Court's judgment would result in the exercise of jurisdiction over "out-of-state consumers to collect payments due on modest personal purchases" and would "sow the seeds of default judgments against franchisees owing smaller debts." We share the Court of Appeals' broader concerns and therefore reject any talismanic jurisdictional formulas; "the facts of each case must [always] be weighed" in determining whether personal jurisdiction would comport with "fair play and substantial justice." The "quality and nature" of an interstate transaction may sometimes be so "random," "fortuitous," or "attenuated" that it cannot fairly be said that the potential defendant "should reasonably anticipate being haled into court" in another jurisdiction. *World-Wide Volkswagen Corp. v. Woodson.* We also have emphasized that jurisdiction may not be grounded on a contract whose terms have been obtained through "fraud, undue influence, or overweening bargaining power" and whose application would render litigation "so gravely difficult and inconvenient that [a party] will for all practical purposes be deprived of his day in court." . . .

For the reasons set forth above, however, these dangers are not present in the instant case. Because Rudzewicz established a substantial and continuing relationship with Burger King's Miami headquarters, received fair notice from the contract documents and the course of dealing that he might be subject to suit in Florida, and has failed to demonstrate how jurisdiction in that forum would otherwise be fundamentally unfair, we conclude that the District Court's exercise of jurisdiction pursuant to Fla.Stat. § 48.193(1)(g) (Supp.1984) did not offend due process. The judgment of the Court of Appeals is accordingly reversed, and the case is remanded for further proceedings consistent with this opinion.

JUSTICE STEVENS, with whom JUSTICE WHITE joins, dissenting.

In my opinion there is a significant element of unfairness in requiring a franchisee to defend a case of this kind in the forum chosen by the franchisor. It is undisputed that appellee maintained no place of business in Florida, that he had no employees in that State, and that he was not licensed to do business there. Appellee did not prepare his French fries, shakes, and hamburgers in Michigan, and then deliver them into the stream of commerce "with the expectation that they [would] be purchased by consumers in" Florida. To the contrary, appellee did business only in Michigan, his business, property, and payroll taxes were payable in that State, and he sold all of his products there.

Throughout the business relationship, appellee's principal contacts with appellant were with its Michigan office. Notwithstanding its disclaimer, the Court seems ultimately to rely on nothing more than standard boilerplate language contained in various documents, to establish that appellee "'purposefully availed himself of the benefits and protections of Florida's laws.'" Such superficial analysis creates a potential for unfairness not only in negotiations between franchisors and their franchisees but, more significantly, in the resolution of the disputes that inevitably arise from time to time in such relationships.

Accordingly, I respectfully dissent.

NOTES AND QUESTIONS

1. *Burger King* differed from prior decisions in three ways. First, the lawsuit was filed in a federal court. The court invoked jurisdiction over the Michigan franchisees based on Federal Rule of Civil Procedure 4, which permits a federal court to use the long-arm statute of the state in which it is sitting to reach nonresident defendants. Rule 4 allows a federal court to exercise personal jurisdiction to the extent the state in which the federal court is sitting can exert jurisdiction under its long-arm statute. See Chapter 6 pt. C for more on service of process.

Second, the decision describes the chronology of due process analysis. Initially, the burden of raising the issue of lack of personal jurisdiction is on the defendant who meets that burden by moving to dismiss the complaint. The burden then moves to the plaintiff to establish that the defendant has the requisite contact(s) with the forum state that put the defendant on notice about the foreseeability of being sued.

If the plaintiff sustains its burden of proof on the minimum contacts issue, the burden of proof on the issue of fair play and substantial justice switches to the defendant. The defendant has the opportunity to show "a compelling case" that even though he has minimum contacts with the forum state, it is nevertheless constitutionally unreasonable for him to defend where the litigation related contacts occurred. In *Burger King*, the Court quickly disposed of the "fair play" analysis by observing that the defendant failed to point "to other factors that can be said persuasively to . . . establish the unconstitutionality of" the forum state's assertion of jurisdiction. Given the Court's articulation of the governing burdens for the first time in *Burger King*, it was not surprising that counsel for the franchisees may have been unaware of their obligations to present a "compelling" case of unreasonableness.

Third, the Court measured the trial court's findings of fact against the Federal Rule 52(a) standard of clearly erroneous, which "requires that '[f]indings of fact . . . must not be set aside unless clearly erroneous.' . . . [N]either Rudzewicz nor the Court of Appeals has pointed to record evidence that would support a 'definite and firm conviction' that the District Court's findings are mistaken." The effect of using the "clearly erroneous" standard is that appellate courts are more deferential to the trial court's findings of fact on issues of foreseeability, purposeful availment, and fair play and substantial justice.

2. A finding that jurisdiction over a nonresident defendant is reasonable effectively means that the defendant failed to present a compelling reason to rebut the presumption of reasonableness of asserting jurisdiction. Because this fact-specific approach lacks predictability and precision, it is subject to strong criticism from lower courts that are bound to apply it. For example, the court in *LAK, Inc. v. Deer Creek Enterprises*, 885 F.2d 1293 (6th Cir. 1989) remarked that:

> If it suggests nothing else, this case may suggest that there is a downside, as well as an upside, to the judicially imposed requirement that each and every question of personal jurisdiction over a non-resident defendant be decided "on its own facts," with counsel and court sifting through each new complex of facts in search of "contacts" demonstrating that the plaintiff's choice of a forum does or does not accord with the notions of "reasonableness" and "fair play" reflected in a vast number of fact-specific judicial opinions. More sharply defined standards might well reduce miscalculations on the part of lawyers who, not surprisingly, normally seek a home court advantage if they think they see some chance of getting it—and it is not inconceivable that clearer standards might lead to more expeditious and efficient resolution of those jurisdictional questions that counsel choose to fight out in court. In this particular case, diligent lawyers have favored us with several hundred case citations; scholarship that comprehensive carries obvious costs, both in time and in money.

3. Since *Burger King*, in contract cases the key evaluative factors in determining whether a nonresident defendant has purposefully established the requisite contacts in the forum state are prior negotiations and contemplated future consequences, the terms of the contract, and the parties' actual course of dealing. What is the meaning of prior negotiations and contemplated future consequences? Courts have considered several factors in the contract situation, such as where the parties contemplated that the work would be performed, where the negotiations were conducted, where payment was made, and whether the defendant initiated the business relationship in some way. The last factor appears to be the strongest factor.

    a. Who initiated the business relationship? Does the record establish that the plaintiff pursued the nonresident defendant? For example, did a representative of the plaintiff travel to the defendant's location in another state to secure the defendant as a developer of a project after arrangements with a first developer fell apart?

b. Prior negotiations. Did all prior face-to-face negotiations between the parties occur in the defendant's state by local counsel for all parties? Were documents executed there as well?

c. Where did the parties contemplate that performance was to occur? For example, was the project designed by an engineer in the defendant's state, constructed by local contractors, and managed by a defendant's state's municipality?

d. Parties' course of dealing. Did the defendant avail itself of the benefits and protections of the law where the lawsuit was filed? Does the franchise agreement include terms regarding regulation of the franchise by the headquarters in the forum state?

e. Does the agreement contain a provision that the laws of the forum state would govern the agreement?

4. If the two franchisees had sued Burger King, what state courts would have jurisdiction over Burger King? Would general jurisdiction enable them to sue in any state where there are franchises?

5. The contract at issue in *Burger King* contained a choice of law clause, meaning that the parties agreed that regardless of where a lawsuit was filed, Florida law would apply to resolve the dispute. A choice of law clause is comparable to the forum selection clause already discussed in conjunction with the *Shute* case, (see the Notes after *International Shoe*). Indeed, many contracts contain both types of clauses, prescribing not only what state's law applies but also where any lawsuit arising from the contract must be filed.

The Supreme Court cases after *Pennoyer* appeared to reverse many of the 19th century territorial principles of jurisdiction over defendants. A court in one state now can assert jurisdiction over defendants who have never physically been in the state, either when the claim arose or when the suit was filed. What happens when a nonresident defendant is served while visiting the forum state? The next decision by the Supreme Court in the area of personal jurisdiction is a reminder that portions of *Pennoyer*'s jurisprudence survive. Although the Court is split on the reason for upholding jurisdiction over a defendant who is served while inside the forum state, there is agreement about the validity of "transient" jurisdiction.

BURNHAM V. SUPERIOR COURT
495 U.S. 604, 110 S.Ct. 2105, 109 L.Ed.2d 631 (1990)

JUSTICE SCALIA announced the judgment of the Court and delivered an opinion in which THE CHIEF JUSTICE and JUSTICE KENNEDY join, and in which JUSTICE WHITE joins with respect to Parts I, II–A, II–B, and II–C.

The question presented is whether the Due Process Clause of the Fourteenth Amendment denies California courts jurisdiction over a nonresident, who was personally served with process while temporarily in that State, in a suit unrelated to his activities in the State.

I

Petitioner Dennis Burnham married Francie Burnham in 1976 in West Virginia. In 1977 the couple moved to New Jersey, where their two children were born. In July 1987 the Burnhams decided to separate. They agreed that Mrs. Burnham, who intended to move to California, would take custody of the children. Shortly before Mrs. Burnham departed for California that same month, she and petitioner agreed that she would file for divorce on grounds of "irreconcilable differences."

In October 1987, petitioner filed for divorce in New Jersey state court on grounds of "desertion." Petitioner did not, however, obtain an issuance of summons against his wife and did not attempt to serve her with process. Mrs. Burnham, after unsuccessfully demanding that petitioner adhere to their prior agreement to submit to an "irreconcilable differences" divorce, brought suit for divorce in California state court in early January 1988.

In late January, petitioner visited southern California on business, after which he went north to visit his children in the San Francisco Bay area, where his wife resided. He took the older child to San Francisco for the weekend. Upon returning the child to Mrs. Burnham's home on January 24, 1988, petitioner was served with a California court summons and a copy of Mrs. Burnham's divorce petition. He then returned to New Jersey.

Later that year, petitioner made a special appearance in the California Superior Court, moving to quash the service of process on the ground that the court lacked personal jurisdiction over him because his only contacts with California were a few short visits to the State for the purposes of conducting business and visiting his children. The Superior Court denied the motion, and the California Court of Appeal denied mandamus relief, rejecting petitioner's contention that the Due Process Clause prohibited California courts from asserting jurisdiction over him because he lacked "minimum contacts" with the State. The court held it to be "a valid jurisdictional predicate for *in personam* jurisdiction" that the "defendant [was] present in the forum state and personally served with process." We granted certiorari.

II

A

... To determine whether the assertion of personal jurisdiction is consistent with due process, we have long relied on the principles traditionally followed by American courts in marking out the territorial limits of each State's authority. That criterion was first announced in *Pennoyer v. Neff*. ... Since *International Shoe*, we have only been called upon to decide whether these "traditional notions" permit States to exercise jurisdiction over absent defendants in a manner that deviates from the rules of jurisdiction applied in the 19th century. We have held such deviations permissible, but only with respect to suits arising out of the absent defendant's contacts with the State. The question we must decide today is whether due process requires a similar connection between the litigation and the defendant's contacts with the State in cases where the defendant is physically present in the State at the time process is served upon him.

B

Among the most firmly established principles of personal jurisdiction in American tradition is that the courts of a State have jurisdiction over nonresidents who are physically present in the State. The view developed early that each State had the power to hale before its courts any individual who could be found within its borders, and that once having acquired jurisdiction over such a person by properly serving him with process, the State could retain jurisdiction to enter judgment against him, no matter how fleeting his visit. ...

Particularly striking is the fact that, as far as we have been able to determine, not one American case from the period (or, for that matter, *not one* American case until 1978) held, or even suggested, that in-state personal service on an individual was insufficient to confer personal jurisdiction. ...

This American jurisdictional practice is, moreover, not merely old; it is continuing. It remains the practice of, not only a substantial number of the States, but as far as we are aware all the States and the Federal Government ... We do not know of a single state or federal statute, or a single judicial decision resting upon state law, that has abandoned in-state service as a basis of jurisdiction. ...

C

Despite this formidable body of precedent, petitioner contends, in reliance on our decisions applying the *International Shoe* standard, that in the absence of "continuous and systematic" contacts with the forum, a nonresident defendant can be subjected to judgment only as to matters that arise out of or relate to his contacts with the forum. This argument rests on a thorough misunderstanding of our cases.

... The short of the matter is that jurisdiction based on physical presence alone constitutes due process because it is one of the continuing traditions of our legal system that define the due process standard of "traditional notions of fair play and substantial justice." That standard was developed by analogy to "physical presence," and it would be perverse to say it could now be turned against that touchstone of jurisdiction.

D

Petitioner's strongest argument, though we ultimately reject it, relies upon our decision in *Shaffer v. Heitner*, 433 U.S. 186 (1977)....

It goes too far to say, as petitioner contends, that *Shaffer* compels the conclusion that a State lacks jurisdiction over an individual unless the litigation arises out of his activities in the State. *Shaffer*, like *International Shoe*, involved jurisdiction over an *absent defendant*, and it stands for nothing more than the proposition that when the "minimum contact" that is a substitute for physical presence consists of property ownership it must, like other minimum contacts, be related to the litigation. Petitioner wrenches out of its context our statement in *Shaffer* that "all assertions of state-court jurisdiction must be evaluated according to the standards set forth in International Shoe and its progeny." ... The logic of *Shaffer*'s holding—which places all suits against absent nonresidents on the same constitutional footing, regardless of whether a separate Latin label is attached to one particular basis of contact—does not compel the conclusion that physically present defendants must be treated identically to absent ones....

It is fair to say, however, that while our holding today does not contradict *Shaffer*, our basic approach to the due process question is different. We have conducted no independent inquiry into the desirability or fairness of the prevailing in-state service rule, leaving that judgment to the legislatures that are free to amend it; for our purposes, its validation is its pedigree, as the phrase "traditional notions of fair play and substantial justice" makes clear. *Shaffer* did conduct such an independent inquiry, asserting that " 'traditional notions of fair play and substantial justice can be as readily offended by the perpetuation of ancient forms that are no longer justified as by the adoption of new procedures that are inconsistent with the basic values of our constitutional heritage.' " ... Where, however, as in the present case, a jurisdictional principle is both firmly approved by tradition and still favored, it is impossible to imagine what standard we could appeal to for the judgment that it is "no longer justified." While in no way receding from or casting doubt upon the holding of *Shaffer* or any other case, we reaffirm today our time-honored approach.... For new procedures, hitherto unknown, the Due Process Clause requires analysis to determine whether "traditional notions of fair play and substantial justice" have been offended. But a doctrine of personal jurisdiction that dates back to the adoption of the Fourteenth Amendment and is still generally observed unquestionably meets that standard.

III

A few words in response to Justice Brennan's opinion concurring in the judgment: It insists that we apply "contemporary notions of due process" to determine the constitutionality of California's assertion of jurisdiction.... The "contemporary notions of due process" applicable to personal jurisdiction are the enduring "*traditional* notions of fair play and substantial justice" established as the test by *International Shoe*. By its very language, that test is satisfied if a state court adheres to jurisdictional rules that are generally applied and have always been applied in the United States.

But the concurrence's proposed standard of "contemporary notions of due process" requires more: It measures state-court jurisdiction not only against traditional doctrines in this country, including current state-court practice, but also against each Justice's subjective assessment of what is fair and just. Authority for that seductive standard is not to be found in any of our personal jurisdiction cases. It is, indeed, an outright break with the test of "traditional notions of fair play and substantial justice," which would have to be reformulated "*our* notions of fair play and substantial justice."

... Because the Due Process Clause does not prohibit the California courts from exercising jurisdiction over petitioner based on the fact of in-state service of process, the judgment is affirmed.

JUSTICE WHITE, concurring in part and concurring in the judgment.

I join Parts I, II–A, II–B, and II–C of Justice SCALIA's opinion and concur in the judgment of affirmance. The rule allowing jurisdiction to be obtained over a nonresident by personal service in the forum State, without more, has been and is so widely accepted throughout this country that I could not possibly strike it down, either on its face or as applied in this case, on the ground that it denies due process of law guaranteed by the Fourteenth Amendment....

JUSTICE BRENNAN, with whom JUSTICE MARSHALL, JUSTICE BLACKMUN, and JUSTICE O'CONNOR join, concurring in the judgment.

I agree with Justice SCALIA that the Due Process Clause of the Fourteenth Amendment generally permits a state court to exercise jurisdiction over a defendant if he is served with process while voluntarily present in the forum State. I do not perceive the need, however, to decide that a jurisdictional rule that " 'has been immemorially the actual law of the land,' " automatically comports with due process simply by virtue of its "pedigree." ... Unlike Justice SCALIA, I would undertake an "independent inquiry into the ... fairness of the prevailing in-state service rule." I therefore concur only in the judgment.

I

I believe that the approach adopted by Justice Scalia's opinion today—reliance solely on historical pedigree—is foreclosed by our decisions in *International Shoe Co. v. Washington* and *Shaffer v. Heitner*.... The critical insight of *Shaffer* is that all rules of jurisdiction, even ancient ones, must satisfy contemporary notions of due process. . . . I agree with this approach and continue to believe that "the minimum-contacts analysis developed in *International Shoe* represents a far more sensible construct for the exercise of state-court jurisdiction than the patchwork of legal and factual fictions that has been generated from the decision in *Pennoyer v. Neff*."

While our *holding* in *Shaffer* may have been limited to *quasi in rem* jurisdiction, our mode of analysis was not. Indeed, that we were willing in *Shaffer* to examine anew the appropriateness of the *quasi in rem* rule—until that time dutifully accepted by American courts for at least a century—demonstrates that we did not believe that the "pedigree" of a jurisdictional practice was dispositive in deciding whether it was consistent with due process. . . . Notwithstanding the nimble gymnastics of Justice Scalia's opinion today, it is not faithful to our decision in *Shaffer*.

II

Tradition, though alone not dispositive, is of course relevant to the question whether the rule of transient jurisdiction is consistent with due process. Tradition is salient not in the sense that practices of the past are automatically reasonable today.

Rather, I find the historical background relevant because, however murky the jurisprudential origins of transient jurisdiction, the fact that American courts have announced the rule for perhaps a century ... provides a defendant voluntarily present in a particular State *today* "clear notice that [he] is subject to suit" in the forum. . . . The transient rule is consistent with reasonable expectations and is entitled to a strong presumption that it comports with due process.

By visiting the forum State, a transient defendant actually "avail[s]" himself, of significant benefits provided by the State. His health and safety are guaranteed by the State's police, fire, and emergency medical services; he is free to travel on the State's roads and waterways; he likely enjoys the fruits of the State's economy as well. Moreover, the Privileges and Immunities Clause of Article IV prevents a state government from discriminating against a transient defendant by denying him the protections of its law or the right of access to its courts. Subject only to the doctrine of *forum non conveniens*, an out-of-state plaintiff may use state courts in all circumstances in which those courts would be available to state citizens. Without transient jurisdiction, an asymmetry would arise: A transient would have the full benefit of the power of the forum State's courts as a plaintiff while retaining immunity from their authority as a defendant.

The potential burdens on a transient defendant are slight.... That the defendant has already journeyed at least once before to the forum—as evidenced by the fact that he was served with process there—is an indication that suit in the forum likely would not be prohibitively inconvenient. Finally, any burdens that do arise can be ameliorated by a variety of procedural devices. For these reasons, as a rule the exercise of personal jurisdiction over a defendant based on his voluntary presence in the forum will satisfy the requirements of due process.

In this case, it is undisputed that petitioner was served with process while voluntarily and knowingly in the State of California. I therefore concur in the judgment.

JUSTICE STEVENS, concurring in the judgment.

As I explained in my separate writing, I did not join the Court's opinion in *Shaffer v. Heitner* because I was concerned by its unnecessarily broad reach. The same concern prevents me from joining either Justice Scalia's or Justice Brennan's opinion in this case. For me, it is sufficient to note that the historical evidence and consensus identified by Justice Scalia, the considerations of fairness identified by Justice Brennan, and the common sense displayed by Justice White, all combine to demonstrate that this is, indeed, a very easy case. Accordingly, I agree that the judgment should be affirmed.

NOTES AND QUESTIONS

1. *Burnham* confirms a fourth basis for the modern exercise of jurisdiction, in addition to domicile, contacts, and consent. As subsequent decisions had eroded *Pennoyer*, lower courts and commentators had questioned the continued viability of transient jurisdiction. When a defendant is personally served with process while physically present (however briefly) in the forum state, personal service is sufficient to confer personal jurisdiction without violating due process.

Justice Scalia said that it is a firmly established principle that a state has jurisdiction over nonresidents who are physically present (however briefly) in the state, regardless of whether the plaintiff's claim is related to the defendant's activities there. Was that principle so firmly established after the cases decided between *Pennoyer* and *Burnham*? Or, did Justice Scalia reinstate the *Pennoyer* idea that each state can automatically exert authority over anyone served within the state borders, and the state retains that authority to enter a judgment against the person?

2. From the nonresident defendant's point of view, how fair is it to be forced to defend in a place where the defendant has no contacts aside from being served during a brief presence there? Your client is a lifelong resident of New York whose commitment to his business never allowed him time for a vacation. A possible buyer of your client's business communicates with him one day from his corporate offices in Texas and insists that he travel to Houston to close the deal. Your client departs for Houston, but to save money instead of a non-stop flight he had booked a one-stop flight there with a brief stop in Miami. When he deplanes, he is served with a summons and complaint to defend a wrongful discharge lawsuit filed by a former employee who has moved to Miami. What is fair to your client about that situation? Is it fair for him to have to choose between finding a lawyer in Florida and taking a default judgment? Did he assume the risk of being served with process and subject to Florida jurisdiction by his stop at the Miami airport? Could you argue for your client that he was not *voluntarily* present when he was served? Would that matter? What interest could Florida possibly have in the outcome of litigation arising in New York and filed by a disgruntled former employee who had been in Florida a short time?

What are the competing arguments? Doesn't your client receive the benefits and protections of Florida law while there, however briefly? Doesn't your client assume the risk of being served when entering the state? Isn't the transient jurisdiction rule far more predictable than the minimum contacts/foreseeability/purposeful availment doctrine for personal jurisdiction?

3. Legislatures and courts have imposed two non-constitutional limits on service of process out of a sense of fairness. One historical restriction on transient jurisdiction is that a defendant is not obligated to defend a lawsuit when she has been fraudulently induced to enter the forum state. In *Wyman v. Newhouse*, 93 F.2d 313 (2d Cir. 1937), Newhouse, a New York resident, received a telegram and a letter from his paramour, Wyman, falsely saying that her mother was ill in Ireland and that she needed to see him before she went to be with her mother permanently. He promised to go to Florida to see her, arriving at 6:00 a.m. at the Miami Airport. Before he could get to her, a deputy sheriff served him with process in a suit for $500,000. A stranger then offered to take him to his home, and stated that he knew a lawyer familiar with her attorney. He did not retain the Florida attorney, but instead returned to New York that evening and consulted his New York counsel, who advised him to ignore the Florida summons. A default judgment was entered against him. Wyman took the Florida judgment to a New York federal court to give the judgment full faith and credit and enforce it. On appeal from denial of the enforcement action, the appellate court concluded that Newhouse was persuaded to enter Florida by a fraud perpetrated upon him by Wyman falsely representing the situation.

> A judgment procured fraudulently, as here, lacks jurisdiction and is null and void. A fraud affecting the jurisdiction is equivalent to a lack of jurisdiction.... A judgment recovered in a sister state,

through the fraud of the party procuring the appearance of another, is not binding on the latter when an attempt is made to enforce such judgment in another state.... The appellee was not required to make out a defense on the merits to the suit in Florida. We are not here concerned with such rule, applicable to alleged fraud in the proceedings after valid jurisdiction of the person and the subject matter has been obtained. Here the court did not duly acquire jurisdiction and no such defense to the merits need be shown.

The other limitation on transient jurisdiction applies to nonresidents who are present in a state in order to participate in a legal proceeding. Whether a party, a witness, or an attorney, the person is generally immune from effective service of process for other lawsuits and claims for a reasonable time before and after the actual time of the proceedings. Thus, a person's presence in a forum to attend another proceeding immunizes her from even transient jurisdiction of the court during the immunity period. See *Stewart v. Ramsay*, 242 U.S. 128, 37 S.Ct. 44, 61 L.Ed. 192 (1916). The primary justification for the immunity is to prevent disruption of the ongoing proceeding and to encourage persons to attend that proceeding.

4. Many domestic relations judges believe that child custody and property disputes surrounding divorce are better resolved by agreement—when possible. Despite the animosity that can accompany divorce, can you imagine why this is so? Who can best understand a family situation and the specific problems that will arise from dissolution of a marriage? Who will have to deal with problems that come up as circumstances change in the future? Many of the earliest court mediation programs were offered, or required, in divorce cases.

When used to foster settlement in divorce cases, the mediation process is intertwined with court procedures. If a divorcing couple is able to reach an agreement, typically the court will enter it as an official part of the divorce decree. This turns the private agreement into an enforceable order of the court. State law also promotes settlement in divorce cases through "no-fault" laws, such as the "irreconcilable differences" ground that the spouses in *Burnham* initially agreed to use for their divorce.

How might the choice of litigation procedures affect the prospects for a successful mediation? Do you think a defendant in a divorce case will feel inclined to reach an agreement after being served with process while a transient? When you study service of process in Chapter 6 pt. C, consider some of the alternatives for providing notice that establishes personal jurisdiction.

J. McIntyre Machinery, Ltd. v. Nicastro
131 S.Ct. 2780 (2011)

JUSTICE KENNEDY announced the judgment of the Court and delivered an opinion, in which THE CHIEF JUSTICE, JUSTICE SCALIA, and JUSTICE THOMAS join.

Whether a person or entity is subject to the jurisdiction of a state court despite not having been present in the State either at the time of suit or at the time of the alleged injury, and despite not having consented to the exercise of jurisdiction, is a question that arises with great frequency in the routine course of litigation. The rules and standards for determining when a State does or does not have jurisdiction over an absent party have been unclear because of decades-old questions left open in *Asahi Metal Industry Co. v. Superior Court of Cal., Solano Cty.*, 480 U.S. 102, 107 S.Ct. 1026, 94 L.Ed.2d 92 (1987).

Here, the Supreme Court of New Jersey, relying in part on *Asahi*, held that New Jersey's courts can exercise jurisdiction over a foreign manufacturer of a product so long as the manufacturer "knows or reasonably should know that its products are distributed through a nationwide distribution system that might lead to those products being sold in any of the fifty states." Applying that test, the court concluded that a British manufacturer of scrap metal machines was subject to jurisdiction in New Jersey, even though at no time had it advertised in, sent goods to, or in any relevant sense targeted the State.

That decision cannot be sustained. Although the New Jersey Supreme Court issued an extensive opinion with careful attention to this Court's cases and to its own precedent, the "stream of commerce" metaphor carried the decision far afield. Due process protects the defendant's right not to be coerced except by lawful judicial power. As a general rule, the exercise of judicial power is not lawful unless the defendant "purposefully avails itself of the privilege of conducting activities within the forum State, thus invoking the benefits and protections of its laws." *Hanson v. Denckla*, 357 U.S. 235, 253, 78 S.Ct. 1228, 2 L.Ed.2d 1283 (1958). There may be exceptions, say, for instance, in cases involving an intentional tort. But the general rule is applicable in this products-liability case, and the so-called "stream-of-commerce" doctrine cannot displace it.

I

This case arises from a products-liability suit filed in New Jersey state court. Robert Nicastro seriously injured his hand while using a metal-shearing machine manufactured by J. McIntyre Machinery, Ltd. (J. McIntyre). The accident occurred in New Jersey, but the machine was manufactured in England, where J. McIntyre is incorporated and operates. The question here is whether the New Jersey courts have jurisdiction over J. McIntyre, notwithstanding the fact that the company at no time either marketed goods in the State or shipped them there. Nicastro was a plaintiff in the New Jersey trial court and is the respondent here; J. McIntyre was a defendant and is now the petitioner.

At oral argument in this Court, Nicastro's counsel stressed three primary facts in defense of New Jersey's assertion of jurisdiction over J. McIntyre.

First, an independent company agreed to sell J. McIntyre's machines in the United States. J. McIntyre itself did not sell its machines to buyers in this country beyond the U.S. distributor, and there is no allegation that the distributor was under J. McIntyre's control.

Second, J. McIntyre officials attended annual conventions for the scrap recycling industry to advertise J. McIntyre's machines alongside the distributor. The conventions took place in various States, but never in New Jersey.

Third, no more than four machines (the record suggests only one), including the machine that caused the injuries that are the basis for this suit, ended up in New Jersey.

In addition to these facts emphasized by petitioner, the New Jersey Supreme Court noted that J. McIntyre held both United States and European patents on its recycling technology. It also noted that the U.S. distributor "structured [its] advertising and sales efforts in accordance with" J. McIntyre's "direction and guidance whenever possible," and that "at least some of the machines were sold on consignment to" the distributor.

In light of these facts, the New Jersey Supreme Court concluded that New Jersey courts could exercise jurisdiction over petitioner without contravention of the Due Process Clause. Jurisdiction was proper, in that court's view, because the injury occurred in New Jersey; because petitioner knew or reasonably should have known "that its products are distributed through a nationwide distribution system that might lead to those products being sold in any of the fifty states"; and because petitioner failed to "take some reasonable step to prevent the distribution of its products in this State."

Both the New Jersey Supreme Court's holding and its account of what it called "[t]he stream-of-commerce doctrine of jurisdiction," were incorrect, however. This Court's *Asahi* decision may be responsible in part for that court's error regarding the stream of commerce, and this case presents an opportunity to provide greater clarity.

II

... As a general rule, neither statute nor judicial decree may bind strangers to the State.

SEC. A EXERCISING JURISDICTION OVER DEFENDANTS 115

A court may subject a defendant to judgment only when the defendant has sufficient contacts with the sovereign "such that the maintenance of the suit does not offend 'traditional notions of fair play and substantial justice.'" *International Shoe Co. v. Washington,* 326 U.S. 310, 316 (1945) (quoting *Milliken v. Meyer,* 311 U.S. 457, 463 (1940)). Freeform notions of fundamental fairness divorced from traditional practice cannot transform a judgment rendered in the absence of authority into law. As a general rule, the sovereign's exercise of power requires some act by which the defendant "purposefully avails itself of the privilege of conducting activities within the forum State, thus invoking the benefits and protections of its laws," *Hanson,* 357 U.S., at 253, 78 S.Ct. 1228, though in some cases, as with an intentional tort, the defendant might well fall within the State's authority by reason of his attempt to obstruct its laws. In products-liability cases like this one, it is the defendant's purposeful availment that makes jurisdiction consistent with "traditional notions of fair play and substantial justice."

A person may submit to a State's authority in a number of ways. There is, of course, explicit consent. Presence within a State at the time suit commences through service of process is another example. Citizenship or domicile—or, by analogy, incorporation or principal place of business for corporations—also indicates general submission to a State's powers. Each of these examples reveals circumstances, or a course of conduct, from which it is proper to infer an intention to benefit from and thus an intention to submit to the laws of the forum State. These examples support exercise of the general jurisdiction of the State's courts and allow the State to resolve both matters that originate within the State and those based on activities and events elsewhere. By contrast, those who live or operate primarily outside a State have a due process right not to be subjected to judgment in its courts as a general matter.

There is also a more limited form of submission to a State's authority for disputes that "arise out of or are connected with the activities within the state." *International Shoe Co.* at 319, 66 S.Ct. 154. Where a defendant "purposefully avails itself of the privilege of conducting activities within the forum State, thus invoking the benefits and protections of its laws," *Hanson* at 253, 78 S.Ct. 1228, it submits to the judicial power of an otherwise foreign sovereign to the extent that power is exercised in connection with the defendant's activities touching on the State. . . .

The imprecision arising from *Asahi,* for the most part, results from its statement of the relation between jurisdiction and the "stream of commerce." The stream of commerce, like other metaphors, has its deficiencies as well as its utility. It refers to the movement of goods from manufacturers through distributors to consumers, yet beyond that descriptive purpose its meaning is far from exact. This Court has stated that a defendant's placing goods into the stream of commerce "with the expectation that they will be purchased by consumers within the forum State" may indicate purposeful availment. But that statement does not amend the general rule of personal jurisdiction. It merely observes that a defendant may in an appropriate case be subject to jurisdiction without entering the forum—itself an unexceptional proposition—as where manufacturers or distributors "seek to serve" a given State's market. The principal inquiry in cases of this sort is whether the defendant's activities manifest an intention to submit to the power of a sovereign. In other words, the defendant must "purposefully avai[l] itself of the privilege of conducting activities within the forum State, thus invoking the benefits and protections of its laws." Sometimes a defendant does so by sending its goods rather than its agents. The defendant's transmission of goods permits the exercise of jurisdiction only where the defendant can be said to have targeted the forum; as a general rule, it is not enough that the defendant might have predicted that its goods will reach the forum State.

In *Asahi*, an opinion by Justice Brennan for four Justices outlined a different approach. It discarded the central concept of sovereign authority in favor of considerations of fairness and foreseeability. As that concurrence contended, "jurisdiction premised on the placement of a product into the stream of commerce [without more] is consistent with the Due Process Clause," for "[a]s long as a participant in this process is aware that the final product is being marketed in the forum State, the possibility of a lawsuit there cannot come as a surprise." 480 U.S., at 117, 107 S.Ct. 1026 (opinion concurring in part and concurring in judgment). It was the premise of the concurring opinion that the defendant's ability to anticipate suit renders the assertion of jurisdiction fair. In this way, the opinion made foreseeability the touchstone of jurisdiction. . . .

Since *Asahi* was decided, the courts have sought to reconcile the competing opinions. But Justice Brennan's concurrence, advocating a rule based on general notions of fairness and foreseeability, is inconsistent with the premises of lawful judicial power. This Court's precedents make clear that it is the defendant's actions, not his expectations, that empower a State's courts to subject him to judgment.

The conclusion that jurisdiction is in the first instance a question of authority rather than fairness explains, for example, why the principal opinion in *Burnham* "conducted no independent inquiry into the desirability or fairness" of the rule that service of process within a State suffices to establish jurisdiction over an otherwise foreign defendant. As that opinion explained, "[t]he view developed early that each State had the power to hale before its courts any individual who could be found within its borders." Furthermore, were general fairness considerations the touchstone of jurisdiction, a lack of purposeful availment might be excused where carefully crafted judicial procedures could otherwise protect the defendant's interests, or where the plaintiff would suffer substantial hardship if forced to litigate in a foreign forum. That such considerations have not been deemed controlling is instructive.

... [P]ersonal jurisdiction requires a forum-by-forum, or sovereign-by-sovereign, analysis. The question is whether a defendant has followed a course of conduct directed at the society or economy existing within the jurisdiction of a given sovereign, so that the sovereign has the power to subject the defendant to judgment concerning that conduct. Personal jurisdiction, of course, restricts "judicial power not as a matter of sovereignty, but as a matter of individual liberty," for due process protects the individual's right to be subject only to lawful power. But whether a judicial judgment is lawful depends on whether the sovereign has authority to render it....

III

In this case, petitioner directed marketing and sales efforts at the United States. It may be that, assuming it were otherwise empowered to legislate on the subject, the Congress could authorize the exercise of jurisdiction in appropriate courts. That circumstance is not presented in this case, however, and it is neither necessary nor appropriate to address here any constitutional concerns that might be attendant to that exercise of power.... Here the question concerns the authority of a New Jersey state court to exercise jurisdiction, so it is petitioner's purposeful contacts with New Jersey, not with the United States, that alone are relevant.

Respondent has not established that J. McIntyre engaged in conduct purposefully directed at New Jersey. Recall that respondent's claim of jurisdiction centers on three facts: The distributor agreed to sell J. McIntyre's machines in the United States; J. McIntyre officials attended trade shows in several States but not in New Jersey; and up to four machines ended up in New Jersey. The British manufacturer had no office in New Jersey; it neither paid taxes nor owned property there; and it neither advertised in, nor sent any employees to, the State. Indeed, after discovery the trial court found that the "defendant does not have a single contact with New Jersey short of the machine in question ending up in this state." These facts may reveal an intent to serve the U.S. market, but they do not show that J. McIntyre purposefully availed itself of the New Jersey market....

* * *

Due process protects petitioner's right to be subject only to lawful authority. At no time did petitioner engage in any activities in New Jersey that reveal an intent to invoke or benefit from the protection of its laws. New Jersey is without power to adjudge the rights and liabilities of J. McIntyre, and its exercise of jurisdiction would violate due process. The contrary judgment of the New Jersey Supreme Court is *Reversed.*

JUSTICE BREYER, with whom JUSTICE ALITO joins, concurring in the judgment.

. . . I do not doubt that there have been many recent changes in commerce and communication, many of which are not anticipated by our precedents. But this case does not present any of those issues. So I think it unwise to announce a rule of broad applicability without full consideration of the modern-day consequences.

In my view, the outcome of this case is determined by our precedents. Based on the facts found by the New Jersey courts, respondent Robert Nicastro failed to meet his burden to demonstrate that it was constitutionally proper to exercise jurisdiction over petitioner J. McIntyre Machinery, Ltd. (British Manufacturer), a British firm that manufactures scrap-metal machines in Great Britain and sells them through an independent distributor in the United States (American Distributor). On that basis, I agree with the plurality that the contrary judgment of the Supreme Court of New Jersey should be reversed.

I

. . . None of our precedents finds that a single isolated sale, even if accompanied by the kind of sales effort indicated here, is sufficient. Rather, this Court's previous holdings suggest the contrary. . . .

Here, the relevant facts found by the New Jersey Supreme Court show no "regular . . . flow" or "regular course" of sales in New Jersey; and there is no "something more," such as special state-related design, advertising, advice, marketing, or anything else. Mr. Nicastro, who here bears the burden of proving jurisdiction, has shown no specific effort by the British Manufacturer to sell in New Jersey. He has introduced no list of potential New Jersey customers who might, for example, have regularly attended trade shows. And he has not otherwise shown that the British Manufacturer "purposefully avail[ed] itself of the privilege of conducting activities" within New Jersey, or that it delivered its goods in the stream of commerce "with the expectation that they will be purchased" by New Jersey users.

There may well have been other facts that Mr. Nicastro could have demonstrated in support of jurisdiction. And the dissent considers some of those facts. But the plaintiff bears the burden of establishing jurisdiction, and here I would take the facts precisely as the New Jersey Supreme Court stated them.

Accordingly, on the record present here, resolving this case requires no more than adhering to our precedents.

II

I would not go further. Because the incident at issue in this case does not implicate modern concerns, and because the factual record leaves many open questions, this is an unsuitable vehicle for making broad pronouncements that refashion basic jurisdictional rules.

A

The plurality seems to state strict rules that limit jurisdiction where a defendant does not "inten[d] to submit to the power of a sovereign" and cannot "be said to have targeted the forum." But what do those standards mean when a company targets the world by selling products from its Web site? And does it matter if, instead of shipping the products directly, a company consigns the products through an intermediary (say, Amazon.com) who then receives and fulfills the orders? And what if the company markets its products through popup advertisements that it knows will be viewed in a forum? Those issues have serious commercial consequences but are totally absent in this case.

B

But though I do not agree with the plurality's seemingly strict no-jurisdiction rule, I am not persuaded by the absolute approach adopted by the New Jersey Supreme Court and urged by respondent and his *amici*. Under that view, a producer is subject to jurisdiction for a products-liability action so long as it "knows or reasonably should know that its products are distributed through a nationwide distribution system that *might* lead to those products being sold in any of the fifty states." In the context of this case, I cannot agree.

. . . A rule like the New Jersey Supreme Court's would permit every State to assert jurisdiction in a products-liability suit against any domestic manufacturer who sells its products (made anywhere in the United States) to a national distributor, no matter how large or small the manufacturer, no matter how distant the forum, and no matter how few the number of items that end up in the particular forum at issue. What might appear fair in the case of a large manufacturer which specifically seeks, or expects, an equal-sized distributor to sell its product in a distant State might seem unfair in the case of a small manufacturer (say, an Appalachian potter) who sells his product (cups and saucers) exclusively to a large distributor, who resells a single item (a coffee mug) to a buyer from a distant State (Hawaii). I know too little about the range of these or in-between possibilities to abandon in favor of the more absolute rule what has previously been this Court's less absolute approach. . . .

Accordingly, though I agree with the plurality as to the outcome of this case, I concur only in the judgment of that opinion and not its reasoning.

JUSTICE GINSBURG, with whom JUSTICE SOTOMAYOR and JUSTICE KAGAN join, dissenting.

A foreign industrialist seeks to develop a market in the United States for machines it manufactures. It hopes to derive substantial revenue from sales it makes to United States purchasers. Where in the United States buyers reside does not matter to this manufacturer. Its goal is simply to sell as much as it can, wherever it can. It excludes no region or State from the market it wishes to reach. But, all things considered, it prefers to avoid products liability litigation in the United States. To that end, it engages a U.S. distributor to ship its machines stateside. Has it succeeded in escaping personal jurisdiction in a State where one of its products is sold and causes injury or even death to a local user?

Under this Court's pathmarking precedent in *International Shoe,* and subsequent decisions, one would expect the answer to be unequivocally, "No." But instead, six Justices of this Court, in divergent opinions, tell us that the manufacturer has avoided the jurisdiction of our state courts, except perhaps in States where its products are sold in sizeable quantities.

Inconceivable as it may have seemed yesterday, the splintered majority today "turn[s] the clock back to the days before modern long-arm statutes when a manufacturer, to avoid being haled into court where a user is injured, need only Pilate-like wash its hands of a product by having independent distributors market it." Weintraub, *A Map Out of the Personal Jurisdiction Labyrinth*, 28 U.C. Davis L.Rev. 531, 555 (1995)....

II

A few points on which there should be no genuine debate bear statement at the outset. First, all agree, McIntyre UK surely is not subject to general (all-purpose) jurisdiction in New Jersey courts, for that foreign-country corporation is hardly "at home" in New Jersey. Second, no issue of the fair and reasonable allocation of adjudicatory authority among States of the United States is present in this case. New Jersey's exercise of personal jurisdiction over a foreign manufacturer whose dangerous product caused a workplace injury in New Jersey does not tread on the domain, or diminish the sovereignty, of any sister State. Indeed, among States of the United States, the State in which the injury occurred would seem most suitable for litigation of a products liability tort claim. Third, the constitutional limits on a state court's adjudicatory authority derive from considerations of due process, not state sovereignty. As the Court clarified in *Insurance Corp. of Ireland v. Compagnie des Bauxites de Guinee,* 456 U.S. 694, 102 S.Ct. 2099, 72 L.Ed.2d 492 (1982):

> "The restriction on state sovereign power described in *World-Wide Volkswagen Corp.* . . . must be seen as ultimately a function

of the individual liberty interest preserved by the Due Process Clause. That Clause is the only source of the personal jurisdiction requirement and the Clause itself makes no mention of federalism concerns. Furthermore, if the federalism concept operated as an independent restriction on the sovereign power of the court, it would not be possible to waive the personal jurisdiction requirement: Individual actions cannot change the powers of sovereignty, although the individual can subject himself to powers from which he may otherwise be protected." *Id.,* at 703, n. 10, 102 S.Ct. 2099.

Finally, in *International Shoe* itself, and decisions thereafter, the Court has made plain that legal fictions, notably "presence" and "implied consent," should be discarded, for they conceal the actual bases on which jurisdiction rests. . . .

III

This case is illustrative of marketing arrangements for sales in the United States common in today's commercial world. A foreign-country manufacturer engages a U.S. company to promote and distribute the manufacturer's products, not in any particular State, but anywhere and everywhere in the United States the distributor can attract purchasers. . . .

The modern approach to jurisdiction over corporations and other legal entities, ushered in by *International Shoe,* gave prime place to reason and fairness. Is it not fair and reasonable, given the mode of trading of which this case is an example, to require the international seller to defend at the place its products cause injury? Do not litigational convenience and choice-of-law considerations point in that direction? On what measure of reason and fairness can it be considered undue to require McIntyre UK to defend in New Jersey as an incident of its efforts to develop a market for its industrial machines anywhere and everywhere in the United States? Is not the burden on McIntyre UK to defend in New Jersey fair, *i.e.,* a reasonable cost of transacting business internationally, in comparison to the burden on Nicastro to go to Nottingham, England to gain recompense for an injury he sustained using McIntyre's product at his workplace in Saddle Brook, New Jersey?

McIntyre UK dealt with the United States as a single market. Like most foreign manufacturers, it was concerned not with the prospect of suit in State X as opposed to State Y, but rather with its subjection to suit anywhere in the United States. If McIntyre UK is answerable in the United States at all, is it not "perfectly appropriate to permit the exercise of that jurisdiction . . . at the place of injury"? See Degnan & Kane, *The Exercise of Jurisdiction Over and Enforcement of Judgments Against Alien Defendants,* 39 Hastings L.J. 799, 813–815 (1988) (noting that "[i]n the international order," the State that counts is the United States, not its component States, and that the fair place of suit within the United States is essentially a question of venue).

In sum, McIntyre UK, by engaging McIntyre America to promote and sell its machines in the United States, "purposefully availed itself" of the United States market nationwide, not a market in a single State or a discrete collection of States. McIntyre UK thereby availed itself of the market of all States in which its products were sold by its exclusive distributor. . . .

Courts, both state and federal, confronting facts similar to those here, have rightly rejected the conclusion that a manufacturer selling its products across the USA may evade jurisdiction in any and all States, including the State where its defective product is distributed and causes injury. They have held, instead, that it would undermine principles of fundamental fairness to insulate the foreign manufacturer from accountability in court at the place within the United States where the manufacturer's products caused injury.

IV

A

While this Court has not considered in any prior case the now-prevalent pattern presented here—a foreign-country manufacturer enlisting a U.S. distributor to develop a market in the United States for the manufacturer's products—none of the Court's decisions tug against the judgment made by the New Jersey Supreme Court. McIntyre contends otherwise, citing *World-Wide Volkswagen,* and *Asahi.* . . .

Notably, the foreign manufacturer of the Audi in *World-Wide Volkswagen* did not object to the jurisdiction of the Oklahoma courts and the U.S. importer abandoned its initially stated objection. And most relevant here, the Court's opinion indicates that an objection to jurisdiction by the manufacturer or national distributor would have been unavailing. To reiterate, the Court said in *World-Wide Volkswagen* that, when a manufacturer or distributor aims to sell its product to customers in several States, it is reasonable "to subject it to suit in [any] one of those States if its allegedly defective [product] has there been the source of injury."

Asahi . . . unlike McIntyre UK, did not itself seek out customers in the United States, it engaged no distributor to promote its wares here, it appeared at no tradeshows in the United States, and, of course, it had no Web site advertising its products to the world. Moreover, Asahi was a component-part manufacturer with "little control over the final destination of its products once they were delivered into the stream of commerce." It was important to the Court in *Asahi* that "those who use Asahi components in their final products, and sell those products in California, [would be] subject to the application of California tort law."

480 U.S., at 115 (majority opinion). To hold that *Asahi* controls this case would, to put it bluntly, be dead wrong.

B

The Court's judgment also puts United States plaintiffs at a disadvantage in comparison to similarly situated complainants elsewhere in the world. Of particular note, within the European Union, in which the United Kingdom is a participant, the jurisdiction New Jersey would have exercised is not at all exceptional. The European Regulation on Jurisdiction and the Recognition and Enforcement of Judgments provides for the exercise of specific jurisdiction "in matters relating to tort . . . in the courts for the place where the harmful event occurred." Council Reg. 44/2001, Art. 5, 2001 O.J. (L.12) 4. . . .

* * *

For the reasons stated, I would hold McIntyre UK answerable in New Jersey for the harm Nicastro suffered at his workplace in that State using McIntyre UK's shearing machine. While I dissent from the Court's judgment, I take heart that the plurality opinion does not speak for the Court, for that opinion would take a giant step away from the "notions of fair play and substantial justice" underlying *International Shoe*, 326 U.S., at 316, 66 S.Ct. 154.

NOTE AND QUESTION

The *Asahi* decision discussed in *McIntyre* sets out three approaches for determining purposeful availment in a stream of commerce case. None of the three approaches commanded a majority of the Court. The most stringent approach for establishing jurisdiction is that placing a product into the stream of commerce must include additional conduct indicating intent or purpose to serve the market in the forum state. "[A] defendant's awareness that the stream of commerce may or will sweep the product into the forum State does not convert the mere act of placing the product into the stream into an act purposefully directed toward the forum State." *Asahi Metal Industry Co., Ltd. v. Superior Court of California, Solano County*, 480 U.S. 102, 112 (1986).

Speaking for himself and three of his colleagues concurring in part, Justice Brennan's view of purposeful availment did not require additional conduct by the defendant. Justice Stevens' concurrence for himself and two colleagues saw no need to reach the issue of purposeful availment because the Court had concluded that California's exercise of jurisdiction over Asahi was "unreasonable and unfair." *Id.* at 121.

If you were general counsel for a corporation that manufactures finished products or component parts for installation in finished products, which view would enable you to advise your client better about predicting where it could be required to defend damage claims or how it could conform its conduct to avoid specific places to defend such claims?

WALDEN v. FIORE
134 S.Ct. 1115 (2014)

JUSTICE THOMAS delivered the opinion of the Court.

This case asks us to decide whether a court in Nevada may exercise personal jurisdiction over a defendant on the basis that he knew his allegedly tortious conduct in Georgia would delay the return of funds to plaintiff with connections to Nevada. Because the defendant had no other contacts with Nevada, and because a plaintiff's contacts with the forum State cannot be "decisive in determining whether the defendant's due process rights are violated," *Rush v. Sawchuk*, 444 U.S. 320, 322 (1980), we hold that the court in Nevada may not exercise personal jurisdiction under these circumstances.

[In August, 2006, Transportation Security Administration agents searched Fiore and Gipson and their carry-on bags at the San Juan, Puerto Rico airport, finding almost $97,000 in cash. Fiore explained that she and Gipson had been gambling in Puerto Rico, and that they had residencies in both California and Nevada (though they produced only California identification). After being cleared for departure to Atlanta, a San Juan official notified the Drug Enforcement Administration at the Atlanta Airport that the two were headed there to catch a connecting flight to Las Vegas, Nevada. In Atlanta, Petitioner Walden, a police officer in Covington, Georgia, working as a deputized DEA agent, seized the cash and advised them that it would be returned if they later proved a legitimate source for the cash. The two gamblers then boarded a flight to Las Vegas. Seven months later, the DEA returned the funds to Fiore and Gipson.

Respondents Fiore and Gipson filed suit against petitioner Walden in the United States District Court for the District of Nevada, seeking money damages under *Bivens v. Six Unknown Fed. Narcotics Agents*, 403 U.S. 388 (1971), i.e., for unconstitutional conduct relating to the seizure of the cash during the seven-month delay in returning the funds.]

The District Court granted petitioner's motion to dismiss. Relying on this Court's decision in *Calder v. Jones*, 465 U.S. 783 (1984), the court determined that petitioner's search of respondents and his seizure of the cash in Georgia did not establish a basis to exercise personal jurisdiction in Nevada. The court concluded that even if petitioner caused harm to respondents in Nevada while knowing they lived in Nevada, that fact alone did not confer jurisdiction. . . .

On appeal, a divided panel of the United States Court of Appeals for the Ninth Circuit reversed.... [T]he court found the District Court's exercise of personal jurisdiction to be proper....

We granted certiorari to decide whether due process permits a Nevada court to exercise jurisdiction over petitioner. We hold that it does not and therefore reverse.

The Due Process Clause of the Fourteenth Amendment constrains a state's authority to bind a nonresident defendant to a judgment of its courts. Although a nonresident's physical presence within the territorial jurisdiction of the court is not required, the nonresident generally must have "certain minimum contacts ... such that the maintenance of the suit does not offend 'traditional notions of fair play and substantial justice.'" *International Shoe Co. v. Washington*, 326 U.S. 310, 316 (1945).

... For a state to exercise jurisdiction consistent with due process, the defendant's suit-related conduct must create a substantial connection with the forum State. Two related aspects of this necessary relationship are relevant to this case.

First, the relationship must arise out of contacts that the "defendant" himself creates with the forum State. Due process limits on the State's adjudicative authority principally protect the liberty of the nonresident defendant—not the convenience of plaintiffs or third parties. [The Court cited *Hanson v. Denckla* and *World-Wide Volkswagen* as examples of how a plaintiff's unilateral activity is an inappropriate consideration when determining whether a defendant has sufficient contacts with a forum State.]

Second, our "minimum contacts" analysis looks to the defendant's contacts with the forum State itself, not the defendant's contacts with persons who reside there. Accordingly, we have upheld the assertion of jurisdiction over defendants who have purposefully "reach[ed] out beyond" their State and into another by, for example, entering a contractual relationship that "envisioned continuing and wide-reaching contacts" in the forum State.... *Burger King v. Rudzewicz*, 471 U.S. 462, 475 (1984). And although physical presence in the forum in not a prerequisite to jurisdiction, physical entry into the State—either by the defendant in person or through an agent, goods, mail, or some other means—is certainly a relevant contact.

... [I]t is the defendant's conduct that must form the necessary connection with the forum State that is the basis for its jurisdiction over him. To be sure, a defendant's contacts with the forum State may be intertwined with his transactions or interactions with the plaintiff or other parties. But a defendant's relationship with a plaintiff or third party, standing alone, is an insufficient basis for jurisdiction. ...

These same principles apply when intentional torts are involved.... A forum State's exercise of jurisdiction over an out-of-state intentional tortfeasor must be based on intentional conduct by the defendant that creates the necessary contacts with the forum.

Calder v. Jones, 465 U.S. 783 (1984) illustrates the application of these principles. In Calder, a California actress brought a libel suit in California state court against a reporter and an editor, both of whom worked for the National Enquirer at its headquarters in Florida. The plaintiff's libel claims were based on an article written and edited by the defendant in Florida for publication in the National Enquirer, a national weekly newspaper with a California circulation of roughly 600,000.

We held that California's assertion of jurisdiction over the defendants was consistent with due process.... [W]e examined the various contacts the defendants had created with California (and not just with the plaintiff) by writing the allegedly libelous story.

We found those forum contacts to be ample: The defendants relied on phone calls to "California sources" for the information in their article; they wrote the story about the plaintiff's activities in California; they caused reputational injury in California by writing an allegedly libelous article that was widely circulated in the State; and the "brunt" of that injury was suffered by the plaintiff in that State. "In sum, California [wa]s the focal point both of the story and of the harm suffered." *Id.* at 789. Jurisdiction over the defendants was "therefore proper in California based on the 'effects' of their Florida conduct in California." *Id.*

The crux of *Calder* was that the reputation-based "effects" of the alleged libel connected the defendant to California, not just to the plaintiff.... [T]he "effects" caused by the defendants' article—i.e., the injury to the plaintiff's reputation in the estimation of the California public—connected the defendants' conduct to California, not just to a plaintiff who lived there. That connection, combined with the various facts that gave the article a California focus, sufficed to authorize the California court's exercise of jurisdiction.[7]

Applying the foregoing principles, we conclude that the petitioner lacks the "minimal contacts" with Nevada that are a prerequisite to the exercise of jurisdiction over him. It is undisputed that no part of petitioner's course of conduct occurred in Nevada. Petitioner approached, questioned, and searched respondents, and seized the cash at issue, in the Atlanta airport.... Petitioner never traveled to, conducted activities within, contacted anyone in, or sent anything or anyone to Nevada. In short, when viewed through the proper lens—whether the *defendant's*

---

[7] Even though the defendants did not circulate the article themselves, they "expressly aimed" "their intentional, and allegedly tortious, actions" at California because they knew the National Enquirer "ha[d] its largest circulation" in California, and that the article would "have a potentially devastating impact" there. *Id.*, at 789–790.

actions connect him to the *forum*—petitioner formed no jurisdictionally relevant contacts with Nevada.

. . . Relying on *Calder*, respondents emphasize that they suffered the "injury" caused by petitioner's allegedly tortious conduct (i.e., the delayed return of their gambling funds) while they were residing in the forum. This emphasis is . . . misplaced. . . . Regardless of where a plaintiff lives or works, an injury is jurisdictionally relevant only insofar as it shows that the defendant has formed a contact with the forum State. The proper question is not where the plaintiff experienced a particular injury or effect but whether the defendant's conduct connects him to the forum in a meaningful way.

. . . Respondents (and only respondents) lacked access to their funds in Nevada not because anything independently occurred there, but because Nevada is where respondents chose to be at a time when they desired to use the funds seized by petitioner. Respondents would have experienced this same lack of access . . . wherever else they might have traveled and found themselves wanting more money than they had. [T]he effects of petitioner's conduct on respondents are not connected to the forum State in a way that makes those effects a proper basis for jurisdiction.[9]

. . . The proper focus of the "minimum contacts" inquiry in intentional torts cases is "'the relationship among the defendant, the forum, and the litigation.'" *Calder*, 465 U.S. at 788. And it is the defendant, not the plaintiff or third parties, who must create contacts with the forum State. . . . Petitioner's relevant conduct occurred entirely in Georgia, and the mere fact that his conduct affected plaintiffs with connections to the forum State does not suffice to authorize jurisdiction. We therefore reverse the judgment of the Court of Appeals.

NOTES AND QUESTIONS

1. How would you advocate that the defendant had some connection with Nevada, the state where Fiore and Gipson lived? The lower court's approach focused on how Walden's post-seizure intentional conduct caused harm to the plaintiffs in Nevada, even though Walden's actions occurred in Georgia. By that reasoning, would a defendant charged with committing an intentional tort be subject to defending the lawsuit wherever the plaintiff lives, regardless of whether the defendant had *any* contacts there? Would that approach be especially difficult for persons interacting with people from

---

[9] Respondents warn that if we decide petitioner lacks minimum contacts in this case, it will bring about unfairness in cases where intentional torts are committed via the Internet or other electronic means (e.g., fraudulent access of financial accounts or "phishing" schemes). . . . In any event, this case does not present the very different questions whether and how a defendant's virtual "presence" and conduct translate into "contacts" with a particular State. To the contrary, there is no question where the conduct giving rise to this litigation took place: Petitioner seized physical cash from respondents in the Atlanta airport, and he later drafted and forwarded an affidavit in Georgia. We leave questions about virtual contacts for another day.

a variety of places? When he seized the money, did Walden "reasonably anticipate being haled into court" in Nevada?

2. *Intentional misconduct.* An important element of the *Walden* analysis is that the defendant committed an intentional tort. From your reading of *Walden*, what is the relevance of the nature of a plaintiff's claim? In other words, is it sufficient to show jurisdiction over the defendant merely by alleging an intentional tort by the defendant? Lower courts have recognized that the *Calder* "effects" test is another way of evaluating the defendant's contacts with the forum, *i.e.*, minimum contacts may be established where the defendants' intentional acts were expressly aimed or purposefully directed at the forum state.

3. *The brunt factor.* A second factor discussed in *Calder* requires that the plaintiff show that it felt the brunt (or effects) of the harm from the defendant's tortious behavior in the forum state. How was this element satisfied in *Walden*? Does it matter where the plaintiff lives in relation to the allegedly unconstitutional conduct?

4. *Defendant's aiming his conduct at the forum.* The third *Calder* factor demands a showing that the defendant "expressly aimed" its tortious conduct at the forum. See footnote 7 in *Walden*. How did the defendant's conduct in *Walden* fail to satisfy this standard? In the context of traditional due process analysis concepts like "purposeful availment" and "foreseeability," what is the significance of the defendant's knowledge about the place where his conduct is directed, e.g., whether the defendant knows the plaintiff resides in the forum state?

5. In *Keeton v. Hustler Magazine, Inc.*, 465 U.S. 770, 104 S.Ct. 1473, 79 L.Ed.2d 790 (1984), decided the same day as *Calder*, the Court held that New Hampshire could exercise jurisdiction over a non-resident corporation, based on allegedly libelous material printed in its magazine. The Court noted that circulation within the state consisted of more than 10,000 copies every month. The corporation's "regular monthly sales of thousands of magazines cannot by any stretch of the imagination be characterized as random, isolated, or fortuitous," and were more than sufficient to satisfy the minimum contacts requirement. The decision also confirms the possibility of bringing a defamation action in any forum with adequate minimum contacts, not only the state in which the plaintiff resides.

6. Using the principles from *Calder* and *Fiore*, decide whether the courts in the following situations have personal jurisdiction over the defendants.

    a. In a Virginia Court, Virginia resident Dave sued an Illinois defendant named Andrew for sending defamatory letters written and mailed from Illinois to Dave's colleagues in Virginia. Does the Virginia court have personal jurisdiction over Andrew by virtue of the effects in Virginia of his conduct? See *First Am. First, Inc. v. National Ass'n of Bank Women*, 802 F.2d 1511 (4th Cir. 1986).

b. A South Carolina corporation sued a New Hampshire company in South Carolina, claiming that the defendant had conspired to steal its customer lists. The co-conspirators were Florida and New Hampshire residents who engaged in a mail order business, but they had not customers in South Carolina. The defendant's only contact that the plaintiff could identify was the defendant's knowledge that possession of the lists could have the effect of lowered sales for the plaintiff. Is that sufficient for jurisdiction over the New Hampshire defendant? See *ESAB Group, Inc. v. Centricut, Inc.*, 126 F.3d 617 (4th Cir. 1997).

DAIMLER AG V. BAUMAN
134 S.Ct. 746 (2014)

JUSTICE GINSBURG delivered the opinion of the Court.

. . .

The question presented is whether the Due Process Clause of the Fourteenth Amendment precludes the [federal] District Court [in California] from exercising jurisdiction over [German corporation] Daimler [using general jurisdiction principles], given the absence of any California connection to the [conduct] described in the complaint.

I

[MB Argentina is Daimler's wholly owned Argentine subsidiary. MBUSA is another Daimler subsidiary and Daimler's exclusive importer and distributor in the United States, with its principal place of business in New Jersey along with multiple California-based facilities. MBUSA is the largest supplier of luxury vehicles in the California market, and its California sales account for 2.4% of Daimler's worldwide sales. Daimler and MBUSA have a General Distributor Agreement establishing MBUSA as an independent contractor, but the distributor Agreement does not make MBUSA an agent of Daimler.]

In 2004, plaintiffs [from Argentina] filed suit in the United States District Court for the Northern District of California, alleging that MB Argentina collaborated with Argentinian state security forces to kidnap, detain, torture, and kill plaintiffs and their relatives during the military dictatorship . . . known as Argentina's "Dirty War." Based on those allegations, plaintiffs asserted claims [under federal law], as well as claims for wrongful death and intentional infliction of emotional distress under the laws of California and Argentina. . . . [N]o part of MB Argentina's alleged collaboration with Argentinian authorities took place in California or anywhere else in the United States.

[The District Court granted Daimler's motion to dismiss, citing 1) Daimler's own affiliations with California as insufficient to support general jurisdiction over Daimler, and 2) the failure of proof that MBUSA acted as Daimler's agent. The Ninth Circuit reversed the District Court, noting that the agency test was satisfied and that jurisdiction over Daimler was reasonable.]

... We granted certiorari to decide whether, consistent with Due Process Clause of the Fourteenth Amendment, Daimler is amendable to suit in California courts for claims involving only foreign plaintiffs and conduct occurring entirely abroad.

II

... Federal courts ordinarily follow state law in determining the bounds of their jurisdiction over persons. See Fed. Rule Civ. Proc. 4(k)(1)(A).... California's long-arm statute allows the exercise of personal jurisdiction to the full extent permissible under the U.S. Constitution. We therefore inquire whether the Ninth Circuit's holding comports with the limits imposed by federal due process.

III

International Shoe distinguished between, on the one hand, exercises of specific jurisdiction ... and on the other, situations where a foreign corporation's "continuous corporate operations within a state [are] so substantial and of such a nature as to justify suit against it on causes of action arising from dealings entirely distinct from those activities." *International Shoe Co. v. Washington*, 326 U.S. 310, 318 (1945). As we have since explained, "[a] court may assert general jurisdiction over foreign (sister-state or foreign-country) corporations to hear any and all claims against them when their affiliations with the State are so 'continuous and systematic' as to render them essentially at home in the forum State." *Goodyear Dunlop Tires Operations, S.A. v. Brown*, 131 S.Ct 2846, 2851 (2011).

Our post-*International Shoe* opinions on general jurisdiction ... are few.... *Helicopteros [Nacionales de Colombia, S.A. v. Hall]*, 466 U.S. 408 (1984) arose from a helicopter crash in Peru. Four U.S. citizens perished in that accident; their survivors and representatives brought suit in Texas state court against the helicopter's owner and operator, a Colombian corporation. That company's contacts with Texas were confined to "sending its chief executive officer to Houston for a contract-negotiation session; accepting into its New York bank account checks drawn on a Houston bank; purchasing helicopters, equipment, and training services from [a Texas-based helicopter company] for substantial sums; and sending personnel to [Texas] for training." *Id.* at 416. Notably, those contacts bore no apparent relationship to the accident that gave rise to the suit. We held that the company's Texas connections did not resemble the "continuous and systematic general business contacts ... found to exist in *Perkins* [*v. Benguet, Consol. Mining Co.*, 342 U.S. 437 (1952)]." "[M]ere purchases, even if occurring at regular intervals," we clarified, "are not enough to warrant a State's assertion of *in personam* jurisdiction over a nonresident corporation in a cause of action not related to those purchase transactions." *Id.* at 418.

Most recently, in *Goodyear*, we answered the question: "Are foreign subsidiaries of a United States parent corporation amendable to suit in state court on claims unrelated to any activity of the subsidiaries in the forum State?" 131 S.Ct. at 2850. That case arose from a bus accident outside Paris that killed two boys from North Carolina. The boys' parents brought a wrongful death suit in North Carolina state court alleging that the bus's tire was defectively manufactured. The complaint named as defendants not only The Goodyear Tire and Rubber Company (Goodyear), an Ohio corporation, but also Goodyear's Turkish, French, and Luxembourgian subsidiaries. Those foreign subsidiaries, which manufactured tires for sale in Europe and Asia, lacked any affiliation with North Carolina. A small percentage of tires manufactured by the foreign subsidiaries were distributed in North Carolina, however, and on that ground, the North Carolina Court of Appeals held that the subsidiaries amendable to the general jurisdiction of North Carolina courts.

We reversed, observing that the North Carolina court's analysis "elided the essential difference between case-specific and all-purpose (general) jurisdiction." Although the placement of a product into the stream of commerce "may bolster an affiliation germane to *specific* jurisdiction," we explained, such contacts "do not warrant a determination that, based on those ties, the forum has *general* jurisdiction over a defendant." [*Goodyear* held that a court may assert jurisdiction over a foreign corporation "to hear any and all claims against [it]" only when the corporation's affiliations with the State in which suit is brought are so constant and pervasive "as to render [it] essentially at home in the forum State."] Because Goodyear's foreign subsidiaries were "in no sense at home in North Carolina," we held, those subsidiaries could not be required to submit to the general jurisdiction of that State's courts. 131 S.Ct. at 2857.

As is evident from ... *Helicopteros* and *Goodyear*, general and specific jurisdiction have followed markedly different trajectories post-*International Shoe*.... As this Court has increasingly trained on the "relationship among the defendant, the forum, and the litigation," general jurisdiction has come to occupy a less dominant place in the contemporary scheme.

IV

With this background, we turn directly to the question whether Daimler's affiliations with California are sufficient to subject it to the general (all-purpose) personal jurisdiction of that State's courts. In the proceedings below, the parties agreed on, or failed to contest, certain points we now take as given. Plaintiffs have never attempted to fit this case into the *specific* jurisdiction category. Nor did plaintiffs challenge on appeal the District Court's holding that Daimler's own contacts with California were, by themselves, too sporadic to justify the exercise of general jurisdiction. . . .

A

[The Court leaves open the question of when general jurisdiction over a subsidiary is enough to sue a parent corporation, but rejects the Ninth Circuit's approach to this question.] The Ninth Circuit's agency finding rested primarily on its observation that MBUSA's services were "important" to Daimler, as gauged by Daimler's hypothetical readiness to perform those services itself if MBUSA did not exist. Formulated this way, the inquiry into importance stacks the deck, for it always will yield a pro-jurisdiction answer. . . . The Ninth Circuit's agency theory thus appears to subject foreign corporations to general jurisdiction whenever they have an in-state subsidiary or affiliate, an outcome that would sweep beyond even the "sprawling view of general jurisdiction" we rejected in *Goodyear*.

B

Even if we were to assume that MBUSA is at home in California, and further to assume MBUSA's contacts are imputable to Daimler, there would still be no basis to subject Daimler to general jurisdiction in California, for Daimler's slim contacts with the State hardly render it at home there.

Goodyear made clear that only a limited set of affiliations with a forum will render a defendant amendable to all-purpose jurisdiction there. "For an individual, the paradigm forum for the exercise of general jurisdiction is the individual's domicile; . . . With respect to a corporation, the place of incorporation and principal place of business are 'paradigm . . . bases for general jurisdiction.'" Those affiliations have the virtue of being unique—that is, each ordinarily indicates only one place—as well as easily ascertainable. These bases afford plaintiff's recourse to at least one clear and certain forum in which a corporate defendant may be sued on any and all claims.

. . . Plaintiffs would have us look beyond the exemplar bases *Goodyear* identified, and approve the exercise of general jurisdiction in every State in which a corporation "engages in a substantial, continuous, and systematic course of business." That formulation, we hold, is unacceptably grasping.

... [T]he inquiry under *Goodyear* is not whether a foreign corporation's in-forum contacts can be said to be in some sense "continuous and systematic," it is whether that corporation's "affiliations with the State are so 'continuous and systematic' as to render [it] essentially at home in the forum State." 131 S.Ct. at 2851.[19]

Here neither Daimler nor MBUSA is incorporated in California, nor does either entity have its principal place of business there. If Daimler's California activities sufficed to allow adjudication of this Argentina-rooted case in California, the same global reach would presumably be available in every other State in which MBUSA's sales are sizable. Such exorbitant exercises of all-purpose jurisdiction would scarcely permit out-of-state defendants "to structure their primary conduct with some minimum assurance as to where that conduct will and will not render them liable to suit." *Burger King Corp. v. Rudzewicz*, 471 U.S. 462, 472 (1985).

It was therefore error for the Ninth Circuit to conclude that Daimler, even with MBUSA's contacts attributed to it, was at home in California, and hence subject to suit there on claims by foreign plaintiffs having nothing to do with anything that occurred or had its principal impact in California.[20]

C

... The Ninth Circuit ... paid little heed to the risks to international comity its expansive view of general jurisdiction posed. Other nations do not share the uninhibited approach to personal jurisdiction advanced by the Court of Appeals in this case. In the European Union, for example, a corporation may generally be sued in the nation in which it is "domiciled," a term defined to refer only to the location of the corporation's "statutory seat," "central administration," or "principal place of business." European Parliament and Council Reg. 1215/2012, Arts. 4(1), and 63(1), 2012 O.J. (L. 351) 7, 18. ... Considerations of international rapport thus reinforce

---

[19] We do not foreclose the possibility that in an exceptional case, a corporation's operations in a forum other than its formal place of incorporation or principal place of business may be so substantial and of such a nature as to render the corporation at home in that State. But this case presents no occasion to explore that question, because Daimler's activities in California plainly do not approach that level. . . .

[20] To clarify in light of Justice SOTOMAYOR's opinion concurring in the judgment, the general jurisdiction inquiry does not "focu[s] solely on the magnitude of the defendant's in-state contacts." General jurisdiction instead calls for an appraisal of a corporation's activities in their entirety, nationwide and worldwide. A corporation that operates in many places can scarcely be deemed at home in all of them. Otherwise, "at home" would be synonymous with "doing business" tests framed before specific jurisdiction evolved in the United States. Nothing in *International Shoe* and its progeny suggests that "a particular quantum of local activity" should give a State authority over a "far larger quantum of ... activity" having no connection to any in-state activity.

Justice SOTOMAYOR would reach the same result, but for a different reason.

our determination that subjecting Daimler to the general jurisdiction of courts in California would not accord with the "fair play and substantial justice" due process demands. *International Shoe*, 326 U.S. at 316.

Reversed.

JUSTICE SOTOMAYOR, concurring in the judgment.

I agree with the Court's conclusion that the Due Process Clause prohibits the exercise of personal jurisdiction over Daimler in light of the unique circumstances of this case. I concur only in the judgment, however, because I cannot agree with the path the Court takes to arrive at that result.

The Court acknowledges that Mercedes-Benz USA, LLC (MBUSA), Daimler's wholly owned subsidiary, has considerable contacts with California. It has multiple facilities in the State, including a regional headquarters. Each year, it distributes in California tens of thousands of cars, the sale of which generated billions of dollars in the year this suit was brought. And it provides service and sales support to customers throughout the State. Daimler has conceded that California courts may exercise general jurisdiction over MBUSA on the basis of these contacts, and the Court assumes that MBUSA's contacts may be attributed to Daimler for the purpose of deciding whether Daimler is also subject to general jurisdiction.

Are these contacts sufficient to permit the exercise of general jurisdiction over Daimler? The Court holds that they are not, for a reason wholly foreign to our due process jurisprudence. The problem, the Court says, is not that Daimler's contacts with California are too few, but that its contacts with other forums are too many. In other words, the Court does not dispute that the presence of multiple offices, the direct distribution of thousands of products accounting for billions of dollars in sales, and continuous interaction with customers throughout a State would be enough to support the exercise of general jurisdiction over some businesses. Daimler is just not one of those businesses, the Court concludes, because its California contacts must be viewed in the context of its extensive "nationwide and worldwide" operations. In recent years, Americans have grown accustomed to the concept of multinational corporations that are supposedly "too big to fail"; today the Court deems Daimler "too big for general jurisdiction."

I

Our personal jurisdiction precedents call for a two-part analysis. The contacts prong asks whether the defendant has sufficient contacts with the forum State to support personal jurisdiction; the reasonableness prong asks whether the exercise of jurisdiction would be unreasonable under the circumstances. As the majority points out, all of the cases in which we have applied the reasonableness prong have involved specific as opposed to general jurisdiction. Whether the reasonableness prong should apply in the general jurisdiction context is therefore a question we have never decided, and it is one on which I can appreciate the arguments on both sides. But it would be imprudent to decide that question in this case given that respondents have failed to argue against the application of the reasonableness prong during the entire 8-year history of this litigation. As a result, I would decide this case under the reasonableness prong without foreclosing future consideration of whether that prong should be limited to the specific jurisdiction context.

... We held in *Asahi* that it would be "unreasonable and unfair" for a California court to exercise jurisdiction over a claim between a Taiwanese plaintiff and a Japanese defendant that arose out of a transaction in Taiwan, particularly where the Taiwanese plaintiff had not shown that it would be more convenient to litigate in California than in Taiwan or Japan.

The same considerations resolve this case. It involves Argentine plaintiffs suing a German defendant for conduct that took place in Argentina. Like the plaintiffs in *Asahi,* respondents have failed to show that it would be more convenient to litigate in California than in Germany, a sovereign with a far greater interest in resolving the dispute. *Asahi* thus makes clear that it would be unreasonable for a court in California to subject Daimler to its jurisdiction.

III

A

Until today, our precedents had established a straightforward test for general jurisdiction: Does the defendant have "continuous corporate operations within a state" that are "so substantial and of such a nature as to justify suit against it on causes of action arising from dealings entirely distinct from those activities"? In every case where we have applied this test, we have focused solely on the magnitude of the defendant's in-state contacts, not the relative magnitude of those contacts in comparison to the defendant's contacts with other States.

B

The majority today concludes otherwise. Referring to the "continuous and systematic" contacts inquiry that has been taught to generations of first-year law students as "unacceptably grasping," the majority announces the new rule that in order for a foreign defendant to be subject to general jurisdiction, it must not only possess continuous and systematic contacts with a forum State, but those contacts must also surpass some unspecified level when viewed in comparison to the company's "nationwide and worldwide" activities.

Neither of the majority's two rationales for this proportionality requirement is persuasive. First, the majority suggests that its approach is necessary for the sake of predictability. Permitting general jurisdiction in every State where a corporation has continuous and substantial contacts, the majority asserts, would "scarcely permit out-of-state defendants 'to structure their primary conduct with some minimum assurance as to where that conduct will and will not render them liable to suit.'" But there is nothing unpredictable about a rule that instructs multinational corporations that if they engage in continuous and substantial contacts with more than one State, they will be subject to general jurisdiction in each one. . . .

Nor is the majority's proportionality inquiry any more predictable than the approach it rejects. If anything, the majority's approach injects an additional layer of uncertainty because a corporate defendant must now try to foretell a court's analysis as to both the sufficiency of its contacts with the forum State itself, as well as the relative sufficiency of those contacts in light of the company's operations elsewhere. . . .

Absent the predictability rationale, the majority's sole remaining justification for its proportionality approach is its unadorned concern for the consequences. "If Daimler's California activities sufficed to allow adjudication of this Argentina-rooted case in California," the majority laments, "the same global reach would presumably be available in every other State in which MBUSA's sales are sizable."

The majority characterizes this result as "exorbitant," but in reality it is an inevitable consequence of the rule of due process we set forth nearly 70 years ago [in *International Shoe*], that there are "instances in which [a company's] continuous corporate operations within a state" are "so substantial and of such a nature as to justify suit against it on causes of action arising from dealings entirely distinct from those activities." In the era of *International Shoe,* it was rare for a corporation to have such substantial nationwide contacts that it would be subject to general jurisdiction in a large number of States. . . . What has changed since *International Shoe* is not the due process principle of fundamental fairness but rather the nature of the global economy. Just as it was fair to say in the 1940's that an out-of-state company could enjoy the benefits of a forum State enough to make it "essentially at home" in the State, it is fair to say today that a multinational conglomerate can enjoy such extensive benefits in multiple forum States that it is "essentially at home" in each one.

C

. . . [T]he rule that [the majority] adopts will produce deep injustice in at least four respects.

First, the majority's approach unduly curtails the States' sovereign authority to adjudicate disputes against corporate defendants who have engaged in continuous and substantial business operations within their boundaries. . . .

Second, the proportionality approach will treat small businesses unfairly in comparison to national and multinational conglomerates. Whereas a larger company will often be immunized from general jurisdiction in a State on account of its extensive contacts outside the forum, a small business will not be. . . .

Third, the majority's approach creates the incongruous result that an individual defendant whose only contact with a forum State is a one-time visit will be subject to general jurisdiction if served with process during that visit [under *Burnham*], but a large corporation that owns property, employs workers, and does billions of dollars' worth of business in the State will not be, simply because the corporation has similar contacts elsewhere (though the visiting individual surely does as well).

Finally, it should be obvious that the ultimate effect of the majority's approach will be to shift the risk of loss from multinational corporations to the individuals harmed by their actions. Under the majority's rule, for example, a parent whose child is maimed due to the negligence of a foreign hotel owned by a multinational conglomerate will be unable to hold the hotel to account in a single U.S. court, even if the hotel company has a massive presence in multiple States. Similarly, a U.S. business that enters into a contract in a foreign country to sell its products to a multinational company there may be unable to seek relief in any U.S. court if the multinational company breaches the contract, even if that company has considerable operations in numerous U.S. forums. Indeed, the majority's approach would preclude the plaintiffs in these examples from seeking recourse anywhere in the United States even if no other judicial system was available to provide relief. I cannot agree with the majority's conclusion that the Due Process Clause requires these results.

NOTES AND QUESTIONS

1. *The Due Process trade-off for individual nonresident defendants.* Under general jurisdiction, an individual nonresident's contacts with the forum state must be "continuous and systematic," rather than the minimal contacts required for specific jurisdiction. So, even though the state can exercise general jurisdiction over a nonresident defendant when the plaintiff's claim does not arise from the defendant's activities there, the due process trade-off is that the plaintiff must prove more than minimal contacts; the plaintiff must prove that the defendant's contacts with the forum state are continuous and systematic.

2. *When a corporation is "essentially at home" in the forum state.* Until *Daimler AG*, most courts and corporations had assumed that a corporation

was subject to the general jurisdiction of any state court when it had continuous and systematic contacts there. Then the *Daimler AG* Court found that a U.S. corporation like MBUSA, even with substantial contacts in every state, was not "at home" in California and thus was not subject to the "general jurisdiction" of California's courts. After *Daimler AG*, the volume of business by the nonresident within the plaintiff's forum State no longer matters to the existence of continuous and systematic contacts. The determining factor generally for whether a corporation is "essentially at home" in the forum State is whether that State is the defendant's principal place of business or state of incorporation. The majority's footnote 19 leaves open the possibility (however slim) that a Plaintiff may counter the simple approach to defining continuous and systematic contacts under exceptional circumstances.

3. In *Shovah v. Roman Catholic Diocese of Albany, New York, Inc.*, 745 F.3d 30 (2d Cir. 2014), the plaintiff sued a Catholic diocese and its former priest, alleging that he had been sexually abused as a minor. The United States District Court for the District of Vermont denied the Diocese's motion to dismiss, finding that the Diocese was "at home" in Vermont and therefore subject to general jurisdiction there, "based on occasional worship services held there by a number of priests associated with the Diocese and other limited contacts." The plaintiff "asserted only general (not specific) jurisdiction over the Diocese: the Diocese's alleged wrongs—breach of fiduciary duty to Shovah by permitting Mercure to hold himself out as a Roman Catholic priest and negligent supervision of Mercure—did not arise from its contacts with Vermont." The diocese then petitioned for a writ of mandamus.

Reversing the district court's analysis as clearly erroneous, the Second Circuit held that it was inconsistent with *Daimler AG*, in which the company had far more contacts with California than the Diocese had with Vermont.

> Unlike Daimler, the Diocese operates no office or facility in Vermont, has no sales in the forum, and the percentage of its contacts with Vermont compared to its activities elsewhere (namely, New York) are trivial. Even imputing the border parishes' contacts with Vermont to the Diocese (which the district court declined to do) would not render the Diocese "at home" there. Considering, for general jurisdiction purposes, those parishes' employment of a small number of Vermont residents and service of a trivial number of Vermont parishioners again reverses the relevant inquiry—it is the Diocese's contacts with the forum, not the forum's residents' contacts with the Diocese in New York, that affect general jurisdiction. Moreover, those parishes' use of twenty-one Vermont vendors (which comprised less than 3.5% of their overall vendors) and acceptance of advertisements from eleven Vermont merchants for publication in church materials over a ten-year period is surely not enough.

Daimler, in contrast, was California's largest supplier of luxury vehicles, and operated offices and facilities in the forum. Moreover, even at 2.4%, Daimler's percentage of worldwide sales conducted in the forum far surpasses the percentage of the Diocese's overall operations attributable to Vermont; yet, the Court unanimously found jurisdiction lacking. Simply put, if California is not Daimler's home, Vermont is not "home" for the Diocese. . . .

If the Diocese is "at home" in Vermont, it begs the question: how many homes might it have? Would the Diocese be "at home" in New Jersey if one of its hundreds of priests were to conduct a wedding or two in that State over a matter of years? Would circulation of *The Evangelist* to a Wyoming resident render the Diocese "at home" there? It is difficult to see where jurisdiction would end; foreign-state and foreign-country corporations could be found "at home" essentially anywhere, based on the briefest and most trivial of contacts.

4. TO THE INTERNET—AND BEYOND!

Should courts be reluctant to apply the traditional due process, personal jurisdiction standards to Internet activity? Are pages on the World Wide Web comparable to postal addresses or phone numbers? Does the creator of a Web page broadcast information on the page to everyone, or does its transmission depend on a request by another? If the mere development of a Web page constitutes a broadcast, a court may be inclined to regard that creation as a type of contact by the Web creator, thereby subjecting the creator of even a passive site to personal jurisdiction in a faraway court.

On the other hand, in order to access a Web page, a person types the Web "address" on a Web browser or clicks on a link, and the computer retrieves the appropriate or desired page from the home computer of the page. Like telephone usage, a Web user obtains information on the Web only by requesting that information. Thus, except for "spam" that appears as electronic mail, viewing Web material depends on the Web user seeking it. Does characterizing Web viewing in this manner expose the Web creator to the jurisdiction of a distant court?

ADVANCED TACTICAL ORDNANCE SYSTEMS, LLC V. REAL ACTION PAINTBALL, INC.

751 F.3d 796 (7th Cir. 2014) (*en banc*)

WOOD, CHIEF JUDGE.

Some readers of our opinions may be familiar with paintball, a type of war game in which the players shoot charges of paint at one another. Paintballs, it turns out, are not the only kind of nonlethal projectile that can be used in this way. Our case concerns a more serious product, known to Advanced Tactical Ordnance Systems (Advanced Tactical) by the name PepperBall (a ball filled with a pepper-spray-like irritant). Police departments, private security firms, and comparable organizations are the primary consumers of these items. This is a trademark infringement action, brought by Advanced Tactical against a company that calls itself Real Action Paintball, Inc., and its president, K.T. Tran. (We refer to both as Real Action, because there is no material difference between the company and its president for purposes of this appeal.) . . . We conclude that the district court lacked personal jurisdiction over defendant Real Action, which preserved its objection on this point. We therefore reverse and remand with directions to dismiss on that basis.

I

Advanced Tactical manufactures and sells PepperBall branded items, including PepperBall projectile irritants. Its headquarters is allegedly in Indiana, though that is less clear than it might be—the company appears to have at least one office in California. It became the manufacturer and seller of PepperBall-branded items in 2012 after it acquired trademarks and other property in a foreclosure sale from a company called PepperBall Technologies Inc. PepperBall Technologies Inc. was located in California. Before the foreclosure, PepperBall Technologies had purchased its irritant projectiles from at least two sources: Perfect Circle, half owner of Advanced Tactical, and a Mexican company called APON. After Advanced Tactical acquired PepperBall Technologies, APON ceased its work as an assembler or manufacturer for PepperBall projectiles.

Around the time of foreclosure, APON's chief operating officer, Conrad Sun, a citizen of California, contacted Real Action Paintball Inc., a California company, to see if Real Action was interested in acquiring irritant projectiles from APON. The answer was yes. The parties concluded their deal in August 2012, after which Real Action posted on its website and sent through its email list an announcement that it had acquired the "machinery, recipes, and materials once used by PepperBall Technologies Inc." That announcement is central to the merits, because it arguably implied that after PepperBall Technologies ceased to exist, Real Action was the only maker of PepperBall irritant projectiles.

Advanced Tactical soon caught wind of Real Action's announcement and fired off a cease-and-desist letter. In response, Real Action added a disclaimer to the original message, stating that it was neither associated nor affiliated with PepperBall Technologies and its brands, and that Real Action projectiles were not made by the current PepperBall Technologies (the name under which Advanced Tactical was doing business). Unsatisfied, Advanced Tactical filed this suit in the District Court for the Northern District of Indiana. It offered a number of different theories of recovery, including intentional violations of the Lanham Act, common law trademark infringement and unfair competition, trade dress infringement, and misappropriation of trade secrets.

The complaint alleged that personal jurisdiction was proper under Indiana's long-arm statute.... Real Action contested personal jurisdiction. In response to the district court's query why Indiana was proper and why California was not preferable, Advanced Tactical pointed to the "blast email" that Real Action sent to all of its customers.... Advanced Tactical also noted that Real Action regularly emailed customers or potential customers from all over the United States, including Indiana, and that it had made at least one sale to an Indiana resident.

The district court ... held an evidentiary hearing on the matter on December 7, 2012, after which it concluded that personal jurisdiction was proper and that Advanced Tactical was entitled to a preliminary injunction. Real Action has appealed, ... contesting both the personal jurisdiction ruling and the injunctive relief....

III

... Because the Lanham Act does not have a special federal rule for personal jurisdiction, ... we look to the law of the forum for the governing rule.... The Supreme Court of Indiana has held that Indiana's long-arm provision "reduce[s] analysis of personal jurisdiction to the issue of whether the exercise of personal jurisdiction is consistent with the Federal Due Process Clause." *LinkAmerica v. Co*, 857 N.E.2d 961, 967 (Ind. 2006)....

Nearly 70 years ago, the Supreme Court held that due process is satisfied for this purpose so long as the defendant had "certain minimum contacts" with the forum state such that the "maintenance of the suit does not offend 'traditional notions of fair play and substantial justice.'" *Int'l Shoe Co. v. Washington*, 326 U.S. 310, 316 (1945)....

Here, the district court found the necessary minimum contacts based on several facts: first, Real Action fulfilled several orders of the allegedly infringing projectiles for purchasers in Indiana; second, it knew that Advanced Tactical was an Indiana company and could foresee that the misleading emails and sales would harm Advanced Tactical in Indiana; third, it sent at least two misleading email blasts to a list that included Indiana residents; fourth, it had an interactive website available to residents of Indiana; and finally, it put customers on its email list when they made a purchase, thereby giving the company some economic advantage. In our view, none of these meets the standards that the Supreme Court has set.

While it is true that Real Action fulfilled a few orders after putting the allegedly infringing message on its website and in emails, Advanced Tactical provides no evidence that those sales had any connection with this litigation. We do not know, for example, whether the Indiana residents saw Real Action's post before making their purchases. There is also nothing to suggest that any Indiana purchaser thought that Advanced Tactical had started selling PepperBalls. Looking at the over 600 sales that Real Action allegedly made to Indiana residents in the two years before suit was filed does not help matters. Specific jurisdiction must rest on the *litigation-specific* conduct of the defendant in the proposed forum state. The only sales that would be relevant are those that were related to Real Action's allegedly unlawful activity. Advanced Tactical—which has the burden of proof here—has not provided evidence of any such sales.

Not only did Advanced Tactical fail to link the few sales to Real Action's litigation-specific activity, but even if it did, it is unlikely that those few sales alone, without some evidence linking them to the allegedly tortious activity, would make jurisdiction proper. To hold otherwise would mean that a plaintiff could bring suit in literally any state where the defendant shipped at least one item. The creation of such *de facto* universal jurisdiction runs counter to the approach the Court has followed since *International Shoe*, and that it reaffirmed as recently as February 2014 in *Walden v. Fiore*, 134 S.Ct. 1115 (2014).

The district court also thought personal jurisdiction proper because Real Action knew that Advanced Tactical was an Indiana company and could foresee that its misleading emails and sales would harm Advanced Tactical in Indiana. *Walden*, however, shows the error of this approach. There the defendant knew that the plaintiffs were going to Nevada, and it was foreseeable that they would want the use of their money there, but the Court squarely rejected this as a permissible basis for jurisdiction. The "mere fact that [defendant's] conduct affected plaintiffs with connections to the forum State does not suffice to authorize jurisdiction." *Walden*, 134 S.Ct. at 1126. The relation between the defendant and the forum "must arise out of contacts that the 'defendant *himself* creates with the forum State." *Id*. at 1118. . . .

The district court also considered Real Action's online activities—the sending of two allegedly misleading emails to a list of subscribers that included Indiana residents and the maintenance of an interactive website. The Supreme Court has not definitively answered how a defendant's online activity translates into "contacts" for purposes of the "minimum contacts" analysis. To the contrary, it expressly "le[ft] questions about virtual contacts for another day" in *Id*. at 1125 n.9. . . . "Our inquiry boils down to this: has [defendant] purposefully exploited the [Indiana] market" beyond simply operating an interactive website accessible in the forum state and sending emails to people who may happen to live there? *Be2 LLC v. Ivanov*, 642 F.3d 555, 558–59 (7th Cir. 2011). Has the defendant, in brief, targeted Indiana somehow? *Id*.

The fact that Real Action maintains an email list to allow it to shower past customers and other subscribers with company-related emails does not show a relation between the company and Indiana. Such a relation would be entirely fortuitous, depending wholly on activities out of the defendant's control. . . . We are not prepared to hold that this alone demonstrates that a defendant made a substantial connection to each state (or country) associated with those persons' "snail mail" addresses. It may be different if there were evidence that a defendant in some way targeted residents of a specific state, perhaps through geographically-restricted online ads. But in such a case the focus would not be on the users who signed up, but instead on the deliberate actions by the defendant to target or direct itself toward the forum state. Advanced Tactical introduced no such evidence in the district court and makes no such argument on appeal.

The interactivity of a website is also a poor proxy for adequate in-state contacts. We have warned that "[c]ourts should be careful in resolving questions about personal jurisdiction involving online contacts to ensure that a defendant is not haled into court simply because the defendant owns or operates a website that is accessible in the forum state, even if that site is 'interactive.'" *Id.* at 558. This makes sense; the operation of an interactive website does not show that the *defendant* has formed a contact with the forum state. And, without the defendant's creating a sufficient connection (or "minimum contacts") with the forum state itself, personal jurisdiction is not proper.

. . . [I]f having an interactive website were enough in situations like this one, there is no limiting principle—a plaintiff could sue everywhere. . . . Having an "interactive website" (which hardly rules out anything in 2014) should not open a defendant up to personal jurisdiction in every spot on the planet where that interactive website is accessible. To hold otherwise would offend "traditional notions of fair play and substantial justice." *Int'l Shoe*, 326 U.S. at 316. . . .

In sum, we see no evidence that the defendant, Real Action, has the necessary minimum contacts with Indiana to support specific jurisdiction. We REMAND the case with instructions to . . . dismiss the complaint for lack of personal jurisdiction.

EXERCISE

You are general counsel for a corporation that has an Internet website, and you recently sent the following memorandum to the CEO of your corporation. Write a follow-up memo to the CEO.

Date: _____, 201_

To: President and Chief Executive Officer

From: General Counsel

Re: Limiting the Corporation's Exposure to Lawsuits

I am writing in response to your recent memorandum of concern about the company's growing litigation costs. After personally reading several recent court decisions, I am planning a meeting with my legal team this morning to explore ways to reduce or eliminate the company's potential exposure to litigation as a result of our Internet Website which the company began to use two years ago.

Thus far, we have been extremely fortunate that very few Website-related lawsuits have been filed against the company. I recognize that my office's suggestions may be outweighed by the need to maximize the company's business/selling efforts. However, that is a business decision that you will ultimately be making in response to my proposal.

I will send you a minimum of five recommendations about changes in the way the company does business. Enjoy your weekend.

B. VENUE

Venue relates to the place or places where a lawsuit may be properly instituted. In state practice, venue may be geared to factors such as the county where a defendant resides or where the claim arose. In federal courts, venue is geared to the federal district or the division (where a district is divided into divisions). Unlike subject matter jurisdiction and personal jurisdiction, which have their source in constitutional law, venue is exclusively statutorily based. Venue connotes locality, and places a limitation on the otherwise free choice a plaintiff has to commence a lawsuit in any court which has both subject matter and personal jurisdiction. In general, venue statutes afford a defendant some protection from being forced to defend in a place remote from her residence or remote from the place where the events underlying the controversy occurred. The venue concept developed from the early concept of a jury trial, i.e., that the case be tried in the vicinity of the events giving rise to the claim.

Federal venue generally is governed by 28 U.S.C. §§ 1390 and 1391. § 1390 defines "venue," and provides that certain types of cases are exempt from the rules set out in § 1391. § 1391(b) provides plaintiffs a list of options for proper venue. Unlike personal jurisdiction, which is analyzed on a state-by-state basis, federal venue is calculated by judicial *district*. Roughly half of the states have only one district, while the other half are divided into two or more districts. For a list of the federal districts, see 28 U.S.C. § 133, which is in your Supplement.

As with personal jurisdiction, venue can be waived, via the Federal Rules (through a failure to raise the issue) or via a contract's forum selection provision (for a forum which otherwise would not be proper under § 1391). Some areas of federal law have their own specialized venue provisions, which explains why § 1391 begins by stating "except as otherwise provided by law . . ." That "law" would be a specialized venue provision such as 28 U.S.C. § 1400(b), dealing with venue in patent cases.

The defendant's remedy for the plaintiff's selection of an improper venue is to file a timely motion to dismiss based on improper venue under Federal Rule 12(b)(3) or 28 U.S.C. § 1406(a). Another remedy available is to seek a transfer due to improper venue, pursuant to 28 U.S.C. § 1406(a). Even if the venue is proper, a defendant can seek a transfer under 28 U.S.C. § 1404(a). The propriety of venue and the alternative remedies is discussed in the following sections.

INTRODUCTORY PROBLEM

Bob Bigelow had an unfortunate accident on July 1, 2013. While cleaning his home with some friends in Dallas, Texas in preparation for a party, the vacuum cleaner he was using exploded. The blast seriously injured Bigelow, sending him to the hospital for almost a month. The vacuum cleaner was a product of the Sucker Corporation of America (SCOA), which sells its wares in hundreds of its own stores in each state throughout the United States. Indeed, Bigelow purchased the vacuum that detonated at one of SCOA's six Dallas stores. SCOA was incorporated in Delaware in 1927, and its national offices and factories are located in Rhode Island.

Shortly after being discharged from the hospital, Bigelow met with his attorney to discuss a lawsuit against SCOA. After numerous unsuccessful negotiation sessions with SCOA, Bigelow decided to sue SCOA for $1,000,000 on product liability theories (negligence, breach of warranty, strict liability) in the state trial court in Dallas, Texas. Following proper service of process on the managing agent of one of its Dallas stores, SCOA's chief corporate and trial attorneys in Rhode Island decided that a trial in the Texas state court would be a nuisance for SCOA. Because the essence of the lawsuit was an attack on the design and manufacture of the vacuum cleaner, SCOA's attorneys concluded that a trial closer to the corporate offices and the available expert witnesses that SCOA always used would be preferable. In addition, a quick trial is a priority in order to minimize the damage to SCOA's nationwide goodwill. Those attorneys also have concluded that there are no substantive or procedural grounds which can result in the lawsuit being thrown out of state court. They have come to you with the following problem—figure out a way for the case to be tried in the federal court in nearby New Hampshire (which has only one federal district and a relatively clear trial docket).

Governing Law: 28 U.S.C. § 1391.

1. FEDERAL VENUE STANDARDS

§ 1391(b) provides parties with several options for venue. The first option is a district in which any defendant resides, if all defendants reside in that state. Note that as long as all defendants reside in the same state, *any* district in which even one of them resides is proper. For individual defendants, § 1391(c)(1) equates residence with the domicile analysis applied in diversity of citizenship subject matter jurisdiction (which you will study in Chapter 4).

The second option under 1391(b) is "a judicial district in which a substantial part of the events or omissions giving rise to the claim occurred, or a substantial part of the property that is the subject of the action is situated." There may be several districts, possibly in multiple states, that qualify under this provision. The fact that more activities took place in one district does not disqualify another district as a proper venue as long as "substantial" activities or omissions took

ASTRO-MED, INC. v. NIHON KOHDEN AMERICA, INC.
591 F.3d 1 (1st Cir. 2009)

WOODCOCK, DISTRICT JUDGE.

Astro-Med, Inc. (Astro-Med) and Nihon Kohden America, Inc. (Nihon Kohden) are rivals in the highly competitive life sciences equipment market, and in October 2006, when Nihon Kohden hired away Kevin Plant, a valuable Astro-Med employee, Astro-Med reviewed its legal options. When first hired at Astro-Med in 2002, Plant signed an employee agreement that contained non-competition and non-disclosure provisions. Relying in large part on those provisions, in December 2006, Astro-Med filed suit against Plant alleging breach of contract and misappropriation of trade secrets. Astro-Med later added a third claim of unfair competition against Plant and joined Nihon Kohden as a defendant, against whom it alleged claims of tortious interference and misappropriation of trade secrets. The lawsuit was especially hard-fought, and Nihon Kohden and Plant were disappointed on April 7, 2008, when a jury returned a verdict against them, awarding $375,800 in damages in favor of Astro-Med. . . .

Astro-Med is a Rhode Island corporation with its principal place of business in West Warwick, Rhode Island. Its Grass Technologies product group manufactures, sells, and distributes instruments for sleep and neurological research and clinical applications of sleep science and brain wave recording and analysis. Although the identity of some of its customers is well known, Astro-Med's financial arrangements with its sales people, its marketing strategy, and its pricing and cost structures are all highly confidential, and Astro-Med makes strenuous efforts to protect its trade secrets and other confidential information.

In October 2002, even though Plant had no prior experience in the medical industry or in medical equipment sales, Astro-Med hired him as a Product Specialist, responsible for the demonstration and training of its Grass Technologies product line. Astro-Med provided Plant with extensive training about its business, products, customers, and competitors, and it was Astro-Med's training that later made him marketable to Nihon Kohden. When Astro-Med hired Plant, he signed an Employee Agreement, which contains a non-competition clause, ..., a trade secrets clause, [and] a choice-of-law and forum-selection clause. ...

Subsequently, Plant asked to be transferred to the state of Florida and become a field sales representative; Astro-Med granted his request and paid to relocate him to Florida. On July 12, 2004, Astro-Med promoted Plant to District Sales Manager for sales of Grass Technologies products. As District Sales Manager, Plant had access to and used Astro-Med's trade secrets, including confidential marketing, pricing, and customer information. He became intimately familiar with Astro-Med's customers and their preferences as well as Astro-Med's pricing strategy and cost data. He also learned about Astro-Med's suppliers, products they supplied, and the customers who purchased these products. Finally, he was informed about Astro-Med's research and development efforts with respect to its Grass Technologies product line.

Nihon Kohden, a California corporation, has its principal place of business in Foothill Ranch, California. As a manufacturer of instrumentation for patient monitoring, sleep assessment, and neurology, Nihon Kohden competes directly with Astro-Med. In 2006, Brian Kehoe, the Florida sales representative for Nihon Kohden, was about to leave the company, and on July 21, 2006, he emailed Gary Reasoner, the Director of the Neurology Business Unit for Nihon Kohden, and informed him that he had met a man, Kevin Plant, who was a potential replacement for the Florida sales territory. ...

In September 2006, Plant sent a resume to Reasoner, and Reasoner interviewed Plant several times over the telephone. In late September 2006, Plant traveled to Foothill Ranch and met with Michael Ohsawa, the Director of Operations for Nihon Kohden, and with Reasoner. Directly after the interview, Nihon Kohden made Plant a job offer, which he accepted. After Plant accepted the Nihon Kohden position, Kehoe emailed Plant: "I will be interested in seeing what you have in the works with Grass [Technologies]." Plant replied, "Sounds good."

Before offering Plant employment, Nihon Kohden became aware of the Astro-Med Employment Agreement with Plant and referred the contract to counsel for review. Nihon Kohden's lawyer advised Nihon Kohden that there was some minimal risk in hiring Plant; notwithstanding that advice, Nihon Kohden hired Plant to sell its products in competition with Astro-Med in the sales territory he had covered for Astro-Med.

* * *

Nihon Kohden argues that Rhode Island was not the proper venue for Astro-Med's lawsuit, and the district court should have either dismissed the claim or transferred the case to a different district in accordance with 28 U.S.C. § 1404.

The applicable venue provision [is] 28 U.S.C. § [1391(b)]. Although Nihon Kohden is a California business, it resides for purposes of venue in Rhode Island. Plant is a resident of Florida. As the defendants reside in different states, subsection (1) does not apply.

Under § [1391(b)(2)], the question becomes whether the District of Rhode Island is "a judicial district in which a substantial part of the events . . . giving rise to the claim occurred." In determining whether Rhode Island is a district in which a substantial part of the events occurred, we look "not to a single 'triggering event' prompting the action, but to the entire sequence of events underlying the claim." *Uffner v. La Reunion Francaise, S.A.*, 244 F.3d 38, 42 (1st Cir.2001). In addition, we do not focus on the actions of one party. Rather, our approach takes a "holistic view of the acts underlying a claim." *Id.* at 43 n. 6. Furthermore, we are not required to determine the best venue, merely a proper venue. See *id.* at 42 (venue may be proper in any number of districts). Thus, even though Plant was a resident of Florida when he was hired by Nihon Kohden, a California corporation, venue in Rhode Island may still be proper.

Astro-Med and Plant entered into an employment contract in Rhode Island, the district in which Astro-Med was headquartered, that contained the non-compete and non-disclosure clauses at issue here. With full knowledge of the Employee Agreement and its contents, Nihon Kohden hired away Plant, thereby interfering with Astro-Med's contract and misappropriating its trade secrets. Because Astro-Med was headquartered in Rhode Island, this district is one of the places where the tortious interference and misappropriation of trade secrets occurred and where the harms from these torts were felt. In addition, Rhode Island was the forum selected by the Employee Agreement to resolve disputes. See *Lambert v. Kysar*, 983 F.2d 1110, 1118 n. 11 (1st Cir. 1993) (upholding forum selection clause). Taken together, these facts constitute a substantial part of Astro-Med's claims against Nihon Kohden.

Further, Plant did not contest venue in Rhode Island and that portion of the lawsuit was, for venue purposes, going to proceed in Rhode Island. Thus, the convenience of the parties strongly militated in favor of retention of venue in Rhode Island. *Uffner*, 244 F.3d at 43 ("[T]he general purpose of the venue rules is 'to protect the defendant against the risk that a plaintiff will select an unfair or inconvenient place of trial.'") Given that a substantial part of Astro-Med's claims involved Rhode Island and proceeding in Rhode Island would not thwart the underlying purpose of the venue statute, we conclude that the district court did not err in refusing to dismiss the claims pending against Nihon Kohden in Rhode Island for improper venue. . . .

The district court judgment is affirmed.

NOTES AND QUESTIONS

1. If tangible property is the subject of the claim—for example, a case seeking title to property or to recover damage to property—proper venue lies in any district where a "substantial part" of the property lies. The physical presence of property can support venue when the property is the subject of the claim, even if the conduct that made the claim actionable took place elsewhere; e.g., a breach of contract for purchase of a yacht when negotiation, signing, and payment occurred in a different district from where the property is located.

Prior to the 2011 revisions to § 1391, a special rule called the *local action* rule applied to certain cases involving land. In such cases, only the district where the land was situated was a proper venue. The 2011 revisions abandoned the local action rule. Most states have also abandoned the rule.

2. § 1391(b)(3) provides that venue is proper in any district in which any defendant is subject to personal jurisdiction. The term "subject" suggests that venue is proper in a district where a defendant could be served, even if she is not actually served there. The good news is that the provision makes venue available merely because personal jurisdiction is available. The bad news is that the provision is available *only* when neither § 1391(b)(1) nor (b)(2) applies. When does § 1391(b)(3) ever apply? The most common situation where the provision applies is when all substantial events or omissions occurred outside the United States and either multiple defendants reside in different states or one or more individual defendants resides outside the United States.

3. How is venue determined in a case involving a corporation or other organization? §§ 1391(c)(2) and (d) govern this situation. Under § 1391(c)(2), a corporation is deemed to reside in any district in which it is subject to personal jurisdiction. Note that this provision is not a separate venue provision for corporations. Rather, it simply defines where a corporate defendant is deemed to "reside" for purposes of applying § 1391(b)(1) (the subsequent language in § 1391(c)(2) about corporate plaintiffs applies only to special venue statutes, not to § 1391). The effect of § 1391(c)(2) is to make it easier to sue corporations, as it merges the personal jurisdiction and venue analyses.

How does § 1391(c)(2) apply in a state with multiple districts? The answer lies in § 1391(d). Under this provision, each district is treated as if it were a separate state. If the defendant corporation's contacts with that *district* would be sufficient to establish personal jurisdiction, defendant is deemed to reside in that district. If this test is satisfied for more than one district in a state, the corporation is a resident of each of those districts. However, if the contacts with a state are sufficient but there is not one district where the contacts are sufficient, the corporation is deemed to reside in the district in that state with the most significant contacts. Note that if a corporation is incorporated in a particular state, defendant will be deemed to reside in *all* districts in that state.

4. As you will see in Chapter 4, a case originally filed in state court may in some situations be "removed" to federal court under 28 U.S.C. § 1441 and other statutes. The venue statutes dictate which federal court can take a removed case. § 1390(c) provides that when a case is properly removed, § 1391 and the other venue statutes do not apply. Thus, if a case is properly removed, a party cannot move to dismiss for lack of venue, even if the federal court that is now hearing the case would not have been a proper venue had the action been originally filed there.

PROBLEMS

After reviewing 28 U.S.C. § 1391, in the following problems identify the districts in which proper venue lies. You may assume that all requirements of federal subject matter jurisdiction are satisfied.

1. Warner, a resident of Virginia, sues Edwards, a resident of the Western District of North Carolina, on a claim arising out of an automobile accident. Edwards has substantial land holdings in New Mexico. The accident occurred in the Northern District of Illinois when Edwards's brakes apparently failed. Edwards's car, usually serviced in western North Carolina, had been checked by a service station in Minnesota a few days before the accident.

2. Warner, a resident of Northern District of Virginia, sues Edwards, a resident of the Western District of North Carolina, on a claim based on a federal civil rights violation occurring in the Northern District of Georgia.

3. Trudeau, a Canadian citizen, sues Stoops, a resident of the Eastern District of Oklahoma, based on a personal injury damage claim arising from an automobile accident in the Western District of Kansas.

4. In #3, suppose that Stoops had sued Trudeau in a federal court. Where is (are) the proper venue(s)?

5. Stoops, a resident of the Eastern District of Oklahoma, sues Dole, a citizen of the Western District of Kansas, alleging personal injury damages from an accident in western Kansas.

6. Clinton, a resident of the Southern District of New York, wants to sue Hillary, Inc., a New York corporation that conducts significant business throughout Virginia and nowhere else. Clinton's claim arises out of that business and is based on federal law.

7. Boxer, a resident of the Central District of California, and Schmidt, a resident of the Eastern District of Colorado, suffer injuries in a boating accident in Oregon. They sue Moboat Corporation, the boat's manufacturer, alleging negligent design of the boat. The boat was purchased in central California after it was manufactured in the Southern District of Florida at its only factory. Moboat Corporation has its headquarters and is incorporated in

Florida. It sells boats in all fifty states, but does continuous and systematic business only in Michigan, Wisconsin, and Pennsylvania.

8. McCain, a resident of the Southern District of Arizona, wants to sue the *New York Times Corporation* and its publisher, A.O. Sulzburger. The *Times* does sufficient business in every district in New York state to be subject to personal jurisdiction there. Sulzburger lives and conducts most business from his home in the Eastern District of New York; he only occasionally visits the offices of the *Times* in the Southern District of New York. McCain's claim is for common law defamation based on an article in the newspaper.

2. TRANSFERRING THE LAWSUIT

a. By Statute

Regardless of whether venue is proper, it may be possible to transfer a case elsewhere within the same court system. For example, a case filed in the Southern District of New York may be transferred to another federal district if statutory requirements are met. A forum shopping plaintiff may file a claim where venue is proper, but the district where it is filed may have little to do with the parties or the litigation, and may be distant from the locale of the key witnesses.

28 U.S.C. § 1404(a) is the most important of the various statutes providing for transfer of a case, allowing transfer of a case on a defendant's motion to either another federal district or to another federal division in the same district. The premise for using § 1404(a) is that venue is proper under § 1391 or some specialized venue statute where the case currently sits. The statute potentially applies to all civil cases, even cases that were initially filed in a state court but were removed properly to a federal court. A § 1404(a) motion for transfer may be made at any time, but delay in filing the motion is an element considered in a ruling on the motion.

One limitation on transferring a case elsewhere in the system is that it can be shifted only to another district "where it might have been brought." The statute bars transfer unless the transferee court would have 1) been a proper venue, usually measured by any provision of § 1391, not just the provision that was used to obtain venue where the case was originally filed; 2) had proper subject matter jurisdiction, which is no problem because the transfer is to another district in the *same court system;* and 3) been a place where the defendant is subject to personal jurisdiction, and specific or general jurisdiction or domicile may be used to satisfy personal jurisdiction in the transferee court.

In addition to whether a case "might have been brought" in the transferee court, § 1404(a) contains three explicit standards for the court to consider and balance in exercising its discretion about whether to grant a motion to transfer: the convenience of the parties, the convenience of the witnesses, and the interest of justice.

The 2011 amendments to the federal jurisdiction and venue provisions relaxed somewhat the strict requirements governing transfer. Now, for transfers under § 1404, the district to which the case may be transferred must either be one that would be a proper venue, or be a district to which all parties consent. The effect of this change is to allow an action to be heard in a district that all parties consider convenient, even if that district would not have venue or personal jurisdiction over some of the defendants.

METEORO AMUSEMENT CORP. V. SIX FLAGS
267 F.Supp.2d 263 (N.D.N.Y. 2003)

McCURN, SENIOR DISTRICT JUDGE.

Plaintiff, Meteoro Amusement Corp. ("Meteoro"), a New Mexico Corporation with its principal place of business in Lansing, New York, filed this civil action against defendant, Six Flags, Inc. ("SFI"), a Delaware corporation, on July 31, 2002. . . .

The following are the facts as set forth in the complaint. Meteoro is the assignee of the patent, entitled "Modularized Amusement Ride and Training Simulation Device", issued on May 14, 2002. The Modularized Amusement Ride and Training Simulation Device is defined in the abstract of the patent as "[a]n amusement device comprising a modular pod, in which one or more riders sit and are restrained, and which spins under power about a horizontal axis according to the passenger's active control" and "may be used in conjunction with many different types of amusement devices, including, but not limited to roller coasters". Meteoro offered to sell SFI, as well as other companies such as Premier Rides and Arrow Dynamics, Inc., the technology embodied in the patent. In 1998, copies of a video which illustrated this technology were distributed to and presumed viewed by Premier Rides, Arrow Dynamics and SFI, and in 1999 the video was made available for public viewing on Meteoro's website.

In December 2000, defendant SFI announced the anticipated debut of a roller coaster called "X" at its theme park, Magic Mountain, located in Valencia, California. The roller coaster was being manufactured by Arrow Communications. Passengers of the X roller coaster are strapped into vehicles that move 360 degrees forward or backward along a central carriage. . . .

In November 2001, the United States Patent and Trademark Office published the application. The following month, X was opened to a limited audience at Magic Mountain, and was opened to the general public in

January 2002. SFI has promoted, and continues to promote X, utilizing, among other things, its website to do so. . . .

Presently before the court [are several preliminary motions to dismiss, which the court denied.] Alternatively, defendant moves this court to transfer venue pursuant to 28 U.S.C. § 1404(a). Plaintiff opposes this motion. . . . The court now . . . exercises its discretion to transfer venue to the Western District of Oklahoma pursuant to 28 U.S.C. § 1404(a).

. . . Defendant moves in the alternative for a transfer of venue pursuant to 28 U.S.C. § 1404(a) to the Western District of Oklahoma, or alternatively to the Central District of California or the Southern District of New York. Defendant has made clear that the foregoing is its order of preference, such that its first choice for venue is the Western District of Oklahoma.

[The court found that the case might have been brought in any of the three districts.]

Once the threshold is met, as it is here, the court has discretion to transfer the case, but such a motion will not be granted absent a clear showing by defendant that the balance of convenience factors weighs in favor of a transfer. Moreover, the burden is on the moving party to establish that there should be a change in venue. In determining whether to grant a motion to transfer venue, the following factors may be considered by the court: the convenience to parties; the convenience of witnesses; the relative ease of access to sources of proof; the availability of process to compel attendance of unwilling witnesses; the cost of obtaining willing witnesses; practical problems that make trial of a case easy, expeditious, and inexpensive; and the interests of justice. Further, in this circuit, when a party seeks a transfer based on convenience of witnesses pursuant to [section] 1404(a) he must clearly specify the key witnesses to be called and must make a general statement of their testimony. . . . [T]he relative financial hardship on the litigants and their respective abilities to prosecute or defend an action in a particular forum are legitimate factors to consider. The consideration of comparative calender conditions is also relevant. Finally, the plaintiff's choice of forum is an additional consideration.

Meteoro argues that their choice of forum should be given great weight. . . . [T]he most substantial weight is given to the convenience of witnesses.

Here, defendant SFI argues that the convenience of witnesses militates in favor of transfer to the Western District of Oklahoma. Since the majority of witnesses will be from Oklahoma City, where SFI's corporate offices are located, and presumably plaintiff will only have two witnesses, SFI argues it will be much more convenient for them to travel to the local federal courthouse than to the Northern District of New York.

. . . Defendant's list includes two categories of witnesses: those who will testify about the purchase of X from Arrow Communications, and those who will testify about its "design, development, structure, function, manufacture and operation". Additionally, defendant expects eight witnesses from Arrow Communications to testify regarding "the design, development, structure, function and manufacture of the X-Coaster ride, the sale of the ride to SFTPI, the documents and circumstances surrounding that sale, the financial and business records of Arrow, the cost, profits, and revenues relating to the sale of the X coaster." These witnesses are all located in Utah.

Plaintiff argues that the majority of "relevant" testimony will come from its witnesses, including its CEO and inventor of the patented devices at issue in this case, John F. Mares. Mr. Mares resides in the Northern District of New York and is the only person active in the operation of the plaintiff corporation. In addition to operating Meteoro, Mr. Mares is employed as a Vice President for a corporation located in Ithaca, New York. Mr. Mares avers that for the foregoing reasons, it would be a severe hardship for him to litigate his claim in another district. At oral argument, plaintiff's counsel identified an additional witness, Bob Perls, who is associated with Meteoro but resides in New Mexico. Counsel for plaintiff also suggested that Meteoro may require expert testimony and would seek to find such an expert within this District.

Defense counsel noted at oral argument that Mr. Mares will be deposed in this district "no matter what." Moreover, defendant argues that for the majority of witnesses, including Mr. Perls and the attorney who prosecuted one of the patents at issue in this case, who also resides in New Mexico, it would be more inconvenient to travel to the Northern District of New York than it would to travel to Oklahoma or California. Plaintiff counters that for most of the potential witnesses defendant identifies, deposition testimony can be taken where they are located, so the inconvenience of travel will be on the parties, not the witnesses. In addition, whichever venue the court chooses, some witnesses will be inconvenienced by travel, and the costs associated with a longer traveling distance are not a substantial enough showing of inconvenience to outweigh the plaintiff's choice of forum.

SFI also argues that the availability of process to compel the testimony of unwilling witnesses is an important factor. Plaintiff contends that any testimony proffered by defendant regarding the design and construction of X is irrelevant, since the roller coaster was built prior to the issuance of the patents defendant allegedly infringed, although defendant counters such testimony is relevant to plaintiff's allegation of willfulness. Moreover, as plaintiff previously argued, and the court tends to agree, non-party witnesses would be deposed where they are located, and defendant failed to identify any reason why this would not be so.

There is also disagreement between the parties as to whether a firsthand viewing of the alleged infringing roller coaster would be necessary, a factor that if proved important would militate in favor of the Central District of California as the proper venue. At oral argument, Defense counsel argued that photographs or design blueprints of the alleged infringing roller coaster will not be sufficient to show a jury whether said coaster, as it currently exists, is infringing plaintiff's patents.

Additionally, defense counsel argues the location of most documents needed for litigation is SFI's headquarters in Oklahoma City. Although the documents can be shipped, this involves an added cost and inconvenience that should weigh in favor of a transfer of venue to the Western District of Oklahoma.

Finally, Meteoro argues that the disparities in the financial means of the parties weighs greatly in favor of denying SFI's motion to transfer. Plaintiff cites the affidavit of its president as evidence of the hardship a transfer would cause, but cites no authority for its allegation that defendant has over one billion dollars in annual revenue. Counsel for plaintiff argues that a transfer to any of the three districts defendant suggests would require that Meteoro retain local counsel, and thereby incur additional costs.

The court finds, after weighing the evidence before it, that venue is most proper in the Western District of Oklahoma. Defendant's headquarters, as well as a near majority of potential witnesses, are located in Oklahoma City. The only factor weighing in favor of the Central District of California, aside from it being the location of a small number of potential witnesses, is that it is the location of the alleged infringing roller coaster. However, there is disagreement as to the evidentiary significance of a viewing of the roller coaster by being in its presence instead of viewing photographs or design blueprints. Further, very little evidence was submitted regarding the appropriateness of the Southern District of New York as a venue, except that defendant has offices there. Finally, the court has already found that the Northern District is an improper venue. Plaintiff's main witness, John Mares, who resides in the Northern District, will be inconvenienced regardless of the forum the Court chooses. The only additional witness specified by plaintiff is located in New Mexico and will likewise be inconvenienced by the Court's choice of forum. . . . Based on the foregoing, defendant's . . . request for a transfer of venue to the Western District of Oklahoma is hereby granted. . . .

NOTES AND QUESTIONS

1. Did the court apply the correct statute? Notice that the court observed that venue in the Northern District of New York was "improper."

2. *Convenience of the parties.* If the transfer's effect would merely shift any inconvenience from the defendant to the plaintiff, the motion to transfer is likely to be denied. The defendant moving for transfer must show that the original forum is inconvenient for it and that the plaintiff would not be substantially inconvenienced by the transfer. The trial court may consider the parties' financial strength as well as their physical condition. Indeed, sometimes it will condition the transfer on the willingness of the defendant to bear specified expenses of the plaintiff to transfer the case.

3. *Convenience of the witnesses.* It is a powerful argument against transfer if the forum chosen by the plaintiff will be the most convenient for the witnesses. The evaluation is based on the convenience for the key witnesses, as opposed to the convenience for all the witnesses. Because a motion to transfer is usually filed early in the life of a lawsuit, the identities of the key witnesses still may be unclear.

What type of proof would persuade a court that a transfer for the "convenience of the witnesses" should be granted? Of what relevance is it to know 1) what helpful testimony a distant witness would provide; 2) the availability of expert witnesses in the transferee district; and 3) the convenience for counsel?

4. *Interest of justice.* Your ability to argue that the interest of justice favors your client should be limited only by your creativity, but most of the case law giving importance to this factor falls into two categories. The "interest of justice" may be served by the avoidance of multiple lawsuits from a single transaction. It may be in the "interest of justice" to transfer a case to a forum where other cases are pending from the same transaction so that the pending cases and the transferred case possibly can be consolidated. If Able sues Baker in the Eastern District of Florida, and Charlie has sued Baker in the Northern District of Tennessee and both cases are based on the same transaction, Baker may attempt to transfer one of the cases to the location of the other case. Or, transfer may be in the "interest of justice" if transfer enables the plaintiff to gain personal jurisdiction over an additional defendant who was not subject to process in the original forum. Able sued Baker in the Eastern District of Florida and Baker moves for a change of venue to the Northern District of Tennessee so that Able would be able to join Charlie as a co-defendant along with Baker.

The second category of case where the "interest of justice" may be served by transfer is where an earlier trial date is easier to obtain because of a less crowded docket in the transferee court. Keep in mind that these three balancing factors are relevant only if the lawsuit "might have been brought" by the plaintiff in the district where your client would like to have the case transferred, or all parties consent to the transfer.

The interest of justice also may relate to a party's inability to obtain a fair trial, e.g., from media attention. See Chapter 12, dealing with the right to trial by jury.

5. As indicated in the introductory text, a case may be transferred under § 1404 to a district that lacks personal jurisdiction and/or venue, provided all parties consent to the transfer. The effect of this amendment is to overrule the Supreme Court's decision in *Hoffman v. Blaski*, 363 U.S. 335, 80 S.Ct. 1084, 4 L.Ed.2d 1254 (1960), which held such transfers improper under the old version of the law. Overruling *Hoffman* affects only transfers under § 1404, not transfers under § 1406.

6. One potential motive for seeking a change of venue is that the defendant would count on a different substantive law applying in a federal district located in another state. The Supreme Court took care of that tactic in *Van Dusen v. Barrack*, 376 U.S. 612, 84 S.Ct. 805, 11 L.Ed.2d 945 (1964) by holding that the same law applies after a transfer as applied prior to the change of venue. The *Van Dusen* principle applies in diversity cases and regardless of which party moves for transfer. *Ferens v. John Deere Company*, 494 U.S. 516, 110 S.Ct. 1274, 108 L.Ed.2d 443 (1990).

The procedural transfer therefore is strictly procedural without any accompanying substantive advantage for the moving party. If the substantive law in the district where the case is filed is unclear, does that argue against transfer? If so, the assumption is that the original judge is better able to figure out the law than a judge would in the transferee state. If the effect of *Van Dusen* is not to change the applicable law after transfer, the "interest of justice" argument that transfer can facilitate consolidation with a case already filed in the transferee district is doubtful.

The effect of *Van Dusen* may raise another concern, though, about the expanded scope of available districts for venue created by the provisions in § 1391(b)(2). Assuming that the "substantial part" standard increases the number of districts where a case could be filed, what prevents a plaintiff from filing in the (proper venue) district that also supplies the preferred substantive law and then not caring much about a defendant's motion to transfer under § 1404(a)? In other words, by the time the motion for transfer is filed, the plaintiff has the benefit of the law that would produce the best result.

7. § 1406(a) transfer is an alternative change of venue statute to § 1404(a). The primary difference between the two provisions is that the premise for using § 1406(a) is that venue where the case currently sits is *improper,* e.g., it violates § 1391. Another difference in the statutes is that the remedy available under § 1406(a) is to either transfer the case or to dismiss it. Why the latter remedy? Because venue in the current district is improper. Both § 1406(a) and Federal Rule 12(b)(3) provide for dismissal of a lawsuit in which the venue is improper. Is a motion to dismiss under § 1406(a) permitted, even when the time for filing a motion under Rule 12(b)(3) to dismiss the complaint has passed? Compare *Steward v. Up North Plastics,*

Inc., 177 F.Supp.2d 953 (D.Minn. 2001) (passage of significant time and motion practice precludes § 1406 motion) with *Ptaszynki v. Ferrell*, 277 F.Supp. 969 (E.D.Tenn. 1967) (transfer permitted even though objection to improper venue was waived).

§ 1406(a) transfer may be used by a court as an alternative remedy to a defendant's motion to dismiss under Federal Rule 12(b)(3). The criteria for granting a motion to transfer under § 1406(a) is the "interest of justice" and whether the lawsuit "could have been brought" in the district where to which transfer is attempted. When might it be in the "interest of justice" to transfer a case to a proper forum rather than dismiss the lawsuit? The main example of the criterion's application occurs when the statute of limitations has already run on the plaintiff's claim. Dismissal would prevent a new lawsuit from being refiled by the plaintiff, but transferring the case is deemed to be a continuation of the original filing.

An assessment of whether a case "could have been brought" in the transferee district under § 1406(a) is comparable to the analysis under § 1404(a): whether the transferee court would have 1) been a proper venue; 2) had proper subject matter jurisdiction; and 3) been a place where the defendant is subject to personal jurisdiction. The main difference between the two provisions is that the parties cannot consent to have the case transferred to an improper venue under § 1406, whereas the parties can waive venue and personal jurisdiction problems in a § 1404 transfer.

8. Does the *Van Dusen* principle mentioned in note 6 apply in the § 1406(a) context? Should the law of the place where the lawsuit was originally filed apply if the case was filed in the wrong place (venue)? Wouldn't that result reward the plaintiff for filing in the wrong court? See, e.g., *Fanselow v. Rice*, 213 F.Supp.2d 1077 (D. Neb. 2002) (law of transferee court applies).

9. As with personal jurisdiction, venue is decided on a party-by-party basis. The trial court may dismiss the lawsuit as to one party as a result of improper venue, and continue the litigation for the other parties for whom venue is proper. Or, in the context of a motion to transfer, a court may transfer a case under § 1404(a) for the defendant for whom venue is proper, and approve the transfer under § 1406 for the party for whom venue is currently improper.

b. By Forum Non Conveniens

Sometimes, a distant and inconvenient forum may have personal jurisdiction over a defendant, but the mere existence of power to adjudicate a claim against a defendant does not necessarily mean that the court should exercise that power. "Forum non conveniens" is a common law doctrine that in its modern conception allows a court to dismiss a claim so that it can be brought in a more appropriate forum *in another court system*. Its application is discretionary with the trial court.

PIPER AIRCRAFT CO. v. REYNO
454 U.S. 235, 102 S.Ct. 252, 70 L.Ed.2d 419 (1981)

JUSTICE MARSHALL delivered the opinion of the Court.

[Five Scottish citizens perished in an air crash in Scotland. Reyno, the legal secretary for the decedents' survivors' attorney brought wrongful-death actions against aircraft and propeller manufacturers from Pennsylvania and Ohio in a California state court. The case was removed to California federal court, and then transferred to United States District Court for the Middle District of Pennsylvania, where the defendants moved to dismiss on the ground of *forum non conveniens*. The District Court granted their motions, noting that an alternative forum existed in Scotland.

The trial court relied on the balancing test from *Gulf Oil Corp. v. Gilbert,* 330 U.S. 501 (1947). There, "to guide trial court discretion, the Court provided a list of 'private interest factors' affecting the convenience of the litigants, and a list of 'public interest factors' affecting the convenience of the forum."

> The factors pertaining to the private interests of the litigants included the "relative ease of access to sources of proof; availability of compulsory process for attendance of unwilling, and the cost of obtaining attendance of willing, witnesses; possibility of view of premises, if view would be appropriate to the action; and all other practical problems that make trial of a case easy, expeditious and inexpensive." The public factors bearing on the question included the administrative difficulties flowing from court congestion; the "local interest in having localized controversies decided at home"; the interest in having the trial of a diversity case in a forum that is at home with the law that must govern the action; the avoidance of unnecessary problems in conflict of laws, or in the application of foreign law; and the unfairness of burdening citizens in an unrelated forum with jury duty.]

After describing our decisions in *Gilbert*, the District Court analyzed the facts of these cases. It began by observing that an alternative forum existed in Scotland; Piper and Hartzell had agreed to submit to the jurisdiction of the Scottish courts and to waive any statute of limitations defense that might be available. It then stated that plaintiff's choice of forum was entitled to little weight. The court recognized that a plaintiff's choice ordinarily deserves substantial deference. It noted, however, that Reyno "is a representative of foreign citizens and residents seeking a forum in the United States because of the more liberal rules concerning products liability law," and that "the courts have been less solicitous when the plaintiff is not an American citizen or resident, and particularly when the foreign citizens seek to benefit from the more liberal tort rules provided for the protection of citizens and residents of the United States."

The District Court next examined several factors relating to the private interests of the litigants, and determined that these factors strongly pointed towards Scotland as the appropriate forum. Although evidence concerning the design, manufacture, and testing of the plane and propeller is located in the United States, the connections with Scotland are otherwise "overwhelming." The real parties in interest are citizens of Scotland, as were all the decedents. Witnesses who could testify regarding the maintenance of the aircraft, the training of the pilot, and the investigation of the accident—all essential to the defense—are in Great Britain. Moreover, all witnesses to damages are located in Scotland. Trial would be aided by familiarity with Scottish topography, and by easy access to the wreckage.

The District Court reasoned that because crucial witnesses and evidence were beyond the reach of compulsory process, and because the defendants would not be able to implead potential Scottish third-party defendants, it would be "unfair to make Piper and Hartzell proceed to trial in this forum." The survivors had brought separate actions in Scotland against the pilot, McDonald, and Air Navigation. "[I]t would be fairer to all parties and less costly if the entire case was presented to one jury with available testimony from all relevant witnesses." Ibid. Although the court recognized that if trial were held in the United States, Piper and Hartzell could file indemnity or contribution actions against the Scottish defendants, it believed that there was a significant risk of inconsistent verdicts.

The District Court concluded that the relevant public interests also pointed strongly towards dismissal. The court determined that Pennsylvania law would apply to Piper and Scottish law to Hartzell if the case were tried in the Middle District of Pennsylvania. As a result, "trial in this forum would be hopelessly complex and confusing for a jury." In addition, the court noted that it was unfamiliar with Scottish law and thus would have to rely upon experts from that country. The court also found that the trial would be enormously costly and time-consuming; that it would be unfair to burden citizens with jury duty when the Middle District of Pennsylvania has little connection with the controversy; and that Scotland has a substantial interest in the outcome of the litigation.

In opposing the motions to dismiss, respondent contended that dismissal would be unfair because Scottish law was less favorable. The District Court explicitly rejected this claim. It reasoned that the possibility that dismissal might lead to an unfavorable change in the law did not deserve significant weight; any deficiency in the foreign law was a "matter to be dealt with in the foreign forum."

On appeal, the United States Court of Appeals for the Third Circuit reversed and remanded for trial. The decision to reverse appears to be based on two alternative grounds. First, the Court held that the District Court abused its discretion in conducting the *Gilbert* analysis. Second, the Court held that dismissal is never appropriate where the law of the alternative forum is less favorable to the plaintiff.

The Court of Appeals began its review of the District Court's *Gilbert* analysis by noting that the plaintiff's choice of forum deserved substantial weight, even though the real parties in interest are nonresidents. It then rejected the District Court's balancing of the private interests. It found that Piper and Hartzell had failed adequately to support their claim that key witnesses would be unavailable if trial were held in the United States: they had never specified the witnesses they would call and the testimony these witnesses would provide. The Court of Appeals gave little weight to the fact that Piper and Hartzell would not be able to implead potential Scottish third-party defendants, reasoning that this difficulty would be "burdensome" but not "unfair," 639 F.2d, at 162. Finally, the court stated that resolution of the suit would not be significantly aided by familiarity with Scottish topography, or by viewing the wreckage.

The Court of Appeals also rejected the District Court's analysis of the public interest factors. It found that the District Court gave undue emphasis to the application of Scottish law: "'the mere fact that the court is called upon to determine and apply foreign law does not present a legal problem of the sort which would justify the dismissal of a case otherwise properly before the court.'" In any event, it believed that Scottish law need not be applied. After conducting its own choice-of-law analysis, the Court of Appeals determined that American law would govern the actions against both Piper and Hartzell. The same choice-of-law analysis apparently led it to conclude that Pennsylvania and Ohio, rather than Scotland, are the jurisdictions with the greatest policy interests in the dispute, and that all other public interest factors favored trial in the United States.

II

The Court of Appeals erred in holding that plaintiffs may defeat a motion to dismiss on the ground of *forum non conveniens* merely by showing that the substantive law that would be applied in the alternative forum is less favorable to the plaintiffs than that of the present forum. The possibility of a change in substantive law should ordinarily not be given conclusive or even substantial weight in the *forum non conveniens* inquiry.

... The Court of Appeals' decision is inconsistent with this Court's earlier *forum non conveniens* decisions in another respect. Those decisions have repeatedly emphasized the need to retain flexibility. ...

In fact, if conclusive or substantial weight were given to the possibility of a change in law, the *forum non conveniens* doctrine would become virtually useless. Jurisdiction and venue requirements are often easily satisfied. As a result, many plaintiffs are able to choose from among several forums. Ordinarily, these plaintiffs will select that forum whose choice-of-law rules are most advantageous. Thus, if the possibility of an unfavorable change in substantive law is given substantial weight in the *forum non conveniens* inquiry, dismissal would rarely be proper. . . .

The Court of Appeals' approach is not only inconsistent with the purpose of the forum non conveniens doctrine, but also poses substantial practical problems. If the possibility of a change in law were given substantial weight, deciding motions to dismiss on the ground of *forum non conveniens* would become quite difficult. Choice-of-law analysis would become extremely important, and the courts would frequently be required to interpret the law of foreign jurisdictions. . . . The doctrine of *forum non conveniens*, however, is designed in part to help courts avoid conducting complex exercises in comparative law. As we stated in *Gilbert*, the public interest factors point towards dismissal where the court would be required to "untangle problems in conflict of laws, and in law foreign to itself."

Upholding the decision of the Court of Appeals would result in other practical problems. At least where the foreign plaintiff named an American manufacturer as defendant, a court could not dismiss the case on grounds of *forum non conveniens* where dismissal might lead to an unfavorable change in law. The American courts, which are already extremely attractive to foreign plaintiffs, would become even more attractive. The flow of litigation into the United States would increase and further congest already crowded courts. . . .

We do not hold that the possibility of an unfavorable change in law should never be a relevant consideration in a *forum non conveniens* inquiry. Of course, if the remedy provided by the alternative forum is so clearly inadequate or unsatisfactory that it is no remedy at all, the unfavorable change in law may be given substantial weight; the district court may conclude that dismissal would not be in the interests of justice. In these cases, however, the remedies that would be provided by the Scottish courts do not fall within this category. Although the relatives of the decedents may not be able to rely on a strict liability theory, and although their potential damages award may be smaller, there is no danger that they will be deprived of any remedy or treated unfairly.

III

The Court of Appeals also erred in rejecting the District Court's *Gilbert* analysis. . . .

A

The District Court acknowledged that there is ordinarily a strong presumption in favor of the plaintiff's choice of forum, which may be overcome only when the private and public interest factors clearly point towards trial in the alternative forum. It held, however, that the presumption applies with less force when the plaintiff or real parties in interest are foreign.

The District Court's distinction between resident or citizen plaintiffs and foreign plaintiffs is fully justified. . . . When the home forum has been chosen, it is reasonable to assume that this choice is convenient. When the plaintiff is foreign, however, this assumption is much less reasonable. Because the central purpose of any *forum non conveniens* inquiry is to ensure that the trial is convenient, a foreign plaintiff's choice deserves less deference.

B

The *forum non conveniens* determination is committed to the sound discretion of the trial court. . . . In examining the District Court's analysis of the public and private interests, however, the Court of Appeals seems to have lost sight of this rule, and substituted its own judgment for that of the District Court.

(1)

In analyzing the private interest factors, the District Court stated that the connections with Scotland are "overwhelming." This characterization may be somewhat exaggerated. Particularly with respect to the question of relative ease of access to sources of proof, the private interests point in both directions. As respondent emphasizes, records concerning the design, manufacture, and testing of the propeller and plane are located in the United States. She would have greater access to sources of proof relevant to her strict liability and negligence theories if trial were held here. However, the District Court did not act unreasonably in concluding that fewer evidentiary problems would be posed if the trial were held in Scotland. A large proportion of the relevant evidence is located in Great Britain. . . .

The District Court correctly concluded that the problems posed by the inability to implead potential third-party defendants clearly supported holding the trial in Scotland. . . . The Court of Appeals rejected this argument. Forcing petitioners to rely on actions for indemnity or contributions would be "burdensome" but not "unfair." Finding that trial in the plaintiff's chosen forum would be burdensome, however, is sufficient to support dismissal on grounds of *forum non conveniens*.

(2)

The District Court's review of the factors relating to the public interest was also reasonable....

Scotland has a very strong interest in this litigation. The accident occurred in its airspace. All of the decedents were Scottish. Apart from Piper and Hartzell, all potential plaintiffs and defendants are either Scottish or English. As we stated in *Gilbert*, there is "a local interest in having localized controversies decided at home." Respondent argues that American citizens have an interest in ensuring that American manufacturers are deterred from producing defective products, and that additional deterrence might be obtained if Piper and Hartzell were tried in the United States, where they could be sued on the basis of both negligence and strict liability. However, the incremental deterrence that would be gained if this trial were held in an American court is likely to be insignificant. The American interest in this accident is simply not sufficient to justify the enormous commitment of judicial time and resources that would inevitably be required if the case were to be tried here.

IV

The District Court ... did not act unreasonably in deciding that the private interests pointed towards trial in Scotland. Nor did it act unreasonably in deciding that the public interests favored trial in Scotland. Thus, the judgment of the Court of Appeals is reversed.

NOTES AND QUESTIONS

1. In the federal system, intra-system transfer provisions like § 1404(a) supersede the common law notion of *forum non conveniens*. However, it is still a tool for dismissal and deference 1) by the courts of one state to another state, e.g., a New York court might dismiss a claim so that it can brought in Colorado; or 2) by a federal or state court to a foreign court, as in *Piper*. The premise for using *forum non conveniens* is that the current venue and jurisdiction of a case are proper, but the only remedy for a finding of *forum non conveniens* is dismissal. Compare that remedy with the motions to transfer under § 1404(a) and § 1406(a).

2. A common rationale for *forum non conveniens* is a concern that foreign cases will flood American courts. As one British judge has stated:

> As a moth is drawn to light, so is a litigant drawn to the United States. If he can only get his case into their courts, he stands to win a fortune. At no cost to himself, and at no risk of having to pay anything to the other side. The lawyers there will conduct the case ... on a "contingency fee" ... There is also in the United States a right to trial by jury. These are prone to award fabulous damages. They are notoriously sympathetic and know that the lawyers will

take their 40 per cent. All this means that the defendant can readily be forced into a settlement. The plaintiff holds all the cards.

Smith Kline & French Laboratories Ltd. v. Bloch, 1 W.L.R. 730 (C.A. 1982).

3. Invoking *forum non conveniens* requires that there is in fact an adequate and alternative court in which the lawsuit can be maintained. What is an "adequate" forum? As you read, *Piper* emphasized that less favorable foreign substantive law does not make the alternative forum "inadequate." An adequate remedy exists when the parties have a remedy available elsewhere, even though it may be less than an American court would grant the plaintiff.

The court will not dismiss a claim unless it lacks the authority to transfer the claim to an alternative forum, e.g., another state court or a foreign court. That alternative court may be the result of the trial court making the defendant's agreement to being subject to personal jurisdiction elsewhere a condition for the dismissal. If the alternative court refuses to take the claim, the original trial court will set aside its order dismissing because it erroneously assumed that another court was willing to adjudicate the case.

4. Not only must there be an adequate alternative forum, there must be an "available" alternative forum where the parties can be within the jurisdiction of a foreign court. *In re Union Carbide Corp. Gas Plant Disaster at Bhopal, India*, 634 F.Supp. 842 (S.D.N.Y. 1986) denied plaintiffs' argument that the legal system of India, which included filing fees of nearly 5% of the damages sought, heavy backlogs, and less favorable tort damages, was inadequate and unavailable. By contrast, the corrupt nature of a foreign court may persuade a federal court that there is no available forum. See, e.g., *Eastman Kodak Co. v. Kavlin*, 978 F.Supp. 1078 (S.D.Fla. 1997) (Bolivian courts deemed "too corrupt to permit fair adjudication of plaintiffs' claims").

5. A court may condition a dismissal on *forum non conveniens* grounds to insure that the lawsuit can be filed in another court, i.e., to be sure that the alternative forum is adequate. For example, if a claim is barred by the statute of limitations under foreign law, the American court will require the defendants to waive any limitations defense in order to make the forum adequate. See *Bank of Credit and Commerce International Ltd. v. State Bank of Pakistan*, 273 F.3d 241 (2d Cir. 2001). Of course, the more certain a court is that a foreign court will hear the case, the fewer conditions if any need to be imposed.

6. Assuming that there is an adequate, available forum, the balancing of the *Gilbert* private and public factors must strongly favor dismissal. You probably noticed that the *Gilbert* factors overlap with the "fair play" factors from personal jurisdiction, leaving you with the impression that if personal jurisdiction is reasonable a court also is unlikely to find that the convenience factors favor dismissal.

Likewise, the balancing of public and private factors for *forum non conveniens* is similar to the considerations in evaluating a change of venue motion under § 1404(a). However, the Court has predictably held that less inconvenience is necessary to obtain a transfer than is necessary to support a dismissal under *forum non conveniens*. *Norwood v. Kirkpatrick*, 349 U.S. 29, 75 S.Ct. 544, 99 L.Ed. 789 (1955).

7. The defendant has the burden of proof, because as *Gilbert* stated, "the plaintiff's choice of forum should rarely be disturbed." On the other hand, when the plaintiff is not American, courts accord less deference to the plaintiff's choice of forum. The choice of forum then is presumed to be less convenient than when an American plaintiff files the claim.

8. If a defendant forgets/neglects to file a timely Rule 12(b)(3) motion to dismiss for improper venue, can she nevertheless file a motion to dismiss based on *forum non conveniens*? One premise for seeking a dismissal under *forum non conveniens* is that venue is currently proper, validating dismissal on *forum non conveniens* in favor of an alternative court. (On the other hand, if venue is *improper*, a court can dismiss the case under a Rule 12(b)(3) motion or can transfer the case under § 1406(a).) While a belated motion is likely to be denied, the fairness and convenience related to the *forum non conveniens* motion inquiry may suggest that a delay could be justified due to the need to investigate alternative jurisdictions, foreign and domestic, in which the case could be heard. See *Jacobs v. Felix Bloch Erben Verlag fur Buhne Film*, 160 F.Supp.2d 722 (S.D.N.Y. 2001).

9. Does a court first need to establish that it has jurisdiction over a case before it can dismiss the case for *forum non conveniens*? The Supreme Court faced that precise issue in *Sinochem International Co., Ltd. v. Malaysia International Shipping Corp.*, 549 U.S. 422, 127 S.Ct. 1184, 167 L.Ed.2d 15 (2007). The Court held that it would defeat the policy reasons supporting *forum non conveniens* dismissal to require the court and parties to devote their attention to other issues like jurisdiction. After all, the purpose of *forum non conveniens* is to spare the court the trouble of dealing with an inconvenient case. Although a court could choose to deal with the other issues first, it has the discretion to decide the *forum non conveniens* question before any other issue.

PROBLEMS

In the following problems, identify which transfer mechanism (§ 1404(a), § 1406(a), *forum non conveniens*, or (if you have already studied removal) § 1441) would be proper to transfer the lawsuit. You need not analyze whether transfer would be allowed under each provision.

1. Shelton, a resident of the Central District of California, sues William, a resident of the Southern District of New York, for injuries suffered in an automobile accident. William owned the vehicle at the time of the accident in the Eastern District of North Carolina. The lawsuit was filed in a federal court in the Central District of California. The defendant wants to transfer the case, and he asks you for your advice on the feasibility of moving the case to:

a. The Eastern District of North Carolina;

b. The Southern District of New York; or

c. A New York state court.

2. Shelton, a resident of the Central District of California, sues William, a resident of the Southern District of New York, and Samuel, a resident of Wales who is in the United States on a student visa, for injuries suffered in an automobile accident. William owned the vehicle which was driven by Samuel at the time of the accident in the Eastern District of North Carolina. The lawsuit was filed in a North Carolina state court which is located in the Eastern District of North Carolina. The defendants want to transfer the case, and they ask you for your advice on the feasibility of moving the case to:

a. The Eastern District of North Carolina;

b. The Southern District of New York;

c. A New York state court; or

d. A court in Wales.

3. Shelton, a resident of the Central District of California, sues William, a resident of the Southern District of New York, for injuries suffered in an automobile accident. William currently attends graduate school in Wales. William drove and owned the vehicle at the time of the accident in the Southern District of New York. The lawsuit was filed in a New York state court which is located in the Southern District of New York. The defendants want to transfer the case, and they ask you for your advice on the feasibility of moving the case to:

a. The Southern District of New York;

b. A California state court; or

c. A court in Wales.

4. Shelton, a resident of the Central District of California, sues William and Samuel, both police officers and both residents of the Southern District of New York, for violation of his federal civil rights which resulted in injuries suffered from a beating during a routine traffic stop. William has retired from the police department and is currently enrolled in graduate school in New Hampshire. William owned the vehicle that was driven by Samuel at the time of the stop in the Northern District of New York. The lawsuit was filed in a New York state court which is located in the Northern District of New York. The defendants want to transfer the case, and they ask you for your advice on the feasibility of moving the case to:

a. The Northern District of New York;

b. The Southern District of New York; or

c. A New Hampshire state court.

c. By Forum Selection Clause

As discussed in section A.1, *supra*, parties explicitly or implicitly include "forum selection" clauses in contracts to identify the federal or state court where any lawsuit arising from the contract must be filed. The next case discusses the preferred approach for raising legal questions about forum selection clauses.

ATLANTIC MARINE CONSTR., CO., INC. v. U.S. DIST. CT. FOR THE WESTERN DISTRICT OF TEXAS
134 S.Ct. 568 (2013)

JUSTICE ALITO delivered the opinion of the Court.

The question in this case concerns the procedure that is available for a defendant in a civil case who seeks to enforce a forum-selection clause [FSC]. We reject petitioner's argument that such a clause may be enforced by a motion to dismiss under 28 U.S.C. § 1406(a) or Rule 12(b)(3). Instead, a forum-selection clause may be enforced by a motion to transfer under § 1404(a). When a defendant files such a motion, we conclude, a district court should transfer the case unless extraordinary circumstances unrelated to the convenience of the parties clearly disfavor a transfer. In the present case, both the District Court and the Court of Appeals misunderstood the standards to be applied in adjudicating a § 1404(a) motion in a case involving a FSC, and we therefore reverse the decision below.

I

[A subcontract between Atlantic Marine Construction Co., a Virginia corporation, and J-Crew Management, Inc., a Texas corporation, included a FSC, stating that all disputes between the parties would be litigated in Virginia. However, J-Crew filed a lawsuit in a Texas federal court when a dispute developed about the enforcement of the contract. Atlantic Marine moved to dismiss, claiming that the FSC made venue improper under 28 U.S.C. § 1406(a) and Federal Rule 12(b)(3). In the alternative, Atlantic Marine moved to transfer venue under 28 U.S.C. § 1404(a). The trial court denied both motions, ruling that, while § 1404(a) is the exclusive mechanism to enforce a FSC, Atlantic Marine had not met its burden of proving that transfer was appropriate. The Fifth Circuit denied Atlantic Marine's petition for a writ of mandamus asking the trial court either to dismiss the case under § 1406(a) or to transfer it a Virginia federal court under § 1404(a). It found that a 12(b)(3) dismissal is the correct mechanism for enforcing a FSC that points to a nonfederal forum. Finally, it ruled that the trial court did not abuse its discretion by refusing to transfer the case. The Supreme Court granted certiorari.]

II

Atlantic Marine contends that a party may enforce a FSC by seeking dismissal of the suit under § 1406(a) and Rule 12(b)(3). We disagree.

§ 1406(a) and Rule 12(b)(3) allow dismissal only when venue is "wrong" or "improper." Whether venue is "wrong" or "improper" depends exclusively on whether the court in which the case was brought satisfies the requirements of federal venue laws, and those provisions say nothing about a FSC.

A

... Whether venue is "wrong" or "improper"—is generally governed by 28 U.S.C. § 1391.... When venue is challenged, the court must determine whether the case falls within one of the three categories set out in § 1391(b). If it does, venue is proper; if it does not, venue is improper, and the case must be dismissed or transferred under § 1406(a). Whether the parties entered into a contract containing a FSC has no bearing on whether a case falls into one of the categories of cases listed in § 1391(b). As a result, a case filed in a district that falls within § 1391 may not be dismissed under § 1406(a) or Rule 12(b)(3).

Petitioner's contrary view improperly conflates the special statutory term "venue" and the word "forum." It is certainly true that, in some contexts, the word "venue" is used synonymously with the term "forum," but § 1391(b) makes clear that venue in "all civil actions" must be determined in accordance with the criteria outlined in that section. That language cannot reasonably be read to allow judicial consideration of other, extrastatutory limitations on the forum in which a case may be brought.

The structure of the federal venue provisions confirms that they alone define whether venue exists in a given forum. In particular, the venue statutes reflect Congress' intent that venue should always lie in *some* federal court whenever federal courts have personal jurisdiction over the defendant. The first two paragraphs of § 1391(b) define the preferred judicial districts for venue in a typical case, but the third paragraph provides a fallback option: If no other venue is proper, then venue will lie in "*any judicial district* in which any defendant is subject to the court's personal jurisdiction" (emphasis added). The statute thereby ensures that so long as a federal court has personal jurisdiction over the defendant, venue will always lie somewhere.... Yet petitioner's approach would mean that in some number of cases—those in which the FSC points to a state or foreign court—venue would not lie in any federal district. That would not comport with the statute's design, which contemplates that venue will always exist in some federal court.

The conclusion that venue is proper so long as the requirements of § 1391(b) are met, irrespective of any FSC, also follows from our prior decisions construing the federal venue statutes. In *Van Dusen v. Barrack*, 376 U.S. 612 (1964), we considered the meaning of § 1404(a), which authorizes a district court to "transfer any civil action to any other district or division where it might have been brought." ... [Section 1406(a)] instructs a court to transfer a case from the "wrong" district to a district "in which it could have been brought." The most reasonable interpretation of that provision is that a district cannot be "wrong" if it is one in which the case could have been brought under § 1391. Under the construction of the venue laws we adopted in *Van Dusen*, a "wrong" district is therefore a district other than "those districts in which Congress has provided *by its venue statutes* that the action 'may be brought.'" *Id.*, at 618. (emphasis added). If the federal venue statutes establish that suit may be brought in a particular district, a contractual bar cannot render venue in that district "wrong." . . .

B

Although a forum-selection clause does not render venue in a court "wrong" or "improper" within the meaning of § 1406(a) or Rule 12(b)(3), the FSC may be enforced through a motion to transfer under § 1404(a). . . . Unlike § 1406(a), § 1404(a) does not condition transfer on the initial forum's being "wrong." And it permits transfer to any district where venue is also proper (*i.e.*, "where [the case] might have been brought") or to any other district to which the parties have agreed by contract or stipulation.

§ 1404(a) therefore provides a mechanism for enforcement of FSC that point to a particular federal district. . . .

[T]he appropriate way to enforce a forum-selection clause pointing to a state or foreign forum is through the doctrine of *forum non conveniens*. § 1404(a) is merely a codification of the doctrine of *forum non conveniens* for the subset of cases in which the transferee forum is within the federal court system; in such cases, Congress has replaced the traditional remedy of outright dismissal with transfer. . . . And because both § 1404(a) and the *forum non conveniens* doctrine from which it derives entail the same balancing-of-interests standard, courts should evaluate a FSC pointing to a nonfederal forum in the same way that they evaluate a FSC pointing to a federal forum. . . .

III

Although the Court of Appeals correctly identified § 1404(a) as the appropriate provision to enforce the FSC in this case, the Court of Appeals erred in failing to make the adjustments required in a § 1404(a) analysis when the transfer motion is premised on a FSC. When the parties have agreed to a valid forum-selection clause, a district court should ordinarily transfer the case to the forum specified in that FSC. Only under extraordinary circumstances unrelated to the convenience of the parties should a § 1404(a) motion be denied. And no such exceptional factors appear to be present in this case.

A

In the typical case not involving a FSC, a district court considering a § 1404(a) motion (or a *forum non conveniens* motion) must evaluate both the convenience of the parties and various public-interest considerations. Ordinarily, the district court would weigh the relevant factors and decide whether, on balance, a transfer would serve "the convenience of parties and witnesses" and otherwise promote "the interest of justice." § 1404(a)

The calculus changes, however, when the parties' contract contains a valid FSC.... The presence of a valid forum-selection clause requires district courts to adjust their usual § 1404(a) analysis in three ways.

First, the plaintiff's choice of forum merits no weight. Rather, as the party defying the FSC, the plaintiff bears the burden of establishing that transfer to the forum for which the parties bargained is unwarranted. Because plaintiffs are ordinarily allowed to select whatever forum they consider most advantageous (consistent with jurisdictional and venue limitations), we have termed their selection the "plaintiff's venue privilege." *Van Dusen*, 376 at 635. But when a plaintiff agrees by contract to bring suit only in a specified forum—presumably in exchange for other binding promises by the defendant—the plaintiff has effectively exercised its "venue privilege" before a dispute arises. Only that initial choice deserves deference, and the plaintiff must bear the burden of showing why the court should not transfer the case to the forum to which the parties agreed.

Second, a court evaluating a defendant's § 1404(a) motion to transfer based on a FSC should not consider arguments about the parties' private interests. When parties agree to a forum-selection clause, they waive the right to challenge the preselected forum as inconvenient or less convenient for themselves or their witnesses, or for their pursuit of the litigation. A court accordingly must deem the private-interest factors to weigh entirely in favor of the preselected forum. As we have explained in a different but "'instructive'" context, "[w]hatever 'inconvenience' [the parties] would suffer by being forced to litigate in the contractual forum as [they] agreed to do was clearly foreseeable at the time of contracting." *The Bremen v. Zapata Off-Shore Co.*, 407 U.S. 1, 17–18 (1972).

As a consequence, a district court may consider arguments about public-interest factors only. Because those factors will rarely defeat a transfer motion, the practical result is that FSC should control except in unusual cases....

Third, when a party bound by a FSC flouts its contractual obligation and files suit in a different forum, a § 1404(a) transfer of venue will not carry with it the original venue's choice-of-law rules—a factor that in some circumstances may affect public-interest considerations. A federal court sitting in diversity ordinarily must follow the choice-of-law rules of the State in which it sits. However, we previously identified an exception to that principle for § 1404(a) transfers, requiring that the state law applicable in the original court also apply in the transferee court. See *Van Dusen*, 376 U.S. at 639. We deemed that exception necessary to prevent "defendants, properly subjected to suit in the transferor State," from "invok[ing] § 1404(a) to gain the benefits of the laws of another jurisdiction...." *Id.* At 638; see *Ferens v. John Deere Co.*, 494 U.S. 516, 522 (1990) (extending the *Van Dusen* rule to § 1404(a) motions by plaintiffs).

When parties have contracted in advance to litigate disputes in a particular forum, courts should not unnecessarily disrupt the parties' settled expectations. A FSC, after all, may have figured centrally in the parties' negotiations and may have affected how they set monetary and other contractual terms; it may, in fact, have been a critical factor in their agreement to do business together in the first place. In all but the most unusual cases, therefore, "the interest of justice" is served by holding parties to their bargain.

B

The District Court's application of § 1404(a) in this case did not comport with these principles. The District Court improperly placed the burden on Atlantic Marine to prove that transfer to the parties' contractually preselected forum was appropriate. As the party acting in violation of the FSC, J-Crew must bear the burden of showing that public-interest factors overwhelmingly disfavor a transfer.

The District Court also erred in giving weight to arguments about the parties' private interests, given that all private interests, as expressed in the FSC, weigh in favor of the transfer. But when J-Crew entered into a contract to litigate all disputes in Virginia, it knew that a distant forum might hinder its ability to call certain witnesses and might impose other burdens on its litigation efforts. It nevertheless promised to resolve its disputes in Virginia, and the District Court should not have given any weight to J-Crew's current claims of inconvenience.

The District Court also held that the public-interest factors weighed in favor of keeping the case in Texas because Texas contract law is more familiar to federal judges in Texas than to their federal colleagues in Virginia. . . .

* * *

We reverse the judgment of the Court of Appeals for the Fifth Circuit. Although no public-interest factors that might support the denial of Atlantic Marine's motion to transfer are apparent on the record before us, we remand the case for the courts below to decide that question.

CHAPTER 4

FEDERAL SUBJECT MATTER JURISDICTION

■ ■ ■

A. THE CONCEPT OF SUBJECT MATTER JURISDICTION

Like Chapter 3, this chapter deals with jurisdiction. But the form of jurisdiction involved here is different. Personal jurisdiction and venue, covered in Chapter 3, focus mainly on the parties and the underlying events. They attempt to locate the litigation in a physical location that is connected to the defendant and relatively convenient for all parties and witnesses. Subject matter jurisdiction, by contrast, deals with institutional rather than individual concerns. The rules governing subject matter jurisdiction determine which of two or more courts, located in the same geographic area, has the authority to hear the particular type of dispute in question.

This Chapter explores the allocation of authority between the state courts and the federal courts. That this question even arises is due to a somewhat unique feature of United States federalism; namely, parallel systems of state and federal courts with substantially overlapping authority. Some federal systems have no federal courts. Others, such as Canada and Australia, operate federal courts, but limit their role to hearing certain narrow categories of cases. Only in the United States do federal and state courts both have the authority to hear a broad array of tort, contract, and property cases between private parties.

Of course, allowing cases to be litigated in federal court diminishes the influence of the state courts. Therefore, it will be no great surprise to learn that the United States Constitution itself sets limits on the subject matter jurisdiction of the federal courts. The main constitutional provision is Article III.[1] This provision establishes the basic paradigm: federal courts are courts of *limited jurisdiction,* with the authority to hear only those categories of cases specifically allocated to them. State courts, by contrast, may hear all cases, unless the U.S. Constitution, Congress, or their state legislature has taken a particular category of case from them.

---

[1] The eleventh amendment, enacted in 1793, also places an important limit on federal court jurisdiction. However, that amendment is beyond the scope of this course. It is usually covered in a course called Federal Courts or Federal Jurisdiction.

Article III confines federal subject matter jurisdiction to nine categories of cases. For our purposes, the most important three are:

- "all Cases, in Law and Equity, arising under this Constitution, the Laws of the United States, and Treaties made, or which shall be made, under their Authority;"
- "Controversies . . . between Citizens of different States;" and
- "Controversies . . . between a State, or the Citizens thereof, and foreign States, Citizens, or Subjects."

Taken together, the nine constitutional categories of Article III cover a wide range of cases. However, two types of cases are notably missing. Unless the case involves claims under federal law, the Constitution, or a treaty, a federal court cannot hear a case where all the parties are either citizens of the same state, or are not citizens of the United States. These cases must be heard in the state courts.

Although it is not apparent from the constitutional text, Article III does not itself grant the lower federal courts jurisdiction over any cases. Instead, Congress allocates that jurisdiction by statute. In fact, Congress has never given the federal courts the full authority authorized by Article III. Because of the need for a statutory enablement, any analysis of subject matter jurisdiction will involve two steps. First, there must be a statute giving the court the authority to hear the dispute in question. Second, even if a statute allows for jurisdiction, the case must fall within one of the nine categories of Article III. As Congress has generally crafted the jurisdiction statutes to fit the limits of Article III, the second question rarely affects whether the court has jurisdiction. Nevertheless, you will encounter one provision—28 U.S.C. § 1441(c), discussed in Part E of this chapter—that arguably exceeds constitutional limits.

This Chapter deals exclusively with the subject matter jurisdiction of the United States District Courts, the trial courts in the federal system. There are many statutes allocating subject matter jurisdiction to these courts. *See, e.g.*, 28 U.S.C. §§ 1330 (actions against foreign nations), 1343 (civil rights cases), and 1344 (election disputes). However, this chapter will concentrate on the four most important provisions. Early in the Chapter (in Parts B and C), you will deal with §§ 1331 and 1332 of the Judicial Code (the "Judicial Code" is title 28 of the United States Code). § 1331 is the general statute implementing the first of the three categories of Article III jurisdiction quoted above, namely, jurisdiction over cases arising under federal law, the Constitution, or a treaty. This type of jurisdiction is commonly called "federal question" jurisdiction. § 1332 implements the second category, and much of the third category, quoted above. Because these categories both turn on the citizenship of the parties, § 1332 is commonly referred to as "diversity of citizenship" or simply "diversity" jurisdiction. However, sometimes a court will refer to

Sec. A The Concept of Subject Matter Jurisdiction

this jurisdiction as "alienage" jurisdiction in a case between a United States citizen and a citizen of another nation.

Part D of the chapter discusses § 1367, which creates a form of jurisdiction called "supplemental." As the name suggests, supplemental jurisdiction adds to other forms of jurisdiction. A party will usually invoke supplemental jurisdiction when some claims in the case qualify for federal question or diversity jurisdiction, and other claims do not. If the claims all arise from the same set of facts, § 1367 may allow the federal court to hear all of them as part of a single case.

One important point to remember about jurisdiction under all of these provisions is that it is usually *concurrent*, not exclusive. This means the federal courts share jurisdiction with the state courts. Because the federal and state courts have concurrent jurisdiction over diversity and alienage cases, those cases may be litigated in either state or federal court. Similarly, state courts usually even have the authority to hear cases arising under federal law. However, there are some claims, which either arise under federal law or involve some strong federal interest, for which the federal courts have exclusive jurisdiction. *See, e.g.,* 28 U.S.C. § 1334 (cases arising under federal bankruptcy laws); § 1338 (patent and copyright infringement claims); and § 1351 (claims (including state-law claims) against foreign diplomats). On the other hand, if the only basis for federal jurisdiction over the claim is § 1331 or § 1332, the federal and state courts will almost always have concurrent jurisdiction.

If jurisdiction is concurrent, plaintiff may choose the court in which to bring her case. But the case may end up in a different system. True, plaintiff alone makes the initial choice of state or federal court. However, another federal statute, 28 U.S.C. § 1441 (discussed in Part E of this Chapter), may give the defendant the option to *remove* a case filed in state court to federal court.

The Judicial Code also contains provisions governing the jurisdiction of the federal Courts of Appeal and the United States Supreme Court. The statutes governing the Courts of Appeal and the Supreme Court are not discussed until Chapter 14, as they usually apply only when the case is being appealed. Nevertheless, it may be useful—both for Procedure and for your other courses—to touch at this juncture upon two important points concerning the United States Supreme Court. Many hold certain misconceptions concerning what we commonly call the "nation's high court." First, the Supreme Court is not really a supreme court. It is instead a supreme *federal* court. Like the lower federal courts, the Supreme Court is bound by the limitations of Article III. Although there are differences between the Supreme Court and the lower federal courts—for example, the Supreme Court's original jurisdiction vests automatically, without the need for a grant from Congress—never forget that the Supreme Court's authority is limited to the nine categories of cases set out in Article III. Second, although the Supreme Court, unlike the lower courts, has the power to hear appeals of cases heard in the state courts, Congress has not given the Supreme Court the authority to hear state-court cases that do not involve some question of federal law, the United States Constitution, or a treaty. As a result, the state courts are the highest authority for interpreting state law.

Finally, the fact that this chapter deals only with the allocation of subject matter jurisdiction between the state and federal courts should not lead you to think the state systems are a monolithic whole. Questions of subject matter jurisdiction also arise frequently in actions heard in the state courts. For example, many states have specialized family courts or probate courts that hear matters such as divorces, child custody, and wills. Many also have small claims courts that provide an abbreviated, simplified procedure for claims involving less than a certain amount. However, because the jurisdiction of state courts is not bound by Article III or any other provision of the Constitution, there will always be one court in a state—often called a district or circuit court—that may hear any claim not assigned to some other court. This court is often referred to as a "court of general jurisdiction."

B. FEDERAL QUESTION JURISDICTION

INTRODUCTORY PROBLEM

Penny owns a large tract of forest land in upstate Vermont. She makes a very good living selling maple syrup, which she extracts from trees located on her property. However, two recent events have threatened Penny's comfortable and profitable living. Unable to remedy the problem by negotiation, Penny has filed two cases in federal district court.

The first case is Penny v. Daniel. Penny sells her maple syrup using the trademark MAPLE LEAF. When Penny discovered that Daniel had begun selling his own maple syrup under the exact same trademark, she sued him for trademark infringement under the federal trademark laws. Daniel admits he used the MAPLE LEAF mark on maple syrup. He also concedes that federal trademark laws clearly impose liability on a party who uses an identical mark on a similar product. Nevertheless, Daniel claims Penny granted him an oral license to use the MAPLE LEAF mark. Penny admits granting an oral license to Daniel, but argues that license is invalid under state contract law because it is not in writing. The sole contested issue in the case is whether the oral license is valid.

Penny's second case is against the giant company Dynamic Dynamos, Inc. ("DDI"). DDI manufactures guidance systems for missiles and other weapons used by the military. Penny sued DDI for trespass when she discovered DDI was constructing a new factory on a remote section of her property. DDI admits it is building the plant on the land described by Penny. However, DDI raises two separate arguments in denying liability. First, although conceding that the land used to belong to Penny, DDI asserts it now owns Penny's land. DDI claims the federal government seized Penny's land for nonpayment of federal income taxes, and later sold the land at a tax sale to DDI. In response to this first argument, Penny alleges the tax sale was invalid under the United States Constitution and federal law because the IRS never gave her notice that she had not paid her taxes.

But DDI is prepared for this response. Second, and in the alternative, DDI claims that even if the tax sale was invalid and Penny owns the land, it is protected by the federal contractor's defense. Under this defense, which is set out in federal statutes and case law, a court cannot impose liability on a federal military contractor that acted in good faith. DDI argues it thought the tax sale was valid.

Penny relies on 28 U.S.C. § 1331 as the sole basis for federal jurisdiction in both cases. Daniel and DDI each file a timely objection to the federal court's jurisdiction in their respective cases. How will the federal courts rule?

Governing Laws: U.S. Const. Article III, § 2, cl. 1; 28 U.S.C. §§ 1331 and 1338.

In some ways, it is redundant for a federal nation to operate separate federal and state court systems. State courts are perfectly competent to deal with cases arising under both state and federal law. Other federal nations such as Canada and Australia operate only a very limited federal court system, and rely on the state courts to handle the vast majority of cases that arise.

The United States, however, has since its inception maintained a comprehensive system of lower federal courts. Every state has at least one federal district court, which often sits in a courthouse just down the street from the state courts. The decision to have federal courts largely reflects a perception that federal courts offer certain advantages that might not be available in the state systems. Those advantages are most readily apparent in situations requiring the interpretation of federal law. First, if most cases arising under federal law go to federal court, federal judges may develop greater expertise in the nuances of federal law. Second, in some cases one might suspect that state judges, who are beholden to their constituencies, might prove hostile to enforcing federal laws. A state judge facing a re-election or retention vote might well be reluctant to enforce a federal civil rights claim or a claim in which an Indian tribe seeks superior rights to scarce water resources. Giving these cases to the federal courts, while not removing politics entirely from the decision, at least provides the appearance of a more neutral forum.

This section focuses almost exclusively on § 1331, the "general" federal question statute. This section gives the federal courts jurisdiction over all matters arising under federal law. However, a quick glance at the statutes following § 1331 will reveal a number of other statutes that allocate jurisdiction over matters arising under specific federal laws. See 28 U.S.C. §§ 1333 (admiralty), 1334 (bankruptcy), 1337 (commerce and antitrust), 1338 (patents, copyrights, trademarks, and other federal intellectual property laws), 1339 (postal matters), 1343 (civil rights), and 1355 (fines and penalties under federal laws). If § 1331 affords jurisdiction over all federal matters, why are these specific provisions necessary? First, as noted above, a few of these statutes make federal jurisdiction exclusive. Jurisdiction under § 1331, however, is shared with the state courts.

Second, until fairly recently § 1331 required a minimum amount in controversy. Many of the specific statutes had a lower threshold, or sometimes no minimum amount at all. For example, Congress created a special jurisdiction provision for federal civil rights claims to allow parties with small claims to avail themselves of federal court. Now that there is no minimum amount in controversy under § 1331, these statutes are redundant.

The following sections explore how courts have interpreted § 1331. Although these same principles often apply to the other federal question statutes, you should not immediately assume the other statutes are interpreted the same way.

1. HOW DOES A PARTY INVOKE FEDERAL QUESTION JURISDICTION?

Suppose you have a case like the Introductory Problem, in which the ultimate outcome depends on how the court interprets the Constitution and federal law. Can such a case automatically go to federal court under § 1331? As the Supreme Court has stated, "How and when a case arises 'under the Constitution or laws of the United States' has been much considered in the books." *Gully v. First National Bank in Meridian*, 299 U.S. 109, 112, 57 S.Ct. 96, 81 L.Ed. 70 (1936). As we will see, the answer depends on exactly who is bringing the underlying claim, as well as the way in which federal law applies to that claim.

LOUISVILLE & NASHVILLE RAILROAD V. MOTTLEY
211 U.S. 149, 29 S.Ct. 42, 53 L.Ed. 126 (1908)

MR. JUSTICE MOODY:

The appellees (husband and wife), being residents and citizens of Kentucky, brought this suit in equity in the circuit court of the United States for the western district of Kentucky against the appellant, a railroad company and a citizen of the same state. . . .

The bill alleged that in September, 1871, plaintiffs, while passengers upon the defendant railroad, were injured by the defendant's negligence, and released their respective claims for damages in consideration of the agreement for transportation during their lives, expressed in ... [a] contract. It is alleged that the contract was performed by the defendant up to January 1, 1907, when the defendant declined to renew the passes. The bill then alleges that the refusal to comply with the contract was based solely upon that part of the act of Congress of June 29, 1906, which forbids the giving of free passes or free transportation. The bill further alleges: First, that the act of Congress referred to does not prohibit the giving of passes under the circumstances of this case; and, second, that, if the law is to be construed as prohibiting such passes, it is in conflict with the 5th Amendment of the Constitution, because it deprives the plaintiffs of their property without due process of law. The defendant demurred to the bill. The judge of the circuit court overruled the demurrer, entered a decree for the relief prayed for, and the defendant appealed directly to this court.

Two questions of law were raised by the demurrer to the bill, were brought here by appeal, and have been argued before us. They are, first, whether that part of the act of Congress of June 29, 1906, which forbids the giving of free passes or the collection of any different compensation for transportation of passengers than that specified in the tariff filed, makes it unlawful to perform a contract for transportation of persons who, in good faith, before the passage of the act, had accepted such contract in satisfaction of a valid cause of action against the railroad; and, second, whether the statute, if it should be construed to render such a contract unlawful, is in violation of the 5th Amendment of the Constitution of the United States. We do not deem it necessary, however, to consider either of these questions, because, in our opinion, the court below was without jurisdiction of the cause. Neither party has questioned that jurisdiction, but it is the duty of this court to see to it that the jurisdiction of the circuit court, which is defined and limited by statute, is not exceeded. This duty we have frequently performed of our own motion.

There was no diversity of citizenship, and it is not and cannot be suggested that there was any ground of jurisdiction, except that the case was a "suit ... arising under the Constitution or laws of the United States." It is the settled interpretation of these words, as used in this statute, conferring jurisdiction, that a suit arises under the Constitution and laws of the United States only when the plaintiff's statement of his own cause of action shows that it is based upon those laws or that Constitution. It is not enough that the plaintiff alleges some anticipated defense to his cause of action, and asserts that the defense is invalidated by some provision of the Constitution of the United States. Although such allegations show that very likely, in the course of the litigation, a question under the Constitution would arise, they do not show that the suit, that is, the plaintiff's original cause of action, arises under the Constitution. In *Tennessee v. Union & Planters' Bank*, 152 U.S. 454, the plaintiff, the state of Tennessee, brought suit in the circuit court of the United States to recover from the defendant certain taxes alleged to be due under the laws of the state. The plaintiff alleged that the defendant claimed an immunity from the taxation by virtue of its charter, and that therefore the tax was void, because in violation of the provision of the Constitution of the United States, which forbids any state from passing a law impairing the obligation of contracts. The cause was held to be beyond the jurisdiction of the circuit court, the court saying, by Mr. Justice Gray: "A suggestion of one party, that the other will or may set up a claim under the Constitution or laws of the United States, does not make the suit one arising under that Constitution or those laws." . . .

The application of this rule to the case at bar is decisive against the jurisdiction of the circuit court.

It is ordered that the judgment be reversed and the case remitted to the circuit court with instructions to dismiss the suit for want of jurisdiction.

NOTES AND QUESTIONS

1. *Mottley* establishes a "well-pleaded complaint" test to determine whether a case qualifies for federal question jurisdiction under § 1331. First, plaintiff's right to recover must come from federal law, the United States Constitution, or a treaty. Second, that issue of federal law must appear in plaintiff's well-pleaded complaint. Which part of this test did the Mottleys fail?

2. The "well-pleaded complaint" rule does not evaluate whether the complaint complies with the procedural rules that govern pleadings. Under current pleading rules, the complaint filed by the Mottleys would be perfectly proper, even though it anticipated defendant's statutory and Constitutional defenses. See Federal Rule 8(a), which is discussed in Chapter 6, pt. B. A complaint is proper under this rule even if it includes superfluous or irrelevant material. However, under the well-pleaded complaint rule, any material that is superfluous or irrelevant to plaintiff's claim(s) will not be considered when determining whether the court has federal question jurisdiction. A well-pleaded complaint, then, is one in which plaintiff says everything it needs to say to plead the claims it is bringing, and nothing more.

3. Note that whether plaintiff ultimately prevails on its claim is also irrelevant to the question of jurisdiction. Federal question jurisdiction is the power to decide a claim arising under federal law. The court does not lose jurisdiction merely because it finds no violation of federal law has occurred.

On the other hand, plaintiff must file a good-faith claim to invoke federal question jurisdiction. If plaintiff's claim is frivolous, the court may refuse to exercise jurisdiction or impose sanctions. See Chapter 6, pt. D.

4. The "well-pleaded complaint" rule means just that: the analysis turns entirely on what plaintiff alleges in her complaint. As discussed in Chapter 2, other parties may also file claims in the case, such as counterclaims and cross-claims. None of these claims are considered in determining whether a case qualifies for federal question jurisdiction under § 1331.

5. The Supreme Court in *Mottley* ordered that the case be dismissed for lack of subject matter jurisdiction. Such dismissals do not prevent the plaintiff from filing the case again in a proper court. Therefore, the Mottleys could—and in fact *did*—file the same action against the railroad in a state court. What issues would the state court decide? The railroad had filed a "demurrer." What is that? Does the railroad deny giving the Mottleys a lifetime pass? Does it deny that it refused to honor that pass? Aren't the only substantive issues in dispute questions of federal and Constitutional law? Does it make sense to say this case does not involve a federal question?

6. The Mottleys' battle with the railroad continued in the state courts. The Kentucky trial court found for the Mottleys, and the state's high court affirmed. The railroad then appealed the case to the United States Supreme Court, which reversed and found for the railroad. *Louisville & Nashville R. Co. v. Mottley*, 219 U.S. 467, 31 S.Ct. 265, 55 L.Ed. 297 (1911). But how could the United States Supreme Court have jurisdiction to decide the merits of the case? Like the lower federal courts, the Supreme Court is a federal court, with jurisdiction limited by Article III of the Constitution. If the case set out above did not involve a federal question, and the second case was framed the same way, how could that second case qualify as a federal question?

The answer requires one to distinguish between Article III and the statutes assigning jurisdiction to the federal courts. Although *Mottley* is not clear on this point, the case is generally interpreted as an interpretation of § 1331, not Article III. The Supreme Court's jurisdiction to review state court decisions comes from § 1257, not § 1331. Moreover, although Article III uses the same language as § 1331—cases "arising under" the Constitution or federal law—the Constitutional language is interpreted far more broadly. A case satisfies Article III as long as its resolution turns on a question of federal law, regardless of whether that federal issue is a necessary part of the complaint. *Mesa v. California*, 489 U.S. 121, 109 S.Ct. 959, 103 L.Ed.2d 99 (1989) (a federal question raised by defendant in its answer is enough to invoke federal question jurisdiction under a different jurisdictional statute). Therefore, because the dispute between the Mottleys and the railroad did turn on questions of federal law, the case qualified as a federal question under Article III, and was within the Supreme Court's power to decide.

Does it make sense that Congress would parrot the language of Article III when drafting § 1331, but intend for that language to mean something considerably narrower in the statute?

7. *Declaratory judgment cases*. Consider a variation on the facts of *Mottley*. Suppose that after the enactment of the federal law mentioned in the

opinion, the Louisville & Nashville Railroad considered adopting a policy telling its conductors to quit accepting lifetime passes. However, the railroad fears that if it adopts this policy, it will be sued by the Mottleys. Historically, there was no legal action the railroad could take to determine whether its proposed policy would withstand a challenge. Its only option was adopt the policy and hope for the best once it was sued.

Today, however, the railroad might be able to sue for a *declaratory judgment*. Under 28 U.S.C. § 2201 and analogous state statutes, a person may ask a court to declare the respective rights of the parties to a potential future dispute. Conceptually, a declaratory judgment is like an ordinary case, except that the court does not grant a money judgment, injunction, or other traditional remedy. The only remedy is the declaration of rights. However, should the parties later get into a dispute involving the same basic legal rights, the result in the earlier declaratory judgment case is binding.

There are a number of limits and special rules dealing with use of the declaratory judgment device. For now, we need only consider how courts analyze a declaratory judgment under the well-pleaded complaint rule. Suppose the railroad brings a declaratory judgment suit against the Mottleys, arguing that the federal statute bars it from honoring lifetime passes, and that the statute is constitutional. Railroad's complaint in this declaratory judgment case must invoke federal law. Do you see why? Does the federal issue appearing in the complaint make the case a federal question? The analysis is not quite that straightforward:

> District courts have original federal question jurisdiction over complaints that contain a claim that arises under federal law. In actions for declaratory judgment, however, the position of the parties is often reversed: the plaintiff asserts a defense to an anticipated action by the declaratory judgment defendant. It is the character of the impending action, not the plaintiff's defense, that determines whether there is federal question jurisdiction. Thus, federal question jurisdiction exists in a declaratory judgment action if the potential suit by the declaratory judgment defendant would arise under federal law.

Cardtoons, L.C. v. Major League Baseball Players Ass'n, 95 F.3d 959 (10th Cir. 1996). Therefore, a court looks beyond the declaratory judgment to the civil action that would otherwise occur to determine if the case involves a federal question. Under this analysis, would Railroad's declaratory judgment case qualify for federal question jurisdiction?

8. What was the underlying reason for the Mottleys' lawsuit? Remember, the Louisville and Nashville Railroad had promised to provide annual passes to the Mottleys in an agreement to settle their claims against the railroad for personal injuries they sustained in an accident. Today, state procedures for enforcing settlement agreements vary, but private settlement agreements are generally enforced in the same way as any contract, by a contract claim brought under state contract law. As in *Mottley*, this claim can

be brought in federal court only if there is a basis for subject matter jurisdiction.

When parties settle a dispute that was filed in court, in some circumstances parties can make enforcement easier and avoid the need for a separate contract suit. For example, they may be able to seek court approval for the agreement and enter it as a consent decree or have the court retain jurisdiction over the case. But these procedures require putting the agreement on the public record and many parties prefer to keep the terms of their settlement private.

2. WHAT TYPES OF CLAIMS PRESENT A "FEDERAL QUESTION?"

The prior case demonstrated that jurisdiction under § 1331 exists only if there is a federal question on the face of the plaintiff's complaint. But what is a federal question? Although usually fairly straightforward, that issue can at times prove to be extraordinarily difficult. The simplest, and most common, example of a federal question case is when a plaintiff sues a defendant for relief afforded by a statute enacted by Congress, e.g., a claim alleging employment discrimination. However, that classic case does not begin to exhaust the scope of what § 1331 means by a federal question. Some cases arising under federal statutes do not qualify as federal questions under § 1331, while other cases involving claims arising under other bodies of law sometimes will qualify. The following discussion summarizes various sources of § 1331 federal questions.

a. United States Constitution

By its very terms, § 1331 also allows federal courts to hear claims asserting rights provided by the United States Constitution. Unlike the Canadian Constitution and those of some other nations, the United States Constitution does not explicitly give people a right to sue in court to enforce its provisions. Nevertheless, courts have for many years assumed that a person may sue for an injunction to prevent a government official from violating the Constitution. See, e.g., *Larson v. Domestic & Foreign Commerce Corp.*, 337 U.S. 682, 69 S.Ct. 1457, 93 L.Ed. 1628 (1949) (federal officials); *Ex parte Young*, 209 U.S. 123, 28 S.Ct. 441, 52 L.Ed. 714 (1908) (state officials). More recently, the Court has held that a party may in certain circumstances also sue for money damages for a violation of Constitutional rights. *Bivens v. Six Unknown Named Agents of Federal Bureau of Narcotics*, 403 U.S. 388, 91 S.Ct. 1999, 29 L.Ed.2d 619 (1971) (victim of search that violated the Fourth Amendment may sue the searching officers under the Constitution).

Note that it is technically inaccurate to refer to constitutional claims as "federal" questions. The United States Constitution is not federal law. Instead, it is a body of national law, created by the states and the people, and amended only with the consent of a supermajority of the states. As a matter of convenience, however, courts and commentators call all claims falling within § 1331 "federal" questions.

b. Treaties

§ 1331 also allows for federal jurisdiction over claims arising under treaties. The main issue to consider when dealing with a treaty is whether the treaty itself creates a legally enforceable claim. Most treaties ratified by the United States are not "self-implementing," which means that the treaty does not have the force of law in the courts. Instead, the treaty must be implemented by a statute. Therefore, the vast majority of claims involving treaties will actually arise under the implementing statute rather than the treaty itself.

c. International Law

International law is the set of rules that govern relations between sovereign nations, as well as human rights rules that limit how sovereigns may treat individuals and groups. It comprises a collection of treaties, conventions, and customary international law. Even though international law does not owe its origin to Congress, international law is treated as federal law for purposes of federal question jurisdiction. Thus, a claim arising under international law qualifies as a federal question under § 1331. An interesting example of this principle is *Kadic v. Karadzic*, 70 F.3d 232 (2d Cir. 1995), which involves claims by Bosnian victims against a Serb leader during the 1990s conflict in the former Yugoslavia. The court held the international human rights claims qualified for federal question jurisdiction under a statute analogous to § 1331.

d. Federal Common Law

As you will discover in Chapter 5, the *Erie* doctrine greatly limits a federal court's ability to fashion independent rules of substantive law. Nevertheless, even after *Erie* there are certain areas in which federal judge-made rules will decide a case. When a party's claim arises under this substantive federal common law, the case presents a federal question. *Illinois v. City of Milwaukee*, 406 U.S. 91, 92 S.Ct. 1385, 31 L.Ed.2d 712 (1972).

e. Special Federal Statutes

The above examples demonstrate that a claim need not arise under a federal statute in order to present a federal question under § 1331. Conversely, there are some situations where a case does not present a federal question even though it clearly arises under a federal statute. The first situation is a case brought to enforce the requirements of the Federal

Arbitration Act, 9 U.S.C. §§ 1–16. The Federal Arbitration Act provides that a provision in a contract that requires disputes to be submitted to arbitration is enforceable in certain circumstances, notwithstanding what state law may provide. The Act also gives a party the right to sue to compel arbitration (§ 4) and to vacate an improper arbitration award (§ 10). Although federal law clearly creates the rights to compel and vacate, the courts have uniformly held that suits to enforce these rights do not create a federal question for purposes of § 1331. *Moses H. Cone Mem. Hosp. v. Mercury Constr. Corp.*, 460 U.S. 1, 25 n. 32, 103 S.Ct. 927, 74 L.Ed.2d 765 (1983); *Kasap v. Folger Nolan Fleming & Douglas, Inc.*, 166 F.3d 1243 (D.C. Cir. 1999). On the other hand, if the underlying dispute being arbitrated itself arises under federal law, a suit brought to enforce the duty to arbitrate may be treated as a federal question. *Vaden v. Discover Bank*, 129 S.Ct. 1262, 173 L.Ed.2d 206 (2009).

Second, although Congress acts as legislature for the District of Columbia, claims arising under federal statutes for the District are not considered federal questions. 28 U.S.C. § 1366; see *Roth v. District of Columbia Courts*, 160 F.Supp.2d 104 (D. D.C. 2001).

f. State Law

As odd as it may seem at first glance, there are even situations where a case that ostensibly turns exclusively on state law may involve a federal question. For example, Congress will often "borrow" state law as governing law for lands and other areas under exclusive federal control, such as military bases. A similar borrowing may occur in suits litigating the rights of the United States. The borrowed rules become the federal law for that area, and can support federal question jurisdiction. See, e.g., *Ten Taxpayer Citizens Group v. Cape Wind Associates, LLC*, 373 F.3d 183 (1st Cir. 2004) (because Congress borrowed state law for the Outer Continental Shelf, suit alleging that construction project was improper because it did not comply with Massachusetts statute was a federal question).

In other situations, a state-law claim will be treated as a federal question because of the interaction between that state law and a federal law. As this second situation most often arises when cases are removed from state to federal court, it is addressed in Part E of this chapter, which deals with removal.

PROBLEMS

1. When P learns that his employee D has been revealing certain sensitive company information, P sues D under state trade secret laws. P brings his action in federal court, seeking $50,000 in damages. D immediately files a $100,000 counterclaim. D's counterclaim arises under the federal "whistleblower" statute, which provides a cause of action for employees who

reveal information showing that their employers are committing a crime. Does the court have subject-matter jurisdiction?

2. P, a pharmaceutical company, produces a drug called Absinthozene. P recently entered into a contract to sell 10,000 lots of Absinthozene to D, a pharmacy distribution company. However, after the contract was entered, the federal government banned the production and sale of Absinthozene based on evidence it could cause brain damage. P obviously does not want to go to the expense of producing the drug if there is no real market. Nevertheless, because D can sell the drug in other nations where it is still legal, P worries D will sue it for breach of contract if it does not honor the terms of the contract. P therefore wants to bring a declaratory judgment action in which it will ask the court for a declaration that the contract is void because of illegality. May P bring this action in federal court, based on federal question jurisdiction?

3. P, a private person, sues the D Tribe of American Indians in federal court for breach of contract. Under federal law, Indian tribes enjoy immunity to most civil actions. In his complaint, however, P argues the immunity should not apply to "commercial activities" such as those that gave rise to the contract between P and D. D moves to dismiss for lack of subject-matter jurisdiction. Will the court grant D's motion?

C. DIVERSITY JURISDICTION

INTRODUCTORY PROBLEM

While preparing her garden for planting, Gardner was seriously injured when her power rototiller malfunctioned. Gardner decides to sue both Cultivate, Inc. (the manufacturer of the rototiller) and Vendor (the individual who sold the rototiller to her) to recover for her injuries. For several reasons she would prefer to bring this action in federal court.

The injury occurred at Gardner's home in Iowa. However, like many others in the Midwest, Gardner prefers to spend her winters in Florida. In fact, Gardner spends seven months of every year at a vacation condominium in Florida. Although Gardner owns the condominium, she considers her house in Iowa as her "true home."

Gardner bought the rototiller from Vendor's lawn supply store in Iowa. At the time of the sale and the injury, Vendor was domiciled in Iowa. Since the accident, however, Vendor has retired to Mexico. Vendor sold both his business and his home in Iowa and bought a new house on a Mexico beach. In addition, he gave up his United States citizenship and acquired Mexican citizenship.

Cultivate, Inc. is a corporation that was incorporated under the laws of the State of Iowa. The company also maintains a small corporate headquarters in that state. Most major decisions emanate from the Iowa office. However, the only factory, as well as the vast majority of the day-today operations of the company, are in New Mexico. All employees live and work in New Mexico.

Gardner suffered injuries of $74,000 in the rototilling accident. She would like to sue both defendants for this injury. In addition, however, Gardner wants to add a second claim to the action. When Gardner bought the rototiller, she was entitled to a $1000 rebate. Under governing law, both Vendor and Cultivate, Inc. are responsible for paying the rebate. Because applicable joinder rules would allow her to join these two claims into a single action, Gardner plans to bring both claims against the two defendants.

May Gardner bring her action in federal court?

Governing Law: 28 U.S.C. § 1332.

1. THE POLICY UNDERLYING DIVERSITY JURISDICTION

Diversity jurisdiction is the second main branch of federal subject matter jurisdiction. Diversity and federal question are alternatives: a party may sue in federal court if the requirements of *either* the federal question statute (§ 1331) *or* the diversity statute (§ 1332) are satisfied. In some cases, both § 1331 and § 1332 may provide jurisdiction. Like federal question jurisdiction, diversity jurisdiction is explicitly authorized by Article III of the Constitution. The "general" diversity statute—the only one with which we will be concerned at this juncture—is § 1332. Unlike federal question jurisdiction, diversity jurisdiction is not concerned with the legal source of the plaintiff's claim. Instead, it looks to the citizenship of the parties. If the parties are citizens of different states, the dispute can possibly be heard in federal court.

As you might expect, the justifications for diversity jurisdiction are quite different than the justifications for federal question jurisdiction. Because federal courts sitting in diversity can hear virtually any claim (with some exceptions to be discussed later), there is no reason to think the federal courts will have any greater expertise with the case. Nor is there any particular national interest in private disputes between citizens of different states. Instead, diversity jurisdiction exists because of a historical fear of state-court bias. State judges are government officials. In many states they are elected by the people of that state, while in the others they are appointed by the state. Therefore, there is some reason to suspect state judges might favor in-state litigants when those litigants are involved in a dispute with someone from out of state. Federal judges, by contrast, are shielded by certain systemic safeguards designed to ensure their neutrality. Federal judges are national appointments; nominated by the President and confirmed by the Senate. Of equal or perhaps even greater importance, federal judges are appointed for life, subject only to impeachment.

Whether federal diversity jurisdiction actually helps prevent state-court bias is subject to some debate. Is a state court in rural southern Illinois more likely to be biased against someone who lives a few miles away in rural Indiana or a fellow Illinoisan who lives 300 miles away in Chicago? State judges today certainly have political leanings, but it is not clear that many have a strong home-state bias. And even if there is home-state loyalty, federal district court judges, like their state-court counterparts, are almost always selected from the bar of the state where they will serve. Moreover, as § 1332 is crafted, diversity jurisdiction exists regardless of whether any of the litigants are citizens of the state where the case is heard. Therefore, a federal court in Alaska has subject-matter jurisdiction over a dispute between a citizen of Florida and a citizen of Georgia. For all of these reasons, there is reason to doubt whether diversity jurisdiction serves its intended purpose.

Nevertheless, diversity jurisdiction is firmly established in the federal courts. In fact, diversity jurisdiction is actually considerably older than general federal question jurisdiction. Congress established diversity jurisdiction in section 11 of the Judiciary Act of 1789, Congress's very first comprehensive federal statute dealing with the federal courts. General federal question jurisdiction, by contrast, dates back only to 1875. Although the federal courts had jurisdiction over narrow categories of federal questions prior to 1875, for the first 85 years of the nation a significant number of federal question claims could be heard only in state courts.

Another difference between diversity and federal question jurisdiction is that diversity has an amount in controversy requirement. Therefore, even if the parties are diverse, the federal courts may hear the case only if the amount at stake exceeds $75,000. Calculating the amount in controversy can be tricky, especially in cases involving interest, multiple claims, or injunctive relief.

Over the past half-century, there have been repeated efforts to abolish diversity jurisdiction. The push for abolition comes from several different sources. First, as noted above, there is some doubt whether state-court bias is a real problem. Second, diversity cases occupy a significant percentage of the federal courts' workload; time that could perhaps be better devoted to cases requiring interpretation of federal law. Compounding this problem is the fact that diversity cases present a number of unique and idiosyncratic issues. As you progress through Civil Procedure, take a moment to make note of the number of special rules that apply to diversity cases. We will see two examples in this chapter— the special rules that apply in supplemental jurisdiction (§ 1367(b)) and removal (§ 1441(b)). Another example is the *Erie* doctrine, discussed in Chapter 5, which arises mainly in diversity cases. Therefore, removing diversity jurisdiction would not only lighten the load on the federal courts, but also significantly simplify certain aspects of federal litigation.

2. DETERMINING DIVERSITY

Because of the wording of § 1332, ascertaining whether diversity jurisdiction exists involves two basic issues. First, you must ensure the litigants are of "diverse citizenship." Second, you must determine whether the amount in controversy exceeds $75,000. This subsection deals with the first step, while subsection 3 deals with the second.

a. Individuals

LUNDQUIST V. PRECISION VALLEY AVIATION, INC.
946 F.2d 8 (1st Cir. 1991)

PER CURIAM.

Plaintiff-appellant Courtney Lundquist filed an action on March 20, 1987 in the District of Massachusetts against defendants-appellees Precision Valley Aviation, Inc., Winnipesaukee Airlines, Inc., Walter Fawcett, and Susan Fawcett, to recover on promissory notes relating to a sale of stock in Winnipesaukee Airlines, Inc., by Lundquist to defendants. Lundquist's complaint alleged federal jurisdiction on the basis of diversity of citizenship under 28 U.S.C. § 1332. The complaint did not allege citizenship but did state that Lundquist resided in Arlington, Massachusetts.

On November 5, 1990, defendants filed a motion to dismiss for lack of subject matter jurisdiction on the ground that complete diversity of citizenship did not exist. The motion, which included affidavits and other evidentiary documents, alleged that Lundquist, like the defendants, was a citizen of New Hampshire. Lundquist filed an objection to the motion to dismiss, including affidavits, in which he alleged that he was a citizen of Florida. Lundquist asked that the district court permit him to amend his complaint to assert Florida citizenship. . . .

Under 28 U.S.C. § 1332(a)(1), there is diversity of citizenship if the plaintiff is a "citizen" of a different state than all of the defendants. *Sweeney v. Westvaco Co.*, 926 F.2d 29, 32–33, 41 (1st Cir. 1991). "Citizenship" in a state is the equivalent of "domicile." *Valedon Martinez v. Hospital Presbiteriano de la Comunidad, Inc.*, 806 F.2d 1128, 1132 (1st Cir. 1986). Where a party changes domicile, "domicile at the time suit is filed [here, March 20, 1987] is the test and jurisdiction once established is not lost by a subsequent change in citizenship." *Id.* Moreover, "the burden of proof is on the plaintiff to support allegations of jurisdiction with competent proof when the allegations are challenged by the defendant." *O'Toole v. Arlington Trust Co.*, 681 F.2d 94, 98 (1st Cir. 1982).

Defendants' primary evidence that Lundquist was a New Hampshire citizen was as follows: (1) that Lundquist owned real property in Melvin Village, New Hampshire and paid taxes on that property; (2) that Lundquist maintained a functioning telephone in Melvin Village; (3) that Lundquist had had a New Hampshire driver's license since 1986; (4) that Lundquist was registered to vote in New Hampshire from 1976 until at least 1990, and has actually voted in New Hampshire during that time; and (5) that Lundquist or Lundquist's wife stated his address to be in Melvin Village, New Hampshire on 1986, 1987, and 1988 annual reports filed with the New Hampshire Secretary of State by Amphibair, Inc., a corporation of which Lundquist was sole director, President, and Treasurer, and Lundquist's wife was Secretary.

Lundquist presented affidavits of himself and his wife setting forth primarily the following evidence that Lundquist was a citizen not of New Hampshire, but of Florida: (1) that Lundquist purchased real property in Florida and moved there in 1984, keeping his New Hampshire property as a summer home; (2) that since 1984 Lundquist has maintained several Florida bank accounts; (3) that Lundquist has a Florida driver's license; (4) that Lundquist's wife has run a horse farm continuously in Florida since 1984; (5) that Lundquist and/or his wife belong to several social organizations in Florida; (6) that Lundquist has summered in New Hampshire, in some years spending as little as two to three weeks there; (7) that all of Lundquist's personal belongings are in Florida except for certain bank accounts and for sparse furnishings in the Melvin Village, New Hampshire residence; and (8) that Lundquist listed a Florida residence on his federal tax returns for 1987, 1988, and 1989.

The district court, in its brief order finding New Hampshire citizenship, noted that Lundquist had lived in Florida at material times. The court placed weight, however, on Lundquist's voting registration in New Hampshire and on Lundquist's representations of New Hampshire residence on corporate filings. . . .

As an initial matter, Lundquist attacks this district court ruling by asserting that the district court applied the wrong legal standard. Lundquist correctly notes that the relevant standard is "citizenship," i.e., "domicile," not mere residence; a party may reside in more than one state but can be domiciled, for diversity purposes, in only one. Because the district court did not expressly use the term "citizenship" or "domicile" in its order, but instead twice stated that Lundquist represented himself to be "a resident of New Hampshire," Lundquist argues that the district court improperly based its ruling on a finding of mere residence in New Hampshire.

The district court's order, however, is silent as to the legal analysis employed by the district court. It discusses only the facts of the case. The district court's references to residence were employed in the course of setting forth findings as to the facts. Since residence is highly relevant to the issue of domicile, the district court's discussion was fully consistent with application of the correct legal standard. Nothing else in the district court's order, beyond this mere accident of language, would suggest that the district court employed the wrong legal standard. We cannot find that the district court committed legal error in the absence of any significant indication that it did so. . . .

The remaining question is whether the district court applied that standard correctly. The district court's determination that Lundquist was a citizen of New Hampshire at the time he commenced the action "is a mixed question of law and fact and as such may not be set aside unless clearly erroneous."

There are, of course, many factors that courts have deemed relevant to the determination of a party's domicile.

> While it is impossible to catalogue all factors bearing on the issue, they include the place where civil and political rights are exercised, taxes paid, real and personal property (such as furniture and automobiles) located, driver's and other licenses obtained, bank accounts maintained, location of club and church membership and places of business or employment.

1 Moore's Federal Practice 3.–3, at 788 (2nd ed. 1991). Just as no single factor is controlling, id. at 787–88, domicile need not be determined by mere numerical comparison of the number of factors that may appear to favor each side of the issue.

In the instant case there is no question that a number of important factors do suggest domicile in Florida. For example, defendants introduced nothing to contradict Lundquist's assertion that most of Lundquist's personal property is in Florida, Lundquist has several bank accounts in Florida, Lundquist belongs to social organizations in Florida, and Lundquist listed a Florida residence on his federal tax returns for relevant years. Although Lundquist stated he had a Florida driver's license, defendants introduced uncontradicted evidence that he also had a New Hampshire license. On the other hand, the factors relied on by the district court—Lundquist's registration to vote and actual voting in New Hampshire, and his representation of New Hampshire residence on corporate reports to the New Hampshire Secretary of State—are also weighty ones.

For example, "some opinions have given special weight to the state in which a party is registered to vote, occasionally stating that such registration raises a presumption of domicile." We need establish no such presumption to agree that Lundquist's voting registration carries weight. The applicable New Hampshire statute provides,

> Every inhabitant of the state, having a fixed and permanent established domicile, ... shall have a right at any meeting or election, to vote in the town, ward, or unincorporated place in which he is domiciled. The determinant of one's domicile is a question of factual physical presence incorporating an intention to reside for an indefinite period. This domicile is the voter's residence to which, upon temporary absence, he has the intention of returning. This domicile is that place in which he dwells on a continuing basis for a significant portion of each year.

N.H. Rev. Stat. Ann. 654:1. Given this statute, Lundquist's voting behavior is tantamount to a representation of New Hampshire domicile to voting officials.

In addition, we have held in *O'Toole*, 681 F.2d at 98, that a party's own representation of domicile on corporate reports is "strong evidence." In *O'Toole*, appellants had filed corporate reports with the state of Massachusetts listing their "domicile" as in Massachusetts. We upheld as not clearly erroneous the district court's determination of Massachusetts domicile, stating,

> Although the term "domicile" on the corporate filing form may not have the exact legal meaning that it has in the § 1332 context, appellants' designation of domicile in Massachusetts on the forms is strong evidence that appellants have the burden of overcoming. The paucity of appellants' presentation of evidence justifies the district court's conclusion that they had not met that burden.

Id.

In the instant case, to be sure, the contrary evidence as to domicile is stronger than it was in *O'Toole*. Also, neither the corporate report forms nor the governing New Hampshire statutes use the word "domicile." New Hampshire law requires that at least one director be an "actual resident" of New Hampshire, N.H. Rev. Stat. Ann. § 296:3, and that the corporation "continuously maintain in this state a secretary, ... who shall be an individual resident in this state...." N.H. Rev. Stat. Ann. § 293–A:12 (emphasis added). Again, Lundquist was the corporation's sole director, and Lundquist's wife held the office of Secretary. Thus, although Lundquist's and his wife's representations on these corporate reports cannot be said to have been representations of "domicile," they were representations not only of mere residence but of continuous, "actual" residence. Accordingly, while *O'Toole* certainly is not on all fours with this case, *O'Toole* does support the proposition that Lundquist's representations to state officials on corporate reports, as well as for voting purposes, are entitled to significant weight.

Given the substantial evidence on both sides of the issue, we cannot say that the district court committed clear error in making the determination that it did. Although Lundquist in his affidavit put forth strong evidence of an intent to remain in Florida, Lundquist's voting registration and representations on corporate reports constitute significant countervailing evidence of intent to remain in New Hampshire and maintain New Hampshire domicile. . . .

The judgment of the district court is affirmed.

NOTES AND QUESTIONS

1. *Lundquist* explores what § 1332 means by a "citizen of a state." In the case of United States citizens, a person's citizenship is measured by her domicile. As the court indicates, domicile is not the same as residence. In one sentence, describe the difference between domicile and residence.

2. Bonnie was born in Oregon to Oregon citizens, and has lived in that state her entire 35-year life. However, for as long as she can remember, she has hated Oregon's gray and dreary climate. In fact, for the past thirty years Bonnie has intended to leave Oregon and relocate to Arizona. Unfortunately, she has not yet saved enough money to make the change. What is Bonnie's domicile? Does she even have a domicile?

Rethink your answers to these questions in light of the following general rules governing domicile:

   a. A person always has one—and only one—domicile.

   b. An infant acquires a domicile at birth, which is almost always the domicile of his parents.

   c. In order to change his domicile, a person must both establish residence in a new state and have the intent to remain in that state. The residence and the intent to remain must exist at the same time, even if only for a moment.

3. *Intent.* Domicile's focus on a person's subjective intent creates special problems in certain situations. Some people do not have the legal capacity to form the required intent. Therefore, a minor will usually keep the domicile of his parents until the age of majority. Of course, the age of majority differs from state to state, which can lead to convoluted analysis, especially in cases where a person moves from a state where he is a minor to one in which he would be old enough to form the required intent. See, e.g., *Rodriguez-Diaz v. Sierra-Martinez*, 853 F.2d 1027 (1st Cir. 1988).

People with diminished mental capacity also cannot themselves form the intent to change domicile. Because people with diminished capacity are limited in their ability to effect a legal transfer of property and enter into contracts, a legal guardian is often appointed to manage their affairs. In some cases, the guardian may move the ward to a new state. Courts are split as to whether the guardian can change the ward's domicile. For an excellent discussion of the competing views, see *Acridge v. The Evangelical Lutheran Good Samaritan Society*, 334 F.3d 444 (5th Cir. 2003).

What about military personnel and prisoners who are serving jail terms in states other than their previous home? For these people, of course, the problem is not capacity. Instead, the problem is that their change of residence is not voluntary. Nevertheless, both military personnel and prisoners may form the intent to remain in their new state of residence. See *Gambelli v. United States*, 904 F.Supp. 494 (E.D. Va. 1995) (military); *Singletary v. Continental Illinois National Bank*, 9 F.3d 1236 (7th Cir. 1993) (prisoner).

b. Corporations and Other "Legal Persons"

The legal concept of a "person" is not limited to human beings. Corporations and government bodies may also have legal rights, and can sue and be sued in court. If a case involves a legal person such as a corporation, how does the court determine the entity's citizenship? After all, a corporation is a legal fiction that does not truly "live" anywhere.

HERTZ CORP. v. FRIEND
130 S.Ct. 1181, 175 L.Ed.2d 102 (2010)

JUSTICE BREYER delivered the opinion of the Court.

The federal diversity jurisdiction statute provides that "a corporation shall be deemed to be a citizen of any State by which it has been incorporated and of the State where it has its principal place of business." 28 U.S.C. § 1332(c)(1). We seek here to resolve different interpretations that the Circuits have given this phrase. . . .

In September 2007, respondents Melinda Friend and John Nhieu, two California citizens, sued petitioner, the Hertz Corporation, in a California state court. They sought damages for what they claimed were violations of California's wage and hour laws. And they requested relief on behalf of a potential class composed of California citizens who had allegedly suffered similar harms.

Hertz filed a notice seeking removal to a federal court.* Hertz claimed that the plaintiffs and the defendant were citizens of different States. Hence, the federal court possessed diversity-of-citizenship jurisdiction. Friend and Nhieu, however, claimed that the Hertz Corporation was a California citizen, like themselves, and that, hence, diversity jurisdiction was lacking.

To support its position, Hertz submitted a declaration by an employee relations manager that sought to show that Hertz's "principal place of business" was in New Jersey, not in California. The declaration

---

* Removal, discussed in Part E of this chapter, allows a defendant sued in state court to move the case to federal court. Generally speaking, a case may be removed only if it could have been filed originally in federal court. [Eds.]

stated, among other things, that Hertz operated facilities in 44 States; and that California—which had about 12% of the Nation's population—accounted for 273 of Hertz's 1,606 car rental locations; about 2,300 of its 11,230 full-time employees; about $811 million of its $4.371 billion in annual revenue; and about 3.8 million of its approximately 21 million annual transactions, *i.e.*, rentals. The declaration also stated that the "leadership of Hertz and its domestic subsidiaries" is located at Hertz's "corporate headquarters" in Park Ridge, New Jersey; that its "core executive and administrative functions . . . are carried out" there and "to a lesser extent" in Oklahoma City, Oklahoma; and that its "major administrative operations . . . are found" at those two locations.

The District Court of the Northern District of California accepted Hertz's statement of the facts as undisputed. But it concluded that, given those facts, Hertz was a citizen of California. In reaching this conclusion, the court applied Ninth Circuit precedent, which instructs courts to identify a corporation's "principal place of business" by first determining the amount of a corporation's business activity State by State. If the amount of activity is "significantly larger" or "substantially predominates" in one State, then that State is the corporation's "principal place of business." If there is no such State, then the "principal place of business" is the corporation's "'nerve center,'" *i.e.*, the place where "'the majority of its executive and administrative functions are performed.'"

Applying this test, the District Court found that the "plurality of each of the relevant business activities" was in California, and that "the differential between the amount of those activities" in California and the amount in "the next closest state" was "significant." Hence, Hertz's "principal place of business" was California, and diversity jurisdiction was thus lacking. The District Court consequently remanded the case to the state courts.

Hertz appealed the District Court's remand order. The Ninth Circuit affirmed in a brief memorandum opinion. Hertz filed a petition for certiorari. And, in light of differences among the Circuits in the application of the test for corporate citizenship, we granted the writ. . . .

Congress first authorized federal courts to exercise diversity jurisdiction in 1789 when, in the First Judiciary Act, Congress granted federal courts authority to hear suits "between a citizen of the State where the suit is brought, and a citizen of another State." The statute said nothing about corporations. In 1809, Chief Justice Marshall, writing for a unanimous Court, described a corporation as an "invisible, intangible, and artificial being" which was "certainly not a citizen." *Bank of United States v. Deveaux*, 3 L.Ed. 38 (1809). But the Court held that a corporation could invoke the federal courts' diversity jurisdiction based on a pleading that the corporation's shareholders were all citizens of a different State from the defendants, as "the term citizen ought to be understood as it is used in the constitution, and as it is used in other laws. That is, to describe the real persons who come into court, in this case, under their corporate name."

In *Louisville, C. & C.R. Co. v. Letson*, 11 L.Ed. 353 (1844), the Court modified this initial approach. It held that a corporation was to be deemed an artificial person of the State by which it had been created, and its citizenship for jurisdictional purposes determined accordingly.... Whatever the rationale, the practical upshot was that, for diversity purposes, the federal courts considered a corporation to be a citizen of the State of its incorporation.

In 1928 this Court made clear that the "state of incorporation" rule was virtually absolute. It held that a corporation closely identified with State A could proceed in a federal court located in that State as long as the corporation had filed its incorporation papers in State B, perhaps a State where the corporation did no business at all. See *Black and White Taxicab & Transfer Co. v. Brown and Yellow Taxicab & Transfer Co.*, 276 U.S. 518, 522–525, (refusing to question corporation's reincorporation motives and finding diversity jurisdiction). Subsequently, many in Congress and those who testified before it pointed out that this interpretation was at odds with diversity jurisdiction's basic rationale, namely, opening the federal courts' doors to those who might otherwise suffer from local prejudice against out-of-state parties. Through its choice of the State of incorporation, a corporation could manipulate federal-court jurisdiction, for example, opening the federal courts' doors in a State where it conducted nearly all its business by filing incorporation papers elsewhere.... Although various legislative proposals to curtail the corporate use of diversity jurisdiction were made, none of these proposals were enacted into law....

At the same time as federal dockets increased in size, many judges began to believe those dockets contained too many diversity cases. A committee of the Judicial Conference of the United States studied the matter. And on March 12, 1951, that committee, the Committee on Jurisdiction and Venue, issued a report.

Among its observations, the committee found a general need "to prevent frauds and abuses" with respect to jurisdiction. Committee Report, at 14. The committee recommended against eliminating diversity cases altogether. Instead it recommended, along with other proposals, a statutory amendment....

[The Committee] proposed that "'a corporation shall be deemed a citizen of the state of its original creation ... [and] shall also be deemed a citizen of a state where it has its principal place of business.'" Judicial Conference of the United States, Report of the Committee on Jurisdiction and Venue 4 (Sept. 24, 1951) (hereinafter Sept. Committee Rept.)—the source of the present-day statutory language....

Subsequently, in 1958, Congress both codified the courts' traditional place of incorporation test and also enacted into law a slightly modified version of the Conference Committee's proposed "principal place of business" language. A corporation was to "be deemed a citizen of any State by which it has been incorporated and of the State where it has its principal place of business." § 2, 72 Stat. 415.

The phrase "principal place of business" has proved more difficult to apply than its originators likely expected. . . .

If a corporation's headquarters and executive offices were in the same State in which it did most of its business, the test seemed straightforward. The "principal place of business" was located in that State.

But suppose those corporate headquarters, including executive offices, are in one State, while the corporation's plants or other centers of business activity are located in other States? In 1959 a distinguished federal district judge, Edward Weinfeld, relied on the Second Circuit's interpretation of the Bankruptcy Act to answer this question in part:

> "Where a corporation is engaged in far-flung and varied activities which are carried on in different states, its principal place of business is the nerve center from which it radiates out to its constituent parts and from which its officers direct, control and coordinate all activities without regard to locale, in the furtherance of the corporate objective. The test applied by our Court of Appeals, is that place where the corporation has an 'office from which its business was directed and controlled'—the place where 'all of its business was under the supreme direction and control of its officers.' " *Scot Typewriter Co.*, 170 F. Supp., at 865.

Numerous Circuits have since followed this rule, applying the "nerve center" test for corporations with "far-flung" business activities.

Scot's analysis, however, did not go far enough. For it did not answer what courts should do when the operations of the corporation are not "far-flung" but rather limited to only a few States. When faced with this question, various courts have focused more heavily on where a corporation's actual business activities are located.

Perhaps because corporations come in many different forms, involve many different kinds of business activities, and locate offices and plants for different reasons in different ways in different regions, a general "business activities" approach has proved unusually difficult to apply. Courts must decide which factors are more important than others: for example, plant location, sales or servicing centers; transactions, payrolls, or revenue generation. . . .

This complexity may reflect an unmediated judicial effort to apply the statutory phrase "principal place of business" in light of the general purpose of diversity jurisdiction, *i.e.*, an effort to find the State where a corporation is least likely to suffer out-of-state prejudice when it is sued in a local court. But, if so, that task seems doomed to failure. After all, the relevant purposive concern—prejudice against an out-of-state party—will often depend upon factors that courts cannot easily measure, for example, a corporation's image, its history, and its advertising, while the factors that courts can more easily measure, for example, its office or plant location, its sales, its employment, or the nature of the goods or services it supplies, will sometimes bear no more than a distant relation to the likelihood of prejudice. At the same time, this approach is at war with administrative simplicity. And it has failed to achieve a nationally uniform interpretation of federal law, an unfortunate consequence in a federal legal system.

In an effort to find a single, more uniform interpretation of the statutory phrase, we have reviewed the Courts of Appeals' divergent and increasingly complex interpretations.... We conclude that "principal place of business" is best read as referring to the place where a corporation's officers direct, control, and coordinate the corporation's activities. It is the place that Courts of Appeals have called the corporation's "nerve center." And in practice it should normally be the place where the corporation maintains its headquarters—provided that the headquarters is the actual center of direction, control, and coordination, *i.e.*, the "nerve center," and not simply an office where the corporation holds its board meetings (for example, attended by directors and officers who have traveled there for the occasion).

Three sets of considerations, taken together, convince us that this approach, while imperfect, is superior to other possibilities. First, the statute's language supports the approach. The statute's text deems a corporation a citizen of the "State where it has its principal place of business." 28 U.S.C. § 1332(c)(1). The word "place" is in the singular, not the plural. The word "principal" requires us to pick out the "main, prominent" or "leading" place. 12 Oxford English Dictionary 495 (2d ed. 1989) (def.(A)(I)(2)). And the fact that the word "place" follows the words "State where" means that the "place" is a place within a State. It is not the State itself.

A corporation's "nerve center," usually its main headquarters, is a single place. The public often (though not always) considers it the corporation's main place of business. And it is a place within a State. By contrast, the application of a more general business activities test has led some courts, as in the present case, to look, not at a particular place within a State, but incorrectly at the State itself, measuring the total amount of business activities that the corporation conducts there and determining whether they are "significantly larger" than in the next-ranking State.

This approach invites greater litigation and can lead to strange results, as the Ninth Circuit has since recognized. Namely, if a "corporation may be deemed a citizen of California on th[e] basis" of "activities [that] roughly reflect California's larger population . . . nearly every national retailer—no matter how far flung its operations—will be deemed a citizen of California for diversity purposes." *Davis v. HSBC Bank Nev., N. A.*, 557 F.3d 1026, 1029–1030 (2009). But why award or decline diversity jurisdiction on the basis of a State's population, whether measured directly, indirectly (say proportionately), or with modifications?

Second, administrative simplicity is a major virtue in a jurisdictional statute. Complex jurisdictional tests complicate a case, eating up time and money as the parties litigate, not the merits of their claims, but which court is the right court to decide those claims. Complex tests produce appeals and reversals, encourage gamesmanship, and, again, diminish the likelihood that results and settlements will reflect a claim's legal and factual merits. Judicial resources too are at stake. Courts have an independent obligation to determine whether subject-matter jurisdiction exists, even when no party challenges it. So courts benefit from straightforward rules under which they can readily assure themselves of their power to hear a case.

Simple jurisdictional rules also promote greater predictability. Predictability is valuable to corporations making business and investment decisions. Predictability also benefits plaintiffs deciding whether to file suit in a state or federal court.

A "nerve center" approach, which ordinarily equates that "center" with a corporation's headquarters, is simple to apply comparatively speaking. The metaphor of a corporate "brain," while not precise, suggests a single location. By contrast, a corporation's general business activities more often lack a single principal place where they take place. That is to say, the corporation may have several plants, many sales locations, and employees located in many different places. If so, it will not be as easy to determine which of these different business locales is the "principal" or most important "place."

Third, the statute's legislative history, for those who accept it, offers a simplicity-related interpretive benchmark. The Judicial Conference provided an initial version of its proposal that suggested a numerical test. A corporation would be deemed a citizen of the State that accounted for more than half of its gross income. The Conference changed its mind in light of criticism that such a test would prove too complex and impractical to apply. That history suggests that the words "principal place of business" should be interpreted to be no more complex than the initial "half of gross income" test. A "nerve center" test offers such a possibility. A general business activities test does not.

We recognize that there may be no perfect test that satisfies all administrative and purposive criteria. We recognize as well that, under the "nerve center" test we adopt today, there will be hard cases. For example, in this era of telecommuting, some corporations may divide their command and coordinating functions among officers who work at several different locations, perhaps communicating over the Internet. That said, our test nonetheless points courts in a single direction, towards the center of overall direction, control, and coordination. Courts do not have to try to weigh corporate functions, assets, or revenues different in kind, one from the other. Our approach provides a sensible test that is relatively easier to apply, not a test that will, in all instances, automatically generate a result.

We also recognize that the use of a "nerve center" test may in some cases produce results that seem to cut against the basic rationale for 28 U.S.C. § 1332. For example, if the bulk of a company's business activities visible to the public take place in New Jersey, while its top officers direct those activities just across the river in New York, the "principal place of business" is New York. One could argue that members of the public in New Jersey would be less likely to be prejudiced against the corporation than persons in New York—yet the corporation will still be entitled to remove a New Jersey state case to federal court. . . .

We understand that such seeming anomalies will arise. However, in view of the necessity of having a clearer rule, we must accept them. Accepting occasionally counterintuitive results is the price the legal system must pay to avoid overly complex jurisdictional administration while producing the benefits that accompany a more uniform legal system.

The burden of persuasion for establishing diversity jurisdiction, of course, remains on the party asserting it. When challenged on allegations of jurisdictional facts, the parties must support their allegations by competent proof. . . . [I]f the record reveals attempts at manipulation—for example, that the alleged "nerve center" is nothing more than a mail drop box, a bare office with a computer, or the location of an annual executive retreat—the courts should instead take as the "nerve center" the place of actual direction, control, and coordination, in the absence of such manipulation.

Petitioner's unchallenged declaration suggests that Hertz's center of direction, control, and coordination, its "nerve center," and its corporate headquarters are one and the same, and they are located in New Jersey, not in California. Because respondents should have a fair opportunity to litigate their case in light of our holding, however, we vacate the Ninth

Circuit's judgment and remand the case for further proceedings consistent with this opinion.

NOTES AND QUESTIONS

1. *Hertz* deals with how one ascertains the citizenship of a corporation. § 1332(c) provides the governing rule. After reviewing that section, do you see why a corporation is often a citizen of two states? Can you conceive of a situation where a corporation could have only one citizenship? Note, however, that a corporation will almost never have more than two citizenships. There can, by definition, be only one "principal" place of business. And a corporation is almost always incorporated under the laws of only one state. If the parties who create the corporation file incorporation papers in more than one state, they will create two separate corporations.

Sometimes you will see reference to a corporation being "chartered" in a state. This is an older term that means the same as "incorporated."

2. The Court never mentions the state in which Hertz was incorporated. A simple internet search reveals that the company, like many others, was incorporated in Delaware. If a corporation may have two citizenships, then why wasn't Hertz diverse from the plaintiffs regardless of its principal place of business? Wasn't Hertz a citizen of Delaware by virtue of its incorporation in that state?

3. *Foreign corporations.* What if a corporation is chartered under the laws of another nation, but has its principal place of business in the United States? If the normal rules applied, such a party would be both an alien (a citizen of the laws of the nation of incorporation) and a citizen of a state. Most courts, however, do not apply the principal place of business test to foreign corporations. Such corporations are citizens only of the nation in which they were incorporated.

4. When a corporation ceases doing business, it is dissolved. However, even after dissolution there may be unresolved claims both by and against the corporation. How does a court determine the citizenship of a dissolved corporation? In one of the first post-*Hertz* cases to deal with the issue, one district court held that a dissolved corporation is a citizen only of its state of incorporation, reasoning that the corporation has *no* principal place of business. *Holston Investments, Inc. B.V.I. v. LanLogistics Corp.*, 766 F.Supp.2d 1327 (S.D. Fla. 2011).

5. *Partnerships and unincorporated associations.* Partnerships and other unincorporated associations present special issues. First, unlike a corporation, these entities are usually not a "person" in the eyes of the law, which means they can neither sue nor be sued in their own name. Second, even if the partnership or unincorporated association is considered a legal person, in determining diversity courts look to the citizenship of all the partners or members of the association. The next case explores this issue, and also deals with another twist on the diversity calculus.

ZAMBELLI FIREWORKS MFG. CO., INC. v. WOOD
592 F.3d 412 (3rd Cir. 2010)

FISHER, CIRCUIT JUDGE.

I

Plaintiff Zambelli Fireworks Manufacturing Co., Inc. d/b/a Zambelli Fireworks Internationale ("Zambelli") is one of the oldest and largest fireworks companies in the United States, doing business in approximately 40 states.... Zambelli is a corporation incorporated under the laws of Pennsylvania, with its principal place of business in New Castle, Pennsylvania.

Defendant Pyrotecnico F/X, LLC ("Pyrotecnico") has been a direct competitor of Zambelli in the fireworks industry for many years. Pyrotecnico is comprised of several related companies, all of which are managed by Stephen Vitale. Pyrotecnico is a limited liability company registered under the laws of Nevada. Its sole member is Pyrotecnico of Louisiana, LLC, another limited liability company registered under the laws of Louisiana. Stephen Vitale, a resident of New Castle, Pennsylvania, is the managing member of Pyrotecnico of Louisiana, LLC.

Defendant Matthew Wood ("Wood"), a resident of Pompano Beach, Florida, works in the fireworks industry as a pyrotechnician and choreographer....

In 2001, Zambelli hired Wood to work in its Florida office pursuant to the terms of an employment agreement containing a two-year non-compete provision....

As Wood assumed increasing responsibilities in the Zambelli company, the Zambelli family considered Wood to be the "next generation" and "future of the company." Thus in 2005, the Zambellis asked Wood to sign an updated employment agreement that would ensure Wood's continued commitment to the company. This later agreement, signed June 2, 2005 (the "2005 Agreement"), superseded the earlier 2001 employment agreement.

In May 2007, a major sale of Zambelli's stock took place, after which the company was no longer wholly owned by Zambelli family members....

In light of the changes in management and the expectation of increased job responsibilities, Wood contacted Stephen Vitale, Pyrotecnico's manager, in October 2007 regarding potential employment with Pyrotecnico....

Wood began working for Pyrotecnico on March 3, 2008....

II

Zambelli filed this action on March 26, 2008, against Wood and Pyrotecnico. Zambelli sought, *inter alia*, to enforce the terms of the restrictive covenant not to compete contained in the 2005 Agreement with Wood. . . .

III

. . .

We begin with the question of whether we have subject matter jurisdiction over this dispute. This case presents us with the opportunity to address, for the first time in this circuit, the rule for determining the citizenship of a limited liability company ("LLC") for diversity jurisdiction purposes. We now join our sister circuits in holding that the citizenship of an LLC is determined by the citizenship of each of its members.

The District Court below premised jurisdiction on the diversity of the parties, based on Zambelli's pleading in its Verified Complaint that it was a corporate citizen of Pennsylvania, Wood was a citizen of Florida, and Pyrotecnico "is a Nevada limited liability company with its principal place of business [in Nevada]." Pyrotecnico admitted this allegation in its Answer. The citizenship of the members of Pyrotecnico was not pled. However, in the course of the trial proceedings, Stephen Vitale, a Pennsylvania resident employed in Pyrotecnico's New Castle, Pennsylvania headquarters, testified that Pyrotecnico was a wholly-owned subsidiary of Pyrotecnico of Louisiana, LLC, of which he was the managing member.

Based on this record, this Court *sua sponte* noted the apparent absence of complete diversity and directed the parties to submit supplemental briefing on the question of this Court's jurisdiction. . . .

Our jurisdiction to hear cases in diversity arises under 28 U.S.C. § 1332(a), which provides that district courts "have original jurisdiction of all civil actions where the matter in controversy exceeds the sum or value of $75,000, exclusive of interest and, and is between . . . citizens of different States." Complete diversity requires that, in cases with multiple plaintiffs or multiple defendants, no plaintiff be a citizen of the same state as any defendant. The key inquiry in establishing diversity is thus the "citizenship" of each party to the action.

Most rules of citizenship are well established. A natural person is deemed to be a citizen of the state where he is domiciled. A corporation is a citizen both of the state where it is incorporated and of the state where it has its principal place of business. 28 U.S.C. § 1332(c). And a partnership, as an unincorporated entity, takes on the citizenship of each of its partners.

We are asked now to resolve the citizenship of an LLC, a relatively new unincorporated business entity possessing some characteristics of both a corporation and a partnership. Although limited liability entities resemble corporations in many respects, including the passive management role performed by both limited liability entity-owners and corporate shareholders, the Supreme Court has flatly rejected arguments in favor of extending the rule of corporate citizenship to analogously formed business entities, *Carden v. Arkoma Assocs.*, 494 U.S. 185 at 189 ("[A]lthough possessing 'some of the characteristics of a corporation' . . . [an unincorporated entity] may not be deemed a 'citizen' under the jurisdictional rule established for corporations[;] . . . [t]hat rule must not be extended.").

For this reason, every federal court of appeals to address the question has concluded that a limited liability company, as an unincorporated business entity, should be treated as a partnership for purposes of establishing citizenship. We now join them in that holding.

As we have held before, the citizenship of partnerships and other unincorporated associations is determined by the citizenship of its partners or members. Accordingly, the citizenship of an LLC is determined by the citizenship of its members. And as with partnerships, where an LLC has, as one of its members, another LLC, "the citizenship of unincorporated associations must be traced through however many layers of partners or members there may be" to determine the citizenship of the LLC. *Hart v. Terminex Int'l*, 336 F.3d 541, 543 (7th Cir. 2003).

In light of this rule, Pyrotecnico's presence defeats complete diversity in this case. On the plaintiff side, Zambelli, as a corporation incorporated under the laws of Pennsylvania and with its principal place of business in New Castle, Pennsylvania, is a citizen of Pennsylvania. On the defendant side, Wood, who is domiciled in Florida, is a citizen of Florida. And Pyrotecnico, despite being a Nevada limited liability company, has a single member: Pyrotecnico of Louisiana, LLC, a Louisiana limited liability company. Tracing its citizenship through the layers, Pyrotecnico takes on the citizenship of the members of Pyrotecnico of Louisiana, including its managing member Stephen Vitale. Because Stephen Vitale is a resident of New Castle, Pennsylvania, Pyrotecnico is a citizen of Pennsylvania and is not diverse from Zambelli, another citizen of Pennsylvania. Complete diversity is therefore lacking.

[The court then dismissed Pyrotecnico from the case, and proceeded to the merits.]

NOTES AND QUESTIONS

1. *Zambelli* deals with two main issues. The first is how to determine the citizenship of a "limited liability company," an increasingly common form of business entity. Do you understand why the court chooses not to treat an

LLC like a corporation? Does the rule adopted by the court make it easier or more difficult for cases involving LLCs to qualify for diversity?

2. The second issue in the case is the complete diversity rule. That rule requires that no plaintiff may share citizenship with any defendant. Like the "well-pleaded complaint" rule that applies in federal question cases, the complete diversity rule is a rule of statutory, not constitutional, interpretation. The courts have interpreted the diversity language in Article III of the Constitution to require only "minimal," rather than complete diversity. Minimal diversity exists when one plaintiff is diverse from any one defendant; the citizenship of the other parties to the case does not matter. Because the Constitution requires only minimal diversity, Congress could change the requirements for diversity jurisdiction under § 1332. In fact, under other specialized diversity statutes Congress sometimes does not require complete diversity. In Chapter 8 you will encounter § 1335, which requires less than complete diversity in interpleader cases.

Similarly, in 2002 Congress enacted the Multiparty, Multiforum Jurisdiction Act of 2002, which gives the district courts subject-matter jurisdiction over certain multi-party cases arising out of an accident in which 75 or more people died. 28 U.S.C. § 1369. The statute explicitly requires only "minimal diversity," which is defined as any situation where at least one plaintiff is diverse from any defendant. 28 U.S.C. § 1369(c)(1). However, if a substantial majority of the plaintiffs are citizens of the same state as the primary defendant or defendants, the federal court must decline to hear the case. In addition, the statute also applies only if the accident did not occur in defendant's home state, or, if there are two or more defendants, at least two reside in different states.

Finally, Congress recently amended § 1332 to give the district courts jurisdiction over large class actions (involving an amount in controversy greater than $5,000,000) in which at least one member of the plaintiff class is diverse from the defendant. This amendment, codified at § 1332(d), is discussed in Chapter 8 in the material dealing with class actions.

3. The complete diversity rule has a long heritage, tracing its roots to the Supreme Court's decision in *Strawbridge v. Curtiss*, 7 U.S. (3 Cranch) 267, 2 L.Ed. 435 (1806). *Strawbridge* has often been criticized. Nevertheless, the rule has never been overturned. One reason cited for retaining the rule is that Congress has amended § 1332 on a number of occasions since 1806, but did nothing in these amendments to overturn the rule. That silence, the courts reason, constitutes acquiescence. Moreover, as we will see in Part D of this chapter, the adoption of § 1367 in 1990 provides more positive proof that Congress is content with the complete diversity rule in ordinary diversity cases.

4. Imagine a case where two plaintiffs sue two defendants. P1 is diverse from both defendants. While P2 is diverse from D1, P2 and D2 are citizens of the same state. However, P2 has not filed a claim against D2. May the case be brought in federal court under diversity jurisdiction? For a

number of years, many lower courts allowed diversity jurisdiction under these circumstances. However, in *Caterpillar Inc. v. Lewis*, 519 U.S. 61, 117 S.Ct. 467, 136 L.Ed.2d 437 (1996), the Supreme Court made it clear that the complete diversity rule applied regardless of whether the non-diverse parties had filed claims against each other. Therefore, in the above example, the case cannot proceed in federal court as long as P2 and D2 are still in the case. Either P2 or D2 must be dropped if the case is to stay in federal court.

5. The complete diversity rule deals with citizenship. What about the other main requirement of § 1332—the amount in controversy? For many years, the courts held that every plaintiff's claim against every defendant had to satisfy the amount in controversy requirement. *Zahn v. International Paper Co.*, 414 U.S. 291, 94 S.Ct. 505, 38 L.Ed.2d 511 (1973). However, the adoption of the supplemental jurisdiction statute, 28 U.S.C. § 1367, has relaxed this requirement to some extent. See *Exxon Mobil Corp. v. Allapattah Services, Inc.* in Part D of this Chapter.

3. THE AMOUNT IN CONTROVERSY

The other primary requirement of § 1332 is that the amount in controversy exceed $75,000. Throughout its history, diversity jurisdiction has been available only for suits involving a minimum amount in controversy. The Judiciary Act of 1789 established a minimum of $500. Congress has periodically increased the floor over the years to its present amount. This increase represents more than inflation. At times, Congress has agreed to increase the amount in controversy as a way to appease those who would abolish diversity jurisdiction altogether. Confining diversity to the larger (and ostensibly more important) cases helps to reduce the demand on federal judicial resources.

What amounts are considered. Generally speaking, a court attempts to ascertain the total value of the dispute. Claims for both compensatory and punitive damages are counted in determining whether the requirement is satisfied. If the plaintiff is allowed by law to recover attorney's fees, those fees are also included. (Of course, as the full amount of fees cannot be calculated at the beginning of the case, courts allow only a claim for reasonably-anticipated fees.) However, other payments that defendant may be required to make to plaintiff may not count. § 1332 makes it clear that the amount in controversy is "exclusive of interest and costs." The term costs means the various expenses charged by the judicial system. Courts often require the losing party to pay the winner's costs.

Contrary to what a literal reading of the statute might suggest, not all interest is excluded from the calculation. As one court restated the rule:

> The purpose of excluding interest is to prevent the delaying of a suit merely to accumulate the necessary amount for federal jurisdiction. Thus, interest is not counted if it "was an incident

arising solely by virtue of a delay in payment" of the underlying amount in controversy. *State Farm Mutual Auto Ins. Co. v. Narvaez*, 149 F.3d 1269 (10th Cir. 1998). Conversely, any interest that is an essential ingredient of the claim does count. *Brown v. Webster*, 156 U.S. 328, 15 S.Ct. 377, 39 L.Ed. 440 (1895). Therefore, a suit to collect $80,000 in unpaid interest coupons on a note would satisfy the amount in controversy, even though the entire amount is made up of interest. However, any additional interest that might be charged due to late payment of the coupons would not count.

Claims for relief other than money. What if the case seeks an injunction or other non-monetary relief? Courts in these situations estimate the cash value of the relief being sought. In the case of an injunction, the courts are split as to how to determine the value. Depending on the jurisdiction, the court will use one of the following tests: (a) the value of injunctive relief to the plaintiff (the majority view), (b) the cost of the injunction to the defendant, (c) the greater of the value to plaintiff or expense to defendant, or (d) the worth of the "object in controversy"; i.e. the subject of the dispute. 1 Moore's Manual, Federal Practice and Procedure § 5.72(3) (2000).

What evidence the court considers. In determining whether the amount in controversy requirement is satisfied, a court usually looks solely to the face of plaintiff's complaint. If plaintiff alleges an amount in excess of $75,000, exclusive of interest and costs, the requirement is usually deemed satisfied. Even if plaintiff's demand for relief seems high, the court will accept it unless it appears to a legal certainty that the plaintiff cannot recover the amount sought. *St. Paul Mercury Indem. Co. v. Red Cab Co.*, 303 U.S. 283, 288–89, 58 S.Ct. 586, 82 L.Ed. 845 (1938). It is very difficult for defendant to overcome the presumption that plaintiff's request is in good faith. For an excellent recent decision applying this principle to several claims, finding some sufficient and others insufficient, see *Rosario Ortega v. Star-Kist Foods, Inc.*, 370 F.3d 124 (1st Cir. 2004), *overturned on other grounds* 545 U.S. 546, 125 S.Ct. 2611, 162 L.Ed.2d 502 (2005).

On the other hand, a plaintiff can keep a case out of court by specifically alleging that she demands "an amount not to exceed $75,000." This is especially helpful when the plaintiff wants to prevent defendant from removing the case, as discussed in Part E of this chapter.

When amount determined. Because the court considers the complaint, a party need only show the amount in controversy is satisfied on the date the case is filed. The court does not lose jurisdiction if it eventually determines plaintiff will actually recover $75,000 or less. However, if plaintiff recovers $75,000 or less, § 1332(b) gives the court the option of requiring plaintiff to pay defendant's costs.

Aggregation. The discussion to this point has been considering only single plaintiff-single defendant-single claim cases. Today, few cases fit that mold. How does the court apply the amount in controversy rules to cases involving multiple claims and parties? The rules governing aggregation are complex, and can require a fairly sophisticated knowledge of both property rights and the substantive law underlying the claim. The following is a brief summary of the basic principles.

1. *Single plaintiff-single defendant.* Generally, a plaintiff may aggregate all claims she has against a single defendant to meet the $75,000 floor. Aggregation is possible regardless of whether the claims are in any way related, and regardless of whether any individual claim by itself exceeds $75,000. However, if a plaintiff seeks recovery for the same injury using two or more claims that present alternate legal theories, the damages sought under each of those claims are not aggregated. Suppose, for example, that plaintiff, who was injured by a defective product, sues defendant for breach of warranty and negligence. Plaintiff seeks $50,000 in damages for each claim. Because these claims are merely alternate ways to recover for the same injury, the $50,000 in damages is counted only once. These two claims would not be aggregated.

2. *Multiple plaintiffs.* Two or more plaintiffs ordinarily cannot aggregate their claims. However, there are two exceptions to this rule. First, as discussed in Part D of this Chapter, to the extent the claims are factually related, a plaintiff with a claim of $75,000 or less may be able to join with a plaintiff whose claim exceeds $75,000 by virtue of the supplemental jurisdiction statute. Second, if two or more plaintiffs hold a joint and undivided interest in property that has a value in excess of $75,000, and their claims involve that property, the court will consider the amount in controversy to be the value of the property rather than the value of each plaintiff's separate share. For a clear discussion of the principles that apply to multiple plaintiffs, see *Allen v. R & H Oil and Gas Co.*, 63 F.3d 1326 (5th Cir. 1995).

3. *Multiple defendants.* A plaintiff may aggregate claims against multiple defendants only if the total injury suffered by plaintiff exceeds $75,000, and under governing law defendants can be held jointly liable for the entire injury. In a jurisdiction that follows the traditional rule of joint and several liability for multiple tortfeasors, aggregation is possible.

4. *Counterclaims.* As discussed above, a court usually considers only the complaint in determining whether the amount in controversy requirement is satisfied. However, several courts have indicated that the requirement may also be met if defendant asserts a compulsory counterclaim that, when added to the prayer in the complaint, totals more than $75,000. Other courts disagree, holding that only the complaint counts for determining the amount in controversy. Compare *Spectacor Mgmt. Group v. Brown*, 131 F.3d 120 (3d Cir. 1997) (considers

counterclaim) with *Oliver v. Haas*, 777 F.S. 1040 (D.Puerto Rico 1991) (counterclaim does not factor into calculation). Even courts like *Spectacor Mgmt.* apply the logic only to compulsory counterclaims, not to permissive counterclaims, cross-claims, or other forms of joinder.

4. ADDITIONAL ISSUES IN DIVERSITY JURISDICTION

a. Alienage Jurisdiction

§ 1332 does not apply only to United States citizens. It also allows the federal courts to exercise jurisdiction over certain cases involving citizens or subjects (technically, a "subject" is a person who lives under a monarchy) of foreign nations. The rationale for this so-called alienage jurisdiction is in many respects the same as that for ordinary diversity jurisdiction; namely, that state courts might favor their own citizens in suits between them and foreign citizens.

1. Review § 1332 and determine whether a federal court may hear the following disputes:

   a. P1 (a citizen of Oregon) and P2 (a citizen of France) sue D, a citizen of Louisiana.

   b. P (a citizen of North Dakota) sues D1 (a citizen of Sweden) and D2 (a citizen of Brazil).

   c. P (a citizen of Indonesia) sues D (a citizen of Norway).

   d. P1 (a citizen of Poland) and P2 (a citizen of Wisconsin) sue D (a citizen of India).

   e. P1 (a citizen of Finland) and P2 (a citizen of Delaware) sue D1 (a citizen of Minnesota) and D2 (a citizen of Finland).

2. Until recently, § 1332 contained language under which an alien who was granted permanent resident alien status (commonly known as a "green card") was always treated as a citizen of the state in which she was domiciled. The 2011 amendments modified this language. Thus, in Problem 1.a above, diversity jurisdiction would exist under § 1332(a)(3) even if the French plaintiff has permanent resident alien status in the United States. However, permanent resident alien status can affect jurisdiction under § 1332(a)(2). In problem 1.b above, if the Swedish defendant had been granted permanent resident alien status, he would be treated as a citizen of the state in which he established domicile. If the Swede's state of domicile was North Dakota, this would destroy complete diversity.

3. Do not forget that state courts may also hear cases involving aliens. In fact, a state court would have subject matter jurisdiction over all the cases set out in Note 1.

4. *Dual citizenship.* Although it is disfavored, the United States does recognize dual citizenship. How do courts treat dual citizenship when calculating diversity jurisdiction? Logic would suggest that the analysis would be the same as that applicable to corporations under § 1332(c), where both of the corporation's citizenships are considered. However, the majority rule is that a court will consider *only the person's American citizenship.* Although the cases are not entirely clear, the rule appears to be the same regardless of whether considering the foreign citizenship would serve to destroy diversity (that is, when the opposing party is also an alien), *Mutuelles Unies v. Kroll & Linstrom*, 957 F.2d 707 (9th Cir. 1992), or to create diversity (that is, where the opposing party is a citizen of the same state as that where the party in question resides), *Von Dunser v. Aronoff*, 915 F.2d 1071 (6th Cir. 1990).

5. As we have seen, § 1332 applies to both United States citizens and people who live in other countries. What about a United States citizen who is domiciled abroad? May that person avail herself of diversity jurisdiction? The somewhat surprising answer is no. Because that person does not have a domicile in any state, she is not a "citizen of a state." And because that person is a citizen of the United States, she is not a citizen or subject of a foreign state. Thus, the United States citizen domiciled abroad may not sue or be sued using diversity jurisdiction. Of course, like anyone else federal question jurisdiction may exist in cases involving that person.

b. Time for Determining Diversity

"[T]he jurisdiction of the Court depends upon the state of things at the time of the action brought." *Mollan v. Torrance*, 22 U.S. (9 Wheat) 537, 6 L.Ed. 154 (1824). As discussed above, the amount in controversy is measured as of the date the complaint is filed. Similarly, for purposes of determining diversity a court will look only to the citizenship of the parties on the date the case begins. Post-filing changes of residence do not affect the court's jurisdiction.

What happens if the requirements for diversity are not satisfied on the date the case is commenced, but no one objects and the problem is cured by the time the case is tried? Under application of the traditional rule, those post-filing events would not matter, and the case would have to be dismissed. However, in *Caterpillar Inc. v. Lewis*, 519 U.S. 61, 117 S.Ct. 467, 136 L.Ed.2d 437 (1996), the Supreme Court held that a federal court could exercise jurisdiction over a case where the complete diversity requirement was not met when the case began in federal court, but the non-diverse defendant had been dismissed before the court considered the jurisdictional issue.

Caterpillar created a potentially significant loophole in the traditional time-of-filing rule, and the Court explained the scope of its earlier decision in 2004. In *Grupo Dataflux v. Atlas Global Group, L.P.*, 541 U.S. 567, 124 S.Ct. 1920, 158 L.Ed.2d 866 (2004), a partnership sued a corporation. Defendant corporation was a citizen of Mexico. As discussed above, a partnership's citizenship is determined by the citizenship of its members. At the time the case was commenced, two of the partners were from Mexico, while the others were citizens of states in the United States. The case accordingly failed the complete diversity requirement because there were aliens on both sides.

Defendant did not challenge jurisdiction in the early stages of the case. A month before trial, the two Mexican partners left the partnership, leaving only United States citizens as partners. The case went to trial, and a judgment was rendered against defendant.

After judgment, defendant challenged subject-matter jurisdiction, invoking the time-of-filing rule. Plaintiff argued that under *Caterpillar*, the jurisdictional defect had been "cured" when the two alien partners left the partnership. The Court disagreed and dismissed the case, distinguishing *Caterpillar*. In *Caterpillar*, there had been a change in the people who were parties to the suit. In *Grupo*, by contrast, the parties remained the same, but meanwhile their citizenship had changed:

> To our knowledge, the Court has never approved a deviation from the rule articulated by Chief Justice Marshall in 1829 that "where there is *no* change of party, a jurisdiction depending on the condition of the party is governed by that condition, as it was at the commencement of the suit." *Conolly*, 27 U.S. 556, 2 Pet., at 556, (emphasis added). Unless the Court is to manufacture a brand-new exception to the time-of-filing rule, dismissal for lack of subject-matter jurisdiction is the only option available in this case. The purported cure arose not from a change in the parties to the action, but from a change in the citizenship of a continuing party. Withdrawal of the Mexican partners from Atlas did not change the fact that Atlas . . . remained a party to the action. True, the composition of the partnership, and consequently its citizenship, changed. But allowing a citizenship change to cure the jurisdictional defect that existed at the time of filing would contravene the principle articulated by Chief Justice Marshall in *Conolly*. We decline to do today what the Court has refused to do for the past 175 years.

c. Manipulating § 1332

In many cases, parties attempt to tinker with the structure of the underlying dispute in an attempt to create or destroy diversity. As you might imagine, legislatures and courts have tried to control such manipulation. A federal court can avail itself of several different tools to deal with attempts to evade the requirements of § 1332.

Nominal and fraudulently joined parties. The easiest way for a party to prevent a federal court from exercising diversity jurisdiction is to make sure that at least one of the plaintiffs is from the same state as one of the defendants. In that case, the complete diversity rule bars jurisdiction. Therefore, a plaintiff who wants to make sure that her case is heard in state court will join with another plaintiff, or add another defendant, who destroys complete diversity.

In most cases, a plaintiff can keep a case out of federal court by joining nondiverse parties. However, if the claim involving the nondiverse party is a frivolous or illegitimate claim brought solely to prevent diversity, the court may exercise jurisdiction. *Junk v. Terminix Intern. Co.*, 628 F.3d 439 (8th Cir. 2010). Similarly, if the additional party is merely a nominal party with no real claim or liability in the matter, the court may ignore that party in determining whether diversity exists. Perhaps the best-known case involving nominal parties is *Rose v. Giamatti*, 721 F.Supp. 906 (S.D. Ohio 1989), in which the famous baseball player Pete Rose sued to challenge his exclusion from baseball. Rose sued the Commissioner of Baseball, the Cincinnati Reds, and Major League Baseball. Although Rose and the latter two defendants were citizens of Ohio, the court held it had diversity jurisdiction. It reasoned that because Rose had no real claim against the Reds or Major League Baseball, the citizenship of those nominal defendants would be ignored.

Realignment of parties. The complete diversity rule requires that no plaintiff be from the same state as any defendant. Whether a plaintiff is from the same state as another plaintiff—or whether a defendant is from the same state as another defendant—is irrelevant. In some situations, the parties may construct a case in which two parties who are at odds with each other nevertheless end up as co-plaintiffs or defendants. This is not always done in bad faith, as in certain types of disputes it may be difficult to ascertain whether a party is properly a plaintiff or a defendant. In situations where a party is wrongly joined, a court has considerable power to realign the parties, putting them into their proper role. As one court stated:

> A plaintiff's alignment of the parties, however, is not determinative. In considering whether there is complete diversity, a federal court must look beyond the nominal designation of the parties in the pleadings and should realign the parties according to their real interests in the dispute.

Safeco Ins. Co. v. City of White House, 36 F.3d 540, 545 (6th Cir. 1994). See also *Indianapolis v. Chase Nat'l Bank*, 314 U.S. 63, 62 S.Ct. 15, 86 L.Ed. 47 (1941). Realignment is especially likely to occur in cases involving declaratory relief. In *Chase Nat'l Bank*, for example, a lender who had been granted a mortgage on certain leased property sued both the landlord and a tenant for a declaration that the lease between the two defendants was valid and enforceable. The Court held that because both the lender and the landlord wanted the lease enforced, the landlord should be realigned as a plaintiff rather than a defendant. However, because the landlord and the tenant were from the same state, the case no longer satisfied the complete diversity rule, defeating diversity jurisdiction.

Collusive joinder. Another powerful tool in the federal court's arsenal is § 1359, which provides that a federal court cannot exercise diversity jurisdiction over a case "in which any party, by assignment or otherwise, has been improperly or collusively . . . joined to invoke the jurisdiction of such court." Note that this statute only applies to acts designed to create diversity, not acts (like the fraudulent joinder described above) done to destroy diversity. Most cases in which the court invokes § 1359 involve assignments of claims. If a party from state A makes a genuine assignment of her claim to a party from state B, the court will consider the citizenship of the assignee. However, if the assignment is a mere sham, the assignment will be ignored, and the court will use the assignor's citizenship. An example of a sham assignment is one where the price paid for the assignment is 95% of whatever assignee recovers when it sues on the obligation. *Kramer v. Caribbean Mills, Inc.*, 394 U.S. 823, 89 S.Ct. 1487, 23 L.Ed.2d 9 (1969).

Legal representatives. In some situations, a party is appointed to represent the rights of another. If the representation involves litigation, the action is brought in the name of the representative. Therefore, a party could create or destroy diversity by the simple expediency of appointing a legal representative who lives in a different state than the represented party. § 1332(c)(2) greatly curtails this "back door" way into federal court. Under that section, the legal representative of an infant, incompetent, or the estate of a decedent is treated as having the same citizenship as the represented party.

Insurance. § 1332(c)(1) contains a special rule that applies to insurance companies. If a plaintiff brings a direct action against an insurance company, the insurance company will be a citizen not only of its state of incorporation and principal place of business, but also a citizen of the same state(s) as the insured (if the insured is a corporation, it may have two citizenships of its own). Like the rule governing personal representatives discussed in the prior note, this provision makes it more difficult for the parties to get a dispute into federal court by a judicious choice of insurance company. Note that this provision only applies to liability insurance. Moreover, not all states allow direct actions against insurance companies. In most states, plaintiffs sue the insured even though the case will actually be defended by—and any judgment paid by—the insurance company.

d. States

Both § 1332 and Article III of the Constitution speak in terms of citizens of a "State." However, the United States includes a number of regions that are not technically states, including the District of Columbia, Puerto Rico, various federal territories, and federal protectorates. May citizens who are domiciled in these areas qualify for diversity jurisdiction? § 1332(e) explicitly addresses this question. It provides that the term "State" in § 1332 "includes the Territories, the District of Columbia, and the Commonwealth of Puerto Rico." Therefore, Congress clearly intends for citizens of these areas to enjoy the benefits of diversity jurisdiction at the same level as citizens of the states.

Whether Congress has the authority to extend diversity to these parties, however, is another matter. After all, Article III limits diversity jurisdiction to disputes between citizens of States. And the notion of a State is a term of art in the Constitution. If the territories, Puerto Rico, and the District are not "States" within the meaning of Article III, Congress has no authority to give the federal courts diversity jurisdiction in state-law suits involving these parties.

The Supreme Court considered the constitutionality of § 1332(e) in *National Mutual Insurance Co. v. Tidewater Transfer Co.*, 337 U.S. 582, 69 S.Ct. 1173, 93 L.Ed. 1556 (1949). Although the Court upheld the statute, the opinion was badly fractured, with no clear majority. Two Justices concluded the District of Columbia was a "State" for purposes of Article III. The remaining seven disagreed. Three other Justices concluded Congress could give the federal courts jurisdiction over the dispute even if the District was not a state. The remaining six rejected this view. Nevertheless, because a total of five Justices voted that § 1332(e) was constitutional, the decision upheld the statute—even though a majority of the Justices rejected each of the two theories offered to sustain the statute.

e. Exceptions to Diversity Jurisdiction

Generally speaking, federal courts sitting in diversity may hear any claim regardless of the nature of the dispute. However, there are exceptions to this rule. The Supreme Court has held that cases involving certain issues fall outside of the diversity jurisdiction of the federal court. These exceptions fall within two broad categories, neither of which appears in the language of § 1332.

The first exception includes domestic relations and probate cases. Federal courts will not exercise diversity jurisdiction over the probate of a will. In addition, in *Ankenbrandt v. Richards*, 504 U.S. 689, 112 S.Ct. 2206, 119 L.Ed.2d 468 (1992), the Court reaffirmed older cases which held that federal courts may not exercise diversity jurisdiction over cases involving core issues of family law. This family law exception applies only to divorce, alimony, and child custody. Thus, although a federal court may not adjudicate a divorce, it may hear a breach of contract or a tort suit between spouses involved in a divorce proceeding, provided the other requirements of § 1332 are satisfied. The Court's rationale in *Ankenbrandt* turned in part on the fact that divorce, alimony, and child custody were historically matters that fell outside the authority of the English Chancery court. Therefore, when Congress granted the federal courts a similar chancery jurisdiction in the Judiciary Act of 1789, it did not intend for the federal courts to hear these cases. Although divorce, alimony, and child custody are now routinely heard in secular courts in the states, the Court noted that Congress had never acted to change § 1332 in a way that would extend federal jurisdiction to these matters.

The Court revisited the probate exception in *Marshall v. Marshall*, 547 U.S. 293, 126 S.Ct. 1735, 164 L.Ed.2d 480 (2006). The case involved the celebrity Anna Nicole Smith (whose real name was Vickie Lynn Marshall). After Smith's quite elderly husband died, Smith and one of her husband's sons disputed who was entitled to receive his vast estate. While the state-court will contest was proceeding, Smith filed for bankruptcy in federal court. The son filed a claim against her in the bankruptcy proceeding, arguing she had defamed him. Smith filed a counterclaim against the son, asserting that the son's challenges to the will tortiously interfered with Smith's expectation of receiving the bulk of the estate under the will. The son argued that the probate exception prevented the federal bankruptcy court from hearing the tortious interference counterclaim. The Supreme Court disagreed. As it had with the domestic relations exception in *Ankenbrandt*, the Court held that the probate exception did not apply to tort claims, even if those claims affected how assets would be distributed following death.

The second exception to diversity jurisdiction involves situations where the federal courts must abstain from exercising jurisdiction. In rare cases, a federal court sitting in diversity may be required to abstain from a case in situations where the underlying state law is unclear and where there are important state interests at stake. See *Railroad Commission v. Pullman Co.*, 312 U.S. 496, 61 S.Ct. 643, 85 L.Ed. 971 (1941); *Louisiana Power and Light Co. v. City of Thibodaux*, 360 U.S. 25, 79 S.Ct. 1070, 3 L.Ed.2d 1058 (1959); *Burford v. Sun Oil Co.*, 319 U.S. 315, 63 S.Ct. 1098, 87 L.Ed. 1424 (1943). Abstention is a complex topic that is far beyond the scope of an introductory Civil Procedure course. Note, however, that unlike the domestic relations and probate exceptions, abstention is a court-created doctrine, not an interpretation of § 1332.

f. Other Diversity Statutes

The discussion in this section focuses on 28 U.S.C. § 1332, the "general" diversity provision. However, § 1332 is not the only provision Congress has enacted to implement the Article III power to have the federal courts hear interstate and international disputes. A number of other provisions deal with other types of "diversity" cases. *See, e.g.*, 28 U.S.C. §§ 1335 (interpleader actions, discussed in Chapter 8); 1348 (actions involving national banks; bank deemed a citizen of a state where it is located); and 1354 (actions between citizens of the same state involving grants to the same land from more than one state; implements Article III, sec. 2, cl. 8, power).

PROBLEMS

1. P, a citizen of Michigan, sues D, a citizen of Wisconsin, for $100,000. P brings her case in state court. Does the state court have jurisdiction to hear the case?

2. P plans to sue D for $100,000 for medical malpractice. At the time of the medical procedure, P and D were citizens of Maryland. After the accident, however, P decided to move to Delaware. P has purchased a new home in Delaware, and a moving van is scheduled to come to P's home tomorrow to pack and move her belongings. If P files her action today, may she sue in federal court?

3. P sues D for $250,000 for breach of contract. When the action was commenced, P was a citizen of the District of Columbia, while D was a citizen of Idaho. The day after the action was commenced, however, P moved to Idaho and established a domicile in that state. D makes a timely request to dismiss the action for lack of subject-matter jurisdiction. How should the court rule?

4. P is a retired salesman. After retiring, P left his home in snowy North Dakota and established domicile in Costa Rica. However, P has kept his United States citizenship. When P fails to receive his commission check for sales he made during his last year on the job, he sues D, his former boss, for $85,000. D is a citizen of North Dakota. May the action be heard in federal court?

5. Same as Problem 4, except that P gave up his United States citizenship and became a citizen of Costa Rica.

6. P, a citizen of Pennsylvania, files a products liability action against D Corp. in federal court. P seeks $150,000 in damages. D Corp. was chartered in the state of Delaware. D Corp. has large factories in Massachusetts, Tennessee, and Nevada. The corporate offices, from which all significant decisions are made, are located in Pennsylvania. However, other than the corporate offices, D Corp. has no facilities in Pennsylvania. Nor does D Corp. sell its product in Pennsylvania (P bought the product while on a business trip to New York). D Corp. files a timely request to have P's case dismissed for lack of subject-matter jurisdiction. How should the court rule?

7. Same as Problem 6, except that P does not sue D Corp., but instead brings a direct action against Umbrella Insurance Company, a corporation that has issued a liability insurance policy covering D Corp. Umbrella is a

Utah corporation with its principal place of business in Texas. Umbrella files a timely request to have P's case dismissed for lack of subject-matter jurisdiction. How should the court rule?

8. Same as Problems 6 and 7, except that (i) P is a citizen of Texas, and (ii) P sues both D Corp. and Umbrella Insurance Company in a single action.

9. Lender sues Borrower for failure to make the final payment on a home loan. Lender is a citizen of Washington, and Borrower is a citizen of Alaska. Lender's complaint asks for the past-due principal payment ($70,000), $6,000 in interest accruing under the terms of the loan agreement prior to default, $5,500 in post-default interest, measured at the judgment rate, and $4,000 in attorneys' fees. After being served with the complaint, Borrower files a counterclaim for $90,000. Borrower claims that because Lender violated federal lending laws by making incorrect disclosures in the loan application process, Lender must return to Borrower all interest payments that Borrower made under the loan. Lender then moves to dismiss the case for lack of subject matter jurisdiction. How should the court rule?

10. P, a citizen of Connecticut, sues D, a citizen of Florida, in federal court. P asserts two claims. In the main claim, P alleges D owes him $70,000 for breach of contract. In the second count, P seeks $8,000 in damages for trespass, based upon the fact that D regularly walks his dog across a corner of the lot of P's Florida vacation home. The contract and trespass claims have nothing to do with each other. Moreover, no court in this state has ever awarded more than $150 in damages for a trespass claim involving someone walking across property. D files a timely request to dismiss the case for lack of subject-matter jurisdiction. How should the court rule?

11. P, a citizen of California, wants to sue D, a citizen of Georgia, for divorce. Because P and D are rich and famous celebrities, the court will be called upon to dispense property worth over ten million dollars. May P file the action in a federal court?

EXERCISE

Just as the federal statutes you have been studying define the types of cases a federal court can hear, there are state standards defining the various types of cases which can be heard by state courts. Typically, a state court of "general jurisdiction" can hear only cases involving a threshold amount of damages, or more. For example, a threshold amount for damages may be $5,000. The enabling statutes for state courts also describe categories of cases which are not heard by the courts of "general jurisdiction." For example, probate cases are commonly excepted from "general jurisdiction" cases.

For the state a) where you intend to practice after graduation, b) where your law school is located, and/or c) your professor assigns, go to that state's annotated statutes and research the standards defining how it is determined which courts hear which types of cases. Based on your research, print the rule and bring it to class for discussion. In addition, answer the following questions.

1. Identify the threshold amount of damages for a court of "general jurisdiction."

2. Identify whether there are certain types of cases recognized as exceptions to cases of "general jurisdiction."

D. SUPPLEMENTAL JURISDICTION

INTRODUCTORY PROBLEM

After he loses his life savings in a bad investment, Ian Investor decides to sue Brenda Broker, the person who recommended the investment. Ian would strongly prefer to sue in federal court. However, because Ian and Brenda are citizens of the same state, and because only state law affords Ian a remedy, Ian's case, standing by itself, would not qualify for either diversity or federal question jurisdiction. Ian comes to you, his attorney, to discuss his options.

During the conversation, Ian tells you about two friends of his who are also about to sue Brenda. Both of these soon-to-be plaintiffs made an investment similar to Ian's, relying on the exact same misleading representations by Brenda. Unlike Ian, however, these other plaintiffs can file in federal court. The first plaintiff, Nancy, is of diverse citizenship from Brenda, and has a claim in excess of $75,000. The second, Robert, can rely on federal question jurisdiction. Because Brenda made the representation to Robert by mail, rather than face-to-face as in the case of Ian and Nancy, Robert has a cause of action under the federal mail fraud provisions.

Ian asks whether he might be able to get his dispute into federal court by joining with either Nancy or Robert to sue Brenda. The cases are, after all, very closely related. Nancy and Robert have each told Ian that they are willing to have him as a co-plaintiff in their respective cases. Your quick review of Rule 20 assures you that Ian could join with either plaintiff. If Ian joins with either Nancy or Robert, may he bring his case in federal court?

Ian also has one other concern. Brenda told Robert that if anyone were to sue her, she would immediately file a counterclaim for any unpaid brokerage fees. Ian owes Brenda $9,000 in brokerage fees. Ian asks you whether the federal court would have jurisdiction over Brenda's state-law counterclaim.

What will you tell Ian?

Governing Law: 28 U.S.C. §§ 1331, 1332, and 1367.

One of the cardinal rules of federal subject-matter jurisdiction is that a federal court must have jurisdiction over every claim presented to it as part of a single case. Therefore, what may have seemed the easy answer to the Introductory problem will not work. The court would not have jurisdiction over Ian's claim—or Brenda's counterclaim—merely because they were part of Nancy's or Robert's proper diversity or federal question action. Instead, the court would have to dismiss Ian's claim and Brenda's counterclaim unless the parties could demonstrate a source of federal jurisdiction.

To this point, we have considered only two bases for federal jurisdiction, federal question and diversity. When determining whether federal question jurisdiction exists, courts analyze each claim separately to see if that claim asserts rights under federal law. In diversity cases, the complete diversity rule requires that no plaintiff can be from the same state as any defendant. Therefore, aside from the aggregation rules in diversity, neither § 1331 nor § 1332 allows a party to piggyback claims that do not qualify for federal jurisdiction with those that do qualify.

This section introduces a third source of federal subject-matter jurisdiction, called "supplemental" jurisdiction. The name is actually quite informative. Supplemental jurisdiction supplements federal question and diversity jurisdiction. In order for supplemental jurisdiction to work, there must be at least one claim by one plaintiff that independently qualifies for federal question or diversity jurisdiction. If such a claim exists, the court may be able to use supplemental jurisdiction to hear other claims in the case that do not by themselves qualify for federal subject-matter jurisdiction. Supplemental jurisdiction will never be the sole basis for jurisdiction in the case; instead, it always works in conjunction with one of the other forms.

If left unchecked, supplemental jurisdiction could undermine the limitations on federal question and diversity jurisdiction discussed in the prior sections. For example, in the Introductory Problem, allowing Ian to use supplemental jurisdiction to join with Nancy would contradict the complete diversity rule. As you will see, Congress has placed important limits on the use of supplemental jurisdiction in order to preserve some of the limits on diversity jurisdiction.

1. THE THEORETICAL BASIS FOR SUPPLEMENTAL JURISDICTION

UNITED MINE WORKERS v. GIBBS
383 U.S. 715, 86 S.Ct. 1130, 16 L.Ed.2d 218 (1966)

JUSTICE BRENNAN delivered the opinion of the Court.

Respondent Paul Gibbs was awarded compensatory and punitive damages in this action against petitioner United Mine Workers of America (UMW) for alleged violations of § 303 of the Labor Management

Relations Act, 1947, as amended, and of the common law of Tennessee. The case grew out of the rivalry between the United Mine Workers and the Southern Labor Union over representation of workers in the southern Appalachian coal fields. Tennessee Consolidated Coal Company, not a party here, laid off 100 miners of the UMW's Local 5881 when it closed one of its mines in southern Tennessee during the spring of 1960. Late that summer, Grundy Company, a wholly owned subsidiary of Consolidated, hired respondent as mine superintendent to attempt to open a new mine on Consolidated's property at nearby Gray's Creek through use of members of the Southern Labor Union. As part of the arrangement, Grundy also gave respondent a contract to haul the mine's coal to the nearest railroad loading point.

On August 15 and 16, 1960, armed members of Local 5881 forcibly prevented the opening of the mine, threatening respondent and beating an organizer for the rival union. The members of the local believed Consolidated had promised them the jobs at the new mine; they insisted that if anyone would do the work, they would. . . . There was no further violence at the mine site; a picket line was maintained there for nine months; and no further attempts were made to open the mine during that period.

Respondent lost his job as superintendent, and never entered into performance of his haulage contract. He testified that he soon began to lose other trucking contracts and mine leases he held in nearby areas. Claiming these effects to be the result of a concerted union plan against him, he sought recovery not against Local 5881 or its members, but only against petitioner, the international union. The suit was brought in the United States District Court for the Eastern District of Tennessee, and jurisdiction was premised on allegations of secondary boycotts* under § 303. The state law claim, for which jurisdiction was based upon the doctrine of pendent jurisdiction, asserted "an unlawful conspiracy and an unlawful boycott aimed at him and (Grundy) to maliciously, wantonly and willfully interfere with his contract of employment and with his contract of haulage." . . .

The jury's verdict was that the UMW had violated both § 303 and state law. . . . On motion, the trial court set aside the award of damages with respect to the haulage contract on the ground that damage was unproved. It also held that union pressure on Grundy to discharge respondent as supervisor would constitute only a primary dispute with Grundy, as respondent's employer, and hence was not cognizable as a claim under § 303. Interference with the employment relationship was cognizable as a state claim, however, and a remitted award was sustained

---

* A "secondary boycott" occurs when a union that has a labor dispute with Employer X pickets, refuses to work for, or refuses otherwise to deal with, Employer Y, if the union is attempting to convince Y to quit dealing with X. Secondary boycotts are illegal under federal labor law. [Eds.]

on the state law claim. The Court of Appeals for the Sixth Circuit affirmed. We granted certiorari. We reverse [on grounds other than pendent jurisdiction].

A threshold question is whether the District Court properly entertained jurisdiction of the claim based on Tennessee law. . . .

The Court held in *Hurn v. Oursler*, 289 U.S. 238, that state law claims are appropriate for federal court determination if they form a separate but parallel ground for relief also sought in a substantial claim based on federal law. The Court distinguished permissible from non-permissible exercises of federal judicial power over state law claims by contrasting "a case where two distinct grounds in support of a single cause of action are alleged, one only of which presents a federal question, and a case where two separate and distinct causes of action are alleged, one only of which is federal in character. In the former, where the federal question averred is not plainly wanting in substance, the federal court, even though the federal ground be not established, may nevertheless retain and dispose of the case upon the nonfederal ground; in the latter it may not do so upon the nonfederal cause of action." The question is into which category the present action fell.

Hurn was decided in 1933, before the unification of law and equity by the Federal Rules of Civil Procedure. At the time, the meaning of "cause of action" was a subject of serious dispute; the phrase might "mean one thing for one purpose and something different for another." *United States v. Memphis Cotton Oil Co.*, 288 U.S. 62, 67–68. The Court in *Hurn* identified what it meant by the term by citation of *Baltimore S.S. Co. v. Phillips*, 274 U.S. 316, a case in which "cause of action" had been used to identify the operative scope of the doctrine of res judicata. In that case the Court had noted that "the whole tendency of our decisions is to require a plaintiff to try his whole cause of action and his whole case at one time," 274 U.S., at 320. It stated its holding in the following language, quoted in part in the *Hurn* opinion:

> A cause of action does not consist of facts, but of the unlawful violation of a right which the facts show. The number and variety of the facts alleged do not establish more than one cause of action so long as their result, whether they be considered severally or in combination, is the violation of but one right by a single legal wrong. The mere multiplication of grounds of negligence alleged as causing the same injury does not result in multiplying the causes of action. "The facts are merely the means, and not the end. They do not constitute the cause of action, but they show its existence by making the wrong appear."

Id., at 321.

With the adoption of the Federal Rules of Civil Procedure and the unified form of action, Fed.Rule Civ.Proc. 2, much of the controversy over "cause of action" abated.... Under the Rules, the impulse is toward entertaining the broadest possible scope of action consistent with fairness to the parties; joinder of claims, parties and remedies is strongly encouraged. Yet because the *Hurn* question involves issues of jurisdiction as well as convenience, there has been some tendency to limit its application to cases in which the state and federal claims are, as in *Hurn*, "little more than the equivalent of different epithets to characterize the same group of circumstances." 289 U.S., at 246.

This limited approach is unnecessarily grudging. Pendent jurisdiction, in the sense of judicial power, exists whenever there is a claim "arising under (the) Constitution, the Laws of the United States, and Treaties made, or which shall be made, under their Authority...," U.S. Const., Art. III, § 2, and the relationship between that claim and the state claim permits the conclusion that the entire action before the court comprises but one constitutional "case." The federal claim must have substance sufficient to confer subject matter jurisdiction on the court. The state and federal claims must derive from a common nucleus of operative fact. But if, considered without regard to their federal or state character, a plaintiff's claims are such that he would ordinarily be expected to try them all in one judicial proceeding, then, assuming substantiality of the federal issues, there is power in federal courts to hear the whole.

That power need not be exercised in every case in which it is found to exist. It has consistently been recognized that pendent jurisdiction is a doctrine of discretion, not of plaintiff's right. Its justification lies in considerations of judicial economy, convenience and fairness to litigants; if these are not present a federal court should hesitate to exercise jurisdiction over state claims.... Needless decisions of state law should be avoided both as a matter of comity and to promote justice between the parties, by procuring for them a surer-footed reading of applicable law. Certainly, if the federal claims are dismissed before trial, even though not insubstantial in a jurisdictional sense, the state claims should be dismissed as well. Similarly, if it appears that the state issues substantially predominate, whether in terms of proof, of the scope of the issues raised, or of the comprehensiveness of the remedy sought, the state claims may be dismissed without prejudice and left for resolution to state tribunals. There may, on the other hand, be situations in which the state claim is so closely tied to questions of federal policy that the argument for exercise of pendent jurisdiction is particularly strong. In the present case, for example, the allowable scope of the state claim implicates the federal doctrine of pre-emption; while this interrelationship does not create statutory federal question jurisdiction, its existence is relevant to the exercise of discretion. Finally, there may be reasons independent of jurisdictional considerations, such as the likelihood of jury confusion in treating divergent legal theories of relief, that would justify separating state and federal claims for trial. If so, jurisdiction should ordinarily be refused.

The question of power will ordinarily be resolved on the pleadings. But the issue whether pendent jurisdiction has been properly assumed is one which remains open throughout the litigation. Pretrial procedures or even the trial itself may reveal a substantial hegemony of state law claims, or likelihood of jury confusion, which could not have been anticipated at the pleading stage.... Once it appears that a state claim constitutes the real body of a case, to which the federal claim is only an appendage, the state claim may fairly be dismissed.

We are not prepared to say that in the present case the District Court exceeded its discretion in proceeding to judgment on the state claim. We may assume for purposes of decision that the District Court was correct in its holding that the claim of pressure on Grundy to terminate the employment contract was outside the purview of § 303. Even so, the § 303 claims based on secondary pressures on Grundy relative to the haulage contract and on other coal operators generally were substantial....

It is true that the § 303 claims ultimately failed and that the only recovery allowed respondent was on the state claim. We cannot confidently say, however, that the federal issues were so remote or played such a minor role at the trial that in effect the state claim only was tried.... The jury returned verdicts against petitioner on those § 303 claims, and it was only on petitioner's motion for a directed verdict and a judgment n.o.v. that the verdicts on those claims were set aside.... Moreover, the question whether the permissible scope of the state claim was limited by the doctrine of pre-emption afforded a special reason for the exercise of pendent jurisdiction; the federal courts are particularly appropriate bodies for the application of pre-emption principles. We thus conclude that although it may be that the District Court might, in its sound discretion, have dismissed the state claim, the circumstances show no error in refusing to do so.

[The Court then reversed the lower court's decision on the merits.]

NOTES AND QUESTIONS

1. *Terminology.* The title of this section is "supplemental jurisdiction." But the Court in *Gibbs* never uses that term, speaking instead in terms of "pendent" jurisdiction. Other cases dealt with what was called "ancillary" jurisdiction. Although there were important differences between pendent and ancillary jurisdiction, those differences are of little more than historical interest. As you will see in the next subsection, Congress eventually passed a statute that merged both pendent and ancillary jurisdiction, and relabeled it "supplemental" jurisdiction.

2. At one level, the Court's decision in *Gibbs* is fairly straightforward. Earlier Supreme Court decisions allowed a federal court to hear state-law claims between non-diverse parties as long as there was a sufficient connection between those claims and claims arising under federal law. These early decisions, including the *Hurn* case discussed in *Gibbs*, justified the rule based on notions of claim preclusion (see Chapter 13). If the non-federal claims would be barred by claim preclusion if not raised in the first action, it certainly makes sense to allow a federal court to hear those non-federal claims along with the federal claim.

In one sense, *Gibbs* merely reflects the evolution of the law of claim preclusion. Courts in the 1800s used a very formalistic approach when dealing with claim preclusion. If the omitted claim involved the same "primary right" as that litigated in the case, the omitted claim would be barred. *Hurn*'s test for supplemental jurisdiction uses this notion of same primary right. By the time of *Gibbs*, however, the law of claim preclusion had changed to the point where an omitted claim would be barred as long as it arose from the same underlying event as the claim presented to the court, regardless of whether the two claims involved the same "primary right." The *Gibbs* test is still based on practical notions of efficiency, but simply applies a more modern test for determining when two claims should be joined.

3. Beneath that simple veneer lie some complex and difficult issues. Federal subject-matter jurisdiction involves much more than efficiency. As noted in the Introduction to this chapter, the Constitution and the Judicial Code keep federal jurisdiction in check in order to preserve the role of the state judiciaries. Is *Gibbs* ignoring these limitations when it concludes that a federal court should be able to exercise jurisdiction over a claim that does not by itself qualify for federal question or diversity jurisdiction? How can "considerations of judicial economy, convenience, and fairness to litigants," which the Court says are the justifications for pendent jurisdiction, override the clear provisions in the Constitution and federal law?

4. *Gibbs* does deal with the Constitution. How does the Court conclude that pendent jurisdiction is consistent with Article III? Compare the Court's brief discussion of Article III with the actual terminology of Article III, § 2. The issue in *Gibbs* is whether the court can exercise jurisdiction over a claim. Notice that Article III does not speak in terms of "claims," but instead gives the federal courts jurisdiction over "cases" and "controversies." According to *Gibbs*, what is the difference between a claim and a case or controversy?

Incidentally, there is a difference between the terms "case" and "controversy" in Article III. A case includes both civil and criminal matters. A controversy is a civil dispute. Article III allows the federal courts to exercise jurisdiction over "all cases" arising under federal law, but only "controversies" involving diverse citizens, or states and the citizens of another state. One practical implication of this difference is that while federal courts may hear criminal prosecutions involving violations of federal law, they may not hear state-law criminal cases, even if brought by a state against a citizen of another state or a foreigner.

2. THE SUPPLEMENTAL JURISDICTION STATUTE

Pendent and ancillary jurisdiction evolved in the federal courts in cases like *Gibbs* and *Hurn v. Ousler*. As a result, there was a sort of tension between pendent and ancillary jurisdiction and the federal statutes allocating jurisdiction to the federal courts, which made no mention of this expanded jurisdiction. However, the long history of pendent and ancillary jurisdiction helped validate it. After all, if Congress did not approve of the doctrines, it could always enact legislation to abolish them.

Congress eventually *did* act—not to overturn the doctrine established in *Gibbs* and the other cases, but expressly to authorize it. In 1990, Congress enacted 28 U.S.C. § 1367, which creates a form of jurisdiction called "supplemental" jurisdiction.[2]

One of Congress's main goals in enacting § 1367 was to unify and simplify the courts' jurisdiction over pendent and ancillary claims. However, Congress also hoped to clean up the law by abolishing some of the limits and distinctions adopted over the years by the courts. Unfortunately, the statute as written is not a model of clarity. Although § 1367 does get rid of some of the problems that arose in the case law, it creates other new problems that courts are still struggling to resolve.

The most obvious change § 1367 makes is in terminology. § 1367 substitutes the single term "supplemental" for both of the older terms "ancillary" and "pendent." More importantly, the statute also abolishes the analytical distinctions that used to exist between pendent and ancillary jurisdiction. Now, a case is dealt with the same way under § 1367 regardless of whether it historically would have been considered a case of pendent or ancillary—or "pendent party," yet another variation—jurisdiction.

Section 1367 establishes a two-part test for supplemental jurisdiction. First, the court applies § 1367(a). This section asks whether the claim in question (that is, the claim that could not be heard by a federal court on its own), and another claim in the case that the federal court can hear, "form part of the same case or controversy under Article III of the United States Constitution." In determining whether two claims form part of the same Article III case, most courts use *Gibbs*'s "common nucleus of operative fact" test. The Court in *Gibbs* used that test in explaining how supplemental jurisdiction fit within the jurisdiction that Article III allows federal courts to exercise.

---

[2] Note that § 1367 is not the only source of "supplemental" jurisdiction. § 1338(b), which gives the federal courts jurisdiction over state-law unfair competition claims brought in connection with claims under federal intellectual property law, is another example. Moreover, the statutes governing appellate court and Supreme Court jurisdiction give those courts the power to hear the entire case being appealed, including not only the federal claims but also the state claims.

The second part of the analysis asks whether the case falls into one of the exceptions listed in § 1367(b) and (c). Although these two subsections are both exceptions, they are very different in nature. § 1367(b) is an issue of power. If a claim is barred by that subsection, a federal court cannot hear it, no matter how efficient it would be to hear the claims in one case. Note, however, that § 1367(b) only applies in multi-party cases. In a case involving only a single plaintiff and defendant, and no additional parties such as third-party defendants, § 1367(b) is not a factor.

The other exception, set out in § 1367(c), reflects the discussion of discretion in *Gibbs*. If the court determines that the state-law claim is the heart and soul of the case, for example, the federal court may refuse to hear the state-law claim. Note that although some of the factors listed in § 1367(c) match those discussed in *Gibbs*, the statute also brings in new factors to consider. Take a moment to review the statute, identifying which of the § 1367(c) factors are mentioned in *Gibbs* and which were added by Congress.

Do §§ 1367(b) and (c) list all the exceptions to supplemental jurisdiction? What about the "family law" exception to diversity jurisdiction discussed in Section C.4.e of this Chapter? One court of appeals has held that the same family law exception precludes a court from exercising supplemental jurisdiction over family law claims, even when they are brought along with a related federal question claim. *United States v. MacPhail*, 149 Fed.Appx. 449 (6th Cir.).

PROBLEMS

1. After a series of highly-publicized cases in which dogs attacked people, Congress enacts the Federal Vicious Dog Act of 2014 ["FVDA"]. FVDA creates a federal cause of action, enabling anyone who suffers personal injury "from a dog bite or otherwise at the hands [*sic*] of a dog" to sue the dog's owner.

Abramson and Cross are neighbors, and live in the same state. Relations between the two are strained, in large part because of Cross's obnoxious terrier "Antoc." Antoc is an avid barker, cheerfully raising his voice to challenge every squirrel or chipmunk (real or perceived) who dares enter his yard. To make matters worse, Cross allows Antoc to roam the neighborhood, and Antoc, being a terrier, naturally views this as an invitation to get into trouble.

One day, while Abramson is doing yard work in his own yard, Antoc runs up to Abramson and nips him on the ankle. Abramson has had enough. He sues Cross in federal court under FVDA for the personal injury, seeking $500 in damages. While he is at it, Abramson decides to bring a claim for the many hours of sleep he has lost due to Antoc's barking. However, as FVDA only creates a claim for "personal injury," Abramson relies on the state law of nuisance for this second claim. Abramson seeks an additional $1000 in damages, together with an injunction, for the nuisance. Will the federal court have subject-matter jurisdiction over both claims?

2. Same facts as Problem 1, except that Abramson does not bring the nuisance claim. Instead, Abramson decides to sue not only for the pain and suffering, but also for the emotional distress and embarrassment that he suffered in the nip incident. However, as FVDA does not allow recovery of emotional distress, Abramson joins a state-law battery claim to his FVDA claim. Abramson seeks $500 under FVDA, and $2000 under the battery claim. Will the federal court have subject-matter jurisdiction over both claims?

3. Same facts as Problem 1, except that Abramson did not bring either a FVDA or nuisance claim. Instead, he brings state-law battery and negligence claims. Abramson seeks $500 in personal injury damages for the bite, and $10,000 for the emotional distress he experienced in the bite incident. However, because negligence law does not allow recovery for emotional harm, only physical, Abramson seeks only $500 under the negligence claim.

4. Same facts as Problem 1, except that Abramson brings a FVDA claim, but not a nuisance claim. During the raid on Abramson's yard, Antoc did not confine his attention to Abramson's ankle. Instead, Antoc also used the occasion to dig up Abramson's flower bed. Abramson therefore decides to add a claim for the damaged flowers to his FVDA suit against Cross. However, because FVDA only deals with personal injuries, Abramson seeks recovery for this damage under a state-law trespass claim. Abramson seeks $500 under FVDA, and $1000 under trespass. Will the federal court have subject-matter jurisdiction over both claims?

5. Same facts as Problem 1, except that Abramson does not sue after the first nip. Instead, he talks to Cross, and politely asks him to "keep that mutt in your yard." Cross blithely ignores Abramson's request. Antoc enters Abramson's yard again one week later, and nips him on the other ankle. Having enough, Abramson decides to sue for both nips in the same action. He sues for the first nip under FVDA. However, the state in which Abramson and Cross live also has its own vicious dog law. This law differs from FVDA in two ways. First, it adopts the common-law "one free bite" rule, under which the owner is not liable unless the dog has bitten once before. Second, it provides for minimum damages of $10,000, regardless of the harm suffered. Because this is Antoc's second attack, Abramson seeks recovery for the second nip only under state law. Will the federal court have subject-matter jurisdiction over both claims?

6. Same facts as Problem 1, except that Abramson does not sue immediately after the first nip. Instead, he talks to Cross in an attempt to resolve the problem amicably. Cross reacts angrily, accusing Abramson of being a dog-hater. To make matters worse, Cross begins to spread rumors about Abramson, telling the neighbors that Abramson is lying about the

supposed nip on the ankle. Abramson has had enough, and sues Cross under FVDA for the nip. He also joins a state-law defamation claim, alleging that Cross's false statements are damaging Abramson's character. Abramson seeks $500 under FVDA, and $2000 for defamation. Will the federal court have subject-matter jurisdiction over both claims?

7. Same facts as Problem 1, except that Abramson seeks only $100 for the dog nip, and $10,000 for the nuisance. Abramson's nuisance claim is admittedly somewhat unusual. State law has so far followed the traditional rule that nuisance is the unreasonable use of someone's land. Although some other states have begun to extend nuisance to the unreasonable use of personal property, the state where Abramson and Cross live has not yet decided the issue. Moreover, no state has yet recognized a claim for nuisance based on the actions of a dog. Will the federal court have subject-matter jurisdiction over both claims?

3. SUPPLEMENTAL JURISDICTION AND JOINDER OF PARTIES

The previous section demonstrated how a plaintiff can use § 1367 to join state-law claims to a case involving an underlying federal claim. But a close reading of the statute makes it clear that supplemental jurisdiction is not limited to joinder of claims. Instead, the statute may also make it possible to join additional parties to the case even without a federal claim against those parties, or allow defendants, third-party defendants and others to file their own non-federal claims as part of the action.

In cases involving multiple parties, § 1367(b) comes into play. That section prevents the use of supplemental jurisdiction for certain specific claims. Unlike § 1367(c), § 1367(b) is not a question of discretion—if one of the listed claims is involved, the federal court has no power to hear the claim.

Section 1367(b) often proves exceptionally difficult to students dealing with it for the first time. Admittedly, the provision is worded in a very technical fashion. However, if you are careful and work through it mechanically, the provision is relatively straightforward. As a bit of advice, you should fight the temptation to paraphrase that section in your own words—the number of tricky permutations makes that approach dangerous. Basically, § 1367(b) uses a three-step analysis to determine if a claim is barred. First, § 1367(b) precludes supplemental jurisdiction only if the *sole* basis for federal jurisdiction over the original claim is § 1332 diversity jurisdiction. If the original federal claim is a federal question, § 1367(b) simply does not apply. Second, the claim in question must be a claim by a plaintiff. Ordinarily, this will be relatively obvious. But you will see that even this issue can be tricky. Third, the claim must be brought against a party joined under the listed rules. Part of the confusion that has arisen in applying § 1367 is that the rules listed do not exhaust all of the joinder provisions in the Federal Rules. The following case illustrates the ambiguity.

EXXON MOBIL CORP. V. ALLAPATTAH SERVICES, INC.
545 U.S. 546, 125 S.Ct. 2611, 162 L.Ed.2d 502 (2005)

JUSTICE KENNEDY delivered the opinion of the Court.

These consolidated cases present the question whether a federal court in a diversity action may exercise supplemental jurisdiction over additional plaintiffs whose claims do not satisfy the minimum amount-in-controversy requirement, provided the claims are part of the same case or controversy as the claims of plaintiffs who do allege a sufficient amount in controversy. Our decision turns on the correct interpretation of 28 U.S.C. § 1367. The question has divided the Courts of Appeals, and we granted certiorari to resolve the conflict.

We hold that, where the other elements of jurisdiction are present and at least one named plaintiff in the action satisfies the amount-in-controversy requirement, § 1367 does authorize supplemental jurisdiction over the claims of other plaintiffs in the same Article III case or controversy, even if those claims are for less than the jurisdictional amount specified in the statute setting forth the requirements for diversity jurisdiction. . . .

I

In 1991, about 10,000 Exxon dealers filed a class-action suit against the Exxon Corporation in the United States District Court for the Northern District of Florida. The dealers alleged an intentional and systematic scheme by Exxon under which they were overcharged for fuel purchased from Exxon. The plaintiffs invoked the District Court's § 1332(a) diversity jurisdiction. After a unanimous jury verdict in favor of the plaintiffs, the District Court certified the case for interlocutory review, asking whether it had properly exercised § 1367 supplemental jurisdiction over the claims of class members who did not meet the jurisdictional minimum amount in controversy.

The Court of Appeals for the Eleventh Circuit upheld the District Court's extension of supplemental jurisdiction to these class members. . . . This decision accords with the views of the Courts of Appeals for the Fourth, Sixth, and Seventh Circuits. The Courts of Appeals for the Fifth and Ninth Circuits, adopting a similar analysis of the statute, have held that in a diversity class action the unnamed class members need not meet the amount-in-controversy requirement, provided the named class members do. These decisions, however, are unclear on whether all the named plaintiffs must satisfy this requirement.

In the other case now before us the Court of Appeals for the First Circuit took a different position on the meaning of § 1367(a). In that case, a 9-year-old girl sued Star-Kist in a diversity action in the United States District Court for the District of Puerto Rico, seeking damages for unusually severe injuries she received when she sliced her finger on a tuna can. Her family joined in the suit, seeking damages for emotional distress and certain medical expenses. The District Court granted summary judgment to Star-Kist, finding that none of the plaintiffs met the minimum amount-in-controversy requirement. The Court of Appeals for the First Circuit, however, ruled that the injured girl, but not her family members, had made allegations of damages in the requisite amount.

The Court of Appeals then addressed whether, in light of the fact that one plaintiff met the requirements for original jurisdiction, supplemental jurisdiction over the remaining plaintiffs' claims was proper under § 1367. The court held that § 1367 authorizes supplemental jurisdiction only when the district court has original jurisdiction over the action, and that in a diversity case original jurisdiction is lacking if one plaintiff fails to satisfy the amount-in-controversy requirement. . . . The Court of Appeals for the First Circuit's view of § 1367 is, however, shared by the Courts of Appeal for the Third, Eighth, and Tenth Circuits, and the latter two Courts of Appeals have expressly applied this rule to class actions.

II

. . . The complete diversity requirement is not mandated by the Constitution, or by the plain text of § 1332(a). The Court, nonetheless, has adhered to the complete diversity rule in light of the purpose of the diversity requirement, which is to provide a federal forum for important disputes where state courts might favor, or be perceived as favoring, home-state litigants. The presence of parties from the same State on both sides of a case dispels this concern, eliminating a principal reason for conferring § 1332 jurisdiction over any of the claims in the action. The specific purpose of the complete diversity rule explains both why we have not adopted [*United Mine Workers v.*] *Gibbs*' expansive interpretive approach to this aspect of the jurisdictional statute and why *Gibbs* does not undermine the complete diversity rule. In order for a federal court to invoke supplemental jurisdiction under *Gibbs*, it must first have original jurisdiction over at least one claim in the action. Incomplete diversity destroys original jurisdiction with respect to all claims, so there is nothing to which supplemental jurisdiction can adhere.

In contrast to the diversity requirement, most of the other statutory prerequisites for federal jurisdiction, including the federal-question and amount-in-controversy requirements, can be analyzed claim by claim. True, it does not follow by necessity from this that a district court has authority to exercise supplemental jurisdiction over all claims provided there is original jurisdiction over just one. Before the enactment of § 1367, the Court declined in contexts other than the pendent-claim instance to follow *Gibbs*' expansive approach to interpretation of the jurisdictional statutes. . . .

Thus, with respect to plaintiff-specific jurisdictional requirements, the Court held in *Clark* v. *Paul Gray, Inc.*, 306 U.S. 583 (1939), that every plaintiff must separately satisfy the amount-in-controversy requirement. Though *Clark* was a federal-question case, at that time federal-question jurisdiction had an amount-in-controversy requirement analogous to the amount-in-controversy requirement for diversity cases. "Proper practice," *Clark* held, "requires that where each of several plaintiffs is bound to establish the jurisdictional amount with respect to his own claim, the suit should be dismissed as to those who fail to show that the requisite amount is involved." *Id.*, at 590. The Court reaffirmed this rule, in the context of a class action brought invoking § 1332(a) diversity jurisdiction, in *Zahn* v. *International Paper Co.*, 414 U.S. 291 (1973). . . .

As the jurisdictional statutes existed in 1989, then, here is how matters stood: First, the diversity requirement in § 1332(a) required complete diversity; absent complete diversity, the district court lacked original jurisdiction over all of the claims in the action. Second, if the district court had original jurisdiction over at least one claim, the jurisdictional statutes implicitly authorized supplemental jurisdiction over all other claims between the same parties arising out of the same Article III case or controversy. Third, even when the district court had original jurisdiction over one or more claims between particular parties, the jurisdictional statutes did not authorize supplemental jurisdiction over additional claims involving other parties. . . .

§ 1367(a) is a broad grant of supplemental jurisdiction over other claims within the same case or controversy, as long as the action is one in which the district courts would have original jurisdiction. The last sentence of § 1367(a) makes it clear that the grant of supplemental jurisdiction extends to claims involving joinder or intervention of additional parties. The single question before us, therefore, is whether a diversity case in which the claims of some plaintiffs satisfy the amount-in-controversy requirement, but the claims of others plaintiffs do not, presents a "civil action of which the district courts have original jurisdiction." If the answer is yes, § 1367(a) confers supplemental jurisdiction over all claims, including those that do not independently satisfy the amount-in-controversy requirement, if the claims are part of the same Article III case or controversy. If the answer is no, § 1367(a) is inapplicable and, in light of our holdings in *Clark* and *Zahn*, the district court has no statutory basis for exercising supplemental jurisdiction over the additional claims.

We now conclude the answer must be yes. When the well-pleaded complaint contains at least one claim that satisfies the amount-in-controversy requirement, and there are no other relevant jurisdictional defects, the district court, beyond all question, has original jurisdiction over that claim. The presence of other claims in the complaint, over which the district court may lack original jurisdiction, is of no moment. If the court has original jurisdiction over a single claim in the complaint, it has original jurisdiction over a "civil action" within the meaning of § 1367(a), even if the civil action over which it has jurisdiction comprises fewer claims than were included in the complaint. Once the court determines it has original jurisdiction over the civil action, it can turn to the question whether it has a constitutional and statutory basis for exercising supplemental jurisdiction over the other claims in the action. . . .

If § 1367(a) were the sum total of the relevant statutory language, our holding would rest on that language alone. The statute, of course, instructs us to examine § 1367(b) to determine if any of its exceptions apply, so we proceed to that section. While § 1367(b) qualifies the broad rule of § 1367(a), it does not withdraw supplemental jurisdiction over the claims of the additional parties at issue here. The specific exceptions to § 1367(a) contained in § 1367(b), moreover, provide additional support for our conclusion that § 1367(a) confers supplemental jurisdiction over these claims. § 1367(b), which applies only to diversity cases, withholds supplemental jurisdiction over the claims of plaintiffs proposed to be joined as indispensable parties under Federal Rule of Civil Procedure 19, or who seek to intervene pursuant to Rule 24. Nothing in the text of § 1367(b), however, withholds supplemental jurisdiction over the claims of plaintiffs permissively joined under Rule 20 or certified as class-action members pursuant to Rule 23. The natural, indeed the necessary, inference is that § 1367 confers supplemental jurisdiction over claims by Rule 20 and Rule 23 plaintiffs. This inference, at least with respect to Rule 20 plaintiffs, is strengthened by the fact that § 1367(b) explicitly excludes supplemental jurisdiction over claims against defendants joined under Rule 20.

We cannot accept the view, urged by some of the parties, commentators, and Courts of Appeals, that a district court lacks original jurisdiction over a civil action unless the court has original jurisdiction over every claim in the complaint. As we understand this position, it requires assuming either that all claims in the complaint must stand or fall as a single, indivisible "civil action" as a matter of definitional necessity—what we will refer to as the "indivisibility theory"—or else that the inclusion of a claim or party falling outside the district court's original jurisdiction somehow contaminates every other claim in the complaint, depriving the court of original jurisdiction over any of these claims—what we will refer to as the "contamination theory."

The indivisibility theory is easily dismissed, as it is inconsistent with the whole notion of supplemental jurisdiction. If a district court must have original jurisdiction over every claim in the complaint in order to have "original jurisdiction" over a "civil action," then in *Gibbs* there was no civil action of which the district court could assume original jurisdiction under § 1331, and so no basis for exercising supplemental jurisdiction over any of the claims....

The contamination theory, as we have noted, can make some sense in the special context of the complete diversity requirement because the presence of nondiverse parties on both sides of a lawsuit eliminates the justification for providing a federal forum. The theory, however, makes little sense with respect to the amount-in-controversy requirement, which is meant to ensure that a dispute is sufficiently important to warrant federal-court attention. The presence of a single nondiverse party may eliminate the fear of bias with respect to all claims, but the presence of a claim that falls short of the minimum amount in controversy does nothing to reduce the importance of the claims that do meet this requirement.

It is fallacious to suppose, simply from the proposition that § 1332 imposes both the diversity requirement and the amount-in-controversy requirement, that the contamination theory germane to the former is also relevant to the latter. There is no inherent logical connection between the amount-in-controversy requirement and § 1332 diversity jurisdiction. After all, federal-question jurisdiction once had an amount-in-controversy requirement as well. If such a requirement were revived under § 1331, it is clear beyond peradventure that § 1367(a) provides supplemental jurisdiction over federal-question cases where some, but not all, of the federal-law claims involve a sufficient amount in controversy. In other words, § 1367(a) unambiguously overrules the holding and the result in *Clark*. If that is so, however, it would be quite extraordinary to say that § 1367 did not also overrule *Zahn*, a case that was premised in substantial part on the holding in *Clark*....

It follows from this conclusion that the threshold requirement of § 1367(a) is satisfied in cases, like those now before us, where some, but not all, of the plaintiffs in a diversity action allege a sufficient amount in controversy. We hold that § 1367 by its plain text overruled *Clark* and *Zahn* and authorized supplemental jurisdiction over all claims by diverse parties arising out of the same Article III case or controversy, subject only to enumerated exceptions not applicable in the cases now before us....

The judgment of the Court of Appeals for the Eleventh Circuit is affirmed. The judgment of the Court of Appeals for the First Circuit is reversed, and the case is remanded for proceedings consistent with this opinion.

[The dissent of JUSTICE STEVENS, joined by JUSTICE BREYER, is omitted.]

JUSTICE GINSBURG, with whom JUSTICE STEVENS, JUSTICE O'CONNOR, and JUSTICE BREYER join, dissenting.

... The Court adopts a plausibly broad reading of § 1367, a measure that is hardly a model of the careful drafter's art. There is another plausible reading, however, one less disruptive of our jurisprudence regarding supplemental jurisdiction. If one reads § 1367(a) to instruct, as the statute's text suggests, that the district court must first have "original jurisdiction" over a "civil action" before supplemental jurisdiction can attach, then *Clark* and *Zahn* are preserved, and supplemental jurisdiction does not open the way for joinder of plaintiffs, or inclusion of class members, who do not independently meet the amount-in-controversy requirement. For the reasons that follow, I conclude that this narrower construction is the better reading of § 1367. ...

The Constitution broadly provides for federal-court jurisdiction in controversies "between Citizens of different States." Art. III, § 2, cl. 1. This Court has read that provision to demand no more than "minimal diversity," *i.e.*, so long as one party on the plaintiffs' side and one party on the defendants' side are of diverse citizenship, Congress may authorize federal courts to exercise diversity jurisdiction. Further, the Constitution includes no amount-in-controversy limitation on the exercise of federal jurisdiction. But from the start, Congress, as its measures have been construed by this Court, has limited federal court exercise of diversity jurisdiction in two principal ways. First, unless Congress specifies otherwise, diversity must be "complete," *i.e.*, all parties on plaintiffs' side must be diverse from all parties on defendants' side. Second, each plaintiff's stake must independently meet the amount-in-controversy specification. ...

The statute today governing federal court exercise of diversity jurisdiction in the generality of cases, § 1332, like all its predecessors, incorporates both a diverse-citizenship requirement and an amount-in-controversy requirement.[5] This Court has long held that, in determining whether the amount-in-controversy requirement has been satisfied, a single plaintiff may aggregate two or more claims against a single defendant, even if the claims are unrelated. But in multiparty cases, including class actions, we have unyieldingly adhered to the nonaggregation rule stated in *Troy Bank* [*v. G.A. Whitehead & Co.*, 222

---

[5] Endeavoring to preserve the "complete diversity" rule first stated in *Strawbridge* v. *Curtiss*, 7 U.S. 267 (1806), the Court's opinion drives a wedge between the two components of 28 U.S.C. § 1332, treating the diversity-of-citizenship requirement as essential, the amount-in-controversy requirement as more readily disposable. § 1332 itself, however, does not rank order the two requirements. What "ordinary principle of statutory construction" or "sound canon of interpretation," allows the Court to slice up § 1332 this way? In partial explanation, the Court asserts that amount in controversy can be analyzed claim-by-claim, but the diversity requirement cannot. It is not altogether clear why that should be so. The cure for improper joinder of a nondiverse party is the same as the cure for improper joinder of a plaintiff who does not satisfy the jurisdictional amount. In both cases, original jurisdiction can be preserved by dismissing the nonqualifying party.

U.S. 39 (1911)]. See *Clark*, 306 U.S., at 589 (reaffirming the "familiar rule that when several plaintiffs assert separate and distinct demands in a single suit, the amount involved in each separate controversy must be of the requisite amount to be within the jurisdiction of the district court, and that those amounts cannot be added together to satisfy jurisdictional requirements"). . . .

These cases present the question whether Congress abrogated the nonaggregation rule long tied to § 1332 when it enacted § 1367. In answering that question, "context [should provide] a crucial guide." *Rosario Ortega* v. *Star-Kist Foods, Inc.*, 370 F.3d 124, 135 (2004). The Court should assume, as it ordinarily does, that Congress legislated against a background of law already in place and the historical development of that law. Here, that background is the statutory grant of diversity jurisdiction, the amount-in-controversy condition that Congress, from the start, has tied to the grant, and the nonaggregation rule this Court has long applied to the determination of the "matter in controversy." . . .

As explained by the First Circuit in *Ortega*, and applied to class actions by the Tenth Circuit in *Leonhardt*, § 1367(a) addresses "civil actions of which the district courts have original jurisdiction," a formulation that, in diversity cases, is sensibly read to incorporate the rules on joinder and aggregation tightly tied to § 1332 at the time of § 1367's enactment. On this reading, a complaint must first meet that "original jurisdiction" measurement. If it does not, no supplemental jurisdiction is authorized. If it does, § 1367(a) authorizes "supplemental jurisdiction" over related claims. In other words, § 1367(a) would preserve undiminished, as part and parcel of § 1332 "original jurisdiction" determinations, both the "complete diversity" rule and the decisions restricting aggregation to arrive at the amount in controversy. § 1367(b)'s office, then, would be "to prevent the erosion of the complete diversity [and amount-in-controversy] requirements that might otherwise result from an expansive application of what was once termed the doctrine of ancillary jurisdiction." See Pfander, *Supplemental Jurisdiction and § 1367: The Case for a Sympathetic Textualism*, 148 U. Pa. L. Rev. 109, 114 (1999). In contrast to the Court's construction of § 1367, which draws a sharp line between the diversity and amount-in-controversy components of § 1332, the interpretation presented here does not sever the two jurisdictional requirements. . . .

The less disruptive view I take of § 1367 also accounts for the omission of Rule 20 plaintiffs and Rule 23 class actions in § 1367(b)'s text. If one reads § 1367(a) as a plenary grant of supplemental jurisdiction to federal courts sitting in diversity, one would indeed look for exceptions in § 1367(b). Finding none for permissive joinder of parties or class actions, one would conclude that Congress effectively, even if unintentionally, overruled *Clark* and *Zahn*. But if one recognizes that the nonaggregation rule delineated in *Clark* and *Zahn* forms part of the determination whether "original jurisdiction" exists in a diversity case, then plaintiffs who do not meet the amount-in-controversy requirement would fail at the § 1367(a) threshold. Congress would have no reason to resort to a § 1367(b) exception to turn such plaintiffs away from federal court, given that their claims, from the start, would fall outside the court's § 1332 jurisdiction. . . .

What is the utility of § 1367(b) under my reading of § 1367(a)? § 1367(a) allows parties other than the plaintiff to assert *reactive* claims once entertained under the heading ancillary jurisdiction. As earlier observed, § 1367(b) stops plaintiffs from circumventing § 1332's jurisdictional requirements by using another's claim as a hook to add a claim that the plaintiff could not have brought in the first instance. . . .

For the reasons stated, I would hold that § 1367 does not overrule *Clark* and *Zahn*. I would therefore affirm the judgment of the Court of Appeals for the First Circuit and reverse the judgment of the Court of Appeals for the Eleventh Circuit.

NOTES AND QUESTIONS

1. Think about what was at stake for the plaintiffs in the two different cases consolidated here. Why would the 10,000 Exxon dealers want to join their claims together? Why do you think the family members claiming damages for emotional distress wanted to join their claims with those of the girl who was severely injured? If it was important to bring the claims in one lawsuit, why did the plaintiffs opt to try to do that in federal court instead of filing in the Florida (*Exxon*) or Puerto Rico (*Ortega*) court system? Would the ability of the plaintiffs to join their claims in federal court make any difference if the case settled without trial, as most cases do?

2. As the Court indicates, when Congress enacted § 1367, it meant to change some of the rules that had applied in pendent and ancillary jurisdiction. One of the reasons Congress enacted § 1367 was to overturn the Supreme Court's decision in *Finley v. United States*, 490 U.S. 545, 109 S.Ct. 2003, 104 L.Ed.2d 593 (1989). In *Finley*, plaintiff had a federal question claim against the United States, and a state-law claim against another, non-diverse defendant. The federal courts had exclusive jurisdiction over the claim against the United States. Therefore, if the federal courts could not hear the state-law claim, plaintiff would be forced to divide her action into two separate suits. The Supreme Court nevertheless refused to allow the courts to exercise pendent jurisdiction, arguing that allowing jurisdiction would be inconsistent with the complete diversity requirements of § 1332. Section 1367 clearly overrules *Finley*. Do you see how? What part of § 1367 overrules *Finley*?

3. Unlike *Finley*, the claims in *Exxon Mobil* were brought in federal court on the basis of diversity jurisdiction. In diversity cases, § 1367(b) adds

SEC. D   **SUPPLEMENTAL JURISDICTION**   **237**

an additional complication to the analysis. At least in part because of that additional factor, it is not clear whether Congress meant to overturn the pre-§ 1367 case law that denied jurisdiction over claims like those in *Zahn* that did not independently meet the requirements of the diversity statute.

   4. The majority and dissents all base their arguments mainly on the language of § 1367(a), not § 1367(b). Restate each of these arguments in your own words. Do you find either argument more faithful to the language of § 1367?

   5. Note that even under the majority's argument, it is essential that all claims involved in the supplemental jurisdiction analysis arise out of a common nucleus of operative fact. However, in the typical case involving joinder of plaintiffs under Federal Rule 20, this requirement will always be satisfied. Why? (If you are unsure, review Federal Rule 20.)

   6. Would the majority allow supplemental jurisdiction in the following cases (assuming in every case that all claims arise from a common nucleus of operative fact)?

   a. P1 and P2 sue D in federal court. P1 and P2 are both citizens of State Alpha, while D is a citizen of State Beta. P1's claim is $60,000, but P2's claim is only $30,000.

   b. P1, from State Alpha, sues D1 and D2, both of whom are from State Beta, in federal court. P's claim against D1 is for $100,000, while her claim against D2 is only for $50,000.

   c. P1 and P2 sue D in federal court. P1 is from State Alpha, while P2 and D are both from State Beta. Each plaintiff claims over $100,000 in damages.

   d. P, from State Alpha, sues D, from State Beta, in federal court. P seeks $100,000 in damages. D impleads 3PD, a citizen of State Alpha. P files a claim against 3PD, as authorized by Federal Rule 14.

   e. P, from State Alpha, sues D, from State Beta, in federal court. P seeks $100,000 in damages. D impleads 3PD, a citizen of State Gamma. 3PD has signed a guaranty under which it is liable for up to $50,000 of D's liability. P accordingly adds a claim against 3PD for $50,000.

   f. P1 and P2, both from State Alpha, sue D, from State Beta, in federal court. P1 then files a $100,000 cross-claim against P2.

   7. Do you understand the majority's distinction (explored in Problem 6c above) between the "amount in controversy" and "complete diversity" requirements of § 1332? According to the majority, why is complete diversity between plaintiffs and defendants required, given that the language of § 1367(a) could be read to dispense with the requirement?

   8. If a court determines that supplemental jurisdiction is unavailable, it dismisses the state-law claim(s). Note, however, that the court does not

dismiss the entire case. Any claims that independently qualify for federal question or diversity jurisdiction remain before the federal court, and the court dismisses *only* the state-law claims that needed supplemental jurisdiction. At that point, what option(s) does the plaintiff have?

9. What happens if the federal court dismisses the state claims after the statute of limitations has expired on those claims? § 1367(d) provides the plaintiff some protection. Under this provision, plaintiff will have at least 30 days to refile the dismissed claims in a state court. The statute of limitations is tolled during this period. Although several commentators have questioned Congress's authority to legislate regarding state statutes of limitations, the Supreme Court upheld the constitutionality of § 1367(d) in *Jinks v. Richland County*, 538 U.S. 456, 123 S.Ct. 1667, 155 L.Ed.2d 631 (2003). In addition, many states have "savings statutes" that toll the statute of limitations whenever a plaintiff mistakenly files her case in a jurisdiction that lacks either subject matter jurisdiction or personal jurisdiction. These savings statutes also give the plaintiff a certain period of time to file the case in a proper forum after the first case is dismissed. If such a savings statute is in force, a plaintiff may not need the protection provided by § 1367(d).

The prior cases and notes demonstrated how supplemental jurisdiction can facilitate bringing a case involving multiple plaintiffs and/or defendants in federal court. Of course, the joinder provisions of the Federal Rules deal with much more than claims by plaintiffs against defendants. Those rules also allow for counterclaims and cross-claims among the plaintiffs and defendants. Moreover, the defendant may add additional parties to the suit through the process of impleader. How does supplemental jurisdiction apply to these other forms of joinder?

At first glance, there may seem to be a discrepancy between what the Federal Rules allow and the limits set out in the supplemental jurisdiction statute. Rule 20, for example, appears to allow a plaintiff to sue multiple defendants as long as the claims arise from the same transaction or occurrence and meet the other requirements of Rule 20. As the prior section demonstrates, however, § 1367(b) does not allow plaintiff to bring claims against a non-diverse defendant.

The key to resolving this seeming contradiction lies in Federal Rule 82. That Rule makes it clear that the Federal Rules do not affect subject-matter jurisdiction. Therefore, all the Federal Rules deal with is the procedural issue of joinder. Whether the federal court can exercise jurisdiction over the various joined claims can only be answered by looking to the jurisdiction statutes, such as §§ 1331, 1332, and 1367.

Although the Federal Rules do not deal with jurisdiction, there nevertheless is a significant parallel between the liberal joinder provisions of the Federal Rules and the concept of supplemental jurisdiction. Many of the joinder rules allow joinder of claims that arise from the "same transaction or occurrence." § 1367(a), the first step in any analysis of supplemental jurisdiction, allows a party to join a claim that the federal court could not hear on its own with another that the federal court could hear, provided the two claims arise from a "common nucleus of operative fact." These two concepts, although worded differently, are construed similarly. Therefore, the analyses of joinder and supplemental jurisdiction will dovetail, at least in part.

As a rule of thumb, if a joinder rule conditions joinder on satisfying the "same transaction or occurrence" test, claims properly joined under that rule will ordinarily satisfy § 1367(a). The only exception, set out in *Exxon Mobil*, is a case involving multiple plaintiffs and/or defendants, where jurisdiction is based solely on diversity but complete diversity is lacking. Aside from that exception, § 1367(a) will be satisfied for all of the following claims:

- joinder of plaintiffs or defendants under Rule 20, when jurisdiction is based on a federal question or there is complete diversity;
- compulsory counterclaims (Rule 13(a));
- any cross-claims that arise from the same transaction or occurrence as plaintiff's claim (a cross-claim is also proper if it arises from the same transaction as a counterclaim; because § 1367(a) requires factual overlap with the plaintiff's claim, these cross-claims may not satisfy § 1367(a)); and
- parties joined to counterclaims or cross-claims under Rule 13(h).

The same logic will also apply to some of the more complex forms of joinder covered in Chapter 8.

But here it is crucial that you keep three *caveats* in mind. First, do not assume that all courts equate "same transaction and occurrence" with the § 1367 "common nucleus" test. A small but growing number view the § 1367 analysis as more inclusive. Therefore, a counterclaim that does not arise from the same transaction as the original claim might nevertheless qualify for supplemental jurisdiction. *Global NAPs, Inc. v. Verizon New England, Inc.*, 603 F.3d 71 (1st Cir. 2010); *Jones v. Ford Motor Credit Co.*, 358 F.3d 205 (2d Cir. 2004). As a practical matter, this reasoning affects mainly permissive counterclaims. Do you see why?

Second, do not assume that supplemental jurisdiction is the only way for a court to obtain jurisdiction over a joined claim. Supplemental jurisdiction is a last resort; to be used only if diversity and federal question jurisdiction do not work for all claims. You should first analyze each claim separately, to see whether diversity or federal question applies. You should turn to supplemental jurisdiction only if you find claims that do not qualify for federal question or diversity jurisdiction. Also, do not forget that § 1367(a) requires that there is at least one claim by plaintiff that does qualify for federal question or diversity.

Using supplemental jurisdiction only as a last resort does more than possibly save you the trouble of undertaking a difficult § 1367 analysis. Remember that § 1367(c) makes jurisdiction over the supplemental claims discretionary. If those claims qualify for federal question or diversity jurisdiction, by contrast, § 1367(c) does not apply.

The third *caveat* is equally important. Too many students try to simplify the analysis by assuming that there will always be supplemental jurisdiction over claims falling within the joinder rules listed above. Concluding that one of the above joinder rules is satisfied only means you have met the requirements of § 1367(a). That is only the first step for supplemental jurisdiction. It is still essential to analyze whether the case satisfies §§ 1367(b) and (c). § 1367(b) in particular will prevent the court from exercising jurisdiction over a number of claims, even though joinder may be proper under the Federal Rules. Under that provision, some claims by a plaintiff in a diversity case—whether brought against a third-party defendant, or a second, nondiverse defendant—will not qualify for supplemental jurisdiction.

Conversely, there are certain situations in which a court may exercise supplemental jurisdiction over claims that do not fall into the above joinder rules. Suppose P sues D in federal court. D has a claim against P that arises out of the same transaction or occurrence. Ordinarily, that claim would be a compulsory counterclaim. However, if D had already filed that claim in a state proceeding, Rule 13(a) provides that the claim is not compulsory (because it is already pending elsewhere). Nevertheless, because the claim is still a permissive counterclaim, most defendants will choose to file it anyway. In this situation, the court may exercise supplemental jurisdiction over the claim (subject always to its discretion to dismiss the state claim under § 1367(c)), even though it is a permissive rather than a compulsory counterclaim.

PROBLEMS

1. P1 and P2 both sue D in federal court. The court clearly has jurisdiction over P1's claim. Although P2's claim arises from the same event as P1's, it would not qualify for federal jurisdiction on its own. May P2 bring her claim in federal court along with P1's claim? What additional information do you need to answer this question?

2. After they were involved in an automobile accident, P sues D in federal court, relying on diversity jurisdiction. P seeks $100,000 in damages.

D files a counterclaim in the action, seeking $15,000 for the injuries that D suffered in the same collision. P moves to dismiss D's counterclaim for lack of subject-matter jurisdiction. How should the court rule?

3. P, a farmer, hired D1 to treat his crops with an herbicide. D1 obtained the herbicide from D2, the manufacturer. Because of a labeling mistake, the herbicide turns out to be Agent Orange, a product that kills every plant, including P's crops. P therefore brings a diversity action against both D1 and D2 in federal court, seeking $250,000 in damages. D1 files a cross-claim against D2 in this action, arguing that D2 must reimburse D1 for any injuries that D1 is required to pay. This cross-claim clearly meets the requirements of Rule 13(g). However, because D1 and D2 are citizens of the same state, D2 moves to dismiss the cross-claim for lack of subject-matter jurisdiction. How should the court rule?

4. P1 and P2 sue D in federal court, relying on diversity jurisdiction. P1 then files a proper cross-claim against P2. Because P1 and P2 are citizens of the same state, P2 moves to dismiss the cross-claim for lack of subject-matter jurisdiction. How should the court rule?

5. P sues D in federal court, relying on diversity jurisdiction, for injuries P suffered in an automobile accident. D files a counterclaim against P for the injuries D suffered in the same accident. D also uses Rule 13(h) to join O, the owner of the automobile driven by P, as an additional party to the counterclaim. Because P and O are from the same state, D's counterclaim qualifies for diversity jurisdiction. P then files a claim against O, arguing that O must reimburse P for any sums P must pay D. O moves to dismiss P's claim for lack of subject-matter jurisdiction. How should the court rule?

E. REMOVAL

INTRODUCTORY PROBLEM

Porthos sues Athos and Aramis in an Arizona state court for injuries Porthos suffered in a swordfight. Porthos is a citizen of Pennsylvania, Athos is a citizen of Nebraska, and Aramis is a citizen of Arizona. Athos and Aramis would rather have the case litigated in federal court. Is there any way they can force the action into federal court?

Governing Law: 28 U.S.C. § 1441.

Sections B–D of this chapter show that in many cases a plaintiff will have the option of suing in either state or federal court. For a variety of reasons—greater familiarity with the state procedural system and plaintiff-favoring juries being perhaps the most common—many plaintiffs will elect to bring their case in state rather than federal court. However, plaintiff does not have absolute control over the choice of forum. The removal statutes may level the playing field by giving defendant the right to move the case to a federal court.

Removal allows defendants to avail themselves of the federal courts to roughly the same extent as plaintiffs. Note that there is no counterpart to removal if plaintiff originally files in federal court. If a plaintiff selects federal court, there is nothing defendant can do to transfer the case to state court.

1. GENERAL RULES GOVERNING REMOVAL

CATERPILLAR INC. V. WILLIAMS
482 U.S. 386, 107 S.Ct. 2425, 96 L.Ed.2d 318 (1987)

JUSTICE BRENNAN delivered the opinion of the Court. . . .

I

At various times between 1956 and 1968, Caterpillar Tractor Company (Caterpillar) hired respondents to work at its San Leandro, California, facility. Initially, each respondent filled a position covered by the collective-bargaining agreement between Caterpillar and Local Lodge No. 284, International Association of Machinists (Union). Each eventually became either a managerial or a weekly salaried employee, positions outside the coverage of the collective-bargaining agreement. Respondents held the latter positions for periods ranging from 3 to 15 years; all but two respondents served 8 years or more.

Respondents allege that, "[d]uring the course of [their] employment, as management or weekly salaried employees," Caterpillar made oral and written representations that "they could look forward to indefinite and lasting employment with the corporation and that they could count on the corporation to take care of them." More specifically, respondents claim that, "while serving Caterpillar as managers or weekly salaried employees, [they] were assured that if the San Leandro facility of Caterpillar ever closed, Caterpillar would provide employment opportunities for [them] at other facilities of Caterpillar, its subsidiaries, divisions, or related companies." Respondents maintain that these "promises were continually and repeatedly made," and that they created "a total employment agreement wholly independent of the collective-bargaining agreement pertaining to hourly employees." In reliance on these promises, respondents assert, they "continued to remain in Caterpillar's employ rather than seeking other employment."

. . . On December 15, 1983, Caterpillar notified respondents that its San Leandro plant would close and that they would be laid off.

On December 17, 1984, respondents filed an action based solely on state law in California state court, contending that Caterpillar "breached

[its] employment agreement by notifying [respondents] that the San Leandro plant would be closed and subsequently advising [respondents] that they would be terminated" without regard to the individual employment contracts. Caterpillar then removed the action to federal court, arguing that removal was proper because any individual employment contracts made with respondents "were, as a matter of federal substantive labor law, merged into and superseded by the ... collective bargaining agreements."* Respondents denied that they alleged any federal claim and immediately sought remand of the action to the state court. In an oral opinion, the District Court held that removal to federal court was proper, and dismissed the case when respondents refused to amend their complaint to attempt to state a claim under § 301 of the LMRA.

The Court of Appeals for the Ninth Circuit reversed, holding that the case was improperly removed. The court determined that respondents' state-law claims were not grounded, either directly or indirectly, upon rights or liabilities created by the collective-bargaining agreement. Caterpillar's claim that its collective-bargaining agreement with the Union superseded and extinguished all previous individual employment contracts alleged by respondents was deemed irrelevant. The court labeled this argument a "defensive allegation," "raised to defeat the [respondents'] claims grounded in those independent contracts." Since respondents' cause of action did not require interpretation or application of the collective-bargaining agreement, the court concluded that the complaint did not arise under § 301 and was not removable to federal court....

II

... Only state-court actions that originally could have been filed in federal court may be removed to federal court by the defendant. Absent diversity of citizenship, federal-question jurisdiction is required. The presence or absence of federal-question jurisdiction is governed by the "well-pleaded complaint rule," which provides that federal jurisdiction exists only when a federal question is presented on the face of the plaintiff's properly pleaded complaint. The rule makes the plaintiff the master of the claim; he or she may avoid federal jurisdiction by exclusive reliance on state law.

Ordinarily federal pre-emption is raised as a defense to the allegations in a plaintiff's complaint. Before 1887, a federal defense such as pre-emption could provide a basis for removal, but, in that year, Congress amended the removal statute. We interpret that amendment to authorize removal only where original federal jurisdiction exists. Thus, it is now settled law that a case may not be removed to federal court on the

---

* A claim for breach of a collective bargaining contract arises under § 301 of the Labor Management Relations Act (LMRA), and is accordingly a federal question. [Eds.]

basis of a federal defense, including the defense of pre-emption, even if the defense is anticipated in the plaintiff's complaint, and even if both parties concede that the federal defense is the only question truly at issue. . . . [The Court then considered a narrow exception to this rule—the "complete preemption" doctrine discussed in pt. 3.b below—but concluded it did not apply.]

It is true that when a defense to a state claim is based on the terms of a collective-bargaining agreement, the state court will have to interpret that agreement to decide whether the state claim survives. But the presence of a federal question, even a § 301 question, in a defensive argument does not overcome the paramount policies embodied in the well-pleaded complaint rule—that the plaintiff is the master of the complaint, that a federal question must appear on the face of the complaint, and that the plaintiff may, by eschewing claims based on federal law, choose to have the cause heard in state court. When a plaintiff invokes a right created by a collective-bargaining agreement, the plaintiff has *chosen* to plead what we have held must be regarded as a federal claim, and removal is at the defendant's option. But a *defendant* cannot, merely by injecting a federal question into an action that asserts what is plainly a state-law claim, transform the action into one arising under federal law, thereby selecting the forum in which the claim shall be litigated. If a defendant could do so, the plaintiff would be master of nothing. Congress has long since decided that federal defenses do not provide a basis for removal.

III

Respondents' claims do not arise under federal law and therefore may not be removed to federal court. The judgment of the Court of Appeals is Affirmed.

NOTES AND QUESTIONS

1. Before evaluating the particular issue of federal question jurisdiction presented by the main case, consider the basic process of removal. What is the threshold test that § 1441(a) establishes for all attempts to remove?

2. Because § 1441(a) makes removal turn on whether the case could have been filed originally in federal court, every removal situation may require application of the rules dealing with federal question, diversity, and/or supplemental jurisdiction. However, removal and original jurisdiction are not perfectly parallel. There are a number of cases that cannot be removed even though they could have been filed originally in federal court. Conversely, there are some cases that can be removed even though they could not have been filed originally in federal court.

3. *Non-removable cases.* § 1441(a) acknowledges Congress may enact exceptions to its general rule. § 1445 lists a few narrow categories of cases

that cannot be removed even if they could have originally been filed in federal court. §§ 1445(a) and (b), dealing with certain actions filed against railroads and other carriers, represent historical political compromises. But what about §§ 1445(c) and (d)? Why would Congress forbid the removal of workers compensation actions? Is there something special about workers compensation that suggests the action should remain in state court? And what might explain § 1445(d), which forbids removal of certain civil actions under the Violence Against Women Act of 1994? Is Congress sending a message that these cases are somehow "beneath" the federal courts? Is it merely a coincidence that the courts have created a "domestic relations" exception to diversity jurisdiction, as discussed in Part C of this chapter?

4. *Preemption.* Now, consider why the plaintiffs' claim in *Caterpillar* was not treated as a federal question. The Court's analysis focuses on the doctrine of preemption, which you will study in greater depth in Constitutional Law. Preemption stems from the "supremacy clause" of Article VI of the United States Constitution, which provides that the United States Constitution and federal statute law are the "Supreme Law of the Land." Therefore, a state law that is inconsistent with the Constitution or federal law is preempted, and has no effect. Do you see why the issue of whether plaintiffs' claims were preempted by federal labor law did not affect the jurisdictional analysis?

5. You may recall that although federal question jurisdiction is ordinarily shared with the state courts, federal courts have exclusive jurisdiction over certain actions arising under federal law, such as antitrust and patent and copyright infringement cases. If a plaintiff mistakenly brings one of those claims in a state court, may defendant remove to federal court? For many years, the surprising answer was often no: many courts refused to allow removal under the argument that if the action was not properly before the state court, it could not be removed. Plaintiff had to file a new action in federal court. Congress remedied this anomaly when it enacted § 1441(f), which allows removal regardless of whether the state court has jurisdiction.

6. Suppose P sues D in state court, alleging both federal and state law claims. P and D are citizens of the same state. If the state and federal claims are sufficiently related, may the case be removed? Could the entire case have been brought in federal court originally?

7. In note 6, suppose D tries to remove based on supplemental jurisdiction. The federal court determines that although the claims satisfy §§ 1367(a) and (b), the state claim presents a novel and complex issue of state law within the meaning of § 1367(c). Does the federal court remand the entire case or only the state claim? See *In re City of Mobile*, 75 F.3d 605 (11th Cir. 1996).

8. Consider again the situation posed in the prior note. What if a removing defendant wants to challenge a district court's decision not to exercise supplemental jurisdiction over a state-law claim based on one of the factors in § 1367(c)? May the party appeal immediately, or must it wait until

the entire case is complete? Section 1447(d) appears to require the party to wait, as it indicates that orders to remand are "not reviewable by appeal or otherwise." However, the Supreme Court has for years read this limitation to apply only to decisions to remand based on lack of subject matter jurisdiction, not remands for other reasons. In *Carlsbad Technology, Inc. v. HIF Bio, Inc.*, 129 S.Ct. 1862, 173 L.Ed.2d 843 (2009), the Court considered whether a remand based on the discretionary factors in § 1367(c) was a decision based on subject matter jurisdiction (in which case appeal would be barred), or a decision based on some other grounds. The Court held that because of the discretion in § 1367(c), the decision was not based on jurisdiction, and could accordingly be appealed immediately.

9. Suppose plaintiff raises both federal and state claims against defendant, and the state claims are *not* sufficiently related to the federal to qualify for supplemental jurisdiction. Can this case be removed? Generally, a defendant must remove the entire case, not merely portions of it. But § 1441(c) creates a limited exception. Under this provision, as revised in 2011, if plaintiff brings both federal question and unrelated state law claims against defendant, defendant may remove the entire case. However, the federal court will then remand the state claims to the state court.

Are the mechanics of § 1441(c) unnecessarily clumsy? Why allow the defendant to remove the entire case, only to have the federal judge automatically remand part of it? Why not just let the defendant remove the federal portions? When answering this question, consider who gets to determine if the state claims are sufficiently related to qualify for supplemental jurisdiction.

10. *Other types of removal*. Although § 1441 is far and away the most-commonly used removal statute, it is by no means the only one. In some situations, Congress passes new legislation, and explicitly provides for removal of state-court actions in that legislation. One example of such a statute is the Price-Anderson Act, 42 U.S.C. § 2014(hh), which allows defendants to remove state court actions involving tort claims stemming from nuclear accidents. In addition to the Price-Anderson Act, 28 U.S.C. §§ 1442, 1442a, 1443, and 1452 are more specialized removal statutes that apply in enumerated situations. These removal provisions are also not always subject to the same rules that apply to removal under § 1441. It is especially interesting to compare the federal officer removal statute, § 1442, to § 1441. Unlike the general statute, § 1442 allows removal of not only civil actions, but also state criminal prosecutions. In addition, on its face § 1442 allows removal regardless of whether the parties are diverse or if a federal question is presented in the complaint.

2. REMOVAL IN DIVERSITY CASES

Application of § 1441 is fairly routine when jurisdiction is based on a federal question. In diversity cases, however, there are a few special rules that often prove to be traps for the unwary. The most obvious special rule is § 1441(b), which prevents removal of a case based on diversity if any of the defendants is a citizen of the state where the state-court action is pending. Can you think of a good policy reason that may have led Congress to include this provision?

Second, the rules governing the time at which diversity is determined differ in removal. When plaintiff files a diversity case originally in federal court, all that matters is that the parties are diverse on the date the case was filed. *Higgins v. E.I. DuPont de Nemours & Co.*, 863 F.2d 1162, 1166 (4th Cir. 1988). Post-filing acts do not affect jurisdiction. In removal cases, by contrast, diversity must be present both on the date the case was filed and the date on which removal occurs. The only exception is a voluntary act by the plaintiff that creates diversity.

To illustrate, suppose P sues D. Both parties are from the same state. If D moves to another state after the case is commenced, the case is not removable. However, if it is P rather than D who moves to another state, D has 30 days to remove, subject to § 1441(b). Other acts by a plaintiff, such as dismissing all non-diverse defendants, may also make the case removable.

What if all the existing parties are diverse, but there are also other potential defendants who would destroy diversity? In *Lincoln Property Co. v. Roche*, 546 U.S. 81, 126 S.Ct. 606, 163 L.Ed.2d 415 (2005), the Supreme Court held that the possible existence of unnamed non-diverse parties did not prevent removal.

Another special rule that applies to diversity removal is the one-year bar of § 1446(b), which is discussed in the section on procedure.

Finally, the amount in controversy requirement can also present problems in diversity removal cases. Many states do not allow a plaintiff to state a specific amount of damages in the complaint. Instead, the court will determine the actual damages based on the evidence adduced at trial. The purpose of this rule is to prevent plaintiffs from trying to win the sympathies of the jury by grossly exaggerating their injuries. However, the absence of any dollar figure makes it difficult for a federal court to determine whether removal was proper. Many courts in this situation presume that the amount in controversy requirement is satisfied unless plaintiff (the party opposing removal) demonstrates that he cannot recover more than $75,000. Others hold that by removing, defendant admits that it might be liable for more than $75,000.

A plaintiff who wants to keep his case in state court may be able to preempt any removal attempts by limiting his prayer for relief in the complaint. For example, if plaintiff's complaint specifically alleges that he is entitled to recover "an amount not to exceed $50,000," a court may not allow the defendant to remove based on diversity.

3. MORE COMPLEX CASES

By this point, you may have developed a rough rule of thumb to use when dealing with questions of federal subject matter jurisdiction. If plaintiff's claim arises under a federal law, a treaty, or the United States Constitution, federal question jurisdiction is the best option. If the claim arises under state law (or the law of another nation), by contrast, your only choice would seem to be diversity—unless of course there are other federal question claims in the litigation, in which case supplemental jurisdiction may be an option.

This subsection demonstrates that this simple dichotomy does not always work. As hinted at in Part B of this chapter, there are certain situations in which state law claims will qualify for federal question jurisdiction. The two cases that follow represent two situations where this may occur. Note that both of these situations arise relatively infrequently, meaning that the rule of thumb described just above can still serve as a starting point in your analysis.

a. State Law Claims with an Essential Federal Element

GRABLE & SONS METAL PRODUCTS, INC. V. DARUE ENGINEERING & MFG.
545 U.S. 308, 125 S.Ct. 2363, 162 L.Ed.2d 257 (2005)

JUSTICE SOUTER delivered the opinion of the Court.

I

In 1994, the Internal Revenue Service seized Michigan real property belonging to petitioner Grable & Sons Metal Products, Inc., to satisfy Grable's federal tax delinquency. Title 26 U.S.C. § 6335 required the IRS to give notice of the seizure, and there is no dispute that Grable received actual notice by certified mail before the IRS sold the property to respondent Darue Engineering & Manufacturing. Although Grable also received notice of the sale itself, it did not exercise its statutory right to redeem the property within 180 days of the sale, and after that period had passed, the Government gave Darue a quitclaim deed.

Five years later, Grable brought a quiet title action in state court, claiming that Darue's record title was invalid because the IRS had failed to notify Grable of its seizure of the property in the exact manner required by § 6335(a), which provides that written notice must be "given by the Secretary to the owner of the property [or] left at his usual place of abode or business." Grable said that the statute required personal service, not service by certified mail.

Darue removed the case to Federal District Court as presenting a federal question, because the claim of title depended on the interpretation of the notice statute in the federal tax law. The District Court declined to remand the case at Grable's behest after finding that the "claim does pose a significant question of federal law," and ruling that Grable's lack of a federal right of action to enforce its claim against Darue did not bar the exercise of federal jurisdiction. . . .

The Court of Appeals for the Sixth Circuit affirmed. On the jurisdictional question, the panel thought it sufficed that the title claim raised an issue of federal law that had to be resolved, and implicated a substantial federal interest (in construing federal tax law). The court went on to affirm the District Court's judgment on the merits. We granted certiorari on the jurisdictional question alone, to resolve a split within the Courts of Appeals on whether *Merrell Dow Pharmaceuticals Inc. v. Thompson*, 478 U.S. 804, 106 S.Ct. 3229, 92 L.Ed.2d 650 (1986), always requires a federal cause of action as a condition for exercising federal-question jurisdiction. We now affirm.

II

Darue was entitled to remove the quiet title action if Grable could have brought it in federal district court originally as a civil action "arising under the Constitution, laws, or treaties of the United States." This provision for federal-question jurisdiction is invoked by and large by plaintiffs pleading a cause of action created by federal law (e.g., claims under 42 U.S.C. § 1983). There is, however, another longstanding, if less frequently encountered, variety of federal "arising under" jurisdiction, this Court having recognized for nearly 100 years that in certain cases federal question jurisdiction will lie over state-law claims that implicate significant federal issues. The doctrine captures the commonsense notion that a federal court ought to be able to hear claims recognized under state law that nonetheless turn on substantial questions of federal law, and thus justify resort to the experience, solicitude, and hope of uniformity that a federal forum offers on federal issues.

The classic example is *Smith v. Kansas City Title & Trust Co.*, 255 U.S. 180, 41 S.Ct. 243, 65 L.Ed. 577 (1921), a suit by a shareholder claiming that the defendant corporation could not lawfully buy certain bonds of the National Government because their issuance was unconstitutional. Although Missouri law provided the cause of action, the Court recognized federal-question jurisdiction because the principal issue in the case was the federal constitutionality of the bond issue. *Smith* thus held, in a somewhat generous statement of the scope of the doctrine, that a state-law claim could give rise to federal-question jurisdiction so long as it "appears from the [complaint] that the right to relief depends upon the construction or application of [federal law]." *Id.*, at 199, 41 S.Ct. 243.

The *Smith* statement has been subject to some trimming to fit earlier and later cases recognizing the vitality of the basic doctrine, but shying away from the expansive view that mere need to apply federal law in a state-law claim will suffice to open the "arising under" door.... It has in fact become a constant refrain in such cases that federal jurisdiction demands not only a contested federal issue, but a substantial one, indicating a serious federal interest in claiming the advantages thought to be inherent in a federal forum.

But even when the state action discloses a contested and substantial federal question, the exercise of federal jurisdiction is subject to a possible veto. For the federal issue will ultimately qualify for a federal forum only if federal jurisdiction is consistent with congressional judgment about the sound division of labor between state and federal courts governing the application of § 1331.... Because arising-under jurisdiction to hear a state-law claim always raises the possibility of upsetting the state-federal line drawn (or at least assumed) by Congress, the presence of a disputed federal issue and the ostensible importance of a federal forum are never necessarily dispositive; there must always be an assessment of any disruptive portent in exercising federal jurisdiction....

III

This case warrants federal jurisdiction.... Grable has premised its superior title claim on a failure by the IRS to give it adequate notice, as defined by federal law. Whether Grable was given notice within the meaning of the federal statute is thus an essential element of its quiet title claim, and the meaning of the federal statute is actually in dispute; it appears to be the only legal or factual issue contested in the case. The meaning of the federal tax provision is an important issue of federal law that sensibly belongs in a federal court. The Government has a strong interest in the "prompt and certain collection of delinquent taxes," *United States v. Rodgers*, 461 U.S. 677, 709, 103 S.Ct. 2132, 76 L.Ed.2d 236 (1983), and the ability of the IRS to satisfy its claims from the property of delinquents requires clear terms of notice to allow buyers like Darue to satisfy themselves that the Service has touched the bases necessary for good title. The Government thus has a direct interest in the availability of a federal forum to vindicate its own administrative action, and buyers (as well as tax delinquents) may find it valuable to come before judges used to federal tax matters. Finally, because it will be the rare state title case that raises a contested matter of federal law, federal jurisdiction to resolve genuine disagreement over federal tax title provisions will portend only a microscopic effect on the federal-state division of labor....

Merrell Dow Pharmaceuticals Inc. v. Thompson, 478 U.S. 804, 106 S.Ct. 3229, 92 L.Ed.2d 650 (1986), on which Grable rests its position, is not to the contrary. *Merrell Dow* considered a state tort claim resting in part on the allegation that the defendant drug company had violated a federal misbranding prohibition, and was thus presumptively negligent under Ohio law. The Court assumed that federal law would have to be applied to resolve the claim, but after closely examining the strength of the federal interest at stake and the implications of opening the federal forum, held federal jurisdiction unavailable. Congress had not provided a private federal cause of action for violation of the federal branding requirement, and the Court found "it would ... flout, or at least undermine, congressional intent to conclude that federal courts might nevertheless exercise federal-question jurisdiction and provide remedies for violations of that federal statute solely because the violation ... is said to be a ... 'proximate cause' under state law." *Id.*, at 812, 106 S.Ct. 3229.

Because federal law provides for no quiet title action that could be brought against Darue, Grable argues that there can be no federal jurisdiction here, stressing some broad language in *Merrell Dow* (including the passage just quoted) that on its face supports Grable's position. But an opinion is to be read as a whole, and *Merrell Dow* cannot be read whole as overturning decades of precedent, as it would have done by effectively adopting the Holmes dissent in *Smith*, and converting a federal cause of action from a sufficient condition for federal-question jurisdiction INTO A NECESSARY ONE....

Merrell Dow should be read in its entirety as treating the absence of a federal private right of action as evidence relevant to, but not dispositive of, the "sensitive judgments about congressional intent" that § 1331 requires. The absence of any federal cause of action affected *Merrell Dow*'s result two ways. The Court saw the fact as worth some consideration in the assessment of substantiality. But its primary importance emerged when the Court treated the combination of no federal cause of action and no preemption of state remedies for misbranding as an important clue to Congress's conception of the scope of jurisdiction to be exercised under § 1331. The Court saw the missing cause of action not as a missing federal door key, always required, but as a missing welcome mat, required in the circumstances, when exercising federal jurisdiction over a state misbranding action would have attracted a horde of original filings and removal cases raising other state claims with embedded federal issues. For if the federal labeling standard without a federal cause of action could get a state claim into federal court, so could any other federal standard without a federal cause of action. And that would have meant a tremendous number of cases.

One only needed to consider the treatment of federal violations generally in garden variety state tort law. "The violation of federal statutes and regulations is commonly given negligence per se effect in state tort proceedings." RESTATEMENT (THIRD) OF TORTS 14. A general rule of exercising federal jurisdiction over state claims resting on federal mislabeling and other statutory violations would thus have heralded a potentially enormous shift of traditionally state cases into federal courts. Expressing concern over the "increased volume of federal litigation," and noting the importance of adhering to "legislative intent," *Merrell Dow* thought it improbable that the Congress, having made no provision for a federal cause of action, would have meant to welcome any state-law tort case implicating federal law "solely because the violation of the federal statute is said to [create] a rebuttable presumption [of negligence] . . . under state law." 478 U.S., at 811–812, 106 S.Ct. 3229. In this situation, no welcome mat meant keep out. *Merrell Dow*'s analysis thus fits within the framework of examining the importance of having a federal forum for the issue, and the consistency of such a forum with Congress's intended division of labor between state and federal courts.

As already indicated, however, a comparable analysis yields a different jurisdictional conclusion in this case. Although Congress also indicated ambivalence in this case by providing no private right of action to Grable, it is the rare state quiet title action that involves contested issues of federal law. Consequently, jurisdiction over actions like Grable's would not materially affect, or threaten to affect, the normal currents of litigation. Given the absence of threatening structural consequences and the clear interest the Government, its buyers, and its delinquents have in the availability of a federal forum, there is no good reason to shirk from federal jurisdiction over the dispositive and contested federal issue at the heart of the state-law title claim.

IV

The judgment of the Court of Appeals, upholding federal jurisdiction over Grable's quiet title action, is affirmed.

[JUSTICE THOMAS concurred]

NOTES AND QUESTIONS

1. What law gave Grable a superior right to possess the property? In twenty-five words or less, restate the Court's reasoning concerning why the state-law claim qualifies as a federal question under 28 U.S.C. § 1331.

2. What if plaintiff's complaint relies on federal law for one element, but that element could be decided in plaintiff's favor without interpreting federal law? For example, suppose plaintiff sues defendant for negligence in the operation of a commercial airplane. Plaintiff alleges defendant is negligent because she violated a federal law prescribing a minimum altitude for operating aircraft. However, plaintiff could also prevail by showing defendant was negligent in some other way (*e.g.*, by operating the airplane in inclement weather). Federal law in this case is an element, but not a necessary element, of the claim. Is the case a federal question? See *Columbia Gas Transmission Corp. v. Drain*, 191 F.3d 552 (4th Cir. 1999) (no jurisdiction).

3. Cases like *Grable* typically arise in the context of removal. Plaintiff for some reason would rather sue in state court, and accordingly couches its complaint as one arising under state law. When it attempts to remove,

defendant asserts that plaintiff has engaged in "artful pleading" to disguise what is really a federal claim in state clothing. This aspect of these cases may temper the analysis, as plaintiff is trying to deny the federal courts their role in interpreting federal law.

4. Attorney obtains a patent for an invention made by Client. When Client attempts to enforce the patent in court, the court declares the patent invalid because of a mistake made in the patent filing. Client accordingly sues Attorney in federal court for malpractice. Client's sole allegation of negligence is the mistake Attorney made in the filing. While malpractice is usually a state-law claim, does the federal element here convert the case into a federal question? Note that if the federal court does have jurisdiction, that jurisdiction would be *exclusive* of the state courts, because the claim would "arise under" federal patent law under 28 U.S.C. § 1338. Does that affect your analysis?

Several lower courts held that patent (and copyright) malpractice claims qualified for federal question jurisdiction, while others disagreed. The Supreme Court took up the question in its 2012–13 term. In *Gunn v. Minton*, 133 S.Ct. 1059 (2013), the Court held in a unanimous opinion that a patent malpractice claim was *not* a federal question. Although the claim would require the court to consider patent law, that question was largely hypothetical, because the patent would already have been declared invalid in a prior action. While *Gunn* involved an attorney who represented a client in patent infringement litigation, the Court's reasoning should also apply to an attorney who represented a client in applying for a patent. *Gunn* also almost certainly applies to copyright malpractice cases.

5. *Federal party theory*. Federal question jurisdiction also exists in suits involving certain corporations and other entities created by Congress. If the statute creating the organization explicitly provides that the organization can "sue and be sued" in federal court, all claims by or against that organization—even state law claims—are considered federal questions. *American National Red Cross v. S.G.*, 505 U.S. 247, 112 S.Ct. 2465, 120 L.Ed.2d 201 (1992). The rationale of these cases seems to be that the issue of the organization's capacity to sue or be sued is an essential issue in the cases, and is controlled by federal law. In that respect, the cases are analogous to federal element cases like *Grable*.

b. Complete Preemption

BENEFICIAL NATIONAL BANK V. ANDERSON
539 U.S. 1, 123 S.Ct. 2058, 156 L.Ed.2d 1 (2003)

JUSTICE STEVENS delivered the opinion of the Court.

The question in this case is whether an action filed in a state court to recover damages from a national bank for allegedly charging excessive interest in violation of both "the common law usury doctrine" and an

Alabama usury statute may be removed to a federal court because it actually arises under federal law. We hold that it may.

I

Respondents are 26 individual taxpayers who made pledges of their anticipated tax refunds to secure short-term loans obtained from petitioner Beneficial National Bank, a national bank chartered under the National Bank Act. Respondents brought suit in an Alabama court against the bank and the two other petitioners that arranged the loans, seeking compensatory and punitive damages on the theory, among others, that the bank's interest rates were usurious. Their complaint did not refer to any federal law.

Petitioners removed the case to the United States District Court for the Middle District of Alabama. In their notice of removal they asserted that the National Bank Act, 12 U.S.C. § 85, is the exclusive provision governing the rate of interest that a national bank may lawfully charge, that the rates charged to respondents complied with that provision, that § 86 provides the exclusive remedies available against a national bank charging excessive interest, and that the removal statute, 28 U.S.C. § 1441, therefore applied. The District Court denied respondents' motion to remand the case to state court but certified the question whether it had jurisdiction to proceed with the case to the Court of Appeals pursuant to 28 U.S.C. § 1292(b).

A divided panel of the Eleventh Circuit reversed. The majority held that under our "well-pleaded complaint" rule, removal is generally not permitted unless the complaint expressly alleges a federal claim and that the narrow exception from that rule known as the "complete preemption doctrine" did not apply because it could "find no clear congressional intent to permit removal under §§ 85 and 86." Because this holding conflicted with an Eighth Circuit decision, we granted certiorari.

II

A civil action filed in a state court may be removed to federal court if the claim is one "arising under" federal law. § 1441(b). To determine whether the claim arises under federal law, we examine the "well pleaded" allegations of the complaint and ignore potential defenses: "a suit arises under the Constitution and laws of the United States only when the plaintiff's statement of his own cause of action shows that it is based upon those laws or that Constitution. It is not enough that the plaintiff alleges some anticipated defense to his cause of action and asserts that the defense is invalidated by some provision of the Constitution of the United States." *Louisville & Nashville R. Co. v. Mottley*, 211 U.S. 149, 152 (1908). . . . As a general rule, absent diversity jurisdiction, a case will not be removable if the complaint does not affirmatively allege a federal claim.

Congress has, however, created certain exceptions to that rule. [Discussion of other case omitted.]

We have also construed § 301 of the Labor Management Relations Act, 1947 (LMRA), 29 U.S.C. § 185, as not only preempting state law but also authorizing removal of actions that sought relief only under state law. *Avco Corp. v. Machinists*, 390 U.S. 557 (1968). We later explained that holding as resting on the unusually "powerful" pre-emptive force of § 301:

> The Court of Appeals held, and we affirmed, that the petitioner's action "arose under" § 301, and thus could be removed to federal court, although the petitioner had undoubtedly pleaded an adequate claim for relief under the state law of contracts and had sought a remedy available only under state law. The necessary ground of decision was that the pre-emptive force of § 301 is so powerful as to displace entirely any state cause of action "for violation of contracts between an employer and a labor organization." Any such suit is purely a creature of federal law, notwithstanding the fact that state law would provide a cause of action in the absence of § 301. *Avco* stands for the proposition that if a federal cause of action completely pre-empts a state cause of action any complaint that comes within the scope of the federal cause of action necessarily "arises under" federal law.

Franchise Tax Bd., 463 U.S., at 23–24 (footnote omitted).

Similarly, in *Metropolitan Life Ins. Co. v. Taylor*, 481 U.S. 58 (1987), we considered whether the "complete pre-emption" approach adopted in *Avco* also supported the removal of state common-law causes of action asserting improper processing of benefit claims under a plan regulated by the Employee Retirement Income Security Act of 1974 (ERISA), 29 U.S.C. § 1001 et seq. For two reasons, we held that removal was proper even though the complaint purported to raise only state-law claims. First, the statutory text in § 502(a), 29 U.S.C. § 1132, not only provided an express federal remedy for the plaintiffs' claims, but also in its jurisdiction subsection, § 502(f), used language similar to the statutory language construed in *Avco*, thereby indicating that the two statutes should be construed in the same way. 481 U.S., at 65. Second, the legislative history of ERISA unambiguously described an intent to treat such actions "as arising under the laws of the United States in similar fashion to those brought under section 301 of the Labor-Management Relations Act of 1947." *Id.*, at 65–66 (internal quotation marks and emphasis omitted).

Thus, a state claim may be removed to federal court in only two circumstances—when Congress expressly so provides, such as in the Price-Anderson Act, or when a federal statute wholly displaces the state-law cause of action through complete pre-emption.[3] When the federal statute completely pre-empts the state-law cause of action, a claim which comes within the scope of that cause of action, even if pleaded in terms of state law, is in reality based on federal law. This claim is then removable under 28 U.S.C. § 1441(b), which authorizes any claim that "arises under" federal law to be removed to federal court. In the two categories of cases where this Court has found complete pre-emption—certain causes of action under the LMRA and ERISA—the federal statutes at issue provided the exclusive cause of action for the claim asserted and also set forth procedures and remedies governing that cause of action.

III

Count IV of respondents' complaint sought relief for "usury violations" and claimed that petitioners "charged . . . excessive interest in violation of the common law usury doctrine" and violated "Alabama Code. § 8–8–1, et seq. by charging excessive interest." Respondents' complaint thus expressly charged petitioners with usury. *Metropolitan Life*, *Avco*, and *Franchise Tax Board* provide the framework for answering the dispositive question in this case: Does the National Bank Act provide the exclusive cause of action for usury claims against national banks? If so, then the cause of action necessarily arises under federal law and the case is removable. If not, then the complaint does not arise under federal law and is not removable.

Sections 85 and 86 serve distinct purposes. The former sets forth the substantive limits on the rates of interest that national banks may charge. The latter sets forth the elements of a usury claim against a national bank, provides for a 2-year statute of limitations for such a claim, and prescribes the remedies available to borrowers who are charged higher rates and the procedures governing such a claim. If, as petitioners asserted in their notice of removal, the interest that the bank charged to respondents did not violate § 85 limits, the statute unquestionably pre-empts any common-law or Alabama statutory rule that would treat those rates as usurious. The section would therefore provide the petitioners with a complete federal defense. Such a federal defense, however, would not justify removal. Only if Congress intended § 86 to provide the exclusive cause of action for usury claims against national banks would the statute be comparable to the provisions that we construed in the *Avco* and *Metropolitan Life* cases.[5]

---

[3] Of course, a state claim can also be removed through the use of the supplemental jurisdiction statute, 28 U.S.C. § 1367(a), provided that another claim in the complaint is removable.

[5] Because the proper inquiry focuses on whether Congress intended the federal cause of action to be exclusive rather than on whether Congress intended that the cause of action be removable, the fact that these sections of the National Bank Act were passed in 1864, 11 years prior to the passage of the statute authorizing removal, is irrelevant, contrary to respondents' assertions.

In a series of cases decided shortly after the Act was passed, we endorsed that approach. . . . In *Evans v. National Bank of Savannah*, 251 U.S. 108 (1919), we stated that "federal law . . . completely defines what constitutes the taking of usury by a national bank, referring to the state law only to determine the maximum permitted rate." See also *Barnet v. National Bank*, 98 U.S. 555, 558 (1879) (the "statutes of Ohio and Indiana upon the subject of usury . . . cannot affect the case" because the Act "creates a new right" that is "exclusive"); *Haseltine v. Central Bank of Springfield*, 183 U.S. 132, 134 (1901) ("[T]he definition of usury and the penalties affixed thereto must be determined by the National Banking Act and not by the law of the State").

In addition to this Court's longstanding and consistent construction of the National Bank Act as providing an exclusive federal cause of action for usury against national banks, this Court has also recognized the special nature of federally chartered banks. Uniform rules limiting the liability of national banks and prescribing exclusive remedies for their overcharges are an integral part of a banking system that needed protection from "possible unfriendly State legislation." *Tiffany v. National Bank of Mo.*, 18 Wall. 409, 412 (1874). The same federal interest that protected national banks from the state taxation that Chief Justice Marshall characterized as the "power to destroy," *McCulloch v. Maryland*, 4 Wheat. 316, 431 (1819), supports the established interpretation of §§ 85 and 86 that gives those provisions the requisite pre-emptive force to provide removal jurisdiction. In actions against national banks for usury, these provisions supersede both the substantive and the remedial provisions of state usury laws and create a federal remedy for overcharges that is exclusive, even when a state complainant, as here, relies entirely on state law. Because §§ 85 and 86 provide the exclusive cause of action for such claims, there is, in short, no such thing as a state-law claim of usury against a national bank. Even though the complaint makes no mention of federal law, it unquestionably and unambiguously claims that petitioners violated usury laws. This cause of action against national banks only arises under federal law and could, therefore, be removed under § 1441.

The judgment of the Court of Appeals is reversed.

JUSTICE SCALIA, with whom JUSTICE THOMAS joins, dissenting.

. . . [T]he Court explains that "[b]ecause §§ 85 and 86 [of the National Bank Act] provide the exclusive cause of action for such claims, there is . . . no such thing as a state-law claim of usury against a national bank." But the mere fact that a state-law claim is invalid no more deprives it of its character as a state-law claim which does not raise a federal question, than does the fact that a federal claim is invalid deprive it of its character as a federal claim which does raise a federal question. The proper response to the presentation of a nonexistent claim to a state court is dismissal, not the "federalize-and-remove" dance authorized by today's opinion. For even if the Court is correct that the National Bank Act obliterates entirely any state-created right to relief for usury against a national bank, that does not explain how or why the claim of such a right is transmogrified into the claim of a federal right. Congress's mere act of creating a federal right and eliminating all state-created rights in no way suggests an expansion of federal jurisdiction so as to wrest from state courts the authority to decide questions of pre-emption under the National Bank Act. . . .

NOTES AND QUESTIONS

1. *Preemption.* Understanding *Beneficial* requires a basic understanding of federal preemption. Basically, the doctrine of preemption provides that federal law will in some situations override state law, rendering the state law of no effect. You will study preemption in greater detail in other law school courses. However, for purposes of federal question jurisdiction there are two categories of preemption: "conflict" and "complete." The vast majority of preemption issues involve what the Court deems "conflict preemption." To the extent that a state law directly clashes with federal law, that state law must give way. You saw this type of preemption in *Caterpillar, Inc. v. Williams* earlier in this chapter. *Caterpillar* makes it clear that conflict preemption is a defense, and therefore cannot satisfy the well-pleaded complaint rule.

So-called "complete preemption" is much rarer, but is far more sweeping in its scope when it does apply. In some situations, Congress intends for federal law to fill up a particular subject area in its entirety. If Congress fills up an area, state law can play no role whatsoever. In cases of complete preemption, state law is preempted not only when it clashes with federal law, but even if it is perfectly consistent with federal law. Complete preemption usually applies in connection with broad federal statutory schemes. As *Beneficial* demonstrates, the Court has explicitly found complete preemption under only three statutes: §§ 85 and 86 of the National Bank Act (*Beneficial*), § 301 of the Labor Management Relations Act (*Avco*), and § 502 of the Employment Retirement Income Security Act of 1974 (ERISA) (*Metropolitan Life*). A case involving the property rights of Indian tribes is probably another category. In *Oneida Indian Nation v. County of Oneida*, 414 U.S. 661, 94 S.Ct. 772, 39 L.Ed.2d 73 (1974), the Court held that a claim by the tribe seeking possession of tribal land would always arise under federal law.

2. The complete preemption rule discussed in *Beneficial* is fundamentally different than the rule discussed in *Grable*. Complete preemption in essence transforms the state-law claim into a federal substantive claim. Once we recognize that federal law replaces state law as the source of the claim, it is easy to see how the claim qualifies as a federal question. Under *Grable*, by contrast, the claim remains primarily a state-law claim, but is nevertheless treated as a federal question claim for purposes of § 1331 due to the federal "ingredient."

3. Isn't Justice Scalia's dissent correct? If federal law preempts state law—regardless of whether it is because of conflict or complete preemption—doesn't that simply mean that there is *no state law claim*? How can the fact of preemption somehow convert a state claim into a federal claim?

4. For a thought-provoking article tracing the development in thought on this topic, and roundly criticizing the approach taken in *Grable*, see Douglas D. McFarland, *The True Compass: No Federal Question in a State Law Claim*, 55 U. KAN. L. REV. 1 (2006).

PROBLEMS

1. In the interest of uniformity, Congress enacts a national speed limit of 65 miles per hour on interstate highways. P is injured by D on an interstate highway. D was driving 70 miles per hour at the time of the accident. P sues D in federal court, alleging that D was negligent *per se* for violating the federal speed limit law. Does the court have federal question jurisdiction?

2. P sues D (a nearby factory) in federal court. P claims that D committed a nuisance by discharging hazardous fumes from its smokestacks. Under state law, nuisance is the unreasonable use of one's property. In his complaint, P alleges that D's use is unreasonable because it exceeds the limits established by the federal Clean Air Act. Although the Clean Air Act does contain a provision allowing aggrieved citizens such as P to sue, the only remedy that provision authorizes is an injunction. P has sued for nuisance in the hope that he can recover damages. Does the court have federal question jurisdiction?

3. Soldier is injured when a military helicopter crashes. Soldier sues Manufacturer, the private company that built the helicopter, alleging negligence. Manufacturer tries to remove the case to federal court. Manufacturer's argument for removal is that the state negligence law is preempted by federal military regulations, which require the helicopter to have the particular feature that caused the injury. Will Manufacturer be able to remove?

4. PROCEDURE FOR REMOVAL

How exactly does a defendant remove a case to federal court? § 1441 itself provides part of the answer. In addition, you should carefully review §§ 1446 and 1447, which set out time constraints, additional requirements, and certain limits, on removal.

Timing. Perhaps the most important limits relate to time. § 1446(b) provides that a defendant has only 30 days following service to remove a case. However, this 30 days only begins to run when the defendant receives a pleading that indicates that the case may be removed. If there are multiple defendants, and defendants are served on different dates, each defendant has 30 days following the date it was served to join the notice of removal. 28 U.S.C. § 1446(b)(2)(B).

In most cases, the plaintiff's original complaint will show that the case qualifies for federal question, diversity, and/or supplemental jurisdiction. However, suppose that the original complaint is based on state law, and one of the plaintiffs is from the same state as the defendant. In this situation, the case could not have originally been filed in federal court because of the complete diversity rule. However, if the non-diverse plaintiff later drops out of the case, and an amended complaint is served that does not name the dropped plaintiff, defendant's 30-day time period begins to run with service of the amended complaint.

The rule stated just above is subject to an important—and often forgotten—exception. The last clause of § 1446(b) provides that no action may be removed based on diversity after one year following *filing* of the *original* complaint. Therefore, a plaintiff in a diversity case may defeat removal by joining both a diverse and a non-diverse defendant, waiting for a year, and then dropping the non-diverse defendant. As long as that non-diverse defendant is not a nominal or fraudulently-joined party, the case cannot be removed.

Multiple defendants. § 1441 provides that an action may be removed by "the defendant or defendants." How does this language operate in the case of multiple defendants? The courts have uniformly held that in a case involving multiple defendants, *all* defendants must join in the removal. If even one defendant refuses to cooperate, the case cannot be removed. However, you do not always need the consent of everyone named as a defendant in the complaint. If a defendant is named in the complaint but has not yet been served, most courts hold that defendant need not join in the removal.

What exactly is a "defendant"? Courts have consistently held that a plaintiff cannot remove even when the defendant files a counterclaim against her. One federal appellate court held that a third-party defendant was not a defendant within the meaning of § 1441, and therefore could not remove. *First National Bank of Pulaski v. Curry*, 301 F.3d 456 (6th Cir. 2002). Third-party defendants are covered in Chapter 8.

Assuming all necessary defendants agree, the case is removed by filing a notice of removal with the proper federal court, serving it on all adverse parties, and filing a copy of the notice with the state court. A "notice" is just what it implies—it is not a request to remove, but instead a statement that defendant is exercising her right to remove the case.

Once the case is properly removed, the state court loses jurisdiction over the case. § 1446(d). In fact, any rulings that the state court issues from that point forward have no effect whatsoever.

Although removal gives the defendant the option of moving the case to the federal system, it gives the defendant no choice as to *which* federal court will hear the case. § 1441 is crystal clear in this regard: the case is removed to "the district and division embracing the place where [the state] action is pending." Thus, a defendant who removes a case from the state courts in Louisville, Kentucky must remove the case to the Western District of Kentucky, Louisville division. In Chapter 3, you studied venue, which in the federal courts comprises various statutes that dictate where an action must be filed. Because the removal statutes specify a particular district, they are treated as overriding the venue statutes. Therefore, if our defendant properly removes the case to the Western District of Kentucky, that court will have venue even if it would have not been a proper venue under the venue statutes had the same action been filed originally in federal court.

If defendant's removal is improper, the federal court may remand the case to state court. Here again, the issue of timing is important. If removal was improper because the underlying case is not one that could have been filed originally in federal court, the objection is actually a challenge to the federal court's subject matter jurisdiction. Thus, like other challenges to subject matter jurisdiction, the motion for remand may be made at any time (even on appeal), and by either side (including the removing defendant itself) or by the court. Similarly, if something happens in the case that causes the federal court to lose subject matter jurisdiction—for example, if the sole federal question in the case is dismissed voluntarily—the federal court may remand. All other objections, however, such as objections to the content of the notice or timeliness, must be raised within 30 days following filing of the notice of removal. 28 U.S.C. § 1447(c).

PROBLEMS

1. P, a citizen of Nebraska, sues D, a citizen of Kansas, in state court. P seeks $500,000 in damages from D for breach of contract and unjust enrichment. D files a timely notice of removal. P moves for a remand. What additional facts do you need before you can determine whether the court will remand the case to the state court?

2. Same facts as Problem 1. Would your analysis differ if P had brought both a federal question claim and a diversity claim against D?

3. P, a citizen of Indiana, sues D1, a citizen of South Dakota, and D2, a citizen of Indiana, in an Indiana state court. P seeks $200,000 in damages from the defendants for conspiring to commit an intentional tort against P. Two weeks after the case is commenced, P and D2 settle. P immediately amends her complaint to drop D2 from the case. May D1 now remove the case? If so, what must D1 do, and when?

4. Same as Problem 3, except that P waits for over a year after the settlement before filing the papers dismissing D2 from the case. Would it matter if P's tardiness was purposeful or merely an oversight?

CHAPTER 5

DETERMINING THE APPLICABLE LAW

■ ■ ■

The United States is a federal nation. Unlike most nations, there is not a single unitary "law" on a given subject, but at least fifty separate laws. In many cases these rules will produce significantly different outcomes for any given dispute.

Further complicating the problem is the possibility that a fifty-first law may apply—namely federal law. Although the legislative power of the federal government is limited by the Constitution, Congress nevertheless has broad authority, especially in matters of national and interstate concern. Federal law today covers a wide range of primary activity, sometimes complementing, sometimes replacing, state law.

The federal nature of the United States system gives rise to a number of interesting and idiosyncratic issues involving how a court determines which law governs a particular civil dispute. This Chapter deals with two of these issues. The first, *choice of law*, focuses on how a court dealing with a multijurisdictional dispute selects which jurisdiction's laws will apply. In most cases, the choice is between two or more states, each of which has some connection with the dispute. In other cases, the laws of different nations may apply. Part A of this Chapter briefly addresses this issue.

The second issue, commonly referred to as "the *Erie* doctrine" after the case that spawned it, is peculiar to a federal system. While all nations must have choice of law rules, only federal nations need to deal with clashes between national law and the laws of the states (or provinces, Länder, or other local term). In the United States, numerous rules govern the interaction between federal and state law. In some situations, federal law overrides, or "preempts", state law. In other situations, federal and state law can co-exist. The *Erie* doctrine is but one of the many rules that deal with this complex interaction. You will deal with most of these rules in other courses. However, because the *Erie* doctrine frequently arises with respect to rules of procedure, it is generally covered in a course in Civil Procedure. Part B of this Chapter deals with the *Erie* doctrine.

A. CHOICE OF LAW

INTRODUCTORY PROBLEM

Corky, a citizen of Connecticut, purchases a purebred Pembroke Welsh Corgi puppy. Corky strongly suspects the puppy will eventually prove to be a champion in the show ring. While vacationing in upstate New York, Corky takes the dog to a local veterinary clinic for routine vaccinations. When he returns later in the day, Corky is horrified to find that his puppy was neutered. Neutering greatly reduces a dog's value, for a neutered dog cannot compete in dog shows. Corky is emotionally devastated that his little friend underwent unnecessary surgery.

Corky's demands for compensation go unanswered. Thirteen months after the incident, Corky sues Violet, the veterinarian who performed the operation, for veterinary malpractice. Although the clinic is located in upstate New York, Violet resides just across the border in Vermont. Corky names only Violet, not the clinic, as defendant. Corky sues Violet in Vermont to prevent any personal jurisdiction challenges.

Violet immediately moves to dismiss, setting out two separate arguments. First, she notes that the Vermont statute of limitations is one year. Because Corky waited 13 months to file his claim, Violet argues that it is time-barred. Second, and in the alternative, Violet points out that under Vermont law, the owner of an animal that is harmed or killed can recover only the decrease in value. Vermont does not allow recovery for any emotional trauma to the owner.

Corky counters Violet's motion by noting that the laws of Connecticut and New York differ from those of Vermont. Both Connecticut and New York would allow recovery for emotional distress. And the statute of limitations on veterinary malpractice claims in Connecticut is two years, while in New York it is three years.

How should the court resolve Violet's motion?

Imagine a dispute between a plaintiff from state A, a defendant from state B, involving an event that occurred in a foreign nation, and which is being litigated in the courts of state C. How does a court determine whether the law of state A, B, C, or the foreign nation, applies? The easiest solution would be for every state simply to apply its own law to all cases in its courts. However, in order to afford the parties some predictability in how they organize their daily activities, no United States court automatically applies forum law on every issue in every case that comes before it. Indeed, the Supreme Court has held that it would violate the United States Constitution for a state to apply its own law to a case that has no significant connection with the state. *Phillips Petroleum Co. v. Shutts*, 472 U.S. 797, 105 S.Ct. 2965, 86 L.Ed.2d 628 (1985).

Because a court does not always apply its own law to multistate disputes, states have been forced to develop rules to deal with selecting a governing law. In the vast majority of states this task of developing rules has fallen on the courts rather than the legislatures. A body of case law called "Conflicts of Law" has developed, which provides rules and considerations for courts to use in determining which law applies.

In many cases the choice is obvious. If plaintiff, defendant, and all significant events giving rise to the claim are situated in the same state, the law of that state will usually govern, regardless of where the case is litigated. But in many other cases, the choice is not immediately clear. For example, good arguments can be made for applying different states' laws in the Introductory Problem.

Choice of law is a complicated field that in most law schools is the subject of an entire upper level course. The case in this section provides a brief overview of this area of the law, and provides a flavor of how choice of law considerations must enter into an attorney's planning process as she selects a forum and frames the complaint. As you will see in *Paul*, different states use different rules to deal with choice of law problems.

PAUL V. NATIONAL LIFE
177 W.Va. 427, 352 S.E.2d 550 (1986)

NEELY, J.

In September of 1977 Eliza Vickers and Aloha Jane Paul, both West Virginia residents, took a weekend trip to Indiana. The two women were involved in a one-car collision on Interstate 65 in Indiana when Mrs. Vickers lost control of the car. That collision took both women's lives. The administrator of Mrs. Paul's estate brought a wrongful death action against Ms. Vickers' estate and the National Life Accident Company in the Circuit Court of Kanawha County. Upon completion of discovery, the defendants below moved for summary judgment. Defendants' motion contended that: (1) the Indiana guest statute, which grants to a gratuitous host immunity from liability for the injury or death of a passenger unless that host was guilty of willful and wanton misconduct at the time of the accident, was applicable; and (2) that the record was devoid of any evidence of willful or wanton misconduct on the part of Ms. Vickers. By order dated 29 October 1984, the Circuit Court of Kanawha County entered summary judgment for the defendants below. The order of the circuit court held that our conflicts doctrine of *lex loci delicti* required that the law of the place of the injury, namely, Indiana, apply to the case, and that the record contained no evidence of willful or wanton misconduct on the part of Ms. Vickers. It is from this order that the plaintiffs below appeal.

The sole question presented in this case is whether the law of Indiana or of West Virginia shall apply. The appellees urge us to adhere to our traditional conflicts doctrine of *lex loci delicti,* while the appellants urge us to reject our traditional doctrine and to adopt one of the "modern" approaches to conflicts questions. Although we stand by *lex loci delicti* as our general conflicts rule, we nevertheless reverse the judgment of the court below.

I

Unlike other areas of the law, such as contracts, torts and property, "conflicts of law" as a body of common law is of relatively recent origin. Professor Dicey has written that he knew of no decisions in England considering conflicts of law points before the accession of James I, and it is generally acknowledged that the first authoritative work on conflicts did not appear until the publication of Joseph Story's *Conflict of Laws* in 1834. Accordingly, no conflicts of law doctrine has ever had any credible pretense to being "natural law" emergent from the murky mists of medieval mysticism. Indeed, the mention of conflicts of law and the *jus naturale* in the same breath would evoke a power guffaw in even the sternest scholastic. In our post-Realist legal world, it is the received wisdom that judges, like their counterparts in the legislative branch, are political agents embodying social policy in law. Nowhere is the received wisdom more accurate than in the domain of conflict of laws.

Conflicts of law has become a veritable playpen for judicial policymakers. The last twenty years have seen a remarkable shift from the doctrine of *lex loci delicti* to more "modern" doctrines, such as the more flexible, manipulable *Restatement* "center of gravity" test. Of the twenty-five landmark cases cited by appellants in which a state supreme court rejected *lex loci delicti* and adopted one of the modern approaches, the great majority of them involved the application to an automobile accident case of a foreign state's guest statute, doctrine of interspousal or intrafamily immunity, or doctrine of contributory negligence. All but one of these landmark cases was decided in the decade between 1963 and 1973, when many jurisdictions still retained guest statutes, the doctrine of interspousal immunity, and the doctrine of contributory negligence. However, in the years since 1970, these statutes and doctrines have all but disappeared from the American legal landscape. . . .

Thus nearly half of the state supreme courts of this country have wrought a radical transformation of their procedural law of conflicts in order to sidestep perceived substantive evils, only to discover later that those evils had been exorcised from American law by other means. Now these courts are saddled with a cumbersome and unwieldy body of conflicts law that creates confusion, uncertainty and inconsistency, as well as complication of the judicial task. This approach has been like that of the misguided physician who treated a case of dandruff with nitric acid, only to discover later that the malady could have been remedied with medicated shampoo. Neither the doctor nor the patient need have lost his head.

The *Restatement* approach has been criticized for its indeterminate language and lack of concrete guidelines. *Restatement (Second) of Conflicts of Law,* Sec. 145–146 (1971)* provides:

§ 145. *The General Principle*

(1) The rights and liabilities of the parties with respect to an issue in tort are determined by the local law of the state which, with respect to that issue, has the most significant relationship to the occurrence and the parties under the principle stated in § 6.

(2) Contacts being taken into account in applying the principle of § 6 to determine the law applicable to an issue include:

    (a) the place where the injury occurred,

    (b) the place where the conduct causing injury occurred,

    (c) the domicile, residence, nationality, place of incorporation, and place of business of the parties, and

    (d) the place where the relationship, if any, between the parties, is centered.

These contacts should be evaluated according to their relative importance with respect to the particular issues.

§ 146. *Personal Injuries.*

In an action for a personal injury, the local law of the state where the injury occurred determines the *rights and liabilities* of the parties, unless, with respect to the particular issue, some other state has a more significant relationship under the principles stated in § 6 to the occurrence and the parties, in which event the local law of the other state will be applied.

Section 6 of the *Restatement* lists the following factors as important choice of law considerations in all areas of law.

    (a) The needs of the interstate and international systems;

    (b) The relevant policies of the forum;

    (c) The relevant policies of other interested states and relative interest of those states in the determination of the particular issue;

    (d) The protection of justified expectations;

---

* *Restatement* provisions Copyright 1971 by the American Law Institute. Reprinted with permission. All rights reserved. [Eds.]

(e) The basic policies underlying the particular field of law;

(f) Certainty, predictability, and uniformity of results; and

(g) Ease in the determination and application of the law to be applied.

As Javolenus once said to Julian, *res ipsa loquitur*. The appellant cites with approval the description of the *Restatement* approach set forth in *Conklin v. Horner,* 38 Wis.2d 468, 473, 157 N.W.2d 579, 581 (1968):

> We emphasized that what we adopted was not a rule, but a method of analysis that permitted dissection of the jural bundle constituting a tort and its environment to determine what elements therein were relevant to a reasonable choice of law.

That sounds pretty intellectual, but we still prefer a rule. The lesson of history is that methods of analysis that permit dissection of the jural bundle constituting a tort and its environment produce protracted litigation and voluminous, inscrutable appellate opinions, while rules get cases settled quickly and cheaply.

The manipulability inherent in the *Restatement* approach is nicely illustrated by two cases from New York, the first jurisdiction to make a clean break with *lex loci delicti*. The cases of *Babcock v. Jackson,* 12 N.Y.2d 473, 191 N.E.2d 279 (1963), and *Kell v. Henderson,* 47 Misc.2d 992, 263 N.Y.S.2d 647 (1965), aff'd, 26 App.Div.2d 595, 270 N.Y.S.2d 552 (1966), are aptly discussed by the Supreme Court of Virginia:

> In *Babcock,* an automobile guest sued her host in New York for injuries sustained in Ontario caused by the defendant's ordinary negligence. Under New York law, the guest could recover for injuries caused by the host's lack of ordinary care, but the Ontario guest statute barred such a recovery. The court abandoned its adherence to the place-of-the-wrong rule and permitted recovery. It decided that, on the guest-host issue, New York had the "dominant contacts" because the parties were domiciled in New York, were on a trip which began in New York, and were traveling in a vehicle registered and regularly garaged in New York. The court noted that Ontario had no connection with the cause of action except that the accident happened to take place there.
>
> *Kell* presented the converse of *Babcock*. There, the question was also whether the New York ordinary negligence rule applied or whether the Ontario guest statute controlled. The guest was injured by the host's ordinary negligence while the parties, both residents of Ontario, were on a trip in New York which was to begin and end in Ontario. The New York court purported to follow *Babcock* but held that Ontario law would not apply.

McMillan v. McMillan, 219 Va. 1127, 253 S.E.2d 662, 664 (1979). It was perhaps recognition of just such gross disparities in result that prompted the Court of Appeals of New York to remark, in a towering achievement in the art of understatement, "candor requires the admission that our past decisions have lacked a precise consistency." *Miller v. Miller,* 22 N.Y.2d 12, 237 N.E.2d 877, 879, 290 N.Y.S.2d 734 (1968).

II

The appellant urges us in the alternative to adopt the "choice-influencing considerations approach" set forth by Professor Leflar in "Choice-Influencing Considerations and Conflicts of Law", 41 N.Y.U.L. Rev. 267 (1966). Professor Leflar has narrowed the list of considerations in conflicts cases to five:

(1) Predictability of results;

(2) Maintenance of interstate or international order;

(3) Simplification of the judicial task;

(4) Advancement of the forum's governmental interests;

(5) Application of the better rule of law.

Professor Leflar's approach has been adopted in the guest statute context in the landmark cases of *Clark v. Clark,* 107 N.H. 351, 222 A.2d 205 (1966); *Milkovich v. Saari,* 295 Minn. 155, 203 N.W.2d 408 (1973); and *Conklin v. Horner,* 38 Wis.2d 468, 157 N.W.2d 579 (1968). In practice the cases tend to focus more on the fourth and fifth considerations than the first three, and the upshot is that the courts of New Hampshire, Minnesota and Wisconsin simply will not apply guest statutes. This seems to us a perfectly intelligible and sensible bright-line rule. However, it seems unnecessary to scrap an entire body of law and dress this rule up in a newfangled five-factor costume when the same concerns can be addressed and the same result achieved through judicious employment of the traditional public policy exception to *lex loci delicti.*

III

Lex loci delicti has long been the cornerstone of our conflict of laws doctrine. The consistency, predictability, and ease of application provided by the traditional doctrine are not to be discarded lightly, and we are not persuaded that we should discard them today. The appellant contends that the various exceptions that have been engrafted onto the traditional rule have made it manipulable and have undermined the predictability and uniformity that were considered its primary virtues. There is certainly some truth in this, and we generally eschew the more strained escape devices employed to avoid the sometimes harsh effects of the traditional rule. Nevertheless, we remain convinced that the traditional rule, for all of its faults, remains superior to any of its modern competitors. Moreover, if we are going to manipulate conflicts doctrine in order to achieve substantive results, we might as well manipulate something we understand. Having mastered marble, we decline an apprenticeship in bronze. We therefore reaffirm our adherence to the doctrine of *lex loci delicti* today.

However, we have long recognized that comity does not require the application of the substantive law of a foreign state when that law contravenes the public policy of this State. West Virginia has never had an automobile guest passenger statute. It is the strong public policy of this State that persons injured by the negligence of another should be able to recover in tort. . . .Today we declare that automobile guest passenger statutes violate the strong public policy of this State in favor of compensating persons injured by the negligence of others. Accordingly, we will no longer enforce the automobile guest passenger statutes of foreign jurisdictions in our courts.[14]

For the foregoing reasons, the order of the circuit granting summary judgment in favor of the appellees is hereby vacated, and the cause remanded for further proceedings not inconsistent with this opinion. . . .

NOTES AND QUESTIONS

1. The *lex loci delicti* rule was applied by all states in negligence cases from the late 1800s to the 1950s. Translating to "the law of the place of the wrong," the rule required courts to determine the outcome of a negligence case by applying the law of the place where the injury occurred. Dissatisfaction with the rule, especially as it applied in certain cases where the parties both lived in one state but the injury occurred in another, led to the development of the alternate choice-of-law regimes discussed in *Paul*.

2. One feature shared by the modern approaches is that they seek to move away from the strict territoriality of the traditional rules. Of course, choice of law cannot escape being territorial to some extent, as laws differ from state to state. But the traditional rules isolated one single event—the injury in the case of a tort, the place a contract was made or to be performed in the case of a contract—and made the choice turn on that single event, without considering other factors. The modern approaches consider a greater number of relevant factors, especially the residence of the parties.

3. The modern approaches to choice of law bear some similarity to the analysis used in the constitutional part of personal jurisdiction analysis, insofar as both consider the connections a given state has with the case. Nevertheless, there are crucial differences. For example, modern choice of

---

[14] Although we intended this to be a rule of general application, we do not intend it as an invitation to flagrant forum shopping. For example, were a resident of a guest statute jurisdiction to sue another resident of a guest statute jurisdiction over an accident occurring in a guest statute jurisdiction, the simple fact that the plaintiff was able to serve process on the defendant within our State borders would not compel us to resist application of any relevant guest statute. This State must have some connection with the controversy above and beyond mere service of process before the rule we announce today will be applied. . . .

law doctrines consider all parties' connections, while personal jurisdiction focuses primarily on the defendant. In addition, a contact need not be purposeful to count in choice of law analysis. Because of these differences and others, it is often true that a forum has jurisdiction, but will not apply its own law. Conversely, a state's law may govern a case even though that state's courts do not have jurisdiction over the defendant.

4. *Paul* is a tort case. Of all the areas of the law, choice of law rules in tort have undergone perhaps the most radical revision during the past fifty years. Although many states employ a similar contact-based analysis in contract cases, see, e.g., *Restatement (Second) of Conflicts of Law* § 188, the choice of law analysis in property cases is not all that different than it was in the early 1900's. Most issues governing ownership of property, for example, are still governed by the law of the place where the property is situated. Similarly, the validity of marriages is still usually governed by the law of the place where the marriage was celebrated.

5. *Procedure*. A decision to apply the law of another state does not mean that that other state's law will govern every aspect of the case. Instead, a court only borrows the other state's substantive law. A forum will almost always apply its own procedural law to a case. Although it is difficult to draw a bright line between substance and procedure, procedural rules, generally speaking, are those rules that deal with the steps a party must take to litigate his claims or defenses in court. Rules governing pleading, joinder, costs, and the like are clearly procedural. Other issues, however, are less obvious. One particular issue that falls on the line between substance and procedure is the statute of limitations. For purposes of choice of law analysis, however, most states consider statutes of limitations procedural. As a result, State X will typically apply the State X limitations period even when it hears a tort or contract claim governed by the law of State Y.

6. As *Paul* points out, choice of law rules differ tremendously between states. Does a forum making a choice of law decision consider the choice of law rules in force in other states when making its decision? In other words, should the court in *Paul* have considered not only Indiana tort law, but also Indiana choice of law rules? If your head is spinning at this point, you will be glad to hear that the answer is no. Choice of law rules are "procedural." A court making a choice of law almost always applies its own choice of law rules, and considers only other states' substantive rules.

7. *Choice of law and settlement*. One of the drawbacks to the modern approaches of the Second Restatement or "choice-influencing considerations" is that their multi-factor analysis makes it more difficult to predict what law a court will choose to apply in a particular case. As illustrated by *Paul*, there can also be some uncertainty even under the traditional *lex loci delicti* rule. As also illustrated by *Paul*, a decision on applicable law can be crucial to the outcome of a case when the law differs among the possible choices. If the parties are uncertain, or disagree, about what state's law will apply, this can block settlement. The parties will either be unable to predict what the outcome would be if the case proceeds, or their different predictions for the

applicable law will lead them to value the case very differently. The parties may need a judicial decision to resolve the legal issue of applicable law before they can agree on how to resolve the underlying dispute, illustrating how litigation can be intertwined with settlement.

B. THE *ERIE* DOCTRINE

INTRODUCTORY PROBLEM

Fred and Ethel Mertz own a small apartment building in New York City. The Mertzes lease one of the apartments in this building to Lucy and Ricky Ricardo. While the Mertzes and Ricardos generally get along swimmingly, Fred's propensity toward parsimony sometimes causes a strain in the relationship.

Given that Lucy does not work outside the home (except for brief stints at a chocolate factory and at a winery), and Ricky works as a nightclub performer, the Mertzes knew they were taking a financial risk leasing to the Ricardos. Indeed, over the years, Ricky has borrowed over $100,000 from Fred to finance his band. In June of this year, Fred's worst fears are realized. Because the "big band" sound has been out of style for decades, Ricky's nightclub is forced to close. Lucy and Ricky are accordingly unable to pay their rent for several months. Seeing no other option, Fred and Ethel sue Lucy and Ricky for both the back rent and the loans. Because the parties are diverse and the amount in controversy exceeds $75,000, Fred and Ethel bring this action in a New York federal district court. The complaint seeks $125,000 in actual damages as well as $300,000 in punitive damages.

Lucy and Ricky immediately file a motion to strike the claim for back rent, or in the alternative to strike the prayer for punitive damages. Their motion is based on two arguments. First, the Ricardos point to a recently-enacted provision in New York's pleading code. This provision, which applies to all claims involving real property, requires the plaintiff to attach to the complaint a copy of the deed or other conveyancing instrument proving plaintiff's ownership of the property. Fred and Ethel attached no such instrument to their complaint—because Fred somehow lost the deed, and there is no copy in the land records.

Second, and in the alternative, Lucy and Ricky ask the court to strike the claim for punitive damages. They correctly point out that New York, like every other state in the nation, does not allow punitive damages for breach of a lease or other contract, even if the breach was intentional.

But Fred and Ethel have a ready response to Lucy and Ricky's motion. First, Fred and Ethel argue that because the case was filed in *federal* court, the state rules of pleading do not apply. Instead, they argue that the required contents of the complaint are governed by the Federal Rules. Fred and Ethel correctly point out that nothing in the applicable Federal Rules (Rules 8, 9, and 10 if you are interested) requires a plaintiff to attach a copy of a conveyancing instrument to a complaint.

SEC. B — THE ERIE DOCTRINE

With respect to the punitive damages issue, Fred and Ethel agree that neither New York nor any other state would allow punitive damages in a case like this. However, the lease contains a choice of law provision, in which the parties agree that all rights and obligations under the lease would be governed by the laws of Albania. Albanian law clearly allows a landlord to recover punitive damages for breach of a lease agreement. Moreover, Fred and Ethel correctly point out that New York courts would honor this choice of law clause and apply Albanian substantive law, even though the lease had absolutely nothing to do with Albania.

How will the court rule on the motion to strike?

As indicated in the text that led off this Chapter, the federal nature of the United States system creates several problems for a court attempting to determine what law governs a case. The first, discussed in the prior section, applies in all courts. Whenever a claim has connections with more than one forum, a court must determine which of those forum's laws will be used to decide the case.

The subject of this section—the *Erie* doctrine—is mainly a concern only when a case is heard in federal court. The basic issue is whether the federal court will use state or federal law to decide the case. At first glance, this issue may seem like little more than a variation on the choice of law question addressed in Part A of this Chapter, the only difference being that in *Erie* one of the candidates is federal law. But that analogy proves overly simplistic. After all, the United States Constitution is clear on how to resolve a clash between state and federal law. Because of the Constitution's Supremacy Clause (Article 6), valid federal law always takes precedence over state law, at least where the two conflict. Therefore, if a court is dealing with a clash between valid federal law and a conflicting state law, it has no real choice: it must apply federal law.

The "choice" of law involved in *Erie* cases is different than that in state/state choice of law cases. In the latter, the court is assuming that all of the candidate laws are valid, and is determining which of the states has a greater "stake" in the dispute. In *Erie*, by contrast, the core issue is determining whether the federal law is (a) valid, and (b) truly governs the dispute at hand. Unlike in choice of law cases, if the federal law is valid and governs the issue in question, the court must apply it. Because *Erie* deals with one particularly vexing branch of federal law—federal judge-made law—it offers a unique insight into some of the basic principles of federal-state relations. Indeed, a study of *Erie* will allow you better to appreciate why some consider the doctrine to be one of the cornerstones of United States federalism.

Determining whether a federal law is "valid" is a complicated issue. A full discussion of the question requires considerable knowledge of

Constitutional Law. In the case of judge-made law, it also requires some knowledge of basic concepts of separation of powers. Because most students who take Civil Procedure do not yet have that in-depth knowledge of constitutional doctrine, the ensuing analysis deals mainly with one particular category of valid federal law; namely, laws that regulate the procedure in federal courts. At the end of the section, however, the discussion briefly touches on other, non-procedural laws.

1. GENESIS OF THE *ERIE* DOCTRINE

The roots of the *Erie* doctrine are almost as old as the United States itself. Congress laid the groundwork in the Judiciary Act of 1789, the first comprehensive statute dealing with the federal court system. Near the end of that Act was a short and little-noticed section, § 34, which provided simply:

> *And be it further enacted,* That the laws of the several states, except where the constitution, treaties or statutes of the United States shall otherwise require or provide, shall be regarded as rules of decision in trials at common law in the courts of the United States in cases where they apply.

Section 34, commonly called the "Rules of Decision Act," is still in force, although it has been amended in certain ways we will consider later. The current version is codified at 28 U.S.C. § 1652. For the first three cases, however, it is important to keep the original language in mind.

The Rules of Decision Act contains an ambiguity, although one that is not obvious to the modern eye. The statute requires federal courts to apply "the laws of the several states." But what exactly is law? The Court answered that question in 1842 in *Swift v. Tyson*, establishing a basic view of law that would last for almost a century.

SWIFT V. TYSON, 41 U.S. (16 Pet.) 1, 10 L.Ed. 865 (1842). Defendant bought land from a person named Norton, giving a "bill of exchange" (a type of negotiable instrument) in return. However, Norton had made several fraudulent representations about the land. Norton later conveyed the bill of exchange to Plaintiff as payment for an existing debt. When Plaintiff presented the bill to Defendant for payment, Defendant refused to pay, arguing that Norton's fraud rendered the bill voidable. The law of negotiable instruments, however, includes a key rule called the "holder in due course" rule. Under this doctrine, a person who acquires a negotiable instrument for value and without knowledge of any problems is not subject to many of the defenses that might otherwise render the instrument unenforceable, including the defense of fraud. If Plaintiff was a holder in due course, he clearly could have recovered on the bill of exchange, even though Norton would have been barred from recovery because of his fraud.

The crucial issue was whether Plaintiff had given "value" for the bill of exchange. Under New York law, it was unclear whether accepting a negotiable instrument in payment of an antecedent debt constituted giving value sufficient to make one a holder in due course. Justice Story, writing for the Court, discussed the New York precedent. However, he then declared that the New York case law was not controlling:

> But, admitting the doctrine to be fully settled in New York, it remains to be considered, whether it is obligatory upon this court, if it differs from the principles established in the general commercial law. It is observable, that the courts of New York do not found their decisions upon this point, upon any local statute, or positive, fixed or ancient local usage; but they deduce the doctrine from the general principles of commercial law. It is, however, contended, that the 34th section of the judiciary act of 1789 furnishes a rule obligatory upon this court to follow the decisions of the state tribunals in all cases to which they apply.... In order to maintain the argument, it is essential, therefore, to hold, that the word "laws," in this section, includes within the scope of its meaning, the decisions of the local tribunals. In the ordinary use of language, it will hardly be contended, that the decisions of courts constitute laws. They are, at most, only evidence of what the laws are, and are not, of themselves, laws. They are often re-examined, reversed and qualified by the courts themselves, whenever they are found to be either defective, or ill-founded, or otherwise incorrect. The laws of a state are more usually understood to mean the rules and enactments promulgated by the legislative authority thereof, or long-established local customs having the force of laws. In all the various cases, which have hitherto come before us for decision, this court have uniformly supposed, that the true interpretation of the 34th section limited its application to state laws, strictly local, that is to say, to the positive statutes of the state, and the construction thereof adopted by the local tribunals, and to rights and titles to things having a permanent locality, such as the rights and titles to real estate, and other matters immovable and intra-territorial in their nature and character. It never has been supposed by us, that the section did apply, or was designed to apply, to questions of a more general nature, not at all dependent upon local statutes or local usages of a fixed and permanent operation, as, for example, to the construction of ordinary contracts or other written instruments, and especially to questions of general commercial law, where the state tribunals are called upon to perform the like functions as ourselves, that is, to ascertain, upon general reasoning and legal analogies, what is the true exposition of the contract or

instrument, or what is the just rule furnished by the principles of commercial law to govern the case. And we have not now the slightest difficulty in holding, that this section, upon its true intendment and construction, is strictly limited to local statutes and local usages of the character before stated, and does not extend to contracts and other instruments of a commercial nature, the true interpretation and effect whereof are to be sought, not in the decisions of the local tribunals, but in the general principles and doctrines of commercial jurisprudence. Undoubtedly, the decisions of the local tribunals upon such subjects are entitled to, and will receive, the most deliberate attention and respect of this court; but they cannot furnish positive rules, or conclusive authority, by which our own judgments are to be bound up and governed. The law respecting negotiable instruments may be truly declared in the languages of Cicero, adopted by Lord MANSFIELD in Luke v. Lyde, 2 Burr. 883, 887, to be in a great measure, not the law of a single country only, but of the commercial world. *Non erit alia lex Romae, alia Athenis; alia nunc, alia posthac; sed et apud omnes gentes, et omni tempore una eademque lex obtinebit.*

It becomes necessary for us, therefore, upon the present occasion, to express our own opinion of the true result of the commercial law upon the question now before us. . . .

The Court then concluded that under the general commercial law Plaintiff was a holder in due course even though he acquired the bill of exchange in satisfaction of an antecedent debt.

NOTES AND QUESTIONS

1. Joseph Story, the author of *Swift*, was one of the most brilliant legal minds in United States history. He was appointed to the Supreme Court in 1811 at the age of 32, the youngest person ever to serve on the Court. He wrote several Commentaries on certain topics in the law, which were frequently cited by the Court even while Story was a sitting Justice.

2. In 50 words or less, explain why, according to *Swift*, common-law rules such as tort and contract are not "state law."

3. Contrary to what seems to have become a modern popular myth, Justice Story's views of the nature of the common law were not universally accepted at the time of *Swift*. Indeed, the Supreme Court stated a very different view in a case decided only eight years prior to *Swift*. *Wheaton v. Peters*, 33 U.S. (8 Pet.) 591, 8 L.Ed. 1055 (1834), was a dispute indirectly involving the Court itself. Wheaton and Peters published reporters containing Supreme Court opinions, references to which (Wheat. and Pet.) still appear in official citations. Wheaton published from 1816 to 1827, and Peters published after that. However, Peters also decided to publish copies of

Wheaton's older reporters. Wheaton sued Peters for violation of both common-law authors' rights and the federal copyright statute.

With respect to the common-law authors' rights, Wheaton argued that English law had recognized such a claim, and that the common-law right continued in the United States after independence. The Court disagreed:

> But, if the common law right of authors were shown to exist in England, does the same right exist, and to the same extent, in this country.
>
> It is clear, there can be no common law of the United States. The federal government is composed of twenty-four sovereign and independent states; each of which may have its local usages, customs and common law. There is no principle which pervades the union and has the authority of law, that is not embodied in the constitution or laws of the union. . . .
>
> When, therefore, a common law right is asserted, we must look to the state in which the controversy originated. . . .
>
> No one will contend, that the common law, as it existed in England, has ever been in force in all its provisions, in any state in this union. It was adopted, so far only as its principles were suited to the condition of the colonies; and from this circumstance we see, what is common law in one state, is not so considered in another. The judicial decisions, the usages and customs of the respective states, must determine, how far the common law has been introduced and sanctioned in each.

Because there was no proof that Pennsylvania (the state where the works were created) recognized authors' rights, the Court held that Wheaton could not recover on that claim. Justice Story did not write an opinion in the case.

4. During the century following *Swift*, the federal courts developed a body of "federal common law." The rules of this federal judge-made law often differed from the rules that would have been applied in the state courts had the same case been heard there. Federal common law grew to encompass not only the general commercial law at issue in *Swift*, but also most issues of contract, tort, and to some extent even property, law.

The next case, *Erie R. Co. v. Tompkins,* started out as a routine application of this federal common law. The plaintiff chose federal court in the hope he would receive the benefit of the more favorable federal common law rule (when you read the case, make sure to identify the clash in governing law). Although the parties disagreed as to the content of the state and federal rules, no one on appeal questioned whether *Swift* ought to apply. And yet, as the first line of the Supreme Court's opinion makes clear, the Court had quite a different agenda in mind.

ERIE R. CO. v. TOMPKINS
304 U.S. 64, 58 S.Ct. 817, 82 L.Ed. 1188 (1938)

MR. JUSTICE BRANDEIS delivered the opinion of the Court.

The question for decision is whether the oft-challenged doctrine of Swift v. Tyson shall now be disapproved.

Tompkins, a citizen of Pennsylvania, was injured on a dark night by a passing freight train of the Erie Railroad Company while walking along its right of way at Hughestown in that state. He claimed that the accident occurred through negligence in the operation, or maintenance, of the train; that he was rightfully on the premises as licensee because on a commonly used beaten footpath which ran for a short distance alongside the tracks; and that he was struck by something which looked like a door projecting from one of the moving cars. To enforce that claim he brought an action in the federal court for Southern New York, which had jurisdiction because the company is a corporation of that state. It denied liability; and the case was tried by a jury.

The Erie insisted that its duty to Tompkins was no greater than that owed to a trespasser. It contended, among other things, that its duty to Tompkins, and hence its liability, should be determined in accordance with the Pennsylvania law; that under the law of Pennsylvania, as declared by its highest court, persons who use pathways along the railroad right of way—that is, a longitudinal pathway as distinguished from a crossing—are to be deemed trespassers; and that the railroad is not liable for injuries to undiscovered trespassers resulting from its negligence, unless it be wanton or willful. Tompkins denied that any such rule had been established by the decisions of the Pennsylvania courts; and contended that, since there was no statute of the state on the subject, the railroad's duty and liability is to be determined in federal courts as a matter of general law. . . .

The Erie had contended that application of the Pennsylvania rule was required, among other things, by section 34 of the Federal Judiciary Act of September 24, 1789, which provides: "The laws of the several States, except where the Constitution, treaties, or statutes of the United States otherwise require or provide, shall be regarded as rules of decision in trials at common law, in the courts of the United States, in cases where they apply."

Because of the importance of the question whether the federal court was free to disregard the alleged rule of the Pennsylvania common law, we granted certiorari.

First. Swift v. Tyson, 16 Pet. 1, 18, held that federal courts exercising jurisdiction on the ground of diversity of citizenship need not, in matters of general jurisprudence, apply the unwritten law of the state as declared by its highest court; that they are free to exercise an independent judgment as to what the common law of the state is—or should be; and that, as there stated by Mr. Justice Story, "the true interpretation of the 34th section limited its application to state laws, strictly local, that is to say, to the positive statutes of the state, and the construction thereof adopted by the local tribunals, and to rights and titles to things having a permanent locality, such as the rights and titles to real estate, and other matters immovable and intra-territorial in their nature and character...."

The Court in applying the rule of section 34 to equity cases, in Mason v. United States, 260 U.S. 545, 559, said: "The statute, however, is merely declarative of the rule which would exist in the absence of the statute." The federal courts assumed, in the broad field of "general law," the power to declare rules of decision which Congress was confessedly without power to enact as statutes. Doubt was repeatedly expressed as to the correctness of the construction given section 34, and as to the soundness of the rule which it introduced. But it was the more recent research of a competent scholar, who examined the original document, which established that the construction given to it by the Court was erroneous; and that the purpose of the section was merely to make certain that, in all matters except those in which some federal law is controlling, the federal courts exercising jurisdiction in diversity of citizenship cases would apply as their rules of decision the law of the state, unwritten as well as written.[5] ...

Second. Experience in applying the doctrine of Swift v. Tyson, had revealed its defects, political and social; and the benefits expected to flow from the rule did not accrue. Persistence of state courts in their own opinions on questions of common law prevented uniformity; and the impossibility of discovering a satisfactory line of demarcation between the province of general law and that of local law developed a new well of uncertainties.

On the other hand, the mischievous results of the doctrine had become apparent. Diversity of citizenship jurisdiction was conferred in order to prevent apprehended discrimination in state courts against those not citizens of the state. Swift v. Tyson introduced grave discrimination by noncitizens against citizens. It made rights enjoyed under the unwritten "general law" vary according to whether enforcement was sought in the state or in the federal court; and the privilege of selecting the court in which the right should be determined was conferred upon the noncitizen. Thus, the doctrine rendered impossible equal protection of the law. In attempting to promote uniformity of law throughout the United States, the doctrine had prevented uniformity in the administration of the law of the state.

---

[5] Charles Warren, *New Light on the History of the Federal Judiciary Act of 1789* (1923) 37 Harv.L.Rev. 49, 51–52, 81–88, 108.

The discrimination resulting became in practice far-reaching. This resulted in part from the broad province accorded to the so-called "general law" as to which federal courts exercised an independent judgment....

In part the discrimination resulted from the wide range of persons held entitled to avail themselves of the federal rule by resort to the diversity of citizenship jurisdiction. Through this jurisdiction individual citizens willing to remove from their own state and become citizens of another might avail themselves of the federal rule. And, without even change of residence, a corporate citizen of the state could avail itself of the federal rule by reincorporating under the laws of another state....

The injustice and confusion incident to the doctrine of Swift v. Tyson have been repeatedly urged as reasons for abolishing or limiting diversity of citizenship jurisdiction. Other legislative relief has been proposed. If only a question of statutory construction were involved, we should not be prepared to abandon a doctrine so widely applied throughout nearly a century. But the unconstitutionality of the course pursued has now been made clear, and compels us to do so.

Third. Except in matters governed by the Federal Constitution or by acts of Congress, the law to be applied in any case is the law of the state. And whether the law of the state shall be declared by its Legislature in a statute or by its highest court in a decision is not a matter of federal concern. There is no federal general common law. Congress has no power to declare substantive rules of common law applicable in a state whether they be local in their nature or "general," be they commercial law or a part of the law of torts. And no clause in the Constitution purports to confer such a power upon the federal courts. As stated by Mr. Justice Field when protesting in Baltimore & Ohio R.R. Co. v. Baugh, 149 U.S. 368, 401, against ignoring the Ohio common law of fellow-servant liability: I am aware that what has been termed the general law of the country—which is often little less than what the judge advancing the doctrine thinks at the time should be the general law on a particular subject—has been often advanced in judicial opinions of this court to control a conflicting law of a state. I admit that learned judges have fallen into the habit of repeating this doctrine as a convenient mode of brushing aside the law of a state in conflict with their views. And I confess that, moved and governed by the authority of the great names of those judges, I have, myself, in many instances, unhesitatingly and confidently, but I think now erroneously, repeated the same doctrine. But, notwithstanding the great names which may be cited in favor of the doctrine, and notwithstanding the frequency with which the doctrine has been reiterated, there stands, as a perpetual protest against its repetition, the constitution of the United States, which recognizes and preserves the autonomy and independence of the states,—independence in their legislative and independence in their judicial departments. Supervision over either the legislative or the judicial action of the states is in no case permissible except as to matters by the constitution specifically authorized or delegated to the United States. Any interference with either, except as thus permitted, is an invasion of the authority of the state, and, to that extent, a denial of its independence.

The fallacy underlying the rule declared in Swift v. Tyson is made clear by Mr. Justice Holmes. The doctrine rests upon the assumption that there is "a transcendental body of law outside of any particular State but obligatory within it unless and until changed by statute," that federal courts have the power to use their judgment as to what the rules of common law are; and that in the federal courts "the parties are entitled to an independent judgment on matters of general law":

> But law in the sense in which courts speak of it today does not exist without some definite authority behind it. The common law so far as it is enforced in a State, whether called common law or not, is not the common law generally but the law of that State existing by the authority of that State without regard to what it may have been in England or anywhere else. . . .
>
> The authority and only authority is the State, and if that be so, the voice adopted by the State as its own (whether it be of its Legislature or of its Supreme Court) should utter the last word.

[Kuhn v. Fairmont Coal Co., 215 U.S. 349 (1910).] Thus the doctrine of Swift v. Tyson is, as Mr. Justice Holmes said, "an unconstitutional assumption of powers by the Courts of the United States which no lapse of time or respectable array of opinion should make us hesitate to correct." In disapproving that doctrine we do not hold unconstitutional section 34 of the Federal Judiciary Act of 1789 or any other act of Congress. We merely declare that in applying the doctrine this Court and the lower courts have invaded rights which in our opinion are reserved by the Constitution to the several states.

Fourth. The defendant contended that by the common law of Pennsylvania as declared by its highest court in Falchetti v. Pennsylvania R. Co., 307 Pa. 203, 160 A. 859, the only duty owed to the plaintiff was to refrain from willful or wanton injury. The plaintiff denied that such is the Pennsylvania law. In support of their respective contentions the parties discussed and cited many decisions of the Supreme Court of the state. The Circuit Court of Appeals ruled that the question of liability is one of general law; and on that ground declined to decide the issue of state law. As we hold this was error, the judgment is reversed and the case remanded to it for further proceedings in conformity with our opinion.

MR. JUSTICE CARDOZO took no part in the consideration or decision of this case.

MR. JUSTICE BUTLER (dissenting).

. . . [Swift v. Tyson] has been followed by this Court in an unbroken line of decisions. So far as appears, it was not questioned until more than 50 years later, and then by a single judge. . . .

It is hard to foresee the consequences of the radical change . . . [this Court has] made. . . . It extends to all matters of contracts and torts not positively governed by state enactments. Counsel searching for precedent and reasoning to disclose common-law principles on which to guide clients and conduct litigation are by this decision told that as to all of these questions the decisions of this Court and other federal courts are no longer anywhere authoritative. . . .

The Court's opinion in its first sentence defines the question to be whether the doctrine of Swift v. Tyson shall now be disapproved; it recites that Congress is without power to prescribe rules of decision that have been followed by federal courts as a result of the construction of section 34 in Swift v. Tyson and since; after discussion, it declares that "the unconstitutionality of the course pursued (meaning the rule of decision resulting from that construction) . . . compels" abandonment of the doctrine so long applied; and then near the end of the last page, the Court states that it does not hold section 34 unconstitutional, but merely that, in applying the doctrine of Swift v. Tyson construing it, this Court and the lower courts have invaded rights which are reserved by the Constitution to the several states. But, plainly through the form of words employed, the substance of the decision appears; it strikes down as unconstitutional section 34 as construed by our decisions; it divests the Congress of power to prescribe rules to be followed by federal courts when deciding questions of general law. In that broad field it compels this and the lower federal courts to follow decisions of the courts of a particular state. . . .

MR. JUSTICE MCREYNOLDS, concurs in this opinion.

MR. JUSTICE REED (concurring in part).

I concur in the conclusion reached in this case, in the disapproval of the doctrine of Swift v. Tyson, and in the reasoning of the majority opinion, except in so far as it relies upon the unconstitutionality of the "course pursued" by the federal courts. . . .

NOTES AND QUESTIONS

1. *Swift* adopted a particular interpretation of the Rules of Decision Act. Does *Erie* change that interpretation? After *Erie*, what does the reference to "laws" in the Rules of Decision Act mean?

2. The Court in *Erie* supports its decision by declaring that *Swift*'s view of the common law was based on a "fallacy." *Erie* substituted a modern view of the common law, a view grounded in the emerging legal philosophy of legal realism. Yet was the view in *Swift* really that outdated? Consider your own studies as a law student. In your courses in Torts, Contracts, and Property, do you study only the law of one state? Moreover, don't courts in one state often cite decisions from *other* states when dealing with new questions? Isn't there in fact a sense of universality to the common law, notwithstanding Justice Brandeis's views?

3. Canada, another federal state with a common-law heritage, has not adopted anything resembling the *Erie* doctrine. There remains in Canada a sense that the common law is a shared body of law (except in Québec), even if the particular rules may on occasion differ between provinces. Could this difference be systemic? To what extent could it be relevant that the Supreme Court of Canada, unlike its American counterpart, is a general court of appeals that can review all decisions rendered by the provinces, even those involving common-law issues? Would it affect your answer to learn that in practice the Supreme Court of Canada rarely reviews cases turning solely on the interpretation of the common law?

4. Even if *Erie*'s view of the common law is correct, is there an internal inconsistency to the decision? If the general common law is purely state law, then isn't the philosophical *nature* of that law also entirely up to the states? Suppose, for example, that a state continues to adhere to *Swift*'s view of the common law. In that state, at least, shouldn't a federal court be free to ignore state-court precedent and determine for itself what the "proper" rule should be? Can the United States Supreme Court change that? Doesn't *Erie* stand for the proposition that federal courts—including the United States Supreme Court—are powerless to change the nature of the common law?

5. Like *Swift* before it, *Erie* deals with the Rules of Decision Act. Suppose Congress were to repeal that statute. Would the federal courts immediately revert to an approach like that in *Swift*? What does the Court mean when it says, "If only a question of statutory construction were involved, we should not be prepared to abandon a doctrine so widely applied throughout nearly a century. But the unconstitutionality of the course pursued has now been made clear, and compels us to do so."?

6. Note that only a bare majority of the Court explicitly signed on to the notion that the rule in *Erie* is constitutionally required. Even Justice Reed, who agreed that *Swift* should be overturned, disavowed the idea that the approach in *Swift* was unconstitutional.

7. *Equal protection?* If *Erie* is a constitutional decision, upon which provision of the Constitution is it based? The only specific provision mentioned by the Court is the equal protection clause (which is in the fourteenth amendment). However, the practice under *Swift* could not violate that clause. Under *Swift*, federal courts would apply a different rule than their state counterparts. There is no equal protection violation merely

because the state and federal governments have two different rules governing the same behavior. (If it were, which government would be violating the clause?) As just one example, both the federal government and some states have laws that regulate unfair trade practices; laws that often differ in several important respects.

8. *Federalism?* The Court's other constitutional references are more subtle. In part *"First"* of the opinion, the Court states that federal courts under *Swift* would "declare rules of decision which Congress was confessedly without power to enact as statutes." In part *"Third"*, the Court indicates that "Congress has no power to declare substantive rules of common law.... And no clause in the Constitution purports to confer such a power upon the federal courts." Finally, later in the same paragraph, the Court mentions how the Constitution "recognizes and preserves the autonomy and independence of the states,—independence in their legislative and independence in their judicial departments." Can you cobble from these quotes—all of which relate to federalism—a constitutional theory supporting *Erie*?

Consider the references to Congressional power in the first two quotes. If you have taken Constitutional Law, you should know that Congress could, under its Article I power to regulate interstate commerce, pass a law regulating the substantive issue in *Erie* (the liability of a railroad), even given the restrictive interpretation of the commerce power that prevailed in 1938. But does it matter that Congress could have passed such a law? In *Erie* itself, would *Congress* be deciding what the standard of care would be? On the other hand, as long as the federal government has the authority to pass a law, does it really matter which branch does so? Who selects Congress? Who selects judges for the federal courts?

9. In certain situations, Congress may delegate some of its lawmaking powers. In fact, the notion of delegation is central to the Court's reasoning in *Hanna v. Plumer*, which is set out later in this Chapter. Of course, in *Erie* itself there was no evidence of a delegation from Congress to the federal courts; indeed, the Rules of Decision Act is clear evidence that Congress had not given the federal courts a general power to make law. But could Congress delegate to the federal courts the power to create governing law for all cases heard in federal court? Although Congress could have passed the rule in *Erie*, could it enact statutes governing every case heard in federal court—especially *diversity* cases? Consider again the quotes set out in note 8 above. Do they make more sense when viewed in this light?

10. Is there something a bit facile about analogizing pre-*Erie* federal common law to a federal statute? If Congress enacts a statute, is there anything a state can do to overcome it? By contrast, did pre-*Erie* federal common law apply in the state courts? And couldn't a state control the result even in federal court merely by enacting a statute?

11. *Erie* is mainly an issue in diversity cases. Do you see why the doctrine has less impact in a federal question case? In a federal question case, what is the source of the law giving rise to the claim?

Many courts and commentators have suggested that *Erie* is an issue *only* in diversity cases. These statements are simply incorrect. The doctrine also applies when a federal court hears the "non-federal" portion of a case heard under its supplemental jurisdiction. Moreover, you will see later in this chapter that the doctrine can apply even in pure federal question cases.

12. The *Erie* case was litigated in a New York federal court. So why does the Supreme Court hold that the federal court should apply *Pennsylvania* law? Given that most *Erie* cases are diversity cases, and accordingly have connections with two or more states, how does a federal court choose *which* state's law to apply?

The Supreme Court answered this question in *Klaxon Co. v. Stentor Electric Mfg. Co.*, 313 U.S. 487, 61 S.Ct. 1020, 85 L.Ed. 1477 (1941). The Court noted that every state had its own "choice of law rules" that dictated what law would be used to decide a case that had connections with more than one jurisdiction. (For an overview of these rules, see the *Paul* case in Part A of this Chapter). These choice of law rules, the Court reasoned, were included among the state laws that federal courts must apply under *Erie*. *Klaxon* requires the federal court to apply the choice of law rules of the state in which the federal court sits.

The *Erie* Court may not even have considered the choice of law issue. Under the dominant choice of law methodology in use in 1938, it was clear that the law of the place of the accident—Pennsylvania—would govern the case. This rule was in force in all states, and would probably also would have represented the federal approach.

13. Must a federal court use the choice of law rules of the state in which it sits even if that state court would not have had jurisdiction to decide the case? If so, it is possible that the federal court could reach a result different than that which would be reached in any state court that might hear the case. In *Griffin v. McCoach*, 313 U.S. 498, 61 S.Ct. 1023, 85 L.Ed. 1481 (1941), a companion case to *Klaxon*, the Court held that the *Klaxon* rule applied even to a case that could not have been heard in any state court. The case involved statutory interpleader, a special form of joinder. As you will learn in Chapter 8, a federal court in a statutory interpleader case may exercise personal jurisdiction over any party who can be served in the United States, even if the party has no contacts with the state in which the federal court sits. Therefore, no state court would have had personal jurisdiction over all the parties in *Griffin*, including the state whose choice of law rules were applied.

The *Erie* opinion paints with a very broad brush. Read literally, it suggests that federal courts are completely powerless to enact rules of law. But a court, by its very nature, makes a number of binding proclamations that are not directly supported by a statute. Suppose, for example, that a judge wants to close a potentially sensitive trial to the media. State judges, however, consistently allow media into all trials. Would the federal court have to follow the state practice and allow the media into the courtroom? Wouldn't a rule barring the media be a form of "federal common law?"

Certainly *Erie* does not go that far. Yet, because the opinion is written in such broad terms, the Court had to revisit the basic issue only seven years after its decision in *Erie*. Before diving into *Guaranty Trust Co. of New York v. York*, however, it is useful to discuss the issue facing the Court. *Guaranty Trust* was a suit in equity. The case involved an action for breach of trust, a historically equitable claim (see Chapter 6). Courts sitting in equity typically do not consider themselves bound by statutes of limitation. Instead, they apply the judge-made doctrine of *laches*. Laches is not a fixed period of time. Instead, a suit is barred by laches only if the defendant was somehow harmed by the plaintiff's delay in bringing the case. The issue in *Guaranty Trust* is whether the federal court should apply laches (under which the action could proceed because defendant had not been harmed by the delay) or, like the state courts, apply the state statute of limitations (under which the action would be barred).

GUARANTY TRUST CO. OF NEW YORK V. YORK
326 U.S. 99, 65 S.Ct. 1464, 89 L.Ed. 2079 (1945)

MR. JUSTICE FRANKFURTER delivered the opinion of the Court.

... In May, 1930, Van Sweringen Corporation issued notes to the amount of $30,000,000. Under an indenture of the same date, petitioner, Guaranty Trust Co., was named trustee with power and obligations to enforce the rights of the noteholders in the assets of the Corporation and of the Van Sweringen brothers. In October, 1930, petitioner, with other banks, made large advances to companies affiliated with the Corporation and wholly controlled by the Van Sweringens. In October, 1931, when it was apparent that the Corporation could not meet its obligations, Guaranty co-operated in a plan for the purchase of the outstanding notes on the basis of cash for 50% of the face value of the notes and twenty shares of Van Sweringen Corporation's stock for each $1,000 note....

Respondent York received $6,000 of the notes as a gift in 1934, her donor not having accepted the offer of exchange....

The suit, instituted [by York] as a class action on behalf of non-accepting noteholders and brought in a federal court solely because of diversity of citizenship, is based on an alleged breach of trust by Guaranty in that it failed to protect the interests of the noteholders in assenting to the exchange offer and failed to disclose its self-interest when sponsoring the offer.... [The lower federal courts held that the action was barred by the New York statute of limitations, even though the suit was in equity.]

We put to one side the considerations relevant in disposing of questions that arise when a federal court is adjudicating a claim based on a federal law. Our problem only touches transactions for which rights and obligations are created by one of the States, and for the assertion of which, in case of diversity of the citizenship of the parties, Congress has made a federal court another available forum.

Our starting point must be the policy of federal jurisdiction which Erie R. Co. v. Tompkins embodies. In overruling Swift v. Tyson, Erie R. Co. v. Tompkins did not merely overrule a venerable case. It overruled a particular way of looking at law which dominated the judicial process long after its inadequacies had been laid bare. Law was conceived as a "brooding omnipresence" of Reason, of which decisions were merely evidence and not themselves the controlling formulations. Accordingly, federal courts deemed themselves free to ascertain what Reason, and therefore Law, required wholly independent of authoritatively declared State law, even in cases where a legal right as the basis for relief was created by State authority and could not be created by federal authority and the case got into a federal court merely because it was "between Citizens of different States" under Art. III, § 2 of the Constitution of the United States. . . .

In relation to the problem now here, the real significance of Swift v. Tyson lies in the fact that it did not enunciate novel doctrine. Nor was it restricted to its particular situation. It summed up prior attitudes and expressions in cases that had come before this Court and lower federal courts for at least thirty years, at law as well as in equity. The short of it is that the doctrine was congenial to the jurisprudential climate of the time. Once established, judicial momentum kept it going. Since it was conceived that there was "a transcendental body of law outside of any particular State but obligatory within it unless and until changed by statute", 276 U.S. 518, 532, 533, State court decisions were not "the law" but merely someone's opinion—to be sure an opinion to be respected— concerning the content of this all-pervading law. Not unnaturally, the federal courts assumed power to find for themselves the content of such a body of law. The notion was stimulated by the attractive vision of a uniform body of federal law. . . .

In exercising their jurisdiction on the ground of diversity of citizenship, the federal courts, in the long course of their history, have not differentiated in their regard for State law between actions at law and suits in equity. Although § 34 of the Judiciary Act of 1789 directed that the "laws of the several States . . . shall be regarded as rules of decision in trials of common law . . .", this was deemed, consistently for over a hundred years, to be merely declaratory of what would in any event have governed the federal courts and therefore was equally applicable to equity suits. . . .

Partly because the States in the early days varied greatly in the manner in which equitable relief was afforded and in the extent to which it was available, Congress provided that "the forms and modes of proceeding in suits . . . of equity" would conform to the settled uses of courts of equity. Section 2, 1 Stat. 275, 276. But this enactment gave the federal courts no power that they would not have had in any event when courts were given "cognizance", by the first Judiciary Act, of equity. From the beginning there has been a good deal of talk in the cases that federal equity is a separate legal system. And so it is, properly understood. The suits in equity of which the federal courts have had "cognizance" ever since 1789 constituted the body of law which had been transplanted to this country from the English Court of Chancery. But this system of equity "derived its doctrines, as well as its powers, from its mode of giving relief". Langdell, Summary of Equity Pleading (1877) xxvii. In giving federal courts "cognizance" of equity suits in cases of diversity jurisdiction, Congress never gave, nor did the federal courts ever claim, the power to deny substantive rights created by State law or to create substantive rights denied by State law.

This does not mean that whatever equitable remedy is available in a State court must be available in a diversity suit in a federal court, or conversely, that a federal court may not afford an equitable remedy not available in a State court. Equitable relief in a federal court is of course subject to restrictions: the suit must be within the traditional scope of equity as historically evolved in the English Court of Chancery; a plain, adequate and complete remedy at law must be wanting; explicit Congressional curtailment of equity powers must be respected; the constitutional right to trial by jury cannot be evaded. That a State may authorize its courts to give equitable relief unhampered by any or all such restrictions cannot remove these fetters from the federal courts. State law cannot define the remedies which a federal court must give simply because a federal court in diversity jurisdiction is available as an alternative tribunal to the State's courts. Contrariwise, a federal court may afford an equitable remedy for a substantive right recognized by a State even though a State court cannot give it. Whatever contradiction or confusion may be produced by a medley of judicial phrases severed from their environment, the body of adjudications concerning equitable relief in diversity cases leaves no doubt that the federal courts enforced State-created substantive rights if the mode of proceeding and remedy were consonant with the traditional body of equitable remedies, practice and procedure, and in so doing they were enforcing rights created by the States and not arising under any inherent or statutory federal law. . . .

And so this case reduces itself to the narrow question whether, when no recovery could be had in a State court because the action is barred by the statute of limitations, a federal court in equity can take cognizance of the suit because there is diversity of citizenship between the parties. Is the outlawry, according to State law, of a claim created by the States a matter of "substantive rights" to be respected by a federal court of equity when that court's jurisdiction is dependent on the fact that there is a State-created right, or is such statute of "a mere remedial character", which a federal court may disregard?

Matters of "substance" and matters of "procedure" are much talked about in the books as though they defined a great divide cutting across the whole domain of law. But, of course, "substance" and "procedure" are the same key-words to very different problems. Neither "substance" nor "procedure" represents the same invariants. Each implies different variables depending upon the particular problem for which it is used. And the different problems are only distantly related at best, for the terms are in common use in connection with situations turning on such different considerations as those that are relevant to questions pertaining to ex post facto legislation, the impairment of the obligations of contract, the enforcement of federal rights in the State courts and the multitudinous phases of the conflict of laws.

Here we are dealing with a right to recover derived not from the United States but from one of the States. When, because the plaintiff happens to be a nonresident, such a right is enforceable in a federal as well as in a State court, the forms and mode of enforcing the right may at times, naturally enough, vary because the two judicial systems are not identic. But since a federal court adjudicating a state-created right solely because of the diversity of citizenship of the parties is for that purpose, in effect, only another court of the State, it cannot afford recovery if the right to recover is made unavailable by the State nor can it substantially affect the enforcement of the right as given by the State.

And so the question is not whether a statute of limitations is deemed a matter of "procedure" in some sense. The question is whether such a statute concerns merely the manner and the means by which a right to recover, as recognized by the State, is enforced, or whether such statutory limitation is a matter of substance in the aspect that alone is relevant to our problem, namely, does it significantly affect the result of a litigation for a federal court to disregard a law of a State that would be controlling in an action upon the same claim by the same parties in a State court?

It is therefore immaterial whether statutes of limitation are characterized either as "substantive" or "procedural" in State court opinions in any use of those terms unrelated to the specific issue before us. Erie R. Co. v. Tompkins was not an endeavor to formulate scientific legal terminology. It expressed a policy that touches vitally the proper distribution of judicial power between State and federal courts. In essence, the intent of that decision was to insure that, in all cases where a federal court is exercising jurisdiction solely because of the diversity of citizenship of the parties, the outcome of the litigation in the federal court should be substantially the same, so far as legal rules determine the outcome of a litigation, as it would be if tried in a State court. The nub of the policy that underlies Erie R. Co. v. Tompkins is that for the same transaction the accident of a suit by a non-resident litigant in a federal court instead of in a State court a block away, should not lead to a substantially different result.... A policy so important to our federalism must be kept free from entanglements with analytical or terminological niceties.

Plainly enough, a statute that would completely bar recovery in a suit if brought in a State court bears on a State-created right vitally and not merely formally or negligibly. As to consequences that so intimately affect recovery or non-recovery a federal court in a diversity case should follow State law.... [I]f a plea of the statute of limitations would bar recovery in a State court, a federal court ought not to afford recovery....

To make an exception to Erie R. Co. v. Tompkins on the equity side of a federal court is to reject the considerations of policy which, after long travail, led to that decision. Judge Augustus N. Hand thus summarized below the fatal objection to such inroad upon Erie R. Co. v. Tompkins: "In my opinion it would be a mischievous practice to disregard state statutes of limitation whenever federal courts think that the result of adopting them may be inequitable. Such procedure would promote the choice of United States rather than of state courts in order to gain the advantage of different laws. The main foundation for the criticism of Swift v. Tyson was that a litigant in cases where federal jurisdiction is based only on diverse citizenship may obtain a more favorable decision by suing in the United States courts." 2 Cir., 143 F.2d 503, 529, 531.

Diversity jurisdiction is founded on assurance to non-resident litigants of courts free from susceptibility to potential local bias.... And so Congress afforded out-of-State litigants another tribunal, not another body of law. The operation of a double system of conflicting laws in the same State is plainly hostile to the reign of law. Certainly, the fortuitous circumstance of residence out of a State of one of the parties to a litigation ought not to give rise to a discrimination against others equally concerned but locally resident. The source of substantive rights enforced by a federal court under diversity jurisdiction, it cannot be said too often, is the law of the States. Whenever that law is authoritatively declared by a State, whether its voice be the legislature or its highest court, such law ought to govern in litigation founded on that law, whether the forum of application is a State or a federal court and whether the remedies be sought at law or may be had in equity....

The judgment is reversed and the case is remanded for proceedings not inconsistent with this opinion.

Mr. Justice Roberts and Mr. Justice Douglas took no part in the consideration or decision of this case.

Mr. Justice Rutledge.

I dissent. . . .

If any characteristic of equity jurisprudence has descended unbrokenly from and within "the traditional scope of equity as historically evolved in the English Court of Chancery," it is that statutes of limitations, often in terms applying only to actions at law, have never been deemed to be rigidly applicable as absolute barriers to suits in equity as they are to actions at law. That tradition, it would seem, should be regarded as having been incorporated in the various Acts of Congress which have conferred equity jurisdiction upon the federal courts. So incorporated, it has been reaffirmed repeatedly by the decisions of this and other courts. It is now excised from those Acts. If there is to be excision, Congress, not this Court, should make it. . . .

The words "substantive" and "procedural" or "remedial" are not talismanic. Merely calling a legal question by one or the other does not resolve it otherwise than as a purely authoritarian performance. But they have come to designate in a broad way large and distinctive legal domains within the greater one of the law and to mark, though often indistinctly or with overlapping limits, many divides between such regions. . . .

It may be true that if the matter were wholly fresh the barring of rights in equity by statutes of limitation would seem to partake more of the substantive than of the remedial phase of law. But the matter is not fresh and it is not without room for debate. A long tradition, in the states and here, as well as in the common law which antedated both state and federal law, has emphasized the remedial character of statutes of limitations, more especially in application to equity causes, on many kinds of issues requiring differentiation of such matters from more clearly and exclusively substantive ones. . . . The tradition now in question is equally long and unvaried. I cannot say the tradition is clearly wrong in this case more than in that. Nor can I say, as was said in the Erie case, that the matter is beyond the power of Congress to control. If that be conceded, I think Congress should make the change if it is to be made. The Erie decision was rendered in 1938. Seven years have passed without action by Congress to extend the rule to these matters. That is long enough to justify the conclusion that Congress also regards them as not governed by Erie and as wishing to make no change. This should be reason enough for leaving the matter at rest until it decides to act. . . .

Mr. Justice Murphy joins in this opinion.

NOTES AND QUESTIONS

1. The state law in question in *Guaranty Trust* was a statute. Even under *Swift*, federal courts would apply state statutes as "state law" under the Rules of Decision Act. Why is *Guaranty Trust* even an *Erie* case?

2. The version of the Rules of Decision Act in effect at the time of *Guaranty Trust* is set out on page 274. Re-read that statute. Do you see why the statute, as written, technically did not apply to the litigation in *Guaranty Trust*? Because the Court nevertheless ordered the federal court to apply state law, *Guaranty Trust* reinforces the notion that the *Erie* doctrine is grounded in the Constitution.

Now read the current version of the Rules of Decision Act, codified at 28 U.S.C. § 1652. Do you see why the current version would apply to a case like *Guaranty Trust* brought today?

3. Consider again the hypothetical set out in the text prior to the case. After *Guaranty Trust*, would a federal court be free to close a case to the media? Why or why not?

4. Why does the Court conclude that a federal court need not apply state "procedural" law? Under *Erie*, a federal court must follow state law by default; *i.e.*, because it is powerless to fashion a contrary rule. If federal courts can ignore state procedural rules, it means that the federal courts have the power to make federal procedural law. Where do the courts get this power?

5. The problem with applying a straightforward substance/procedure analysis in *Guaranty Trust* is that for many purposes statutes of limitation are considered procedural. For example, courts generally consider statutes of limitation procedural for purposes of choice of law, which means that a court applies its own state's limitations period even when applying some other state's law to the other issues in the case. *C.f. Restatement of the Law (Second), Conflicts* § 142. The Court in *Guaranty Trust*, however, does not consider itself bound by this precedent. Because the Court says that the considerations underlying *Erie* are different than issues such as choice of law, the definition of "substance" and "procedure" might also be different. The Court devotes much of the opinion to defining substance and procedure in the *Erie* context. It ends up adopting what is commonly referred to as the "outcome determinative" test. Under this test, when is a rule procedural?

6. Do you agree with the Court that the considerations underlying *Erie* and choice of law are different? Isn't *Erie* merely a type of choice of law rule that applies in federal court? On the other hand, is a court faced with an *Erie* issue really choosing one of two valid but competing laws?

7. Apply the outcome determinative test to the following situation: State X has a maniacal obsession with its state university's athletic program. The school colors are an obnoxious shade of blue. To show its school spirit, the state legislature passes a statute that requires all state judges to wear blue robes. In addition, the law provides that no pleadings will be accepted

unless printed in blue ink. Does a federal judge in State X have to replace her black robe with an obnoxious blue one when she hears a diversity case? May the federal court clerk accept a complaint printed in black ink for such a case?

8. The Court in *Guaranty Trust* explicitly reserves judgment on whether a federal court must apply a state limitations period when adjudicating a case arising under federal law. Today, the rule is that the limitations period on a federal claim is a question of *federal* law, although in some cases the court will borrow the most analogous state limitations period. 28 U.S.C. § 1658; *Reed v. United Transp. Union*, 488 U.S. 319, 109 S.Ct. 621, 102 L.Ed.2d 665 (1989).

9. *Remedies*. The Court also indicates that a federal court is not bound by state law when it is called upon to fashion an appropriate equitable remedy. Is that consistent with the rest of the opinion? Isn't the remedy the heart and soul of the "outcome" in a case, insofar as different remedies change the outcome?

For a discussion of how *Erie* applies to equitable remedies and other issues in equity, see John T. Cross, *The* Erie *Doctrine in Equity*, 60 LA. L. REV. 173 (1999). The author concludes that federal courts do in fact have a significant, albeit limited, power to ignore state laws governing equitable remedies.

As the discussion above suggests, *Guaranty Trust*'s "outcome determinative" test is problematic. Many matters that on their face seem clearly procedural can nevertheless change the outcome of a particular case. For the next twenty years, the Court continued to struggle with how to define the federal courts' power to regulate their procedure, as the following case demonstrates.

BYRD V. BLUE RIDGE RURAL ELECTRIC CO-OPERATIVE, INC., 356 U.S. 525, 78 S.Ct. 893, 2 L.Ed.2d 953 (1958). Plaintiff worked for a construction contractor. Plaintiff's employer was retained by Defendant, an electric utility, to install new power lines. While working on this job, Plaintiff was injured. Plaintiff sued Defendant for negligence in federal court, based on diversity. Defendant argued that because Plaintiff was injured on the job, his sole remedy lay under the South Carolina Workmen's Compensation Act.

One of the key issues in the case was who would decide whether Plaintiff was a "statutory employee" of Defendant. If Plaintiff was a statutory employee, his sole right to monetary relief would be workmen's compensation. In the South Carolina courts, the judge would decide that threshold issue. Plaintiff, however, wanted the federal court to try that issue to a jury. The Supreme Court held that the state practice of having the judge decide did not apply in the federal courts. Its analysis turned on three factors. First, the Court found the state practice of using a judge was not an integral part of the right to recover against the employer:

> We find nothing to suggest that this rule was announced as an integral part of the special relationship created by the statute. Thus the requirement appears to be merely a form and mode of enforcing the immunity, *Guaranty Trust Co. of New York v. York*, 326 U.S. 99, and not a rule intended to be bound up with the definition of the rights and obligations of the parties.

Second, the Court found a countervailing federal interest: the federal custom of using juries to decide contested factual issues. Although the Court in footnote 10 declined to hold that the Seventh Amendment required a jury in this case, that federal "tradition" nevertheless entered the calculus:

> It may well be that in the instant personal-injury case the outcome would be substantially affected by whether the issue of immunity is decided by a judge or a jury. Therefore, were "outcome" the only consideration, a strong case might appear for saying that the federal court should follow the state practice.

> But there are affirmative countervailing considerations at work here. The federal system is an independent system for administering justice to litigants who properly invoke its jurisdiction. An essential characteristic of that system is the manner in which, in civil common-law actions, it distributes trial functions between judge and jury and, under the influence—if not the command—of the Seventh Amendment, assigns the decisions of disputed questions of fact to the jury. The policy of uniform enforcement of state-created rights and obligations, cannot in every case exact compliance with a state rule—not bound up with rights and obligations—which disrupts the federal system of allocating functions between judge and jury.

Third, the Court also noted that the state law was not "outcome determinative" to the same degree as the rules in *Erie* and *Guaranty Trust*:

> We have discussed the problem upon the assumption that the outcome of the litigation may be substantially affected by whether the issue of immunity is decided by a judge or a jury. But clearly there is not present here the certainty that a different result would follow, cf. *Guaranty Trust Co. of New York v. York, supra*, or even the strong possibility that this would be the case. There are factors present here which might reduce that possibility. The trial judge in the federal system has powers denied the judges of many States to comment on the weight of evidence and credibility of witnesses, and discretion to grant a

new trial if the verdict appears to him to be against the weight of the evidence. We do not think the likelihood of a different result is so strong as to require the federal practice of jury determination of disputed factual issues to yield to the state rule in the interest of uniformity of outcome.

NOTES AND QUESTIONS

1. The Court's analysis invokes the Seventh Amendment. However, the Court dodges the issue of whether the Amendment actually requires a jury. But isn't that the crucial issue? If the Seventh Amendment requires a jury to decide the issue, of course, that specific requirement overrides the general federalism concerns of *Erie*. If the Seventh Amendment does not require a jury in the particular case, how is it even relevant to the analysis?

2. Can you think of any other areas where there is a federal interest strong enough to affect the *Erie* analysis?

3. Does *Byrd* modify the *Guaranty Trust* test, or does it simply create an exception? Try to restate the rule of *Byrd* as a three-step exception, based on the three excerpts set out above.

4. How would your three-part test apply to the blue robe/blue ink example set out in note 7 following *Guaranty Trust*?

HANNA V. PLUMER
380 U.S. 460, 85 S.Ct. 1136, 14 L.Ed.2d 8 (1965)

MR. CHIEF JUSTICE WARREN delivered the opinion of the Court.

The question to be decided is whether, in a civil action where the jurisdiction of the United States district court is based upon diversity of citizenship between the parties, service of process shall be made in the manner prescribed by state law or that set forth in Rule 4(d)(1) of the Federal Rules of Civil Procedure.

On February 6, 1963, petitioner, a citizen of Ohio, filed her complaint in the District Court for the District of Massachusetts, claiming damages in excess of $10,000 for personal injuries resulting from an automobile accident in South Carolina, allegedly caused by the negligence of one Louise Plumer Osgood, a Massachusetts citizen deceased at the time of the filing of the complaint. Respondent, Mrs. Osgood's executor and also a Massachusetts citizen, was named as defendant. On February 8, service was made by leaving copies of the summons and the complaint with respondent's wife at his residence, concededly in compliance with Rule 4(d)(1). . . .

Respondent filed his answer on February 26, alleging, *inter alia*, that the action could not be maintained because it had been brought "contrary to and in violation of the provisions of Massachusetts General Laws Chapter 197, Section 9." That section provides:

> Except as provided in this chapter, an executor or administrator shall not be held to answer to an action by a creditor of the deceased which is not commenced within one year from the time of his giving bond for the performance of his trust, or to such an action which is commenced within said year unless before the expiration thereof the writ in such action has been served by delivery in hand upon such executor or administrator or service thereof accepted by him or a notice stating the name of the estate, the name and address of the creditor, the amount of the claim and the court in which the action has been brought has been filed in the proper registry of probate. . . .

On October 17, 1963, the District Court granted respondent's motion for summary judgment, . . . [concluding] that the adequacy of the service was to be measured by § 9, with which, the court held, petitioner had not complied. On appeal, petitioner admitted noncompliance with § 9, but argued that Rule 4(d)(1) defines the method by which service of process is to be effected in diversity actions. The Court of Appeals for the First Circuit, finding that "(r)elatively recent amendments (to § 9) evince a clear legislative purpose to require personal notification within the year," concluded that the conflict of state and federal rules was over "a substantive rather than a procedural matter," and unanimously affirmed. Because of the threat to the goal of uniformity of federal procedure posed by the decision below, we granted certiorari.

We conclude that the adoption of Rule 4(d)(1), designed to control service of process in diversity actions, neither exceeded the congressional mandate embodied in the Rules Enabling Act nor transgressed constitutional bounds, and that the Rule is therefore the standard against which the District Court should have measured the adequacy of the service. Accordingly, we reverse the decision of the Court of Appeals.

The Rules Enabling Act, 28 U.S.C. § 2072, provides, in pertinent part:

> The Supreme Court shall have the power to prescribe, by general rules, the forms of process, writs, pleadings, and motions, and the practice and procedure of the district courts of the United States in civil actions.
>
> Such rules shall not abridge, enlarge or modify any substantive right and shall preserve the right of trial by jury. . . .

Under the cases construing the scope of the Enabling Act, Rule 4(d)(1) clearly passes muster. Prescribing the manner in which a defendant is to be notified that a suit has been instituted against him, it relates to the "practice and procedure of the district courts."

The test must be whether a rule really regulates procedure,—the judicial process for enforcing rights and duties recognized by substantive law and for justly administering remedy and redress for disregard or infraction of them. *Sibbach v. Wilson & Co.*, 312 U.S. 1, 14. . . .

Thus were there no conflicting state procedure, Rule 4(d)(1) would clearly control. However, respondent, focusing on the contrary Massachusetts rule, calls to the Court's attention another line of cases, a line which—like the Federal Rules—had its birth in 1938. *Erie R. Co. v. Tompkins*, 304 U.S. 64, overruling *Swift v. Tyson*, 16 Pet. 1, held that federal courts sitting in diversity cases, when deciding questions of "substantive" law, are bound by state court decisions as well as state statutes. The broad command of *Erie* was therefore identical to that of the Enabling Act: federal courts are to apply state substantive law and federal procedural law. However, as subsequent cases sharpened the distinction between substance and procedure, the line of cases following *Erie* diverged markedly from the line construing the Enabling Act. *Guaranty Trust Co. of New York v. York*, 326 U.S. 99, made it clear that *Erie*-type problems were not to be solved by reference to any traditional or common-sense substance-procedure distinction. . . .

Respondent . . . suggests that the *Erie* doctrine acts as a check on the Federal Rules of Civil Procedure, that despite the clear command of Rule 4(d)(1), *Erie* and its progeny demand the application of the Massachusetts rule. Reduced to essentials, the argument is: (1) *Erie*, as refined in *York*, demands that federal courts apply state law whenever application of federal law in its stead will alter the outcome of the case. (2) In this case, a determination that the Massachusetts service requirements obtain will result in immediate victory for respondent. If, on the other hand, it should be held that Rule 4(d)(1) is applicable, the litigation will continue, with possible victory for petitioner. (3) Therefore, *Erie* demands application of the Massachusetts rule. The syllogism possesses an appealing simplicity, but is for several reasons invalid.

In the first place, it is doubtful that, even if there were no Federal Rule making it clear that in-hand service is not required in diversity actions, the *Erie* rule would have obligated the District Court to follow the Massachusetts procedure. "Outcome-determination" analysis was never intended to serve as a talisman. Indeed, the message of *York* itself is that choices between state and federal law are to be made not by application of any automatic, "litmus paper" criterion, but rather by reference to the policies underlying the *Erie* rule.

The *Erie* rule is rooted in part in a realization that it would be unfair for the character of result of a litigation materially to differ because the suit had been brought in a federal court. . . .

The decision was also in part a reaction to the practice of "forum-shopping" which had grown up in response to the rule of *Swift v. Tyson*. That the *York* test was an attempt to effectuate these policies is demonstrated by the fact that the opinion framed the inquiry in terms of "substantial" variations between state and federal litigation. Not only are nonsubstantial, or trivial, variations not likely to raise the sort of equal protection problems which troubled the Court in *Erie*; they are also unlikely to influence the choice of a forum. The "outcome-determination" test therefore cannot be read without reference to the twin aims of the *Erie* rule: discouragement of forum-shopping and avoidance of inequitable administration of the laws.

The difference between the conclusion that the Massachusetts rule is applicable, and the conclusion that it is not, is of course at this point "outcome-determinative" in the sense that if we hold the state rule to apply, respondent prevails, whereas if we hold that Rule 4(d)(1) governs, the litigation will continue. But in this sense every procedural variation is "outcome-determinative." For example, having brought suit in a federal court, a plaintiff cannot then insist on the right to file subsequent pleadings in accord with the time limits applicable in state courts, even though enforcement of the federal timetable will, if he continues to insist that he must meet only the state time limit, result in determination of the controversy against him. So it is here. Though choice of the federal or state rule will at this point have a marked effect upon the outcome of the litigation, the difference between the two rules would be of scant, if any, relevance to the choice of a forum. Petitioner, in choosing her forum, was not presented with a situation where application of the state rule would wholly bar recovery; rather, adherence to the state rule would have resulted only in altering the way in which process was served. Moreover, it is difficult to argue that permitting service of defendant's wife to take the place of inhand service of defendant himself alters the mode of enforcement of state-created rights in a fashion sufficiently "substantial" to raise the sort of equal protection problems to which the *Erie* opinion alluded.

There is, however, a more fundamental flaw in respondent's syllogism: the incorrect assumption that the rule of *Erie R. Co. v. Tompkins* constitutes the appropriate test of the validity and therefore the applicability of a Federal Rule of Civil Procedure. The *Erie* rule has never been invoked to void a Federal Rule. It is true that there have been cases where this Court has held applicable a state rule in the face of an argument that the situation was governed by one of the Federal Rules. But the holding of each such case was not that *Erie* commanded displacement of a Federal Rule by an inconsistent state rule, but rather that the scope of the Federal Rule was not as broad as the losing party urged, and therefore, there being no Federal Rule which covered the point in dispute, *Erie* commanded the enforcement of state law.... (Here, of course, the clash is unavoidable; Rule 4(d)(1) says—implicitly, but with unmistakable clarity—that inhand service is not required in federal courts.) At the same time, in cases adjudicating the validity of Federal Rules, we have not applied the *York* rule or other refinements of *Erie*, but have to this day continued to decide questions concerning the scope of the Enabling Act and the constitutionality of specific Federal Rules in light of the distinction set forth in *Sibbach*.

Nor has the development of two separate lines of cases been inadvertent. The line between "substance" and "procedure" shifts as the legal context changes. "Each implies different variables depending upon the particular problem for which it is used." *Guaranty Trust Co. of New York v. York, supra*, 326 U.S. at 108. It is true that both the Enabling Act and the *Erie* rule say, roughly, that federal courts are to apply state "substantive" law and federal "procedural" law, but from that it need not follow that the tests are identical. For they were designed to control very different sorts of decisions. When a situation is covered by one of the Federal Rules, the question facing the court is a far cry from the typical, relatively unguided *Erie* Choice: the court has been instructed to apply the Federal Rule, and can refuse to do so only if the Advisory Committee, this Court, and Congress erred in their prima facie judgment that the Rule in question transgresses neither the terms of the Enabling Act nor constitutional restrictions.

We are reminded by the *Erie* opinion that neither Congress nor the federal courts can, under the guise of formulating rules of decision for federal courts, fashion rules which are not supported by a grant of federal authority contained in Article I or some other section of the Constitution; in such areas state law must govern because there can be no other law. But the opinion in *Erie*, which involved no Federal Rule and dealt with a question which was "substantive" in every traditional sense (whether the railroad owed a duty of care to Tompkins as a trespasser or a licensee), surely neither said nor implied that measures like Rule 4(d)(1) are unconstitutional. For the constitutional provision for a federal court system (augmented by the Necessary and Proper Clause*) carries with it congressional power to make rules governing the practice and pleading in those courts, which in turn includes a power to regulate matters which, though falling within the uncertain area between substance and procedure, are rationally capable of classification as either. Neither *York* nor the cases following it ever suggested that the rule there laid down for coping with situations where no Federal Rule applies is coextensive with the limitation on Congress to which *Erie* had adverted. . . .

---

* U.S. Const. Art. 1, § 8, gives Congress the power to enact laws that are "necessary and proper" for implementing any of its enumerated powers. This clause, commonly referred to as the "Necessary and Proper Clause," augments Congress's powers not only under Article I, but also under any other provision of the Constitution. [Eds.]

Erie and its offspring cast no doubt on the long-recognized power of Congress to prescribe housekeeping rules for federal courts even though some of those rules will inevitably differ from comparable state rules. . . . To hold that a Federal Rule of Civil Procedure must cease to function whenever it alters the mode of enforcing state-created rights would be to disembowel either the Constitution's grant of power over federal procedure or Congress' attempt to exercise that power in the Enabling Act. Rule 4(d)(1) is valid and controls the instant case.

Reversed.

 MR. JUSTICE BLACK concurs in the result.

 MR. JUSTICE HARLAN, concurring. . . .

Erie was something more than an opinion which worried about "forum-shopping and avoidance of inequitable administration of the laws," although to be sure these were important elements of the decision. I have always regarded that decision as one of the modern cornerstones of our federalism, expressing policies that profoundly touch the allocation of judicial power between the state and federal systems. *Erie* recognized that there should not be two conflicting systems of law controlling the primary activity of citizens, for such alternative governing authority must necessarily give rise to a debilitating uncertainty in the planning of everyday affairs. And it recognized that the scheme of our Constitution envisions an allocation of law-making functions between state and federal legislative processes which is undercut if the federal judiciary can make substantive law affecting state affairs beyond the bounds of congressional legislative powers in this regard. Thus, in diversity cases *Erie* commands that it be the state law governing primary private activity which prevails. . . .

To my mind the proper line of approach in determining whether to apply a state or a federal rule, whether "substantive" or "procedural," is to stay close to basic principles by inquiring if the choice of rule would substantially affect those primary decisions respecting human conduct which our constitutional system leaves to state regulation. If so, *Erie* and the Constitution require that the state rule prevail, even in the face of a conflicting federal rule.

The Court weakens, if indeed it does not submerge, this basic principle by finding, in effect, a grant of substantive legislative power in the constitutional provision for a federal court system, and through it, setting up the Federal Rules as a body of law inviolate. . . . So long as a reasonable man could characterize any duly adopted federal rule as "procedural," the Court, unless I misapprehend what is said, would have it apply no matter how seriously it frustrated a State's substantive regulation of the primary conduct and affairs of its citizens. Since the members of the Advisory Committee, the Judicial Conference, and this

Court who formulated the Federal Rules are presumably reasonable men, it follows that the integrity of the Federal Rules is absolute. Whereas the unadulterated outcome and forum-shopping tests may err too far toward honoring state rules, I submit that the Court's "arguably procedural, *ergo* constitutional" test moves too fast and far in the other direction. . . .

It remains to apply what has been said to the present case. The Massachusetts rule provides that an executor need not answer suits unless in-hand service was made upon him or notice of the action was filed in the proper registry of probate within one year of his giving bond. The evident intent of this statute is to permit an executor to distribute the estate which he is administering without fear that further liabilities may be outstanding for which he could be held personally liable. If the Federal District Court in Massachusetts applies Rule 4(d)(1) of the Federal Rules of Civil Procedure instead of the Massachusetts service rule, what effect would that have on the speed and assurance with which estates are distributed? As I see it, the effect would not be substantial. It would mean simply that an executor would have to check at his own house or the federal courthouse as well as the registry of probate before he could distribute the estate with impunity. As this does not seem enough to give rise to any real impingement on the vitality of the state policy which the Massachusetts rule is intended to serve, I concur in the judgment of the Court.

NOTES AND QUESTIONS

1. Like all *Erie* cases, *Hanna* involves a clash between state and federal law. What is the federal law involved in the case? Did any of the earlier cases involve this type of federal law?

2. Although the Federal Rules are codified, they are nevertheless a type of judge-made law. The Supreme Court, with the help of an Advisory Committee, promulgates the Rules pursuant to the authority granted in the Rules Enabling Act, 28 U.S.C. § 2072. Unless Congress rejects or modifies a proposed Rule, it automatically takes effect on December 1 of the year it was promulgated. 28 U.S.C. § 2074(a).

3. Review the Rules Enabling Act. Does it give the Supreme Court the power to enact a wide variety of rules? What explicit limits does the Act place on the Court's authority to enact laws?

4. Conceptually, both *Guaranty Trust* and *Byrd* dealt with the federal courts' inherent ability to regulate their own procedure. The issue in *Hanna* is fundamentally different. Because the Rules Enabling Act represents a delegation to the Supreme Court of some of Congress's lawmaking powers, the issue in a case like *Hanna* is not the courts' inherent power, but rather whether the Supreme Court has acted within the scope of the Congressional delegation.

5. With this background, consider the portion of *Hanna* that discusses whether a federal court should apply a Federal Rule in lieu of state law (which oddly enough comes at the end of the opinion). What test does the Court adopt? Is that test anything more than a restatement of the restrictions imposed by the Rules Enabling Act?

6. Note that when considering whether to apply a Federal Rule, a court does not ask whether the difference in state and federal law would be outcome determinative. If the Rule is valid under the Rules Enabling Act, it automatically applies. Why is outcome determination not relevant to the Rules? Recall that the Rules Enabling Act delegates Congressional power. Does Congress have the ability to change the outcome of cases?

7. Justice Harlan's concurrence criticizes the majority's test for evaluating the Federal Rules. How does he propose a court should deal with a Federal Rule? Do you find his argument persuasive? Does Justice Harlan's approach gauge the federal court's inherent or delegated power to make law?

8. *Other Rules*. The Federal Rules of Civil Procedure are not the only body of law promulgated by the federal courts pursuant to a delegation by Congress. 28 U.S.C. § 2075 allows the Supreme Court to promulgate procedural rules for the Bankruptcy Courts. Section 2071 allows all federal courts to enact local rules governing practice in those courts. The analysis of rules promulgated under these statutes is similar to the Rules Enabling Act analysis in *Hanna*.

The Federal Rules of Evidence are a special case. Although the Rules Enabling Act specifically allows the Supreme Court to enact rules of evidence, the current Federal Rules of Evidence were actually enacted by Congress rather than the Supreme Court. Because of this different origin, at least one federal appellate court has held that the Rules of Evidence are not governed by the *Hanna* analysis. *Sims v. Great American Life Insurance Co.*, 469 F.3d 870 (10th Cir. 2006). Other courts disagree.

9. Suppose that the federal law at issue in *Hanna*—the rule allowing service at the defendant's abode—was not codified in the Federal Rules, but was instead a common practice followed by the federal courts. Now, the "arguably procedural" test would not apply. Under *Guaranty Trust* and *Byrd*, the court would have to apply the state law requiring in-hand service, because to apply the federal "law" would change the outcome. Does *Hanna* offer any insight into this situation? According to the Court, would a federal court in our hypothetical apply the federal custom or state law? Why?

10. Although the Court's "likely to cause forum shopping" test is technically *dictum*, it has become the accepted way to deal with *Erie* issues involving federal rules established by precedent, as opposed to rules promulgated pursuant to the Rules Enabling Act or similar laws. Apply that test to the federal laws in *Erie*, *Guaranty Trust*, and *Byrd*. Would the outcome of any of these cases have changed?

11. *Hanna*, then, essentially sets out two separate analyses for determining if a rule is "procedural"—one for the Federal Rules of Civil

Procedure and similar written rules, and another for all other judge-made law. Restate the tests for each of these two situations. Under which of the tests is a given federal judge-made rule more likely to be applied?

12. Why should there be two separate tests? Regardless of whether the rule is a Federal Rule or ordinary judge-made law, the question is the same: is the rule "procedural?" Why should the analysis differ? The Supreme Court's analysis relies on the fact that the Federal Rules were created pursuant to the Rules Enabling Act. To understand why that matters, consider who enacted the Rules Enabling Act. Does Congress have the authority to enact substantive law? On the other hand, doesn't the Rules Enabling Act explicitly provide that the Supreme Court may enact only rules of "procedure and evidence?"

13. Consider the following two hypothetical situations:

Situation One. A state legislature enacts a statute imposing a special $10,000 filing fee for complaints in malpractice cases. The filing fee for federal courts in that state is $150. The federal fee is set by the district clerk, not by the Federal Rules or any local rule. Must the federal court charge a $10,000 filing fee for federal diversity malpractice cases?

Situation Two. The judges in State X have proven to be extremely biased against out-of-state litigants, at least when those litigants are suing or being sued by citizens of State X. Plaintiff, from State Y, sues Defendant, from State X, in a federal court in State X. Must the federal judge adopt a bias against Plaintiff?

In both of these situations, won't the difference in federal and state practice lead to forum shopping? Does that mean the federal court should ape the state court? If so, does that make sense?

Re-read the portion of *Hanna* dealing with judge-made law. What is the Court trying to say when it talks about the "twin aims" of *Erie*? What is the "inequitable administration of the laws?" Does that second aim affect how one applies the likely to cause forum shopping test? Is all forum shopping equally objectionable?

2. POST-*HANNA* CASES APPLYING THE *ERIE* DOCTRINE

The Supreme Court has decided a number of *Erie* doctrine cases since 1965. Nevertheless, most of these cases follow the basic analysis set out in *Hanna*, while at times borrowing from the logic of the earlier decisions. This section briefly discusses some of the more important decisions. Taking its guidance from *Hanna*, the discussion is divided based on the source of the federal "law" at issue in the cases.

a. Rules Promulgated Under the Rules Enabling Act

Most of the significant post-*Hanna* decisions have involved rules enacted under 28 U.S.C. § 2072, the Rules Enabling Act. As indicated above, the Rules Enabling Act is the source not only of the Federal Rules of Civil Procedure, but also other bodies of Federal Rules. *Hanna* indicates that the core issue in the case is whether the rule in question complies with the limitations enacted by the Rules Enabling Act itself. This analysis has two parts. First, the Rule must be one that can rationally be characterized as a rule of "procedure." Second, the Rule cannot abridge, enlarge, or modify the underlying substantive right.

To date, the Supreme Court has not found any Federal Rule invalid under this analysis. Nevertheless, the Court's opinions also point out that there is another issue involved in these cases. Before determining whether a particular Federal Rule is valid under the two-step analysis, a court must determine that the rule truly applies to the issue at hand.

***Walker*: When a case commences for purposes of a statute of limitations.** Both *Hanna* and *Guaranty Trust* make it clear that *Erie* applies to state statutes of limitations, at least when the case is based on state law. Does it follow that the federal court must calculate the limitations period in exactly the same way? In many states, the statute of limitations is tolled not when the case is filed, but only once the defendant is served. By contrast, Federal Rule 3 provides, "A civil action is commenced by filing a complaint with the court." Does Federal Rule 3 allow a plaintiff to beat out a state statute of limitations in federal court merely by filing the complaint? In *Walker v. Armco Steel Corp.*, 446 U.S. 740, 100 S.Ct. 1978, 64 L.Ed.2d 659 (1980), the Court held that Federal Rule 3 did not govern when a case was deemed commenced for purposes of applying a state statute of limitations. Instead, the Rule simply was an internal timing device for purposes of applying other Federal Rules. Because Rule 3 did not apply, the Court in *Walker* applied the "likely to cause forum shopping" analysis of *Hanna*, finding that state law controlled the issue of what a plaintiff must do to satisfy the state statute of limitations.

Does the Court's argument in *Walker* make sense? Why—other than for purposes of the statute of limitations—do we care about when a case commences? Are any of the time periods in the Federal Rules measured by the date the action is commenced?

Note that when a case is governed by a *federal* limitations period, courts look to the date of filing rather than service to determine whether the complaint is timely. Does this undermine the Court's argument that Rule 3 is nothing more than an internal timing mechanism? Consider this question again after reading the next case.

***Semtek*: Effect of an involuntary dismissal.** The Court's 2001 decision in *Semtek International Inc. v. Lockheed Martin Corp.*, 531 U.S. 497, 121 S.Ct. 1021, 149 L.Ed.2d 32 (2001), also involved a state statute of limitations, albeit in a more oblique way. *Semtek* involved various state-law tort claims. The Central District of California had dismissed those claims because they were barred by the state statute of limitations. Plaintiff then refiled the same claims in a Maryland state court, relying on the longer Maryland limitations period. Defendant moved to dismiss the claims based on claim preclusion. Defendant's argument relied on Federal Rule 41(b), which indicates that most involuntary dismissals operate as an "adjudication on the merits." Defendant argued that that language meant that the dismissal had full claim preclusion effect, barring plaintiff from ever bringing the claims again in any court.

The Court rejected defendant's argument, reading Federal Rule 41(b) narrowly. Under the Court's interpretation, Rule 41(b) only would bar plaintiff from refiling the same claims in the *same federal court*—that is, in the Central District of California. The Federal Rule did not apply when plaintiff sued again in state court, or even in any other federal district. To justify this narrow reading, the Court suggested that a reading that would prevent plaintiff from suing in other courts might render the Federal Rule invalid:

> Moreover, as so interpreted, the Rule would in many cases violate the federalism principle of *Erie R. Co. v. Tompkins*, by engendering "'substantial' variations [in outcomes] between state and federal litigation" which would "[l]ikely ... influence the choice of a forum," *Hanna v. Plumer*, 380 U.S. 460, 467–468 (1965). With regard to the claim-preclusion issue involved in the present case, for example, the traditional rule is that expiration of the applicable statute of limitations merely bars the remedy and does not extinguish the substantive right, so that dismissal on that ground does not have claim-preclusive effect in other jurisdictions with longer, unexpired limitations periods. Out-of-state defendants sued on stale claims in California and in other States adhering to this traditional rule would systematically remove state-law suits brought against them to federal court—where, unless otherwise specified, a statute-of-limitations dismissal would bar suit everywhere.

Having concluded that Federal Rule 41(b) did not apply to a situation where plaintiff refiled in a different court, the Court had to determine what law *did* govern that question. Interestingly, the Court did not automatically turn to state law. It instead held that the issue was governed by a "federal common law" that might vary from court to court. While the particular rule would ordinarily be borrowed from the law in which the court that dismissed the action sat (in *Semtek*, California law), the federal court could ignore a particular state law if it conflicted with some federal interest:

> This federal reference to state law will not obtain, of course, in situations in which the state law is incompatible with federal interests. If, for example, state law did not accord claim-preclusive effect to dismissals for willful violation of discovery orders, federal courts' interest in the integrity of their own processes might justify a contrary federal rule. No such conflict with potential federal interests exists in the present case. Dismissal of this state cause of action was decreed by the California federal court only because the California statute of limitations so required; and there is no conceivable federal interest in giving that time bar more effect in other courts than the California courts themselves would impose.

Read literally, the ruling in *Semtek* is extremely broad. Involuntary dismissals are not limited to cases where the statute of limitations has expired. Instead, Federal Rule 41(b) applies to a wide array of situations, including failure to prosecute, failure to comply with court orders, lack of jurisdiction or venue, and failure to state a claim. If *Semtek* means what it says, the preclusive effect of all of these dismissals will ordinarily be governed by "borrowed" state law whenever plaintiff refiles the same claim in any other court.

A second troubling aspect of *Semtek* is the Court's reasoning. Recall that the case deals with a Federal Rule. So why, in the first excerpt set out above, is the Court suggesting that forum shopping might be a concern? Under *Hanna*, does it matter whether application of a Federal Rule would lead to forum shopping? While this portion of the opinion is technically *dictum*, it may suggest that the Court is not entirely comfortable with the strictly compartmentalized approach of *Hanna*.

***Burlington Northern*: Sanctions for unsuccessful appeals.** *Walker* and *Semtek* are evidence that a court will sometimes construe a Federal Rule narrowly so as to avoid a clash with state law. In other situations, however, the Court will take the Federal Rule at face value. Consider *Burlington Northern Railroad v. Woods*, 480 U.S. 1, 107 S.Ct. 967, 94 L.Ed.2d 1 (1987). In that case, state law required a party who appealed a trial court's money judgment to pay an additional penalty of ten percent of that judgment if she also lost the appeal. Federal Rule of Appellate Procedure 38, by contrast, gives a federal appellate court the ability to impose sanctions in cases involving "frivolous" appeals. Plaintiff argued that the rules did not conflict, as the federal court could impose both the ten percent penalty called for by state law, and, if it found the appeal frivolous, an additional amount under the Federal Rule. The Supreme Court disagreed, holding that the rules clashed. Because the

Federal Rule was a valid procedural rule under the Rules Enabling Act analysis, the Court held that it applied.

***Shady Grove*: Class actions and state tort reform.** In the push to enact "tort reform," some states have enacted laws that limit the use of class actions in tort cases. In *Shady Grove Orthopedic Associates v. Allstate Insurance Co.*, 130 S.Ct. 1431, 176 L.Ed.2d 311 (2010), the Court determined whether these limits applied in federal court. At issue was a New York law that prevented a party from maintaining as a class action any suit seeking statutory damages or a penalty. Plaintiff sued Allstate in federal court for failing to pay the statutorily-mandated interest on certain insurance benefits. As Allstate had allegedly also refused to pay interest to others in similar circumstances, plaintiff sought to have the case certified as a class action under Federal Rule 23. Concluding that the interest was a form of "penalty," the lower federal courts held that the case could not proceed as a class action because of the New York law.

The Supreme Court reversed. To the majority, Federal Rule 23 clearly governed the case. That Rule sets out explicit requirements concerning what sorts of cases may be certified as class actions, which the plaintiff's action satisfied. Because the availability of the class action device clearly qualified as a matter of "procedure" for purposes of the Rules Enabling Act, and did not abridge, enlarge, or modify any substantive right, Rule 23 was a valid Federal Rule. In so finding, the majority rejected the dissent's argument that the New York law was a limitation on *remedy* rather than the right to use a certain procedural device.

The majority and dissent also differed concerning what factors a court may consider in determining whether a Federal Rule is procedural. The majority indicated the court should consider only the Federal Rule itself. As long as the Federal Rule was designed to regulate procedure in the Federal Courts, it is valid. The dissent disagreed, arguing that the purpose of the competing *state* law is also an important factor. If the purpose of the state law is to regulate the substantive right, the federal court should apply it.

b. Other Federal Judge-Made Law

Other cases have dealt with the application of federal judge-made rules not promulgated under the Rules Enabling Act. In these situations, *Hanna* adopts a "likely to cause forum shopping" analysis. If ignoring state law (and applying contrary federal law) would cause a reasonable litigant to favor either federal or state court, the state law is "substantive" and must be applied by the federal court.

***Challoner*: State choice of law rules.** In the *Klaxon* and *Griffin* cases discussed in the notes following *Erie*, the Court held that a federal court hearing a state law claim must apply the choice of law rules of the state in which the federal court sits—even if the courts of that state could not themselves have heard the case. Those decisions predate both *Guaranty Trust* and *Hanna*. However, in *Day & Zimmermann, Inc. v. Challoner*, 423 U.S. 3, 96 S.Ct. 167, 46 L.Ed.2d 3 (1975), a post-*Hanna* decision, the Court reaffirmed the basic rule of *Klaxon*. *Challoner* involved a case filed by a soldier who was a citizen of Wisconsin, against a company incorporated under the laws of Maryland and with its principal place of business in Pennsylvania, involving a military mishap that occurred in Cambodia. The case was filed in a federal district court in Texas. Under Texas choice of law rules, Cambodian law would govern liability, as the harm had occurred in Cambodia. Cambodian law, however, was less favorable to plaintiff. The court of appeals refused to apply Texas choice of law rules, arguing that they resulted in the application of the law of a forum—Cambodia—with no real interest in the dispute. The Supreme Court reversed in a per curiam opinion. Failure to apply Texas choice of law rules, the Court reasoned, would cause the federal court in Texas to reach a different result than a Texas state court would reach.

While *Klaxon* is still good law, does *Griffin* survive *Hanna*? Recall that *Griffin* held that a federal court must apply state law even if the state courts could not have heard the particular case. Is there any chance of forum shopping when the state courts could not have heard the case? *See* John T. Cross, *State Choice of Law Rules in Bankruptcy*, 42 Okla. L. Rev. 531 (1989), which argues that both *Klaxon* and *Griffin* are still good law.

***Gasperini*: Standard for reviewing a jury verdict on appeal.** A New York statute required a court of appeals to overturn a judgment based on a jury verdict "if it deviates materially from what would be reasonable compensation." In *Gasperini v. Center for Humanities, Inc.*, 518 U.S. 415, 116 S.Ct. 2211, 135 L.Ed.2d 659 (1996), the Court considered whether this standard applied in federal court. After a jury rendered a significant money judgment against it in the federal trial court, defendant appealed, invoking the New York "deviates materially" standard. The victorious plaintiff argued the regular federal appellate standard should apply, under which a jury verdict can be overturned only if the result "shocks the conscience"—a far more difficult standard to satisfy.

The Court first held that the New York standard, not the federal standard, governed. The Court likened the New York standard to a cap on damages, a rule that would clearly be substantive under *Hanna*:

> We think it a fair conclusion that CPLR § 5501(c) differs from a statutory cap principally "in that the maximum amount recoverable is not set forth by statute, but rather is determined by case law." *Brief for City of New York as Amicus Curiae* 11. In

sum, § 5501(c) contains a procedural instruction, but the State's objective is manifestly substantive.

It thus appears that if federal courts ignore the change in the New York standard and persist in applying the "shock the conscience" test to damage awards on claims governed by New York law, "'substantial' variations between state and federal [money judgments]" may be expected. See *Hanna*, 380 U.S., at 467–468. We therefore agree with the Second Circuit that New York's check on excessive damages implicates what we have called *Erie*'s "twin aims." . . . *Erie* precludes a recovery in federal court significantly larger than the recovery that would have been tolerated in state court.

However, the Court also concluded that the state-law standard should be applied by the *trial* court, rather than the court of appeals as would have been the case in the New York state courts. Its reasoning turned on the Seventh Amendment, and resembles the reasoning in the pre-*Hanna* decision in *Byrd*:

> The Seventh Amendment, which governs proceedings in federal court, but not in state court, bears not only on the allocation of trial functions between judge and jury, the issue in *Byrd*; it also controls the allocation of authority to review verdicts, the issue of concern here. . . .
>
> *Byrd* involved the first Clause of the Amendment, the "trial by jury" Clause. This case involves the second, the "Reexamination" Clause. In keeping with the historic understanding, the Reexamination Clause does not inhibit the authority of trial judges to grant new trials "for any of the reasons for which new trials have heretofore been granted in actions at law in the courts of the United States." Fed. Rule Civ. Proc. 59(a). That authority is large. "The trial judge in the federal system," we have reaffirmed, "has . . . discretion to grant a new trial if the verdict appears to [the judge] to be against the weight of the evidence." *Byrd*, 356 U.S., at 540. . . .
>
> In contrast, appellate review of a federal trial court's denial of a motion to set aside a jury's verdict as excessive is a relatively late, and less secure, development. Such review was once deemed inconsonant with the Seventh Amendment's Reexamination Clause. . . .
>
> New York's dominant interest can be respected, without disrupting the federal system, once it is recognized that the federal district court is capable of performing the checking function, i.e., that court can apply the State's "deviates

materially" standard in line with New York case law evolving under CPLR § 5501(c). . . .

District court applications of the "deviates materially" standard would be subject to appellate review under the standard the Circuits now employ when inadequacy or excessiveness is asserted on appeal: abuse of discretion. . . .

c. Federal Statutes

All of the *Erie* decisions to this point have involved the issue of whether a federal court can apply federal judge-made law. Of course, most federal law comes from Congress, not the courts. How does *Erie* apply when a federal court is asked to apply a federal statute? Does *Erie* apply at all?

STEWART ORGANIZATION V. RICOH CORPORATION
487 U.S. 22, 108 S.Ct. 2239, 101 L.Ed.2d 22 (1988)

JUSTICE MARSHALL delivered the opinion of the Court.

This case presents the issue whether a federal court sitting in diversity should apply state or federal law in adjudicating a motion to transfer a case to a venue provided in a contractual forum-selection clause.

The dispute underlying this case grew out of a dealership agreement that obligated petitioner company, an Alabama corporation, to market copier products of respondent, a nationwide manufacturer with its principal place of business in New Jersey. The agreement contained a forum-selection clause providing that any dispute arising out of the contract could be brought only in a court located in Manhattan.[1] Business relations between the parties soured under circumstances that are not relevant here. In September 1984, petitioner brought a complaint in the United States District Court for the Northern District of Alabama. The core of the complaint was an allegation that respondent had breached the dealership agreement, but petitioner also included claims for breach of warranty, fraud, and antitrust violations.

Relying on the contractual forum-selection clause, respondent moved the District Court either to transfer the case to the Southern District of New York under 28 U.S.C. § 1404(a) or to dismiss the case for improper venue under 28 U.S.C. § 1406. The District Court denied the motion. It reasoned that the transfer motion was controlled by Alabama law and

---

[1] Specifically, the forum-selection clause read: "Dealer and Ricoh agree that any appropriate state or federal district court located in the Borough of Manhattan, New York City, New York, shall have exclusive jurisdiction over any case or controversy arising under or in connection with this Agreement and shall be a proper forum in which to adjudicate such case or controversy."

that Alabama looks unfavorably upon contractual forum-selection clauses. . . .

On appeal, a divided panel of the Eleventh Circuit reversed the District Court. The panel concluded that questions of venue in diversity actions are governed by federal law, and that the parties' forum-selection clause was enforceable as a matter of federal law. . . .

A district court's decision whether to apply a federal statute such as § 1404(a) in a diversity action . . . involves a considerably less intricate analysis than that which governs the "relatively unguided *Erie* choice." *Hanna v. Plumer*, 380 U.S. 460 (1965). Our cases indicate that when the federal law sought to be applied is a congressional statute, the first and chief question for the district court's determination is whether the statute is "sufficiently broad to control the issue before the Court." *Walker v. Armco Steel Corp.*, 446 U.S. 740, 749–750 (1980). This question involves a straightforward exercise in statutory interpretation to determine if the statute covers the point in dispute.

If the district court determines that a federal statute covers the point in dispute, it proceeds to inquire whether the statute represents a valid exercise of Congress' authority under the Constitution. If Congress intended to reach the issue before the District Court, and if it enacted its intention into law in a manner that abides with the Constitution, that is the end of the matter. . . . Thus, a district court sitting in diversity must apply a federal statute that controls the issue before the court and that represents a valid exercise of Congress' constitutional powers.

Applying the above analysis to this case persuades us that federal law, specifically 28 U.S.C. § 1404(a), governs the parties' venue dispute. . . .

Section 1404(a) is intended to place discretion in the district court to adjudicate motions for transfer according to an "individualized, case-by-case consideration of convenience and fairness." *Van Dusen v. Barrack*, 376 U.S. 612, 622 (1964). A motion to transfer under § 1404(a) thus calls on the district court to weigh in the balance a number of case-specific factors. The presence of a forum-selection clause such as the parties entered into in this case will be a significant factor that figures centrally in the district court's calculus. In its resolution of the § 1404(a) motion in this case, for example, the District Court will be called on to address such issues as the convenience of a Manhattan forum given the parties' expressed preference for that venue, and the fairness of transfer in light of the forum-selection clause and the parties' relative bargaining power. The flexible and individualized analysis Congress prescribed in § 1404(a) thus encompasses consideration of the parties' private expression of their venue preferences. . . .

It is true that § 1404(a) and Alabama's putative policy regarding forum-selection clauses are not perfectly coextensive. Section 1404(a) directs a district court to take account of factors other than those that bear solely on the parties' private ordering of their affairs. The district court also must weigh in the balance the convenience of the witnesses and those public-interest factors of systemic integrity and fairness that, in addition to private concerns, come under the heading of "the interest of justice." It is conceivable in a particular case, for example, that because of these factors a district court acting under § 1404(a) would refuse to transfer a case notwithstanding the counterweight of a forum-selection clause, whereas the coordinate state rule might dictate the opposite result. But this potential conflict in fact frames an additional argument for the supremacy of federal law. Congress has directed that multiple considerations govern transfer within the federal court system, and a state policy focusing on a single concern or a subset of the factors identified in § 1404(a) would defeat that command. . . . The forum-selection clause, which represents the parties' agreement as to the most proper forum, should receive neither dispositive consideration (as respondent might have it) nor no consideration (as Alabama law might have it), but rather the consideration for which Congress provided in § 1404(a). . . .

Because § 1404(a) controls the issue before the District Court, it must be applied if it represents a valid exercise of Congress' authority under the Constitution. The constitutional authority of Congress to enact § 1404(a) is not subject to serious question. As the Court made plain in *Hanna*, "the constitutional provision for a federal court system . . . carries with it congressional power to make rules governing the practice and pleading in those courts, which in turn includes a power to regulate matters which, though falling within the uncertain area between substance and procedure, are rationally capable of classification as either." 380 U.S., at 472. See also *id.*, at 473 ("*Erie* and its offspring cast no doubt on the long-recognized power of Congress to prescribe housekeeping rules for federal courts"). Section 1404(a) is doubtless capable of classification as a procedural rule. . . . It therefore falls comfortably within Congress' powers under Article III as augmented by the Necessary and Proper Clause.

We hold that federal law, specifically 28 U.S.C. § 1404(a), governs the District Court's decision whether to give effect to the parties' forum-selection clause and transfer this case to a court in Manhattan.[11] We therefore affirm the Eleventh Circuit order reversing the District Court's application of Alabama law. The case is remanded so that the District Court may determine in the first instance the appropriate effect under

---

[11] Because a validly enacted Act of Congress controls the issue in dispute, we have no occasion to evaluate the impact of application of federal judge-made law on the "twin aims" that animate the *Erie* doctrine.

federal law of the parties' forum-selection clause on respondent's § 1404(a) motion.

[The concurring opinion of JUSTICE KENNEDY, joined by JUSTICE O'CONNOR, is omitted.]

JUSTICE SCALIA, dissenting.

... The Court largely attempts to avoid acknowledging the novel scope it gives to § 1404(a) by casting the issue as how much *weight* a district court should give a forum-selection clause as against other factors when it makes its determination under § 1404(a). I agree that if the weight-among-factors issue were before us, it would be governed by § 1404(a). That is because, while the parties may decide who between them should bear any inconvenience, only a court can decide how much weight should be given under § 1404(a) to the factor of the parties' convenience as against other relevant factors such as the convenience of witnesses. But the Court's description of the issue begs the question: what law governs whether the forum-selection clause is a *valid* or *invalid* allocation of any inconvenience between the parties. If it is invalid, *i.e.*, should be voided, between the parties, it cannot be entitled to any weight in the § 1404(a) determination. Since under Alabama law the forum-selection clause should be voided, in this case the question of what weight should be given the forum-selection clause can be reached only if as a preliminary matter federal law controls the issue of the validity of the clause between the parties.

Second, § 1404(a) was enacted against the background that issues of contract, including a contract's validity, are nearly always governed by state law. It is simply contrary to the practice of our system that such an issue should be wrenched from state control in absence of a clear conflict with federal law or explicit statutory provision.

[After concluding that § 1404 did not apply to the issue, Justice Scalia argued that the federal courts could not, under *Erie*, fashion a judge-made rule to govern the question of forum selection clauses.]

NOTES AND QUESTIONS

1. The Court in *Stewart* finds that 28 U.S.C. § 1404 clashes with state law. Review that statute. Does it say anything about forum selection clauses? If not, how can the Court conclude that it applies? What motion was presented to the trial court?

2. Is Justice Scalia correct when he argues it is logically necessary to determine if the forum selection clause is valid and enforceable? Does the Court need to find the clause valid in order to give it any weight in a § 1404 analysis? Even if the clause is invalid, how might it be relevant to a court's decision whether to transfer the case?

3. According to *Stewart*, how does a court deal with an *Erie* dispute involving a federal statute? Does it ask whether the statute would cause forum shopping? Whether the statute is "arguably procedural?" Why is the analysis different?

4. Suppose the Court had concluded that § 1404 did not apply. How would it have analyzed the case? Would Alabama's rule refusing to enforce forum selection clauses apply in federal court?

5. Note that defendant had also moved to dismiss under 28 U.S.C. § 1406 based on the forum selection clause. The Court did not deal with that issue. If it had, how should it have ruled? Does § 1406 itself govern whether the forum selection clause is valid? Does any other federal statute or rule deal with the issue? What about 28 U.S.C. § 1391?

3. FEDERAL COMMON LAW

The *Semtek* case in the prior section holds that "federal common law" governs the preclusive effect of a federal involuntary dismissal. This reference to a federal common law may have surprised you. A number of sources (including many student aids) declare that *Erie* abolished federal common law. But if you reread *Erie* itself, you will see that the Court did not paint with so broad a brush. Instead, *Erie* says, "There is no federal *general* common law." (emphasis added) Use of the qualifier "general" suggests that there could be *specific* pockets of federal judge-made law.

In fact, there is a considerable amount of federal common law. Moreover, you already know about one category of this law. Many of the Supreme Court cases set out above explore the federal courts' ability to fashion a body of *procedural* law to govern proceedings in the federal courts. This procedural common law remains the largest body of federal common law. However, it is not the only category. The following case indicates that there are also areas in which the federal courts can create rules that would clearly be substantive under any definition of that word.

TEXAS INDUSTRIES, INC. V. RADCLIFF MATERIALS, INC.
451 U.S. 630, 101 S.Ct. 2061, 68 L.Ed.2d 500 (1981)

CHIEF JUSTICE BURGER delivered the opinion of the Court.

This case presents the question whether the federal antitrust laws allow a defendant, against whom civil damages, costs, and attorney's fees have been assessed, a right to contribution from other participants in the unlawful conspiracy on which recovery was based....

I

Petitioner and the three respondents manufacture and sell ready-mix concrete in the New Orleans, La., area. In 1975, the Wilson P. Abraham Construction Corp., which had purchased concrete from petitioner, filed a civil action in the United States District Court for the Eastern District of Louisiana naming petitioner as defendant; the complaint alleged that petitioner and certain unnamed concrete firms had conspired to raise prices in violation of § 1 of the Sherman Act, 15 U.S.C. § 1....

Through discovery, petitioner learned that Abraham believed respondents were the other concrete producers that had participated in the alleged price-fixing scheme. Petitioner then filed a third-party complaint against respondents seeking contribution from them should it be held liable in the action filed by Abraham. The District Court dismissed the third-party complaint for failure to state a claim upon which relief could be granted, holding that federal law does not allow an antitrust defendant to recover in contribution from co-conspirators....

On appeal, the Court of Appeals for the Fifth Circuit affirmed, holding that, although the Sherman and the Clayton Acts do not expressly afford a right to contribution, the issue should be resolved as a matter of federal common law. The court then examined what it perceived to be the benefits and the difficulties of contribution and concluded that no common-law rule of contribution should be fashioned by the courts.

II

The common law provided no right to contribution among joint tortfeasors.... Since the turn of the century, however, 39 states and the District of Columbia have fashioned rules of contribution in one form or another, 10 initially through judicial action and the remainder through legislation. Because courts generally have acknowledged that treble-damages actions under the antitrust laws are analogous to common-law actions sounding in tort, we are urged to follow this trend and adopt contribution for antitrust violators.

The parties and *amici* representing a variety of business interests—as well as a legion of commentators—have thoroughly addressed the policy concerns implicated in the creation of a right to contribution in antitrust cases. With potentially large sums at stake, it is not surprising that the numerous and articulate *amici* disagree strongly over the basic issue raised: whether sharing of damages liability will advance or impair the objectives of the antitrust laws....

III

The contentions advanced indicate how views diverge as to the "unfairness" of not providing contribution, the risks and trade-offs perceived by decisionmakers in business, and the various patterns for contribution that could be devised. In this vigorous debate over the advantages and disadvantages of contribution and various contribution schemes, the parties, *amici*, and commentators have paid less attention to a very significant and perhaps dispositive threshold question: whether courts have the power to create such a cause of action absent legislation and, if so, whether that authority should be exercised in this context.

Earlier this Term, in *Northwest Airlines, Inc. v. Transport Workers*, 451 U.S. 77, we addressed the similar question of a right to contribution under the Equal Pay Act of 1963 and Title VII of the Civil Rights Act of 1964. We concluded that a right to contribution may arise in either of two ways: first, through the affirmative creation of a right of action by Congress, either expressly or by clear implication; or, second, through the power of federal courts to fashion a federal common law of contribution.

A

[The Court held that the antitrust laws did not create a right to contribution, either expressly or by implication.] . . .

B

There is, of course, "no federal general common law." *Erie R. Co. v. Tompkins*, 304 U.S. 64, 78 (1938). Nevertheless, the Court has recognized the need and authority in some limited areas to formulate what has come to be known as "federal common law." These instances are "few and restricted," *Wheeldin v. Wheeler*, 373 U.S. 647, 651 (1963), and fall into essentially two categories: those in which a federal rule of decision is "necessary to protect uniquely federal interests," *Banco Nacional de Cuba v. Sabbatino*, 376 U.S. 398, 426 (1964), and those in which Congress has given the courts the power to develop substantive law.

(1)

The vesting of jurisdiction in the federal courts does not in and of itself give rise to authority to formulate federal common law, nor does the existence of congressional authority under Art. I mean that federal courts are free to develop a common law to govern those areas until Congress acts. Rather, absent some congressional authorization to formulate substantive rules of decision, federal common law exists only in such narrow areas as those concerned with the rights and obligations of the United States, interstate and international disputes implicating the conflicting rights of States or our relations with foreign nations, and admiralty cases. In these instances, our federal system does not permit the controversy to be resolved under state law, either because the authority and duties of the United States as sovereign are intimately involved or because the interstate or international nature of the controversy makes it inappropriate for state law to control.

In areas where federal common law applies, the creation of a right to contribution may fall within the power of the federal courts. For example, in *Cooper Stevedoring Co. v. Fritz Kopke, Inc.*, 417 U.S. 106 (1974), we held that contribution is available among joint tortfeasors for injury to a longshoreman. But that claim arose within admiralty jurisdiction, one of the areas long recognized as subject to federal common law.... *Copper Stevedoring* thus does not stand for a general federal common-law right to contribution.

The antitrust laws were enacted pursuant to the power of Congress under the Commerce Clause, Art. I, § 8, cl. 3, to regulate interstate and foreign trade, and the case law construing the Sherman Act now spans nearly a century. Nevertheless, a treble-damages action remains a private suit involving the rights and obligations of private parties. Admittedly, there is a federal interest in the sense that vindication of rights arising out of these congressional enactments supplements federal enforcement and fulfills the objects of the statutory scheme. Notwithstanding that nexus, contribution among antitrust wrongdoers does not involve the duties of the Federal Government, the distribution of powers in our federal system, or matters necessarily subject to federal control even in the absence of statutory authority. In short, contribution does not implicate "uniquely federal interests" of the kind that oblige courts to formulate federal common law.

(2)

Federal common law also may come into play when Congress has vested jurisdiction in the federal courts and empowered them to create governing rules of law. In this vein, this Court has read § 301(a) of the Labor Management Relations Act, not only as granting jurisdiction over defined areas of labor law but also as vesting in the courts the power to develop a common law of labor-management relations within that jurisdiction. *Textile Workers v. Lincoln Mills*, 353 U.S. 448 (1957). A similar situation arises with regard to the first two sections of the Sherman Act, which in sweeping language forbid "[e]very contract, combination . . . , or conspiracy, in restraint of trade" and "monopoliz[ing], or attempt[ing] to monopolize, . . . any part of the trade or commerce. . . ." 15 U.S.C. §§ 1, 2. We noted in *National Society of Professional Engineers v. United States*, 435 U.S. 679, 688 (1978):

> Congress, however, did not intend the text of the Sherman Act to delineate the full meaning of the statute or its application in concrete situations. The legislative history makes it perfectly clear that it expected the courts to give shape to the statute's broad mandate by drawing on common-law tradition.

It does not necessarily follow, however, that Congress intended to give courts as wide discretion in formulating remedies to enforce the provisions of the Sherman Act or the kind of relief sought through contribution. The intent to allow courts to develop governing principles of law, so unmistakably clear with regard to substantive violations, does not appear in debates on the treble-damages action created in § 7 of the original Act. . . .

In contrast to the sweeping language of §§ 1 and 2 of the Sherman Act, the remedial provisions defined in the antitrust laws are detailed and specific....

The presumption that a remedy was deliberately omitted from a statute is strongest when Congress has enacted a comprehensive legislative scheme including an integrated system of procedures for enforcement.

Northwest Airlines, Inc. v. Transport Workers Union, supra, 451 U.S., at 97. That presumption is strong indeed in the context of antitrust violations; the continuing existence of this statutory scheme for 90 years without amendments authorizing contribution is not without significance. There is nothing in the statute itself, in its legislative history, or in the overall regulatory scheme to suggest that Congress intended courts to have the power to alter or supplement the remedies enacted....

We are satisfied that neither the Sherman Act nor the Clayton Act confers on federal courts the broad power to formulate the right to contribution sought here.

IV

The policy questions presented by petitioner's claimed right to contribution are far-reaching. In declining to provide a right to contribution, we neither reject the validity of those arguments nor adopt the views of those opposing contribution. Rather, we recognize that, regardless of the merits of the conflicting arguments, this is a matter for Congress, not the courts, to resolve....

Because we are unable to discern any basis in federal statutory or common law that allows federal courts to fashion the relief urged by petitioner, the judgment of the Court of Appeals is *Affirmed*.

NOTES AND QUESTIONS

1. Federal common law is actually as old as the *Erie* doctrine itself. On a case decided on the same day as *Erie*, the Supreme Court applied a rule that it called "federal common law" to resolve a dispute involving the allocation of water in an interstate stream. *Hinderlider v. La Plata River & Cherry Creek Ditch Co.*, 304 U.S. 92, 58 S.Ct. 803, 82 L.Ed. 1202 (1938). Such a rule is clearly substantive.

2. Part III.B of the *Texas Industries* opinion suggests there are two broad categories of substantive federal common law. In fact, these two categories correspond nicely to the two categories of *procedural* common law discussed after *Hanna*. In the first category (where federal common law is "necessary to protect uniquely federal interests"), the federal courts have the *inherent* power to make law. In the second, Congress has *delegated* part of its lawmaking power to the federal courts.

3. The second category is the easier of the two to understand. If Congress has delegated authority to the courts, the only real issues are whether Congress had the power to begin with, and whether the court is acting within the scope of the delegation (a third issue—constitutional limits on Congress's authority to delegate its legislative power—is best left to a course in Constitutional or Administrative Law). When you dealt with the Rules Enabling Act, you were basically analyzing the scope of the delegation. That Act places explicit limits on the Supreme Court's rulemaking power, limiting the Rules to those that do not abridge, enlarge, or modify substantive rights.

Determining the scope of delegation in areas of substantive federal common law, by contrast, is a far trickier proposition. Unlike the Rules Enabling Act, there is almost never a statute that explicitly delegates substantive lawmaking authority to the courts. Instead, the courts typically find such a delegation by implication. In *Textile Workers v. Lincoln Mills*, 353 U.S. 448, 77 S.Ct. 912, 1 L.Ed.2d 972 (1957), a case discussed in *Texas Industries*, the Court found a delegation of lawmaking authority in a statute that simply gave the federal courts exclusive jurisdiction over certain labor contracts. Similarly, the power to fashion equitable remedies described in *Guaranty Trust* may stem from the grant of equity jurisdiction to the federal courts.

4. Although *Texas Industries* lists it as an area of inherent power, could admiralty law actually be an area where lawmaking power has been delegated? To what extent is it relevant that federal courts have always had exclusive jurisdiction in admiralty? *See* Judiciary Act of 1789, § 9. If *Erie* applied in admiralty, would there be any state judge-made maritime law for the federal courts to apply?

5. Turn now to the first category of substantive federal common law: situations where there is a strong federal interest. The cases finding federal common law in this area are summarized in Part III.B(1) of the opinion. Is there a thread that ties them together?

6. There is little doubt that a uniform national law would usually be desirable in the first category of federal common law. But does it necessarily follow that federal *courts* should have the ability to make law in such areas? If there is truly a strong federal interest in areas such as foreign affairs, isn't the usual solution for *Congress* to enact a statute setting out a nationwide rule? Why shouldn't the same be required in the areas listed by the Court?

In fact, in many situations Congress *will* react to a question of national importance by enacting legislation. If Congress passes a law, the Supreme Court has indicated the legislation "displaces" any federal common law on the subject. *American Elec. Power Co., Inc. v. Connecticut*, 131 S.Ct. 2527 (2011). Following displacement, the case is governed by the statute rather than a common law rule.

7. Like a federal statute, substantive federal common law is a federal question. Therefore, a claim arising under federal common law can be heard

in the federal courts regardless of the citizenship of the litigants or amount in controversy. *Illinois v. City of Milwaukee*, 406 U.S. 91, 92 S.Ct. 1385, 31 L.Ed.2d 712 (1972).

PROBLEMS

1. Defendant, a Michigan citizen, has a 20-year-old son who attends the University of Northern Florida. Every spring break, students from the University travel to Daytona Beach, Florida. While driving to Daytona Beach last spring, Defendant's son negligently collided with a car driven by Plaintiff, a Florida citizen, in a small town in northern Florida.

Since Defendant's son has no assets, Plaintiff decides to sue Defendant. To avoid a battle over personal jurisdiction, Plaintiff brings the action in the federal district court for the Western District of Michigan. Defendant immediately files a motion to dismiss under Federal Rule of Civil Procedure 12(b)(6), citing a recent case of the Michigan Supreme Court holding that a parent may not be held vicariously liable for the actions of a non-minor child. A person reaches majority in Michigan at age 18.

How will the district court rule on Defendant's motion to dismiss?

2. Because of the substantial variation in filing fees among the federal district courts, the Supreme Court recently amended Federal Rule of Civil Procedure 3 to read as follows:

> A civil action is commenced by (a) filing a complaint with the court, and (b) paying a $100.00 filing fee to the clerk of court.

Plaintiff is contemplating bringing a class action against Defendant in the state of Dakota. Upon reviewing state law, however, she discovers that Dakota Rule of Civil Procedure 6.02 imposes a special filing fee of $20,000 for all lawsuits brought in the form of a class action. Dakota adopted this special fee because of the tremendous burden that class actions place on the courts. In order to avoid this expense, Plaintiff brings her suit in the federal district court for the District of Dakota by filing her complaint and paying the $100.00 fee. Defendant moves to dismiss, claiming that Plaintiff's lawsuit was not properly commenced because she failed to comply with the filing fee requirements of Dakota law.

How should the court rule on Defendant's motion?

3. You are the attorney for Defendant in a breach of contract action currently pending in the district court for the District of Superior. Plaintiff filed the lawsuit back in 1999, and has done nothing since serving the summons and complaint upon your client. Therefore, you file a motion to dismiss the case "for failure to prosecute."

Under Federal Rule of Civil Procedure 41(b), all involuntary dismissals are deemed to be "with prejudice," unless the court specifically says otherwise. This means that, following dismissal, Plaintiff would be barred from ever bringing the breach of contract claim against your client.

The hearing on your motion is scheduled for 8:00 a.m. tomorrow. At 10:30 in the evening, your client calls and says, "Isn't this motion just a waste of my money? I just talked to my cousin, a Superior state court judge. She said that under Superior law all dismissals are deemed to be *without prejudice* unless the court indicates otherwise [you may assume that this is a correct statement of Superior law]. Even if we win tomorrow, can't Plaintiff simply sue me again for the breach of contract claim?"

What do you tell your client?

4. The legislature of the state of Carolina has become extremely concerned about the profusion of personal injury litigation in that state. To combat this problem, the legislature passes a statute that requires a plaintiff who *loses* a personal injury lawsuit to pay the attorney's fees of the prevailing defendant. This new statute is clearly at variance with the traditional American common-law rule in effect in the other 49 states, which requires each party to pay his own attorney's fees.

Plaintiff sues Defendant in a federal district court in Carolina for injuries sustained when Plaintiff slipped and fell on the sidewalk in front of Defendant's house. The jury finds for Defendant. Defendant moves for an order requiring Plaintiff to pay Defendant's attorney's fees in the action. How will the judge rule?

5. Bugs lives in Iowa, on the Iowa/Missouri state line. Just across the state line lives Elmer Fudd, a small-time farmer who ekes out a living growing carrots. To increase his profits, Elmer quits growing carrots and takes up raising horseradish. Infuriated, Bugs immediately sues Elmer in a federal district court in Missouri, asking for an injunction ordering Elmer to sell his horseradish and resume growing carrots.

Under the law of most states, a jury will not be empaneled in a suit involving solely equitable relief [recall that an injunction is equitable relief]. The federal courts follow this practice. Under the Missouri constitution, however, all parties in a civil lawsuit have the right to a jury trial, even when the case involves equitable relief.

Bugs requests a jury trial in his case with Elmer. Elmer resists Bugs' request. How should the district judge rule?

6. Same facts as Problem 5. Elmer has asked the district court to dismiss Bugs's suit under the equitable doctrine of "unclean hands." Historically, courts of equity would only hear cases in which the plaintiff had not acted improperly. If the plaintiff came to court with unclean hands, the court would refuse to lend any assistance to the plaintiff.

Elmer claims that Bugs has unclean hands because he has been pilfering Elmer's carrots. Bugs, however, cites a recent decision of the Missouri Supreme Court which holds that that the doctrine of unclean hands does not apply in Missouri actions in equity.

How should the judge rule on Elmer's motion to dismiss?

7. The St. Croix river defines part of the boundary between the states of Minnesota and Wisconsin. In areas where the river forms the boundary, all land east of the river is in the state of Wisconsin; while all land to the west is in Minnesota.

After a particular snowy winter, the April thaw causes the St. Croix to "jump its banks;" thereby carving out a new channel. As a result, 3,000 acres of land (the "3,000 acres") which were formerly located east of the St. Croix are now on the west side of the river.

Although Wisconsin and Minnesota are neighbors, they differ in the celebration of one very important religious holiday. In Wisconsin, the walleye fishing season begins on the first of May. In Minnesota, it begins on the second Saturday in May.

On May 1st, Wally Fisher, a Wisconsin citizen, is fined by the Minnesota Department of Natural Resources (the "DNR") for reeling in a walleye from a small lake situated on the 3,000 acres. Infuriated, the state of Wisconsin immediately sues the DNR in a federal district court in Minnesota, asking for a declaratory judgment that the 3,000 acres is still a part of the state of Wisconsin. The DNR, citing Minnesota law, moves to dismiss Wisconsin's complaint.

Under the law of Minnesota and 24 other states, the new river channel would be used to establish the boundary. Under the law of Wisconsin and 24 other states, however, the doctrine of "avulsion" would apply, and the sudden change in the river's course would not serve to redefine the boundary.

How should the court rule on the DNR's motion?

Variation: What if Wisconsin had sued the DNR in a Minnesota *state* court? Is there any reason for Minnesota not to follow its own law?

Chapter 6

Pleading Claims

■ ■ ■

Pleading is the process by which the litigants inform each other and the court of the claims and defenses they intend to present at trial. Although the governing rules have been relaxed over the years, there is still a certain formalism to the pleading process. The Federal Rules of Civil Procedure, for example, require pleadings to be in writing, dictate a certain basic form, and limit the parties' ability to amend their pleadings. The Rules likewise limit the number of pleadings that may be filed and give each pleading a particular name.

This Chapter explores how parties plead claims. Chapter 7 turns to the defendant, and discusses the various ways defendant may respond. The main focus in both chapters is pleading in the federal courts. Nevertheless, this Chapter begins with a brief discussion of how pleading developed in the Anglo-American legal system. That historical overview is important, for it sets the stage. You cannot really appreciate the pleading system created by the Federal Rules without understanding the systems it replaced. Although the federal pleading rules are by no means a panacea, they were adopted to cure perceived deficiencies in prior pleading systems. The Federal Rules did much more than change the technical rules of pleading. They instead represent a quantum shift in the philosophy underlying pleading.

A. PHILOSOPHY AND HISTORY OF PLEADING

There is no *a priori* reason why a legal system should require formal pleading of claims and defenses. In fact, outside the Anglo-American systems pleadings play a much less significant role. Many nations use pleadings merely to give the adjudicator a general idea of what happened. Those pleadings do not necessarily limit the course of the proceedings in the case. The adjudicator is not bound by the claims or defenses—or even the version of the facts—set forth in the pleadings, but may instead decide what matters bear looking into and what legal theories might apply.

In Anglo-American systems, by contrast, the pleadings serve two basic functions. First, as in other systems, they provide information for both the court and the other side. Second, however, pleadings also serve a constraining function. Even if a plaintiff could, under the facts, have recovered under theory X, the parties may through the pleadings preclude the court from deciding for plaintiff under that theory. Therefore, pleading gives the parties a degree of control over their case that does not exist in other systems. But with that control comes responsibility. It is up to the parties to make sure they do not overlook viable claims or defenses.

The history of pleadings in the Anglo-American systems reflects a shift from the constraining function of pleadings to the notice function. Historically, pleadings provided very little in the way of factual information to the court or the other side. Their role was instead to narrow the case down to a single issue for trial. Today, pleadings focus on the facts, and do not necessarily limit the party to one issue or legal theory.

Generally speaking, the rules that have governed pleading in Anglo-American lay[1] courts since the eleventh century fall into one into one of three paradigms: historical English pleading, Code pleading, and Federal or "notice" pleading. Each of these will be discussed in turn.

1. HISTORICAL ENGLISH PLEADING

Following independence, courts in the United States quite naturally borrowed extensively from the rules and customs of English civil practice. Key among these rules were those governing pleading. Starting in the eleventh century, and continuing over a span of several centuries, England developed a complex, if sometimes Byzantine, set of rules governing pleading. These rules were transplanted across the Atlantic Ocean, and dominated pleading in the United States courts until the latter part of the nineteenth century.

Today, no court in the United States uses rules that are anywhere close to the historical English rules. Nevertheless, study of the old pleading rules is of much more than historical interest. Although the historical rules no longer apply directly, they established a basic paradigm of pleading that still dominates our thought today. First, pleadings in the Anglo-American systems follow a certain prescribed order, with each step serving a different role. Plaintiff must commence the action. Plaintiff's pleading must do more than merely advise the court as to what happened to give rise to a dispute. It must also both show that plaintiff is entitled to recover under the law, and demonstrate that the court has authority to hear the case. Defendant's response must deal with all of the allegations of the complaint. Moreover, defendant is limited in the ways in which it can respond.

Second, in the early 1800s pleading was a very important, if not the most important, aspect of procedure, at least in the common-law courts. Cases were often won or lost based on technical mistakes in pleading.

---

[1] The ecclesiastical courts, which applied church or canon law, used their own method of pleading.

Even if a party survived the pleading stage, strict pleading rules could force a party into a difficult tactical position by requiring him to adopt one strategy instead of another. Today, by contrast, pleading does not play nearly as significant a role in litigation as it did in the past. Nevertheless, it would be a fundamental mistake to conclude that pleading is not important today. Although the pleading rules have been relaxed, courts still take pleading seriously. As the cases in Part B of this Chapter demonstrate, cases can still be won or lost solely on the pleadings.

Third, the historical pleading system played a key role in establishing the basic structure of the substantive law. Consider your courses in Contracts and Torts. As you have already seen, there are substantial differences between the rules that govern a breach of contract claim and a tort claim, including differences in the standard for liability and damages that can be recovered. And yet, reduced to their essence, contracts and torts are both concerned with whether defendant breached a duty to plaintiff. The only core difference between the claims is that while in tort the law establishes and defines the duty, in contract the parties agree on the scope of any duty. The differences that exist between tort and contract today are attributable in large part to historical procedural rules. The English courts used different types of pleading for tort and contract claims. Because the differences in pleading were also accompanied by differences in the procedure used in the case, litigation of what we would today call a tort claim differed significantly from litigation of a case involving an agreed-upon duty. Over the years, these differences in procedure led judges and attorneys to view tort and contract as completely separate areas of law.

There is a great deal of discussion of historical pleading in the case law and literature. Unfortunately, there is considerably more chaff than wheat. Many discussions of the old pleading rules are little more than a caricature. These discussions portray the historical rules as the work of some mad scientist, a hopelessly complex system with myriad arbitrary rules, filled with traps for the unwary. What these discussions fail to point out is that there was a method to the madness. The historical pleading rules reflected certain basic principles and assumptions about the proper role of pleading. Although the rules are admittedly complex—and yes, at times seemingly arbitrary—they make more sense when viewed in light of the basic principles. The following excerpts illustrate how the core principles and assumptions evolved into the historical system.

CHARLES E. CLARK, HANDBOOK OF THE LAW OF CODE PLEADING
10–14 (1928)

COMMON-LAW PLEADING

The two great characteristics of common-law pleading were the issue-forming process and the system of forms of action. The parties by successive steps of affirmation or denial were expected eventually to reach an issue which formed the sole point to be tried in the case. Under the system of forms of action a party seeking judicial relief was compelled to bring his claim within the limits of one of the existing forms or he was denied relief.

The common-law system of pleading came into vogue in England after the Norman Conquest. It developed as a more or less gradual process; the beginnings of most of the common-law actions cannot be stated with absolute precision. By the time of Edward I it had become a science to be formulated and cultivated. From that time until the time of the reforms of the nineteenth century the "science of special pleading" was of the utmost importance and among its devotees are included the great legal names of all but the most recent English lawyers.

Since the facts were passed upon by a body of laymen, not by a trained judge, it was felt necessary to ascertain clearly the points of dispute between the parties before the trial was begun. The institution of trial by jury, which meant so much to our ancestors in their efforts to secure a free and impartial justice, is therefore responsible for this striking characteristic of common-law pleading—the development of an issue. Unlike the Roman formulary system the issue was to be made by the parties themselves, not by a judicial officer of the government. Hence under the original idea of common-law pleading each party must in turn answer the previous pleading of his adversary by either denying, or affirming and adding new matter (*confessing and avoiding*) until there is ultimately reached a stage where one side has affirmed and the other has denied a single material point in the case. This was the issue, and, except as modified by later rules, provision was made for only one such issue. It was thought to be the glory of the system that the parties themselves would thus in advance of the trial single out and disclose the one material point as to which they were in dispute, thus eliminating all extraneous or agreed matter. The highly technical rules so characteristic of the system of common-law pleading were in the main designed either to aid or to force the parties in this matter to formulate the issue.

The other great characteristic feature of common-law pleading—the forms of action—had a close connection with the triumph of the king's courts over the local courts, a history too long to be traced in detail here. Whenever a litigant desired to sue in the king's court, he was required to procure a writ from the king through the office of the chancellor; that is, from the clerks in chancery. The writ was the king's command, directing the sheriff to summon the defendant before one of the king's courts. It served the further important purpose of giving jurisdiction to the court named in it. The process of issuing writs came to be strictly limited to cases where precedents existed, so that a litigant had to bring his claim within the limits set by some former precedent. Many writs were developed in reference to land, but because of the cumbersome nature of the procedure gradually fell into disuse. Actions for money damages—called personal actions—were the actions in general use under this system of pleading. At its later development, due to the restrictions on the issuance of new writs, these were limited to the famous forms of action—trespass, trespass on the case, trover, replevin, and detinue, in tort; and covenant, debt, account, and assumpsit in contract. The action of ejectment came to be practically a substitute for all the actions concerning land.

The practice of the clerks in chancery of *forming* new writs had ceased by the middle of the thirteenth century.... Hence the common-law system was limited in the extent of the relief which it could grant and the manner of granting it to the arbitrary units comprising the forms of action. Coupled with this were the refinements enforced to induce the production of an issue, resulting in a highly technical system which afforded none too complete relief. The rise of the courts of equity served, however, to postpone the necessity of reform for some time.

Equity Pleading

Pleadings in the equity courts consisted of detailed statements of the contentions of the parties. There were no formed actions in equity and little emphasis on the formation of an issue. The proceedings were more flexible than those at law in such matters as the joining of parties and the rendering of split judgments....

The equity courts developed from the exercise by the king of his royal prerogative through the chancellor to do justice where the courts failed to do so. [Key aspects of the system included] the absence of a separate body for the trial of facts and hence the absence of emphasis upon the formation of an issue. Likewise there were no forms of action in equity, the complainant stated his case at large in the form of a petition to the chancellor. The pleadings in equity were, however, quite detailed, since, being sworn to, they gave the facts upon which the case was decided. No formal trial with witnesses was ordinarily had, at least until modern times.

... The equity procedure itself was designed as a flexible system to meet varying claims and hence was of a kind to appeal to those who were attempting to change the harshness and inflexibility of the common law. But equity jurisprudence too had tended to become rigid; the procedure seems to have aggravated the delays apparently natural in all systems of law, and hence it also came to the point where it was not fulfilling the needs of a growing and developing system of law. The division of remedial justice into two systems with two courts entirely distinct from each other intensified the defects inherent in each system. A litigant not infrequently would have to be sent out of court to bring his action in another tribunal simply because he had chosen the wrong one. Since the rules governing the choice of tribunal were not always clear and easy of application, the harm to innocent seekers for justice was great.

NOTES

1. As the excerpt makes clear, you cannot understand English pleading without understanding the English court system. A defining feature of that system was that judicial authority was spread among several different courts. The most important of these systems were the "common law" or "law" courts, and the "Chancery" or courts of "equity." A large majority of civil disputes involving private parties would be heard in one of these two courts. However, there were important differences between the procedure in these courts, including fundamental differences in the process of pleading. Most discussion of historical pleading focuses on the rules that applied in the common law courts. The complexity and seeming arbitrariness of these rules, as compared to the relative flexibility of pleading in equity, was a major impetus for development of the modern pleading regimes.

2. The reading also illustrates three historical features of the common law courts that played a crucial role in the development of the complex pleading rules used by those courts. The first was the use of *lay juries*. Only the common law courts used juries. Because important issues in the case would be decided by people untrained in the law, the pleading system in the common law courts tried to keep the case in a form that could be managed by the jury. Thus, one overriding goal of pleading in the common law courts was to "form the issue"—to reduce the case to a single issue that the jury could both fathom and decide.

The second feature was the *writ system*. A party could not sue in the king's courts without obtaining a writ. At first, the writ system was designed to make the claimant show why the king's courts, rather than local courts, should hear the case. As one of the king's main roles was to preserve peace in the realm, obtaining a writ often required the claimant to show how the dispute threatened breach of the peace. Thus, much of the language in the traditional writs speaks of acts done "with force of arms." Often, this allegation had nothing to do with what actually happened, but was merely a talismanic statement designed to fit the case into the writ.

As the excerpt indicates, the writ system soon became highly rigid. The number of writs was fixed. If a party could not make his case fit into one of the writs, he could not obtain relief from the common law courts. In that situation, only equity could afford relief.

The final distinguishing feature—the *forms of action*—relates directly to the fixing of the writs. The writs did more than define the situations in which a party could obtain relief. Each writ also had its own unique procedure and remedies. Under some writs, for example, a party was required to produce twelve "oath helpers" who would swear that his allegations were true. If all of the oath helpers recited the oath in precisely the prescribed form, the party automatically won. Because procedures under some writs were more advantageous, claimants would often try to bend their case to fit it into a certain writ. Writs with cumbersome or onerous procedures eventually fell into disuse.

Similarly, courts of law were extremely limited with respect to the remedies they could provide. Depending on the writ, the primary remedies available in law were damages, ejectment, replevin, mandamus, and prohibition. The court could not grant other remedies, such as an injunction or specific performance.

3. At first, the overlapping jurisdiction of common law and equity caused a power struggle between the two systems. During the reign of James I, however, the English lawmakers reached a compromise that gave the common law courts primacy over private disputes. From that point forward, a party could sue in equity only if he could demonstrate that he could not obtain adequate relief in the common law courts. How could a party make such a showing? Often, a party turned to equity because of one of the constraining features of common law pleading and procedure.

    a. *Remedy*. The first situation was where the party sought a remedy that was unavailable in law. Suppose, for example, that A wants to sue B for breach of a contract to perform a service at which B is particularly skilled. A does not want damages; she wants B to do what he promised. Because a court of law could not grant the remedy of specific performance, A could not obtain the relief she wanted in law. Courts of equity, by contrast, had considerable discretion in fashioning a remedy to fit the needs of the parties. Specific performance was one of many remedies available in equity but not common law.

    Similarly, suppose C wants to sue D, a large factory, for nuisance based on D's continued emission of noxious fumes. C would prefer an injunction to damages because a damages award would require C to keep suing every time D emits more fumes. As injunctions were not available in law, C could only obtain the desired relief in equity.

    b. *Substantive Rights*. A second situation where a party would sue in equity is where the case did not fit within one of the writs. The writs, as eventually fixed, did not begin to cover all situations where a party should be able to recover. However, a party could go to equity—which was not constrained by the writ system—in order to obtain recovery. Several causes of action, including the actions for cancellation of a contract based on fraud and for breach of fiduciary duty, originated in this fashion in the courts of equity.

c. *Procedure*. The procedural facets of the writs could also prove unduly restraining. For example, a party who sued in common law could not force the other side to divulge information that might be useful in preparing the case. The modern concept of discovery owes its origins to the bill of discovery, a form of relief available in equity that allowed a party to obtain information from other parties. Similarly, modern procedural devices such as the class action originated in the courts of equity.

4. Courts in the United States did not slavishly mirror the English system. United States courts were never as rigidly compartmentalized as their English forerunners. For example, although most states originally had separate courts of law and equity, the United States federal courts assigned the same judges to hear both cases at law and in equity. Nor did United States courts necessarily follow all of the pleading rules and limitations on the writs applied in the English courts. Nevertheless, the English rules did establish a basic model that applied to varying degrees in the early United States courts.

5. Most jurisdictions in the United States have merged common law and equity into a single system. In the federal courts, this merger occurred in 1938. Federal Rule 1 indicates that the Rules apply with equal force in all cases, regardless of whether they would historically have been heard in law or in equity. Federal Rule 2 provides for a unitary action known simply as a "civil action." As a result, many of the procedural tools traditionally available only in equity, such as the class action and discovery, are now available in any type of action.

However, the procedural merger of common law and equity did not entirely erase the distinctions between the two systems. Vestigial remnants of the old division remain to this day. For example, although a party may obtain either legal or equitable relief from a single court, many courts still require a party to show that his legal remedy (typically damages) is inadequate before he may obtain an equitable remedy such as an injunction or specific performance. Similarly, special defenses such as laches and unclean hands may apply to claims in equity, but not to claims in law.

2. CODE PLEADING

The historical system only grew more complex—and foreign to the layperson—as it developed. Greater complexity fomented increased discontent. In the common-law courts, cases were too often resolved on technicalities instead of the merits. Although equity involved fewer technicalities, proceedings in equity were so flexible and fact oriented that they proved inordinately time-consuming and expensive.

As the system grew more cumbersome and arcane, courts, attorneys, and eventually legislatures began to push for reform. William Blackstone, a noted British jurist, published a work in 1765 entitled "Commentaries on the Law of England." This work severely criticized several aspects of the English system, including the complex pleading system. Blackstone's work strongly influenced the philosopher Jeremy Bentham, who was at that time Blackstone's pupil. Bentham spearheaded a movement to change the English legal system to make it more just. Bentham's efforts bore fruit on both sides of the Atlantic. In England, a series of promulgations beginning in 1834 effected significant changes in that system. The American states began their reform process shortly thereafter, but in some important ways the American reforms were more profound than the English reforms.

CHARLES E. CLARK, HANDBOOK OF THE LAW OF CODE PLEADING
17–19 (1928)

In this country the movement for pleading reform resulted in the adoption of the New York Code of 1848, the model and forerunner of all the practice codes in states which have adopted code pleading. By this act a single combined system of law and equity administered through the form of the one civil action was substituted for the two separate law and equity systems previously existing, and the forms of action at law and the separate suit in equity were abolished. It was further provided that the pleadings should state the facts, and the forming of the issue was less stressed....

The New York Code of 1848

In New York the movement for reform which had been making some real strides in England, became especially strong just prior to the middle of the nineteenth century. By a new constitution, adopted in that state in 1846, the court of chancery was abolished, and there was created in its place a court having general jurisdiction in law and equity. Further, the next legislature was directed to provide for the appointment of three commissioners "to revise, reform, simplify, and abridge" the practice and pleadings of courts of record of the state.... The commission speedily went to its task and the following year reported a code which with some amendments was passed on April 12, 1848, and became operative on the following first of July. The code was in large measure the work of David Dudley Field, one of the commissioners, and is generally referred to as the "Field Code." Though so expeditiously prepared and enacted, it has served as the model of all succeeding codes in this country.

Characteristics of the Code

Probably the most important characteristics of the code were the one form of action and the system of pleading the facts. The first still remains as the crowning achievement of the codes.... The forms of action were abolished, the separation of law and equity was done away with, and in its place the codifiers planned a *blended* system of law and equity with only a single form of action to be known as the *civil action*. As to the second characteristic, it was planned that the parties should in their pleadings state the facts in simple and concise form. Instead of the *issue pleading* of the common law there was to be *fact pleading*. . . . [However,] this part of the plan has worked least successfully of all the reforms made, since the codifiers and the courts failed to appreciate that the difference between statements of facts and statements of law is almost entirely one of degree only.

Among other important changes may be noted the adoption of the equity principles of greater freedom of joining parties and of rendering judgments in part for or against the various parties as the justice of the case may require (the *split judgment* of equity).

NOTES AND QUESTIONS

1. "Code" pleading caught on quickly, in part because of a perception that it simplified the pleading process. Missouri followed New York in 1849, and California in 1850. Within 25 years of adoption of the Field Code, twenty four states had adopted code pleading. Moreover, although the federal courts did not abolish the distinction between law and equity until 1938, the rules used in federal equity cases were amended in 1912 to borrow many of the principles of the codes.

Most of the jurisdictions that originally adopted Code pleading eventually replaced it with the notice pleading system of the Federal Rules. Nevertheless, Code pleading remains in force in a few states, including California and Nebraska. Although these states have borrowed other aspects of the Federal Rules, they still require a claimant to follow the fact pleading standards of the Field Code.

Because this book deals primarily with *federal* procedure, it will not deal with Code pleading in any depth. Should you find the need to study the topic further, there are a number of detailed books on the subject, many focusing on California's system.

2. The "fact pleading" standard of the Codes was the polar opposite of that employed in common-law pleading. Pleadings in the common-law courts focused on stating a claim in a particular preordained form. Because these forms were created to fit exactly the elements of the limited number of causes of action, the pleadings provided very little real information about the underlying event. Code pleading, by contrast, required the party to focus on the actual facts. In fact, a pleading under the Codes would be deemed insufficient if it contained "legal conclusions" instead of facts. As the excerpt points out, however, the line between law and facts is not always clear. As just one example, is a statement that "plaintiff and defendant entered into a contract" a statement of fact or one of law?

3. Even though the Codes required the parties to plead facts rather than law, a party could not simply file a complaint that detailed everything that happened. Instead, the Codes required a complaint to contain "a statement of facts *constituting a cause of action*." The attorney therefore had to pick and choose among the facts, focusing on those that were most pertinent to the theory under which the plaintiff hoped to recover.

This feature is a crucial feature of both Code pleading and notice pleading, but one often not apparent to the newcomer. Code and notice pleading purport to focus on the facts rather than the law. But the law always lurks just beneath the surface. Unless the facts fit into a recognized theory of recovery, a plaintiff cannot prevail even if she sets out the most compelling facts. Therefore, notwithstanding their genesis and stated standards, Code and notice pleading still require a claimant to plead the facts in a way that tracks the elements of the claim or claims she is bringing.

4. Do you think pleading standards play any role in the ability of parties to settle their disputes? Or in the timing of settlement? If you were designing a civil procedure system to encourage settlement as early as possible in the life of a case, what pleading requirements might maximize this goal? Would you emphasize a constraining function as in common-law pleading or a notice function? What are some competing goals that might affect your design?

B. PLEADING A CLAIM UNDER THE FEDERAL RULES

The Federal Rules of Civil Procedure, adopted in 1938, represent the third main theory of pleading in United States history. The Federal Rules' system of "notice" pleading is in force not only in the federal courts, but also in the majority of state courts. Even states like Illinois, New York, and Texas, which have retained other elements of the Codes, have basically adopted this form of pleading, primarily because it is even more forgiving than the Codes. Notice pleading is somewhat similar to Code pleading insofar as it concentrates on the facts rather than the underlying legal claim. Nevertheless, there are significant differences between the two, especially in the extent to which a party may include legal conclusions in her pleading.

1. THE FORM OF THE COMPLAINT

Most discussions of pleading focus on what a party must say in order to state a claim. But the Federal Rules also contain some requirements concerning the *form* of the complaint. Most of these requirements can be found in Rule 10.

Before reviewing these requirements, make sure you understand the difference between a *pleading* and a *motion*. Although attorneys and judges understand the difference intuitively, it can be difficult for a first-year student to distinguish the two. Like pleadings, most motions are in writing. Both must also meet most of the rules governing form set out in Federal Rule 10. Both ask the court to do something. So what is the difference?

Pleadings are usually comprehensive documents that recite all the party's claims or defenses. A case in federal court will involve a very limited number of pleadings. If there is a single plaintiff and a single defendant, the only pleadings will be a complaint (by plaintiff), an answer (by defendant), and possibly an answer to the answer and/or a reply (both by plaintiff). Additional pleadings may occur in a case involving multiple parties, as there may be pleadings for the cross-claims and third-party claims. Even so, the number of pleadings is strictly limited by Rule 7(a).

All other requests to the court are made by motion, as provided in Rule 7(b). Motions are best thought of as a "silver bullet." They are both more specific and more immediate than a pleading. While a pleading sets out a roadmap for the entire trial, a motion seizes on one or more issues in that case, and asks the court to resolve them quickly. For example, if defendant thinks the court lacks subject-matter jurisdiction over one or more claims, it can ask the court to dismiss the case immediately.

Note that a party can raise the same issues in either a pleading or a motion. For example, a defendant may assert lack of venue either in a pre-answer motion, or as one of the defenses in her answer, a pleading. If defendant chooses to assert the defense in her answer, she will probably file a motion asking the court to dismiss the case for that very reason. In this latter case, the motion brings the issue to resolution.

Rule 10 sets out a certain basic form that all pleadings must follow. The following hypothetical complaint illustrates how Rule 10 applies in practice. This complaint will also serve as the basis for further discussion.

UNITED STATES DISTRICT COURT for the DISTRICT OF VERMONT

PABLO PICASSO, Plaintiff   )
)
            v.   )   Civil Action No. 15–1234
)
VINCENT VAN GOGH,   )
Defendant

Complaint

Plaintiff for his Complaint against Defendant states as follows:

Parties

1. Plaintiff, Pablo Picasso, is a citizen of the Commonwealth of Pennsylvania, residing in the city of Pittsburgh.

2. Defendant, Vincent van Gogh, is a citizen of the State of Vermont, residing in the Town of Brattleboro.

Jurisdiction

3. This Court has subject matter jurisdiction pursuant to 28 United States Code §§ 1338 and 1367. Plaintiff's First and Second Claims for Relief arise under a federal statute, 17 United States Code § 501(a). Because both claims are federal copyright claims, this Court has subject matter jurisdiction exclusive of the state courts under 28 United States Code § 1338(a).

4. Plaintiff's Third Claim for Relief arises under state law. However, because Plaintiff's federal and state claims arise from a common nucleus of operative fact, comprising the same Article III case or controversy, this Court has supplemental jurisdiction over the state-law claim under 28 United States Code § 1367.

5. Defendant resides and is domiciled within the State of Vermont, and is therefore subject to the personal jurisdiction of this Court.

6. Venue is proper in this Court pursuant to 28 United States Code § 1391(b) because Defendant resides in the District of Vermont.

Factual Background

7. Until February 1, 2015, Plaintiff was a painter who earned his living creating and selling oil paintings.

8. One of the works that Plaintiff produced during his career as a painter was an oil painting entitled "Guernica", which Plaintiff completed in the spring of 2009. Plaintiff owns the copyright in this painting.

9. On February 1, 2015, Plaintiff retired from painting and took up another profession.

10. On February 2, 2015, Plaintiff entered into a written contract with Defendant for the sale of Plaintiff's studio in Pittsburgh. The purchase price in the contract was $10,000.

11. Plaintiff vacated the Pittsburgh studio on February 4, 2015. In his haste to depart, Plaintiff accidentally left behind the painting "Guernica."

12. On or about May 15, 2015, Plaintiff attended an art fair in Vermont. Defendant had a booth at this fair. While visiting Defendant's

booth, Plaintiff saw that Defendant was offering for sale a painting that looked exactly like Plaintiff's "Guernica" painting.

First Claim for Relief—Copyright Infringement

13. Plaintiff readopts and realleges the allegations set out in paragraphs 1 to 12 of this Complaint.

14. Sometime between February 4, 2009, and May 15, 2015, Defendant copied Plaintiff's "Guernica" painting.

15. By producing a work that is substantially similar to Plaintiff's copyrighted painting, Defendant violated Plaintiff's exclusive right to reproduce the work under 17 United States Code § 106(1), and thereby infringed Plaintiff's copyright.

Second Claim for Relief—Violation of Attribution Right

16. Plaintiff readopts and realleges the allegations set out in paragraphs 1 to 12 of this Complaint.

17. The work that Defendant was exhibiting at the May 15, 2015 art fair was the original "Guernica" work produced by Plaintiff.

18. However, sometime between February 4, 2015, and May 15, 2015, Defendant had altered the painting by removing Plaintiff's name from the surface of the painting and substituting the name of Defendant.

19. By displaying the altered work without any reference to Plaintiff, Defendant violated Plaintiff's 17 United States Code § 106A(a)(1)(A) right of attribution in the work, and thereby infringed Plaintiff's rights.

Third Claim for Relief—Conversion

20. Plaintiff readopts and realleges the allegations set out in paragraphs 1 to 12, 17, and 18 of this Complaint.

21. The contract between Plaintiff and Defendant was only for the sale of the studio and the underlying land, and did not include any paintings or other personal property that might be located in the studio.

22. By taking possession of, and offering for sale, Plaintiff's "Guernica" painting, Defendant converted the painting.

23. As a result of the intentional exercise of dominion over Plaintiff's property, Defendant is liable for punitive damages in an amount to be determined at trial.

Prayer for Relief

WHEREFORE, Plaintiff demands:

1. A judgment and order of this Court against Defendant for ordinary damages in the amount of $200,000;

2. A judgment and order of this Court against Defendant for punitive damages in the amount of $4,000,000;

Sec. B Pleading a Claim Under the Federal Rules   337

3. A judgment and order of this Court requiring Defendant to return the painting "Guernica" to Plaintiff; and

4. All other relief, in law and equity, as may be found proper.

Prayer for relief (cont.)

Al Gonzalez
Atty. Lic. No. 8080
Ashcroft and Gonzalez
601 South Main St.
Burlington, VT 05401
Counsel for Pablo Picasso

Demand for Jury Trial

Pursuant to Federal Rule of Civil Procedure 38(b), Plaintiff demands a trial by jury on all claims raised in this Complaint which may be tried by a jury.

Al Gonzalez
Counsel for Plaintiff

DATE: December 1, 2015

NOTES AND QUESTIONS

1. The above complaint really merges two separate documents into one. First, the complaint sets out plaintiff's claims and asks the court to grant recovery. Second, plaintiff demands a jury trial. As you will see in Chapter 12 pt. B, a plaintiff does not have to demand a jury in the complaint to preserve his right to a jury trial. Nevertheless, as there is no reason to delay the request, most parties file the demand with their original pleading.

Note that the plaintiff's attorney signs twice; once after the complaint, and again after the demand for a jury. This seeming redundancy reflects Rule 11, which is discussed in greater detail later in this Chapter. Rule 11 requires every pleading and motion to be signed by an attorney of record. Because the plaintiff is using a single document to serve two functions, the attorney signs twice, as if it were two documents.

2. Rule 10(a) requires a caption setting out the name of the court, the title of the action, the nature of the pleading (that is, complaint, answer, or reply), and the file number. The heading of the above complaint contains the required information. The "title of the action" is simply the name of the plaintiff and the defendant. If a case involves more than one plaintiff or defendant, all must be named in the complaint, but subsequent pleadings and motions need only state the first named plaintiff and defendant, and refer generally to the remaining parties. In other words, if A, B, and C sue X and Y, the complaint would list all five parties, but in all other pleadings and motions the title of the action would be simply "A et al. v. X et al."

3. Rule 10(b) requires that the paragraphs in the complaint be numbered. In addition, it indicates that the pleader should limit each paragraph "as far as practicable to a single set of circumstances." Note that using narrow, numbered fact allegations allows a pleader to incorporate earlier statements by reference, as the drafter of this hypothetical complaint has done.

4. The description of the parties in Paragraphs One and Two is not technically required. Nevertheless, it is very commonly included. This information provides the court a quick "who's who" in the case. Given that most judges do not immediately review the pleadings when the case is assigned to them, the information provided in this overview is very useful when the court is called upon to deal with preliminary challenges to jurisdiction and venue.

5. Federal Rule 17(a) requires that all actions "be prosecuted in the name of the real party in interest." Although located outside the portion of the Rules dealing with pleadings, this Rule directly affects how a party drafts its complaint. In essence, Rule 17(a) requires the complaint to name the person who will actually benefit from any judgment for the plaintiff. To see how the Rule applies, consider a situation where an insurance company has fully compensated its insured for a tortious injury caused by another. By law, the insurance company is *subrogated* to the rights of the insured, and can bring an action against the tortfeasor. Under Rule 17, the action must be brought in the name of the insurance company rather than the insured, as any judgment would be paid to the insurance company. Similarly, where the insured has been compensated for only part of the injury, the case should be brought in the names of both the insured and the insurance company. Can you see why the insurance company would prefer to leave its name off the complaint? Courts often enforce the real party in interest rule even when there are strong policy reasons for allowing "anonymous" pleadings, such as in sexual harassment cases. *Doe v. Del Rio*, 241 F.R.D. 154 (S.D.N.Y. 2006); *Rose v. Beaumont School District*, 240 F.R.D. 264 (E.D. Tex. 2007).

Failure to name the real party in interest is rarely fatal to a case. The Rule explicitly provides that a case will not be dismissed for failure to name the real party in interest until plaintiff has been given a reasonable time to join or substitute the real party in interest, or have the real party in interest ratify the claim.

Note that Rule 17(a) does not require that the action be litigated *by* the real party in interest. Subject to the rules of ethics, an unnamed party (often an insurance company) may actually control litigation of the case. Rule 17 only deals with how the case is captioned.

6. Paragraphs Three to Six comprise the statement of jurisdiction, the first of Rule 8(a)'s three basic elements. (Many of the state versions of Rule 8(a) do not require the claimant to plead the basis for jurisdiction.) Although a statement of subject-matter jurisdiction is required for most claims (including counterclaims, cross-claims, and third-party claims) filed in federal

SEC. B   PLEADING A CLAIM UNDER THE FEDERAL RULES

court, allegations concerning personal jurisdiction and venue are not required. Nevertheless, because these issues are likely to arise at a fairly early stage of the case, it makes sense to include them in the complaint.

7. Rule 10(b) requires that different claims be stated in separate "counts." The hypothetical complaint uses the more recognizable phrase "claims for relief." Technically, two claims must be phrased as two counts only when they arise from different underlying transactions or occurrences. Therefore, the plaintiff in the hypothetical complaint was not required to list his claims separately. As a matter of convenience, however, most attorneys treat each claim as a separate count or claim for relief.

8. It is extremely rare for a case to be dismissed for failure to number the paragraphs or divide the claims into separate counts. Nor is a court likely to impose sanctions on the attorney. A court may require that the pleading be amended, but even that is rare.

2. THE BASIC PLEADING STANDARD OF FEDERAL RULE 8(a)

The prior section discussed the typical format of a complaint. Federal Rule 8(a) sets the standard for the language a party must use to state its actual claims:

(a) Claim for Relief. A pleading that states a claim for relief must contain:

(1) a short and plain statement of the grounds for the court's jurisdiction, unless the court already has jurisdiction and the claim needs no new jurisdictional support;

(2) a short and plain statement of the claim showing that the pleader is entitled to relief; and

(3) a demand for the relief sought, which may include relief in the alternative or different types of relief.

Note that Rule 8(a) by its very terms applies not only to complaints by plaintiffs, but to *all* claims for relief. Therefore, its basic notice pleading standard also applies to counterclaims, cross-claims, and claims by and against third-party defendants. Although most of the case law and literature focuses on the plaintiff's claim, do not forget that other claims are analyzed the same way.

The first element of a proper claim is a statement about jurisdiction, as discussed in note 6 in the prior subsection. Most disputes involving Rule 8(a) turn on the second criterion, the "short and plain statement of the claim." At first glance, this may not seem appreciably different than the standard used in the Codes, which required the pleader to state facts constituting a cause of action. Nevertheless, there is an important difference, although one admittedly difficult to appreciate in the abstract.

Code pleading required the claimant to "show his cards" by divulging what facts he had to support his claim. Federal notice pleading, by contrast, requires the claimant to reveal very few of the facts she has to support her claim. Instead, the claimant must only give the other side a rough idea—that is, put the other side "on notice"—of why he is being sued. This standard requires the claimant to disclose not only the legal claim or claims, but also to give the defendant some clue as to the events that gave rise to that claim. Armed with that information, the other side can decide how to respond.

For many years, the Federal Rules also contained an "Appendix of Forms," which provided hypothetical examples of various pleadings and other documents. Pleadings based on the Forms were considered *per se* valid. However, the Supreme Court abolished the Forms and the presumption of validity in 2015.

In actual practice, very few attorneys file pleadings as brief as Federal Rule 8(a) would allow. Most include considerably more information. If a two-page pleading would suffice, why do firms bother? One reason is the persistence of tradition. Another may be a sense that clients should feel that they are getting their money's worth. However, there may also be valid litigation-related reasons to include a great deal of specific information in a complaint. As you will see in Chapter 10, for example, a party who files a highly specific pleading may have a tactical advantage in the mandatory disclosure stage of discovery.

3. APPLYING THE RULE 8(a) STANDARD

In essence, all Federal Rule 8(a) requires is that a party put the other side on notice of the claim or claims it plans on pursuing. Given that low threshold, you may wonder how a complaint could ever fail to meet the standards of the rule. The following three Supreme Court cases consider what qualifies as a "short and plain statement of the claim." Because the cases are arguably inconsistent, be sure to read the opinions in light of both the language of, and the policy underlying, Federal Rule 8(a).

SWIERKIEWICZ V. SOREMA, N. A.
534 U.S. 506, 122 S.Ct. 992, 152 L.Ed.2d 1 (2002)

JUSTICE THOMAS delivered the opinion of the Court.

This case presents the question whether a complaint in an employment discrimination lawsuit must contain specific facts establishing a prima facie case of discrimination . . . . We hold that an employment discrimination complaint need not include such facts and instead must contain only "a short and plain statement of the claim showing that the pleader is entitled to relief." Fed. Rule Civ. Proc. 8(a)(2).

Petitioner Akos Swierkiewicz is a native of Hungary, who at the time of his complaint was 53 years old.¹ In April 1989, petitioner began working for respondent Sorema N. A., a reinsurance company headquartered in New York and principally owned and controlled by a French parent corporation. Petitioner was initially employed in the position of senior vice president and chief underwriting officer (CUO). Nearly six years later, Francois M. Chavel, respondent's Chief Executive Officer, demoted petitioner to a marketing and services position and transferred the bulk of his underwriting responsibilities to Nicholas Papadopoulo, a 32-year-old who, like Mr. Chavel, is a French national. About a year later, Mr. Chavel stated that he wanted to "energize" the underwriting department and appointed Mr. Papadopoulo as CUO. Petitioner claims that Mr. Papadopoulo had only one year of underwriting experience at the time he was promoted, and therefore was less experienced and less qualified to be CUO than he, since at that point he had 26 years of experience in the insurance industry.

Following his demotion, petitioner contends that he "was isolated by Mr. Chavel . . . excluded from business decisions and meetings and denied the opportunity to reach his true potential at SOREMA." Petitioner unsuccessfully attempted to meet with Mr. Chavel to discuss his discontent. Finally, in April 1997, petitioner sent a memo to Mr. Chavel outlining his grievances and requesting a severance package. Two weeks later, respondent's general counsel presented petitioner with two options: He could either resign without a severance package or be dismissed. Mr. Chavel fired petitioner after he refused to resign.

Petitioner filed a lawsuit alleging that he had been terminated on account of his national origin in violation of Title VII of the Civil Rights Act of 1964, as amended, 42 U.S.C. § 2000e *et seq.*, and on account of his age in violation of the Age Discrimination in Employment Act of 1967 (ADEA), as amended, 29 U.S.C. § 621 *et seq.* The United States District Court for the Southern District of New York dismissed petitioner's complaint because it found that he "had not adequately alleged a prima facie case, in that he had not adequately alleged circumstances that support an inference of discrimination." The United States Court of Appeals for the Second Circuit affirmed the dismissal. . . .

Applying Circuit precedent, the Court of Appeals required petitioner to plead a prima facie case of discrimination in order to survive respondent's motion to dismiss. In the Court of Appeals' view, petitioner was thus required to allege in his complaint: (1) membership in a protected group; (2) qualification for the job in question; (3) an adverse employment action; and (4) circumstances that support an inference of discrimination. . . .

---

¹ Because we review here a decision granting respondent's motion to dismiss, we must accept as true all of the factual allegations contained in the complaint.

This Court has never indicated that the requirements for establishing a prima facie case . . . [at trial] also apply to the pleading standard that plaintiffs must satisfy in order to survive a motion to dismiss. . . . Consequently, the ordinary rules for assessing the sufficiency of a complaint apply. See, *e.g.*, *Scheuer* v. *Rhodes,* 416 U.S. 232, 236 (1974) ("When a federal court reviews the sufficiency of a complaint, before the reception of any evidence either by affidavit or admissions, its task is necessarily a limited one. The issue is not whether a plaintiff will ultimately prevail but whether the claimant is entitled to offer evidence to support the claims"). . . .

Furthermore, imposing the Court of Appeals' heightened pleading standard in employment discrimination cases conflicts with Federal Rule of Civil Procedure 8(a)(2), which provides that a complaint must include only "a short and plain statement of the claim showing that the pleader is entitled to relief." Such a statement must simply "give the defendant fair notice of what the plaintiff's claim is and the grounds upon which it rests." *Conley* v. *Gibson,* 355 U.S. 41, 47 (1957). This simplified notice pleading standard relies on liberal discovery rules and summary judgment motions to define disputed facts and issues and to dispose of unmeritorious claims. . . .

Other provisions of the Federal Rules of Civil Procedure are inextricably linked to Rule 8(a)'s simplified notice pleading standard. Rule 8(e)(1) states that "no technical forms of pleading or motions are required," and Rule 8(f) provides that "all pleadings shall be so construed as to do substantial justice." Given the Federal Rules' simplified standard for pleading, "[a] court may dismiss a complaint only if it is clear that no relief could be granted under any set of facts that could be proved consistent with the allegations." *Hishon* v. *King & Spalding,* 467 U.S. 69, 73 (1984). . . .

Applying the relevant standard, petitioner's complaint easily satisfies the requirements of Rule 8(a) because it gives respondent fair notice of the basis for petitioner's claims. Petitioner alleged that he had been terminated on account of his national origin in violation of Title VII and on account of his age in violation of the ADEA. His complaint detailed the events leading to his termination, provided relevant dates, and included the ages and nationalities of at least some of the relevant persons involved with his termination. These allegations give respondent fair notice of what petitioner's claims are and the grounds upon which they rest. In addition, they state claims upon which relief could be granted under Title VII and the ADEA.

Respondent argues that allowing lawsuits based on conclusory allegations of discrimination to go forward will burden the courts and encourage disgruntled employees to bring unsubstantiated suits. Whatever the practical merits of this argument, the Federal Rules do not contain a heightened pleading standard for employment discrimination suits. A requirement of greater specificity for particular claims is a result that "must be obtained by the process of amending the Federal Rules, and not by judicial interpretation." *Leatherman* [*v. Tarrant County Narcotics Intelligence and Coordination Unit*, 507 U.S. 163 (1993)] at 168. Furthermore, Rule 8(a) establishes a pleading standard without regard to whether a claim will succeed on the merits. "Indeed it may appear on the face of the pleadings that a recovery is very remote and unlikely but that is not the test." *Scheuer*, 416 U.S. at 236.

For the foregoing reasons, we hold that an employment discrimination plaintiff need not plead a prima facie case of discrimination and that petitioner's complaint is sufficient to survive respondent's motion to dismiss. Accordingly, the judgment of the Court of Appeals is reversed, and the case is remanded for further proceedings consistent with this opinion. . . .

BELL ATLANTIC CORP. V. TWOMBLY
550 U.S. 544, 127 S.Ct. 1955, 167 L.Ed.2d 929 (2007)

SOUTER, J., delivered the opinion of the Court, in which ROBERTS, C. J., and SCALIA, KENNEDY, THOMAS, BREYER, and ALITO, JJ., joined. STEVENS, J., filed a dissenting opinion, in which GINSBURG, J., joined, except as to Part IV.

I

The upshot of the 1984 divestiture of the American Telephone & Telegraph Company's (AT & T) local telephone business was a system of regional service monopolies (variously called "Regional Bell Operating Companies," "Baby Bells," or "Incumbent Local Exchange Carriers" (ILECs)), and a separate, competitive market for long-distance service from which the ILECs were excluded. More than a decade later, Congress [completely changed the law, allowing competition for local service, while simultaneously] . . . authorizing ILECs to enter the long-distance market.

"Central to the [new] scheme [was each ILEC's] obligation . . . to share its network with competitors," *Verizon Communications Inc. v. Law Offices of Curtis v. Trinko*, LLP, 540 U.S. 398, 402, 124 S.Ct. 872, 157 L.Ed.2d 823 (2004), which came to be known as "competitive local exchange carriers" (CLECs). . . .

Respondents William Twombly and Lawrence Marcus (hereinafter plaintiffs) represent a putative class consisting of all "subscribers of local telephone and/or high speed internet services . . . from February 8, 1996 to present." In this action against petitioners, a group of ILECs, plaintiffs seek treble damages and declaratory and injunctive relief for claimed violations of § 1 of the Sherman Act, which prohibits "[e]very contract, combination in the form of trust or otherwise, or conspiracy, in restraint of trade...."

The complaint alleges that the ILECs conspired to restrain trade in two ways, each supposedly inflating charges for local telephone and high-speed Internet services. Plaintiffs say, first, that the ILECs "engaged in parallel conduct" in their respective service areas to inhibit the growth of upstart CLECs. Their actions allegedly included making unfair agreements with the CLECs for access to ILEC networks, providing inferior connections to the networks, overcharging, and billing in ways designed to sabotage the CLECs' relations with their own customers. According to the complaint, the ILECs' "compelling common motivatio[n]" to thwart the CLECs' competitive efforts naturally led them to form a conspiracy....

Second, the complaint charges agreements by the ILECs to refrain from competing against one another. These are to be inferred from the ILECs' common failure "meaningfully [to] pursu[e]" "attractive business opportunit[ies]" in contiguous markets where they possessed "substantial competitive advantages"....

The complaint couches its ultimate allegations this way:

> In the absence of any meaningful competition between the [ILECs] in one another's markets, and in light of the parallel course of conduct that each engaged in to prevent competition from CLECs within their respective local telephone and/or high speed internet services markets and the other facts and market circumstances alleged above, Plaintiffs allege upon information and belief that [the ILECs] have entered into a contract, combination or conspiracy to prevent competitive entry in their respective local telephone and/or high speed internet services markets and have agreed not to compete with one another and otherwise allocated customers and markets to one another.

The United States District Court for the Southern District of New York dismissed the complaint for failure to state a claim upon which relief can be granted. The District Court acknowledged that "plaintiffs may allege a conspiracy by citing instances of parallel business behavior that suggest an agreement," but emphasized that "while '[c]ircumstantial evidence of consciously parallel behavior may have made heavy inroads into the traditional judicial attitude toward conspiracy[, . . .] "conscious parallelism" has not yet read conspiracy out of the Sherman Act entirely.'" Thus, the District Court understood that allegations of parallel business conduct, taken alone, do not state a claim under § 1; plaintiffs must allege additional facts that "ten[d] to exclude independent self-interested conduct as an explanation for defendants' parallel behavior." The District Court found plaintiffs' allegations of parallel ILEC actions to discourage competition inadequate because "the behavior of each ILEC in resisting the incursion of CLECs is fully explained by the ILEC's own interests in defending its individual territory." As to the ILECs' supposed agreement against competing with each other, the District Court found that the complaint does not "alleg[e] facts . . . suggesting that refraining from competing in other territories as CLECs was contrary to [the ILECs'] apparent economic interests, and consequently [does] not rais[e] an inference that [the ILECs'] actions were the result of a conspiracy."

The Court of Appeals for the Second Circuit reversed, holding that the District Court tested the complaint by the wrong standard. It held that "plus factors are not required to be pleaded to permit an antitrust claim based on parallel conduct to survive dismissal." 425 F.3d 99, 114 (2005). Although the Court of Appeals took the view that plaintiffs must plead facts that "include conspiracy among the realm of 'plausible' possibilities in order to survive a motion to dismiss," it then said that "to rule that allegations of parallel anticompetitive conduct fail to support a plausible conspiracy claim, a court would have to conclude that there is no set of facts that would permit a plaintiff to demonstrate that the particular parallelism asserted was the product of collusion rather than coincidence." *Ibid.*

We granted certiorari to address the proper standard for pleading an antitrust conspiracy through allegations of parallel conduct, and now reverse.

II

Because § 1 of the Sherman Act "does not prohibit [all] unreasonable restraints of trade . . . but only restraints effected by a contract, combination, or conspiracy," *Copperweld Corp. v. Independence Tube Corp.*, 467 U.S. 752, 775, 104 S.Ct. 2731, 81 L.Ed.2d 628 (1984), "[t]he crucial question" is whether the challenged anticompetitive conduct "stem[s] from independent decision or from an agreement, tacit or express," *Theatre Enterprises*, 346 U.S., at 540, 74 S.Ct. 257. While a showing of parallel "business behavior is admissible circumstantial evidence from which the fact finder may infer agreement," it falls short of "conclusively establish[ing] agreement or . . . itself constitut[ing] a Sherman Act offense." *Id.*, at 540–541, 74 S.Ct. 257. Even "conscious parallelism," a common reaction of "firms in a concentrated market [that] recogniz[e] their shared economic interests and their interdependence with respect to price and output decisions" is "not in itself unlawful." *Brooke Group Ltd. v. Brown & Williamson Tobacco Corp.*, 509 U.S. 209, 227, 113 S.Ct. 2578, 125 L.Ed.2d 168 (1993). . . .

This case presents the antecedent question of what a plaintiff must plead in order to state a claim under § 1 of the Sherman Act. Federal Rule of Civil Procedure 8(a)(2) requires only "a short and plain statement of the claim showing that the pleader is entitled to relief," in order to "give the defendant fair notice of what the . . . claim is and the grounds upon which it rests," *Conley v. Gibson*, 355 U.S. 41, 47, 78 S.Ct. 99, 2 L.Ed.2d 80 (1957). While a complaint attacked by a Rule 12(b)(6) motion to dismiss does not need detailed factual allegations, a plaintiff's obligation to provide the "grounds" of his "entitle[ment] to relief" requires more than labels and conclusions, and a formulaic recitation of the elements of a cause of action will not do. Factual allegations must be enough to raise a right to relief above the speculative level,³ on the assumption that all the allegations in the complaint are true (even if doubtful in fact).

In applying these general standards to a § 1 claim, we hold that stating such a claim requires a complaint with enough factual matter (taken as true) to suggest that an agreement was made. Asking for plausible grounds to infer an agreement does not impose a probability requirement at the pleading stage; it simply calls for enough fact to raise a reasonable expectation that discovery will reveal evidence of illegal agreement. And, of course, a well-pleaded complaint may proceed even if it strikes a savvy judge that actual proof of those facts is improbable. . . . Without more, parallel conduct does not suggest conspiracy, and a conclusory allegation of agreement at some unidentified point does not supply facts adequate to show illegality. Hence, when allegations of parallel conduct are set out in order to make a § 1 claim, they must be placed in a context that raises a suggestion of a preceding agreement, not merely parallel conduct that could just as well be independent action. . . .

Plaintiffs do not, of course, dispute the requirement of plausibility and the need for something more than merely parallel behavior . . . , and their main argument against the plausibility standard at the pleading stage is its ostensible conflict with an early statement of ours construing Rule 8. Justice Black's opinion for the Court in *Conley v. Gibson* spoke not only of the need for fair notice of the grounds for entitlement to relief but of "the accepted rule that a complaint should not be dismissed for failure to state a claim unless it appears beyond doubt that the plaintiff can prove no set of facts in support of his claim which would entitle him to relief." 355 U.S., at 45–46, 78 S.Ct. 99. This "no set of facts" language can be read in isolation as saying that any statement revealing the theory of the claim will suffice unless its factual impossibility may be shown from the face of the pleadings; and the Court of Appeals appears to have read *Conley* in some such way when formulating its understanding of the proper pleading standard.

---

³ The dissent greatly oversimplifies matters by suggesting that the Federal Rules somehow dispensed with the pleading of facts altogether. While, for most types of cases, the Federal Rules eliminated the cumbersome requirement that a claimant "set out in detail the facts upon which he bases his claim," *Conley v. Gibson*, 355 U.S. 41, 47, 78 S.Ct. 99, 2 L.Ed.2d 80 (1957), Rule 8(a)(2) still requires a "showing," rather than a blanket assertion, of entitlement to relief. Without some factual allegation in the complaint, it is hard to see how a claimant could satisfy the requirement of providing not only "fair notice" of the nature of the claim, but also "grounds" on which the claim rests.

On such a focused and literal reading of *Conley*'s "no set of facts," a wholly conclusory statement of claim would survive a motion to dismiss whenever the pleadings left open the possibility that a plaintiff might later establish some "set of [undisclosed] facts" to support recovery. . . .

Conley's "no set of facts" language has been questioned, criticized, and explained away long enough. To be fair to the *Conley* Court, the passage should be understood in light of the opinion's preceding summary of the complaint's concrete allegations, which the Court quite reasonably understood as amply stating a claim for relief. But the passage so often quoted fails to mention this understanding on the part of the Court, and after puzzling the profession for 50 years, this famous observation has earned its retirement. The phrase is best forgotten as an incomplete, negative gloss on an accepted pleading standard: once a claim has been stated adequately, it may be supported by showing any set of facts consistent with the allegations in the complaint. *Conley*, then, described the breadth of opportunity to prove what an adequate complaint claims, not the minimum standard of adequate pleading to govern a complaint's survival.

III

When we look for plausibility in this complaint, we agree with the District Court that plaintiffs' claim of conspiracy in restraint of trade comes up short. To begin with, the complaint leaves no doubt that plaintiffs rest their § 1 claim on descriptions of parallel conduct and not on any independent allegation of actual agreement among the ILECs. Although in form a few stray statements speak directly of agreement, on fair reading these are merely legal conclusions resting on the prior allegations. Thus, the complaint first takes account of the alleged "absence of any meaningful competition between [the ILECs] in one another's markets," "the parallel course of conduct that each [ILEC] engaged in to prevent competition from CLECs," "and the other facts and market circumstances alleged [earlier]"; "in light of" these, the complaint concludes "that [the ILECs] have entered into a contract, combination or conspiracy to prevent competitive entry into their . . . markets and have agreed not to compete with one another." The nub of the complaint, then, is the ILECs' parallel behavior, consisting of steps to keep the CLECs out and manifest disinterest in becoming CLECs themselves, and its sufficiency turns on the suggestions raised by this conduct when viewed in light of common economic experience.

We think that nothing contained in the complaint invests either the action or inaction alleged with a plausible suggestion of conspiracy. As to the ILECs' supposed agreement to disobey the 1996 Act and thwart the CLECs' attempts to compete, we agree with the District Court that nothing in the complaint intimates that the resistance to the upstarts was anything more than the natural, unilateral reaction of each ILEC intent on keeping its regional dominance. . . .

[The Court also held that the allegations pertaining to the second theory did not suggest a conspiracy.] . . . We agree with the District Court's assessment that antitrust conspiracy was not suggested by the facts adduced under either theory of the complaint, which thus fails to state a valid § 1 claim.

Plaintiffs say that our analysis runs counter to *Swierkiewicz v. Sorema N. A.*, 534 U.S. 506, 508, 122 S.Ct. 992, 152 L.Ed.2d 1 (2002), which held that "a complaint in an employment discrimination lawsuit [need] not contain specific facts establishing a prima facie case of discrimination.". . . . As the District Court correctly understood, however, "*Swierkiewicz* did not change the law of pleading, but simply re-emphasized . . . that the Second Circuit's use of a heightened pleading standard for Title VII cases was contrary to the Federal Rules' structure of liberal pleading requirements." 313 F.Supp.2d, at 181. Even though *Swierkiewicz*'s pleadings "detailed the events leading to his termination, provided relevant dates, and included the ages and nationalities of at least some of the relevant persons involved with his termination," the Court of Appeals dismissed his complaint for failing to allege certain additional facts that *Swierkiewicz* would need at the trial stage to support his claim in the absence of direct evidence of discrimination. We reversed on the ground that the Court of Appeals had impermissibly applied what amounted to a heightened pleading requirement by insisting that *Swierkiewicz* allege "specific facts" beyond those necessary to state his claim and the grounds showing entitlement to relief.

Here, in contrast, we do not require heightened fact pleading of specifics, but only enough facts to state a claim to relief that is plausible on its face. Because the plaintiffs here have not nudged their claims across the line from conceivable to plausible, their complaint must be dismissed.

JUSTICE STEVENS, with whom JUSTICE GINSBURG joins except as to Part IV, dissenting.

. . . Does a judicial opinion that the charge is not "plausible" provide a legally acceptable reason for dismissing the complaint? I think not. . . .

The Court and petitioners' legal team are no doubt correct that the parallel conduct alleged is consistent with the absence of any contract, combination, or conspiracy. But that conduct is also entirely consistent with the presence of the illegal agreement alleged in the complaint. And the charge that petitioners "agreed not to compete with one another" is not just one of "a few stray statements," it is an allegation describing unlawful conduct. As such, the Federal Rules of Civil Procedure, our longstanding precedent, and sound practice mandate that the District

Court at least require some sort of response from petitioners before dismissing the case. . . . .

If *Conley*'s "no set of facts" language is to be interred, let it not be without a eulogy. That exact language, which the majority says has "puzzl[ed] the profession for 50 years," has been cited as authority in a dozen opinions of this Court and four separate writings. In not one of those 16 opinions was the language "questioned," "criticized," or "explained away." Indeed, today's opinion is the first by any Member of this Court to express any doubt as to the adequacy of the *Conley* formulation. Taking their cues from the federal courts, 26 States and the District of Columbia utilize as their standard for dismissal of a complaint the very language the majority repudiates: whether it appears "beyond doubt" that "no set of facts" in support of the claim would entitle the plaintiff to relief.

Petitioners have not requested that the *Conley* formulation be retired, nor have any of the six amici who filed briefs in support of petitioners. I would not rewrite the Nation's civil procedure textbooks and call into doubt the pleading rules of most of its States without far more informed deliberation as to the costs of doing so. Congress has established a process—a rulemaking process—for revisions of that order. . . .

Whether the Court's actions will benefit only defendants in antitrust treble-damages cases, or whether its test for the sufficiency of a complaint will inure to the benefit of all civil defendants, is a question that the future will answer. . . .

The transparent policy concern that drives the decision is the interest in protecting antitrust defendants—who in this case are some of the wealthiest corporations in our economy—from the burdens of pretrial discovery. Even if it were not apparent that the legal fees petitioners have incurred in arguing the merits of their Rule 12(b) motion have far exceeded the cost of limited discovery, or that those discovery costs would burden respondents as well as petitioners, that concern would not provide an adequate justification for this law-changing decision. For in the final analysis it is only a lack of confidence in the ability of trial judges to control discovery, buttressed by appellate judges' independent appraisal of the plausibility of profoundly serious factual allegations, that could account for this stark break from precedent. . . .

ASHCROFT V. IQBAL

556 U.S. 662, 129 S.Ct. 1937, 173 L.Ed.2d 868 (2009)

JUSTICE KENNEDY delivered the opinion of the Court.

Respondent Javaid Iqbal is a citizen of Pakistan and a Muslim. In the wake of the September 11, 2001, terrorist attacks he was arrested in the United States on criminal charges and detained by federal officials.

Respondent claims he was deprived of various constitutional protections while in federal custody. To redress the alleged deprivations, respondent filed a complaint against numerous federal officials, including John Ashcroft, the former Attorney General of the United States, and Robert Mueller, the Director of the Federal Bureau of Investigation (FBI). Ashcroft and Mueller are the petitioners in the case now before us. As to these two petitioners, the complaint alleges that they adopted an unconstitutional policy that subjected respondent to harsh conditions of confinement on account of his race, religion, or national origin. . . .

Respondent's account of his prison ordeal could, if proved, demonstrate unconstitutional misconduct by some governmental actors. But the allegations and pleadings with respect to these actors are not before us here. This case instead turns on a narrower question: Did respondent, as the plaintiff in the District Court, plead factual matter that, if taken as true, states a claim that petitioners deprived him of his clearly established constitutional rights. We hold respondent's pleadings are insufficient.

I

. . . [In November 2001 respondent was arrested and held on immigration charges in Brooklyn, N.Y. Subsequently, he] was designated a person "of high interest" to the September 11 investigation and in January 2002 was placed in a section of the MDC known as the Administrative Maximum Special Housing Unit (ADMAX SHU). As the facility's name indicates, the ADMAX SHU incorporates the maximum security conditions allowable under Federal Bureau of Prison regulations. ADMAX SHU detainees were kept in lockdown 23 hours a day, spending the remaining hour outside their cells in handcuffs and leg irons accompanied by a four-officer escort. . . .

The allegations against petitioners are the only ones relevant here. The complaint contends that petitioners designated respondent a person of high interest on account of his race, religion, or national origin, in contravention of the First and Fifth Amendments to the Constitution. The complaint alleges that "the [FBI], under the direction of Defendant MUELLER, arrested and detained thousands of Arab Muslim men . . . as part of its investigation of the events of September 11." It further alleges that "[t]he policy of holding post-September-11th detainees in highly restrictive conditions of confinement until they were 'cleared' by the FBI was approved by Defendants ASHCROFT and MUELLER in discussions in the weeks after September 11, 2001." Lastly, the complaint posits that petitioners "each knew of, condoned, and willfully and maliciously agreed to subject" respondent to harsh conditions of confinement "as a matter of policy, solely on account of [his] religion, race, and/or national origin and for no legitimate penological interest." The pleading names Ashcroft as the "principal architect" of the policy, and identifies Mueller as "instrumental in [its] adoption, promulgation, and implementation."

Petitioners moved to dismiss the complaint for failure to state sufficient allegations to show their own involvement in clearly established unconstitutional conduct. [The District Court denied their motion.] Accepting all of the allegations in respondent's complaint as true, the court held that "it cannot be said that there [is] no set of facts on which [respondent] would be entitled to relief as against" petitioners.... [P]etitioners filed an interlocutory appeal in the United States Court of Appeals for the Second Circuit. While that appeal was pending, this Court decided *Bell Atlantic Corp. v. Twombly*, 550 U.S. 544 (2007), which discussed the standard for evaluating whether a complaint is sufficient to survive a motion to dismiss. . . .

III

In *Twombly*, the Court found it necessary first to discuss the antitrust principles implicated by the complaint. Here too we begin by taking note of the elements a plaintiff must plead to state a claim of unconstitutional discrimination against officials entitled to assert the defense of qualified immunity.

. . . Based on the rules our precedents establish, respondent correctly concedes that Government officials may not be held liable for the unconstitutional conduct of their subordinates under a theory of respondeat superior. . . . Because vicarious liability is inapplicable . . . , a plaintiff must plead that each Government-official defendant, through the official's own individual actions, has violated the Constitution.

The factors necessary to establish a . . . [constitutional] violation will vary with the constitutional provision at issue. Where the claim is invidious discrimination in contravention of the First and Fifth Amendments, our decisions make clear that the plaintiff must plead and prove that the defendant acted with discriminatory purpose. Under extant precedent purposeful discrimination requires more than "intent as volition or intent as awareness of consequences." *Personnel Administrator of Mass. v. Feeney*, 442 U.S. 256, 279 (1979). It instead involves a decisionmaker's undertaking a course of action " 'because of,' not merely 'in spite of,' [the action's] adverse effects upon an identifiable group." *Ibid*. It follows that, to state a claim based on a violation of a clearly established right, respondent must plead sufficient factual matter to show that petitioners adopted and implemented the detention policies at issue not for a neutral, investigative reason but for the purpose of discriminating on account of race, religion, or national origin.

Respondent disagrees. He argues that, under a theory of "supervisory liability," petitioners can be liable for "knowledge and acquiescence in their subordinates' use of discriminatory criteria to make classification decisions among detainees." That is to say, respondent believes a supervisor's mere knowledge of his subordinate's discriminatory purpose amounts to the supervisor's violating the Constitution. We reject this argument.... In the context of determining whether there is a violation of clearly established right to overcome qualified immunity, purpose rather than knowledge is required to impose ... liability on the subordinate for unconstitutional discrimination; the same holds true for an official charged with violations arising from his or her superintendent responsibilities.

IV

A

We turn to respondent's complaint. Under Federal Rule of Civil Procedure 8(a)(2), a pleading must contain a "short and plain statement of the claim showing that the pleader is entitled to relief." As the Court held in *Twombly*, the pleading standard Rule 8 announces does not require "detailed factual allegations," but it demands more than an unadorned, the-defendant-unlawfully-harmed-me accusation. A pleading that offers "labels and conclusions" or "a formulaic recitation of the elements of a cause of action will not do." 550 U.S., at 555. Nor does a complaint suffice if it tenders "naked assertion[s]" devoid of "further factual enhancement." *Id.*, at 557.

To survive a motion to dismiss, a complaint must contain sufficient factual matter, accepted as true, to "state a claim to relief that is plausible on its face." *Id.*, at 570. A claim has facial plausibility when the plaintiff pleads factual content that allows the court to draw the reasonable inference that the defendant is liable for the misconduct alleged. The plausibility standard is not akin to a "probability requirement," but it asks for more than a sheer possibility that a defendant has acted unlawfully. Where a complaint pleads facts that are "merely consistent with" a defendant's liability, it "stops short of the line between possibility and plausibility of 'entitlement to relief.'" *Id.*, at 557 (brackets omitted).

Two working principles underlie our decision in *Twombly*. First, the tenet that a court must accept as true all of the allegations contained in a complaint is inapplicable to legal conclusions. Threadbare recitals of the elements of a cause of action, supported by mere conclusory statements, do not suffice.... Rule 8 marks a notable and generous departure from the hyper-technical, code-pleading regime of a prior era, but it does not unlock the doors of discovery for a plaintiff armed with nothing more than conclusions. Second, only a complaint that states a plausible claim for relief survives a motion to dismiss. Determining whether a complaint states a plausible claim for relief will, as the Court of Appeals observed, be a context-specific task that requires the reviewing court to draw on its judicial experience and common sense. But where the well-pleaded facts do not permit the court to infer more than the mere possibility of misconduct, the complaint has alleged—but it has not "show[n]"—"that the pleader is entitled to relief." Fed. Rule Civ. Proc. 8(a)(2).

In keeping with these principles a court considering a motion to dismiss can choose to begin by identifying pleadings that, because they are no more than conclusions, are not entitled to the assumption of truth. While legal conclusions can provide the framework of a complaint, they must be supported by factual allegations. When there are well-pleaded factual allegations, a court should assume their veracity and then determine whether they plausibly give rise to an entitlement to relief.

Our decision in *Twombly* illustrates the two-pronged approach. . . .

The Court held the plaintiffs' complaint deficient under Rule 8. In doing so it first noted that the plaintiffs' assertion of an unlawful agreement was a " 'legal conclusion' " and, as such, was not entitled to the assumption of truth. Had the Court simply credited the allegation of a conspiracy, the plaintiffs would have stated a claim for relief and been entitled to proceed perforce. The Court next addressed the "nub" of the plaintiffs' complaint-the well-pleaded, nonconclusory factual allegation of parallel behavior-to determine whether it gave rise to a "plausible suggestion of conspiracy." Acknowledging that parallel conduct was consistent with an unlawful agreement, the Court nevertheless concluded that it did not plausibly suggest an illicit accord because it was not only compatible with, but indeed was more likely explained by, lawful, unchoreographed free-market behavior. Because the well-pleaded fact of parallel conduct, accepted as true, did not plausibly suggest an unlawful agreement, the Court held the plaintiffs' complaint must be dismissed.

B

Under *Twombly*'s construction of Rule 8, we conclude that respondent's complaint has not "nudged [his] claims" of invidious discrimination "across the line from conceivable to plausible."

We begin our analysis by identifying the allegations in the complaint that are not entitled to the assumption of truth. Respondent pleads that petitioners "knew of, condoned, and willfully and maliciously agreed to subject [him]" to harsh conditions of confinement "as a matter of policy, solely on account of [his] religion, race, and/or national origin and for no legitimate penological interest." . . . These bare assertions, much like the pleading of conspiracy in *Twombly*, amount to nothing more than a "formulaic recitation of the elements" of a constitutional discrimination claim, namely, that petitioners adopted a policy " 'because of,' not merely 'in spite of,' its adverse effects upon an identifiable group." *Feeney*, 442 U.S., at 279. As such, the allegations are conclusory and not entitled to be assumed true. . . . It is the conclusory nature of respondent's allegations, rather than their extravagantly fanciful nature, that disentitles them to the presumption of truth.

We next consider the factual allegations in respondent's complaint to determine if they plausibly suggest an entitlement to relief. The complaint alleges that "the [FBI], under the direction of Defendant MUELLER, arrested and detained thousands of Arab Muslim men . . . as part of its investigation of the events of September 11." It further claims that "[t]he policy of holding post-September-11th detainees in highly restrictive conditions of confinement until they were 'cleared' by the FBI was approved by Defendants ASHCROFT and MUELLER in discussions in the weeks after September 11, 2001." Taken as true, these allegations are consistent with petitioners' purposefully designating detainees "of high interest" because of their race, religion, or national origin. But given more likely explanations, they do not plausibly establish this purpose.

. . . Respondent's constitutional claims against petitioners rest solely on their ostensible "policy of holding post-September-11th detainees" in the ADMAX SHU once they were categorized as "of high interest." To prevail on that theory, the complaint must contain facts plausibly showing that petitioners purposefully adopted a policy of classifying post-September-11 detainees as "of high interest" because of their race, religion, or national origin.

This the complaint fails to do. Though respondent alleges that various other defendants, who are not before us, may have labeled him a person of "of high interest" for impermissible reasons, his only factual allegation against petitioners accuses them of adopting a policy approving "restrictive conditions of confinement" for post-September-11 detainees until they were "'cleared' by the FBI." Accepting the truth of that allegation, the complaint does not show, or even intimate, that petitioners purposefully housed detainees in the ADMAX SHU due to their race, religion, or national origin. All it plausibly suggests is that the Nation's top law enforcement officers, in the aftermath of a devastating terrorist attack, sought to keep suspected terrorists in the most secure conditions available until the suspects could be cleared of terrorist activity. Respondent does not argue, nor can he, that such a motive would violate petitioners' constitutional obligations. He would need to allege more by way of factual content to "nudg[e]" his claim of purposeful discrimination "across the line from conceivable to plausible." *Twombly*, 550 U.S., at 570.

. . . Yet respondent's complaint does not contain any factual allegation sufficient to plausibly suggest petitioners' discriminatory state of mind. His pleadings thus do not meet the standard necessary to comply with Rule 8.

It is important to note, however, that we express no opinion concerning the sufficiency of respondent's complaint against the defendants who are not before us. Respondent's account of his prison ordeal alleges serious official misconduct that we need not address here. Our decision is limited to the determination that respondent's complaint does not entitle him to relief from petitioners.

C

Respondent offers three arguments that bear on our disposition of his case, but none is persuasive.

1

Respondent first says that our decision in *Twombly* should be limited to pleadings made in the context of an antitrust dispute. This argument is not supported by *Twombly* and is incompatible with the Federal Rules of Civil Procedure.... Our decision in *Twombly* expounded the pleading standard for "all civil actions," and it applies to antitrust and discrimination suits alike.

2

Respondent next implies that our construction of Rule 8 should be tempered where, as here, the Court of Appeals has "instructed the district court to cabin discovery in such a way as to preserve" petitioners' defense of qualified immunity "as much as possible in anticipation of a summary judgment motion." We have held, however, that the question presented by a motion to dismiss a complaint for insufficient pleadings does not turn on the controls placed upon the discovery process. *Twombly*, at 559 ...

We decline respondent's invitation to relax the pleading requirements on the ground that the Court of Appeals promises petitioners minimally intrusive discovery. That promise provides especially cold comfort in this pleading context, where we are impelled to give real content to the concept of qualified immunity for high-level officials who must be neither deterred nor detracted from the vigorous performance of their duties. Because respondent's complaint is deficient under Rule 8, he is not entitled to discovery, cabined or otherwise.

3

Respondent finally maintains that the Federal Rules expressly allow him to allege petitioners' discriminatory intent "generally," which he equates with a conclusory allegation....

It is true that Rule 9(b) requires particularity when pleading "fraud or mistake," while allowing "[m]alice, intent, knowledge, and other conditions of a person's mind [to] be alleged generally." But "generally" is a relative term. In the context of Rule 9, it is to be compared to the particularity requirement applicable to fraud or mistake. Rule 9 merely excuses a party from pleading discriminatory intent under an elevated pleading standard. It does not give him license to evade the less rigid—though still operative—strictures of Rule 8. And Rule 8 does not empower respondent to plead the bare elements of his cause of action, affix the label "general allegation," and expect his complaint to survive a motion to dismiss.

V

We hold that respondent's complaint fails to plead sufficient facts to state a claim for purposeful and unlawful discrimination against petitioners. The Court of Appeals should decide in the first instance whether to remand to the District Court so that respondent can seek leave to amend his deficient complaint.

The judgment of the Court of Appeals is reversed, and the case is remanded for further proceedings consistent with this opinion.

JUSTICE SOUTER, with whom JUSTICE STEVENS, JUSTICE GINSBURG, and JUSTICE BREYER join, dissenting.

This case . . . comes to us with the explicit concession of petitioners Ashcroft and Mueller that an officer may be subject to *Bivens* liability as a supervisor on grounds other than *respondeat superior*. The Court apparently rejects this concession and, although it has no bearing on the majority's resolution of this case, does away with supervisory liability . . . [for constitutional claims] The majority then misapplies the pleading standard under *Bell Atlantic Corp. v. Twombly* to conclude that the complaint fails to state a claim. I respectfully dissent from both the rejection of supervisory liability as a cognizable claim in the face of petitioners' concession, and from the holding that the complaint fails to satisfy Rule 8(a)(2) of the Federal Rules of Civil Procedure. . . .

Given petitioners' concession, the complaint satisfies Rule 8(a)(2). Ashcroft and Mueller admit they are liable for their subordinates' conduct if they "had actual knowledge of the assertedly discriminatory nature of the classification of suspects as being 'of high interest' and they were deliberately indifferent to that discrimination." Iqbal alleges that after the September 11 attacks the Federal Bureau of Investigation (FBI) "arrested and detained thousands of Arab Muslim men," that many of these men were designated by high-ranking FBI officials as being " 'of high interest,' " and that in many cases, including Iqbal's, this designation was made "because of the race, religion, and national origin of the detainees, and not because of any evidence of the detainees' involvement in supporting terrorist activity." The complaint further alleges that Ashcroft was the "principal architect of the policies and practices challenged," and that Mueller "was instrumental in the adoption, promulgation, and implementation of the policies and practices challenged." According to the complaint, Ashcroft and Mueller "knew of, condoned, and willfully and maliciously agreed to subject [Iqbal] to these conditions of confinement as a matter of policy, solely on account of [his] religion, race, and/or national origin and for no legitimate penological interest." The complaint thus alleges, at a bare minimum, that Ashcroft and Mueller knew of and condoned the discriminatory policy their subordinates carried out. Actually, the complaint goes further in alleging that Ashcroft and Muller affirmatively acted to create the discriminatory detention policy. If these factual allegations are true, Ashcroft and Mueller were, at the very least, aware of the discriminatory policy being implemented and deliberately indifferent to it.

Ashcroft and Mueller argue that these allegations fail to satisfy the "plausibility standard" of *Twombly*. They contend that Iqbal's claims are implausible because such high-ranking officials "tend not to be personally involved in the specific actions of lower-level officers down the bureaucratic chain of command." But this response bespeaks a fundamental misunderstanding of the enquiry that *Twombly* demands. *Twombly* does not require a court at the motion-to-dismiss stage to consider whether the factual allegations are probably true. We made it clear, on the contrary, that a court must take the allegations as true, no matter how skeptical the court may be. . . . The sole exception to this rule lies with allegations that are sufficiently fantastic to defy reality as we know it: claims about little green men, or the plaintiff's recent trip to Pluto, or experiences in time travel. That is not what we have here.

Under *Twombly*, the relevant question is whether, assuming the factual allegations are true, the plaintiff has stated a ground for relief that is plausible. That is, in *Twombly*'s words, a plaintiff must "allege facts" that, taken as true, are "suggestive of illegal conduct." 550 U.S., at 564, n. 8. In *Twombly*, we were faced with allegations of a conspiracy to violate § 1 of the Sherman Act through parallel conduct. The difficulty was that the conduct alleged was "consistent with conspiracy, but just as much in line with a wide swath of rational and competitive business strategy unilaterally prompted by common perceptions of the market." *Id.*, at 554. We held that in that sort of circumstance, "[a]n allegation of parallel conduct is . . . much like a naked assertion of conspiracy in a § 1 complaint: it gets the complaint close to stating a claim, but without some further factual enhancement it stops short of the line between possibility and plausibility of 'entitlement to relief.'" *Id.*, at 557 (brackets omitted). Here, by contrast, the allegations in the complaint are neither confined to naked legal conclusions nor consistent with legal conduct. The complaint alleges that FBI officials discriminated against Iqbal solely on account of his race, religion, and national origin, and it alleges the knowledge and deliberate indifference that, by Ashcroft and Mueller's own admission, are sufficient to make them liable for the illegal action. Iqbal's complaint therefore contains "enough facts to state a claim to relief that is plausible on its face."

I do not understand the majority to disagree with this understanding of "plausibility" under *Twombly*. Rather, the majority discards the allegations discussed above with regard to Ashcroft and Mueller as conclusory, and is left considering only two statements in the complaint: that "the [FBI], under the direction of Defendant MUELLER, arrested and detained thousands of Arab Muslim men . . . as part of its investigation of the events of September 11," and that "[t]he policy of holding post-September-11th detainees in highly restrictive conditions of confinement until they were 'cleared' by the FBI was approved by Defendants ASHCROFT and MUELLER in discussions in the weeks after September 11, 2001." I think the majority is right in saying that these allegations suggest only that Ashcroft and Mueller "sought to keep suspected terrorists in the most secure conditions available until the suspects could be cleared of terrorist activity," and that this produced "a disparate, incidental impact on Arab Muslims." And I agree that the two allegations selected by the majority, standing alone, do not state a plausible entitlement to relief for unconstitutional discrimination.

But these allegations do not stand alone as the only significant, nonconclusory statements in the complaint, for the complaint contains many allegations linking Ashcroft and Mueller to the discriminatory practices of their subordinates. See Complaint ¶ 10, (Ashcroft was the "principal architect" of the discriminatory policy); ¶ 11 (Mueller was "instrumental" in adopting and executing the discriminatory policy); ¶ 96, at 172a–173a (Ashcroft and Mueller "knew of, condoned, and willfully and maliciously agreed to subject" Iqbal to harsh conditions "as a matter of policy, solely on account of [his] religion, race, and/or national origin and for no legitimate penological interest").

The majority says that these are "bare assertions" that, "much like the pleading of conspiracy in *Twombly*, amount to nothing more than a 'formulaic recitation of the elements' of a constitutional discrimination claim" and therefore are "not entitled to be assumed true." The fallacy of the majority's position, however, lies in looking at the relevant assertions in isolation. The complaint contains specific allegations that, in the aftermath of the September 11 attacks, the Chief of the FBI's International Terrorism Operations Section and the Assistant Special Agent in Charge for the FBI's New York Field Office implemented a policy that discriminated against Arab Muslim men, including Iqbal, solely on account of their race, religion, or national origin. Viewed in light of these subsidiary allegations, the allegations singled out by the majority as "conclusory" are no such thing. Iqbal's claim is not that Ashcroft and Mueller "knew of, condoned, and willfully and maliciously agreed to subject" him to a discriminatory practice that is left undefined; his allegation is that "they knew of, condoned, and willfully and maliciously agreed to subject" him to a particular, discrete, discriminatory policy detailed in the complaint. Iqbal does not say merely that Ashcroft was the architect of some amorphous discrimination, or that Mueller was instrumental in an ill-defined constitutional violation; he alleges that they helped to create the discriminatory policy he has described. Taking the complaint as a whole, it gives Ashcroft and Mueller "'fair notice of what the ... claim is and the grounds upon which it rests.'" *Twombly*, 550 U.S., at 555 (quoting *Conley v. Gibson*, 355 U.S. 41, 47 (1957)).

... By my lights, there is no principled basis for the majority's disregard of the allegations linking Ashcroft and Mueller to their subordinates' discrimination.

I respectfully dissent.

[JUSTICE BREYER also filed a dissenting opinion].

NOTES AND QUESTIONS

1. It is easier to understand the Court's reasoning in these three cases if you understand something about the substantive law that applies in each. Consider *Swierkiewicz*, which deals with a discrimination claim, first. Generally speaking, discrimination law is designed to protect negative treatment of people based on their race, religion, sex, national origin, or age. However, a claimant bringing a discrimination claim cannot prevail merely by showing he is a member of a protected group who suffered negative treatment. Instead, he must show *causation*: that his race, religion, gender, national origin, or age was a factor behind the negative treatment.

Of course, the best way to prove causation is with direct proof: a statement or memorandum from a defendant directly showing that the decision was made on an improper basis. But such direct evidence is rarely available. Most employers who do discriminate are savvy enough not to tell employees that they have been treated a particular way because of their race or gender. To counteract this situation, the courts also allow a discrimination plaintiff to establish a "prima facie" case of discrimination through the use of indirect or circumstantial evidence.

The issue in *Swierkiewicz* is whether the rules governing how a party *proves* a discrimination case at trial also affect what a party must *plead* in the complaint.

2. Now consider *Twombly*. The plaintiff in that case was bringing an antitrust claim under § 1 of the Sherman Act, which prohibits any "contract, combination, ... or conspiracy" in restraint of trade. To prevail under that section, plaintiff must show some form of agreement between defendant and at least one other person. The issue the Supreme Court wrestles with is what a party must allege in its complaint concerning a conspiracy.

3. The plaintiff in *Twombly* did specifically allege an "agreement" between the parties. But the Supreme Court holds that allegation insufficient. What more would the Court require plaintiff to say? Is a typical antitrust plaintiff likely to have sufficient information at its disposal to be able to state what the Court requires? Remember that a party cannot ordinarily use discovery until after it has successfully filed a proper complaint.

4. The key to *Twombly* is the Court's notion of plausibility. It is not enough for a claimant to base its claim on a legal conclusion. Rather, the claimant must include in the pleading enough facts to demonstrate the conclusion is plausible. Do you understand what it means to be "plausible?" Is plausible the same as possible? As probable? See the second paragraph in Part II of the majority opinion.

5. Do you agree with the *Twombly* Court that it is not plausible to conclude, based on the facts in the complaint, that defendants had entered into some sort of agreement? Does it matter that each actor had an economic incentive to engage in the same conduct by itself, even absent an agreement? If the actors were all merely engaging in the same sort of "parallel behavior," without an agreement, there would be no violation of § 1 of the Sherman Act.

On the other hand, what does the majority mean when it says the facts in the complaint suggest "parallel conduct that *could just as well be* independent action?" Is the Court confusing plausibility with probability? Does this statement suggest plaintiff must show that the conclusion that supports its claim is the most likely?

6. Now consider *Iqbal*, which elaborates at great length on the notion of plausibility. First, the Court makes it clear the plausibility standard applies to all pleadings, not only those alleging allegations of a conspiracy under the federal antitrust laws.

7. Like *Swierkiewicz*, *Iqbal* deals with a claim of discrimination. One of the important holdings in *Iqbal* concerns the substantive law applicable in claims arising directly under the U.S. Constitution (which are sometimes called *Bivens* claims). Because Ashcroft and Mueller did not themselves physically detain Iqbal, they could not be directly liable. Instead, plaintiff alleges they were secondarily liable for the actions of their underlings. The Court clarifies the standard that applies to this secondary liability, holding that mere knowledge of what a subordinate is doing is not enough to hold a party liable for the acts of the subordinate. Instead, the plaintiff must demonstrate that the party adopted a policy with the purpose of causing the effects on the plaintiff's group.

Note that, as the dissent points out, Ashcroft and Mueller had *conceded* that they could be held liable if they knew of the illegal conduct and were deliberately indifferent to it. The majority refuses to be bound by this concession, and goes on to hold that a showing of purpose is required. Is it proper for the majority to refuse to honor the concession? Did the majority overlook the "constraining" function of pleadings, discussed in Part A of this Chapter?

8. Is *Iqbal* consistent with *Swierkiewicz*? The majority appears to think the cases can be reconciled. But consider the following observations. Both cases deal with claims of discrimination. While the governing law is different, under both laws plaintiff is trying to show that defendant purposefully discriminated against plaintiff based on improper grounds (age and national origin in *Swierkiewicz*, religion, race, and national origin in

Iqbal). Both plaintiffs tried to make that showing by alleging that one or more members of their group were disproportionately subject to unfavorable treatment, as compared to others not in the group. How can such allegations make the claim plausible in *Swierkiewicz*, but not in *Iqbal*? Indeed, is there any meaningful difference between the Court's conclusion in *Swierkiewicz* that the complaint allowed an "inference of discrimination" and the notion of "plausibility" in *Iqbal*?

9. *Iqbal* states that all facts alleged in a pleading are presumed true (at least when the court is gauging the sufficiency of that pleading), while legal conclusions are entitled to no such presumption. In twenty-five words or less, explain the difference between a statement of fact and a legal conclusion. Would both the majority and dissenting judges agree with your explanation?

10. *Twombly*, and especially *Iqbal*, have caused a considerable upheaval among the lower federal courts and the attorneys who practice in those courts. There is also extensive discussion of the cases in the legal literature, much of it highly critical. As the dissent in *Twombly* points out, most courts prior to these two cases applied a far more lenient standard (the *Conley* standard). These courts have struggled to determine exactly what the Supreme Court means by plausibility, and how it applies to the myriad different claims filed in federal court.

11. What is the penalty for filing an insufficient complaint? If a court determines plaintiff's complaint is insufficient, the remedy is ordinarily not to dismiss outright, but to give plaintiff at least one additional opportunity to remedy the situation. Does this temper the holdings in *Twombly* and *Iqbal*? On the other hand, are the plaintiffs in those cases likely to have enough facts to draft claims that satisfy the court's plausibility standard?

12. *Swierkiwicz*, *Twombly*, and *Iqbal* deal with the pleading of facts. Of course, a party must also provide notice of the legal basis for its claim. *Daniels v. USS Agri-Chemicals*, 965 F.2d 376 (7th Cir. 1992) presents an interesting twist on how much latitude a party has in stating its legal claim. In that case, plaintiff's husband was killed when a container exploded. Because the product had been manufactured in Illinois, plaintiff sued for wrongful death in an Illinois federal court. Plaintiff's complaint specifically stated that defendant was liable under *Illinois* wrongful death law. However, the court held that because the decedent had lived in Indiana, and because the explosion had occurred in Indiana, *Indiana* rather than Illinois law applied. Plaintiff then sought to amend her complaint to state a claim under Indiana law. Because plaintiff's amendment occurred more than two years following the decedent's death, defendant objected to the amendment, citing a provision of Indiana law requiring wrongful death claims to be filed within two years of the death.

The court allowed the action to proceed. In the court's view, no amendment was necessary. Because the *facts* that plaintiff had stated in her complaint would also state a claim under the Indiana wrongful death statute, the court held that the original complaint actually stated a claim under Indiana law, even though it referenced only Illinois law.

Did the complaint in *Daniels* really put the defendant on notice that it was being sued under Indiana law? How important is it that the Illinois and Indiana wrongful death acts were functionally equivalent?

Suppose you represent the defendant in a case like *Daniels*. How do you respond to the complaint? Can you simply deny liability? Do you have to research the laws of every state with even a minimal connection to the case to see whether plaintiff's facts state a claim under the laws of any of those states? Reconsider this question after you have studied the rules governing the answer in Chapter 7.

4. HEIGHTENED PLEADING STANDARDS

While the "notice pleading" standard of Rule 8(a) applies to the vast majority of civil claims filed with a federal court, it does not apply to all. In a few situations, a party is required to plead a claim with greater specificity. The following cases describe two such situations.

WALLACE V. TESORO CORP.
796 F.3d 468 (5th Cir.)

SMITH, CIRCUIT JUDGE.

Kevin Wallace appeals the dismissal of his retaliation claim against Tesoro Corporation ("Tesoro"). He contends that Tesoro terminated his employment for engaging in protected activity under the Sarbanes-Oxley Act of 2002 ("SOX") in violation of 18 U.S.C. § 1514A. The district court held in part that Wallace had failed to state a claim . . . .

I.

. . . Wallace was the Vice President of Pricing and Commercial Analysis at Tesoro. He contends that before he was fired in March 2010, he engaged in protected activity relating to four categories of suspected unlawful activity: Tesoro counted taxes as revenues on certain financial forms, including the company's Forms 10–K and 10–Q filings, even though that money was collected just for transmittal to the Treasury; [discussion of other three claims omitted] . . . .

On the claim of booking taxes as revenue, Wallace states that, at an unspecified time in 2009, he began investigating a discrepancy between Tesoro's financial forecasts and cash performance. He discovered that Tesoro was reporting taxes as revenue, making some segments of the company look more profitable than they really were. Wallace brought the problem to the attention of his supervisor, Claude Moreau; the Vice President of Internal Audit, Tracy Jackson; and the Director of Commercial Accounting, Greg Belisle.

Belisle told Wallace that the system would no longer book taxes as revenue as of April 2010. At some later time, Wallace learned that Moreau had dissuaded Belisle from implementing that change. Wallace also met with Moreau a week before his termination and told him the results of a study that included the practice of booking taxes as revenue....

Wallace was fired on March 12, 2010. He contends that his activities relating to the foregoing suspected wrongful activities motivated the termination.

II.

Wallace filed a complaint against Tesoro with OSHA in May 2010, stating that Tesoro had retaliated against him for engaging in protected activity....

Tesoro moved to dismiss, and the magistrate judge ("MJ") recommended granting the motion....

The district court accepted the MJ's recommendations.... The court accepted the MJ's reasoning: Wallace was objectively unreasonable in believing that booking taxes as revenue violated SEC rules [discussion of reasoning concerning other three claims omitted] ....

Wallace contends that the dismissal was improper....

The district court erred, however, in dismissing Wallace's claim regarding his investigating Tesoro's allegedly booking taxes as revenue. He has adequately pleaded that he engaged in protected activity relating to that practice.

III.

SOX protects employees from retaliation for engaging in protected activity, which is

> any lawful act done by the employee to provide information, cause information to be provided, or otherwise assist in an investigation regarding any conduct which the employee reasonably believes constitutes a violation of section 1341 [mail fraud], 1343 [wire fraud], 1344 [bank fraud], or 1348 [securities fraud], any rule or regulation of the Securities and Exchange Commission, or any provision of Federal law relating to fraud against shareholders....

18 U.S.C. § 1514A(a). Essentially, the employee has to provide information or assist in an investigation that he reasonably believes relates to one or more of six categories of laws and regulations....

An employee's reasonable belief that conduct violates one of those six categories must be evaluated under both an objective and a subjective standard. *Allen v. Admin. Review Bd.*, 514 F.3d 468, 477 (5th Cir.2008).

The objective standard examines whether the belief would be held by "a reasonable person in the same factual circumstances with the same training and experience as the aggrieved employee." *Id.* . . .

We review de novo a dismissal for failure to state a claim. We accept all well-pleaded facts as true and view them in the light most favorable to the plaintiff. . . .

VII.

Wallace challenges the holding that he had not engaged in protected activity in reporting that Tesoro was booking taxes as revenue. He advances two contentions: The district court relied on an incorrect legal standard and erred in holding that his belief was not reasonable. The first contention fails because the court did not base its dismissal on the allegedly erroneous standard. The court did err, however, in holding as a matter of law, at the Rule 12(b)(6) stage, that Wallace had not pleaded an objectively reasonable belief of a SOX violation.

. . . There is no doubt that SOX protects only those employees who reasonably believed they were investigating or reporting a violation of one of the six SOX categories. Wallace has sufficiently pleaded, however, that he thought the accounting practice violated SEC rules. The objective reasonableness of an employee's belief under SOX cannot be resolved as a matter of law "if there is a genuine issue of material fact." Wallace has adequately alleged that he believed the practice at least violated SEC rules. The basis for that belief in this case, including the level and role of Wallace's accounting expertise and how that should weigh against him, are grounded in factual disputes that cannot be resolved at this stage of the case.

Tesoro offers several alternative grounds for affirming the dismissal, but none has merit. Wallace was not required to plead with particularity in accordance with Federal Rule of Civil Procedure 9(b). . . .

A.

The parties dispute whether the plaintiff in a SOX retaliation suit must plead fraud with particularity in accordance with Rule 9(b). Although the MJ at one point recommended such a holding, the district court did not dismiss any part of the complaint for failing to plead with particularity. Although Tesoro maintains that the dismissal can be affirmed for failing to satisfy Rule 9(b), it is plain from the rule's text that it does not apply to this retaliation suit.

Rule 9(b) states, "In alleging fraud or mistake, a party must state with particularity the circumstances constituting fraud or mistake." Tesoro urges that a plaintiff claiming retaliation under § 1514A(a)(1) for reporting suspected fraud must therefore plead the factual circumstances of that fraud with particularity. What that overlooks is that § 1514A(a)(1) protects an employee who "reasonably believes" that conduct violates an enumerated statute. An employee who assists in an investigation regarding conduct he reasonably believes to be wire fraud is protected from adverse action for that assistance, even if the conduct turns out not to be fraudulent.

An employee's reasonable belief is determined by an objective and subjective inquiry examining whether he actually believed that fraud was taking place and whether a reasonable person, in the same situation and with the same training, would have reached a like conclusion. There is no reason to think that the information necessary for an employee to form a reasonable belief of fraud is the same information a complaint must include to survive Rule 9(b).

The requirements of Rule 9(b) show how poorly it would work as a benchmark for reasonable belief that fraud is occurring. "At a minimum, Rule 9(b) requires allegations of the particulars of time, place, and contents of the false representations, as well as the identity of the person making the misrepresentation and what he obtained thereby." *Benchmark Elecs., Inc. v. J.M. Huber Corp.*, 343 F.3d 719, 724 (5th Cir.2003). But an employee who is providing information about potential fraud or assisting in a nascent fraud investigation might not know who is making the false representations or what that person is obtaining by the fraud; indeed, that may be the point of the investigation. Leaving those employees unprotected would have grave consequences for the statutory scheme of employee protection embodied in § 1514A and would do so in a way that appears completely unrelated to whether a belief actually is reasonable. . . .

Nothing in SOX or Rule 9(b) suggests that a reasonable belief of fraud must be pleaded with particularity. To say otherwise not only would contravene the statutory text and the regime of notice pleading but also would alter the substantive requirements of a reasonable belief in a way completely divorced from caselaw and the goals of SOX.

Even after multiple rounds of amendment, Wallace's complaint remains garbled, and we express no view on the ultimate merits. At this preliminary stage, however, Wallace has cleared the low hurdle of pleading a plausible case for relief. The district court erred only in dismissing the portion of the complaint alleging protected activity relating to the reporting of taxes as revenues.

The judgment of dismissal is therefore AFFIRMED in part, REVERSED in part, and REMANDED for further proceedings as appropriate.

NOTES AND QUESTIONS

1. Do you understand how the heightened pleading standard of Rule 9(b) actually differs in practice from the notice pleading standard of Rule 8(a)? If the court had determined Rule 9(b) did apply, what additional language would Wallace have needed to include?

2. Wallace alleges he was fired for reporting that his employer committed wire fraud. Rule 9(b) applies whenever a party alleges fraud. So how can the court conclude that rule does *not* apply to Wallace's allegations?

3. Rule 9(b) indicates that the heightened pleading standard applies to fraud and to mistake. Note, however, that courts also regularly apply the standard to allegations of intentional misrepresentation. See *Alternative System Concepts, Inc. v. Synopsys, Inc.*, 374 F.3d 23 (1st Cir. 2004).

4. Does the Supreme Court's "plausibility" standard (discussed in the prior section in connection with Rule 8(a)) also apply to heightened pleading under Rule 9(b)? The Supreme Court confirmed that it does apply in *Matrixx Initiatives, Inc. v. Siracusano*, 563 U.S. 27, 131 S.Ct. 1309 (2011). However, under the facts of the case, the Court found the plausibility standard satisfied. In a case brought under the Private Securities Litigation Reform Act of 1995, defendant argued plaintiff had failed to properly allege either a "material misrepresentation" or scienter. More particularly, defendant argued plaintiff had no statistically significant evidence demonstrating that investors viewed the false information distributed by defendant as material. The Court rejected defendant's argument, finding that a plaintiff may demonstrate the causal link between the false information and reliance by using other sorts of evidence such as expert opinions. Similarly, the Court held that plaintiff may make a plausible allegation of scienter by evidence that was not statistically significant.

5. Unlike the basic standard of Rule 8(a), Rule 9(b) applies to all assertions of fraud or mistake, not only those forming part of a claim for relief. Claims of fraud or mistake are often asserted by defendants as defenses to contract claims. If plaintiff induced defendant to enter into the contract by fraud, or if the parties were mistaken as to a core underlying fact, the contract is unenforceable.

6. Why does Rule 9(b) single out certain claims for a higher pleading standard? Many courts and commentators suggest the purpose is to protect reputation. Because an allegation of fraud could damage defendant's reputation (and because any judgment exonerating the defendant would not occur for some time, and not receive as much media coverage), a complaint alleging fraud must show that it is well-grounded in fact before plaintiff will even be allowed in court.

If protecting reputation is the rationale behind the rule, why does the heightened pleading standard also apply to *mistake*? Allegations that one has made a mistake, after all, are not likely to besmirch one's good name. And why are other damning accusations such as the intentional torts of battery expenses incurred . . . , loss of goodwill, [and] emotional distress and mental anguish." According to Browning, these allegations satisfy Rule 9(g) because they "notify the defendant as to the nature of the claimed damages." Amplifying this point at oral argument, counsel insisted that "the standard of pleading special damages has been relegated to notice pleading." We find no support for this proposition. Indeed, it runs counter to the very case Browning cites, *Schoen v. Washington Post*, which expressly requires that disparagement of property claims set forth "the precise nature of the losses as well as the way in which the special damages resulted from the allegedly false publication." 246 F.2d 670, 672 (D.C. Cir. 1957). The plaintiff in *Schoen* specified his business receipts before and after defendant's disparaging publication, alleged that the publication caused "many customers to withdraw their custom," and identified three such customers. Browning's amended complaint contains no allegations remotely like those in *Schoen*. She neither quantifies her loss nor identifies any lost business relationships. She alleges no facts suggesting causation. While it may not be "necessary . . . to provide . . . the *maximum* degree of detail that plaintiff might be capable of providing," Browning merely asserts in general terms that *The New Yorker* article cost her financially. We agree with the district court that Rule 9(g) requires more. . . .

NOTES AND QUESTIONS

1. In *Browning*, a showing of special damages was an element of the claim itself. Plaintiff could not recover for disparagement of property unless she could prove actual pecuniary loss. Because of Rule 9(g), she must include specific information about that loss in her complaint. Ordinary damages, by contrast, may be alleged in general terms.

2. Several claims require a showing of special damages as an element of the claim itself. Most are claims that evolved from libel and slander. However, this does not mean that Rule 9(g) issues arise only in that *genre* of case. Courts interpret special damages to include any injury that would not be expected to flow from the underlying event. As a result, Rule 9(g) can apply to any substantive claim.

To illustrate, consider an automobile accident in which plaintiff suffered whiplash and a heart attack. Whiplash would constitute general damages, as it is easily foreseeable. Therefore, the complaint would not have to mention the whiplash specifically. However, Rule 9(g) requires plaintiff to mention the heart attack in the complaint. Failure to include special damages precludes plaintiff from introducing evidence of that injury at trial, although courts may allow the plaintiff to amend. Under this broader interpretation, special damages can more accurately be thought of as special *injury*—any injury that would come as a surprise to defendant.

received no "positive responses, offers to publish, or contracts from any of the publishers that she contacted." Appellant Direct Outstanding Creations Corporation, a business created by Browning's husband, subsequently "acquired . . . rights to . . . the manuscript . . . [but] has not been able to sell [those] rights to . . . any publisher[ ]."

Appellee *The New Yorker* ran an article in 1997 by appellee Jane Mayer attributing comments to publisher Alfred S. Regnery about "a memoir by a putative Presidential mistress." According to the article, although "it seemed plausible . . . that [such] a memoir . . . would find a home at Regnery [Publishing Co.][,]" Regnery said he "wouldn't touch [the book] with a ten-foot pole" because it wasn't "particularly newsworthy" and was "far below [Regnery's] standards." Browning claims that she never sent her manuscript to Regnery, and that Regnery never made these statements. . . .

Based on the foregoing, Browning asserts eight common and federal law claims: (1) tortious interference with prospective business opportunity (against all appellees); (2) disparagement of property (against *The New Yorker* and Mayer); . . . Concluding that Browning failed to state a claim with respect to each count and denying leave to amend, the district court dismissed the complaint with prejudice under Federal Rules of Civil Procedure 12(b)(6) and 15(a). Browning appeals. . . .

[Discussion of other claims omitted.]

As support for her disparagement of property claim against *The New Yorker* and Mayer, Browning relies on the article reporting Regnery's negative comments. A disparagement of property claim requires that the plaintiff plead "special damages," *Fowler v. Curtis Publ'g Co.*, 182 F.2d 377, 378 (D.C. Cir. 1950), that is, "pecuniary harm resulting from the defendant's unprivileged publication of false statements, with knowledge or reckless disregard of the falsity, concerning the plaintiff's property or product," *Art Metal-U.S.A., Inc. v. United States*, 753 F.2d 1151, 1155 n.6 (D.C. Cir. 1985). Federal Rule of Civil Procedure 9(g) requires that special damages be "specifically stated," *i.e.*, the plaintiff must allege actual damages with "particularity" and specify " 'facts showing that such special damages were the natural and direct result' " of the defendant's conduct (here, the alleged false and disparaging article). *Fowler*, 182 F.2d at 379. . . . A plaintiff can satisfy this pleading obligation by identifying either particular customers whose business has been lost or facts showing an established business and the amount of sales before and after the disparaging publication, along with evidence of causation.

Browning's amended complaint states that "as a proximate result of the publication of [Mayer's article], . . . neither [ ] Browning nor Direct Outstanding Creations Corporation were [*sic*] able to sell the publishing and other rights in the manuscript," and therefore that they suffered damages "including but not limited to marketing and other business

BROWNING V. CLINTON
292 F.3d 235 (D.C. Cir. 2002)

TATEL, CIRCUIT JUDGE.

In this appeal, we review the district court's Rule 12(b)(6) dismissal of eight common and federal law claims against former President Clinton, two of his lawyers, one of his aides, *The New Yorker*, and a journalist. Construing the complaint liberally and giving appellant the "benefit of all inferences that can be derived from the facts alleged," *Kowal v. MCI Communications Corp.*, 16 F.3d 1271, 1276 (D.C. Cir. 1994), we affirm as to all appellees except Mr. Clinton; with respect to Mr. Clinton, we affirm the dismissal of six claims and reverse two.

This case involves appellant Dolly Kyle Browning's "longstanding friendship" with former President Clinton—a friendship she alleges "included an extramarital, sexual relationship"—and her "semi-autobiographical novel" in which the female protagonist has a longstanding extramarital affair with the governor of a southern state. Browning copyrighted her novel in 1988 and sent it to Warner Books, where an editor "encouraged [her] to continue to work on [it]." Thereafter, Browning charges, Clinton and the other appellees engaged in a scheme to prevent publication of her book and defame her. According to the amended complaint, the scheme involved the following:

In 1992, Browning's own brother, allegedly at Clinton's direction, telephoned to "warn[ ] [Browning], 'if you cooperate with the media we will destroy you.'" Clinton's brother also "threatened [her]" by phone. The following year, appellee Bruce Lindsey, then serving as Deputy White House Counsel, "threatened [ ] Browning by telling her sister[,] 'we've read your sister's book and we don't want it published.'"

In 1994, Browning and Clinton met at their thirtieth high school reunion where, according to Browning, Clinton "apologized to [her] for the threat that had been made against her." Shortly thereafter, Browning's sister and Lindsey, acting as intermediaries, reached an "understanding" about what Browning could say: She "was permitted to say publicly that she and Clinton had a thirty-three year relationship that from time to time included sex," but "agreed not to tell the true story" and "not to use . . . the 'A words' . . . adultery and affair"; Clinton agreed "not [to] tell any lies about [her]."

Browning retained a literary agent in the summer of 1995. Later that year, *Esquire* magazine published an article about Browning and her book, and in early 1996, *Publisher's Weekly* reported that Browning was "ready to go public in a big way via the book business[,] . . . assuming, that is, that a publisher bites. This month, [Browning's literary agent] will begin shopping around a bombshell *roman a clef* that could knock *Primary Colors* right out of the headlines." In the end, however, Browning and conversion of property governed by mere notice pleading? In truth, Rule 9(b) is a historical accident; a carryover from pre-Federal Rules pleading regimes. An excellent discussion of the evolution of the Rule can be found in William M. Richman, Donald E. Lively, and Patricia Mell, *The Pleading of Fraud: Rhymes Without Reason*, 60 S. CAL. L. REV. 959 (1987). Although the reputation argument may not be historically correct, it does provide some *post hoc* justification for keeping the rule the way it is.

7. In many cases the facts necessary to prove fraud are known only to defendant. Some courts have proven willing to relax the standards of Rule 9(b) when plaintiff has no access to the facts. *See In re Rockefeller Center Properties, Inc. Securities Litigation*, 311 F.3d 198 (3d Cir. 2002). By allowing plaintiff to file the complaint, the court makes it possible for plaintiff to avail itself of discovery to unearth the necessary facts.

8. Note that Rule 9(b) does not require that all elements of a fraud or mistake claim be pleaded with particularity. Other matters, including malice, intent, and knowledge, may be pleaded generally.

9. Are there other areas in which claims are subject to a heightened pleading standard? For a number of years, some courts held civil rights claims to a heightened standard, perhaps because of the disproportionately high percentage of such claims found to be frivolous. The Supreme Court ended this practice in *Leatherman v. Tarrant County Narcotics Intelligence and Coordination Unit*, 507 U.S. 163, 113 S.Ct. 1160, 122 L.Ed.2d 517 (1993). The Court in *Leatherman* held that Rules 8(a) and 9(b) mean what they say, and that lower courts had no authority to export Rule 9(b)'s higher standards to claims other than fraud and mistake. Does *Iqbal* suggest a return to pre-*Leatherman* practice?

Notwithstanding *Leatherman*, some scholars have argued that courts routinely impose heightened pleading standards on certain types of claims. *See, e.g.*, Christopher M. Fairman, *The Myth of Notice Pleading*, 45 ARIZ. L. REV. 987 (2003). One recent example of such a case is *Hawkins v. Kiely*, 250 F.R.D. 73 (D. Me. 2008), which involved a defamation claim. The court in that case granted defendant's motion for a more definite statement because the complaint did not specify the actual content of the allegedly defamatory statements, did not indicate when the statements were made, and did not specify where and to whom the statements were published. Are these details necessary to put defendant on notice of the claim against it?

The prior case and notes show how Rule 9(b) requires a party to provide more detail than would otherwise be required by Rule 8(a). The following case discusses another subsection of Rule 9 that similarly requires a party to be more specific.

Rules 9(b) and (g) require more of a claimant for certain issues. Other provisions in Rule 9, however, have just the opposite effect. Rule 9(a), for example, provides that a party need not allege either her or the other side's capacity to sue or be sued. Rules 9(c), (d), and (e) allow a party to allege conditions precedent (such as conditions to performance of a contract), official documents and acts, and judgments in general terms. When attempting to recover on a judgment from one state in a different state, for example, the judgment victor does not have to allege that the rendering court had jurisdiction. If defendant wants to argue that the judgment is void because of lack of jurisdiction, he must raise that issue in his answer.

5. THE PRAYER FOR RELIEF

In addition to the jurisdictional statement and statement of the claim, Rule 8(a) requires a party to include "a demand for the relief sought." This enables the pleader to inform the court what she hopes to gain from the case, whether it be an award of damages or an injunction. The Rule specifically allows a pleader to seek several different remedies, or even to plead for alternative, inconsistent remedies. Therefore, a plaintiff in a breach of contract case could ask the court for both an order of specific performance and damages for nonperformance. Although it would constitute double recovery for a court to grant both, plaintiff can make its preferences as to remedy known.

A party who asks for damages must include a specific figure in the request. If the party also seeks punitive damages, the prayer usually lists the figures for compensatory and punitive damages separately. Note that the specific damages figure is not the same as an allegation of special damages, discussed just above. Special damages involve a specific, enumerated harm. The damages request in the prayer for relief is usually merely a dollar figure, with little if any explanation of how it is calculated.

Some *state* pleading rules do not allow a claimant to state a damages figure, because of a fear that exaggerated damages requests might unduly influence the jury. This difference between state and federal practice can prove to be an issue in cases that are removed from the state to the federal courts based on diversity, as the court cannot immediately determine the amount in controversy. The federal court in a removal case will often ask for additional information on the damages being sought. Others will treat defendant's removal as an admission that the amount in controversy exceeds $75,000.

The prayer for relief mainly serves as a rough guide. Under Federal Rule 54(c), the court is not limited by the prayer for relief when awarding judgment for a party. Therefore, the court can grant damages even when the claimant sought only an injunction. By the same token, if the court or jury determines plaintiff suffered one million dollars of damage, the court can enter judgment for that amount even though plaintiff asked for only eighty thousand. (For an example from pop culture that drives this point home, watch the film "The Verdict" with Paul Newman.)

There is, however, one situation where the prayer for relief is binding. If defendant chooses not to defend the case and thereby defaults, the default judgment cannot exceed, or be different in kind from, the relief requested in the prayer. Therefore, it is important for a plaintiff to ask for enough to satisfy the claim.

Problems

1. P sues D for breach of contract. The operative language of plaintiff's complaint reads simply, "D owes P $100,000 for goods that P delivered to D on August 9, 2011." D objects to this language, arguing that it does not meet the standards of Rules 8 and 9. Will D prevail on her objection?

2. Same as Problem 1, except that D received several large shipments of different goods from P on the date in question.

3. P sues D, a car dealer, for rescission of a contract for the sale of a used car. P's complaint states that "D's salesman purposefully lied to P about the condition of the car in question." D objects to this language, arguing that it does not meet the standards of Rules 8 and 9. Will D prevail on her objection?

4. P sues D, a car dealer, for rescission of a contract for the sale of a used car. P's complaint goes into great detail about how D's salesman lied about the condition of the car, providing not only the dates upon which the representations occurred, but also the gist of what the salesman said and how it was false. However, because P is suing D rather than the salesman, P also includes the following language in the complaint, "Because D knew of the salesman's activities, D is also liable." D objects to the quoted language, arguing that it fails to provide enough detail about what D knew and how she learned of it. Will D prevail on her objection?

5. Same as Problem 4, except assume that the language set out in that paragraph is sufficient. When the car in question would not start, P could not make it to the local convenience store to buy his weekly lottery ticket, and accordingly did not win the lottery. In his prayer for relief, P does not mention anything about the lottery ticket, but does state that "as a consequence of the false statement, P suffered $10,000,000 in damages." D objects to the quoted language, arguing that it does not meet the standards of Rules 8 and 9. Will D prevail on her objection?

6. P sues D for conversion of P's personal property. In her prayer for relief, P asks the court both to order D to return the property, and to pay P the market value of the property. D objects, pointing out that plaintiff is not entitled to both the property and its value in damages. Will D prevail on his objection?

EXERCISE

For the state a) where you intend to practice after graduation, b) where your law school is located, and/or c) your professor assigns, go to that state's annotated rules and research the procedural rules by which service of process is made. Based on your research, print the rule and bring it to class for discussion. In addition, answer the following questions.

1. Identify the minimum requirements for stating a claim.
2. Identify the topics which are required to be pled with specificity.
3. Identify the requirement for demanding judgment.
4. Do the rules prescribe the format for a pleading?
5. Is pleading in the alternative permitted?

C. NOTIFYING OPPOSING PARTIES: SERVICE OF PROCESS

Service of process relates to the notice a defendant receives about the filing of a lawsuit. Historically, service was satisfied by placing a copy of the complaint and a summons in the hands of the defendant. Over time, the law recognized that there are circumstances when a defendant is deemed to have been notified through "substituted" service or "constructive" service of process. With any method of service, the goal is to ensure that the party being served acquires the relevant documents.

Service is intimately connected with personal jurisdiction, which you studied in Chapter 3. In order for a court to exercise jurisdiction over a defendant in the case, defendant must both be properly served, and the exercise of jurisdiction must satisfy the minimum contacts standard. A "long arm" statute—which you studied in connection with exercising personal jurisdiction over defendants who could not be found in the state—is actually nothing more than a service statute governing out-of-state service (although a statute increasingly tailored to meet the due process limits on personal jurisdiction). Constitutional issues also arise in connection with service of process. Unless defendant waives service, — *rule* service must satisfy both constitutional and rule standards.

The federal rules do not address issues about whether the defendant can be served within the federal district where the lawsuit was filed, or whether a particular type of service of process satisfies the Due Process Clause of the United States Constitution. The federal rule merely describes the procedure for serving the papers, and assumes that the defendant can be served in a constitutionally acceptable manner.

"constructive" service: service that is not actual but deemed effective on account of the circumstances or the performance of acts in compliance w/ a specified method

374 PLEADING CLAIMS CH. 6

INTRODUCTORY PROBLEM

Kennedy, a citizen of Massachusetts, sued four Virginia defendants (Harrison, Tyler, Taylor, and Wilson) in a Virginia federal court for breach of contract connected with purchase of a large local business. The United States Marshal notified Harrison by delivering a summons and a copy of the complaint to him personally. She notified Tyler by sending him a copy of those two documents by first class mail. She attempted to notify Taylor about the lawsuit by going to his home, but when she realized he was out of town, she left the documents with the person who answered the door. Wilson proved to be difficult to notify. When the Marshal attempted to leave the documents at the address listed by Kennedy as Wilson's residence on the complaint, she could not find such a street listing anywhere within the commonwealth of Virginia, much less within the boundaries of the federal district and division where the complaint was filed. Knowing that defendants should be notified about lawsuits brought against them, the Marshal called the cellphone providers and found a cell number under Wilson's name. She called him and told him that he had been sued and that he could pick up the papers at her office in the local federal building.

Assess whether the defendants were provided with proper notice about the filing of the complaint.

Governing Law: Federal Rule 4.

1. CONSTITUTIONAL STANDARDS

MULLANE V. CENTRAL HANOVER BANK & TRUST CO.
339 U.S. 306, 70 S.Ct. 652, 94 L.Ed. 865 (1950)

MR. JUSTICE JACKSON delivered the opinion of the Court.

[A petition was filed in a New York court to settle the 113 accounts of the trustee of a common trust fund. A number of the beneficiaries were nonresidents of New York and their addresses were unknown. Pursuant to New York law which was the legal basis for establishing the trusts, notice about the proceeding was by publication in a local newspaper. The guardian appointed by the court on behalf of some of the trust beneficiaries appeared specially and objected to the assertion of jurisdiction on the ground that the nonresidents had not been served personally.]

Personal service of written notice within the jurisdiction is the classic form of notice always adequate in any type of proceeding. But the vital interest of the State in bringing any issues as to its fiduciaries to a final settlement can be served only if interests or claims of individuals who are outside of the State can somehow be determined. A construction of the Due Process Clause which would place impossible or impractical obstacles in the way could not be justified.

Against this interest of the State we must balance the individual interest sought to be protected by the Fourteenth Amendment. This is defined by our holding that "The fundamental requisite of due process of law is the opportunity to be heard." *Grannis v. Ordean*, 234 U.S. 385, 394 (1914). This right to be heard has little reality or worth unless one is informed that the matter is pending and can choose for himself whether to appear or default, acquiesce or contest.

The Court has not committed itself to any formula achieving a balance between these interests in a particular proceeding or determining when constructive notice may be utilized or what test it must meet. Personal service has not in all circumstances been regarded as indispensable to the process due to residents, and it has more often been held unnecessary as to nonresidents. We disturb none of the established rules on these subjects. No decision constitutes a controlling or even a very illuminating precedent for the case before us. But a few general principles stand out in the books.

An elementary and fundamental requirement of due process in any proceeding which is to be accorded finality is notice reasonably calculated, under all the circumstances, to apprise interested parties of the pendency of the action and afford them an opportunity to present their objections. The notice must be of such nature as reasonably to convey the required information, and it must afford a reasonable time for those interested to make their appearance. But if with due regard for the practicalities and peculiarities of the case these conditions are reasonably met the constitutional requirements are satisfied. . . .

But when notice is a person's due, process which is a mere gesture is not due process. The means employed must be such as one desirous of actually informing the absentee might reasonably adopt to accomplish it. The reasonableness and hence the constitutional validity of any chosen method may be defended on the ground that it is in itself reasonably certain to inform those affected, or, where conditions do not reasonably permit such notice, that the form chosen is not substantially less likely to bring home notice than other of the feasible and customary substitutes.

It would be idle to pretend that publication alone as prescribed here, is a reliable means of acquainting interested parties of the fact that their rights are before the courts. It is not an accident that the greater number of cases reaching this Court on the question of adequacy of notice have been concerned with actions founded on process constructively served through local newspapers. Chance alone brings to the attention of even a local resident an advertisement in small type inserted in the back pages of a newspaper, and if he makes his home outside the area of the newspaper's normal circulation the odds that the information will never reach him are large indeed. The chance of actual notice is further reduced when as here the notice required does not even name those whose attention it is supposed to attract, and does not inform acquaintances who might call it to attention. In weighing its sufficiency on the basis of equivalence with actual notice we are unable to regard this as more than a feint.

Nor is publication here reinforced by steps likely to attract the parties' attention to the proceeding. It is true that publication traditionally has been acceptable as notification supplemental to other action which in itself may reasonably be expected to convey a warning. The ways of an owner with tangible property are such that he usually arranges means to learn of any direct attack upon his possessory or proprietary rights. Hence, libel of a ship, attachment of a chattel or entry upon real estate in the name of law may reasonably be expected to come promptly to the owner's attention. When the state within which the owner has located such property seizes it for some reason, publication or posting affords an additional measure of notification. A state may indulge the assumption that one who has left tangible property in the state either has abandoned it, in which case proceedings against it deprive him of nothing, or that he has left some caretaker under a duty to let him know that it is being jeopardized. . . .

In the case before us there is, of course, no abandonment. On the other hand these beneficiaries do have a resident fiduciary as caretaker of their interest in this property. But it is their caretaker who in the accounting becomes their adversary. Their trustee is released from giving notice of jeopardy, and no one else is expected to do so. Not even the special guardian is required or apparently expected to communicate with his ward and client, and, of course, if such a duty were merely transferred from the trustee to the guardian, economy would not be served and more likely the cost would be increased.

This Court has not hesitated to approve of resort to publication as a customary substitute in another class of cases where it is not reasonably possible or practicable to give more adequate warning. Thus it has been recognized that, in the case of persons missing or unknown, employment of an indirect and even a probably futile means of notification is all that the situation permits and creates no constitutional bar to a final decree foreclosing their rights.

Those beneficiaries represented by appellant whose interests or whereabouts could not with due diligence be ascertained come clearly within this category. As to them the statutory notice is sufficient. However great the odds that publication will never reach the eyes of such unknown parties, it is not in the typical case much more likely to fail than any of the choices open to legislators endeavoring to prescribe the best notice practicable.

Nor do we consider it unreasonable for the State to dispense with more certain notice to those beneficiaries whose interests are either conjectural or future or, although they could be discovered upon investigation, do not in due course of business come to knowledge of the common trustee. Whatever searches might be required in another situation under ordinary standards of diligence, in view of the character of the proceedings and the nature of the interests here involved we think them unnecessary. We recognize the practical difficulties and costs that would be attendant on frequent investigations into the status of great numbers of beneficiaries, many of whose interests in the common fund are so remote as to be ephemeral; and we have no doubt that such impracticable and extended searches are not required in the name of due process. The expense of keeping informed from day to day of substitutions among even current income beneficiaries and presumptive remaindermen, to say nothing of the far greater number of contingent beneficiaries, would impose a severe burden on the plan, and would likely dissipate its advantages. These are practical matters in which we should be reluctant to disturb the judgment of the state authorities.

Accordingly we overrule appellant's constitutional objections to published notice insofar as they are urged on behalf of any beneficiaries whose interests or addresses are unknown to the trustee.

As to known present beneficiaries of known place of residence, however, notice by publication stands on a different footing. Exceptions in the name of necessity do not sweep away the rule that within the limits of practicability notice must be such as is reasonably calculated to reach interested parties. Where the names and post office addresses of those affected by a proceeding are at hand, the reasons disappear for resort to means less likely than the mails to apprise them of its pendency.

The trustee has on its books the names and addresses of the income beneficiaries represented by appellant, and we find no tenable ground for dispensing with a serious effort to inform them personally of the accounting, at least by ordinary mail to the record addresses. Certainly sending them a copy of the statute months and perhaps years in advance does not answer this purpose. The trustee periodically remits their income to them, and we think that they might reasonably expect that with or apart from their remittances word might come to them personally that steps were being taken affecting their interests.

We need not weigh contentions that a requirement of personal service of citation on even the large number of known resident or nonresident beneficiaries would, by reasons of delay if not of expense, seriously interfere with the proper administration of the fund. Of course personal service even without the jurisdiction of the issuing authority serves the end of actual and personal notice, whatever power of compulsion it might lack. However, no such service is required under the circumstances. This type of trust presupposes a large number of small interests. The individual interest does not stand alone but is identical with that of a class. The rights of each in the integrity of the fund and the fidelity of the trustee are shared by many other beneficiaries. Therefore notice reasonably certain to reach most of those interested in objecting is likely to safeguard the interests of all, since any objections sustained would inure to the benefit of all. We think that under such circumstances reasonable risks that notice might not actually reach every beneficiary are justifiable. . . .

The statutory notice to known beneficiaries is inadequate, not because in fact it fails to reach everyone, but because under the circumstances it is not reasonably calculated to reach those who could easily be informed by other means at hand. However it may have been in former times, the mails today are recognized as an efficient and inexpensive means of communication. Moreover, the fact that the trust company has been able to give mailed notice to known beneficiaries at the time the common trust fund was established is persuasive that postal notification at the time of accounting would not seriously burden the plan.

In some situations the law requires greater precautions in its proceedings than the business world accepts for its own purposes. In few, if any, will it be satisfied with less. Certainly it is instructive, in determining the reasonableness of the impersonal broadcast notification here used, to ask whether it would satisfy a prudent man of business, counting his pennies but finding it in his interest to convey information to many persons whose names and addresses are in his files. We are not satisfied that it would. Publication may theoretically be available for all the world to see, but it is too much in our day to suppose that each or any individual beneficiary does or could examine all that is published to see if something may be tucked away in it that affects his property interests. We have before indicated in reference to notice by publication that, "Great caution should be used not to let fiction deny the fair play that can be secured only by a pretty close adhesion to fact." *McDonald v. Mabee*, 243 U.S. 90 (1917).

We hold the notice of judicial settlement of accounts required by the New York Banking Law is incompatible with the requirements of the Fourteenth Amendment as a basis for adjudication depriving known persons whose whereabouts are also known of substantial property rights. Accordingly the judgment is reversed and the cause remanded for further proceedings not inconsistent with this opinion.

NOTES AND QUESTIONS

1. What did the Court hold? Why is the Court willing to validate a mode of service (first-class mail) that is not the best available? Why does the Court conclude that it is unnecessary for every beneficiary to receive notice about the lawsuit? Is service by publication ever sufficient, and if so, under what circumstances? How can notice never received comply with due process?

2. People living in the United States speak many different languages. Is it consistent with due process for the notice about a lawsuit to be in English? When a non-English speaking defendant receives a summons and complaint in English, does the face of the "official looking" documents convey enough information for the defendant to be on notice to have it translated? What problems would be created if court systems began to print forms in languages other than English?

3. In *Greene v. Lindsey*, 456 U.S. 444, 102 S.Ct. 1874, 72 L.Ed.2d 249 (1982), a Kentucky statute permitted service of process in a landlord-tenant eviction proceeding by posting a summons "in a conspicuous place on the premises," if the defendant or a member of the defendant's family over 16 years of age could not be located. The landlord posted the summons in a public housing project on the door of each of the tenants' apartments. The tenants claimed they never saw the summonses and did not know of the eviction proceedings until after default judgments had been entered against them and the time for filing an appeal had expired. The tenants filed a federal civil rights class action against public officials, claiming in part that the notice procedures used violated due process.

The Supreme Court held that under *Mullane* the procedures failed to afford the tenants adequate notice of the proceedings against them under the circumstances of the case. Because the notices were often removed from the doors before the tenants could see them, merely posting the notices on the doors failed to satisfy minimum standards of due process. The Court, though, did not hold that posting notices were always an inappropriate method of service under due process. The Court endorsed notice by mail to ensure that the tenants would have the opportunity to present a defense. Wouldn't the lack of mail box security in a public housing project present potentially the same due process problems for missing or stolen notices as the posting procedures? Some jurisdictions reacted to *Greene* by requiring that the notice in eviction cases be both posted *and* mailed to the tenant.

4. In *Baidoo v. Blood-Dzraku*, 48 Misc.3d 309 (N.Y.Cty. 2015), a plaintiff in a divorce proceeding was unable to serve her husband by customary methods such as personal service or substitute service. Under state procedures, she asked the trial court to permit her to propose an alternative method to fit the circumstances of the case. After the court ruled that the aforementioned methods were "impracticable," the court focused on whether serving the divorce summons by the novel and non-traditional method of Facebook was reasonably calculated under due process to apprise the defendant that he was being sued for divorce.

The court explored whether when "the summons for divorce is sent to what plaintiff represents to be defendant's Facebook account, is there a good chance he will receive it?" The plaintiff persuaded the court that 1) the Facebook account she was aware of belonged to the defendant, 2) the defendant regularly logged on to his account, and 3) the typical backup means of supplementing Facebook service by email service was itself impracticable because the plaintiff could not find an email address for the defendant. The court also rejected service by publication because "it is almost guaranteed *not* to provide a defendant with notice of the action for divorce, or any other law suit for that matter."

2. PROCEDURAL STANDARDS FOR SERVICE OF PROCESS

The notice function of service of process is essential to ensuring that a defendant has a fair opportunity to respond to the complaint and to raise defenses and objections. Federal Rule 4 requires that the defendant be served, i.e., receive a copy of a summons and a copy of the complaint.

An objection to the method of service and/or to the process itself can occur in two contexts. First, defendant can ask the court to dismiss the complaint due to insufficient service of process or insufficient process, using one of the tools you will study in the next Chapter. The second way to challenge occurs outside the case. A plaintiff often obtains a default judgment against a defendant who never answered the complaint. After plaintiff tries to enforce the judgment, e.g., by garnishing defendant's wages, defendant may learn about the lawsuit for the first time and file a motion with the court to vacate the default judgment. The premise for the motion is that the default judgment was improper because the court lacked jurisdiction over defendant due to the improper service of process.

While an important goal of service of process is to notify defendant that a lawsuit has been filed, defendant's actually knowledge about the lawsuit does not relieve plaintiff from the service of process requirements. For example, in *Ayres v. Jacobs & Crumplar,* 99 F.3d 565, 568–70 (3d Cir. 1996), the court held that a defendant's actual notice about the lawsuit, as shown by the defendant's later participation in discovery, failed to confer jurisdiction on the court, because no proper summons was issued and signed by the clerk or stamped with the seal of the court. The formal requirements of Rule 4 for proper service must be satisfied, and actual knowledge of the lawsuit does not cure a defective service of process. Not all courts agree with that judicial approach. See, e.g., note 2, after *Cox v. Quigley,* infra.

Several requirements apply to the summons. It must 1) be issued by the clerk of court, bearing the court's seal and the clerk's signature; 2) identify the district court, name the parties, and list the name and address of plaintiff or plaintiff's attorney; 3) be directed to the specific defendant; 4) state the time within which defendant must appear and defend the lawsuit; and 5) caution about the consequences of defendant's failure to appear.

At or about the same time a complaint is filed, plaintiff must prepare a summons and submit it to the clerk for signing and sealing. In multiple defendant cases, copies of the summons must be issued for each defendant. The summons and complaint are served together, and plaintiff is responsible for effective service. In federal court, because plaintiff himself cannot serve the papers on defendant, plaintiff selects an appropriate person, typically a commercial process server who works for a fee, to serve the defendant. A United States Marshal serves process only when ordered by the court.

Federal Rule 4(d) imposes a duty on defendants to avoid unnecessary costs of formal service of process. To avoid costs, plaintiff can notify the defendant about filing the lawsuit and ask defendant to waive service. The plaintiff must make an explicit request to defendant to waive formal service of process. The request must be in writing, conform to the approved form, identify the court, describe the consequences of both waiver and the refusal to waive, include a copy of the complaint, be sent by first-class mail or "other reliable means," and be addressed directly to defendant. The next case illustrates potential problems with relying on the waiver procedure.

LARSEN V. MAYO MEDICAL CENTER
218 F.3d 863 (8th Cir. 2000)

HEANEY, CIRCUIT JUDGE.

Patricia Larsen contracted an illness from medication administered to her during her hospitalization at the Mayo Medical Center ("Mayo"). She sued Mayo for medical malpractice. Mayo moved for summary judgment on the basis that Larsen's claim was time-barred. The district court granted the motion, and Larsen appeals. Because Larsen failed to serve Mayo within the two-year statute of limitations, we affirm.

... Larsen filed her complaint against Mayo on May 29, 1998 wherein she alleged medical malpractice. On June 1, 1998, Larsen attempted to serve Mayo by mailing a copy of the summons and complaint and enclosing an Acknowledgment of Service form for Mayo to return. Mayo received the materials two days later, but did not sign and return the acknowledgment form. On June 15, 1998, Larsen's counsel contacted Mayo's in-house counsel, who informed him that Mayo would not admit service or assist Larsen in any way in suing his client.

On June 22, 1998, Larsen filed an amended complaint, which she again mailed to Mayo with an Acknowledgment of Service form. Mayo did not return the form, and on September 3, 1998, Larsen's counsel again contacted Mayo's counsel, who again told him that Mayo would not execute the form.

On September 4, 1998, Larsen mailed copies of the amended summons and complaint to the Olmstead County Sheriff's Department. The Sheriff's Department received the materials on September 8, 1998 and served Mayo the following day.

... [T]he district court considered whether service was timely. It concluded that service was not effective until September 8, 1998, the date the Olmstead County Sheriff's Department received the summons and complaint for service on Mayo, and thus that Larsen's claims were time-barred. Larsen appeals the district court's grant of Mayo's summary judgment motion. . . .

Larsen contends that service was timely even if the limitations period began to run on July 24, 1996. She argues that under the Federal Rules of Civil Procedure a civil action is commenced by filing a complaint with the court, see Fed.R.Civ.P. 3, and that since she filed her complaint on May 29, 1998, her action is timely. This argument fails to recognize the case law of both the Supreme Court and our court.

Larsen correctly points out that the Federal Rules of Civil Procedure determine the date from which various timing requirements begin to run. They do not, however, affect the commencement of a lawsuit. See *Walker v. Armco Steel Corp.*, 446 U.S. 740, 750–52 (1980). Rather, state commencement rules apply because they are "part and parcel of the statute of limitations." *Walker*, 446 U.S. at 752. Accordingly, Minnesota's commencement rule, rather than the federal commencement rule, governs in this case.

Under Minnesota's Rules of Civil Procedure, a civil action is commenced:

(a) when the summons is served upon that defendant, or

(b) at the date of acknowledgment of service if service is made by mail, or

(c) when the summons is delivered to the sheriff in the county where the defendant resides for service. . . .

Minn. R. Civ. P. 3.01.

Although Minnesota law controls the commencement of a lawsuit, service of process in federal diversity actions is procedural, and therefore, governed by the Federal Rules. Under the Federal Rules, a plaintiff may, among other things, notify the defendant of the commencement of the action and request that the defendant waive service of the summons. See Fed.R.Civ.P. 4(d)(2). If the defendant returns the waiver and the plaintiff files the waiver with the court, "the action shall proceed . . . as if a summons and complaint had been served at the time of filing the waiver." *Id.* at 4(d)(4). However, if the defendant does not waive service, service has not been effected.

In this case, Larsen twice mailed copies of the summons and complaint to Mayo, first on June 1, 1998 and again on June 22, 1998. Both times she enclosed an acknowledgment form, and both times, Mayo refused to execute the form. Because Mayo did not waive service by returning the acknowledgment form, the requirements for service by mail were not met. Mayo then was not served until the Olmstead County Sheriff's Department received a copy of the summons and complaint on September 8, 1998, more than a month after the two-year limitations period expired.

Larsen makes two alternative arguments, both of which are without merit. She claims that service was effective under Fed.R.Civ.P. 4(m), which states:

> **Time Limit for Service.** If service of the summons and complaint is not made upon a defendant within [90] days after the filing of the complaint, the court, upon motion or on its own initiative after notice to the plaintiff, shall dismiss the action without prejudice as to that defendant or direct that service to be effected within a specified time. . . .

Larsen argues that Rule 4(m) conflicts with Minnesota's commencement rule, and thus, that the federal rule, not the state rule, governs.

First, Fed.R.Civ.P. 4(m) is irrelevant. The rule is only a time restriction that requires the summons and complaint to be served within [90] days of the filing of the complaint. It does not address how or when a lawsuit is properly commenced.

Second, even if relevant, Fed.R.Civ.P. 4(m) does not conflict with Minnesota's commencement rule. In *Walker*, the Supreme Court interpreted a state commencement rule identical to that of Minnesota and held that the state rule did not conflict with the Federal Rules. See 446 U.S. at 752 ("[Each] can exist side by side, therefore, each controlling its own intended sphere of coverage without conflict."). Because the rules do not conflict, Minn. R.Civ.P. 3.01 governs the commencement of Larsen's lawsuit.

Finally, Larsen argues that service was effective under Fed.R.Civ.P. 4(h), which provides for service on a corporation by delivering a copy of the summons and complaint to an officer, manager or authorized agent of the corporation. This argument also is meritless because the summons and complaint were mailed and not personally served on anyone during the limitations period. Further, they were not even mailed to an officer, manager or authorized agent of Mayo Clinic, but addressed to "Medical/Legal Department, Mayo Clinic." Thus, service was ineffective under Rule 4(h).

The statute of limitations began to run in this case no later than July 24, 1996. The lawsuit was not commenced until September 8, 1998, over a month after the limitations period expired. Thus, the district court correctly concluded that Larsen's medical malpractice claim against Mayo is time-barred, and we affirm its decision to grant summary judgment.

NOTES AND QUESTIONS

1. As in *Larsen*, if a defendant refuses to waive service of process under Rule 4(d), plaintiff must proceed with normal service of process using Rules 4(e), (f), and (h). The case also makes the point that Rule 4(m)'s 90-day period for completing service continues to run while the waiver of service request is made. That Rule gives plaintiff 90 days after filing to serve the defendant with the summons and complaint. When the 90 days have passed, the lawsuit can be dismissed. Dismissal may be harmful to plaintiff because the statute of limitations may prevent plaintiff from filing again.

However, the period may be extended for "good cause." The trial court has discretion to determine whether "good cause" exists. For example, if the plaintiff can show that the limitations period has run, the court has the discretion to decide against dismissal and instead grant a motion to extend the time for service.

2. Carefully reading Rule 4(d) discloses the non-economic inducement to waive formal service of process: a longer time for responding to the complaint. While a defendant has 21 days to answer a complaint following personal service, a defendant with a United States address has 60 days to answer the complaint following a waiver of service.

3. If the defendant agrees to waive service of process, he is expected to return the waiver form. When a defendant has agreed to waive service and returns the waiver form, the date of service is deemed the date when the plaintiff files the form with the court. Regardless of which procedure is used, the waiver of service or formal service must occur within the 90-day period after filing the complaint. In *Larsen*, even if the defendant had returned the waiver of service form, if the 90-day time period had passed before the form was filed, the case would have to be dismissed, thereby creating a risk that refiling the lawsuit could occur after expiration of the limitations period.

4. Did Patricia Larsen have alternatives to filing a complaint against the Mayo Medical Center? Would she have been successful in recovering any money in a settlement if, as with filing her complaint, she did not initiate the process until after July 24, 1998?

In an effort to control the cost of tort suits, many states have enacted tort reform statutes that limit recoveries in medical malpractice cases. Some large health care providers have taken an alternative approach and successfully reduced medical malpractice lawsuits and the costs associated with them by using voluntary dispute resolution programs such as Sorry Works! and MEDIC+OM. These programs provide patients and doctors an opportunity to discuss the medical situation directly with each other in a structured process that shares some elements with mediation.

Federal Rule 4 governs most of the service of process standards in federal courts. Specifically, Rule 4(e) and (h) regulate service on individuals, corporations and other associations. It is important to remember, though, that the methods enumerated in Rule 4 are merely one option. The Rule also indicates that service on defendants may be effected by the law of the state in which the federal district court is held or in which service occurs. State rules, for example, may authorize service by mail—certified, registered, first-class, express, or electronic.

The most desirable method of service for individuals is to serve them personally. Personal service avoids any question about whether defendant has received notice about the lawsuit, and it is unlikely to produce due process objections. In-hand delivery is not always essential. What happens if defendant attempts to evade service, or refuses to accept delivery after being informed by the process server of the nature of the papers? Service is sufficient it the process server touches the party to be served with the papers, or, if touching is impossible, leaves the papers in the defendant's physical proximity. The defendant does not have to possess the papers for effective service.

International Controls Corp. v. Vesco, 593 F.2d 166 (2d Cir. 1979), is an example of the difficulties posed by a possession requirement. The process server came across a bolted gate and two bodyguards in front of the defendant's home, and the defendant refused to come outside so he could be served. The process server attached the papers to a blue ribbon and threw them over the defendant's fence on the front lawn. The papers were also mailed to the defendant at his residence. The court found that the defendant had actual notice of the proceedings against him, and upheld the service.

The federal rules also permit substituted service of process alternatives to personal delivery. One option for the process server under Federal Rule 4(e)(2) is to leave the papers at the defendant's "dwelling or usual place of abode with someone of suitable age and discretion who resides there."

COX V. QUIGLEY
141 F.R.D. 222 (D.Me. 1992)

HORNBY, DISTRICT JUDGE.

Where is the dwelling house or usual place of abode of a young person who has recently graduated from college, has left home and is serving on board ship in the Military Sealift Command for most of the year and spends his time off visiting various relatives and vacationing in different parts of the country or abroad? That is the question on this motion to vacate default judgment. Concluding that at the time service was attempted the defendant had no dwelling house or usual place of abode except perhaps for his ship, I find that the plaintiff failed to make proper service of process under [current Rule 4(e)] when the process server left the papers with the defendant's father at his parents' home. As a result, the court never obtained personal jurisdiction over the defendant and the default judgment must be vacated.

Growing up, Joseph Quigley lived with his family on Cayuga Heights Road in Ithaca, New York. He attended Maine Maritime Academy in Castine, Maine and graduated in the spring of 1987. Earlier that year, his parents moved to a new house in Ithaca on Iradell Road where there was no bedroom for their son. When he returned to Ithaca after graduation and took a summer job, Quigley slept on a cot in the basement. In the fall of 1987, he obtained a position with the Military Sealift Command and went to sea. In May, 1988, he notified his employer that he was changing his address to Florida, specifically Port Richie, his grandparents' address. At the same time he registered to vote in Florida and proceeded to cast a Florida absentee ballot. He has only voted once. He also filed his federal income tax return listing a Florida address in May, 1988. All of these events occurred before the relevant developments in this lawsuit.

In June, 1988, the plaintiff's lawyer attempted to serve process on Quigley in connection with this lawsuit. The plaintiff's lawyer had a sheriff deliver the process to Quigley's parents' home on Iradell Road in Ithaca. Quigley's father, who has the same first name and middle initial as his son, declined to accept the process after determining that the lawsuit did not involve him. He told the deputy sheriff that his son was at sea for several months. The lawyer's secretary next wrote the deputy sheriff to determine if Quigley's parents' home was his usual place of abode and, if so, to leave the process there. This time the deputy sheriff left the process with Quigley's father and apparently also sent a copy by mail. Quigley's father took the process to his own lawyer who returned it by mail to the plaintiff's lawyer informing him that Quigley did not reside with his father and that his father did not accept service on his behalf.

[Current Rule 4(e)(2)] provides that service can be made upon an individual by serving him personally "or by leaving copies [of the summons and complaint] at the individual's dwelling house or usual place of abode. . . ." The issue, therefore, is whether Iradell Road was Quigley's dwelling house or usual place of abode in June, 1988. The parties also presented evidence to me concerning events that occurred after June, 1988. My decision is limited to Quigley's status as of June, 1988. Nevertheless, his later activities may shed light on what took place earlier and may also affect his credibility.

Quigley's later activities include the following: He continued to hold his New York driver's license until it was stolen from him in Greece in the summer of 1988. On October 14, 1988, Quigley obtained a replacement Virginia license while his ship was in port in Norfolk, Virginia. Apparently Virginia makes such licenses available to nonresidents because of the large number of Navy personnel stationed there. The

Virginia license listed New York as Quigley's residence. I draw no conclusions from these driver's licenses. The original New York license did not expire until March, 1989, and it is not unusual that a graduating college student in the process of locating a job and ultimately a place to live does not immediately obtain a new driver's license. The apparent New York residence on the Virginia license is also explainable as a reference to the pre-existing New York license.

Quigley arranged for his grandmother in Florida to forward all his financial and business mail to his mother in New York and gave his mother a power-of-attorney. His mother was the joint account holder of his bank accounts and paid his bills. Through his father, a real estate broker, Quigley engaged in real estate transactions, buying a house, accepting a mortgage and renting property. All the documents reflecting these transactions listed Iradell Road as his address. I draw no conclusion from the real estate transactions carried on by Quigley's parents in his absence. His parents would logically use their own New York address for ease of payments.

When Quigley was arrested for OUI in Maine in the spring of 1989, he gave both his sister's Maine address and his ship as his address. During leave periods, Quigley spent approximately equal amounts of time with his parents, his grandparents and his sister. Most of his leave time was spent elsewhere, however, such as Virginia or Brazil. When Quigley upgraded his Coast Guard license in April, 1989, he gave his Iradell Road address. Most of Quigley's employment-related documents were addressed to the Florida address. His federal tax returns filed in 1989 and 1990 listed Florida as his address. Quigley maintains that when his mother became seriously ill he moved back to Iradell Road in late 1990. His New York driver's license issued on August 30, 1991, lists Iradell Road as his address but his interrogatory answers signed in this case on September 3, 1991, list Florida as both his residence and post office address.

In fact, I do not find Quigley to be a particularly credible witness when it comes to statements about his dwelling house and place of abode or about his contacts with New York. Several of his previous statements in affidavits or interrogatory answers were equivocal or made material omissions in failing to reveal that his financial mail was forwarded by his grandmother unopened to his mother in New York, in understating the number of times he visited Ithaca and in later referring to his residence as Florida when he had already changed it back to New York. Confronted with the default in this lawsuit, I conclude that Quigley has been at best cavalier in his statements seeking to avoid the default judgment. Nevertheless, many of the factors that control my decision whether Iradell Road is his dwelling house or usual place of abode are based on documentary evidence and, in many cases, predate his notice of the lawsuit.

I conclude from the evidence that Quigley's goal in May, 1988, was to change his tax residence to Florida in order to avoid New York income taxes. Although tax residence alone is not determinative of the location of a dwelling house or usual place of abode, I conclude for that and other reasons that Quigley was no longer dwelling or maintaining a usual place of abode at Iradell Road in Ithaca, New York by June, 1988. The obvious purpose of [current Rule 4(e)(2)'s] provision for service upon a responsible person at a defendant's dwelling house or usual place of abode is to provide some assurance that timely notice of the lawsuit will reach a defendant who has not been served personally. Leaving the process with a responsible person where the defendant is living is a good way to accomplish this objective. But in no sense was Quigley dwelling at Iradell Road or maintaining a place of abode there any longer in June, 1988. He had left home the fall after graduation and had taken up a new tax and voting residence. He maintained only a minimal connection to his parents' home. Quigley visited Iradell Road only briefly and treated his parents on his off-duty time to the same share of his time as his sister and grandmother. His grandmother at his Florida address forwarded certain categories of mail to his mother. But Quigley's parents had no effective way of reaching him at sea except through the Red Cross in case of a medical emergency. Thus, Iradell Road was not a location where process would reach Quigley in a timely manner. Quigley's father told the deputy sheriff that Quigley no longer lived there and the lawyer's letter to the plaintiff's lawyer confirmed the situation.

By the same token, I do not suggest that Florida had become Quigley's dwelling or usual place of abode. Quigley had no particular connection with his grandparents' house except the ability to sleep there when he was in the United States, a privilege he seldom used after May, 1988, and to use the address for his mail and to have his grandmother forward financial and business mail to his mother. He was obviously not dwelling there or maintaining an abode in Florida. If Quigley had a dwelling house or usual place of abode in June, 1988, it was his ship while he was not on leave. I do not mean to suggest that the ship furnished the plaintiff with an attractive option for service. As Quigley testified, he was often at sea for months at a time in the Military Sealift Command and his destinations and the dates of returning to port were often secret. I recognize that [current Rule 4(e)(2)] is designed to provide plaintiffs an alternative method to serve a defendant who is avoiding personal service. Its permission for service at a dwelling house or usual place of abode is probably based on the assumption that these are usually not quickly or easily moved. Therefore, even though a defendant may avoid the process server in person, some other responsible person in the house can receive the papers. Courts and commentators have referred to our society's mobility and affluence as grounds for enlarging this method of service by recognizing that defendants may have two or more dwelling houses or places of abode for purposes of service. But there is a limit to the scope of this service option. Unfortunately, our mobile and affluent society has a large number of transient or homeless people. For them, there may be no dwelling house or usual place of abode. Although they are not the object of a lawsuit as frequently as the affluent, the Rule's language covers all categories. The last shelter at which a homeless person slept will often not furnish reasonable assurance that process will reach the defendant. For such defendants service at the dwelling house or place of abode is unavailable; personal service may be a plaintiff's only option then, no matter how difficult.

Quigley, of course, was not homeless. He was, however, transient. As the plaintiff has conceded, it is her burden of proof to show that Iradell Road in Ithaca was his dwelling house or usual place of abode in June, 1988. I conclude that under the circumstances here that was no longer the case. Quigley had graduated from college, left home, found a job, obtained a new tax residence, voted in a different state, and maintained employment records with a new Florida address. Although he used his parents' address in some other respects, such as to obtain financial documents and have his mother manage his financial affairs (there is no suggestion that the power-of-attorney authorized her to accept service of process or answer a complaint), and although his behavior with his driver's and Coast Guard licenses was inconsistent, I conclude that these factors are not sufficient to show that he was dwelling or maintaining a place of abode at Iradell Road. This conclusion may mean that it will be difficult for plaintiffs to serve some highly mobile or transient defendants. But ease of service cannot displace the need to find a method that will reasonably assure timely notice of the lawsuit.

Finally, the plaintiff has not satisfied me that Quigley had timely notice of this lawsuit. Although it seems incomprehensible that Quigley's father did not notify him of the lawsuit even later when he ultimately did visit home, family and father-son relationships encompass many possibilities. I do find credible Quigley's parents' failure to contact him while he was at sea given the difficulties of using the mail and ship-to-shore phone with a person in the Military Sealift Command.

Default judgment is therefore vacated.

NOTES AND QUESTIONS

1. In *Jaffe and Asher v. Van Brunt*, 158 F.R.D. 278 (S.D.N.Y. 1994), defendant tried to vacate a default judgment obtained in a lawsuit by a law firm suing him to collect an attorney's fee. The court denied the motion, concluding that the law firm "properly effected service at Van Brunt's usual

place of abode" in Connecticut at his parents' residence, which also was the site where defendant asked for the law firm's bill to be sent.

Defendant argued that he had resided in California for several years preceding the lawsuit, supporting his contention with copies of his California driver's license and his income tax returns. The law firm argued that his parents' home was defendant's "usual place of abode," because he maintained a private phone line and fax machine there, he used a private bedroom and clothing he kept there when he visited the New York metropolitan area, and he received mail there.

> Our highly mobile and affluent society has relegated to history the days when an individual had but a single residence. Thus, as the Second Circuit acknowledged, "it is unrealistic to interpret [the federal rule] so that the person to be served has only one dwelling house or usual place of abode at which process may be left." *National Development Co. v. Triad Holding Corp.*, 930 F.2d 253, 257 (2d Cir.1991). A strictly literal interpretation of the rule may thwart the purpose of [the federal rule]—to insure that service is reasonably calculated to provide a defendant with actual notice of the action. Hence, for purposes of effecting service under Rule 4(e), an individual can have multiple " 'dwelling houses or usual places of abode,' provided each contains sufficient indicia of permanence." *Id.*, 930 F.2d at 257.

The court found "sufficient indicia of permanence" at his parents' home to make service there reasonably calculated to provide their son with actual notice of the action. "[E]ven if the parents' home were not one of defendant's 'usual places of abode,' his numerous representations that that location was his address estop him from challenging service there."

2. Under the Federal Rule, abode service is proper on anyone of suitable age and discretion who "resides" in defendant's usual residence or place of abode. In *Franklin America, Inc. v. Franklin Cast Products,* 94 F.R.D. 645 (E.D. Mich. 1982), service was made on the defendant's part-time housekeeper, Mrs. Bannon. Defendant Schwartz claimed "that service was invalid because (1) Mrs. Bannon was not "residing" in the Schwartz home in January 1982; and (2) Mrs. Bannon was not appointed by Schwartz as his agent to receive service of process." In granting the defendant's motion to dismiss, the court made several observations.

> The term "residing therein" has been broadly and naturally interpreted to apply to a landlord, an apartment manager, a housemaid whose usual place of residence was the defendant's home, and a live-in maid. On the other hand, the term "resides there" has been held not to encompass a janitor or a ranch employee.

> It appears the common theme in the cases is not only whether the defendant is reasonably likely to receive the papers served, but

whether the person to whom they are handed is a full-time resident of the defendant's dwelling house or usual place of abode.

"Resides there" has long been held to require the recipient of the papers to be actually living in the same place as defendant. Thus, service on an employee of defendant who spends only a part of his time at defendant's residence is defective.

Here it is undisputed that Mrs. Bannon was a part-time housekeeper who did not live in the Schwartz home. She cannot be deemed to have been "residing therein" without placing an artificial construction on the language of the rule. Thus Mrs. Bannon was not "residing" in the Schwartz home to properly accept service intended for Schwartz.

While [the federal rule] authorizes service upon "an agent authorized by appointment ... to receive service of process", it is undisputed that Schwartz never so appointed Mrs. Bannon. Whether or not his wife appointed Mrs. Bannon as an agent for her husband by virtue of her telephone conversation with the Deputy United States Marshal is immaterial, since there is simply no evidence to indicate Schwartz ever gave his wife that power and an appointment must be made or authorized by the defendant. Thus the service cannot be upheld on the theory that Mrs. Bannon was an agent authorized to accept service of process for Schwartz....

The trial judge granted the plaintiff thirty days in which to "re-serve" the defendant. Why?

By contrast, in *Limon-Hernandez v. Lumbreras*, 171 F.R.D. 271 (D. Or. 1997), the process server gave the papers to an adult male who answered the door at the home of the defendant. After quoting from Federal Rule 4(e)(2), the court upheld the propriety of service by stating simply that the papers were left "with an adult male who was inside of the Lumbreras residence." The court failed to inquire into whether the person who received the papers actually resided there. And in *Howard Johnson International, Inc. v. Wang*, 7 F.Supp.2d 336 (S.D.N.Y. 1998), the court found it to be a "minor point" that the recipient of service did not actually live at the defendant's residence or place of abode.

3. Federal Rule 4(e)(2)(C) also authorizes substituted service on a defendant by delivery of a copy of the summons and complaint to an agent of the defendant. The rule applies only to service on individuals, and should be distinguished from Rule 4(h)(1)(B)'s service on an organization's managing or general agent. Courts look to whether an agency relationship exists, *i.e.*, there must be evidence that the defendant intended to confer authority to receive process on an agent. For example, an agency relationship may be implied from the terms of a power of attorney or from other circumstances.

Rule 4(e)(2)(C) also permits service on an agent authorized by law. For example, a statute may provide that a nonresident corporation which registers to do business in a state can (or must) designate an agent for service, or if none is appointed the Secretary of State becomes the agent who accepts service on behalf of the business. Operation of a long-arm statute is another example of an agent authorized by law, because the Secretary of State is designated as the defendant's agent who mails the papers by certified mail to the defendant at the address listed on the complaint.

4. Service within the United States on a corporation, partnership, or unincorporated association subject to being sued under a common name is made by 1) the waiver of service provision; or 2) delivery of the summons and complaint to an officer, managing or general agent, or to any other agent appointed to receive service or authorized by law to receive service. Because the summons and complaint must be served on the designated person, it is insufficient merely to mail the papers to the corporation generally. As the *Larsen* case indicated, mailing the legal papers to the "Medical/Legal Department, Mayo Clinic" was ineffective service under the federal rules.

For effective service of a corporate officer or managing or general agent, specific authorization by the corporation to accept service is unnecessary. Whether a person is regarded as a managing or general agent depends on the person's duties and authority rather than the name of the office. The governing principle is that service is to be made on someone who realizes her responsibilities to the corporation and knows what to do with the legal papers she receives. To uphold service of process, the person served must fit within the personnel categories listed in Rule 4(h)(1)(B) and therefore has the authority to accept service of process on the defendant's behalf. The record should show that the recipient of the summons and complaint had discretion in the operation of the defendant business, and that the recipient recognized the obligation to deliver the summons promptly to the defendant's appropriate personnel.

Service upon corporations and other entities is separate from considerations of service on individuals. For example, while it is permissible to serve an individual at his usual place of abode with a person of suitable age and discretion, the same type of service is not specifically authorized in the federal rules for corporations. Thus, service on a corporation is improper when a copy of the summons and complaint are left with a person (who is not a managing agent or a designated person for service of process) at the corporation's headquarters.

5. Some courts adopt a flexible approach to personal service upon corporations, known as "redelivery." Service on a corporation is upheld if: (a) the process server acts with due diligence in trying to meet the statutory requirements by establishing that the recipient is a company employee; (b) the process server nevertheless serves a person not authorized to accept service; and (c) the recipient then redelivers the papers to one who *is* authorized to accept service. The redelivery must be close in time and space so that it can be classified as part of the same act. See, e.g., *Melkaz International Inc. v. Flavor Innovation Inc.*, 167 F.R.D. 634 (E.D.N.Y. 1996).

6. Rule 4 sets forth a series of methods for serving process on individuals in a foreign country. As with other provisions, Rule 4(f) addresses only the *manner* of service and not whether a particular defendant is subject to suit. Rule 4(f)(1) allows service of process pursuant to the 1969 Hague Convention on the Service Abroad of Judicial and Extrajudicial Documents in Civil or Commercial Matters for international litigation in actions governed by the federal rules. Because it specifically refers to the Hague Convention as among the permissible means of service of process in a foreign country, service made pursuant to that treaty is within the foreign service exception to the 90-day time limit for completing process in Rule 4(m). The Hague Convention, however, does not preempt all other methods of service on defendants residing in another signatory nation.

Articles 2 through 7 of the Hague Convention set out the manner in which service should be executed in a signatory nation. Article 2 requires that all signatory nations must designate a "Central Authority" whose responsibility is to accept requests of service from any other signatory nation. The Hague Convention provides for alternate methods of service: 1) service through the Central Authority of member states; 2) service through consular channels; 3) service by mail if the receiving nation does not object; and 4) service pursuant to the internal laws of the nation.

Article 10(a) of the Hague Convention states that, if the "state of destination does not object," the Convention "shall not interfere with the freedom to send judicial documents, by postal channels, directly to persons abroad." For a discussion of Article 10(a) cases permitting and prohibiting service by mail on foreign corporations, see *Brockmeyer v. May*, 383 F.3d 798 (9th Cir. 2004).

The ability to request a waiver of service under Rule 4(d) may be particularly beneficial for service that is to occur outside the United States. If a foreign defendant waives service, the costs associated with serving process abroad can be reduced or eliminated. Waiver of service also eliminates the risk that the costs of service will be taxed against him for being unsuccessful in the lawsuit. A foreign defendant has ninety days following the mailing date to submit its defenses instead of the twenty-one days a defendant has to answer a complaint.

Rule 4(f)(2)(A)–(C) sets forth several methods for serving process in a foreign country that are neither signatories to the Hague Convention nor parties to any other applicable international agreement: 1) the manner prescribed by the law of the foreign country for service in an action in that nation in any of its courts of general jurisdiction; 2) as directed by the foreign authority in response to a formal letter of request from the forum court that proceeds through diplomatic channels and invokes the aid of the addressee court in the country in which service would take place (a time consuming, cumbersome and expensive method of service); and 3) personal delivery upon an individual in a foreign country by any form of mail requiring a signed receipt, to be addressed and dispatched to the party to be served by the clerk of the court.

Rule 4(f)(3) gives the court discretion to order service by any method that is not prohibited by international agreement. For all of the methods, due process requirements of reasonable notice and opportunity to be heard must be satisfied. Courts have approved alternative methods of service such as first-class mail, electronic mail, publication, and telex. See, e.g., *Rio Properties, Inc. v. Rio International Interlink*, 284 F.3d 1007 (9th Cir. 2002) (service by electronic mail was reasonably calculated to inform the defendant about the pendency of the lawsuit as well as the method most likely to reach the defendant). The flexibility of Rule 4(f)(3) is illustrated by *Levin v. Ruby Trading Corporation*, 248 F.Supp. 537 (S.D.N.Y. 1965). The defendant was Canadian, and the plaintiff had tried unsuccessfully to serve him under Rule 4(f)(2) by registered mail and by personal service. Pursuant to a court order, service was then attempted by ordinary mail to the defendant at his Canadian residence. The court upheld the service under the existing version of Rule 4(f)(3), because it provided an alternative to the signed receipt mailing in Rule 4(f)(2).

PROBLEMS

1. Adams sues Bursen in federal court. Must or may the process server give the complaint and summons to Bursen personally?

2. Adams sues Bursen in federal court, and Adams personally takes the papers to Bursen's home, leaving them with a 10-year-old girl who answers the door. Was service of process proper?

3. Adams sues Bursen in federal court for an injury that occurred while Adams was visiting Bursen's large estate, but the process server hands the papers to Bursen at his weekend lakefront cottage in a nearby county. Was service of process proper?

4. Adams sues Bursen in federal court, and the process server leaves the papers with Bursen's limousine driver who answered the door at Bursen's home, because she mistook the driver for Bursen. The driver does not live at Bursen's home. Was service of process proper?

5. Adams sues Bursen in federal court. A procedural rule in the state where the federal court is located permits a process server to leave the papers at the defendant's home, regardless of whether anyone is present at the time. The process server leaves the papers at Bursen's house when no one was at home. Was service of process proper?

6. A state rule allows service by publication if personal service and substituted service methods are unsuccessful. Bursen has avoided numerous attempts by a privately-retained process server to serve him. Adams then invokes the service by publication rule for the required time period, receives no response from Bursen, and then obtains a default judgment against Bursen. When Adams seeks to enforce the judgment by garnishing Bursen's wages, Bursen moves to set aside the default judgment, arguing the notice by publication procedure violates due process. Applying *Mullane*, how should the court rule?

7. Adams sues Bursen in federal court, and Adams properly solicits Bursen to waive service of process. If Bursen fails to respond to Adams's request, is Adams obligated to do anything further?

8. After filing a federal claim against the defendant, Adams attempted to serve Bursen by sending him copies of the summons and complaint, along with the proper forms for waiver of service under Rule 4(d). Bursen fails to return the acknowledgment required by Rule 4. Now that Bursen is aware of the lawsuit, he also manages to avoid Adams's various attempts to have him served under Rule 4(e). However, Adams knows that a procedural rule in his state permits service by publication for defendants who seek to avoid service. Can Adams serve Bursen under the state rule and obtain a default judgment if Bursen fails to answer?

9. Adams sues Bursen, who does business as Bursen's Bike Shop. The process server leaves the papers with Cohn at one of the three bike shops owned by Bursen. Cohn is the manager of the store where he receives the papers intended for Bursen. Was service of process proper?

10. Adams sues Bikes 'R Me, Inc., in federal court. Bursen is President of the corporation. The process server leaves the papers with Bursen's father at the home they share. Was service of process proper?

11. Adams sues Bikes 'R Me, Inc., in federal court. Bursen is President of the corporation. The process server leaves the papers with Cohn at the corporate office. Was service of process proper?

12. Describe the difference between the defense of insufficiency of service of process under Rule 12(b)(5) and the defense of insufficiency of process under Rule 12(b)(4).

EXERCISE

Because the federal rules permit a plaintiff to serve a defendant under the methods described in the federal rules as well as using the techniques allowed by the state encompassing the federal district where the case is filed or where service is made, it is important to be familiar with the service of process standards in state courts as well. For the state where a) you intend to practice after graduation, b) your law school is located, and/or c) your professor assigns, go to that state's annotated statutes and research the procedural rules by which service of process is made. Based on your research, print the rule and bring it to class for discussion. In addition, answer the following questions.

1. Identify the minimum requirements for who can serve process.

2. Identify the methods of service described by rule for serving individuals.

a. Is personal service required?

b. Is substituted (some method other than personal) service permitted? If so, by what method?

                    i. First-class mail?

                    ii. Electronic mail?

                    iii. Registered or certified mail?

                    iv. Facsimile transmission?

                    v. Serving another person? If so, who, where, and how is the service to be accomplished?

        c. Is service by publication permitted? If so, under what circumstances?

                    i. Must plaintiff show that attempts to serve by other means were unsuccessful?

                    ii. Must the papers also be mailed to the defendant to increase likelihood of receipt of the notice?

                    iii. What types of notice? Posting? Newspaper? Certain types of cases?

    3. Identify the methods of service described by the rule for serving corporations. Are specific persons associated with the corporate entity designated for service, or can anyone in the corporation be served? If the former is true, which corporate positions are designated?

    4. Is waiver of service of process addressed specifically with a set of procedures similar to Federal Rule 4(d)?

    5. Find the governing long-arm statute. Many long-arm statutes specify the method by which service of process using the long-arm must be achieved. Identify the method for service of process under your long-arm statute, and compare it to the methods in your state for serving individuals and corporations.

D. VERACITY STANDARDS FOR PLEADINGS AND OTHER FILED DOCUMENTS

While a court has inherent authority to impose sanctions, *Chambers v. NASCO*, 501 U.S. 32, 111 S.Ct. 2123, 115 L.Ed.2d 27 (1991), in federal courts Rule 11 is the primary source of power for sanctioning attorneys and their clients. Under the federal rules, an attorney's signature originally constituted a certification that "good grounds" existed for a pleading. Sweeping changes to Rule 11 were made in 1983 and again in 1993. The certification of a signer under the 1983 version of the rule guaranteed that the signer had read the paper to be filed and that to the best of the signer's knowledge, information and belief it was "well grounded in fact and warranted by existing law or a good faith argument" for changing existing law. Sanctions for violations were mandatory.

The 1993 (and current) version of Rule 11 was a response to the widespread criticism of the 1983 rule. The 1983 version apparently affected plaintiffs more severely than defendants, created problems for the party who alleged a novel legal theory, rarely was enforced with non-monetary sanctions, provided little incentive to discontinue a legal or factual position after it had lost its legal or factual support, and created conflicts between the attorney and client. Despite the view of Justices Scalia and Thomas, dissenting from the order transmitting rule amendments to Congress, that the "proposed revision [of Rule 11] would render the Rule toothless," the amended rule took effect on December 1, 1993.

The Rule has a dual purpose: it 1) establishes the standards for attorneys and parties who file pleadings, motions or other documents in court; and 2) regulates the situations in which court may impose sanctions for rule violations. It is important to remember that the Rule applies to all filed documents, not just complaints. State procedural systems follow their own versions of Rule 11 for filed documents, and every jurisdiction maintains ethical standards for attorneys who take frivolous positions.

Rule 11 requires that a document must be signed by an attorney or by the party, if there is no attorney. Unless preserved by statute or rule, the Rule 11 signature requirement eliminates verification requirements, by which the client had to co-sign certain documents along with the attorney. If the document is not signed, by Rule 11(a) the court must strike the paper unless the paper is signed promptly after the attorney or party becomes aware of the problem. The following paragraphs summarize the significance of the Rule 11 signature requirement and the sanctions that may be imposed for its violation.

The duty of candor. Litigants are subject to sanctions for advocating a position after it is no longer tenable. The rule protects litigants against sanctions if they withdraw or correct contentions after being notified about a potential violation.

When does the duty of candor apply? It applies only to assertions in papers filed with the court, but does not cover matters arising for the first time during oral presentations to the court when an attorney may make a statement that would not have been made had there been more time for research and thought. A litigant's obligations regarding contents of filed papers include continuing to advocate positions contained in pleadings and motions after learning that the positions no longer are meritorious.

What happens when a litigant realizes the lack of merit in a position already taken in writing? Sometimes a litigant may have good reason to believe that a fact is true, but may need time to develop the facts from the opposition or third parties to confirm the basis for the allegation. Even if support for the fact does not exist after reasonable investigation, it is unnecessary to amend the pleading. However, the attorney can no longer advocate the fact as part of the claim or defense.

Are sanctions mandatory? Under Rule 11, the trial court has discretion to determine whether to apply sanctions. It also has significant discretion to decide what sanctions should be imposed for a Rule 11 violation. However, the Rule states that sanctions should be no more severe than reasonably necessary to deter repetition of the conduct by the offending attorney or party or comparable conduct by similarly situated persons.

How does the Rule indicate that its primary purpose is to deter counsel from advocating meritless positions? If a court imposes a monetary sanction, it is ordinarily to be paid to the court as a penalty. If requested, monetary sanctions may be awarded to another party. Any sanction may be imposed on attorneys, law firms, or parties who violate the rule or are deemed to be responsible for the rule violation. A person who signs, files, submits, or advocates a document has a nondelegable responsibility to the court.

Are sanctions imposed automatically? Before sanctions are imposed, litigants must receive notice about an alleged violation and a chance to respond. If the court imposes sanctions, it generally must express its reasons for the sanction in a written order or on the record.

What is a "safe harbor" provision and how is it expressed in Rule 11? Most motions are filed with the court and then served on opposing parties. Rule 11 motions work differently. The motion for sanctions is first served on the party allegedly committing the violation. However, it cannot be filed until at least 21 days after service. During that period, if the violation is corrected by for example withdrawing an allegation, the motion should not be filed with the court.

Are any writings exempt from the Rule's coverage? Rule 11 explicitly is inapplicable to discovery and disclosure requests, responses, objections and motions under the discovery provisions in Rules 26–37. Note however that the discovery rules contain their own veracity requirement in Rule 26(g).

RUSZALA V. WALT DISNEY WORLD CO.
132 F.Supp.2d 1347 (M.D. Fla. 2000)

GLAZEBROOK, UNITED STATES MAGISTRATE JUDGE.

... On January 16, 1996, Corporal Robert Stephens, of the Orange County Sheriff's Office, responded to a request for service from Walt Disney World Company ("Walt Disney"). Upon his arrival at the Walt Disney offices, Corporal Stephens obtained the following information. Walt Disney was investigating possible employee theft at Walt Disney's Ohana restaurant. Plaintiff Bill R. Ruszala was a server at Walt Disney's Ohana restaurant. A documented analysis of the restaurant's computerized transaction log revealed a discrepancy between the number of guests that Ruszala "rung up" on the register and the number of guests actually served by Ruszala. Walt Disney security investigators, Phillip McNab and Dennis J. Ramos, interviewed Ruszala at the Walt Disney security offices. During the interview, Ruszala confessed to stealing money from Walt Disney's Ohana Restaurant.

After obtaining the foregoing information, Corporal Stephens entered the room where Ruszala was located. Before asking Ruszala any questions, Corporal Stephens advised Ruszala of his right to an attorney. When Ruszala asked for an attorney, Corporal Stephens ceased questioning him and placed Ruszala under arrest on the charge of employee theft.

On June 29, 1998, Ruszala brought this action against defendants Walt Disney, Dennis Ramos, and Kevin Beary as Sheriff of Orange County, Florida, in connection with his arrest on January 16, 1996. In total, Ruszala alleged six causes of action including: false imprisonment, false arrest, malicious prosecution, defamation, violating of civil rights, and conspiracy to violate civil rights. Specific to Sheriff Beary, Ruszala alleged false arrest and conspiracy to violate civil rights in violation of 42 U.S.C. § 1983. The only basis for adding Sheriff Beary as a defendant was that Corporal Stephens purportedly did not have personal knowledge of the facts purporting to constitute probable cause for Ruszala's arrest. Ruszala claimed that Corporal Stephens impermissibly relied solely on Walt Disney's private security personnel to provide him information to support Ruszala's arrest.

On March 20, 2000, Sheriff Beary moved for summary judgment on Ruszala's claims of false arrest and conspiracy to violate civil rights. On April 25, 2000, the Honorable G. Kendall Sharp granted Sheriff Beary's motion for summary judgment as against Ruszala. On that same date, the Court ordered Ruszala and his attorney, Scott Sterling, to show cause within 2 days why they should not be held jointly liable for Sheriff Beary's attorney's fees and costs incurred in defending this action. On May 4, 2000, Beary filed a motion to tax costs and entitlement to attorneys' fees, together with his bill of costs. On May 5, 2000, the Clerk of Court taxed costs in the amount of $726.02. On May 10, 2000, Ruszala filed a response to this Court's show cause order and defendant Kevin Beary's motion to tax costs and entitlement to attorney's fees. Ruszala did not object to the costs requested by Sheriff Beary and previously taxed by the Clerk of Court. . . .

Rule 11(b) of the Federal Rules of Civil Procedure imposes a duty upon attorneys and parties to refrain from filing or pursuing frivolous claims. Fed.R.Civ.P. 11(b). Rule 11 sanctions are proper: (1) when a party files a pleading that has no reasonable factual basis; (2) when the party files a pleading that is based on a legal theory that has no reasonable chance of success and that cannot be advanced as a reasonable argument to change existing law; and (3) when the party files a pleading in bad faith for an improper purpose. Rule 11(c) allows a court to "impose an appropriate sanction upon the attorneys, law firms, or parties that have violated subdivision (b) or are responsible for the violation," which may include "part or all of the reasonable attorneys' fees and other expenses directly resulting from the violation." Fed.R.Civ.P. 11(c)(4).

The objective standard for testing conduct under Rule 11 is "reasonableness under the circumstances" and "what was reasonable to believe at the time" the pleading was submitted. This court requires a two-step inquiry as to: 1) whether the party's claims are objectively frivolous; and 2) whether the person who signed the pleadings should have been aware that they were frivolous. Although sanctions are warranted when the claimant exhibits a "deliberate indifference to obvious facts," they are not warranted when the claimant's evidence is merely weak but appears sufficient, after a reasonable inquiry, to support a claim under existing law. The purpose of Rule 11 is to deter frivolous lawsuits and not to deter novel legal arguments or cases of first impression. The grant of summary judgment, in and of itself, does not mean that an action is frivolous or warrants the imposition of sanctions.

As amended in December 1993, Rule 11 makes clear the continuing nature of a litigant's responsibility under Rule 11. Under the 1993 amendment:

> It [Rule 11] also, however, emphasizes the duty of candor by subjecting litigants to potential sanctions for insisting upon a position after it is no longer tenable. . . .
>
> [A] litigant's obligations with respect to the contents of these papers are not measured solely of the time they are filed with or submitted to the court, but include reaffirming to the court and advocating positions contained in those pleadings and motions after learning that they cease to have any merit.

Fed.R.Civ.P. 11, advisory committee's note. Thus, Rule 11 sanctions are appropriate when a party pursues a claim after it is no longer tenable in fact or law. . . .

This Court carefully evaluates Sheriff Beary's claim of frivolity given that the Court granted summary judgment before trial on the ground that no genuine issue of material fact remains as to whether Corporal Stephens had probable cause to arrest Ruszala. Finding that Ruszala's arrest was made pursuant to probable cause, the district court decided the action in Ruszala's favor on a dispositive motion rather than at a trial on the merits. Sheriff Beary is clearly a prevailing defendant.

Nevertheless, Congress has determined that success on summary judgment is not alone sufficient to require an assessment of attorney's fees. Congress could have enacted legislation mandating an award of attorney's fees to all prevailing parties, but instead opted to leave such an award to the Court's discretion.

The undersigned is unable to determine from the record whether Ruszala brought the claim in subjective bad faith, and therefore presumes that he did not. Nevertheless, in applying the stringent standard established by current case law, defendant Sheriff Beary has established that as of Ruszala's February 26, 1999 deposition, Ruszala's and his counsel's actions in litigating through summary judgment was frivolous, unreasonable, and without foundation. . . .

At the February 26, 1999 deposition, Ruszala admitted that he previously confessed to stealing money from Walt Disney's Ohana Restaurant. Ruszala also said that Corporal Stephens acted in a very professional manner and that Corporal Stephens "wouldn't violate my civil rights." Ruszala further admitted that Corporal Stephens had no reason not to believe the Walt Disney security people when they advised Corporal Stephens that Ruszala had confessed to committing a theft. Additionally, Ruszala stated that Corporal Stephens "arrested me because I confessed to something. Like I said, I knew he had a job to do, so apparently I believed he was doing his job as he though he was suppose to." By Ruszala's own admissions, Corporal Stevens had probable cause to arrest Ruszala.

Subsequent to Ruszala's February 26, 1999 deposition, Sheriff Beary's counsel, Bruce R. Bogan, sent two letters to Ruszala's counsel on June 24, 1999 and on December 28, 1999. In those letters, Bogan asked Ruszala to withdraw his claims against Sheriff Beary. In the December 28, 1999 letter, Bogan warned counsel that if Sheriff Beary was not voluntarily dismissed from this suit, Sheriff Beary would seek attorney's fees and costs on the basis that the action was frivolous.

In light of these factors, the Court finds that the false arrest claim and the conspiracy to violate civil rights claim stemming from an arrest without probable cause were unreasonable and without foundation. . . .

It is clear to the undersigned that after Ruszala's deposition Ruszala and his attorney were clearly on notice that Ruszala's claims lacked any basis in fact or law. Yet, it is equally clear that Ruszala and his attorney continued the pursuit of their claims against Sheriff Beary even when it became patently clear that Ruszala's claims had no chance of success. In applying the objective standard of reasonableness test, the Court finds that Ruszala and his counsel violated Rule 11 by pursuing claims that were not tenable despite overwhelming evidence of probable cause—an absolute defense to the claims asserted in the complaint.

In considering the nature of sanctions to be imposed, the Court finds that monetary penalty in the form of attorney's fees is the minimum necessary to deter such future conduct. As already discussed, Ruszala's claims against Sheriff Beary lacked any merit. The primary evidence presented in support of this conclusion was Ruszala's own testimony. This action did not turn on subtle, unsettled issues of law, nor did it involve close questions of facts. Under these circumstances, Sheriff Beary is entitled to attorney's fees expended in the defense of this case under Rule 11.

NOTES AND QUESTIONS

1. Since the 1980s, politicians have tried to use the issue of frivolous lawsuits for political gain. For example, in 1995, the Congress adopted the Private Securities Litigation Reform Act of 1995, which in part cross-referenced parts of Rule 11 and amended Rule 11 *exclusively* for securities cases. See 15 U.S.C. § 78u. According to the Conference Committee:

> Existing Rule 11 has not deterred abusive securities litigation. Courts often fail to impose Rule 11 sanctions even where such sanctions are warranted. When sanctions are awarded, they are generally insufficient to make whole the victim of a Rule 11 violation: the amount of the sanction is limited to an amount that the court deems sufficient to deter repetition of the sanctioned conduct, rather than imposing a sanction that equals the costs imposed on the victim by the violation. Finally, courts have been unable to apply Rule 11 to the complaint in such a way that the victim of the ensuing lawsuit is compensated for all attorneys' fees and costs incurred in the entire action.

The Act made sanctions mandatory and presumed that the opposing party's attorneys' fees would be the sanction, rejecting the deterrence rationale in Rule 11. Upon final adjudication of each securities case, the trial court is required to make specific findings on the parties' compliance with Rule 11. This requirement thereby dispenses with the filing of a motion, as well as the safe harbor provision.

Recent Congressional attempts to deal with the issue of frivolous lawsuits have failed. For example, the U.S. House of Representatives approved the Lawsuit Abuse Reduction Act of 2005 to amend Rule 11. Specifically, the bill inter alia (1) disallowed withdrawal or correction of pleadings to avoid sanctions, and (2) prescribed a one-year suspension from law practice for lawyers found to have violated Rule 11 three or more times. The bill was received in the Senate, but was never voted out of the Judiciary Committee. In 2009, for the third time a lone Senate sponsor introduced the Frivolous Lawsuit Prevention Act of 2009 to amend Federal Rule 11 to (1) change from discretionary to mandatory the authority of a court to impose sanctions, and (2) permit monetary sanctions to be awarded against a party's attorneys. The bill was referred to the Senate Judiciary Committee, where it died at the end of the session.

2. All filed pleadings, motions and other papers must be signed by the individual attorney of record or by the party who is unrepresented. In either

situation, the signer's address must be included. When a team of attorneys is conducting the litigation, the attorney who signs the paper may not necessarily be the one responsible for either the decision to file it or its preparation. For example, an associate in a law firm may prepare, sign, and file a paper at the direction of a partner. The rule's emphasis on the responsibility of the attorney suggests that the potential scope of the obligation under the rule might extend to attorneys who share responsibility for the filing of a paper even though they may not have signed the document in question.

When is a represented party responsible for problems with a filed document? Does it matter whether the party signs the document? In *Business Guides, Inc. v. Chromatic Communications, Enters., Inc.*, 498 U.S. 533, 111 S.Ct. 922, 112 L.Ed.2d 1140 (1991), the Court applied the reasonable inquiry standard to a represented party who signed a document along with counsel. Because the rule concentrates on the person who signs the document, a represented party who does not sign a document does not appear to be subject to Rule 11. *Aetna Ins. Co. v. Meeker*, 953 F.2d 1328 (11th Cir. 1992). Even if a party does not sign the document, should the party nevertheless be liable for providing false facts to the attorney?

"Absent exceptional circumstances, a law firm shall be held jointly responsible for violations committed by its partners, associates, and employees." That language from Rule 11(c)(1) overruled *Pavelic & LeFlore v. Marvel Entertainment Group*, 493 U.S. 120, 110 S.Ct. 456, 107 L.Ed.2d 438 (1989), which had held that sanctions could be imposed only on the signing attorney.

3. Like the warranties in Rule 11(b), the American Bar Association Model Rules of Professional Conduct require analogous guarantees for attorneys in civil litigation. Consistent with Rule 11(b)(1), Rule 3.2 requires a lawyer to "make reasonable efforts to expedite litigation consistent with the interests of the client." Also, Rule 4.4 prohibits actions when the "means . . . have no substantial purpose other than to embarrass, delay, or burden a third person . . ." The analogous ethical standards for Rule 11(b)(2)–(4) are found in Rule 3.1, which addresses the issue of nonfrivolous legal and factual assertions. "A lawyer shall not bring or defend a proceeding, or assert or controvert an issue therein, unless there is a basis for doing so that is not frivolous, which includes a good faith argument for an extension, modification or reversal of existing law." Having devoted so much attention to concerns about frivolous lawsuits, notice that neither the procedural nor the ethical standards are willing or able to define the term "nonfrivolous." Which is more demanding of attorneys, the ethical standard or the legal standard?

EXERCISE

For the state a) where you intend to practice after graduation, b) where your law school is located, and/or c) your professor assigns, go to that state's annotated rules and research the procedural rules for veracity standards relating to documents filed with the court. Based on your research, print the portion of the rule and bring it to class for discussion. In addition, answer the following questions.

1. What is the scope of the standard, e.g., documents only, exempting discovery documents?

2. What does an attorney's signature certify?

3. Define the scope of the attorney's obligation, i.e., is it a continuing duty or is it restricted to the attorney's knowledge at the time the document is filed?

4. Who may be responsible for violations, e.g., the signing attorney, the attorney's law firm, the client?

5. Regarding sanctions:

a. What does the moving party have to prove in order for sanctions to be imposed?

b. Are sanctions mandatory or discretionary?

c. What types of sanctions are available?

d. What ordinarily happens to collected sanctions, e.g., paid to the court?

e. Can the court initiate sanctions, without a motion from a party?

6. Are the tests for a violation objective or subjective?

CHRISTIAN V. MATTEL, INC.
286 F.3d 1118 (9th Cir. 2002)

MCKEOWN, CIRCUIT JUDGE.

It is difficult to imagine that the Barbie doll, so perfect in her sculpture and presentation, and so comfortable in every setting, from "California girl" to "Chief Executive Officer Barbie," could spawn such acrimonious litigation and such egregious conduct on the part of her challenger. In her wildest dreams, Barbie could not have imagined herself in the middle of Rule 11 proceedings. But the intersection of copyrights on Barbie sculptures and the scope of Rule 11 is precisely what defines this case.

James Hicks appeals from a district court order requiring him, pursuant to Federal Rule of Civil Procedure 11, to pay Mattel, Inc. $501,565 in attorneys' fees that it incurred in defending against what the district court determined to be a frivolous action. Hicks brought suit on behalf of Harry Christian, claiming that Mattel's Barbie dolls infringed Christian's Claudene doll sculpture copyright. In its sanctions orders, the district court found that Hicks should have discovered prior to commencing the civil action that Mattel's dolls could not have infringed Christian's copyright because, among other things, the Mattel dolls had been created well prior to the Claudene doll and the Mattel dolls had clearly visible copyright notices on their heads. After determining that Hicks had behaved "boorishly" during discovery and had a lengthy rap sheet of prior litigation misconduct, the district court imposed sanctions.

We hold that the district court did not abuse its discretion in determining that the complaint filed by Hicks was frivolous under Rule 11. In parsing the language of the district court's sanctions orders, however, we cannot determine with any degree of certainty whether the district court grounded its Rule 11 decision on Hicks' misconduct that occurred outside the pleadings, such as in oral argument, at a meeting of counsel, and at a key deposition. This is an important distinction because Rule 11 sanctions are limited to misconduct regarding signed pleadings, motions, and other filings. Consequently, we vacate the district court's orders and remand for further proceedings consistent with this opinion. In so doing, we do not condone Hicks' conduct or suggest that the district court did not have a firm basis for awarding sanctions. Indeed, the district court undertook a careful and exhaustive examination of the facts and the legal underpinnings of the copyright challenge. Rather, the remand is to assure that any Rule 11 sanctions are grounded in conduct covered by Rule 11 and to ensure adequate findings for the sizeable fee award.

As context for examining the district court's determination that the underlying copyright action was frivolous, we begin by discussing the long history of litigation between Mattel and Hicks' past and current clients: Harry Christian; Christian's daughter, Claudene; and the Collegiate Doll Company ("CDC"), Claudene's proprietorship.

Mattel is a toy company that is perhaps best recognized as the manufacturer of the world-famous Barbie doll. Since Barbie's creation in 1959, Mattel has outfitted her in fashions and accessories that have evolved over time. In perhaps the most classic embodiment, Barbie is depicted as a slender-figured doll with long blonde hair and blue eyes. Mattel has sought to protect its intellectual property by registering various Barbie-related copyrights, including copyrights protecting the doll's head sculpture. Mattel has vigorously litigated against putative infringers.

In 1990, Claudene Christian, then an undergraduate student at the University of Southern California ("USC"), decided to create and market a collegiate cheerleader doll. The doll, which the parties refer to throughout their papers as "Claudene," had blonde hair and blue eyes and was outfitted to resemble a USC cheerleader.

Mattel soon learned about the Claudene doll. After concluding that it infringed certain Barbie copyrights, Mattel brought an administrative action before the United States Customs Service in 1996 in which it alleged that the Claudene doll, manufactured abroad, had pirated the head sculpture of the "Teen Talk" and "SuperStar" Barbies. The Customs Service ruled in CDC's favor and subsequently released a shipment of Claudene dolls. Undaunted, Mattel commenced a federal court action in 1997 in which it once again alleged that CDC infringed various of Mattel's copyrights. At the time, Claudene Christian was president of CDC and Harry Christian was listed as co-founder of the company and chief financial officer. CDC retained Hicks as its counsel.

After the court dismissed CDC's multiple counterclaims, the case was settled. Mattel released CDC from any copyright infringement liability in exchange for, among other things, a stipulation that Mattel was free to challenge CDC's alleged copyright of the Claudene doll should CDC "or any successor in interest" challenge Mattel's right to market its Barbie dolls.

Seizing on a loophole in the parties' settlement agreement, within weeks of the agreement, Harry Christian, who was not a signatory to the agreement, retained Hicks as his counsel and filed a federal court action against Mattel. In the complaint, which Hicks signed, Christian alleged that Mattel obtained a copy of the copyrighted Claudene doll in 1996, the year of its creation, and then infringed its overall appearance, including its face paint, by developing a new Barbie line called "Cool Blue" that was substantially similar to Claudene. Christian sought damages in the amount of $2.4 billion and various forms of injunctive relief. . . .

Two months after the complaint was filed, Mattel moved for summary judgment. In support of its motion, Mattel proffered evidence that the Cool Blue Barbie doll contained a 1991 copyright notice on the back of its head, indicating that it predated Claudene's head sculpture copyright by approximately six years. Mattel therefore argued that Cool Blue Barbie could not as a matter of law infringe Claudene's head sculpture copyright. . . .

At a follow-up counsel meeting required by a local rule, Mattel's counsel attempted to convince Hicks that his complaint was frivolous. During the videotaped meeting, they presented Hicks with copies of various Barbie dolls that not only had been created prior to 1996 (the date of Claudene's creation), but also had copyright designations on their heads that pre-dated Claudene's creation. Additionally, Mattel's counsel noted that the face paint on some of the earlier-created Barbie dolls was virtually identical to that used on Claudene. Hicks declined Mattel's invitation to inspect the dolls and, later during the meeting, hurled them in disgust from a conference table.

Having been unsuccessful in convincing Hicks to dismiss Christian's action voluntarily, Mattel served Hicks with a motion for Rule 11 sanctions. In its motion papers, Mattel argued, among other things, that

Hicks had signed and filed a frivolous complaint based on a legally meritless theory that Mattel's prior-created head sculptures infringed Claudene's 1997 copyright. Hicks declined to withdraw the complaint during the 21-day safe harbor period provided by Rule 11, and Mattel filed its motion.

Seemingly unfazed by Mattel's Rule 11 motion, Hicks . . . sought information regarding the face painting on certain Barbie dolls and the face paint/head sculpture combinations used by Mattel after 1996. The district court summarily denied the motion. It later noted, in the context of its summary judgment order, that "it is unclear what [Christian] is requesting when he seeks access to post-1996 Barbies." . . .

The district court granted Mattel's motions for summary judgment and Rule 11 sanctions. . . .

As for Mattel's Rule 11 motion, the district court found that Hicks had "filed a meritless claim against defendant Mattel. A reasonable investigation by Mr. Hicks would have revealed that there was no factual foundation for [Christian's] copyright claim." Indeed, the district court noted that Hicks needed to do little more than examine "the back of the heads of the Barbie dolls he claims were infringing, . . ."

> The district court awarded Mattel $501,565 in attorneys' fees. At the outset of its order, the court summarized the findings in its earlier order, namely that it had "predicated its [Rule 11] decision" on Hicks' filing a frivolous complaint and "further found" that he had " 'behaved boorishly, misrepresented the facts and misstated the law.' " . . .

The district court next considered various arguments that Hicks had advanced in opposition to Mattel's fee application. Hicks first contended, without much elaboration, that a fee award would have a "ruinous" effect on his finances and ability to practice law. The district court held, however, that "repeated reprimands and sanctions" imposed in prior litigations "clearly have not had the desired deterrent effect on his behavior," and it concluded that Hicks would not be punished sufficiently if the court were to impose mere "non-monetary sanctions." Hicks also argued (somewhat ironically) that Mattel's fees request was excessive in light of how simplistic it should have been to defend against Christian's action. The district court disagreed, reasoning that like the court in *Brandt v. Schal Assocs., Inc.*, 960 F.2d 640, 648 (7th Cir.1992), the judiciary has " 'little sympathy for the litigant who fires a big gun, and when the adversary returns fire, complains because he was firing blanks.' " . . .

The court is satisfied that the other attorneys' fees Mattel has claimed are both reasonable and proximately caused by Mr. Hicks' pursuit of this frivolous action. [T]he Court grants Mattel its attorneys' fees in the amount of $501,565.00.

... We review the district court's decision to impose Rule 11 sanctions—and, if they are warranted, the reasonableness of the actual amount imposed—for abuse of discretion. *Cooter & Gell v. Hartmarx Corp.*, 496 U.S. 384, 401, 405 (1990). In conducting our review of the district court's factual findings in support of the sanctions, we "would be justified in concluding that [the court] had abused its discretion in making [the findings] only if [they] were clearly erroneous." The district court's legal findings must be affirmed unless they result from a "materially incorrect view of the relevant law."

The district court found that Hicks "filed a meritless claim against defendant Mattel. A reasonable investigation by Mr. Hicks would have revealed that there was no factual foundation for plaintiff's copyright claim." Hicks challenges these findings, arguing that the issues were "more complex" than the district court recognized. Before considering this operative issue, we first consider Rule 11 principles that guide our review.

Filing a complaint in federal court is no trifling undertaking. An attorney's signature on a complaint is tantamount to a warranty that the complaint is well grounded in fact and "existing law" (or proposes a good faith extension of the existing law) and that it is not filed for an improper purpose.

The attorney has a duty prior to filing a complaint not only to conduct a reasonable factual investigation, but also to perform adequate legal research that confirms whether the theoretical underpinnings of the complaint are "warranted by existing law or a good faith argument for an extension, modification or reversal of existing law." *Golden Eagle Distrib. Corp. v. Burroughs Corp.*, 801 F.2d 1531, 1537 (9th Cir. 1986). One of the fundamental purposes of Rule 11 is to "reduce frivolous claims, defenses or motions and to deter costly meritless maneuvers, . . . [thereby] avoid[ing] delay and unnecessary expense in litigation." Nonetheless, a finding of significant delay or expense is not required under Rule 11. Where, as here, the complaint is the primary focus of Rule 11 proceedings, a district court must conduct a two-prong inquiry to determine (1) whether the complaint is legally or factually "baseless" from an objective perspective, and (2) if the attorney has conducted "a reasonable and competent inquiry" before signing and filing it.

Hicks filed a single claim of copyright infringement against Mattel. The complaint charges that the Cool Blue Barbie infringed the copyright in the Claudene doll head. In addition, in a subsequent letter to Mattel's counsel, he claimed that Virginia Tech Barbie also infringed Claudene. Hicks cannot seriously dispute the district court's conclusions that, assuming the applicability of the doctrine of prior creation, Christian's complaint was legally and factually frivolous. Indeed, as a matter of copyright law, it is well established that a prior-created work cannot infringe a later-created one. See *Grubb v. KMS Patriots, L.P.*, 88 F.3d 1, 5 (1st Cir.1996) (noting that "prior creation renders any conclusion of access or inference of copying illogical."). . . .

Recognizing the futility of attacking prior creation, Hicks argues that the paint on the Claudene doll's face features a light makeup that is distinctive and that the two Barbie dolls thus infringe Claudene's overall appearance and presentation. This argument fails because, among other things, Mattel used the light face paint on the Pioneer Barbie, which was created two years before the Claudene doll, thus defeating once again any claim of copying. It also bears noting that Mattel has been repainting various doll heads for decades. . . .

The district court concluded that Hicks "filed a case without factual foundation." Hicks, having argued unsuccessfully that his failure to perform even minimal due diligence was irrelevant as a matter of copyright law, does not contest that he would have been able to discover the copyright information simply by examining the doll heads. Instead he argues that the district court did not understand certain "complex" issues. Simply saying so does not make it so. The district court well understood the legal and factual background of the case. It was Hicks' absence of investigation, not the district court's absence of analysis, that brought about his downfall.

The district court did not abuse its discretion in concluding that Hicks' failure to investigate fell below the requisite standard established by Rule 11.

Hicks argues that even if the district court were justified in sanctioning him under Rule 11 based on Christian's complaint and the follow-on motions, its conclusion was tainted because it impermissibly considered other misconduct that cannot be sanctioned under Rule 11, such as discovery abuses, misstatements made during oral argument, and conduct in other litigation.

Hicks' argument has merit. . . .

The laundry list of Hicks' outlandish conduct is a long one and raises serious questions as to his respect for the judicial process. Nonetheless, Rule 11 sanctions are limited to "paper[s]" signed in violation of the rule. Conduct in depositions, discovery meetings of counsel, oral representations at hearings, and behavior in prior proceedings do not fall within the ambit of Rule 11. Because we do not know for certain whether the district court granted Mattel's Rule 11 motion as a result of an impermissible intertwining of its conclusion about the complaint's frivolity and Hicks' extrinsic misconduct, we must vacate the district court's Rule 11 orders.

We decline Mattel's suggestion that the district court's sanctions orders could be supported in their entirety under the court's inherent authority. To impose sanctions under its inherent authority, the district court must "make an explicit finding [which it did not do here] that counsel's conduct constituted or was tantamount to bad faith." *Primus Auto. Fin. Serv., Inc. v. Batarse*, 115 F.3d 644, 648 (9th Cir.1997). We acknowledge that the district court has a broad array of sanctions options at its disposal: Rule 11, 28 U.S.C. § 1927, and the court's inherent authority. Each of these sanctions alternatives has its own particular requirements, and it is important that the grounds be separately articulated to assure that the conduct at issue falls within the scope of the sanctions remedy. On remand, the district court will have an opportunity to delineate the factual and legal basis for its sanctions orders.

Hicks raises various challenges to the quantum of attorneys' fees. Because we are vacating the district court's Rule 11 orders on other legal grounds, we express no opinion at this stage about the particular reasonableness of any of the fees the district court elected to award Mattel. We do, however, encourage the district court on remand to ensure that the time spent by Mattel's attorneys was reasonably and appropriately spent in relation to both the patent frivolousness of Christian's complaint and the services directly caused by the sanctionable conduct.[12] See Fed.R.Civ.P. 11, advisory committee notes, 1993 Amendments, Subdivisions (b) and (c) (noting that attorneys' fees may only be awarded under Rule 11 for those "services directly and unavoidably caused" by the sanctionable conduct).

We vacate the district court's Rule 11 orders and remand for further proceedings consistent with this opinion.

NOTES AND QUESTIONS

1. Use of the words "reasonable under the circumstances" in Rule 11 codifies the previous judicial conclusion that the thoroughness of the inquiry required by Rule 11 depends in part upon the time available for investigation. Rule 11(b). The Supreme Court held under the 1983 rule, that "[a]n inquiry that is unreasonable when an attorney has months to prepare a complaint may be reasonable when he has only a few days before the statute of limitations runs." *Cooter & Gell v. Hartmarx Corp.*, 496 U.S. 384, 401–2, 110 S.Ct. 2447, 110 L.Ed.2d 359 (1990).

---

[12] For example, because the action was frivolous on its face, why would Mattel's attorneys need to spend 700 hours ($173,151.50 in fees) for the summary judgment motion and response? Although Hicks clearly complicated the proceedings through multiple filings, Mattel's theory and approach was stunningly simple and required little explication: (1) Mattel's Barbie dolls and face paint were prior copyright creations that could not infringe the after-created Claudene doll and (2) Christian was neither a contributor to nor owner of the copyright. This is not to say that Hicks' defense of the motion necessarily called for a timid response, but neither does it compel a bazooka approach.

2. Absent time pressures, what should a reasonable factual inquiry include? For example, must counsel interview the available witnesses? May counsel rely on a document reciting the state of incorporation of a party to a lease? Or, must counsel review the relevant "original source" documents that are available to the client? See, e.g., *Belleville Catering Co. v. Champaign Market Place, L.L.C.*, 350 F.3d 691 (7th Cir. 2003) (counsel's reliance on lease's erroneous description of state of incorporation does not satisfy reasonable inquiry requirement when document showing certificate of incorporation is available).

On the other hand, because Rule 11 does not require the impossible, what if the evidence to prove or disprove a claim is in an opponent's exclusive possession? Rule 11 permits a claim or answer to be based on information and belief. However, Rule 11(b)(3) requires a party to state when their factual contentions depend on an opportunity for further investigation or discovery.

Can counsel rely upon a client's statements to show a reasonable factual inquiry? In *Hadges v. Yonkers Racing Corp.*, 48 F.3d 1320, 1329–30 (2d Cir. 1995), the court stated that, in deciding whether an attorney may be sanctioned for relying on a client's statements, courts must determine whether there was "evidentiary support" corroborating factual misrepresentations. By contrast, is it unreasonable to file a paper based on the client's knowledge if the client is relying on second-hand assertions?

3. Does an attorney's inexperience in a particular area of law reduce the Rule 11 obligations? In *Zuk v. Eastern Pa. Psychiatric Inst. of the Med. College of Pa.*, 103 F.3d 294 (3d Cir. 1996), the attorney claimed that the case at bar was the first copyright case which he had handled, pointing out that a practitioner has to begin somewhere. The court responded that,

> [w]hile we are sympathetic to this argument, its thrust is more toward the nature of the sanctions to be imposed rather than to the initial decision whether sanctions should be imposed. Regrettably, the reality of appellant's weak grasp of copyright law is that it caused him to pursue a course of conduct which was not warranted by existing law and compelled the defendant to expend time and money in needless litigation.

4. When is a claim warranted by existing law per Rule 11(b)(2) (i.e., must the law clearly support the attorney's position on behalf of the client)? In *Anderson v. Smithfield Foods, Inc.*, 353 F.3d 912 (11th Cir. 2003), a group of landowners sued the world's largest hog producer and pork processor, alleging that the defendants "polluted land and water in violation of numerous laws and regulations, and lied about and profited from these environmental transgressions. Plaintiffs alleged that this conduct gives rise to liability under" the Racketeer Influenced and Corrupt Organizations Act for business practices amounting to racketeering because it constituted a pattern of money laundering and wire and mail fraud. The appellate court reversed the award of Rule 11 sanctions, noting that

there is scant on-point authority to guide the reasonable lawyer to the conclusion that, with the RICO claims . . . , he either had no reasonable chance of success or was advancing an unreasonable argument to change existing law. Though we have concluded that the . . . Amended Complaint does not state viable RICO claims, we are unable to conclude that only an unreasonable lawyer would have made these claims.

Similarly, what happens when the state of the law is unsettled or involves a case of first impression? Sanctions are unlikely to be imposed, i.e., a court is not going to conclude that the claim is unwarranted by existing law.

5. When do you know that a paper you filed is warranted by existing law? To be warranted under existing law, does an argument contained in the paper have to ultimately prevail? No, what is relevant is whether the attorney presented an objectively reasonable argument in support of the view of what the law is or should be. Rule 11 sanctions are not merited on the grounds of frivolousness merely because the court disagrees with an attorney's position on behalf of a client and rules for the opposing side.

Should a dismissal for failure to state a claim for relief automatically justify Rule 11 sanctions for filing a paper that is unwarranted under existing law? *Tahfs v. Proctor*, 316 F.3d 584 (6th Cir. 2003) found that:

> At the pleading stage in the litigation, ordinarily there is little or no evidence before the court at all, and such facts as are alleged, must be interpreted in favor of the nonmovant. While a party is bound by Rule 11 to refrain from filing a complaint "for any improper purpose," from making claims "[un]warranted by existing law," or from making "allegations and other factual contentions [without] evidentiary support," making those determinations is difficult when there is nothing before the court except the challenged complaint. . . . "Rule [11] must be read in light of concerns that it will spawn satellite litigation and chill vigorous advocacy." [*Cooter & Gill*] Rule 11 "is not intended to chill an attorney's enthusiasm or creativity in pursuing factual or legal theories." . . . While we agree that the magistrate judge's Report and Recommendation provides a forceful argument for dismissal of Tahfs's complaint pursuant to Rule 12(b)(6) for lack of factual specificity, it does not follow, therefrom, that "the claims . . . therein are [un]warranted by existing law," as the expression is used in Rule 11(b)(2). If that were so, almost any complaint dismissed under Rule 12(b)(6) would warrant the imposition of sanctions. Had the district court read Tahfs's complaint in a light most favorable to her, as it was obligated to do, we are convinced it would have seen that the filing of a federal complaint was not "unreasonable" under the circumstances. Tahf's complaint was dismissed because it failed to provide the defendants sufficient notice regarding the actors who allegedly were corrupt and their allegedly corrupt actions. A complaint alleging conspiracy, whose essential deficiency is that it

is lacking in sufficient factual detail and specificity, is not, perforce, "[un]warranted by existing law" or frivolous. A complaint does not merit sanctions under Rule 11 simply because it merits dismissal pursuant to Rule 12(b)(6).

On the other hand, is a legal position unwarranted by existing law if it is contrary to clear precedent? When the attorney knew or should have known that the position taken on behalf of a client has no chance of success under the existing case law, sanctions are likely. But where does that leave the pleader who seeks to overturn long-standing precedents on an issue? How do you argue that Rule 11 would have permitted you to attack public school segregation in 1950? Wouldn't Rule 11 have chilled your enthusiasm for pursuing a novel legal theory like desegregation?

Rule 11 permits you to argue for an extension or modification of existing law. Under what circumstance is that argument likely to be most successful? Suppose that you have raised an issue of first impression in your jurisdiction. Even if courts elsewhere have ruled against your position, it would appear unreasonable to sanction you assuming that you have made a good faith argument for a change in the law. The important question is how to resolve the apparent conflict between the duty to represent your client zealously and Rule 11's purpose of reducing frivolous claims. Can you accommodate both goals?

6. Rule 11 explicitly requires notice and an opportunity to respond to allegations of a Rule 11 violation. In addition, it contains a 21-day "safe harbor" provision. By sending a Rule 11 motion to the opposition, those attorneys and parties opposing sanctions have 21 days in which to correct or withdraw a challenged paper. Under Rule 11(c)(2) after the 21 days expire, a separate Rule 11 motion must be filed describing the specific conduct that allegedly violated the rule. Most courts require strict compliance with the safe harbor provision and deny Rule 11 motions which fail to comply. The safe harbor provision is inapplicable to the court's imposition of sanctions on its own initiative.

Before the recent amendments, the Federal Rules required an answer to be filed within 20 days of service. In *Religious Tech. Ctr. v. Gerbode*, 1994 WL 228607 (C.D. Cal. 1994), the court in fn. 6 raised the following conflict between the time within which to answer and the safe harbor provision:

> It would appear to be problematical to comply with the "safe harbor" provision in any case involving a challenge to a complaint. Even if the frivolousness is immediately apparent on the face of the pleading at the time of service, does service of a motion for sanctions under Rule 11 toll the 20-day period to answer under Rule 12(a)(1)(A)? If not, what purpose does compliance with the "safe harbor" provision serve if the complaint must be responded to before the 21-day waiting period expires? If the frivolousness is not immediately apparent and the Rule 11 motion is not made until after the complaint is dismissed, what useful purpose is served by

compliance with the "safe harbor" provision at that point? Certainly, by that juncture, it is too late for the complaint to be "withdrawn or appropriately corrected."

By extending the time period for the answer to 21 days, the recent amendments at least partially ameliorate this problem. However, issues may still arise. Do you see how?

7. Does the safe harbor provision encourage a "threat and retreat" behavior whereby a plaintiff could file a series of complaints, and then withdraws them when faced with possible Rule 11 sanctions? Dissenting from adoption of the 1993 safe harbor amendment to Rule 11, Justice Scalia expected parties to "file thoughtless, reckless, and harassing pleadings, secure in the knowledge that they have nothing to lose." 146 F.R.D. 507, 508 (1993). See Carl Tobias, "Civil Rights Plaintiffs and the Proposed Revision of Rule 11," 77 Iowa L. Rev. 1775 (1992).

8. Despite Rule 11 and the Model Rules of Professional Conduct, cases like *Ruszala* and *Christian* show that there are still attorneys and parties who file frivolous claims. Some of the legislative activity extending Rule 11 has been motivated by the perception that frivolous claims may be "strike suits." This is a term for a lawsuit that lacks merit but is filed as an attempt to extract a settlement. This strategy sometimes works because even if a case is frivolous it can be costly to defend. Hence some defendants may be willing to settle at "nuisance value" in order to avoid the cost to dispose of the case through the Civil Procedure system. In *Ruszala*, Sheriff Beary incurred the cost for his attorney to take a deposition and draft a motion for summary judgment. Did the Rule 11 sanctions reimburse all his costs? In *Christian*, Mattel claimed attorney's fees in excess of $500,000. Do you think Mattel will recover all these costs on remand? The repeated revisions of Rule 11 suggest the difficulty in reaching a balance that prevents strike suits but does not deter meritorious claims. Rather than relying on Rule 11 sanctions as a deterrent, some defendants that deal with large volumes of litigation refuse to settle any suits they deem frivolous as a way of driving up costs for the plaintiff and sending a message that deters suits filed to recover only a nuisance value.

PROBLEMS

1. Prior to filing a Rule 11 motion for sanctions against Chumbley and Associates, plaintiff Boyer sent an e-mail to Chumbley warning her that he would file a Rule 11 motion against her unless she withdrew her "obviously groundless motion to dismiss his complaint." How should Chumbley respond?

2. Defendant Chumbley responds to plaintiff Boyer's complaint by filing one document with the court, containing an answer, a motion to dismiss, and a motion for sanctions under Rule 11. How should Boyer respond?

3. After Carrell Corp.'s motion to dismiss Lerner's good faith complaint was granted for the first time for failure to state a claim for relief,

Carrell notified Lerner about its intent to seek sanctions and three weeks later moved for sanctions under Federal Rule 11. Should the court grant or deny the motion for sanctions?

4. Same as #3, except that Carrell Corp. filed its Rule 11 motion for sanctions when Lerner's identical complaint was dismissed for the third time within a ten-month period under Rule 12(b)(6), based on the current law. Should the court grant or deny the motion for sanctions?

5. The Waldman Partnership sued Davis, Inc. for breach of contract. After two years of discovery and an unsuccessful motion to dispose of the case on its merits, the parties settled the case. A month later, the judge in the case issued an order for Davis, Inc. to pay the plaintiffs more than $40,000 in attorney fees and court costs for Rule 11 violations. Was the order proper?

6. Abramson is serving as local counsel for the firm of Cross and Deason, a law partnership with forty partners and sixty associates located in another federal district. Cross is the plaintiffs' lead counsel in *The Waldman Partnership v. Davis, Inc.*, a breach of contract action. Three associates are working on the case with Cross. Cross and the three associates work on a pretrial motion to dismiss for lack of subject matter jurisdiction, and one of the associates signs it and sends it to Abramson to file it. The motion can only be termed a legally groundless motion. Assuming that defendant has followed the Rule 11 procedures, who is liable for sanctions if the court agrees that monetary sanctions are appropriate in reaction to the subject matter motion?

7. Same as #6, except that the motion is not only legally deficient. It also reflects numerous factual misstatements by the clients who were in a position to investigate and report accurately the facts supporting the motion. Can the client now be sanctioned?

8. In #6, the court is inclined to impose monetary sanctions against the attorneys, instead of other sanctions. What criteria determine when monetary sanctions are appropriate? What alternative non-monetary sanctions are available?

E. AMENDED AND SUPPLEMENTAL PLEADINGS

What is the purpose of a rule allowing pleadings to be amended? Given the relative flexibility of the federal rules, the purpose seems to be to provide a maximum opportunity for each claim to be decided on its merits rather than on procedural technicalities. Generally, Rule 15 emphasizes a permissive approach that courts are to approve amendment requests regardless of their nature. The rule also reflects the fact that the federal rules assign the pleadings a limited role of providing notice of both the nature of the pleader's claim or defense and the transaction or event that has been called into question. The purpose of the later discovery process is to develop the factual and legal issues.

Rule 15 relates to amended and supplemental pleadings. There are four sub-rules which set forth when and under what circumstances pleadings may be amended, and provide for amendments to conform to the evidence, the relation back of amendments, and the presentation of supplemental matters.

INTRODUCTORY PROBLEM

There are two Stan's Stereo Stores in Champaign-Urbana, Illinois—Stan's Stereo, Inc. (Champaign) and Stan's Stereo Corp. (Urbana). Stock in each separate corporation is owned by the same persons in the same proportion. Kelly slipped in the Champaign store while shopping for a stereo and brought suit mistakenly against Stan's Stereo Corp. (the Urbana store). Service was made upon Stan's brother, Bill, who managed the Urbana store, at Bill's home. After the statute of limitations had run, Kelly's counsel moved to amend the complaint to name Stan's Stereo, Inc. as the defendant. As the judge, what additional information do you need before ruling on Kelly's motion?

Governing Law: Rule 15.

1. AMENDING PLEADINGS WITH (OR WITHOUT) THE COURT'S PERMISSION

Rule 15(a) enables a party to assert new information that was overlooked or unknown to the pleader at the time the complaint or answer was filed. It also establishes a time period during which the pleadings may be amended automatically and by granting the court broad discretion to allow amendments to be made after that period has expired.

BEECK V. AQUASLIDE 'N' DIVE CORP.
562 F.2d 537 (8th Cir. 1977)

[This case is set out on page 1.]

NOTES AND QUESTIONS

1. While *Beeck* deals with amendment of an answer (the pleading defendant files in response to the complaint), the court's basic analysis would also apply to amendment of a complaint.

2. As indicated by Federal Rule 15(a)(1), a pleading may be amended once without leave of court (as a matter of course) within twenty-one days after it is served (Rule 15(a)(1)(A)), or if the pleading is one to which a responsive pleading is required, within twenty-one days after the responsive pleading is served (or twenty-one days following a Rule 12 motion, if one is served prior to the responsive pleading). What constitutes a responsive pleading? A Rule 12(b)(6) motion to dismiss is not a responsive pleading, according to Rule 7(a) which defines pleadings. Instead, in a single-plaintiff, single-defendant case, the only responsive pleadings will be (a) defendant's answer, (b) plaintiff's answer to any counterclaim filed by defendant, and (c)

SEC. E   AMENDED AND SUPPLEMENTAL PLEADINGS   417

if the court orders one, a reply by plaintiff. You will study answers and replies in Chapter 7.

3. What is the policy of Rule 15(a)(1)'s liberal approach to early amendments? Why does the rule permit only one amendment without the court's permission?

4. Except for amendments as a matter of course, all amendments require leave of court or consent of the adverse party. Rule 15(a)(2) provides that leave to amend shall be freely given when justice so requires. The motion to amend may be stated with some generality. For example, it could be stated "justice requires the amendment in order that the actual issues between the parties be tried" or "the amendment is necessary to clarify and simplify the issues", or "the proposed amendment was inadvertently omitted", etc.

In *Beeck*, what arguments could be made that the plaintiff would be prejudiced by allowing the amendment? What does prejudice mean in this case? Why was there no bad faith in *Beeck*? If the court had rejected the amendment, how could the defendant have defended the lawsuit?

The decision as to whether justice requires the amendment is within the court's discretion, and is liberally construed. In *Dennis v. Dillard Dept. Stores, Inc.*, 207 F.3d 523 (8th Cir. 2000), the appellate court found that the trial court had abused its discretion by denying defendant employer's motion for permission to amend its answer under Rule 15(a). The defendant employer claimed that "it inadvertently omitted the 'factor other than sex' defense [to an employee's Equal Pay Claim], and that the omission was an oversight, unrealized until Dennis pointed it out in her response to Dillard's summary judgment motion." Dillard argued that granting its motion for leave to amend would not have unfairly prejudiced Dennis. While discovery had closed when the employer sought to amend, the trial court could reopen discovery for the limited purpose of exploring the added defense. Moreover, almost three months remained until trial when the employer filed its motion to amend, and the Eighth Circuit found that the defendant did not omit the defense in bad faith.

5. Likewise, Rule 15(a)(2) allows a party to amend a pleading "with the opposing party's written consent," even after the time for amending as a matter of course has passed. If the parties consent, the usual motion procedure need not be followed. The right to amend is not subject to the court's discretion and the court must permit the amendment to be filed. See, e.g., *American States Insurance Company v. Dastar Corp.*, 318 F.3d 881 (9th Cir. 2003).

6. A court may impose conditions when granting leave to amend. The statement in Rule 15(a)(2) that the court should freely give permission when justice so requires presupposes that the court may use its discretion to impose conditions on the grant of a proposed amendment as an appropriate way of balancing the interests of the party seeking the amendment and those of the objecting party. The most common condition imposed on the amending

party is costs for other parties to assume additional preparation in order to meet the new issues or theories that are asserted in the amended pleading. The trial court also may grant a continuance to provide additional time for the opposing party to prepare for trial. On the other hand, a trial court may deny permission to amend when the amendment would cause the opposing party to bear additional costs litigating a new issue and the moving party does not offer to reimburse the nonmoving party for its expenses. See, e.g., *Campania Management Co. v. Rooks, Pitts & Poust*, 290 F.3d 843 (7th Cir. 2002).

7. There is no fixed time limit for making a motion to amend a pleading. That matter too is within the discretion of the court. What are the relevant considerations in deciding the timeliness of a motion to amend a pleading? Prejudice to the other party? Mistake or excusable neglect?

8. Rule 15 does not require that an amended pleading restate the entire original pleading to be amended. The amendment may be accomplished by service of the amendment itself, or, if leave is granted, even by interlineation or by striking a part of the pleading to be amended. However, the better way to request leave to amend under Rule 15 is to attach a copy of the amended pleading to the motion so that it becomes part of the record at that time, regardless of what action the trial court takes or fails to take on it. This ensures that the appellate courts know exactly what amendment the trial court was asked to allow. It is only with such knowledge that the trial court's decision can be reviewed.

9. A pleading that has been amended under Rule 15(a) supersedes [takes the place of] the pleading it modifies. The superseded pleading has no legal effect unless its successor pleading specifically refers to it and adopts or incorporates it by reference. Per Rule 15(a), when a complaint is amended, the defendant is entitled to amend the answer to meet the content of the new complaint.

2. AMENDMENTS TO ADD ISSUES AT TRIAL

OTNESS V. UNITED STATES
23 F.R.D. 279 (D. Alaska Terr. 1959)

KELLY, DISTRICT JUDGE.

Plaintiff brought suit against the United States of America under the Federal Tort Claims Act for damages suffered to his vessel while navigating in the Wrangell Narrows south of Petersburg, Alaska, as a result of an alleged collision with a navigation aid maintained by the United States Coast Guard. During the course of the trial evidence was introduced showing that the navigation aid, of great dimensions in size and weight, submerged and disappeared beneath the surface of the channel waters leading into Petersburg. Plaintiff in his complaint alleged that the Coast Guard was negligent in its operations to locate the submerged navigation structure, and that the Coast Guard negligently

SEC. E   AMENDED AND SUPPLEMENTAL PLEADINGS   419

issued a bulletin to mariners to the effect that dragging operations revealed that the structure was not present above the contour of the natural bottom of the Wrangell Narrows. The plaintiff further alleged that these acts of negligence of the Coast Guard proximately caused injury to the plaintiff, who collided with the submerged navigation aid while navigating in the area where the structure disappeared.

After the presentation of all testimony in the case and while the court still had the decision under advisement, plaintiff filed a motion for leave to file a second amended complaint wherein he seeks to amend his complaint under Rule 15(b) of the Federal Rules of Civil Procedure, raising the additional claim to relief based on the "willful, wanton, or reckless conduct" of the Coast Guard in the circumstances surrounding its efforts to locate the submerged structure. Before decision can be made in the case itself, this motion must be disposed of.

Rule 15(b)(2) provides that:

> When issues not raised by the pleadings are tried by express or implied consent of the parties, they shall be treated in all respects as if they had been raised in the pleadings. Such amendment of the pleadings as may be necessary to cause them to conform to the evidence and to raise these issues may be made upon motion of any party at any time, even after judgment; but failure so to amend does not affect the result of the trial of these issues . . .

The plaintiff contends that "the amendment goes to matters which have already been in proof and the defendant cannot possibly be prejudiced by this amendment, since any effort which it would make to show lack of willful, wanton or reckless care would be no different than its efforts already made to show lack of negligence on the part of the defendant." While the contention of the plaintiff may have some merit if the issues of the case were limited solely to the negligence of the defendant, the prejudicial effect of granting such a motion would be underscored in the defendant's selection of affirmative defenses. The plaintiff by his pleadings confined the issues solely to negligence, and it is to be presumed that the defendant planned his defense of ordinary care and contributory negligence in reliance on the plaintiff's complaint. If the requested amendment were allowed and the issue thereunder were now to be resolved in plaintiff's favor, defendant's affirmative defense would be of no avail, since contributory negligence is not generally regarded as a defense to wanton or willful conduct. To overcome the motion it would be necessary for the defendant to have proved willful or wanton contributory conduct by the plaintiff. However, in the trial of the case, the defendant had no duty to go further than to allege and prove ordinary care or contributory negligence as a bar to recovery by the plaintiff under the plaintiff's complaint. Since the defendant had no notice of plaintiff's intention to request an amendment, and since a different defense would be required under the amendment, which the defendant may or may not have been capable of proving, the defendant cannot be said to have had a fair opportunity to defend against the issue raised by the motion.

In filing his motion under Rule 15(b), the plaintiff has apparently assumed that the issue of willful or wanton conduct was tried by the implied consent of the parties. There is no authorization within the above rule to allow an amendment to the pleadings to conform to proof merely because evidence presented which is competent and relevant to the issue created by the pleadings may incidentally tend to prove another fact not in issue. Where proof is taken only under the claim of the complaint, there is no proper case for amendment even though the proof may prove another issue. The plaintiff gave no indication of, or intention to claim, additional grounds for relief during the course of the trial. The line of demarcation as to what evidence might go no further than proving mere negligence and that which may tend to prove willful or wanton conduct is not so clear and capable of recognition as to warrant a holding that if evidence submitted under a complaint of negligence may also tend to prove willful, wanton or reckless conduct by the defendant, the defendant impliedly consents to its introduction for that purpose if he had made no objection, even though the plaintiff has not made his additional purpose clear during the trial. No consent to the trial of the issue created by the motion has been shown.

Furthermore, this case was fully tried and the evidence was quite complete, and it appears to this court that as a matter of fact there was no evidence in the case which would indicate that there was any 'willful, wanton or reckless conduct' on the part of the Coast Guard or any of its personnel in any particular whatsoever.

It follows, therefore, that the motion of the plaintiff must be denied.

NOTES AND QUESTIONS

1. Why did the court deny the plaintiff's motion? Do you believe that the plaintiff's counsel was acting deviously in not raising the willful claim until the defendant could not respond? (A court in a bench trial can reopen the proof to hear additional evidence.) Was the issue proposed relevant to an issue already in the case? Was there any indication at trial that the plaintiff was seeking to raise a new issue?

2. Rule 15(b) provides for amendments necessary to cause the pleadings to conform to the evidence. One of the reasons for permitting such amendments is to insure that the pleadings support the judgment. Another is to take cognizance of the issues that were actually tried. The Rule goes further than authorizing amendments to conform to the evidence. It provides that if issues not raised by the pleadings are tried by express or implied consent, they are treated as if they had been raised.

During trial, when an objection to evidence is made on the ground that it is not within the issues presented by the pleadings, the court may permit amendments freely if the presentation of the merits of the action will be served and the objecting party will not be actually prejudiced or seriously disadvantaged. Under such circumstances the court is authorized to grant a continuance of the trial to enable the objecting party to meet such evidence.

PROBLEMS

1. Hillary files her complaint against Bill. Before Bill answers, Hillary files an amended complaint adding new claims and seeking an additional $10 million in damages. Why did Hillary have a right to do this?

2. Hillary files her complaint against Bill, who files a motion to dismiss. Hillary realizes that Bill is correct. Before the hearing on Bill's motion, Hillary files an amended complaint fixing the problem raised by Bill's motion (thereby mooting the motion). Why did Hillary have a right to do this?

3. Hillary files her complaint against Bill, who is served on September 15. Bill files his answer to the complaint and has it served on Hillary on October 3. His answer contains no counterclaims. On October 20, Bill files an amended answer, correcting some errors in the original answer. Why does Bill have a right to do this?

4. If Hillary in #1 or Bill in #3 had waited too long to take advantage of filing an amendment as a matter of right, what showing would either have to make to be allowed to amend?

5. Hillary sues for breach of Contract #1 and at trial introduces evidence regarding Bill's breach of both Contract #1 and Contract #2. If the trial court finds implied consent by Bill to have tried the second contract claim, how should the court treat the proof relating to the second contract?

6. Hillary sues for breach of Contract #1 and at trial introduces evidence regarding Bill's breach of both Contract #1 and Contract #2. Bill objects to introduction of evidence on the Contract #2 claim. What is the basis of the objection?

7. In #6, how should Hillary respond to Bill's objection?

3. AMENDMENTS FILED AFTER THE LIMITATIONS PERIOD HAS EXPIRED

ERWIN V. MCDERMOTT
284 F.R.D. 40 (D. Mass. 2012)

GORTON, DISTRICT JUDGE.

This case arises from the alleged use of excessive force against plaintiff Dustin Erwin outside of The Foxy Lady nightclub in Brockton, Massachusetts on the night of August 9, 2008. Currently before the Court are plaintiff's motion to amend and defendant's motions for summary judgment and to strike.

I. Background

On the evening of August 9, 2008, Erwin attended a bachelor party held in his honor at the Foxy Lady nightclub. By his own account, Erwin became intoxicated and was asked to leave. He and his friends complied and, as they reached the parking lot, were pursued by Christopher McDermott, an off-duty Brockton Police Officer working a paid security detail for the Foxy Lady nightclub. McDermott allegedly chased Erwin to the adjacent Walgreens parking lot, sprayed him with mace and then radioed for backup. Soon thereafter, Officer Darvin Anderson of the Brockton Police Department arrived on the scene with his K–9 dog officer Gomo. Erwin alleges that Anderson intentionally struck him with a police cruiser and then ordered Gomo to attack him. Erwin sustained injuries in the form of puncture wounds, scrapes and bruises for which he was later hospitalized. McDermott and Anderson then handcuffed Erwin and placed him under arrest for resisting arrest and assault and battery on a police officer. Erwin was prosecuted in state court for those crimes but found not guilty by a jury.

II. Procedural History

On July 26, 2011, Erwin filed suit in this Court against McDermott and Anderson ("the Officers"), the City of Brockton and Foxy Lady, Inc. ("The Foxy Lady Corporation"). . . .

Plaintiff named The Foxy Lady Corporation as a defendant after corporate records indicated that it 1) had offices near Brockton, Massachusetts, 2) was in the business of owning and operating nightclubs and 3) was run by Thomas Tsoumas; and an internet search revealed that 4) the Foxy Lady nightclub has locations in Brockton and Providence and 5) Tsoumas runs the Providence branch. The Complaint was served upon The Foxy Lady Corporation in August 2011 and it appears that Attorney David Berman was hired soon thereafter to represent its interests. . . .

In January 2012, Attorney Berman filed a motion for summary judgment . . . on the behalf of The Foxy Lady Corporation, alleging for the first time that Frank's of Brockton, Inc. ("Frank's of Brockton"), not The Foxy Lady Corporation, is the true owner of the Foxy Lady nightclub and the real party in interest in this case. Attorney Berman did not explain why the alleged misidentification was not raised in [an earlier] motion to dismiss.

Seeking to cure the apparent misnomer, plaintiff moved to dismiss without prejudice "Foxy Lady, Inc." and to amend the Complaint to substitute "Frank's of Brockton, Inc." Attorney Berman has filed an opposition to the motion to amend, this time on behalf of Frank's of Brockton, opposing the proposed amendment on two grounds. First, he

SEC. E AMENDED AND SUPPLEMENTAL PLEADINGS 423

argues that the proposed amendment is untimely because the deadline for amendments set by the pretrial order has passed. Second, he claims that the amendment would be futile because the statute of limitations has already run on an action against Frank's of Brockton. In response, plaintiff represents that there is good cause to amend the Complaint and submits that the amendment will relate back to the filing date of the Complaint. . . .

Attorney Berman, now apparently at the behest of The Foxy Lady Corporation, follows up . . . with a motion to strike paragraph 14 of the affidavit of Attorney Michael Harriman, an associate with Sinsheimer & Associates, the firm representing the plaintiff. Attorney Harriman filed the subject affidavit to explain the actions he took on behalf of the plaintiff to ascertain the owner of the Foxy Lady nightclub. The paragraph to which Attorney Berman objects states:

> Following these inquires and the conversations which resulted therefrom, I infer that "Frank's of Brockton, Inc." has a large role in the operation and ownership of "The Foxy Lady." I cannot, however, decipher with absolute clarity that "Frank's of Brockton, Inc." is the sole corporate entity involved in owning and operating "The Foxy Lady" at 265 N. Pearl Street.

In his motion to strike that paragraph, Attorney Berman claims that the foregoing inference is unreasonable. He goes on to claim that "Frank's of Plymouth" owns the Foxy Lady nightclub and in the next breath that "Frank's of Brockton" is the true owner.

III. Analysis

Plaintiff's motion for leave to amend presents two issues: 1) whether the Court should exercise its discretion to allow plaintiff leave to amend the Complaint and 2) if so, whether the Amended Complaint "relates back" to the filing date of the Complaint.

A. Federal Rule of Civil Procedure 15

A court "should freely give" a party leave to file an amended pleading "when justice so requires." Fed.R.Civ.P. 15(a)(2). The decision to allow leave to amend is entrusted to the discretion of the court.

An amendment adding or correcting the identity of a party against whom a claim is asserted relates back to the date of the original pleading if:

> 1) the amendment asserts a claim or defense that arose out of the conduct, transaction, or occurrence set out—or attempted to be set out—in the original pleading; and
>
> 2) within [90 days], the party to be brought in by amendment:

(i) received such notice of the action that it will not be prejudiced in defending on the merits; and

(ii) knew or should have known that the action would have been brought against it, but for a mistake concerning the proper party's identity.

See Fed.R.Civ.P. 15(c)(1)(C). Unlike the decision to allow leave to amend, which is left to the discretion of the court, relation back is mandatory if an amended pleading meets the foregoing criteria.

The "relation back" provisions expressed in Rule 15 were intended to balance a defendant's interest in repose with the systemic interest in resolving disputes on their merits. If a defendant knew or should have known that, "absent some mistake, the action would have been brought against him," relation back should be allowed. Such an interpretation of Rule 15(c)(1)(C) strikes an appropriate balance between those two interests:

> A prospective defendant who legitimately believed that the limitations period had passed without any attempt to sue him has a strong interest in repose. But repose would be a windfall for a prospective defendant who understood, or who should have understood, that he escaped suit during the limitations period only because the plaintiff misunderstood a crucial fact about his identity.

Krupski v. Costa Crociere S. p. A., 130 S.Ct. 2485, 2496 (2010).

B. Application

The criteria set forth in Rule 15(c)(1)(C) are met here. First, the Amended Complaint adds no new claims or defenses; the sole change is to the name and identity of the owner of the Foxy Lady nightclub. Second, the only prejudice Frank's of Brockton would suffer from amendment is the inability to benefit from its deceptive litigation strategy. A defendant who obscures its identity to take advantage of a statute of limitation forfeits any interest he might have had in repose. Finally, Frank's of Brockton has been on notice of this litigation from the outset. In the motion to dismiss, Attorney Berman argued that the owner of the nightclub was not vicariously liable for the actions of the Officers. If Attorney Berman was representing the interests of an unaffiliated entity named "Foxy Lady, Inc.", he would have had no reason to address the merits of the dispute. It would have been sufficient for him to say, "you sued the wrong company." In fact, had Attorney Berman actually represented The Foxy Lady Corporation, he would have done his client a disservice in failing to raise the misnomer argument in the motion to dismiss. To the contrary, it is clear that Attorney Berman has been representing Frank's of Brockton all along and it is disingenuous if not fraudulent of him to suggest otherwise.

Contrary to Attorney Berman's apparent belief,

[a] suit at law is not a children's game, but a serious effort on the part of adult human beings to administer justice; and the purpose of process is to bring parties into court. If it names them in such terms that every intelligent person understands who is meant, as is the case here, it has fulfilled its purpose.

United States v. A.H. Fischer Lumber Co., 162 F.2d 872, 873 (4th Cir.1947). Plaintiff's naming of The Foxy Lady Corporation as a defendant was a good-faith effort to provide notice to the owner of the Foxy Lady nightclub of the pendency of this action. Plaintiff apparently named the wrong entity but accomplished his purpose nevertheless. Soon after the service of the Complaint, Attorney Berman was retained to represent the interests of the Foxy Lady nightclub. He has been doing so overzealously ever since.

The circumstances indicate that Attorney Berman knew from the beginning that Frank's of Brockton was the true owner of the nightclub but obscured that fact from the Court and the plaintiff until the statute of limitations had run. Plaintiff's counsel twice requested in writing that the defendant disclose the real party in interest. Attorney Berman demurred. When plaintiff's counsel filed an affidavit documenting its efforts to ascertain the owner of the Foxy Lady nightclub, Attorney Berman, apparently under the misapprehension that continued obfuscation would allow his client to avoid liability, responded with a frivolous motion to strike.

Under the circumstances, this Court will exercise its discretion to allow the plaintiff leave to file an Amended Complaint substituting "Frank's of Brockton, Inc." for "Foxy Lady, Inc." as the real party in interest. The Amended Complaint will relate back to the filing date of the Complaint, as provided for by Fed.R.Civ.P. 15(c)(1)(C). Attorney Berman and the true owner of the Foxy Lady nightclub, whoever it may be, are forewarned that their unscrupulous tactics are counterproductive and, if continued, will result in the imposition of sanctions and/or reference to the Massachusetts Board of Bar Overseers. . . .

NOTES AND QUESTIONS

1. *Erwin* deals with two separate issues governed by Rule 15: (a) whether the amendment should be allowed in the first place (which you studied earlier in this Chapter), and (b) whether the amendment should relate back. Be very careful not to conflate these two separate issues. An amendment does not necessarily relate back merely because it is an amendment of right, or allowed by the court. Similarly, if the time for amending as of right has expired, the court may deny an amendment even if it would otherwise have related back.

As a practical matter, however, there is some relationship between the two issues. If court permission is required for an amendment, a court is unlikely to grant permission to amend to change the defendant if there is a statute of limitations problem and the amendment would not relate back. Allowing the amendment in such a case would be an exercise in futility.

2. Relation back is a legal fiction. If an amendment can be said to "relate back," it is treated as if it were filed along with the original pleading even though it was actually filed after the limitations period.

3. Rule 15(c)(1)(A) provides that if the statute of limitations governing a claim for relief allows relation back of amended pleadings, relation back is permitted. This provision ensures that the more restrictive language of Rule 15 does not override statutes of limitations that themselves specifically allow relation back. Rule 15(c)(1)(A) defers to a statute of limitations only when it is more generous on relation back, but it is inapplicable if the statute is *more* restrictive. When that happens, Rule 15(c)(1)(B) or 15(c)(1)(C) governs whether an amended pleading relates back.

4. Where there is no statute allowing amendment, relation back cases fall into two basic categories. In the first, the claimant wants to add a claim against an *existing* party. In the second, the claimant wants to add a *new* party (or substitute a new party for an existing party). The standard applicable to the two situations is not exactly the same. Adding new claims is governed by Rule 15(c)(1)(B), which only requires the amended claim to arise from the same transaction or occurrence as the original claim or claims. Amendments adding or changing a party must meet not only this requirement, but also the additional standards established by subsection (C).

Do you see why *Erwin* involved a change in parties, and plaintiff accordingly had to satisfy parts (B) and (C)?

5. Rule 15(c)(1)(C), dealing with amendments adding or changing parties, sets out two requirements. First, the new party must have received notice of the action within 90 days of the date that action was filed (the "period provided by Rule 4(m)" is ordinarily 90 days). In addition, the defendant must either have known, or should have known, also within that 90-day period that but for a mistake concerning the identity of the proper party, it would have been named in the action.

6. Under Rule 15(c)(1)(C), the notice received by the newly named party must ensure that no prejudice will result in presenting a defense on the merits. The focus of the prejudice requirement is on the proposed defendant's ability to obtain sufficient evidence that he may properly prepare his case to defendant against the plaintiff's allegations. The case law is split about whether the notice received by the party to be added may be formal or informal.

7. Suppose plaintiff knows of a potential defendant, but initially elects not to join that defendant to its suit. If plaintiff later changes its mind, would an amendment adding that defendant relate back (assuming the notice and knowledge requirements of Rule 15(c) are satisfied)? In *Nelson v. Adams*

USA, Inc., 529 U.S. 460, 120 S.Ct. 1579, 146 L.Ed.2d 530 (2000), the Court held the amendment would not relate back because plaintiff had not made a "mistake" concerning the defendant's identity.

What if plaintiff has no way to know the identity of one or more of the people who caused him harm? Is relation back available once plaintiff learns who they are? See, e.g., *Garrett v. Fleming*, 362 F.3d 692 (10th Cir. 2004) (lack of knowledge is not a mistake).

4. SUPPLEMENTAL PLEADINGS

STEWART V. SHELBY TISSUE, INC.
189 F.R.D. 357 (W.D. Tenn. 1999)

DONALD, DISTRICT JUDGE.

Before the court is the plaintiff's, Dennis Stewart (hereinafter "Stewart"), motion for leave to file counts VII and VIII of his First Amended Verified Complaint. The defendants, Shelby Tissue, Inc. (hereinafter "Shelby") and General Electric Capital Corporation (hereinafter "GE") have filed a joint response opposing the motion.

Stewart was employed by Shelby and its parent, GE, starting in November of 1997, as Chief Executive Officer. A contract of employment was entered into between the parties. In November of 1998, apparently disagreements started to arise between the parties, resulting in Stewart's demotion to Sales Manager. Stewart resigned from Shelby/GE on January 8, 1999. Subsequently, he began work with Kruger, Inc., which, at some point in time, became associated with Global Tissue, LLC. On January 8, 1999, Stewart filed this complaint.

On or about January 22, 1999, Shelby/GE sent a letter to Kruger concerning Stewart claiming that he could not compete with Shelby based upon an alleged employment agreement. Further, Shelby/GE wrote Stewart and advised him he was in violation of that alleged employment agreement. Stewart was terminated from Kruger/Global Tissue in March 1999. Stewart alleges that Shelby/GE's efforts resulted in his termination from Kruger/Global Tissue.

On April 26, 1999, Stewart filed his First Amended Verified Complaint. This complaint included Count VII, alleging unlawful inducement of breach of contract, and Count VIII, alleging tortious interference with contractual relations. At the time Stewart filed his First Amended Verified Complaint, neither Shelby nor GE had filed an answer. Both of these counts are based on the actions of Shelby/GE subsequent to Stewart's initial filing of his complaint.

On May 6, 1999, Stewart filed a Motion for Leave to File Counts VII and VIII. Shelby/GE have filed a response in opposition.

Fed.R.Civ.P. 15 permits a party to either amend or supplement a pleading. There are two fundamental purposes for permitting a party to amend or supplement a pleading. The first is the policy of deciding a complaint on its merits rather than dismissing it on technical reasons. The second is that pleadings, in the federal system, generally serve the limited purpose of notice to the opposing party.

[The court's discussion of amendment principles under Rule 15(a) and 15(c) is omitted.]

Amendment of a pleading only applies concerning facts and circumstances which occurred prior to the date of filing of the original complaint. For transactions, occurrences or events arising after the date of filing a complaint, a supplemental pleading must be filed. Thus, a supplemental pleading may include new facts, new claims, new defenses, and new parties. Supplemental pleadings may be used to bring in additional parties when the subsequent events alleged in the new pleadings make it necessary. However, a supplemental pleading will only be allowed upon reasonable notice and terms that are just.

The granting of a motion to file a supplemental pleading is within the discretion of the trial court. Factors such as undue delay, trial inconvenience, and prejudice to the parties should be considered when evaluating a motion to file a supplemental pleading. Even if the original pleading is defective, the court may permit a supplemental pleading. However, as a general rule, applications for leave to file a supplemental pleading are normally granted.

Like motions to amend under Fed.R.Civ.P. 15(a), motions to supplement under Fed.R.Civ.P. 15(d) must be presented within a reasonable period of time. See *McHenry v. Ford Motor Co.*, 269 F.2d 18, 24 (6th Cir.1959) (denying a motion to amend which was brought four years after the commencement of the case). Generally, they can be brought at any time the action is before the trial court.

Although Fed.R.Civ.P. 15 does not provide for the application of the "relation back" provision under Fed.R.Civ.P. 15(c) to Fed.R.Civ.P. 15(d), the courts have generally recognized that it does apply. Thus, there is protection for supplemental pleadings against responses claiming statutes of limitations.

In his brief, Stewart claims that the factual bases for Counts VII and VIII are of a continuing nature since the filing of his initial complaint and, as such, amendment of his complaint concerning these two counts should fall within the scope of Fed.R.Civ.P. 15(a). It is evident from the record that the factual bases for these claims, unlawful inducement of breach of contract and tortious interference with contractual relations, only arose after the filing of the initial complaint. Thus, Fed.R.Civ.P. 15(d) applies.

Stewart acknowledges in his motion that Fed.R.Civ.P. 15(d) may apply and argues for leave to file a supplemental pleading for the two claims in question, after the fact. In support, Stewart claims that Shelby/GE will not be prejudiced by the granting of such leave and that because of the early filing of this request to file a supplemental pleading, there will be no undue delay or inconvenience. Further, Stewart argues that these two additional counts involve a common nucleus of facts with the other claims which would promote the speedy and economic disposition of the entire controversy. Stewart's arguments have merit.

In response, Shelby/GE argues that Stewart is actually bringing these additional claims to protract the litigation and complicate the defense. Shelby/GE, however, presents precious little in support of these arguments. Shelby/GE does not refer to any evidence or facts which would support the contention that Stewart is attempting to protract the litigation or complicate the defense. Indeed, a brief review of Stewart's allegations concerning Shelby/GE's activities since Stewart filed his original complaint indicates that his claim may very well have merit.

Shelby/GE also argues that because Stewart's claim is without merit, as discussed in Shelby/GE's motion to dismiss filed March 26, 1999, Stewart should not be permitted to file a supplemental pleading. However, Shelby/GE's motion was filed well before Stewart's First Amended Verified Complaint and the motion does not directly address Counts VII and VIII. Further, this court has already addressed Shelby/GE's motion to dismiss by order dated June 9, 1999, and found that the majority of the claims raised in Stewart's complaint should not be dismissed. Thus, this argument of Shelby/GE is also without merit.

The court is not unmindful of the fact that Stewart has filed his supplemental pleading before asking the court's leave, in violation of Fed.R.Civ.P. 15(d). However, the court finds that Shelby/GE had reasonably timely notice of the facts and circumstances underlying the supplemental pleading and that no prejudice will result.

Shelby/GE has not demonstrated that any undue delay, trial inconvenience, or prejudice would result if Stewart's motion was granted. Further, not granting Stewart's motion would require him to file a separate action, which would be a waste of judicial resources. Thus, the court finds that the motion should be granted.

NOTES AND QUESTIONS

1. Rule 15(d) allows a supplemental pleading to set forth transactions or events that have occurred *since* the filing of the original pleading, thereby bringing the case up to date. The supplemental pleading may set forth new facts in order to update the earlier pleading or change the amount or nature of the relief sought in the original pleading.

2. As *Stewart* indicates, amended and supplemental pleadings differ. Amended pleadings relate to matters that occurred prior to the filing of the original pleading and replace them entirely. A supplemental pleading relates to events that have occurred subsequent to the pleading to be altered. The discretion exercised by the court in deciding to grant leave to file a supplemental pleading is similar to that applied in passing on a motion to amend. Unlike an amendment pursuant to Rule 15(a), a supplemental pleading is never allowed as a matter of right, but only by leave of court.

3. Why did Stewart believe that Counts VII and VIII could be filed as amendments to the original complaint? Did Stewart's counsel err by filing the First Amended Verified Complaint without obtaining the court's permission?

4. As stated previously, leave of court is required before filing a supplemental pleading. If a supplemental pleading is filed without obtaining a court order, the opposing party may file a Rule 12(f) motion to strike. Before ruling on the motion to strike the court determines if any prejudice has occurred. If there is none, the court orders the supplemental pleading filed as though a proper petition for leave had been filed.

Exercise

For the state a) where you intend to practice after graduation, b) where your law school is located, and/or c) your professor assigns, go to that state's annotated rules and research the procedural rules for amending and supplementing pleadings. Based on your research, print the portion of the rules and bring them to class for discussion. In addition, answer the following questions.

1. Identify whether, and if so under what circumstances, the following types of amendments are recognized in the rules:

a. Amendments "as a matter of course," which do not require the court's approval;

b. Amendments with consent of the court;

c. Amendments conforming to the evidence at trial, or tried by express or implied consent; and

d. Amendments which are filed after the limitations period has expired, but are allowed to relate back.

2. Identify whether, and if so when, supplemental pleadings are permitted.

Chapter 7

Responding to Claims

■ ■ ■

A. DISMISSALS

Introductory Problem

Alpha and Beta bring a complex antitrust claim against MegaCorp. Following discovery, Alpha becomes concerned about the bills for attorney's fees and for court costs that he has incurred. He concludes that by the end of trial the cost of the litigation would approach the damages he seeks from MegaCorp. Alpha decides he needs to move on with his personal and business life, because there is no guarantee he will prevail at trial. Meanwhile, Beta, who had incurred the same bills as Alpha, has not been able to pay her share of the attorney's fees. As a result, plaintiffs' counsel has stopped preparing for trial and done nothing to pursue the case for eight months.

Two motions are filed in the case on the same day. First, against the advice of his counsel and his co-plaintiff Beta, Alpha voluntarily dismisses his complaint against MegaCorp. Second, sensing that plaintiffs had overextended themselves financially in the case, MegaCorp moves to dismiss the case because plaintiffs seemed to have lost their nerve to prosecute their claim.

Is either Alpha or MegaCorp entitled to relief from the trial court?

Governing Rule: Rule 41(a)–(b)

The Federal Rules control the procedure for and the effects of dismissals. Rule 41(a) deals with voluntary dismissals, which are essentially a plaintiff's remedy. For example, if a plaintiff decides that, upon further reflection, she does not want her claim to go forward, she may have the case dismissed by the trial court. Rule 41(b) concerns involuntary dismissals, which constitute a defendant's remedy. The involuntary dismissal may occur as a result of plaintiff's failure to comply with rules like Rule 12(b)(6) or a failure to move the case at a pace satisfactory to the court.

1. VOLUNTARY DISMISSALS

MARQUES V. FEDERAL RESERVE BANK OF CHICAGO
286 F.3d 1014 (7th Cir. 2002)

POSNER, CIRCUIT JUDGE.

The plaintiffs brought suit against the Federal Reserve Bank of Chicago and the Federal Deposit Insurance Corporation, plus the shareholders of the federal reserve bank (the other national banks in the bank's federal reserve district), which are individually liable for the bank's debts "to the extent of the amount of their subscriptions to [the bank's] stock at the par value thereof in addition to the amount subscribed." 12 U.S.C. § 502. The plaintiffs claim to be the agents for the owners of $25 billion in bearer bonds that the bank had issued back in 1934 in exchange for 1665 metric tons of gold. They want the bank ordered to redeem the bonds for face value plus simple interest at 4 percent since 1934 (although the bonds matured in 1965); the total amount of money they are seeking is thus close to $100 billion.

The suit is preposterous. There is no record of any such bond issue, and as the national debt of the United States was only $28 billion in 1934, as a year later the entire stock of gold owned by the United States had a value of only $9 billion, and as no securities issue by a U.S. government entity exceeded $100 million before 1940, the claim that in 1934 a federal reserve bank issued bonds that virtually doubled the national debt and added $25 billion in gold to the government's gold holdings can only cause one to laugh. What is more (not that more is needed), although the price at which the government bought gold was fixed at $35 an ounce effective at the beginning of that year, the plaintiffs are claiming that the federal reserve bank bought gold from their predecessors at a price of $467.02 an ounce. The plaintiffs further undermine their case by arguing that there is an international conspiracy to deny the validity of these bonds, a conspiracy pursuant to which the plaintiffs' documents expert, who certified the genuineness of the bonds (in an unsworn and evasive report), has been repeatedly arrested and then released without charges being filed.

The bank's lawyer told us without being contradicted that the Department of Justice has declined to prosecute the persons involved in the fraud because no one could possibly be deceived by such obvious nonsense. We are puzzled by this suggestion. The Treasury has established a Website warning the public against the class of frauds (called "Morgenthaus," after Henry Morgenthau, Jr., the Secretary of the Treasury in 1934) of which the bond issue alleged in this suit is one (the others also involve supposed $25 billion bond issues). See http://www.publicdebt.treas.gov/cc/ccphony3.htm. There is no ceiling on gullibility.

Mr. Portman, the plaintiff who argued the appeal pro se, is one of the deceived—if he is not one of the deceivers, another and perhaps more plausible possibility, Portman having recently submitted a demand to the Federal Reserve Bank of Cleveland that it pay him $125 billion to redeem a similar set of fictitious 1934 vintage "Federal Reserve Bonds." We are sending this opinion to the Justice Department for whatever further consideration the Department may wish to give the fraud.

... The plaintiffs attempted to dismiss their suit voluntarily under Fed.R.Civ.P. 41(a)(1). Had they succeeded in their attempt, the dismissal would have been without prejudice, and so they could reinstate the suit without facing the bar of res judicata. They can't do that if the judgment granting the bank's motion for summary judgment—a judgment on the merits and therefore with prejudice—stands.

The reason they give for having wanted to dismiss their suit is, naturally, preposterous—that they were in serious negotiations in Spain with the U.S. Government and hoped that the government would acknowledge the legitimacy of their claim so that they could sell the bonds to Russia. But one doesn't need a good reason, or even a sane or any reason, to dismiss a suit voluntarily. The right is absolute, as Rule 41(a)(1) and the cases interpreting it make clear, until, as the rule states, the defendant serves an answer or a motion for summary judgment. The plaintiffs filed their notice of voluntary dismissal, and the bank served a motion to dismiss the suit under Rule 12(b)(6), on the same day. A motion under Rule 12(b)(6) becomes a motion for summary judgment when the defendant attaches materials outside the complaint, as the bank did, and the court "actually considers" some or all of those materials. But the judge did not convert the bank's motion to a motion for summary judgment until later.

And anyway we do not know which document, the plaintiffs' notice of voluntary dismissal or the defendant's motion to dismiss, came first. The plaintiffs argue that the bank acknowledged in the district court that the notice of voluntary dismissal was filed before the motion to dismiss was served, but the only record of this acknowledgment is a transcript that the parties neglected to make a part of the appellate record. However, the district judge, rather than make a finding on which document came first, appears to have believed that as long as they were on the same day, it didn't matter. (It is unquestioned that the plaintiffs did succeed in dismissing the FDIC as a defendant under Rule 41(a)(1), and it is not a party to this appeal.) We cannot find an appellate case on who has the burden of proving the sequence of the submissions, but *Keal v. Monarch Life Ins. Co.*, 126 F.R.D. 567 (D.Kan.1989), places the burden on the defendant, sensibly, as it seems to us, since it is the defendant that is asserting the right to prevent the plaintiff from dismissing the suit.

... There is ... considerable and unchallenged case authority (including decisions by this court) that a judgment on the merits that is entered after the plaintiff has filed a proper Rule 41(a)(1) notice of dismissal is indeed void. . . .

We are therefore compelled to reverse the judgment and direct the dismissal of the suit, without prejudice, under Rule 41(a)(1). Should the plaintiffs attempt to bring a new suit similar to the one they are dismissing, namely a fraudulent and possibly a criminal suit, they will be subject to appropriate sanctions. Reversed.

NOTES AND QUESTIONS

1. Federal Rule 41(a) addresses the circumstances in which a plaintiff can voluntarily dismiss a claim prior to adjudication. The purpose of the rule is to give the plaintiff the right to take a case out of court if no other party will be prejudiced by the dismissal. Why *should* a plaintiff be allowed to dismiss her claim before it is resolved on the merits? Why *would* a plaintiff voluntarily dismiss her own case? One possibility may be that the plaintiff has identified a more convenient forum, but why did that not occur to the plaintiff when she first filed her claim? Can you think of other reasons?

2. Rule 41(a)(1) provides two methods by which a plaintiff has an "absolute right" to dismiss a claim without having to obtain the consent of the trial court. First, prior to service of an answer or a motion for summary judgment, a plaintiff by her own unilateral act can dismiss her claim merely by filing a notice (not a motion, which invites a response by the opposing side) that informs the court and all other parties that she is dismissing her claim. Filing the notice itself effects dismissal, without regard to the effort already expended by the court and/or the defendant on the case. See *American Soccer Co., Inc. v. Score First Enterprises*, 187 F.3d 1108 (9th Cir. 1999).

3. What is the effect of a voluntary dismissal by notice? A corollary point to the *Marques* holding is that once a notice of dismissal is filed, the trial court loses jurisdiction over the case. See, e.g., *Commercial Space Management Co., Inc. v. The Boeing Co., Inc.*, 193 F.3d 1074 (9th Cir. 1999). Filing the notice:

> ... closes the file. There is nothing the defendant can do to fan the ashes of that action into life and the court has no role to play. This is a matter of right running to the plaintiff and may not be extinguished or circumscribed by adversary or court. There is not even a perfunctory order of court closing the file. Its alpha and omega was the doing of the plaintiff alone. He suffers no impairment beyond his fee for filing.

American Cyanamid Co. v. McGhee, 317 F.2d 295 (5th Cir.1963).

4. The notice rule is explicitly subject to the provision of Rule 23(e), whereby a plaintiff cannot voluntarily dismiss a class action by this notice procedure. What is the purpose of that provision? What effect would a

voluntary dismissal have on the absent members of a class that has already been certified by the court? Courts commonly are willing to approve class action dismissals under Rule 23(e) that have been settled between the parties.

5. Unilateral dismissals by the plaintiff are subject to the so-called "Two Dismissal Rule." The first voluntary dismissal of a claim is without prejudice to bringing the claim again. However, as you read in Rule 41(a)(1), a notice dismissal operates as an adjudication on the merits when the plaintiff already had dismissed the claim (with or without the consent of the court) in any state or federal court. The effect of the "Two Dismissal Rule" is that when the plaintiff tries to file the claim a *third* time, the defendant can refer to Rule 41(a)(1)(B) to support his assertion that the third filing is precluded.

6. The second type of voluntary dismissal has no time restriction. Under Rule 41(a)(1)(ii), a case may be dismissed *at any time* by a signed agreement of all the parties. Dismissals by stipulation are presumed to be without prejudice unless they specify otherwise.

7. Alex Attorney, who represents Dora Defendant, is drafting a settlement agreement based on a successful negotiation with Clara Counsel, who represents Patrick Plaintiff. What should Alex include in the draft about dismissing the suit Patrick filed against Dora? Would a voluntary dismissal without prejudice under Rule 41(a) be sufficient from Dora's perspective? How can Patrick be sure that Dora will fulfill her obligations under the settlement agreement if the case is dismissed?

Under Rule 41(a)(2) if a party cannot dismiss unilaterally or with the consent of the opposing party, a plaintiff must file a motion to obtain the court's consent to dismiss. Whether a trial court grants or denies the motion is within the court's discretion, and some courts have suggested relevant factors for the exercise of that discretion. In addition, a dismissal granted by the court is without prejudice to the case being filed again.

HINFIN REALTY CORP. v. PITTSTON CO.
206 F.R.D. 350 (E.D.N.Y. 2002)

SPATT, JUDGE.

[Landowners brought a claim to recover the costs of environmental cleanup. During discovery, the landowners moved to voluntarily dismiss action without prejudice and the defendant opposed the motion.]

The Second Circuit has delineated a number of factors that courts should consider when determining whether a defendant will be prejudiced by a voluntary dismissal. See *Zagano v. Fordham Univ.*, 900 F.2d 12 (2d Cir. 1990). These factors include: (1) the plaintiff's diligence in bringing the motion; (2) any "undue vexatiousness" on the plaintiff's part; (3) the extent to which the suit has progressed, including the defendant's efforts and expense in preparation for trial; (4) the duplicative expense of relitigation; and (5) the adequacy of the plaintiff's explanation for a need to dismiss.

The Court finds that the plaintiffs were diligent in bringing their motion to dismiss the action without prejudice because they filed it immediately after the events that led to their decision not to pursue the action at this time. The complaint was initially filed on July 24, 2000, but no proceedings occurred during the remainder of that year. The plaintiffs filed their amended complaint on February 1, 2001, and Judge Orenstein held an initial conference four days later. The plaintiffs litigated the action throughout 2001, responding to Pittston's motion to stay the proceeding and to Pittston's discovery demands.

In early January 2002, the plaintiffs determined that they no longer wished to proceed with the action. First, they had begun responding to Pittston's discovery demands and realized that they wished to conserve their limited finances rather than pursue this action. In addition, Donald Death, Sr., had fallen ill, his prognosis was not good, and he was the individual who knew the most about the history of the premises, which goes back many years. In this kind of environmental case, the so-called "ancient" history is extremely important in determining the source of pollution. Therefore, in a letter dated January 11, 2002, the plaintiffs informed the Court that they wished to withdraw their opposition to the defendant's motion to stay the proceedings because the defendant had presented them with documentary evidence showing that Pittston was the incorrect defendant. The plaintiffs also advised the Court that they had asked Pittston to stipulate to a dismissal without prejudice so that the plaintiffs could investigate whether Pittston was the proper defendant, but Pittston declined to consent to the dismissal.

Had the plaintiffs prosecuted this case more vigorously, they might have reached this conclusion earlier in the action. Nevertheless, the Court finds that as soon as the plaintiffs made the decision to dismiss the action without prejudice, they informed Pittston. In addition, immediately after Pittston declined to consent to the withdrawal, the plaintiffs' withdrew their opposition to Pittston's motion to stay the action. When that tactic failed to halt the proceedings, the plaintiffs promptly filed the present motion. Accordingly, the Court finds that the plaintiffs were diligent in moving to dismiss the action without prejudice, and thus, the first *Zagano* factor weighs in their favor.

In addition, the Court finds no evidence of vexatiousness on the part of the plaintiff. Although the plaintiff could have pursued the action with more vigor, there is no evidence to suggest that the case was brought to harass the defendant. To the contrary, the plaintiffs have made few, if any, requests of the defendant after filing this lawsuit. Therefore, the Court finds that this factor also weighs in favor of granting the plaintiffs' motion.

The Court finds that the third *Zagano* factor, the extent to which the suit has progressed, is neutral. The fact that the case is approximately 21-months old weighs against granting the motion to dismiss without prejudice. However, when the plaintiffs first asked Pittston to agree to a dismissal without prejudice in January 2002, virtually no discovery had been conducted. Indeed, in an order dated November 2, 2001, Judge Orenstein stated, "Little or no discovery done." In the two months following that order, Pittston served extensive interrogatories, a notice to admit 188 facts, and a request for documents. On the other hand, the plaintiffs have not made any discovery requests. Importantly, as of the date of this order, no depositions have been conducted. Further, the Court notes that the defendant chose not to move to dismiss the case, and neither party has moved for summary judgment. In addition, a trial date has not been set. Thus, in light of the fact that the case is now 21-months old, but little action has been taken, the Court finds the third *Zagano* factor to be neutral.

In their memorandum in opposition, Pittston claims that absent the plaintiffs' conduct, the case would be ready for summary disposition. The Court finds this argument unpersuasive in light of the fact that Pittston seeks to file a third-party action, which would require additional trial preparation. Accordingly, the defendants' argument does not alter the Court's conclusion that the third *Zagano* factor is neutral.

Pittston contends that if it is forced to relitigate this case, it faces the prospect of duplicative expenses. The defendant states that it has spent significant sums propounding and compelling discovery in this case and avers that if the plaintiffs re-file the lawsuit, Pittston will be required to "re-answer the complaint, re-exchange Rule 26(a) disclosures, re-retain its environmental experts, attend status hearings, and re-issue discovery." If the plaintiffs choose to file another lawsuit against Pittston, the grounds likely will be the same, and much of the work already done by Pittston will be easy to duplicate. Certainly, Pittston can use some of the material discovered and the legal work already done, if the case is renewed in the future. Further, this is not a case in which substantial discovery has been conducted, and the Court does not perceive a large amount of duplicative expenditures. As such, the fourth *Zagano* factor does not weigh against dismissal without prejudice.

The Court finds that the explanations for the plaintiffs' application are sufficient to support the motion. Donald Death, Jr., the president of the plaintiff corporations, needs time to settle his late father's affairs. He also requires time to review the companies' documents, some of which are over 40 years old. In addition, the plaintiffs' environmental consultant must devise a remediation plan to be approved by the DEC. Donald Death, Jr., wishes to gather all of this relevant information before deciding whether to recoup the cost of remediation through litigation. While he investigates this matter, he does not want to spend additional money to continue an action that he might find to be unnecessary. In doing so, he is sparing the defendants from expending additional monies in the defense of this lawsuit. The plaintiffs have limited assets and, apparently, wish to spend the money they have remediating their land, rather than litigating this matter.

Economic concerns, such as those raised by the plaintiff, almost always dictate the course of litigation, and this case is no exception. The Court is not persuaded by Pittston's argument that the plaintiffs' motion is an attempt to avoid the discovery cutoff date. Accordingly, the Court finds that the plaintiffs' explanation for their request weighs heavily in favor of dismissing this action without prejudice.

Thus, an application of the *Zagano* factors leads the Court to conclude that the plaintiffs' motion to dismiss the action without prejudice should be granted. However, Pittston argues that it will suffer prejudice if the plaintiffs are permitted to refile this case at a later date because the witnesses will die, such as Donald Death, Sr., for example, memories will continue to fade, and the land may be sold. The defendant is not the only party who may suffer the consequences of the passage of time. The memories of witnesses for both sides may fade and the witnesses for both sides might become unavailable. Indeed, the unavailability of Donald Death, Sr., who was an important witness for the plaintiffs, is a main reason that the plaintiffs seek to discontinue this action. As both parties could suffer due to the passage of time, the Court finds that the defendant's argument against dismissing the action is not determinative. Indeed, the prospect of "starting a litigation all over again does not constitute legal prejudice." *D'Alto v. Dahon Cal., Inc.*, 100 F.3d 281 (2d Cir. 1996). As such, the Court grants the plaintiffs' motion to dismiss the action without prejudice.

However, this does not end the inquiry. Pittston asks the Court to condition the dismissal upon an award of its costs, including attorney's fees, in the amount of $135,000. Where a plaintiff successfully dismisses a suit without prejudice under Rule 41(a)(2), courts often grant the defendant an award of costs or fees. See *Colombrito v. Kelly*, 764 F.2d 122, 133 (2d Cir.1985) ("Fee awards are often made when a plaintiff dismisses a suit without prejudice."). "The purpose of such awards is generally to reimburse the defendant for the litigation costs incurred, in view of the risk (often the certainty) faced by the defendant that the same suit will be refiled and will impose duplicative expenses upon him." *Colombrito*, 764 F.2d at 133. By contrast, courts rarely award fees and costs when an action is dismissed voluntarily with prejudice.

Applying these guidelines, the Court must seriously consider the application to award reasonable attorney's fees and costs to the defendant. Of course, if the plaintiffs were to agree to dismiss the action with prejudice, the Court would deny the defendant's motion for attorney's fees and costs because the risk of duplicative expenses will be moot. However, even if the Court were to grant this application, Pittston has not submitted billing time sheets or affidavits in support of its claim that it has incurred over $135,000 in attorney's fees and costs defending this suit since July 24, 2000. In addition, the plaintiffs have not had an opportunity to respond to a detailed accounting of Pittston's claim. Accordingly, the Court denies the defendant's motion for attorney's fees and costs, without prejudice and with leave to renew with the proper documentation and in accordance with the Court's Individual Rules.

By making this decision, the Court is not indicating that it has, as yet, decided to grant this application for attorney's fees and costs. Indeed, if the plaintiffs submit a notice to the Court, within ten days of the date of this decision, indicating that they are dismissing the action with prejudice, the Court will deny an application for attorney's fees and costs, because Pittston will no longer bear the risk of duplicative litigation and expense. However, if the plaintiffs decide not to submit a notice indicating that they are dismissing the action with prejudice, the defendant is permitted to file an application for attorney's fees and costs and is instructed to submit the appropriate documentation in support of its application. The Court notes that with reasonable certainty, it will reduce the defendant's fee application by the amount of work the defendant will be able to use in a subsequent litigation. . . .

NOTES AND QUESTIONS

1. Can you explain the meaning of each *Zagano* factor and how each contributes to the overall exercise of the court's discretion? In circuits that do not follow *Zagano*, a court typically will grant a Rule 41(a)(2) motion for voluntary dismissal unless the defendant can show that the dismissal will result in some legal prejudice to him other than the prospect of a second lawsuit. The purpose of requiring a court order to dismiss is to prevent voluntary dismissals which unfairly affect the opposing party. Can you explain how examining a list of factors is preferable to deciding merely whether the defendant will experience prejudice from the dismissal?

2. Courts cannot set conditions on Rule 41(a)(1) dismissals by notice or stipulation. For dismissals by notice by contrast, Rule 41(a)(2) allows the court to condition dismissal "on terms that the court considers proper." What is the purpose of imposing such conditions? In *Hinfin Realty*, the defendant sought payment of its attorney's fees and costs as a condition for the dismissal. What are some other conditions that could be attached to a dismissal? As you might expect, the plaintiff can decline the dismissal if it is dissatisfied with the conditions imposed by the court. If a plaintiff accepts a

dismissal but fails to meet the condition, the court's order of dismissal may be modified so that the claim is dismissed "with prejudice."

3. What happens to a defendant's counterclaim after the plaintiff seeks voluntary dismissal of her claim? The second sentence of Rule 41(a)(2) precludes the court from dismissing the plaintiff's claim unless the defendant's counterclaim can remain pending for independent adjudication. By itself, a compulsory counterclaim may or may not have an independent basis for subject matter jurisdiction. If it does have an independent basis, dismissal of the plaintiff's claim has no effect on the counterclaim's continued viability. If it does not have an independent basis, it is likely the court is hearing the compulsory counterclaim under its supplemental jurisdiction. When the dismissal occurs, the trial court has to decide whether it wants to exercise its discretion to continue to hear the claim under the criteria in 28 U.S.C. § 1367(c), one of which relates to the dismissal of all claims which had an independent basis for subject matter jurisdiction. See, e.g., *Piedra v. Mentor Graphics Corp.*, 979 F.Supp. 1297 (D. Or. 1997) (court dismisses compulsory counterclaim as well as the plaintiff's claim).

2. INVOLUNTARY DISMISSALS

Rule 41(b) codifies the inherent authority to dismiss a claim against the wishes of the plaintiff and with prejudice to the plaintiff bringing the claim again. The Rule is often used to authorize dismissals for failure to prosecute, but it is actually far broader. Rule 41(b) governs *all* involuntary dismissals, ranging from lack of venue and improper service, through failure to state a claim, to failure to comply with a court order in discovery or at trial. In *LeSane v. Hall's Security Analyst*, 239 F.3d 206 (2d Cir. 2001), the court identified several criteria for deciding whether to grant an involuntary dismissal for violating a court order:

> the duration of the plaintiff's failures, whether plaintiff had received notice that further delays would result in dismissal, whether the defendant is likely to be prejudiced by further delay, whether the district judge has take[n] care to strik[e] the balance between alleviating court calendar congestion and protecting a party's right to due process and a fair chance to be heard . . . and whether the judge has adequately assessed the efficacy of lesser sanctions.

239 F.3d at 209. Rule 41(b), providing for involuntary dismissals, is a defendant's remedy. What is meant by an involuntary dismissal when the plaintiff "fails to prosecute"?

AURA LAMP & LIGHTING INC. v. INTERNATIONAL TRADING CORP.
325 F.3d 903 (7th Cir. 2003)

ILANA DIAMOND ROVNER, CIRCUIT JUDGE.

The district court dismissed this case for want of prosecution and the plaintiff, Aura Lamp & Lighting Inc. ("Aura Lamp"), appeals. . . .

I

Because the district court dismissed the case for want of prosecution and for violations of discovery orders, the salient facts are few. Aura Lamp and International Trading Corporation ("ITC") allegedly entered into a number of contracts relating to lighting products and their components. The details of these agreements are unnecessary to the resolution of this appeal. Aura Lamp sued ITC in a six-count complaint. Five of the counts allege breach of contract. The sixth claim seeks to invalidate a patent held by ITC. Aura Lamp filed the complaint on April 6, 2000. A few weeks later, the district court ordered Aura Lamp to amend its complaint by May 19, 2000 to cure jurisdictional defects related to certain diversity jurisdiction allegations in the complaint. That date came and went without any amendment to the complaint by Aura Lamp. ITC then moved to dismiss the complaint or in the alternative to transfer the case. The district court set a briefing schedule, ordering Aura Lamp to reply by July 5, 2000. Again the date passed without any action by Aura Lamp. ITC complied with the district court's scheduling order by filing its reply brief even though no responsive brief had been filed by Aura Lamp. Aura Lamp then belatedly filed a response brief which the district court accepted over ITC's objection. The district court denied the motion to dismiss, ordered Aura Lamp once again to amend its complaint to cure the jurisdictional defect and threatened dismissal if Aura Lamp continued to ignore the court's orders. Aura Lamp then amended the complaint.

On December 21, 2000, the court ordered the close of written discovery by March 21, 2001 and the close of all other discovery by August 1, 2001. Approximately one week later, ITC served interrogatories, document requests and requests for admission on Aura Lamp. Under the Federal Rules of Civil Procedure, Aura Lamp was to respond to this discovery within thirty days. The thirty days passed without a response from Aura Lamp and without any request for an extension of time to respond. Numerous calls and letters from ITC's counsel followed, and Aura Lamp failed to meet two agreed extension dates. ITC then moved to compel discovery, asking that the requests for admission be deemed admitted, and also seeking sanctions. The case was scheduled for a status conference on March 22, 2001, and the court took up the motion to compel at that time. When asked to explain the delays in responding to discovery, Aura Lamp's counsel replied that he was solely responsible for the case, stating, "I wish I had somebody else to go through this stuff." [Transcript references are deleted.] He explained that his client was a "one-man operation" that did not have the resources to sort through the documents requested. Over ITC's objection, the district court elected to grant one final extension to Aura Lamp, allowing counsel for Aura Lamp to pick the date on which all discovery was to be produced. Several times during the status conference, the court threatened dismissal of the case if Aura Lamp failed to meet the deadline. ("I'll set a deadline, if the case [sic] isn't met, the case is going away."); ("I want to set a date that is going to be real so that if it isn't met, I'm going to take severe action in this case."); ("Due to the amount of time it's taken the plaintiff to respond to these discovery requests, and given the enormous amount of time I'm giving you to respond over the objection of the defendants, if there is not good faith compliance by that date, I am going to seriously consider a motion to dismiss for want of prosecution."). *See also* ("I'm going to have to take some severe action."); ("[I]f I set a deadline, given all that's transpired, it's going to have to be it."); ("I'm setting a deadline, and I want it to be a real deadline, and I want there to be consequences if it isn't followed."). Aura Lamp's counsel asked to set the deadline to the last working day in April, amounting to an additional one and a half month extension. Shortly thereafter, ITC served a second set of document requests on Aura Lamp.

On the very last day of April 2001, Aura Lamp served ITC with responses that ITC characterized as incomplete and defective. According to ITC, Aura Lamp failed to produce a single page of documents and filed specious objections to both the document and interrogatory requests. Aura Lamp filed no response to ITC's second request for the production of documents. ITC's counsel again tried to resolve the matter with a letter requesting compliance. When Aura Lamp did not respond, ITC moved to dismiss the case for repeated violations of court orders, failure to comply with discovery, and failure to prosecute. On June 15, 2001, the court held a status hearing on the motion. Counsel for Aura Lamp informed the court he wanted to reply to the motion in writing and that he intended to file two motions of his own. Remarkably (given the tenor of the prior hearing), he intended to move to extend time to propound the plaintiff's discovery requests and also for additional time to respond to ITC's request for the production of documents. After setting out a deadline for Aura Lamp to file these new motions and briefing schedules for all pending motions, the court set a hearing date of July 11, 2001.

At the July 11 hearing, the court learned that, in addition to missing several other deadlines, Aura Lamp had failed to comply with the briefing schedule set on June 15. Counsel for Aura Lamp explained that the most recent delays were due to secretarial difficulties, computer problems, and scheduling challenges posed by an ongoing trial in chancery court. He insisted that his conduct was not wilful and wanton but rather due to unforeseen circumstances beyond his control. The district court replied, "I don't think I have to find wilful and wanton." Ultimately, the court found that Aura Lamp repeatedly missed court-ordered deadlines and failed to prosecute the case. She noted that Aura Lamp had been granted numerous extensions both by the court and by counsel for ITC to no avail. Aura Lamp had also failed to follow basic court procedures by failing to sign many of the documents filed with the court. The court concluded, "[Y]ou brought the case, and the plaintiff has to prosecute a case when they bring it, and the plaintiff hasn't. And I think to allow this to go on anymore would just compound all the problems that have occurred by really doing something that's unfair to the defendants." The court then dismissed the case for want of prosecution and denied all other motions as moot. Aura Lamp appeals.

II

On appeal, Aura Lamp maintains that the district court erred in dismissing the case under Federal Rule of Civil Procedure 37 because that rule requires a finding of wilful and wanton misconduct, and the court thus applied the wrong standard. Aura Lamp also contends that dismissal under Rule 37 or Rule 41 requires specific warnings prior to dismissal and also requires that the court consider lesser sanctions before dismissing. Aura Lamp argues that the court's warnings were inadequate and that no lesser sanctions were considered before the court dismissed the case....

B

ITC moved to dismiss the complaint with prejudice "pursuant to Fed.R.Civ.Proc. ... 41(b)." The district judge ultimately dismissed the case for want of prosecution pursuant to Rule 41(b) but she also discussed and may have relied upon Aura Lamp's violations of orders related to discovery.... In our Circuit, we review for abuse of discretion the district court's decision to sanction a plaintiff by dismissing a suit. Our review of a dismissal for want of prosecution is highly deferential. *Ball v. City of Chicago,* 2 F.3d 752, 760 (7th Cir.1993). In order to find an abuse of discretion, the district court's decision must strike us as fundamentally wrong.

Certain principles guide the district court in determining whether to dismiss a case for want of prosecution pursuant to Rule 41. Ideally, the district court should consider the frequency and magnitude of the plaintiff's failure to comply with deadlines for the prosecution of the suit, the apportionment of responsibility for those failures between the plaintiff and his counsel, the effect of those failures on the judge's calendar and time, the prejudice if any to the defendant caused by the plaintiff's dilatory conduct, the probable merits of the suit, and the consequences of dismissal for the social objectives of the type of litigation that the suit represents. *Ball,* 2 F.3d at 759–60. "There is no 'grace period' before dismissal for failure to prosecute is permissible and no requirement of graduated sanctions, but there must be an explicit warning before the case is dismissed." *Ball,* 2 F.3d at 760. Aura Lamp asks us to find the district court abused its discretion in dismissing the case because (1) the court did not adequately warn Aura Lamp that the case would be dismissed; (2) the court failed to consider whether lesser sanctions would be effective; (3) Aura Lamp's violations were not of sufficient frequency or magnitude to warrant dismissal; (4) in apportioning the fault between the parties, the district court should have found that ITC's conduct was responsible for more egregious delays than Aura Lamp's; (5) neither the court nor the defendant suffered prejudice due to Aura Lamp; (6) Aura Lamp's claims are meritorious.

We begin with the issue of warning. The district judge is not obliged to warn the plaintiff repeatedly nor is the court required to issue a formal rule to show cause before dismissing a case. *Ball,* 2 F.3d at 755. "A judge is not obliged to treat lawyers like children" *Ball,* 2 F.3d at 755. All that is required is explicit warning. Here, the court repeatedly and expressly warned Aura Lamp that it was contemplating dismissal during the March 22 status conference. ("I'll set a deadline, if the case [sic] isn't met, the case is going away."); ("I want to set a date that is going to be real so that if it isn't met, I'm going to take severe action in this case."); ("Due to the amount of time it's taken the plaintiff to respond to these discovery requests, and given the enormous amount of time I'm giving you to respond over the objection of the defendants, if there is not good faith compliance by that date, I am going to seriously consider a motion to dismiss for want of prosecution."). This is by no means a complete list of the court's warnings but is merely a representative sample. These warnings are more than adequate. Aura Lamp was on notice of the consequences of further failures to respond to the court's orders.

Aura Lamp also faults the court for failing to consider the efficacy of lesser sanctions first. Although we recommend that courts consider sanctioning a misbehaving lawyer before the sanction of dismissal is imposed on a possibly faultless plaintiff, we do not require that courts do so. *Ball,* 2 F.3d at 758. At the July 11 hearing, as the court was ruling on the motion to dismiss, counsel for Aura Lamp asked the court to allow him to resign from the case and find someone else who could handle the case properly. The court replied that it was too late for such a maneuver. The district judge acknowledged that both counsel and his client had difficulties in prosecuting the case but that ultimately the plaintiff was responsible for prosecuting the case and had failed to do so. Clearly the court believed this was the only effective sanction at the time. Especially in light of counsel's earlier admission that his client was a "one-man operation" without the resources to respond to discovery, it would appear that the court did not abuse its discretion in refusing to impose lesser sanctions. See also *Dickerson v. Board of Educ. of Ford Heights, Ill.,* 32

F.3d 1114, 1117 (7th Cir.1994) (where a pattern of dilatory conduct is clear, dismissal need not be preceded by the imposition of less severe sanctions).

Aura Lamp next argues that its violations were not sufficiently egregious and were too infrequent to warrant such a harsh sanction. This claim is easily answered by merely listing the violations. In addition to failing to sign pleadings filed with the court, Aura Lamp repeatedly missed court-imposed deadlines for both discovery and motion practice, ignored agreed extensions, and failed to amend its complaint to cure a jurisdictional defect for several months after the court ordered it do so. Moreover, Aura Lamp asked permission to propound discovery on the defendant after the court-ordered discovery cut-off date, a date that Aura Lamp's counsel had himself selected at the court's invitation. We have upheld dismissals in cases where the violations were comparable to or less severe than they are here, and no court would find an abuse of discretion in these circumstances.

Aura Lamp maintains that ITC caused at least some of the delay. But in apportioning the fault between Aura Lamp and ITC, Aura Lamp offers no valid evidence of dilatory conduct by ITC that contributed to any of Aura Lamp's failures. The sum and substance of Aura Lamp's argument on this point is that ITC did not tell Aura Lamp's counsel that his extraordinarily late responses to discovery were evasive and incomplete. Aura Lamp also complains that ITC did not contact its counsel concerning responses to ITC's request for production of documents. Aura Lamp claims it made the documents available for inspection and ITC did not take advantage of the opportunity to review them. However, Aura Lamp fails to mention that ITC specifically requested that Aura Lamp photocopy the documents and forward them to ITC. This argument is frivolous. So too is Aura Lamp's claim that neither the court nor the defendant suffered any prejudice at its hands. The district court specifically listed the motions that ITC was forced to bring to protect its interests in the case, adding needless expense to the case and clogging the court's docket. We conclude that this is not a close question. On the Rule 41 issues, the appeal is doomed. . . .

NOTES AND QUESTIONS

1. The Supreme Court reviewed a dismissal for want of prosecution in *Link v. Wabash Railroad Company*, 370 U.S. 626, 82 S.Ct. 1386, 8 L.Ed.2d 734 (1962). After the case had been pending for six years, the court set a date for a pretrial conference. Two hours before the time for the conference, plaintiff's attorney called the judge's office to say that he could not attend the pretrial conference. When the lawyer did fail to appear at the conference, the judge exercised his inherent power to dismiss the case for want of prosecution. The Supreme Court affirmed the dismissal.

> Neither the permissive language of the Rule which merely authorizes a motion by the defendant nor its policy requires us to conclude that it was the purpose of the Rule to abrogate the power of courts, acting on their own initiative, to clear their calendars of cases that have remained dormant because of the inaction or dilatoriness of the parties seeking relief. The authority of a court to dismiss *sua sponte* for lack of prosecution has generally been considered an "inherent power," governed not by rule or statute but by the control necessarily vested in courts to manage their own affairs so as to achieve the orderly and expeditious disposition of cases. . . . It would require a much clearer expression of purpose than Rule 41(b) provides for us to assume that it was intended to abrogate so well-acknowledged a proposition.

Link, 370 U.S. at 630–31. The Court then concluded that the judge's exercise of inherent power was not an abuse of discretion. Counsel's absence at the pretrial conference, in the light of the whole history of the litigation, supported a reasonable inference that the plaintiff deliberately had been intentionally trying to delay the progress of the case. The Court also rejected the argument that counsel's absence would penalize his client.

> There is certainly no merit to the contention that dismissal of petitioner's claim because of his counsel's unexcused conduct imposes an unjust penalty on the client. Petitioner voluntarily chose this attorney as his representative in the action, and he cannot now avoid the consequences of the acts or omissions of this freely selected agent. Any other notion would be wholly inconsistent with our system of representative litigation, in which each party is deemed bound by the acts of his lawyer-agent and is considered to have "notice of all facts, notice of which can be charged upon the attorney."

Link, 370 U.S. at 633–34. *Link* is clear that a trial court has the inherent authority to dismiss for want of prosecution. Rule 41(b) codifies that authority in part. Even though the rule speaks of a motion by the defendant, the cases make it clear that the court may act on its own without a motion.

    2. As the *Aura Lamp* court noted, the appellate standard of review for an involuntary dismissal due to delay is abuse of discretion. While that is a difficult burden for an appellant to satisfy, involuntary dismissals are sometimes set aside because the dismissal under Rule 41(b) is with prejudice to the plaintiff refiling the claim. Contrary to *Aura Lamp*, though, some appellate courts may be concerned about whether the trial court could have imposed less severe sanctions to move the case to trial. See, e.g., *Mann v. Lewis*, 108 F.3d 145 (8th Cir. 1997) (dismissal with prejudice excessive when dilatory conduct of counsel was not attributable to plaintiff). What are some examples of less serious sanctions?

    3. No fixed time limits control involuntary dismissals. A court should examine the totality of the circumstances in each case in deciding whether

failure to pursue the case is serious enough to require dismissal under Rule 41(b). A lengthy period of inaction may justify a dismissal for failure to prosecute if it is the plaintiff who appears to be at fault, e.g., failing to follow an earlier warning to act with more diligence.

4. Most trial courts maintain a set of local rules, which often include a provision about the failure to prosecute. The typical local rule provides that if a case has been pending for a given length of time, or if no action has been taken in the case for a particular period, the case must be reviewed to determine whether there is an adequate excuse for past delays.

PROBLEMS

1. Peter sues Donald in federal court, but before Donald is even served with process, Peter wants to withdraw his complaint. How could you as Peter's attorney accomplish his goal?

2. Same facts as Problem 1. In addition, Peter tells you that last year he filed the same claim against Donald in a state court and also withdrew that claim almost as soon as he filed it. Does this change the situation for Peter seeking a dismissal with this second lawsuit?

3. Same facts as Problem 1, except that by the time Peter wants to withdraw his claim Donald has filed an answer as well as a motion for summary judgment. Is Peter's goal of dismissal less likely to be met?

4. Same facts as Problem 3, except that Donald has filed a counterclaim against Peter. What happens to Donald's counterclaim if the court grants Peter's motion to dismiss his claim?

5. Same facts as Problem 3, except that Donald wants Peter to pay for the money he has spent to pay his attorney. Is Peter's goal of dismissal still likely to be met?

6. Peter sues Donald in a federal court. For the next two years, Peter obtains a series of continuances. The trial judge grants the last continuance, saying that it will dismiss Peter's claim if he is not ready for trial in sixty days. At the end of the sixty-day period, Peter requests another continuance. What can Donald do?

EXERCISE

For the state where a) you intend to practice after graduation, b) your law school is located, and/or c) your professor assigns, go to that state's annotated statutes and research the procedural rules by which dismissals are governed. Based on your research, print the rule and bring it to class for discussion. In addition, answer the following questions.

1. Can voluntary dismissals be made by notice?

2. Identify whether there is a point in time beyond which notice dismissals are disallowed.

3. Is there a limitation on the number of dismissals that may occur before a dismissal is deemed to be an adjudication on the merits?

4. Do certain types of cases require a court's consent before dismissing?

5. If a court must approve at least some types of voluntary dismissals, what are the criteria for the court to follow in granting such dismissals?

6. What are the stated grounds for involuntary dismissals?

7. Are there stated criteria for determining whether a dismissal (voluntary or involuntary) is with prejudice or without prejudice?

B. OBJECTING TO THE COMPLAINT BY MOTION

A defendant can respond to the complaint either by motion or an answer. The answer, discussed in Part C of this Chapter, must address all of the allegations in the complaint, and either deny or admit liability for each. A motion, by contrast, focuses on one particular problem defendant has identified in the complaint, and asks the court to resolve that issue quickly. Motions are particularly useful when the problem might cause the court to dismiss the complaint, such as when the chosen court lacks jurisdiction or venue. If defendant can have the case dismissed by motion, it need not go to the trouble (and potential embarrassment) of having to deal with the substantive allegations in the complaint.

Not all defenses and objections can be raised by motion. For example, a party cannot use a pre-answer motion to ask the court to rule that the party did not commit the acts alleged in the opposing party's pleading. That issue must be raised in the answer, or after the answer by a motion such as summary judgment (discussed in Chap. 11 pt. A). Federal Rule 12 allows only seven specified defenses and objections to be raised by pre-answer motion. Review Rule 12(b) in your Supplement. Many of the listed defenses involve jurisdiction (including service) and venue. Other defenses, such as failure to join a necessary party, you will encounter later. In actual practice, attorneys tend to refer to the defenses by their number. Therefore, the defense of failure to state a claim is commonly referred to as a "12(b)(6)."

Note that a party is not *compelled* to raise these defenses in a pre-answer motion. The Rule explicitly provides that all defenses "must be asserted in a responsive pleading", but then, in the following sentences, allows the seven defenses to be made by pre-answer motion. Therefore, a party who objects to the court's venue need not raise a pre-answer motion, but can instead wait to include that defense in her answer. However, special timing rules govern when a party may raise some of these defenses, especially if the party raises some, but not all, of the Rule 12(b) defenses in a pre-answer motion. These timing rules are discussed just below.

SEC. B OBJECTING TO THE COMPLAINT BY MOTION

Rule 12(b) does not stand alone. First, Rules 12(e) and (f) also allow a party to object to allegations of the complaint by motion. Second, Rule 12(c) allows a party to ask the court to rule on the merits of the case once the pleadings are complete. All three of these rules focus on the substantive allegations, not defenses like jurisdiction and venue.

Third, and perhaps most often overlooked by first-year students, Rule 12 does not contain an exhaustive list of issues that can be raised by motion. Suppose, for example, defendant feels the judge assigned to the case has a conflict of interest because her nephew is married to plaintiff's daughter. Defendant need not wait until the answer to raise this issue. Instead, he can file a pre-answer motion to ask the judge to recuse herself from the case. Although this claim is not listed anywhere in Rule 12, it is not one of the "defenses" governed by Rule 12(b) because it does not deal with the complaint, service of the complaint, or the court's authority to decide the case. It is instead a procedural matter that has nothing to do with the merits or the court's (as opposed to the individual judge's) authority to adjudicate.

This section focuses on Rule 12 motions, especially those motions listed in Rule 12(b). Part 1 discusses the timing rules governing when a party much raise each defense. As you will see, the timing rules vary widely depending on the defense in question. Part 2 focuses on motions challenging the substantive allegations in a claim, which raise a number of unique considerations.

1. TIMING RULES GOVERNING RULE 12 MOTIONS

a. Defenses Other than Subject-Matter Jurisdiction

INTRODUCTORY PROBLEM

ACME, Inc. and Fisk's Disks are engaged in a life-and-death struggle. Both companies sell recordable compacts discs ("CDRs") for use in computers. Because demand for CDRs has fallen off dramatically during the past few years, both companies have had difficulties eking out a profit. ACME and Fisk's both need to divert business from the other in order to survive.

Over the past few months, ACME's sales have fallen precipitously. When ACME discovers that Fisk's has been engaged in some arguably shady activities to win over ACME's customers, ACME sues Fisk's in a federal district court in Oregon. ACME's complaint contains three claims for relief. The first is a false advertising claim under federal law. ACME alleges that Fisk's sales staff has been making false and derogatory statements about ACME's product to customers, therefore convincing them to switch brands. Claim number two is a common-law tortious interference with contract claim. The third claim alleges "sales below cost," arguing that Fisk's sold its product at a price below its total production costs, thereby winning over additional customers. Jurisdiction is based on federal question, coupled with supplemental jurisdiction.

Fisk's does no business in Oregon, and is accordingly confident the Oregon court lacks personal jurisdiction and venue. How may Fisk's bring this to the court's attention? If Fisk's raises the issue and loses, may it go ahead and deny liability on the merits?

Governing Law: Federal Rules 12(b), (g), and (h).

Rules 12(g) and (h) set specific timing requirements for various Rule 12 defenses. If a defendant moves to dismiss under Rule 12(b), Rule 12(g) requires the motion to include certain other defenses and objections then available that Rule 12 permits to be raised by motion. Any defenses subject to this Rule that are not raised are lost: defendant can neither make a second pre-answer motion raising the other defenses or objections, or raise them in his answer. For example, a defendant who makes a motion to dismiss a complaint for failure to state a claim on which relief can be granted cannot thereafter raise, either by motion or in its answer, defenses such as lack of personal jurisdiction, improper venue, insufficiency of process, or insufficiency of service of process.

Rule 12(h) makes it clear that not all Rule 12(b) defenses are waived if not included in a pre-answer motion. The defenses of 1) failure to state a claim for relief on which relief can be granted, 2) failure to join an indispensable party, and 3) failure to state a legal defense to a claim do not have to be asserted at the earliest opportunity. Under Rule 12(h)(2), they may be made in a later pleading, a motion for judgment on the pleadings, or at trial. After trial, the three objections cannot be raised. By contrast, the defense of lack of *subject matter* jurisdiction is never waived, per Rule 12(h)(3).

A defendant choosing to assert defenses and objections in an answer rather than by raising them in a Rule 12(b) motion waives most defenses or objections that are not included in the answer. If a subsequent judgment in a case is taken to another jurisdiction to be enforced, *i.e.*, to be collected, the latter jurisdiction's viewpoint about whether to permit the judgment-loser in the first state to raise a jurisdictional issue in the enforcement action depends on what happened in the first case. For example, if an objection to personal jurisdiction was raised in the first case, the court where the judgment is taken to be enforced will not permit the issue of the first court's jurisdiction to be retried.

Rule 12(h)(1)(B)(ii) requires a party to raise certain defenses no later than the answer, or an amendment to an answer allowed under Rule 15(a) "as a matter of course." This latter reference is to amendments a party may make without the court's permission, which you studied in Chapter 6(E)(1). Therefore, even if a defendant fails to include lack of

SEC. B   OBJECTING TO THE COMPLAINT BY MOTION   451

venue in its answer, it can preserve the defense by amending the answer within 21 days.

If all this seems unfathomable, rest assured you are not alone. These timing rules often prove tricky to the newcomer. One way to make better sense of the technical language is to avoid the common practice of referring to defenses by their Rule 12(b) number. In other words, rather than referring to lack of venue as a "Rule 12(b)(3) defense", think of it as "a defense that Rule 12 allows to be raised by pre-answer motion." This usage better matches the language of the Rule, and accordingly helps avoid two common mistakes. First, it recognizes that the timing rules also apply to Rule 12(c), (e), and (f) motions, not only those made under Rule 12(b). Second, it takes into account that there are objections, such as conflict of interest, that can be raised by motion completely independently of Rule 12. These latter motions do not trigger the Rule 12(g) and (h) timing Rules, and the objections are not subject to waiver under those rules.

In brief, Rule 12(g)(2) bars successive pre-answer motions raising many of the defenses and objections listed anywhere in Rule 12. Rule 12(h)(1)(A) bars successive Rule 12 pre-answer motions and/or successive Rule 12 motions in the answer. Rule 12(h)(1)(B)(i) prohibits a Rule 12 objection altogether if it is not made either as a pre-answer motion or as a Rule 12 motion in the answer. All of these timing rules are subject to the explicit exceptions in Rule 12(h)(2) and 12(h)(3).

PROBLEMS

1. Colbert sues Fallon for defamation. Before answering the complaint, Fallon files a motion to dismiss the complaint for insufficient process. The judge denies the motion. Can Fallon then move to dismiss for lack of personal jurisdiction?

2. Colbert sues Fallon for defamation. Before answering the complaint, Fallon files a motion to dismiss the complaint for lack of subject matter jurisdiction. The judge denies the motion. Can Fallon then move to dismiss for lack of personal jurisdiction?

3. Colbert sues Fallon for defamation. Before answering the complaint, Fallon files a motion to dismiss the complaint for insufficient process. The judge denies the motion. Can Fallon then move to dismiss for lack of subject matter jurisdiction?

4. Colbert sues Fallon for defamation. Before answering the complaint, Fallon files a motion to dismiss the complaint for insufficient process. The judge denies the motion. Can Fallon answer, raising the defense of lack of personal jurisdiction?

5. Colbert sues Fallon for defamation. If Fallon decides to answer the complaint rather than filing a Rule 12(b) motion to dismiss, can Fallon include a defense of insufficient process in the answer?

6. Colbert sues Fallon for defamation. If Fallon moves to dismiss the complaint for insufficiency of service of process, may or must Fallon move at the same time to dismiss for lack of personal jurisdiction?

7. Colbert sues Fallon for defamation in Missouri. Fallon files a timely motion to dismiss the complaint for lack of personal jurisdiction. The judge grants the motion. What is the effect of granting the motion?

8. Colbert sues Fallon for defamation in Missouri. Fallon answers the complaint and defends the case on its merits. Before trial begins Fallon files a motion to dismiss the complaint for lack of personal jurisdiction. How should the court react?

9. Colbert sues Fallon for defamation in Missouri. Fallon answers the complaint and defends the case on its merits and loses. Colbert files suit in Illinois to enforce the Missouri judgment. Fallon moves to dismiss the Illinois action, saying that the Missouri court lacked personal jurisdiction over him. How should the court react?

10. Colbert sues Fallon for defamation in Missouri. Fallon ignores the complaint and the Missouri court issues a default judgment for Colbert. Colbert takes the Missouri judgment to Illinois to enforce. Fallon defends against the enforcement action on the ground that Missouri lacked personal jurisdiction over him. How should the court react?

11. Colbert sues Fallon for defamation in Missouri. Before answering the complaint, Fallon files a motion to dismiss the complaint for lack of personal jurisdiction. The judge denies the motion. Fallon does nothing else in the lawsuit and the court awards Colbert a default judgment. Colbert takes the Missouri judgment to Illinois for enforcement. How should the Illinois court react to any motion by Fallon to dismiss the Illinois enforcement action?

b. Subject-Matter Jurisdiction

NORTH CENTRAL F.S., INC. V. BROWN, 951 F.Supp. 1383 (N.D. Iowa 1996). North Central operated grain elevators in various locations in Iowa. North Central had entered into "hedge-to-arrive" ("HTA") agreements with grain producers, under which the producers would sell grain to North Central. The producers declared that the HTA agreements violated federal law, and were therefore unenforceable. North Central then sued the producers in a federal district court in Iowa. Neither of the parties challenged the court's subject-matter jurisdiction. The court nevertheless raised the question of its own jurisdiction *sua sponte*, stating:

> The federal district courts have always been courts of limited jurisdiction. "Federal courts are not courts of general jurisdiction and have only the power that is authorized by Article III of the

Constitution and the statutes enacted by Congress pursuant thereto." *Marine Equip. Management Co. v. United States*, 4 F.3d 643, 646 (8th Cir.1993). A federal court therefore has a duty to assure itself that the threshold requirement of subject matter jurisdiction has been met in every case.

The parties ... may not confer subject matter jurisdiction upon the federal courts by stipulation, and lack of subject matter jurisdiction cannot be waived by the parties or ignored by the court. Even where "'the parties did not raise any jurisdictional issues[, t]his court is obligated to raise such jurisdictional issues if it perceives any.'" *White v. Nix*, 43 F.3d 374, 376 (8th Cir.1994). The federal courts have a duty to examine the substantiality of the federal claim throughout the litigation, and must dismiss all claims if the federal claim proves patently meritless even after the trial begins. . . .

The court eventually held that it lacked jurisdiction over North Central's claims.

NOTES AND QUESTIONS

1. *North Central* illustrates one of the most important features of subject matter jurisdiction: unlike every other defense in a case, subject matter jurisdiction cannot be waived by the parties. As Federal Rule 12(h)(3) makes clear, any party may raise the issue at any time during the course of a proceeding, even on appeal. Not only may either party raise the issue of subject matter jurisdiction at any time, but a court may raise it of its own accord, or "sua sponte." As a result, a court may dismiss a case for lack of subject matter jurisdiction even though both parties are willing to have it heard in that court. Nor can the parties create subject matter jurisdiction where it would not otherwise exist by consenting in a contract to have claims under that contract heard by a particular court.

2. *Challenges by plaintiff.* Even more unusual is that plaintiff may challenge subject matter jurisdiction. This result makes sense in a removal case, where the defendant has taken the case to federal court. But plaintiff may also challenge subject matter jurisdiction in cases where plaintiff himself has chosen federal court. Moreover, plaintiff may challenge jurisdiction at any time. In other words, a party can bring a case in federal court, lose on the merits at trial, and then move to dismiss the action for lack of jurisdiction. If the court dismisses, the unfavorable judgment is not binding. *Capron v. Van Noorden*, 6 U.S. (2 Cranch) 126, 2 L.Ed. 229 (1804).

3. Whether the parties may by agreement *deprive* a court of the power to hear a dispute is a more complicated matter. Courts typically treat the issue as a question of venue rather than subject matter jurisdiction.

4. The *North Central* opinion discusses why the rule governing challenges to subject matter jurisdiction is so accommodating. Do these same arguments apply to *diversity* cases? Although diversity jurisdiction is an allocation of authority, the justifications for diversity jurisdiction are

noticeably different than for other types of cases. Diversity jurisdiction exists not to ensure the supremacy of federal law, but because the framers feared that the state courts might tend to side with in-state litigants when those parties were embroiled in litigation with out-of-staters. Given this different justification, should parties from the same state be able to litigate their state law claims in federal court if both are willing to do so? Construct an argument that even this situation presents a threat to state authority.

5. The above principles only apply to *direct attacks*, i.e., challenges made while the case in question is still pending at the trial court or on appeal. Once that case is entirely complete (either because no appeal was taken or because the appellate courts have finished with the case), a party's ability to challenge the subject matter jurisdiction of the court that decided the case is more limited. A situation in which a person challenges a prior case in a separate and distinct case is referred to as a "*collateral attack*." If a party actually litigated the court's subject matter jurisdiction in the first proceeding, that party is bound by the court's determination, even if that determination later proves to be clearly incorrect. *Durfee v. Duke*, 375 U.S. 106, 84 S.Ct. 242, 11 L.Ed.2d 186 (1963) (*Durfee* is in Chap. 13 pt. F).

The law is less clear when the issue of subject matter jurisdiction was not litigated in the first case. If a party shows up and litigates the case, but never raises the question of subject-matter jurisdiction, she will usually be precluded from challenging the court's jurisdiction in a collateral proceeding. *Chicot County Drainage Dist. v. Baxter State Bank*, 308 U.S. 371, 60 S.Ct. 317, 84 L.Ed. 329 (1940). However, the Supreme Court has never directly ruled on the issue of where the party simply never shows up at all in the action. Although several commentators have suggested that collateral attack would be available in this case, the law is not clear.

2. CHALLENGING THE SUBSTANTIVE ALLEGATIONS OF A CLAIM

INTRODUCTORY PROBLEM

Same facts as the Introductory Problem for the prior section. Fisk's files a timely pre-answer motion to dismiss for lack of personal jurisdiction and venue. The court denies the motion to dismiss. Fisk's then files an answer. In this answer, Fisk's argues that the second and third claims should be dismissed because they do not state claims on which relief can be granted. With respect to the tortious interference claim, Fisk's argues that the complaint is insufficient. ACME alleged only that "Fisk's intentionally contacted some of ACME's regular customers to convince them to buy Fisk's products." The tort of tortious interference with contract, however, requires proof that defendant caused someone *who had a binding contract* with plaintiff to breach that contract. Because ACME did not allege the existence of a contract between the customers and ACME, Fisk's argues the complaint is deficient.

With respect to the sales below cost claim, Fisk's acknowledges that the complaint contains plenty of background facts. However, Fisk's points out that under governing law, a competitor cannot be held liable for selling its products on the retail level at a price below the cost of production. Therefore, Fisk's claims, ACME cannot prevail on this claim. Fisk's answer asks the court to dismiss the tortious interference and sales below cost claims.

Before the court rules on Fisk's request to dismiss the second and third claims, the parties conduct discovery. In the discovery process, Fisk's learns that ACME has no evidence whatsoever that Fisk's sales personnel made any false statements to ACME's customers. Fisk's then files a post-answer motion which it captions "motion to dismiss for failure to state a claim." Although Fisk's acknowledges that the wording of the false advertising claim meets the pleading requirements of the Federal Rules, Fisk's argues that the court should dismiss the false advertising claim because ACME cannot prove its claim.

ACME objects to both the timing and substance of the motions. First, ACME argues that Fisk waived the defense of failure to state a claim by failing to include it along with its personal jurisdiction and venue challenges, and, in the case of the post-answer motion, by failing to include it in the answer. Second, ACME argues that even if the challenges were timely, all three of its claims do state claims upon which relief can be granted.

How will the court rule?

Governing Law: Federal Rules 12(b)(6), 12(e), (g), and (h).

In all the pleading cases in Chapter 6, defendant or defendants moved to dismiss plaintiff's complaint for failure to state a claim upon which relief can be granted. Each of the defendants claimed that the respective complaints were so inadequate that plaintiff should not be allowed to proceed any further with its case. In footnote 1 of *Swierkiewicz*, however, the Supreme Court states that the Court will "accept as true all of the factual allegations contained in the complaint." If a court must accept everything the plaintiff says as true, how can it ever dismiss a complaint for failure to state a claim?

The answer lies in the nature of the motion to dismiss for failure to state a claim. This motion, often called a "12(b)(6)" motion to reflect its location in the Federal Rules, tests only whether the plaintiff has drafted a legally and technically proper complaint. It does not ask whether the claimant is telling the truth or whether it has evidence to support its claim. Nor does it consider any defenses or denials that defendant may include in its answer. As long as the complaint seeks recovery under a theory recognized by governing law, and provides enough detail to comply with Federal Rules 8 and 9, it will survive a 12(b)(6) challenge.

a. When a Pleading "Fails to State a Claim"

Logically, there are two basic forms a Rule 12(b)(6) challenge can take. First, the challenged pleading may be missing some key language. The claimant may not have provided enough detail to satisfy the plausibility standard of *Twombly* and *Iqbal* (or the heightened standard of Rule 9(b) or 9(g)), or failed specifically to allege a crucial element of a claim. Second, the pleading may contain ample facts, but those facts do not state a claim recognized at law. Although in both of these situations the pleading fails to state a claim, courts treat these two situations quite differently. In the former, the court rarely dismisses. Instead, it will usually give the claimant at least one opportunity to amend the pleading to add the missing details. In the latter, however, the court is more likely to dismiss. Unless plaintiff can show that the complaint can be modified to allow recovery under a different legal theory, it would waste both the court's and defendant's time to allow plaintiff to amend when she simply has no chance of recovery under even the most prolix complaint.

Sometimes defendant will need to add a fact or two in order to prove plaintiff cannot prevail. For example, plaintiff's breach of contract claim might be based on an oral contract that violates the statute of frauds. In some of these cases, plaintiff's complaint will supply the missing fact; *e.g.*, plaintiff could specify the contract was oral. If plaintiff does not provide the crucial fact, however, the complaint is sufficient on its own, and will survive a 12(b)(6) challenge. Defendant's proper recourse in this situation is to file either a Federal Rule 12 motion for judgment on the pleadings (covered later in this section) or a motion for summary judgment under Federal Rule 56 (covered in Chapter 11). Nevertheless, many defendants will file a 12(b)(6), but attach affidavits or other proof of the missing facts to the motion. In these situations, Rule 12(d) provides that the 12(b)(6) motion will be converted into a motion for summary judgment, and treated under the provisions of Rule 56.

b. Procedural Aspects of the Rule 12(b)(6) Motion

The Federal Rules are quite flexible concerning how a party raises the defense of failure to state a claim. The defense can be raised by pre-answer motion just like a motion to dismiss for lack of subject matter jurisdiction or improper service. The defendant can combine the Rule 12(b)(6) motion with any other defenses it can raise by pre-answer motion.

Moreover, unlike the personal jurisdiction, service, and venue defenses, a party who files a pre-answer motion under Rule 12 does not waive the defense of failure to state a claim by failing to include it in that motion. Recall from the prior section that Rule 12(g)(2), which requires many other Rule 12(b) defenses to be joined in pre-answer motions, makes an exception for those defenses listed in Rules 12(h)(2) and

Sec. B Objecting to the Complaint by Motion

12(h)(3). Failure to state a claim is listed in Rule 12(h)(2). Therefore, the defense of failure to state a claim to be raised at any point in the case, including at the trial itself. The defense cannot be waived by any other motion (except, of course, a previous unsuccessful motion to dismiss for failure to state a claim). Note, however, that Rule 12(h)(2) also dictates how the defense must be raised. Therefore, a defendant who makes a pre-answer motion based on some other ground, and then later decides to challenge the sufficiency of the complaint, does not make a second pre-answer motion. Instead, he raises the defense of failure to state a claim in his answer, by a Rule 12(c) motion for judgment on the pleadings (which occurs after pleading is complete), or by motion at the trial itself.

A Rule 12(b)(6) motion does not operate as an admission of any facts. If the court finds that the complaint properly states a claim, defendant can then deny one or more of plaintiff's facts in her answer, and force plaintiff to prove those facts at trial.[1]

Cases involving multiple claims have at times caused courts some concern. Suppose plaintiff alleges two claims against defendant. One of the claims is not recognized under governing law, but the other is. Should a court grant a 12(b)(6) dismissal in this situation? Most courts will simply dismiss the improper claim, leaving the other in place. A few, however, interpret Rule 12(b)(6) to require dismissal of the entire case. These courts typically turn to the Rule 12(f) motion to strike (discussed immediately below) when they need to dismiss fewer than all the claims.

c. Motion for a More Definite Statement and Motion to Strike

Rules 12(e) and (f) give a defendant additional options. Rule 12(e) allows a party against whom a claim has been asserted to move for a more definite statement if the pleading "is so vague or ambiguous that a party cannot reasonably prepare a response." If the motion is granted, plaintiff has fourteen days to amend the complaint to make it clearer. In theory, this provision gives defendant an alternative in that category of cases where the facts set out in the complaint are so sparse that defendant cannot determine exactly what plaintiff is actually claiming. In practice, however, Rule 12(e) is rarely invoked. If a complaint is indeed so vague or ambiguous that it does not fairly apprise defendant of what plaintiff is claiming, defendant will succeed on a Rule 12(b)(6) motion to dismiss for failure to state a claim. A vague or ambiguous complaint, after all, does not comply with Rule 8(a)'s notice pleading requirements. The Rule 12(b)(6) motion is preferable from defendant's standpoint because it tests both the wording and the underlying law, and can result in outright

---

[1] This flexibility in Rule 12(b)(6) motion stands in stark contrast to the rules that applied under the common-law pleading regime. Common-law pleading's counterpart to the 12(b)(6) was the *demurrer*. The demurrer required the defendant to make a difficult choice, as it formed the issue. A defendant who demurred was deemed to have admitted that all the factual allegations of the complaint were true. Thus, if defendant lost the demurrer, it had essentially lost the case.

dismissal. At the very worst, the court will give the plaintiff the opportunity to amend the complaint, leaving defendant no worse off than it would have been had it filed a Rule 12(e) motion.

The Rule 12(f) motion to strike serves two basic purposes. First, as discussed above, it allows a party to strike specific claims or allegations in a pleading. This often occurs when defendant wants to strike fewer than all claims or when plaintiff wants to strike portions of defendant's answer.

Second, the Rule also mentions striking "redundant, immaterial, impertinent, or scandalous matter." Mere redundancy or immateriality by itself rarely supports a motion to strike. However, in a few cases courts have struck particularly inflammatory allegations, or those that intrude too greatly on a party's privacy. Note, however, that a court will usually strike an allegation as "scandalous" only if it is both beyond the pale and of little relevance to the dispute. Scandalous allegations that are highly relevant are rarely struck.

d. Objecting to the Statement of a Claim and Settlement

By objecting in a pre-answer motion or an answer that a complaint does not state a claim recognized at law, a defendant can test the strength of a case prior to investing large sums to defend against the claim. A court's decision on a motion to dismiss can be a key point for determining a settlement strategy. If a defendant thinks there is a good chance that its 12(b)(6) motion will be granted and the improper claim dismissed, it may be unwilling to consider paying anything to settle the case before the court rules on the motion. If the claim survives the 12(b)(6) motion, however, defendant may decide to assess the level of risk in the case and engage in settlement discussions. Plaintiff will be in a stronger position at that point, having won the motion. But if defendant can settle the case within an acceptable monetary range, it will avoid the costs of proceeding with discovery.

PROBLEMS

1. P sues D for personal injuries sustained in an automobile accident. P's complaint fails to mention that P previously sued D for property damage suffered in the same accident. Because P's claim is barred by claim preclusion, D moves to dismiss for failure to state a claim. How will the court rule?

2. Same as Problem 1, except that P's complaint discusses the prior case, and that the court found D liable. Because P's claim is barred by claim preclusion, D moves to dismiss for failure to state a claim. How will the court rule?

3. P sues D for fraud. D moves to dismiss the case for lack of subject-matter jurisdiction. The court denies the motion. D files an answer denying

liability. Later, before the trial commences, D then moves to dismiss the case for failure to plead fraud with particularity. Assuming that D is correct that P's complaint is insufficient, how should the court rule?

4. Same as Problem 3, except D titles his motion a "motion for judgment on the pleadings."

5. P sues D for fraud. D answers. D's answer contains a counterclaim in which D alleges that P libeled D by accusing D of fraud in the complaint. Under governing law, statements in a court pleading cannot give rise to a cause of action for libel or slander. What should P do?

C. RESPONDING TO THE COMPLAINT: THE ANSWER

INTRODUCTORY PROBLEM

The National Park Service has sued four Virginia defendants (Jefferson, Madison, Monroe, and Washington) in a Virginia federal court for civil trespass at Shenandoah National Park in Luray, Virginia on or about July 4, 2005. (A trespasser is a person who enters or remains upon or in possession of the land of another without the possessor's consent.) Jefferson answered the federal complaint by stating that he was in the Park on July 4, 2005. Madison's Answer to the complaint contains no reference to his whereabouts on or about July 4, 2005. Monroe responds to the United States' complaint by stating that he celebrated the Fourth of July holiday energetically by getting a lot of exercise and by drinking alcoholic beverages heavily, but he does not believe that he has enough information to know whether he was at the Park on or about that day. In his Answer, Washington admits that he was at the Park on July 4, 2005, but only because someone intentionally and falsely misrepresented to him that Bono was having a concert there that evening. Assess the effect of each defendant's Answer to the Plaintiff's Complaint.

Governing Law: Federal Rule 8(b)–(d).

After a plaintiff has filed a complaint, it seems only fair for the person sued to have the opportunity to respond to that complaint. After a defendant has had the chance to digest the allegations of the complaint, to take a few deep breaths to try and relax, and to contact an attorney, the defendant and counsel can determine how to respond to the complaint. Defendant's response may serve multiple purposes: to admit certain allegations, to deny allegations, to accompany the response with a defendant's counterclaim, and to bring in other parties to the lawsuit. Defendant's response to the complaint is called the "answer." The response to defendant's answer is called an "answer" or a "reply," and is discussed later in this Chapter. This portion of the Chapter will focus on the methods available to defendant in responding to plaintiff's complaint.

Federal Rule 8(b) informs a defendant how to challenge and require a plaintiff to prove some or all of the allegations in the complaint. Defendant is to state in short and plain terms defenses to each claim and to admit or deny plaintiff's allegations. Failure to deny an allegation when an answer is required results in the allegation being treated as admitted. Rule 8(b) informs a defendant that the answer to the complaint should notify plaintiff of the allegations in the complaint that defendant admits and will not be in issue at trial. It also alerts plaintiff about which allegations are denied and therefore will require proof to be established at trial to enable plaintiff to succeed. Pleading of affirmative defenses, as opposed to denials, is governed by Rule 8(c) and will be discussed in the next section. As previously discussed for claims for relief in a complaint, the answer should notify plaintiff of the issues contested by defendant. Later discovery and pretrial procedures provide factual development of the facts applicable to the claims and defenses.

1. MENU OF RESPONSES

Defendant has a variety of devices to use in answering a complaint. Defendant can *admit* each and every allegation in the complaint. Any defendant in that position is probably better off to begin a course of negotiations with plaintiff to settle the case for less than plaintiff has sought in the complaint. Negotiation is preferable to admitting all the allegations immediately, which subjects defendant to a judgment for all the relief sought by plaintiff.

A more likely and preferred alternative is for defendant to *deny all or part* of the allegations in the complaint. Rule 8(b) requires that denials fairly respond to the substance of the allegation. This standard potentially applies to any type of denial, whether it is a general denial, a specific denial, or a qualified denial. How can an answer fail to meet the substance of what is being denied? Suppose defendant states in the answer, "Prove whatever you alleged" or "Your allegations do not even justify a response." Even though Rule 8(b) does not prescribe a proper model to deny allegations and even though these statements may characterize defendant's initial reaction to the complaint, they neither admit nor deny plaintiff's allegations and therefore cannot be said to meet fairly the substance of the allegation. A denial that does not meet the substance of the statements being denied is treated under Rule 8 as admitted.

General denial. What happens if defendant selects the responsive alternative of denying every one of the complaint's allegations, also known as a general denial and recognized in Rule 8(b)? How does defendant say this? While there is no set formula for making a general denial, it would be typical for defendant to state simply, "Defendant denies each and every allegation of the complaint." The tactical advantage of a general denial is that it forces plaintiff to prove every matter of fact alleged in the complaint.

Can a defendant justify this response? Even though the rules allow a defendant to make a general denial, its use is limited. First, because the complaint included jurisdictional statements as well as the claims for relief, it is unlikely that plaintiff incorrectly stated all matters relating to the matters such as the parties' identities and addresses. Situations are rare when a defendant can completely deny the complaint's allegations. In the language of Rule 8(b), can a general denial fairly respond to the substance of the allegation?

Second, as with all pleadings, a defendant's general denial of all allegations must have a good faith factual and legal basis under Rule 11. Recall that Rule 11 (discussed in Chap. 6 pt. D) applies to all arguments made in documents filed with the court, not merely the plaintiff's complaint. If plaintiff moves under Rule 12(f) to strike defendant's answer because defendant has failed to deny plaintiff's allegations in good faith, all plaintiff has to show is one defect in order for the entire answer to be stricken. True, the court granting the motion is likely to permit defendant to file another answer, but the court may well question defendant's credibility. A more specific answer will compel defendant to admit some matters, which means that plaintiff will not have so many things to prove at trial. Third, issues relating to a party's capacity or the performance or occurrence of a condition precedent require specific denials, per Rule 9(c).

Specific denials. Because it is unlikely that a defendant can make a general denial in good faith, Rule 8(b) permits defendant to specifically deny designated allegations. A specific denial is the most common method of answering a complaint when all allegations in a complaint's paragraph can be controverted. There is no magic formula for making a specific denial, other than for defendant to be clear about which allegations are being denied and which are not, e.g., "Defendant denies all the allegations in Paragraph 3."

Qualified denials. A defendant may prefer to admit some of the allegations in a paragraph but deny others. A general or specific denial is inappropriate because some allegations are being admitted. Rule 8(b) authorizes defendant to generally deny all allegations except those specifically admitted. This denial often is called a qualified denial, because it has the effect of a specific denial but is subject to express qualifications, e.g., "Defendant denies all the allegations in Paragraph 5, except those relating to identity and residential address."

Denial based on lack of knowledge or information to form a belief. Rule 8(b) states that if defendant lacks knowledge or information sufficient to form a belief as to the truth of an allegation, defendant shall so state and this statement has the effect of a denial. Who can use this denial? A defendant can use this type of denial when there is insufficient data to justify either an honest admission or a denial of plaintiff's allegation. When can the denial be used? Within the time for a defendant to answer the complaint (usually 21 days unless service of process was waived), defendant lacks both first-hand knowledge of important facts and the ability to find out about those facts in order to form a belief, e.g., "For lack of knowledge or information sufficient to form a belief, Defendant can neither affirm nor deny the Plaintiff's domicile."

Denial based upon information and belief. A defendant who lacks first-hand or personal knowledge about the validity of one or more of the allegations in the complaint, *but* has sufficient information to form a belief about the truth or falsity of the allegations may assert a denial upon "information and belief." This type of denial is not explicitly authorized by Rule 8(b), unlike the denial based upon a lack of knowledge or information sufficient to form a belief. However, federal courts have permitted allegations on information and belief, presumably because of the language in Rule 11 stating that an attorney's signature on a pleading certifies "that to the best of the person's knowledge, information, and belief, formed after an inquiry reasonable under the circumstances" it is well grounded in fact and warranted by existing law.

A denial upon information and belief is most appropriate when the denial is based upon information from a third person, such as the party's attorney. Denials by corporate defendants are typical examples, because the corporation lacks first-hand or personal knowledge. A denial upon information and belief is not available if the statements in the complaint address matters within defendant's personal knowledge, matters within the general knowledge of the community, or matters of public record. Any use of a denial on information and belief in this context is subject to a motion to strike under Rule 12(f).

Negative pregnant. Sometimes, a denial, if read literally and interpreted against defendant, actually denies only an immaterial part of the complaint and leaves admitted the key allegations by plaintiff. At common law this pleading defect was called a negative pregnant, i.e., the "negative" was said to be "pregnant" with an admission. Although the answer was in the form of a denial, it was uncertain whether defendant intended to deny all the elements of the allegation or to deny only some elements. An example of one form of a negative pregnant occurs when a plaintiff claims that the value of a car exceeds $15,000, and defendant denies that the value exceeded that sum. Taken literally, defendant denied only the immaterial word "exceeded" but admitted that the value of the car at least equaled $15,000.

A negative pregnant may be the result of defendant framing the denial in exactly the same language as plaintiff's affirmative allegation, e.g., a defendant attempts to deny an allegation that he "negligently drove his automobile causing injury to plaintiff" with the statement that he "did not negligently drive his automobile causing injury to the plaintiff." At common law, defendant only denied that he acted negligently but admitted having driven the car when it struck and injured the plaintiff.

Failure to deny. Under Rule 8(b)(6), a failure to deny allegations in the complaint constitutes an admission of the facts alleged. The sentence applies even in cases where no answer is filed. There are two limitations on the application of the basic rule. First, allegations concerning the amount of damages specifically are exempted from the effect of Rule 8(b) and are not admitted by a failure to deny. Second, the rule makes it clear that an admission by failure to deny only applies to allegations in pleadings to which a responsive pleading is required. According to the second sentence of Rule 8(b), allegations contained in a pleading (like an answer) to which no response is required or permitted are deemed denied and thus contested automatically without the necessity of a denial.

To avoid the effect of the first sentence of Rule 8(b), a pleader must do more than make a passing reference to the allegations in the preceding pleading or interpose an ambiguous response to them. As discussed under Rule 8(b) a denial must fairly respond to the substance of the allegations; otherwise the response will be treated as an admission. Rule 8(b) should be read in conjunction with Rule 7(a), which lists those pleadings that are required or permitted to be interposed under the federal rules. For example, any affirmative defense raised in an answer automatically is deemed denied and at issue because no responsive pleading is permitted to an affirmative defense in the absence of a court order. Similarly, because no responsive pleading to an answer is permitted, facts raised for the first time in an answer are considered denied. However, if the trial court orders a reply to the answer, which is permitted by Rule 7(a), an allegation in the answer that is not denied in the reply is deemed admitted under Rule 8(b).

KING VISION PAY PER VIEW, LTD. v. J.C. DIMITRI'S RESTAURANT, INC.
180 F.R.D. 332 (N.D. Ill. 1998)

SHADUR, SENIOR DISTRICT JUDGE.

J.C. Dimitri's Restaurant, Inc. ("Dimitri's") and James Chelios ("Chelios") have filed what purports to be a Response to Complaint that addresses the Complaint filed against them by King Vision Pay Per View, Ltd. This *sua sponte* opinion is triggered by the Response's pervasive and impermissible flouting of the crystal-clear directive of Fed.R.Civ.P.

("Rule") 8(b) as to how any responsive pleading to a federal complaint must be drafted.[1]

This is it. For too many years and in too many hundreds of cases this Court has been reading, and has been compelled to order the correction of, allegedly responsive pleadings that are written by lawyers who are either unaware of or who choose to depart from Rule 8(b)'s plain roadmap. It identifies only three alternatives as available for use in an answer to the allegations of a complaint: to admit those allegations, to deny them or to state a disclaimer (if it can be made in the objective and subjective good faith demanded by Rule 11) in the express terms of the second sentence of Rule 8(b), which then entitles the pleader to the benefit of a deemed denial.

Here Dimitri's' and Chelios' counsel has engaged in a particularly vexatious violation of that most fundamental aspect of federal pleading. It is hard to imagine, but fully 30 of the Response's 35 paragraphs (its express statements in Response ¶¶ 6–12, 17, 25–26 and 33–34, plus the incorporation by reference of such earlier paragraphs in Response ¶¶ 19 and 28) contain this nonresponse, in direct violation of Rule 8(b)'s express teaching: Neither admit nor deny the allegations of said Paragraph—, but demand strict proof thereof.

. . . [A] a host of this Court's unpublished opinions . . . speak not only of the unacceptability of any such Rule 8(b) violation but also to the equally unacceptable "demand" for "strict proof," a concept that to this Court's knowledge is unknown to the federal practice or to any other system of modern pleading.

This Court's efforts at lawyer education through the issuance of repeated brief opinions or oral rulings, or through faculty participation in seminars and symposia on federal pleading and practice,[4] have proved unavailing. It is time for this Court to follow the Rules itself, in this instance Rule 8(b):

> Averments in a pleading to which a responsive pleading is required, other than those as to the amount of damage, are admitted when not denied in the responsive pleading.

Accordingly all of the allegations of Complaint ¶¶ 6–12, 17, 25–26 and 33–34 are held to have been admitted by Dimitri's and Chelios, and this action will proceed on that basis. And although the same phenomenon referred to in n. 4 probably makes it quite unlikely that the lawyers who are most prone to commit the same offense will be lawyers

---

[1] "Drafted" is really too fancy a label for a task that, in this respect, requires no drafting skills at all—merely the ability to read and to comply with instructions that the Rule's drafters have set out in plain and simple English.

[4] Unfortunately those seminars and symposia usually turn out to involve preaching to the converted. Lawyers who really need such continuing legal education rarely attend (they must be too busy making mistakes).

who are regular (or even sporadic) readers of F.Supp. or F.R.D., this opinion is being sent to West Publishing Company for publication. Future Rule 8(b) violators are hereby placed on constructive notice that their similarly defective pleadings will encounter like treatment.

PROBLEMS

1. Constant sues Mocerf for breach of contract. In his Answer, the defendant in ¶¶ 3 through 7 responds to corresponding allegations in the Complaint that allege the terms of provisions in documents. Instead of providing direct responses to the allegations, Mocerf asserts that the documents "speak for themselves." Is this a proper response under Rule 8?

2. In addressing later paragraphs of the same Complaint, for his Answer, Mocerf states: "Defendant is without sufficient knowledge to admit the allegations contained in paragraphs 8–12, and therefore denies same." Is this a proper response under Rule 8?

3. Podoll's Complaint stated that on July 1, 2015, the insured property was completely destroyed by fire. Defendant Singlust answers that "on July 1, 2015, the insured property was not completely destroyed by fire." Is this a proper response under Rule 8? How can you improve the response?

4. Podoll's Complaint also stated that "Defendant Singlust made, executed and delivered" an insurance contract. Singlust's Answer denied that he had "made, executed and delivered" an insurance contract. Is there a problem with that response?

EXERCISE

In response to the complaint filed by Picasso in Chap. 6 pt. B.1, defendant van Gogh filed the following answer. After reading the answer, determine which of its paragraphs are illustrative of the material discussed above. Specifically, do any parts of the answer illustrate a general denial, specific denial, qualified denial, denial based on lack of information, denial based on information and belief, negative pregnant, or a failure to deny?

UNITED STATES DISTRICT COURT for the
DISTRICT OF VERMONT

PABLO PICASSO, Plaintiff)
)
v.) Civil Action 15–1234
)
VINCENT VAN GOGH, Defendant)

ANSWER

Defendant for his Answer to Plaintiff's Complaint states as follows:

1. Defendant admits the allegations contained in Paragraphs 1, 2, 4, 6, 10, and 21.

2. Defendant denies the allegations contained in Paragraphs 14, 15, 17, 18, 19, and 22.

3. With respect to the allegations contained in Paragraph 3, Defendant admits that this Court has subject matter jurisdiction over Plaintiff's first two claims, but denies that the cited statutory provisions support subject matter jurisdiction over those claims.

4. With respect to Paragraph 5, Defendant admits that he resides in Vermont, and denies the remainder of the Paragraph.

5. With respect to Paragraphs 7, 8, 9, and 11, Defendant is without knowledge and belief as to the truth of those allegations, and therefore denies all of the allegations in those Paragraphs.

6. With respect to Paragraph 12, Defendant admits that Plaintiff attended the Art Fair, but is without knowledge and belief as to whether Defendant's painting looked like any work Plaintiff may have produced, and accordingly denies the allegation of similar appearance.

7. With respect to Paragraphs 13, 16, and 20, Defendant incorporates to the same force and effect his responses to the assertions that Plaintiff readopts and realleges in these Paragraphs.

8. With respect to Paragraph 23, Defendant denies that he is liable for punitive damages.

9. Plaintiff's Second and Third Claims fail to state a claim upon which relief can be granted.

10. Plaintiff's Third Claim, which arises under state law, is preempted by federal Copyright law.

11. In the alternative, if Defendant's acts might have made him liable to Plaintiff, Plaintiff is barred by laches from bringing the action at this time.

WHEREFORE, Defendant Vincent van Gogh demands that Plaintiff's complaint be dismissed with prejudice, that he recover his costs from this case, and that he be granted all further relief to which he may be entitled.

Howdy Doody
Bar Wars, P.S.C.
6000 Seventh National Tower
Passivity, KY 44444
COUNSEL FOR DEFENDANT

CERTIFICATE OF SERVICE

I certify that on the 20th day of December, 2015, a copy of the foregoing Answer was mailed to Al Gonzalez, 601 South Main Street, Burlington, VT 05401, Counsel for Plaintiff.

Counsel for Defendant

2. AFFIRMATIVE DEFENSES

An affirmative defense is usually described as an avoidance of plaintiff's allegations in the complaint. Information contained in an affirmative defense does not necessarily negate any allegations in the complaint, but it avoids those allegations by adding new information. The purpose of requiring an affirmative defense under Rule 8(c) is to give plaintiff notice of defendant's intent to introduce new matter as a defense.

Access of the parties to the facts, types of defenses, mere convenience, and the nature of the substantive law involved are all factors to determine whether a matter is an affirmative defense. The usual test for whether a matter should be pleaded as an affirmative defense is whether the matter is directly inconsistent or contrary to allegations in the complaint. If so, it is not a matter to be pleaded affirmatively.

When in doubt about whether a certain defense not listed in Rule 8(c) should be pleaded as an affirmative defense, the safe course is to plead it affirmatively, and in addition, deny any relevant allegations in the complaint. It is relatively common to plead affirmative defenses generally, but the particularity provisions of Rule 9 concerning the pleading of fraud, denials of capacity, and denials of occurrence of conditions should be noted. What happens if a defendant fails to plead an affirmative defense? Because Rule 8(c)(1) is mandatory, principles of statutory construction suggest that failure to raise the defense results in a waiver and exclusion of the defense from the case.

RED DEER v. CHEROKEE COUNTY, IOWA
183 F.R.D. 642 (N.D. Iowa 1999)

BENNETT, DISTRICT JUDGE.

[Plaintiff is a female, Native American who unsuccessfully applied for a deputy sheriff's job and then sued the county alleging age, race, and sex discrimination and retaliation. She filed a motion to exclude "after-acquired" evidence of her prior employment records. The court addressed the issue of whether such "after-acquired evidence" constitutes an affirmative defense.]

... The plaintiff ... seeks to exclude evidence from her prior employment records, because she contends those records were not considered by the county at the time it decided not to hire her, but the county contends those records are admissible "after-acquired evidence" of misrepresentations in the plaintiff's job application. Although the court must resolve these evidentiary questions, they have been overshadowed by pleading and trial readiness questions that have arisen as a consequence of the motions in limine. Those questions include whether "after-acquired evidence" is an affirmative defense that must be pleaded and proved by the defendant, and if the defense is an affirmative one. . . .

. . . The County contends that Red Deer misrepresented the reasons for her departures from two of her previous jobs, and characterizes her termination from one of those jobs as a discharge for "dishonest conduct." Dishonest conduct, the County points out, is a ground for termination of a deputy sheriff and prior dishonest conduct would have constituted a ground not to hire Red Deer at all. Thus, the County asserts that, had it known about Red Deer's misrepresentations on her job application at the time of its decision not to hire her, the County would not have hired Red Deer regardless of her race, sex, or age. . . .

The court finds that Red Deer's motion in limine, which seeks to exclude evidence of her prior employment records on the ground that such records were not considered by the County in making its decision not to hire her, must . . . be denied. In *McKennon v. Nashville Banner Pub. Co.*, 513 U.S. 352 (1995), the Supreme Court considered the impact of "after-acquired evidence" of an employee's wrong-doing upon the relief the employee may obtain for discrimination by the employer. . . .

The one black letter rule established in *McKennon* is that where an employer seeks to rely upon after-acquired evidence of wrongdoing by the employee during his or her employment—and this court concludes where the employer seeks to rely on evidence of wrongdoing in the application process—the employer "must first establish that the wrongdoing was of such severity that the employee in fact would have been terminated on those grounds alone if the employer had known of it at the time of the discharge." *Id.* at 362–63. In the circumstances of the case now before the court, a failure-to-hire case not a discharge case, this court reads the rule to be that the County must first establish that the wrongdoing was of such severity that Red Deer in fact would not have been hired on those grounds alone if the County had known of the wrongdoing at the time of the decision not to hire her. . . .

The question under *McKennon* is not whether the County actually relied on the evidence in making its decision, but what the County would have done had the evidence come to light at the time of Red Deer's applications. Indeed, the Supreme Court was aware of Red Deer's concern, because it specifically noted that "[t]he employer could not have been motivated by knowledge it did not have and it cannot now claim that the employee was fired [or not hired] for the nondiscriminatory reason." *Id.* at 360. . . .

In these circumstances, the evidence of Red Deer's past employment is relevant to the availability and success of the County's after-acquired evidence defense, and is not unfairly prejudicial. . . .

. . . Scant case law considers whether "after-acquired evidence" is an affirmative defense that must be pleaded as well as proved by the defendant. Indeed, no court appears to have considered the question directly. . . .

In *McKennon*, the Supreme Court clearly placed the burden of proving the "after-acquired evidence" defense upon the defendant. For example, the Court stated that "[w]here an employer seeks to rely upon after-acquired evidence of wrongdoing, *it must first establish* that the wrongdoing was of such severity that the employee in fact would have been terminated [or not hired] on those grounds alone if the employer had known of it at the time of the discharge." *McKennon*, 513 U.S. at 362–63 (emphasis added). The Court did not, however, specifically identify the defense as an "affirmative" one, and said nothing whatever about the defendant's obligation to plead the defense. Unfortunately, more general guidance on what constitutes an affirmative defense is also sparse, but what suggestions this court has discovered are discussed in the next subsection.

. . . The purpose of the pleading requirement for affirmative defenses in Rule 8(c) "is to give the opposing party notice of the plea of [the affirmative defense] and a chance to argue, if he can, why the imposition of [the affirmative defense] would be inappropriate." *Blonder-Tongue Lab. v. University of Illinois Found.*, 402 U.S. 313, 350 (1971). . . .

"[A]fter-acquired evidence" plainly is not among the affirmative defenses specifically enumerated in Rule 8(c). Where a defense is not one of the enumerated defenses, whether or not it comes within the ambit of Rule 8(c) depends upon whether it falls within the "catchall" for "any other" defenses. . . .

In *Sayre v. Musicland Group, Inc.*, 850 F.2d 350 (8th Cir.1988), a diversity case, the Eighth Circuit Court of Appeals stated that "[t]he pleading of affirmative defenses is a procedural matter" to which federal rules of procedure apply. *Sayre*, 850 F.2d at 352. Therefore, in determining whether mitigation of damages was an affirmative defense that must be pleaded and proved, the Eighth Circuit Court of Appeals looked first to federal decisions, which had uniformly found mitigation of damages to be an affirmative defense that must be pleaded and proved. Id. Such guidance from federal decisions is lacking here.

. . . The case now before the court is not a diversity case, but a federal question case. However, this court can think of no reason why allocation of the burden of proof, if it is the pertinent factor to be drawn from state decisions for determining what is an affirmative defense within the meaning of Fed.R.Civ.P. 8(c) in a diversity case, should not also be a pertinent factor for determining what is an affirmative defense in a federal question case. Thus, to the extent federal cases establish the burden of proof for the defense in question here, the allocation of that burden of proof is relevant to the determination of what is an affirmative defense.

... The test in the First Circuit is "whether the defense 'shares the common characteristic of a bar to the right of recovery even if the general complaint were more or less admitted to.'" *Wolf v. Reliance Standard Life Ins. Co.*, 71 F.3d 444, 449 (1st Cir.1995) (quoting *Jakobsen v. Massachusetts Port Auth.*, 520 F.2d 810, 813 (1st Cir.1975)).

... [T]he various authorities considered so far do suggest a number of factors that may be pertinent to the question of whether a particular defense is an affirmative one within the meaning of Rule 8(c). This court finds it unnecessary to select any one test of what constitutes an affirmative defense over another or to consider one suggested factor to the exclusion of others. This is so, because—at least in the absence of a definitive test from the Eighth Circuit Court of Appeals—perhaps the best manner in which the court can analyze the question of what constitutes an affirmative defense within the meaning of Rule 8(c) is to consider each of the suggested factors or tests.

Therefore the court will consider here each of the following factors. First, the court will consider the allocation of the burden of proof, reasoning that if the defendant bears the burden of proof on the defense, it is an affirmative defense. Second, the court will consider whether the defense simply controverts the plaintiff's proof, or instead "avoids" the plaintiff's claim. To put it another way, the court will consider "whether the defense 'shares the common characteristic of a bar to the right of recovery even if the general complaint were more or less admitted to,'" not simply controverted. *Wolf*, 71 F.3d at 449 (quoting *Jakobsen*, 520 F.2d at 813). If so, the defense is an affirmative one. Third, the specific purposes of Rule 8(c) must not be overlooked. Thus, the court should consider the need for notice of the defense to avoid surprise and undue prejudice to the plaintiff. ...

The court now turns to application of these factors or analyses to the defense in question here. As to allocation of the burden of proof, the Supreme Court has made clear that the burden of proof on the "after-acquired evidence" defense is allocated to the defendant. *McKennon*, 513 U.S. at 362–63. Thus, under this test, the defense is an affirmative one that must also be pleaded pursuant to Rule 8(c). The "after-acquired evidence" defense is also one that does not controvert the plaintiff's proof, but instead "avoids" the plaintiff's claim, or at least part of the plaintiff's potential relief. As the Supreme Court explained in *McKennon*, the defense, if proved, limits the plaintiff's relief, generally precluding frontpay or reinstatement, and limiting backpay to the period from the date of the unlawful discharge or failure to hire to the date the new information was discovered. *McKennon*, 513 U.S. at 361–62.... In other words, the "after-acquired evidence" defense "'shares the common characteristic of a bar to the right of recovery even if the general complaint were more or less admitted to,'" *Wolf*, 71 F.3d at 449 (emphasis added) (quoting *Jakobsen*, 520 F.2d at 813), or the claim was otherwise in fact proved.

Treating the "after-acquired evidence" defense as an affirmative one that must be pleaded and proved also is consonant with the purposes of Rule 8(c), because it is a defense for which the need for notice to avoid surprise and undue prejudice to the plaintiff is particularly apparent.... For example, here, Red Deer must frame legal arguments concerning what constitutes a "misrepresentation" and what constitutes "misconduct" of sufficient gravity that it meets the *McKennon* standard of misconduct for which the County would not have hired her on those grounds alone. She must also establish relevant facts concerning the applicability of the defense, including whether she did indeed make any "misrepresentations" and what were the actual circumstances under which she left the two jobs that are at the focus of the County's assertion of the defense.

Therefore, the court concludes that "after-acquired evidence" is an affirmative defense that must indeed be pleaded and proved pursuant to Rule 8(c). [The court proceeded to permit the County to amend its answer to include the affirmative defense.]

NOTES AND QUESTIONS

1. What is an affirmative defense? Instead of being regarded as denials, the defenses listed in Rule 8(c) are analogous to confessions or avoidances that exonerate the defendant because of circumstances that occurred before, during, or after the alleged wrong. By asserting an affirmative defense, defendant introduces new matter that constitutes an excuse or justification if the defense is valid.

However, the rule provides no help in identifying the essential characteristics of an affirmative defense. Rule 8(c) does not specifically define what is meant by an "affirmative defense." Instead, it provides a non-exhaustive list of affirmative defenses. Some recognized affirmative defenses not mentioned in Rule 8(c) are alteration of an instrument, condition subsequent, impossibility of performance, infancy, insanity, mistake, novation, privilege in defamation actions, rescission, and breach of warranty.

2. The assertion of an affirmative defense may involve three related burdens: the burden of pleading, the burden of production (or going forward

with the evidence), and the burden of persuasion (or risk of nonpersuasion). The rule does not state which, if any, of the three burdens are essential characteristics for describing an affirmative defense.

In *Gomez v. Toledo*, 446 U.S. 635, 639–40, 100 S.Ct. 1920, 64 L.Ed.2d 572 (1980), the Court held that a defendant has the burden of pleading an affirmative defense, because whether an affirmative defense exists depends on facts peculiarly within the knowledge and control of the defendant. For example, the applicable test for immunity focuses on whether defendant has an objectively reasonable basis for his belief that his conduct was lawful and whether he has a subjective belief.

Burdens of production may shift between the parties. For example, once plaintiff produces sufficient evidence to establish a prima facie case, the burden of production shifts to defendant to produce evidence either conclusively rebutting one or more elements of plaintiff's prima facie case, or establishing an affirmative defense.

Finally, defendant has the burden of proof on an affirmative defense to establish every essential element of the defense so that he would be entitled to a directed verdict if the evidence went unchallenged at trial. For example, for the affirmative defense of a statute of limitation, defendant has the burden of demonstrating by prima facie proof that the limitations period has expired since plaintiff's claims accrued.

3. Suppose defendant fails to plead an affirmative defense, but at trial introduces evidence relevant to that defense (e.g., evidence that a particular contract was oral rather than in writing). If plaintiff does not object to that evidence, the parties will be deemed to have agreed to try the issue by implied consent, and the court may allow amendment of the answer under Rule 15(b). Rule 15(b), which you studied in Chap. 6 pt. E, applies to all pleadings, not just the complaint. The test for allowing an amendment to conform pleadings to issues impliedly tried is whether the opposing party would be prejudiced by the implied amendment. The focus is on whether evidence was introduced without objection.

4. Rule 8(c)(2) provides that "If a party mistakenly designates a defense as a counterclaim or a counterclaim as a defense, the court must, if justice requires, treat the pleading as though it were correctly designated . . . ." The purpose of the rule is to protect a defendant against designation errors in pleading matters such as fraud and mistake leading to reformation or cancellation of a written instrument like a contract. The question is one primarily of name and form, and the rule is designed to protect a party who has made a wrong choice in that respect.

5. *Motion to strike.* When the merits or lack of merits of defendant's affirmative defense depends on a legal question, a Rule 12(f) motion to strike can test the legal sufficiency of the defense. Once defendant has raised an affirmative defense by answer, plaintiff may move for the defense to be stricken from the pleadings. A motion to strike a defense which is insufficient in law has the same function with respect to an affirmative defense that a

motion to dismiss for failure to state a claim performs with respect to the complaint. Thus a motion to strike an insufficient defense assumes the truth of the allegations of the defense. The test for a motion to strike on this ground is similar to the test for a motion to dismiss on the ground that the complaint does not state a claim entitling the plaintiff to relief: do the allegations of the defense authorize defendant to prove any state of facts which would constitute an affirmative defense?

3. RESPONDING TO THE ANSWER

The terms of Federal Rule 7(a) require a court order authorizing a reply to any part of an answer other than a counterclaim. Without a court order, an answer to a counterclaim is the only reply authorized. That response in effect "answers" the claim stated in the counterclaim, and is subject to the same rules as defendant's original answer. Assuming that there is a complaint and an answer containing affirmative defenses, the case law indicates that an affirmative defense in the answer does not generally merit a reply. Thus, ordinarily, some unusual reason must be urged, e.g., the complaint and answer with new matter do not cover the issues in the case, or the availability or expense of discovery procedures or the possibility of summary judgment justify a reply.

REYES v. SAZAN
168 F.3d 158 (5th Cir. 1999)

PATRICK E. HIGGINBOTHAM, CIRCUIT JUDGE.

This lawsuit alleges that various officials violated the plaintiffs' constitutional rights by conspiring to enforce selectively the traffic laws and damaging a pickup truck in a fruitless search for contraband. We conclude the district court abused its discretion by not requiring a Rule 7 reply to the defense of qualified immunity. . . .

As we must, we assume the plaintiffs' story: Florentino and Elizabeth Martinez, brother and sister, were driving with Elizabeth's minor daughter in Ramiro Reyes's pickup truck on Interstate 12 in St. Tammany Parish, Louisiana, en route to Alabama. The truck had Texas plates. When they passed a marked Louisiana State Police vehicle, Carl Sazan, a Louisiana State Trooper, pulled them over. They were driving under the speed limit. [Everyone got out of the truck. A police dog arrived with another trooper, but no drugs were found. Nevertheless, Sazan ordered the plaintiffs to follow him to headquarters where a more thorough search occurred which damaged the vehicle at a cost exceeding $2,000. Again the police found no drugs and brought no charges against any of the vehicles occupants. During the search, plaintiffs were forced to stand in a cold rain. The plaintiffs sued Sazan and the supervisory officers for federal civil rights violations and state damage claims. All defendants asserted qualified immunity as an affirmative defense.]

The plaintiffs replied that their suits were against the defendants in their individual capacities and that these defendants were not entitled to qualified immunity. They explained that [the supervising officers] conspired with Sazan to enforce traffic laws selectively against Hispanics and out-of-state residents.

While the district court agreed that Reyes could not maintain his claims under §§ 1983 and 1985(3), it denied the motion to dismiss in other respects. It also decided that it had supplemental jurisdiction over plaintiffs' state law claims. . . .

The complaint alleges specific facts detailing plaintiffs' personal experience with Sazan. It offers no similar detail for the claim that [the supervising officers] conspired to deny them and other Hispanic drivers their civil rights. The district court concluded that the plaintiffs had "plead with particularity that this was part of a policy to stop and search those of Hispanic origin and/or that the supervisors failed to adequately train and/or monitor the Troopers." The court did not dismiss the suit, suggesting that it would grant summary judgment to the supervisors absent evidence raising a genuine issue of material fact. As we will explain, we do not agree that the claim was plead with particularity against the supervisory officers, and we conclude that the district court moved too quickly.

Faced with sparse details of claimed wrongdoing by officials, trial courts ought routinely require plaintiffs to file a reply under Federal Rule of Civil Procedure 7(a) to qualified immunity defenses. See *Schultea v. Wood*, 47 F.3d 1427, 1430, 1432 (5th Cir.1995) (en banc). The *Schultea* court held that "the [district] court may, in its discretion, insist that a plaintiff file a reply tailored to an answer pleading the defense of qualified immunity." *Id.* at 1433–44. The district court need not allow any discovery at this point unless the "plaintiff has supported his claim with sufficient precision and factual specificity to raise a genuine issue as to the illegality of defendant's conduct at the time of the alleged acts." *Id.* at 1434.

Plaintiffs did not allege their claims against the supervisory defendants with particularity. Their pleading was little more than a bare conclusion, and the district court erred in finding the complaint to be sufficient. Rather, it should first have ordered a reply, and if the required detail was not forthcoming, dismiss the complaint. . . .

The district court abused its discretion in failing to require a Rule 7 reply. As the *Schultea* court made clear, "Vindicating the immunity doctrine will ordinarily require such a reply, and a district court's discretion not to do so is narrow indeed when greater detail might assist." *Id.* at 1434.

The Supreme Court since *Schultea* has attempted to clarify the jurisdiction of the courts of appeal to review a denial of qualified immunity. At present, the rule of jurisdiction comes to this: Legal conclusions are immediately appealable, but not the sufficiency of the evidence to support the denial. The appellate court can consider the materiality of disputed issues of fact, but not contentions that there are factual disputes.

The Supreme Court's refinement of qualified immunity jurisdiction has only made the more important *Schultea*'s emphasis upon the reply as a tool of the trial court insisting on particularity in pleading. Indeed, the Court's vigorous adherence to the distinction between fact and law—or genuine issues and material issues—underscores the strength of the *Schultea* approach. Whether the complaint is insufficiently particular, and thus a reply to the defense of qualified immunity is needed, is a question of law. Similarly, we can examine afresh whether a reply is "tailored to the assertion of qualified immunity and fairly engage[s] its allegations," *Schultea*, 47 F.3d at 1433, a look that does not require reviewing the record to determine if the reply's factual assertions are true.

We vacate the district court's denial of qualified immunity to [the supervising officers], and remand with instructions to require that the plaintiffs file a reply to the defense. . . .

NOTES AND QUESTIONS

1. *Reyes* and *Schultea* state that a court-ordered reply can be useful to test the sufficiency of an affirmative defense. *Schultea* noted that its rule creates an incentive for a defendant "to plead his defense with some particularity because it has the practical effect of requiring particularity in the reply." How does the language of Rules 7(a)(7), 8(b)(1)(A), and 8(e) require a particularized reply?

2. The three-step pleading process recommended in *Reyes* is 1) plaintiff files a short and plain statement asserting a civil rights claim; 2) defendant then pleads qualified immunity as an affirmative defense in its answer; and 3) the trial judge has the discretion to insist that plaintiff file a reply responding to the affirmative defense.

3. Are there any strategic or financial reasons why a defendant would try to obtain a court order directing plaintiff to reply to defendant's answer? If indeed there are good reasons for a defendant to seek a reply by plaintiff, are there valid reasons for Rule 7(a) being so restrictive when defendant asserts an affirmative defense?

4. When should plaintiff be denied a court order to file a reply to defendant's answer and affirmative defense? In *Beckstrom v. Coastwise Line*, 13 F.R.D. 480 (D. Alaska 1953), the plaintiff sought permission to reply to an answer containing a number of affirmative defenses. Although it denied the

plaintiff's request, the court responded to the contention that a motion of this type was impermissible in the following manner:

> Defendants suggest that the plaintiff may not be ordered to file a reply upon its own motion because Rule 7(a) gives the power to order a reply to the defendants' answer and it would be inappropriate for a plaintiff to ask the Court to order him to reply, and that if the rule had been intended to permit the plaintiff to seek leave to reply, the rule would not have contained its present phraseology.
>
> That conclusion is not inevitable. It is usually the defendant who requests the reply but . . . the Court, in each instance, denied plaintiff's motion for leave to file a reply . . . without questioning the right of the plaintiff to make such a motion or to have the motion granted in the proper case. The liberal construction required of the rules would permit the granting of plaintiff's motion for leave to file a reply, and an order accordingly.

In *Beckstrom*, the plaintiff was attempting to revive his right to demand a jury trial, which had been lost by his failure to file a timely demand, by obtaining permission to interpose a reply and then demanding a jury trial within ten days thereafter (that time period is now fourteen days). Was the court correct to deny the motion to file a reply?

EXERCISE

For the state a) where you intend to practice after graduation, b) where your law school is located, and/or c) your professor assigns, go to that state's annotated rules and research the procedural rules for answering complaints, asserting affirmative defenses, and filing replies. Based on your research, print the rules and bring them to class for discussion. In addition, answer the following questions.

1. Identify the types of responses (e.g., denials) that are:

a. Recognized explicitly in the rules; and

b. Recognized by the courts as methods for responding to a complaint.

2. Identify whether affirmative defenses (e.g., statute of limitations) are:

a. Recognized explicitly in the rules; and

b. Recognized by the courts as valid affirmative defenses.

3. Identify whether a motion to strike a pleading is recognized, and if so, how it compares to Federal Rule 12(f).

4. Identify whether a reply to an answer is recognized, and if so, how it compares to Federal Rule 7(a).

D. FAILURE TO RESPOND: DEFAULT JUDGMENT

INTRODUCTORY PROBLEM

Carter, a citizen of Georgia, loaned Clinton, a citizen of New York, approximately $1,000,000 for one year at five percent interest. Clinton signed a promissory note to signify her debt to Carter. At the end of the one-year period, Clinton refuses to pay and Carter immediately sues Clinton in a New York federal court requesting $1,050,000 in damages. Clinton does not answer Carter's summons and complaint, appear in court, or otherwise defend the claim against her. The court clerk enters Clinton's default and subsequently enters a default judgment against Clinton, awarding Carter $1,050,000.

May a court clerk enter a judgment with such serious consequences to a defendant?

Governing Rule: Rule 55(a)–(b).

KPS & ASSOCIATES, INC. v. DESIGNS BY FMC, INC.
318 F.3d 1 (1st Cir. 2003)

LIPEZ, CIRCUIT JUDGE.

[A sales agent, KPS & Associates, Inc. ("KPS"), sued in September, 1999, to recover commissions owing from a vendor, Designs by FMC, Inc. ("Designs"), whose products the agent promoted. The trial court entered a default judgment based on the defendant's failure to answer the complaint. Thereafter, the court refused to set aside the default judgment and entered a damage award for $367,154 against the defendant, which it doubled pursuant to Massachusetts unfair trade practices law (Chapter 93A).] . . .

For the reasons stated below, we affirm the district court in all respects save one—the computation of the base quantum of damages after the entry of default. In fixing that amount, the district court erred in its application of Rule 55(b)(2) of the Federal Rules of Civil Procedure (dealing with the determination of damages after an entry of default).

Following the filing of the complaint in this case, the litigation quickly bogged down in a messy motion practice. Both parties and their attorneys accused each other of misconduct and filed numerous motions for sanctions, to strike, to quash, to compel, and to disqualify.

. . . [O]n March 1, 2000, [KPS's counsel] Hurvitz submitted to the court a request for an entry of default since Designs had yet to file its answer. This request was served on Designs' New York and local counsel. On March 10, 2000, the clerk entered a notice of default against Designs pursuant to Rule 55(a) of the Federal Rules of Civil Procedure. Copies of the notice were served on all counsel. On March 17, 2000, KPS filed a request for the entry of default judgment, which was likewise served on all counsel.

On March 21, 2000, [Designs' counsel] Schrader finally took action, faxing a letter to the court in which he asserted that he had sent a timely answer on March 1, 2000, by Federal Express. Shortly thereafter, Designs filed a motion to set aside the default, and the district court conducted a hearing on May 17, 2000. At the close of the hearing, the district court ruled from the bench, denying Designs' motion to set aside the entry of default. The court characterized Schrader's behavior over the course of the litigation as "stonewalling" and explicitly disbelieved Schrader's proffered explanation with regard to the filing of the answer. She told Schrader: "We have had trouble with you from the very beginning." She concluded: "And because I do not credit these stories, because I do not find there to be good cause to remove the default, the motion to remove the default is denied." . . .

Subsequently, on July 27, 2000, the court issued a brief written order on damages which stated, in part:

> No further hearing is necessary to ascertain the compensatory damages claimed as the verified complaint and plaintiff's affidavit attached thereto set forth a sum certain based on sales and commission figures there detailed, and, a default having been entered, each of plaintiff's allegations of fact are established as a matter of law. [citations omitted]

The district court then referred the matter to a magistrate judge for the sole purpose of determining whether Designs should be held liable for double or treble damages under Chapter 93A—i.e., to determine whether Designs' unlawful conduct was "willful or knowing." The magistrate judge permitted no evidence on the base quantum of damages, which the court had fixed as the "sum certain" contained in the complaint and a supporting affidavit.

Following the hearing on 93A liability, the magistrate judge issued a Report and Recommendation finding that Designs had willfully and knowingly engaged in conduct prohibited by Chapter 93A and that KPS should be awarded double damages. Designs filed its objections to the Report and Recommendation with the district judge, who overruled those objections. Judgment was entered on September 28, 2001, for $367,154— twice the $183,577 recited in the *ad damnum* clause of KPS's complaint— plus prejudgment interest. On October 23, 2001, Designs filed a timely notice of appeal. . . .

Designs argues that the district court erred in denying its motion to set aside the entry of default. *See* Fed.R.Civ.P. 55(c). . . .

Rule 55(c) provides that a court may set aside an entry of default "for good cause shown." We review the district court's denial of a Rule 55(c) motion for abuse of discretion, while we review any factual findings underlying that decision for clear error. We will not disturb the district court's decision unless it is "clearly wrong." *Bond Leather Co. v. Q.T. Shoe Mfg. Co.,* 764 F.2d 928, 938 (1st Cir.1985).

. . . In *McKinnon v. Kwong Wah Restaurant,* 83 F.3d 498 (1st Cir.1996), we identified no fewer than seven factors a district court may consider:

> (1) whether the default was willful; (2) whether setting it aside would prejudice the adversary; (3) whether a meritorious defense is presented; (4) the nature of the defendant's explanation for the default; (5) the good faith of the parties; (6) the amount of money involved; (7) the timing of the motion [to set aside entry of default].

Id. at 503. Thus Rule 55(c), as an "express[ion of] the traditional inherent equity power of the federal courts," 10A Wright, Miller & Kane, Federal Practice and Procedure: Civil 3d § 2692 (1998), permits the consideration of a panoply of "relevant equitable factors." *Enron Oil Corp. v. Diakuhara,* 10 F.3d 90, 96 (2d Cir.1993). The "Rule 55(c) determinations are case-specific" and "must, therefore, be made in a practical, commonsense manner, without rigid adherence to, or undue reliance upon, a mechanical formula." *Gen. Contracting & Trading Co. [v. Interpole, Inc.,* 899 F.2d 109], 112 (1st Cir.1990). . . . [T]he decision of the district court to accord dispositive weight to one of the familiar factors or other relevant equitable factors does not necessarily mean an abuse of discretion.

This flexibility is necessitated by the competing policies and values that underlie the concept of default. On the one hand, it "provide[s] a useful remedy when a litigant is confronted by an obstructionist adversary," and "play[s] a constructive role in maintaining the orderly and efficient administration of justice." *Enron,* 10 F.3d at 96. It furnishes an invaluable incentive for parties to comply with court orders and rules of procedure. *See* Fed.R.Civ.P. 37(b)(2)(C). It encourages the expeditious resolution of litigation and promotes finality. On the other hand, countervailing considerations include the goals of "resol[ving] cases on the merits," *Key Bank of Me. v. Tablecloth Textile Co.,* 74 F.3d 349, 356 (1st Cir.1996), and avoiding "harsh or unfair result[s]." *Enron,* 10 F.3d at 96. Since "default judgments implicate sharply conflicting policies . . . the trial judge, who is usually the person most familiar with the circumstances of the case and is in the best position to evaluate the good faith and credibility of the parties, is entrusted with the task of balancing these competing considerations." *Eagle Assocs. v. Bank of Montreal,* 926 F.2d 1305, 1307 (2d Cir.1991) (internal quotation marks omitted).

Eleven days after the clerk had entered the default against Designs, Schrader faxed a letter to the court in which he asserted that he had submitted a timely answer via Federal Express. In that letter, Schrader stated that the answer had been sent by a "temporary secretary" and that he had been told by Federal Express that "the packages were likely rejected because the federal express [sic] slip filled out was an **International** Air Waybill" (original emphasis). Schrader indicated that he had been trying to get an affidavit from the temporary secretary who had been working that day. He also told the court that he would submit to the clerk that same day a motion to vacate the default, along with an explanatory affidavit. The motion and affidavit were not filed until one week later.

. . . The district court held a hearing on May 17, 2000, on Designs' motion to remove the default. . . . At the hearing, Schrader argued that the default should be set aside because (a) the default was not willful, (b) Designs had a meritorious defense, and (c) KPS could not show any prejudice. Schrader focused on the willfulness factor. . . .

The district court was not impressed. First, commenting on the procedural history to that point, the court characterized Schrader's behavior as "stonewalling," and she admonished him in open court: "We have had trouble with you from the beginning." She noted his previous failures to meet deadlines and remarked on his duplicitousness, referencing his earlier representation that he could not attend the hearing and then his sudden appearance. She noted inconsistencies and implausibilities in Schrader's representations during the hearing about the late answer, and she found other representations he had made in affidavits to be incredible. . . . These findings led to the dispositive ruling from the bench: "And because I do not credit these stories, because I do not find there to be good cause to remove the default, the motion to remove the default is denied."

. . . By the time the district court denied Designs' motion to set aside the default, it had become well acquainted with the parties and circumstances in this case. It had conducted two motion hearings and one pretrial conference. It had received numerous written communications from counsel and had taken several motions (with supporting materials) under advisement. Given the district court's familiarity with the case, and on the record developed in connection with the hearing, we cannot say that the district court clearly erred in its assessment of Schrader's credibility, nor did it clearly err in rejecting his proffered explanation for the default.

The burden of demonstrating good cause for the removal of a default rested with Designs. Thus, Designs had the burden to demonstrate a lack of willfulness. When the district court rejected Schrader's explanation, Designs was effectively left with *no* explanation for the default. Hence

Designs' argument that the default was not willful lacked any factual predicate and was properly disregarded by the district court.

At the default hearing, Schrader also argued that Designs had a meritorious defense which weighed in favor of setting aside the default. The district court, however, had once before taken a dim view of Designs' asserted defenses .... Thus we take the district court's comment on "stonewalling" to imply that it adhered to its prior skepticism about the defenses, and that it felt that Designs was merely trying to postpone the inevitable. We cannot say that the court erred in its evaluation of Designs' defense. All of the materials offered by Designs in support of its defense were internally generated balance sheets, reports, and the like. KPS, on the other hand, attached copies of actual customer invoices and purchase orders to its complaint. Moreover, over the course of this dispute, the amount Designs claims it is due from KPS has varied wildly: at one time nothing ("a wash"), at another $6,000, at another $30,000, at another $60,000, and finally over $74,000 (not including the $10 million claimed in the New York lawsuit).

Schrader also argued before the district court that KPS would suffer no prejudice if the default were to be set aside. Schrader was correct on this point. ... We have stated elsewhere that in the context of a Rule 55(c) motion, delay in and of itself does not constitute prejudice. "The issue is not mere delay, but rather its accompanying dangers: loss of evidence, increased difficulties of discovery, or an enhanced opportunity for fraud or collusion." *FDIC v. Francisco Inv. Corp.,* 873 F.2d 474, 479 (1st Cir.1989). There is no indication that any of these dangers were present or considered by the district judge when she ruled on the Rule 55(c) motion.

The district court, however, correctly gave significant weight to two other factors—the nature of Designs' explanation for the default, and the good faith of the parties. The district court determined that Schrader had fabricated his explanation regarding the filing of an answer—a finding that goes to the nature of the explanation as well as to Designs' good faith. ... In light of these determinations of fabrication and bad faith, and its consideration of other salient factors, the district court did not abuse its discretion in refusing to set aside the default.

... In its order of July 27, 2000, the district court indicated that no hearing was necessary to determine the base quantum of damages since "the verified complaint and plaintiff's affidavit attached thereto set forth a sum certain based on sales and commission figures there detailed." The order also referred the matter to the magistrate judge for a hearing on Chapter 93A liability. The order did not, however, identify the amount of this "sum certain." The district court subsequently clarified the amount of damages on September 28, 2001, when it overruled Designs' objections to the magistrate judge's Report and Recommendation on the doubling of damages under Chapter 93A: "Judgment may be entered for plaintiff in double the amount of its damages of $183,577." The district court apparently arrived at this sum by looking to the *ad damnum* clause of the complaint.

Designs argues two related points with respect to the district court's calculation of damages. First, Designs argues that KPS's claim was not for a "sum certain" and that the district court erred in thereby fixing the base quantum of damages on the basis of the complaint, without a hearing. Second, Designs argues that the district court erred in limiting the scope of the hearing before the magistrate judge to the issue of liability for multiple damages under Chapter 93A. Designs maintains that it was entitled to an evidentiary hearing to determine the base quantum of damages, notwithstanding any admissions made as result of its default or the amount claimed in the *ad damnum* clause.

The district court's order of July 27, 2000, as clarified by its memorandum and order of September 28, 2001, was entered pursuant to Rule 55(b). . . .

On the basis of its conclusion that "the verified complaint and plaintiff's affidavit attached thereto set forth a sum certain," the district court determined that no evidentiary inquiry was necessary to calculate the amount of damages to be set forth in the default judgment. We review the district court's refusal to inquire further for abuse of discretion.

We conclude that the district court abused its discretion in failing to conduct further inquiry before fixing the base quantum of damages. There are two reasons why further inquiry was required. First, there are obvious discrepancies between the damages claimed in the body of the complaint and the damages requested in the *ad damnum* clause, as well as serious arithmetical errors in the affidavit filed with the complaint. Second, even without these errors and discrepancies, there would still be a need for further inquiry given the nature of KPS's claim.

According to the face of the complaint, KPS claims that it is entitled to $67,238 in base commissions and $63,795 in "sales price differentials," i.e., price mark-ups beyond cost. Adding these two figures results in a total of $131,033. However, in the enumerated counts and *ad damnum* clause, the complaint states that KPS is entitled to judgment against Designs in the amount of $183,577—an unexplained difference of over $50,000. Likewise, KPS's affidavit filed in support of its complaint contains several computational errors. . . . Moreover, many of the accountings and purchase orders attached as exhibits to the complaint's supporting affidavit are illegible or incomprehensible. Given these inconsistencies and errors, the district court erred in simply fixing the base quantum of damages at the amount stated in the complaint's *ad damnum* clause.

Even if KPS's complaint and affidavit were free from the discrepancies and errors detailed above, the district court could not have determined damages without a further evidentiary inquiry. Following the entry of default, a district court can enter a final judgment without requiring further proof of damages only in limited situations. For example, no evidentiary inquiry is necessary if the claim is for a "sum certain."

Contrary to the district court's statement, this is not a sum certain case. In the Rule 55 context, a claim is not a sum certain unless there is no doubt as to the amount to which a plaintiff is entitled as a result of the defendant's default....

As with a "sum certain," a hearing is not normally required if the claim is "liquidated." " 'Liquidated' means adjusted, certain, settled with respect to amount, fixed. A claim is liquidated when the amount thereof has been ascertained and agreed upon by the parties or fixed by operation of law." *Hallett Constr. Co. v. Iowa State Highway Comm'n*, 258 Iowa 520, 139 N.W.2d 421, 426 (1966). The classic example is an enforceable liquidated damages clause in a contract. Another example would be a delinquent tax assessment. KPS and Designs, however, vigorously dispute the issue of damages. Likewise, KPS's damages have not been fixed by operation of law. Finally, as the inconsistencies and inaccuracies in the complaint and the supporting affidavit amply demonstrate, KPS's claims are not capable of simple mathematical computation. Thus, KPS's complaint and its supporting affidavit do not state a liquidated claim.

Relying on the erroneous conclusion that KPS's claim stated a claim for a sum certain, the district court did not look beyond the complaint's *ad damnum* clause and an internally inconsistent supporting affidavit in fixing the base quantum of damages. For the reasons explained above, this limited approach was an abuse of discretion requiring that we remand the matter to the district court for further consideration of the damages issue....

NOTES AND QUESTIONS

1. Federal Rule 55 establishes the process for obtaining default judgments, as well as setting aside those judgments. Before a default or a default judgment can be entered, the court must have jurisdiction over the party against whom the judgment is sought, which means that the party was effectively served with process. See *Peralta v. Heights Medical Center*, 485 U.S. 80, 108 S.Ct. 896, 99 L.Ed.2d 75 (1988) ("a judgment entered without notice or service is constitutionally infirm"). Rule 55(a) permits a party to file a motion asking the clerk of the court to enter a default against an opposing party who "failed to plead or otherwise defend" against the moving party's claim. "Otherwise defend" refers to attacks on service of process, motions to

dismiss, or Rule 12(e) motions for more specificity, any of which may prevent entry of a default without having to answer on the merits.

Is the entry of a default limited to complaints, or may defaults be entered on other claims for relief? The entry of a default for failure "to plead or otherwise defend" is not limited to situations involving a failure to answer a complaint, but instead applies to any pleading. For example, a plaintiff's failure to answer a counterclaim may entitle the defendant to an entry of default on the counterclaim.

When the requirements of Rule 55(a) are satisfied, an entry of default is made by the court clerk without any action by the court. An entry of default is simply a notation of the fact of default, and cuts off the party's right to further notice about the proceedings unless the party has appeared. The entry of a default serves as an intermediate step in anticipation of a final judgment by default by the clerk under Rule 55(b)(1). Thus, compliance with Rule 55(a) is always a prerequisite to a default judgment under Rule 55(b)(1), but it is not necessarily required as a prerequisite for a default judgment under Rule 55(b)(2). For example, when a default is entered as a sanction, the judge, not the clerk, will enter the default.

After a default is entered under Rule 55(a) and upon request of the party seeking the default judgment, the clerk may enter a default judgment under Rule 55(b)(1) when the claim "is for a sum certain." and the defaulting party has not made any appearance in the case. Rule 55(b)(1) applies only when a party has never appeared in the case to defend; it does not apply when a party appears and then merely fails to participate further. Rule 55(b)(1) gives the court clerk authority to enter a default judgment only when the defendant has clearly defaulted by showing no interest in participating in the case.

Under Rule 55(b)(1), the plaintiff submits an affidavit to establish that the amount due is certain or easily can be computed and is reasonable under the circumstances. By contrast, if the relief sought is for an unliquidated sum of money or if some other relief (e.g., injunctive relief, specific performance) is sought, the judge must decide whether that relief is appropriate following a hearing.

2. Any situation not covered by Rule 55(b)(1) falls within Rule 55(b)(2) and must be examined by a judge. Rule 55(b)(2) applies to a defendant who has filed a procedural or legal challenge to the complaint that does not address the merits of the plaintiff's claim. For a default judgment, the defaulting party's appearance must be unrelated to the merits of the case. Conversely, if a defendant has been served and appeared on the merits by, for example, filing an answer, the court cannot grant a default judgment and a trial proceeds in the defendant's absence.

The trial judge has discretion whether to enter a default judgment, and the judge may hold hearings to aid in the exercise of that discretion. The judge's ability to exercise discretion is made effective by the requirement that the motion for a default judgment be sent to the defaulting party, enabling that party to appear and show cause why a default judgment should not be entered. At a hearing, the judge can require proof of the facts that must be proved to establish liability. If the sum of damages is not certain or capable of easy computation, the hearing may include that issue. Once the judge determines that a default judgment should be entered, he or she determines the amount and character of the recovery that should be awarded. Rule 54(c) limits the amount of relief to the amount sought in the plaintiff's demand for judgment.

3. Rule 55(c) provides relief from either an entry of default or a default judgment. A court may set aside an entry of default for "good cause." A default judgment is set aside for the same reasons as a motion for relief from a judgment found in Rule 60(b). See Chap. 13, pt. G. In either situation, it is within the trial court's discretion to set aside the entry of default or the default judgment. A court is more likely to grant a motion under Rule 55(c) after a showing that if relief is granted the outcome of the lawsuit may be different than if the default judgment is allowed to stand, i.e., the potential injustice of allowing the case to be disposed of by default. The trial judge will often require the party in default to show a meritorious defense to the claim as a prerequisite to vacating the judgment.

PROBLEMS

1. For problems a.–d., decide who enters the default and who enters the default judgment.

   a. Paul (from a different state than the defendant) sues the City of Davenport in federal court for trespass for an uncertain amount of damages. The city is served with process.

   b. Same as a., except that the amount of damages is a sum certain.

   c. Same as a., except that the city moves to dismiss for improper service of process, but after losing the motion does nothing in the case, which involves a sum certain.

   d. Same as a., except that the city answers the complaint, and then does nothing else in the case, which involves a sum certain.

2. Paul sues the City of Davenport in federal court for a federal civil rights violation. Inexplicably, the city is never served with process and Paul moves for a default judgment a month after filing his claim. Can a default judgment be granted?

3. Pam sues Daphne Temporary Employees, Inc. in federal court for a Fair Labor Standards violation, which is valued for a sum certain. The defendant is served with process, but never files an answer or any motions in the case. Can Pam seek a default judgment? If so, how?

4. Pat sues Dan in federal court in a diversity action for breach of a contract that clearly states a sum certain in case a court finds a breach. The trial court denies Dan's motion to dismiss the complaint for improper venue,

and Dan fails to file an answer or any other motions. Pat wants to file a motion for a default judgment. Can she, and if so, by what method under Federal Rule 55?

5. Six months ago, Pablo sued Doris and obtained a default judgment. Doris recently learned that the default judgment had been granted, because her wages were being garnished (as often happens after a default judgment). She is mad about the situation, and wants your help. What, is anything, can you do under Rule 55 to stop Doris's wages from being garnished?

EXERCISE

For the state where a) you intend to practice after graduation, b) your law school is located, and/or c) your professor assigns, go to that state's annotated statutes and research the procedural rules by which default judgments are governed. Based on your research, print the rule and bring it to class for discussion. In addition, answer the following questions.

1. Can a court clerk enter a default? If so, on what grounds?

2. When can a court clerk enter a default judgment?

3. When can a judge grant a default judgment?

4. Under what circumstances, if any, can a default judgment be set aside?

E. JUDGMENT ON THE PLEADINGS

INTRODUCTORY PROBLEM

Bailey and Givens are first-year law students who sit together in every class. One day, Givens has a job interview scheduled immediately following Civil Procedure. However, Professor Droan is waxing particularly eloquent that day, and keeps the class well past the scheduled dismissal time. Worried that she will be late—and not wanting to lug her notebook computer to the interview—Givens asks Bailey if he will keep her notebook for the afternoon as a "favor." Bailey agrees.

Later that day, Bailey and friends decide to use the notebook as a substitute Frisbee. The non-aerodynamic notebook crashes to the ground and is ruined. Understandably furious, Givens sues Bailey for the cost of replacing the notebook. Givens's complaint argues that Bailey was a "bailee" of the notebook, and that Bailey's gross negligence caused the damage to the notebook.

Bailey files a timely answer. Although he admits all the facts alleged by Givens in her complaint (including Givens's assertion that he acted with gross negligence), Bailey denies that he is liable. Bailey asserts in his answer that he received no consideration for acting as a bailee. Therefore, he claims, he owed no duty whatsoever to Givens to care for her notebook.

It is no surprise that Givens had an interview and Bailey didn't . . . for under governing law, no consideration is required to establish a bailment. Although a bailee who receives no benefit from the bailment is held to a lesser standard of care, such a bailee can be held liable if he acted in a grossly negligent fashion.

Givens would like to resolve this case without the time and expense of discovery and trial. What motion should she bring? Is she likely to prevail on that motion?

Governing Law: Federal Rules 12(b)(6) and (c).

Part B of this Chapter discusses the motion to dismiss for failure to state a claim. That discussion focused mainly on how a defendant uses that motion to deal with an insufficient complaint. If the complaint is insufficient, and plaintiff cannot cure the defects, the obvious solution is for the court to dismiss the case. A 12(b)(6) dismissal operates as an adjudication on the merits unless the court specifies otherwise, preventing the plaintiff from suing again on the same claim or any other claim arising from the same basic set of facts. Federal Rule 41(b); *Federated Department Stores v. Moitie*, 452 U.S. 394, 101 S.Ct. 2424, 69 L.Ed.2d 103 (1981). Therefore, from the defendant's perspective, a 12(b)(6) dismissal effectively ends the case.

In situations like that posed in the Introductory Problem, however, a 12(b)(6) motion does not produce the desired result. Now it is plaintiff who should prevail. Dismissing the case, however, leaves plaintiff with nothing. What plaintiff wants is a way for the court to decide the case on the pleadings alone, granting judgment to plaintiff for the relief requested. The Federal Rule 12(c) motion for judgment on the pleadings is one way for plaintiff to achieve this goal.

Notwithstanding this difference in outcome, a 12(c) motion is conceptually similar to a 12(b)(6). In both cases, the court *does not consider the evidence*, but looks only at the pleadings. A court dealing with a defendant's motion to dismiss for failure to state a claim looks only at the complaint. In a 12(c) motion, by contrast, the court looks at *all* the pleadings. If the pleadings, taken together, indicate that one party should prevail, the court can grant judgment without considering the actual evidence.

Note that plaintiff is not the only party who can use the Federal Rule 12(c) motion. Suppose plaintiff sues defendant for alienation of affection. Defendant files an answer in which she denies she committed the facts alleged by plaintiff. Later, however—perhaps because the higher courts cleared up the law—defendant realizes that the law in that jurisdiction does not allow recovery for alienation of affection. Defendant in such a case can file a Federal Rule 12(c) motion for judgment on the pleadings.

In this situation, the Rule 12(c) motion serves basically as a delayed motion to dismiss for failure to state a claim. See also Federal Rule 12(h)(2), which requires a party who wants to raise the defense of failure to state a claim after the pleadings are closed to use a Federal Rule 12(c) motion for judgment on the pleadings.

A judgment on the pleadings is a final judgment. If plaintiff is the judgment winner, it may collect on that judgment once 14 days have elapsed following entry of the judgment. Federal Rule 62(a). The party who loses the judgment may appeal immediately.

CHAPTER 8

ADVANCED JOINDER

■ ■ ■

The materials for this chapter are at www.crosscivilprocedure.com.

CHAPTER 9

ALTERNATIVE DISPUTE RESOLUTION AND SETTLEMENT

■ ■ ■

The materials for this chapter are at www.crosscivilprocedure.com.

CHAPTER 10

DISCOVERY

■ ■ ■

In Chapters 6 and 7, we noted that the primary function of modern pleading rules is to provide notice to the opposing party about the nature of the claim or answer. The general requirements for pleading, though, postpone the development of the claims' and defenses' underlying facts. The discovery rules thus play a vital role in trial preparation. The Supreme Court in *United States v. Procter & Gamble Company,* 356 U.S. 677, 78 S.Ct. 983, 2 L.Ed.2d 1077 (1958) stated that discovery devices "together with pretrial procedures make a trial less a game of blind man's bluff and more a fair contest with the basic issues and facts disclosed to the fullest practicable extent."

At a minimum, the purposes of the discovery rules are:

- to narrow the issues, so that it may be unnecessary to produce evidence at trial for issues that are not disputed;
- to obtain evidence for use at trial;
- to learn about evidence that may be used at the trial and to determine how and from whom it may be obtained;
- to promote negotiated settlements through observation of the demeanor and responses of witnesses and through verification of documents which facilitate a practical assessment of the value of a case;
- to further trial verdicts based upon accurate presentations, instead of surprise; and
- to provide an economical method of resolving disputes, presuming that attorneys use the rules appropriately.

The rationale for discovery is that every party to a civil action is entitled to pretrial disclosure of all relevant information in the control of any person, unless the information is privileged. Pretrial discovery is not bound by the evidentiary rules of admissibility applicable at trial. The discovery rules provide several devices for use under varying circumstances to acquire information. Federal Rules 30 and 32 govern depositions; Rule 33 authorizes interrogatories to parties; Rule 34 provides for the production of documents and things and entry upon land for inspection and other purposes; Rule 35 permits physical and mental examination of persons; Rule 36 governs requests for admissions.

Rule 26 is the basic rule applicable to all the federal discovery devices. It contains the principal provisions on the scope of discovery for all discovery devices. By the use of one or more of the discovery mechanisms, a party can prepare for trial in a manner that promotes the just, speedy, and inexpensive determination of the case as prescribed in Rule 1. Courts recognize the value of the discovery rules and generally construe them liberally. The goal of flexible discovery is to end the "sporting theory of justice," by which the result depends on the fortuitous availability of evidence or the skill and strategy of counsel. Concerns about discovery abuse, e.g., excessive discovery, have produced specific rules mandating exchange of certain information, as well as Rule 26(g), which is analogous to Federal Rule 11.

A. THE SCOPE OF DISCOVERY

1. MANDATORY DISCLOSURE

INTRODUCTORY PROBLEM

Grant and Hayes (doing business as City Cycle) sue Harding Cycle in an Ohio federal court over a contract dispute involving a bicycle franchise agreement. The legal basis of the plaintiffs' claim is a violation of the Federal Franchisee Protection Act of 1962. Plaintiffs for several years sold more bicycles in the United States than any other retailer. Harding Cycle was plaintiffs' wholesaler, renting the store to the plaintiffs and supplying the bikes for the plaintiffs' retail operation. The plaintiffs allege that Harding Cycle became jealous of their success, broke the lease, and persuaded the manufacturer not to renew the franchise agreement with them because it told the manufacturer that it could sell even more bicycles than City Cycle.

Following the filing of the pleadings, what information must the parties exchange with each other under the Federal Rules?

Governing Rule: Rule 26(a).

In 1993, following years of controversy about discovery abuses such as the failure to turn over even the most basic of information, the Supreme Court drafted Rule 26(a), mandating the disclosure by each party of certain types of information that otherwise would and should be exchanged by the parties in any civil litigation. Rule 26(a) requires disclosure of certain information at three periods during litigation, without the need for a discovery request from an opposing party. First, following a discovery meeting under Rule 26(f), the parties must make broad initial disclosures under Rule 26(a)(1). Second, 90 days before trial, the parties must disclose information about expert testimony, pursuant to

Rule 26(a)(2). Finally, 30 days before trial, the parties must make specific pretrial disclosures, under Rule 26(a)(3).

What is the normal order of initial discovery events in federal litigation? First, the court schedules a Rule 26(f) scheduling conference, before which the parties conduct a discovery meeting to explore the possibility of a settlement, arrange for the Rule 26(a) mandatory disclosures, and develop a proposal for a discovery plan. Second, the parties make their mandatory disclosures and then meet with the trial judge for the scheduling conference at which a discovery timetable is established.

Rule 26(a) requires automatic, initial disclosure, without the need for a request, of four categories of information that are then "reasonably available": 1) names of witnesses "likely to have discoverable information . . . that the disclosing party may use to support its claims or defenses" and the subjects of such information; 2) copies (or at least categories and locations) of "documents, electronically stored information, and tangible things that the disclosing party has in its possession, custody, or control" which the disclosing party may use in support of its claims or defenses; 3) damage computations of any category of damage claimed by the disclosing party, including non-privileged documents supporting the computation and the nature and extent of injuries; and 4) all insurance policies that may provide coverage for all or part of a later judgment in the case. Disclosure of information or documents to be used exclusively for impeachment is unnecessary at this point. (Impeachment refers to questioning which discredits a witness by showing that the witness is not telling the truth or does not have a reliable basis for the offered testimony.)

Failing to disclose the information can result in the exclusion of the witness's testimony or the document from evidence. For example, in *Gould Paper Corp. v. Madisen Corp.*, 614 F.Supp.2d 485, 490 (S.D.N.Y. 2009), the defendants were prohibited from proving damages in support of their counterclaim because they failed to provide a damages calculation. They could not use an expert in the future to prove damages because they did not provide a damage calculation or disclose an expert witness during discovery, as required. A party can object to making the disclosures at the conference, because they "are not appropriate in this action. . . ." By stipulation or court order, the initial disclosure process may be modified or eliminated.

Unless otherwise ordered or stipulated, ninety days before trial the parties must disclose information about expert testimony, per Rule 26(a)(2). The content of the disclosure is the identity of any person who "may" testify as an expert witness, along with the disclosure of a report for each expert witness. The written report must be signed by the expert, and state: 1) all of the expert's opinions as well as the basis and reasons for the opinions; 2) any information considered by the expert in forming those opinions; 3) any exhibits which support or summarize the opinions; and 4) the expert's qualifications, publications, compensations and cases during the past four years where she testified or was deposed. If the expert is not required to provide a written report, the disclosure still must state the subject matter of the testimony and a summary of the facts and opinions about which the expert is expected to testify. See Section A.4 of this Chapter.

Unless otherwise ordered by the trial court under Rule 26(a)(3), thirty days before trial every party must make a written disclosure of the identity of each witness who may testify, as well as deposition testimony and exhibits that may be offered at trial. Again, impeachment witnesses and other information do not have to be disclosed. Any opponent objecting to a deposition or exhibit must express an objection within two weeks of the disclosure of the intent to use it.

2. DISCOVERY OF RELEVANT AND NON-PRIVILEGED INFORMATION

INTRODUCTORY PROBLEM 1

In *Grant and Hayes v. Harding Cycle* (referred to in pt. 1, *supra*), the defendant sent interrogatories and a request for production of documents to the plaintiffs. Defendant seeks information for the previous five years about plaintiffs' business income, business and personal expenses, financial worth, tax returns, the identities of all legal counsel employed, the advice sought from them, and any oral and written statements about this litigation made to legal counsel by plaintiffs or anyone else.

Upon defendant's request, what is the obligation of plaintiffs to disclose the information to the defendant?

Governing Rule: Rule 26(b).

INTRODUCTORY PROBLEM 2

Pete Lilly sits forlornly in his prison dormitory, thinking of happier days in Las Vegas or selling his wares on cable television. Lilly misses playing baseball, too, and he contacts attorney Ruben Feline about whether a lawsuit can be filed to install a baseball diamond at the prison. Feline files a civil rights claim in federal court in Indianapolis against the United States Bureau of Prisons, seeking to require prison officials to institute a baseball rehabilitation training program at Lilly's prison. Feline has a letter from Lilly outlining the benefits of such a program as well as the logistical difficulties of installing a diamond at the prison. Pretrial discovery ensues.

Ned Mice is the attorney for the U.S. Bureau of Prisons. He serves a timely request upon Lilly for production of copies of "all information in your files pertaining to the justification for this lawsuit." Must Lilly or Feline produce a copy of the letter or provide this information to Mice?

Governing Rule: Federal Rule 26(b)–(c).

For purposes of discovery, "relevant" information may be broader than the information that would be admissible at trial.. Without judicial intervention using Rule 26(b)(1), a party may discover information "relevant to any party's claim or defense."

THOMPSON V. DEPARTMENT OF HOUSING AND URBAN DEVEL.
199 F.R.D. 168 (D. Md. 2001)

GRIMM, UNITED STATES MAGISTRATE JUDGE.

Plaintiffs are class representatives of African American residents of Baltimore's public housing developments. They filed suit in January, 1995 against the U.S. Department of Housing and Urban Development and its secretary (the "federal defendants") and the Housing Authority of Baltimore City ("HABC"), its executive director and the Mayor and City Council of Baltimore (the "local defendants"). The class action lawsuit alleged that the defendants and their predecessors, from 1933 through the present, established and perpetuated *de jure* racial segregation in Baltimore's public housing, in violation of the 5th, 13th, and 14th Amendments to the United States Constitution, as well as Title VI of the Civil Rights Act of 1964, Title VIII of the Civil Rights Act of 1968, 42 U.S.C. Sections 1981, 1982, and 1983, the U.S. Housing Act of 1937 and the Housing and Community Development Act of 1974. Plaintiffs seek declaratory, injunctive, and equitable relief, and attorneys' fees.

... [I]n mid-2000 the plaintiffs initiated discovery against the defendants, and the undersigned was referred the case for resolution of discovery disputes. Pending is the motion by the plaintiffs to compel the local defendants to provide responsive answers to Rule 33 and 34 discovery requests.

... For purposes of applying the above test the definition of relevance in Fed.R.Evid. 401 was most helpful; Rule 26(b)(5) and Discovery Guidelines 5 and 9 of this court required that privileges be identified with particularity in order to justify a refusal to disclose requested information, and courts were quick to add that unparticularized claims of burden or expense were insufficient. Moreover, application of the cost-benefit factors identified in Rule 26(b)(2) enabled the court to allocate the costs of discovery between the parties, thereby, in appropriate cases, requiring a party seeking contested discovery to pay all or part of the expenses of obtaining it.

Despite the obvious utility of the Rule 26(b)(2) factors in tailoring discovery to accommodate fair disclosure without imposing undue burden or expense, they have tended largely to be ignored by litigants, and, less frequently than desirable, used by the courts, *sua sponte*, to manage discovery. Instead, particularly with respect to disputes involving Rule 33 and Rule 34 discovery, the focus of the litigants tends to be the party seeking discovery's perceived "right" to all information relating to the broad "subject matter" of the litigation, without any reflection as to the real usefulness of the information sought, or the burden or expense required to produce it, countered by the party resisting the discovery's unparticularized claims of burden, expense, irrelevance, and privilege. Further, despite the requirements of Local Rule 104.7 and Discovery Guideline 1(d) of this court, the efforts of the litigants to resolve their disputes before seeking court intervention infrequently demonstrated that, during their discussions, the parties themselves attempted to evaluate the Rule 26(b)(2) factors to reach a common ground.

The most recent revisions to the discovery rules imposed changes intended to reach lingering concerns about the overbreadth and expense of discovery, and remind the courts and litigants of the fact that in determining what discovery should take place in a particular case, Rule 26(b)(1) is but the first step, necessarily followed by balancing the Rule 26(b)(2) factors. Accordingly, the December 1, 2000 changes to Rule 26(b)(1) restricted the scope of discovery to unprivileged facts relevant to "the claim or defense of any party...." ... Furthermore, they emphasize that "all discovery is subject to the limitations imposed by Rule 26(b)(2)(C)", the cost-benefit balancing factors.

... [W]hen confronted with a difficult scope of discovery dispute, the parties themselves should confer, and discuss the Rule 26(b)(2) factors, in an effort to reach an acceptable compromise, or narrow the scope of their disagreement.

For example, if the plaintiff seeks discovery of information going back 20 years, and the defendant objects on the grounds of burden, a possible solution may be to agree first to produce information going back 5 years. Then, depending on the results of a review of the more recent information, if more extensive disclosure can be justified, based on the results of the initial, more limited, less burdensome, examination, it should be produced. Similarly, if the burden and expense of searching for and producing all documents that fall within the scope of a broad Rule 34 request is objected to, the party objecting might agree to spend up to a stated amount of time looking for the records, and producing them for inspection, with the understanding that if, following review of the documents produced, the requesting party can justify a request for more, under the Rule 26(b)(2) factors, it would be produced, perhaps under a cost sharing, or shifting agreement. The court, too, if called upon to resolve discovery disputes, may find such an incremental, phased approach useful, as a result of evaluating the Rule 26(b)(2) factors.

The pending discovery dispute illustrates the points raised above. The plaintiffs have filed a sweeping lawsuit alleging discriminatory action by the defendants covering three-quarters of a century, and involving all aspects of the public housing programs in Baltimore. Within a year or so of suit being filed, the parties entered into a comprehensive partial consent decree, itself broad in scope, which settled many, but by no means all, of the claims originally filed. After a hiatus in discovery of several years, plaintiffs initiated renewed discovery requests, under Rules 33 and 34. The local defendants objected to certain of these requests, asserting: overbreadth and burden, without giving particulars to permit either plaintiffs or the court meaningfully to evaluate this claim; and that the challenged requests exceeded the scope of permissible discovery as they were not tailored to the existing "claims and defenses" remaining in the litigation following the consent decree. Plaintiffs, justifying their discovery requests, argue their broad entitlement to discovery relating to the whole of the dispute that is the basis for the litigation, without once attempting to identify which claims that survived the partial consent decree will be furthered by the requested information, or addressing the burden to the local defendants to produce it. Both parties seem content to leave it to the court to sift through the 56-page complaint and the 74-page partial consent decree to determine what discovery should be allowed. Moreover, although counsel for the parties undoubtedly have conferred in an effort to resolve or narrow the dispute, they have provided the court with nothing to show whether they have attempted to apply the Rule 26(b)(2) balancing factors to try to reach common ground, at least as to some of the areas of dispute. This will not do.

I am returning this dispute to the parties with guidance as to how they should meet and confer to attempt to resolve or narrow their differences.... In this regard, it seems clear that the challenged requests are too broad as stated, and need to be narrowed by a good faith analysis of which claims that survived the partial consent decree will be furthered by the discovery sought. Additionally, the local defendants are cautioned that, provided the plaintiffs accommodate legitimate concerns of the local defendants regarding burden and expense, it is likely that for each of the discovery requests challenged on the basis of scope or burden, some discovery will be appropriate. However, unparticularized claims of burden or expense ... will not suffice. If the local defendants claim that they cannot produce requested information because of burden, they must justify this claim with specific details that can be evaluated by the plaintiffs, and, if necessary, the court.

This means that the parties must set aside their differences as adversaries and make a good faith effort to reach common ground on the disputes. It strikes me that this case is a perfect example of how creative counsel can employ the phasing methods [described] by the Court . . . to permit the plaintiffs to have access to some, but less than all, of the information they seek, with the understanding that if, following the initial, limited review, additional discovery would make sense under the Rule 26(b)(2) factors, it will be provided. Cost shifting or sharing also should be considered.

If, following their consultations, counsel find that there still are differences that cannot be overcome by negotiation, as likely will be the case, they will contact me, and a discovery conference will be set promptly. While I am mindful of the fact that the commentary to the recent rule changes emphasizes the need for the court actively to be involved in applying the Rule 26(b)(2) factors, this involvement necessarily must follow, not precede, the parties own good faith efforts to do so. Therefore, if there is to be a discovery conference, the court will expect counsel to demonstrate that they have fully considered the cost/benefit factors, and made reasonable modifications of their positions to accommodate them.

Accordingly, it is . . . ordered that the plaintiffs' motion to compel discovery from the local defendants is denied, without prejudice, and the parties are to take further action in accordance with this order.

NOTES AND QUESTIONS

1. *Any matter . . . relevant to the claim or defense.* Rule 26(b)(1) begins with a general statement that "[p]arties may obtain discovery regarding any nonprivileged matter." What is a "matter"? Does it include information about the party's own case? About the opponent's case?

Rules 26(b)(1) also states that information sought through discovery does not have to be admissible at a judicial proceeding to be relevant. The discovery meaning of relevance thus is potentially broader than the evidentiary standard for trial, but it does not define the breadth of relevancy. *Thompson* shows how a judge works through discovery requests to impose limits on the scope of what constitutes relevant discovery.

To assist a judge in assessing the scope of relevant discovery, Rule 26(b)(1) further requires that discovery requests must be

> proportional to the needs of the case considering the importance of the issues at stake in the action, the amount in controversy, the parties' relative access to relevant information, the parties' resources, the importance of the discovery in resolving the issues, and whether the burden or expense of the proposed discovery outweighs its likely benefit.

2. *What can be discovered.* Even for information that is privileged and thus is not itself discoverable, it is still proper to request whether, for example, documents exist which may contain such privileged information or

the identities of persons who may have privileged information. An example of such discovery could be phrased: "State whether documents were written to plaintiff's counsel by the plaintiff", *or* "State the identity of any person from whom a statement was taken."

3. *Attorney-client privilege.* Generally, the attorney-client privilege applies to communications between an attorney and the client, to whom the privilege belongs. The privilege protects communications made in confidence to an attorney (or the attorney's agent) whose legal advice is sought by a person who is or is attempting to become a client. The purpose of the privilege is to encourage complete and honest communication between the attorney and client. A person claiming the privilege must raise it in response to a discovery request and will have the burden of proving that the privilege applies. For corporations, the privilege applies to all corporate employees (not just upper-level managers) who seek or receive legal advice from an attorney. *Upjohn Co. v. United States*, 449 U.S. 383, 101 S.Ct. 677, 66 L.Ed.2d 584 (1981).

If correctly stated, a request for discovery should not create an issue that privileged information is being sought by a party. For example, in a personal injury case, an interrogatory that asks, "What color was the traffic signal when you went through the intersection?" properly seeks relevant information and ordinarily must be answered. However, an interrogatory which asks, "What did you tell your attorney about the color of the traffic signal at the intersection?" seeks information that was the subject of an exchange between the party and the party's attorney. The party receiving the interrogatory should object to answering this interrogatory because it seeks privileged information. If the party answers the interrogatory, she has voluntarily waived the claim of privilege.

4. *Rule 26(b)(5)'s requirements.* An attorney withholding information based on a claim of privilege or based on attorney work product protection is supposed to maintain a document index, or "privilege log," which expressly states the basis of her claim and describes in detail the nature of the information of the document withheld so that the opposing party can evaluate the claim. Specifically, a party objecting to discovery must describe the documents without having to disclose the information that is privileged and provide "precise reasons" for the objection to the discovery. The information provided in the privilege log also must be sufficient to enable the court to determine whether each element of the asserted privilege is satisfied. See, e.g., *McCoo v. Denny's Inc.*, 192 F.R.D. 675 (D. Kan. 2000).

5. *Protective orders.* Does a party or witness have a remedy when she has a problem with the type or manner of discovery? Rule 26(c) governs protective orders, which are intended to protect parties and witnesses during discovery from having to disclose information under the requested circumstances. A protective order may be sought because either 1) the information sought falls outside the rules, or 2) though the information can be discovered under the rules, some aspect of the discovery of that information is troubling to the responding party. Prior to seeking a protective

order, a party must in good faith confer or attempt to confer with the other party to try to resolve the discovery dispute without the trial court's intervention.

Either a party or a witness may file a motion for a protective order, which issues only on a showing of "good cause" to shield her "from annoyance, embarrassment, oppression, or undue burden or expense." For example, when the frequency or extent of discovery sought violates the proportionality rules of Rule 26(b)(1), the court has the discretion to grant a motion for a protective order. Courts may also issue protective orders to address automatic disclosure or other types of requested discovery. Rule 26(c)(1)(A)–(H) specifies eight examples of protective orders, but the list is not exhaustive.

6. *Supplementing disclosure or discovery.* Under the conditions described in Rule 26(e)(1)(A)–(B), parties have a duty to supplement automatic disclosure and discovery responses when the information has not already been provided. "[I]n a timely manner," a party must supplement initial, expert and pretrial disclosures in interrogatories, requests for production, and requests for admission that a party learns are incomplete or incorrect in a material respect. In *United States v. Boyce*, 148 F.Supp.2d 1069 (S.D.Cal. 2001), the court suggested that a party cannot wait until just before trial to supplement a discovery response. The duty only applies to parties; non-party witnesses need not supplement their depositions.

7. *Phased discovery.* The judge in *Thompson* suggested phased discovery starting with 5 years of information as a means to avoid burden and expense and to determine if it was necessary to go back 20 years. A phased discovery plan can also be useful in integrating litigation and settlement processes. For example, if the parties plan on using mediation, it may be possible to limit initial discovery to basic information. They will need to learn enough to estimate the likely recovery at trial in order to be able to evaluate settlement proposals. But because there is no formal presentation of evidence in mediation, they may not need full discovery unless they are unable to settle the case.

8. *Discovery disputes.* The discovery rules are designed to be applied by the parties with the court in a supervisory role only. For example, in producing documents, the parties exchange them directly and do not file them with the court. Judges often have to resolve disagreements about discovery, but many attorneys prefer to avoid bringing frequent discovery squabbles to busy judges. Can you imagine why? In addition, what effect does filing frequent motions about discovery disputes have on the cost of litigating a case?

The Rule 26(f) requirement for the parties to confer early in the case and attempt to agree on a discovery plan is a mechanism in the rules to avoid litigation of discovery disputes and to encourage an autonomous process. It illustrates one way in which dispute resolution principles are applied within the Civil Procedure process. Who is more likely to have the information needed to craft an efficient discovery plan tailored to the parties' needs in a complicated case, the judge or counsel? Later in this Chapter you will see another way in which the discovery rules try to keep discovery disputes out of court. Under Rule 37(a)(1), any party filing a motion requesting an order to compel disclosure or discovery must certify that it has first conferred, or made a good faith effort to confer, with the party that has failed to make the disclosure.

9. *Stipulations about discovery procedures.* Despite what may appear to be the rigidity in the discovery rules, Rule 29 generally permits the parties to agree to conduct discovery outside the rules. As long as an agreement is in writing and the trial court has not directed them otherwise, the parties may stipulate to modify discovery procedures provided the agreements do not interfere with hearing or trial dates or a discovery deadline. The 1970 Advisory Committee Notes to Rule 29 state that the trial court can override any stipulation by the parties.

PROBLEMS

1. Paulin and Vesely witnessed an intersection vehicle collision at the corner of Third Street and Eastern Parkway. In the subsequent case of *Smith v. Jones*, Jones takes Paulin's deposition and asks, "Based on your observations at the time of the accident, who was at fault—the driver of the VW Beetle or the driver of the Jaguar convertible?" Under Rule 26(b)(1), is that information discoverable?

2. Same facts as #1, and the next question at Paulin's deposition is, "Did you hear Vesely express an opinion about whom she believed was at fault?" Paulin's answer would constitute hearsay, and would not be admissible at a trial. Is the information sought discoverable?

3. In the same *Smith v. Jones* case, Smith sends Jones an interrogatory asking, "State whether you have automobile insurance." Is the information sought discoverable?

4. In *Smith v. Jones*, plaintiff Smith is seeking both compensatory damages for lost wages and punitive damages. Can Smith send an interrogatory to Jones seeking his tax returns and other information about his assets, to prepare for the punitive damages claim? Can Jones send an interrogatory to Smith seeking his tax returns and other information about his assets, to prepare for the lost wages claim?

5. Again, in *Smith v. Jones*, Jones wants to file a motion to dismiss Smith's complaint because it fails to state a claim upon which relief can be granted. Jones has a copy of a statement from Smith that directly contradicts one of Smith's claims. Can Jones send Smith an interrogatory asking, "State all facts which you have disclosed to your attorney and to all other persons about your claim." How should Smith respond?

6. In a product liability case, *Abadu v. National Motors*, the plaintiff sends the following interrogatory: "State whether defendant has made any

subsequent changes in the product after the accident which gave rise to this litigation." Is the information sought discoverable?

7. In a Title VII employment discrimination case, law student Greenidge claims that he suffered racial discrimination when he did not receive an offer of employment from Dewey, Cheatham and Howe, a law firm he clerked for during the summer between his second and third years of law school. As his attorney, what is the scope of discoverable relevant information about the hiring practices at Dewey and other law firms?

3. DISCOVERY OF ATTORNEY WORK PRODUCT

INTRODUCTORY PROBLEM

When the buyer of a recreational vehicle (RV) returned it to the seller (Dixie RV) because of alleged defects and breaches of warranties, the seller sued the buyer for breach of contract. During discovery, the defendant-buyer sent several requests for information to Dixie RV.

    a. All written statements made by the buyer to any employee of Dixie RV preceding and following the buyer's purchase of the RV.

    b. The law that governs Dixie's view that it is entitled to recover damages from the buyer.

    c. Memoranda by any Dixie employee to any other Dixie employee about the buyer's problems with the RV purchased by the buyer.

Is the buyer entitled to discover any of the preceding information?

Governing Law: Federal Rule 26(b).

HICKMAN V. TAYLOR
329 U.S. 495, 67 S.Ct. 385, 91 L.Ed. 451 (1947)

MR. JUSTICE MURPHY delivered the opinion of the Court.

[The tugboat "J.M. Taylor" sank in 1943, drowning five of the nine crew members. Several days later, the tug boat owners and their insurers hired a law firm to investigate and defend against future claims. One of the lawyers, Fortenbaugh, interviewed the four survivors and took statements from them. He also interviewed others who knew about the accident; he wrote memoranda of his interviews in some cases. At a later public hearing, all the witnesses testified and their testimony was made available to the general public. A representative of one of the drowning victims sued and requested "copies of all [written] statements" of the [witnesses] along with the "exact provisions" of the oral statements. The defendants refused to produce or summarize the materials on the grounds that the requests were for "privileged matter obtained in preparation for litigation." After the trial court ordered discovery, and the Third Circuit reversed, the Supreme Court granted certiorari.]

In urging that he has a right to inquire into the materials secured and prepared by Fortenbaugh, petitioner emphasizes that the deposition-discovery portions of the Federal Rules of Civil Procedure are designed to enable the parties to discover the true facts and to compel their disclosure wherever they may be found. It is said that inquiry may be made under these rules, epitomized by Rule 26, as to any relevant matter which is not privileged; and since the discovery provisions are to be applied as broadly and liberally as possible, the privilege limitation must be restricted to its narrowest bounds. On the premise that the attorney-client privilege is the one involved in this case, petitioner argues that it must be strictly confined to confidential communications made by a client to his attorney. And since the materials here in issue were secured by Fortenbaugh from third persons rather than from his clients, the tug owners, the conclusion is reached that these materials are proper subjects for discovery under Rule 26.

. . . We agree, of course, that the deposition-discovery rules are to be accorded a broad and liberal treatment. No longer can the time-honored cry of 'fishing expedition' serve to preclude a party from inquiring into the facts underlying his opponent's case. Mutual knowledge of all the relevant facts gathered by both parties is essential to proper litigation. To that end, either party may compel the other to disgorge whatever facts he has in his possession. The deposition-discovery procedure simply advances the stage at which the disclosure can be compelled from the time of trial to the period preceding it, thus reducing the possibility of surprise. But discovery, like all matters of procedure, has ultimate and necessary boundaries. . . .

We also agree that the memoranda, statements and mental impressions in issue in this case fall outside the scope of the attorney-client privilege and hence are not protected from discovery on that basis. . . . [T]his privilege does not extend to information which an attorney secures from a witness while acting for his client in anticipation of litigation. Nor does this privilege concern the memoranda, briefs, communications and other writings prepared by counsel for his own use in prosecuting his client's case; and it is equally unrelated to writings which reflect an attorney's mental impressions, conclusions, opinions or legal theories.

But the impropriety of invoking that privilege does not provide an answer to the problem before us. Petitioner has made more than an ordinary request for relevant, non-privileged facts in the possession of his adversaries or their counsel. He has sought discovery as of right of oral and written statements of witnesses whose identity is well known and whose availability to petitioner appears unimpaired. He has sought production of these matters after making the most searching inquiries of his opponents as to the circumstances surrounding the fatal accident, which inquiries were sworn to have been answered to the best of their information and belief. Interrogatories were directed toward all the events prior to, during and subsequent to the sinking of the tug. Full and honest answers to such broad inquiries would necessarily have included all pertinent information gleaned by Fortenbaugh through his interviews with the witnesses. Petitioner makes no suggestion, and we cannot assume, that the tug owners or Fortenbaugh were incomplete or dishonest in the framing of their answers. In addition, petitioner was free to examine the public testimony of the witnesses taken before the United States Steamboat Inspectors. We are thus dealing with an attempt to secure the production of written statements and mental impressions contained in the files and the mind of the attorney Fortenbaugh without any showing of necessity or any indication or claim that denial of such production would unduly prejudice the preparation of petitioner's case or cause him any hardship or injustice. For aught that appears, the essence of what petitioner seeks either has been revealed to him already through the interrogatories or is readily available to him direct from the witnesses for the asking.

The District Court, after hearing objections to petitioner's request, commanded Fortenbaugh to produce all written statements of witnesses and to state in substance any facts learned through oral statements of witnesses to him. Fortenbaugh was to submit any memoranda he had made of the oral statements so that the court might determine what portions should be revealed to petitioner. All of this was ordered without any showing by petitioner, or any requirement that he make a proper showing, of the necessity for the production of any of this material or any demonstration that denial of production would cause hardship or injustice. The court simply ordered production on the theory that the facts sought were material and were not privileged as constituting attorney-client communications.

In our opinion, neither Rule 26 nor any other rule dealing with discovery contemplates production under such circumstances. That is not because the subject matter is privileged or irrelevant, as those concepts are used in these rules. Here is simply an attempt, without purported necessity or justification, to secure written statements, private memoranda and personal recollections prepared or formed by an adverse party's counsel in the course of his legal duties. As such, it falls outside the arena of discovery and contravenes the public policy underlying the orderly prosecution and defense of legal claims. Not even the most liberal of discovery theories can justify unwarranted inquiries into the files and the mental impressions of an attorney.

Historically, a lawyer is an officer of the court and is bound to work for the advancement of justice while faithfully protecting the rightful interests of his clients. In performing his various duties, however, it is essential that a lawyer work with a certain degree of privacy, free from unnecessary intrusion by opposing parties and their counsel.... This work is reflected, of course, in interviews, statements, memoranda, correspondence, briefs, mental impressions, personal beliefs, and countless other tangible and intangible ways—aptly though roughly termed by the Circuit Court of Appeals in this case as the "Work product of the lawyer." Were such materials open to opposing counsel on mere demand, much of what is now put down in writing would remain unwritten. An attorney's thoughts, heretofore inviolate, would not be his own. Inefficiency, unfairness and sharp practices would inevitably develop in the giving of legal advice and in the preparation of cases for trial. The effect on the legal profession would be demoralizing. And the interests of the clients and the cause of justice would be poorly served.

We do not mean to say that all written materials obtained or prepared by an adversary's counsel with an eye toward litigation are necessarily free from discovery in all cases. Where relevant and non-privileged facts remain hidden in an attorney's file and where production of those facts is essential to the preparation of one's case, discovery may properly be had. Such written statements and documents might, under certain circumstances, be admissible in evidence or give clues as to the existence or location of relevant facts. Or they might be useful for purposes of impeachment or corroboration. And production might be justified where the witnesses are no longer available or can be reached only with difficulty.... But the general policy against invading the privacy of an attorney's course of preparation is so well recognized and so essential to an orderly working of our system of legal procedure that a burden rests on the one who would invade that privacy to establish adequate reasons to justify production through a subpoena or court order....

No attempt was made to establish any reason why Fortenbaugh should be forced to produce the written statements. There was only a naked, general demand for these materials as of right and a finding by the District Court that no recognizable privilege was involved. That was insufficient to justify discovery under these circumstances and the court should have sustained the refusal of the tug owners and Fortenbaugh to produce.

But as to oral statements made by witnesses to Fortenbaugh, whether presently in the form of his mental impressions or memoranda, we do not believe that any showing of necessity can be made under the circumstances of this case so as to justify production. Under ordinary conditions, forcing an attorney to repeat or write out all that witnesses have told him and to deliver the account to his adversary gives rise to grave dangers of inaccuracy and untrustworthiness. No legitimate purpose is served by such production. The practice forces the attorney to testify as to what he remembers or what he saw fit to write down regarding witnesses' remarks. Such testimony could not qualify as evidence; and to use it for impeachment or corroborative purposes would make the attorney much less an officer of the court and much more an ordinary witness. The standards of the profession would thereby suffer.

Denial of production of this nature does not mean that any material, non-privileged facts can be hidden from the petitioner in this case.... Searching interrogatories directed to Fortenbaugh and the tug owners, production of written documents and statements upon a proper showing and direct interviews with the witnesses themselves all serve to reveal the facts in Fortenbaugh's possession to the fullest possible extent consistent with public policy. Petitioner's counsel frankly admits that he wants the oral statements only to help prepare himself to examine witnesses and to make sure that he has overlooked nothing. That is insufficient under the circumstances to permit him an exception to the policy underlying the privacy of Fortenbaugh's professional activities....

We therefore affirm the judgment of the Circuit Court of Appeals.

SPIRIT MASTER FUNDING, LLC v. PIKE NURSERIES ACQUISITION, LLC
287 F.R.D. 680 (N.D.Ga. 2012)

AMY TOTENBERG, DISTRICT JUDGE.

[Spirit (the Landlord) sued Pike (the Tenant), alleging breach of lease for retail property as result of Pike's failure to maintain and repair property and failure to pay rent. Pike moved for production of documents relating to property inspections performed for Spirit by Hercules and Ramos.]

The Court conducted a telephonic hearing on November 8, 2012, to resolve several discovery disputes between the parties. Subsequent to the hearing the parties submitted supplemental authority, and the sole remaining issue before the Court is whether Plaintiff is entitled to assert the work product privilege over documents prepared by and communications with its non-testifying consulting experts.

I. BACKGROUND

... Plaintiff objects to the production of documents by and communications with its non-testifying consulting experts on the basis that such information is subject to the work-product privilege.

II. DISCUSSION

The work product privilege provides a qualified immunity for materials prepared in anticipation of litigation by a party, an attorney, or other representatives of the party. Two provisions of Federal Rule of Civil Procedure 26 are relevant here: Rule 26(b)(3)(A) governing the limitations on discovering materials prepared in anticipation of litigation and Rule 26(b)(4)(D) governing the limitations on discovery related to non-testifying experts specially retained in anticipation of litigation. Rule 26(b)(3)(A)(ii) protects from discovery "documents and tangible things that are prepared in anticipation of litigation or for trial by or for another party or its representative (including the other party's attorney, consultant, surety, indemnitor, insurer, or agent)" unless the requesting party "shows that it has substantial need for the materials to prepare its case and cannot, without undue hardship, obtain their substantial equivalent by other means." *See* Fed.R.Civ.P. 26(b)(3)(A)(ii). Similarly, Rule 26(b)(4)(D)(ii) protects from disclosure "facts known or opinions held by an expert who has been retained or specially employed by another party in anticipation of litigation or to prepare for trial and who is not expected to be called as a witness at trial," except where there exist "exceptional circumstances under which it is impracticable for the [requesting] party to obtain facts or opinions on the same subject by other means." *See* Fed.R.Civ.P. 26(b)(4)(D)(ii).

A. Shifting Burdens Under Fed.R.Civ.P. 26

As the party asserting the work product privilege, Plaintiff bears the burden of establishing that the documents it seeks to protect were prepared in anticipation of litigation.... This burden may be satisfied through a detailed privilege log and affidavits from counsel, the party, or the expert, and also by any of the traditional ways in which proof is produced in pretrial proceedings. Once Plaintiff has shown the application of the work product privilege, the burden shifts to Defendant to demonstrate the existence of exceptional circumstances for the discovery of otherwise privileged documents. Defendant, as the party seeking to show exceptional circumstances under Rule 26(b)(4)(B) carries a heavy burden.

B. Dual Purpose: Anticipation of Litigation vs. Ordinary Course of Business

Pike asserts that the documents at issue here, i.e. communications with and reports prepared by consulting experts, were prepared "in the ordinary course of business ... unrelated to litigation, or for other nonlitigation purposes" and are thus not protected by the work product privilege. *See Adams v. City of Montgomery*, 282 F.R.D. 627, 633 (M.D.Ala. 2012). "It is possible for a witness to wear two hats: one as a specially employed expert in anticipation of litigation and one as an ordinary witness." *Essex Builders Group, Inc. v. Amerisure Ins. Co.*, 235

F.R.D. 703 (M.D. Fla. 2006). Thus, "it is admittedly difficult to reduce to a neat general formulation the relationship between preparation of a document and possible litigation necessary to trigger the protection of the work product doctrine." *Adams*, 282 F.R.D. at 634.

The Court must thus determine when the contested documents were created, and why the documents were created in assessing the applicability of the work product doctrine. Courts universally agree that a document whose purpose is to assist in preparation for litigation is within the scope of Rule 26's work product protection. However, as the Second Circuit aptly noted in *U.S. v. Adlman*, 134 F.3d 1194, 1197–98 (2d Cir. 1998), "the issue is less clear . . . as to documents which, although prepared because of expected litigation, are intended to inform a business decision influenced by the prospects of litigation." The *Adlman* Court held that, in light of the plain language of Rule 26 and the policies underlying the work product doctrine,[3] where a document is created because of the prospect of litigation it does not lose protection merely because it was also created in order to assist with a business decision. Accordingly, it is now well recognized that documents that serve a dual purpose are covered by the work product protection if they were produced "with the 'motivating purpose' for or 'because of' anticipated litigation." *Adams*, 282 F.R.D. at 634.

Pike has introduced argument, but no evidence to controvert the affidavits and documents provided by Spirit demonstrating that Messrs. Ramos and Hercules were retained in anticipation of litigation rather than as part of Spirit's ordinary course of business. Spirit has submitted the Affidavits of Mr. Samuels and Mr. Hercules both attesting that the experts were retained specifically in anticipation of litigation, along with a detailed timeline surrounding the retention of these experts and the developing dispute between the parties that led to this lawsuit being filed within a few months. The Court finds that Plaintiff's counsel's anticipation that litigation would ensue when he retained Messrs. Ramos and Hercules to investigate the condition of the property was objectively reasonable. Pike had begun copying its lawyers on emails between the parties' representatives and sent the "Too Bad" email on August 19, 2011, threatening that a "federal bankruptcy judge" would sort out the parties'

---

[3] Courts have recognized four interests weighing against allowing an opposing party to depose or call at trial a consultative, non-testifying expert witness: (1) an "important interest in allowing counsel to obtain the expert advice they need in order properly to evaluate and present their clients' position without fear that every consultation with an expert may yield grist for the adversary's mill," which the court found underlies Fed.R.Civ.P.26(b)(4)(B)'s limitation on discovery of consultative, as opposed to testifying experts; (2) unfairness of allowing an opposing party to benefit from a party's effort and expense incurred in preparing its case; (3) fear of restraint on the willingness of experts to serve as consultants if their testimony could be compelled; and (4) the substantial risk of "explosive" prejudice stemming from the fact of the prior retention of any expert by the opposing party. *Pickett v. IBP, Inc.*, 2000 U.S. Dist. LEXIS 19500 (M.D.Ala. Oct. 16, 2000) (quoting House v. Combined Ins. Co. of America, 168 F.R.D. 236 (N.D.Iowa 1996)).

dispute "so told by [its] attorney." Therefore, the Court concludes that the consulting experts' investigative findings and opinions provided to Spirit's counsel are protected work product pursuant to Fed.R.Civ.P. 26(b)(4)(D).

Even if Spirit retained Ramos and Hercules and their investigations were undertaken in part to assist Spirit in determining Pike's compliance with its lease obligations, the work product privilege does not vanish merely because the communications and reports were created in order to assist with a business decision unless the documents would have been created in essentially similar form irrespective of the litigation. *See* 8 WRIGHT, MILLER, AND MARCUS, FEDERAL PRACTICE & PROCEDURE § 2024, at 512–14 (2012) ("[D]ual purpose documents may be protected even though a nonlitigation purpose can also be ascertained.").

[The remainder of the court's opinion is discussed in the next section about discovery regarding experts.]

NOTES AND QUESTIONS

1. What are the justifications for the work product doctrine? After you read the first paragraph of current Rule 26(b)(3), compare it with the holding in *Hickman*. Which is broader? If you find that the scope of the federal rule is broader, why does the rule cover more issues than *Hickman*?

2. *Prepared in anticipation of litigation or for trial.* A document or thing is defined as work product only if it was "prepared in anticipation of litigation or for trial." A document or thing that existed before the claim or defense in your case was asserted is outside that definition, although it is possible that it may have constituted work product in a prior case. Several courts have adopted the test enunciated in Wright, Miller & Marcus, 8 *Fed. Practice & Procedure,* § 2024 at 343 (1994): documents are "prepared for litigation" and therefore within the scope of the work product rule if, "in light of the nature of the document and the factual situation in the particular case, the document can be fairly said to have been prepared or obtained because of the prospect of litigation." Does the fact that a party ultimately was sued contribute to what the thoughts of the party were at the time of the material's preparation?

Does work product protection apply to documents prepared in anticipation of other litigation, rather than only the pending claims? See 8 Wright, Miller & Marcus, § 2024, at 350–51 (collecting cases and concluding that most courts consider the work product doctrine to protect material prepared in anticipation of previous litigation).

3. *By or for another party, etc.* Rule 26(b)(3) qualifies the definition of a work product as a document or thing prepared in anticipation of litigation by the requirement that such a document or thing was prepared "by or for another party or its representative." The rule lists examples of a party's

representative as "including the other party's attorney, consultant, surety, indemnitor, insurer, or agent."

4. *Obtaining statements of parties and witnesses.* Would you like to have copies of all the statements that the opposing party has taken, both before and after the claim was filed? The problem is that statements obtained by attorneys from party-opponents and witnesses qualify as trial preparation materials. After a plaintiff files a claim, the work product doctrine in Rule 26(b)(3) can shield a diligent attorney from having to disclose all statements taken by the diligent attorney.

Two types of existing statements are discoverable under Rule 26(b)(3)(C) merely for the asking. First, a party can obtain a copy of her own statement from another party. As counsel for that person, you definitely want to read anything that your client already has told the opposing party's attorney or agents. Second, a witness also can obtain her own statement from any party. The witness can authorize you to request her statement and have it mailed to the witness, in care of your office, i.e., address the envelope to Wally Witness, c/o Clarence Darrow.

The definition of a "statement" in Rule 26(b)(3)(C)(i)–(ii) is broad, applying to a written statement that the person has signed or otherwise adopted or approved; or a contemporaneous stenographic, mechanical, electrical, or other recording—or a transcription of it—that recites substantially verbatim the person's oral statement.

What about all other statements? Assuming that there is no voluntary disclosure, they can be obtained from the party-opponent only upon a showing of substantial need and undue hardship. Otherwise, a party may ask in an interrogatory: "Name any person from whom you have taken a statement." That request is legitimate; work product only prohibits the disclosure of the statement itself. With the person's identity, the party's attorney can attempt to talk to that person or depose her. In addition, a party may ask for the identity of the custodian of the statement and/or its location.

5. *Attorney's mental impressions and legal evaluations.* Why do an attorney's mental impressions have almost absolute protection from disclosure under Rule 26(b)(3)(B)? An attorney's notes or memoranda from a meeting or an interview reveal her mental processes. Notes also indicate her legal conclusions. Why? When she is taking notes, an attorney (any person, for that matter) focuses on the facts and the documents that she deems legally significant. In the case of documents, the work product doctrine historically applies. It may also apply, though, to an attorney or her agent being asked in a deposition to recall conversations with witnesses, because what she recalls is likely to be what she regards as important. Of course, even the opinion work product concept does not prevent an attorney from learning the identities of who has been interviewed and later deposing those persons. Other than a fraud exception for opinion work product, it cannot be overcome by a showing of substantial need and undue hardship to obtain a

substantial equivalent document, as is possible with ordinary work product—the topic of the next case.

GUTSHALL V. NEW PRIME, INC.
196 F.R.D. 43 (W.D. Va. 2000)

MICHAEL, SENIOR DISTRICT JUDGE.

This case presents the questions of whether surveillance evidence conducted by a defendant in a personal injury case is discoverable if the defendant only intends to use the evidence for impeachment purposes, and whether such evidence is protected by the attorney work product doctrine. Finding that the federal discovery rules require discovery of such evidence, and that it is not protected by the work product doctrine, the court shall grant the plaintiff's motion to compel.

On June 10, 1998, the plaintiff was operating a tractor-trailer on Interstate 80 in Lake County, Indiana, when he allegedly was rear-ended by another tractor-trailer, owned by defendant New Prime, Inc. ("New Prime"), and operated by defendant Robert Tapper ("Tapper"). The plaintiff sued on April 8, 1999, claiming that Tapper was operating his tractor-trailer within the course and scope of employment with New Prime, that Tapper's negligence caused back injuries the plaintiff suffered as a result of the accident, and that New Prime is liable under the doctrine of *respondeat superior*.

On April 15, 1999, the plaintiff served the following interrogatory on New Prime: "Please state whether or not you have conducted and/or obtained any surveillance of the plaintiff." On November 17, 1999, the plaintiff requested production of: "Documents and things . . . relating to any . . . visual depiction . . . of . . . any person involved in the collision, which is in your possession, to which you have access or of which you have knowledge." An accompanying interrogatory contains the same language.

As of the date of New Prime's initial responses to these requests, New Prime had not conducted any surveillance, and properly responded that it had not. New Prime subsequently arranged for surveillance of the plaintiff from May 1 to June 1, 2000. The plaintiff noticed the surveillance on May 26, and so informed his attorney. Claiming that New Prime failed to supplement its discovery responses in compliance with Federal Rule of Civil Procedure 26(e)(1) by not producing the surveillance evidence, the plaintiff filed a "Motion to Compel Discovery Responses" on June 30, and a motion to exclude that evidence. Trial was scheduled to begin less than a month later, on July 26.

... New Prime argues that because Rule 26(a)(3) excludes information that will be used solely for impeachment purposes, which is the only purpose for which New Prime claims it intends to use the surveillance evidence, it was not required to produce that evidence pursuant to the document requests.

Rule 26(a)(3) does not describe the scope of discovery or exclude impeachment evidence therefrom; it describes the scope of automatic initial disclosure requirements. The plaintiff does not assert that the evidence should have been produced because it fell within automatic initial disclosure requirements, but because it was responsive to two interrogatories and a request for production of documents. Therefore, New Prime's reliance on Rule 26(a)(3) is misplaced. The scope of discovery is described in Rule 26(b). . . .

Unlike subsection (a), subsection (b) does not distinguish between substantive and impeachment evidence. . . .

New Prime prepared, or commissioned the preparation of, the surveillance materials in anticipation of trial in this case. Consequently, those materials constitute "work product" that New Prime ordinarily would not be compelled to produce. However, even work product materials are discoverable if the plaintiff "has substantial need of the materials in the preparation of [his] . . . case and that [he] . . . is unable without undue hardship to obtain the substantial equivalent of the materials by other means." Fed.R.Civ.P. 26(b)(3). . . . Most other federal courts have not found surveillance tapes to be protected work product. *See, e.g., Smith v. Diamond Offshore Drilling, Inc.,* 168 F.R.D. 582 (S.D.Tex.1996) (surveillance evidence must be produced notwithstanding its work product status); *Snead v. American Export-Isbrandtsen Lines, Inc.,* 59 F.R.D. 148, 151 (E.D.Pa.1973) (observing that even though the plaintiff may be unable to bend without pain, "under some particular circumstances he may have done so and this may be the very incident the camera recorded. . . . there is substantial need to have knowledge of the films for the preparation of the plaintiff's case").

The court agrees with the majority of courts that considered the issue, and finds that a plaintiff alleging claims for personal injury has a substantial need for surveillance evidence in preparing his case for trial, due to the relevance and importance of such evidence, and the substantial impact it may have at trial. Further, it is impossible to procure the substantial equivalent of such evidence without undue hardship, as videotape "fixes information available at a particular time and a particular place under particular circumstances, and therefore cannot be duplicated." *Smith,* 168 F.R.D. at 586. Notwithstanding the work product status of the surveillance evidence, it therefore must be produced by New Prime pursuant to Federal Rule of Civil Procedure 26(e)(1). The plaintiff's motion to compel shall be granted. However, the plaintiff having cited no legal basis for excluding the surveillance evidence, his motion to exclude shall be denied. . . .

PROBLEMS

1. Long before one of Paulin Electronics's drills malfunctioned in Vesely's hand in 2015, other Paulin drills had injured consumers in 2008. Several months after they were injured but before Vesely was injured, Paulin's President asked the production supervisor (Prewitt) and the product designer (Christian) to send her memoranda detailing the decision making process by which the specific drill design was selected and the drill was produced. Each of them drafted a long memorandum detailing the meetings with employees and outside consultants.

Vesely's counsel now sends interrogatories to Paulin seeking all "notes, records, letters, memoranda, or other communications concerning the Paulin Deluxe electric drill in issue." May Paulin use Rule 26(b)(3) to avoid producing Prewitt's and Christian's memoranda?

2. Prewitt's first assistant, Henn, actually drafted the memo attributed to Prewitt. Henn no longer works for Paulin and cannot be located. Vesely's attorney sends an interrogatory to Paulin's President asking her to "relate the substance of any interviews you and/or your counsel conducted with Henn concerning the Paulin Deluxe electric drill in issue." Paulin's lawyer, Prizant, in fact had interviewed Henn before she left, but he did not record the meeting or take notes. Must Prizant provide the requested information?

3. Assume that Prizant met with Henn after Vesely's attorney had filed a lawsuit against Paulin Electronics. Prizant took extensive notes during the interview with Henn. The notes include factual statements made by Henn about the drill, Prizant's evaluative notes about the credibility of Henn's statements, other evidence that might contradict what Henn said, and problems with admissibility of the evidence. Vesely's interrogatories seek production of "any notes, memoranda, recordings, or other records of discussions with Henn concerning the Paulin Deluxe electric drill." Are the notes protected under Rule 26(b)(3)?

4. Vesely sends the following interrogatory to Paulin Electronics: "During the time President Paulin sought the Prewitt and Christian memos, did Prewitt, Christian, or Henn give oral or written assurances that the Paulin Deluxe electric drill was free of any defects?" In fact, Henn had told Prizant and Christian that the drill was free of defects. Prizant refuses to answer, on the ground that the information is protected by the work product privilege. Does Rule 26(b)(3) apply?

5. Assume that in #1 above, the memoranda are ordinary work product. Can work product be overcome if:

a. Vesely's counsel proves to the court that she wants the memoranda to ensure that she has not overlooked anything of value in preparing her case?

b. Neither Prewitt nor Christian can be found?

c. Vesely did not hire an attorney until two years after he was injured, i.e., 2008, and both Prewitt and Christian have retired from Paulin Electronics, relocating in a distant state?

d. Vesely's counsel tried unsuccessfully to speak personally to Prewitt and Christian but both refused to answer her questions?

e. Vesely's counsel tried unsuccessfully to speak personally to Prewitt and Christian after their retirements but neither could remember anything about the time period surrounding the writing of the memos?

6. Consider whether any of the following meets the definition of a "statement" under Rule 26(b)(3)(C), and must be provided on request to the person who made the statement.

a. An attorney's two-page memorandum, contemporaneously summarizing a one-hour interview with a witness to a vehicle collision.

b. Same as A, except that the witness signed the page on which the attorney had taken notes of the interview.

c. A ten-minute tape recording, by an attorney, memorializing a one-hour interview with a witness. The attorney's recording was made the day after the witness interview.

4. DISCOVERY ABOUT EXPERTS

INTRODUCTORY PROBLEM

Vicki Victim was seriously hurt when a lawnmower manufactured by Lucky Lawnmower, Inc. and operated by Vicki, exploded. Vicki contacted Arnold Attorney who began an investigation of the case. Lucky Lawnmower's investigation consists of the following:

1. A report of a design engineer who was hired to determine the cause of the accident. She was the first person to look at the lawnmower after the accident. She disassembled the lawnmower and concluded that the accident was probably caused by an improperly installed carburetor. Being a kind soul, she reassembled the lawnmower correctly. The report itself was inconclusive as to the cause of the accident and Lucky does not plan to use the design engineer at trial. Somehow, Arnold found out about the disassembly process, even though he does not know the engineer's identity.

2. A report of a products safety engineer/expert who works for Lucky in the quality control department. The report states that there have been two other reported explosions of the model involved in the lawsuit but, in his

opinion, the other explosions were caused by improper consumer use of the lawnmower. The products safety expert will testify at trial.

    a.   May Arnold take the deposition of the design engineer to find out about both the opinions of the engineer and the re-assembly of the lawnmower?

    b.   Arnold wants to know about all prior complaints regarding the particular lawnmower model in controversy. May Arnold require the products safety engineer/expert to appear for a deposition and bring with him all prior complaints and any reports he has prepared concerning other accidents?

Governing Rule: Rule 26(b).

As noted earlier in this Chapter, the Federal Rules address the mandatory pretrial (ninety days before trial, unless otherwise ordered or agreed) disclosure of expert witnesses whose opinions "may be presented at trial." Every party must disclose the identity of its experts and present an expert report for each expert witness, per Rule 26(a)(2) which also describes the contents of the expert report. In addition, those experts may be deposed about their opinions. The disclosure is subject to the Rule 26(e)(2) duty to supplement, also discussed earlier.

Based on the expert's special knowledge, skill, experience or training, parties offer expert testimony to assist the fact finder in comprehending information about the case and reaching conclusions about the issues. Having just studied work product, you may be wondering about the nature of the identity of an expert and the expert's report. Is the identity of an expert work product? The person's name and the report prepared by the expert surely was obtained by the party in anticipation of trial. Indeed, the first phrase of the work product rule, Rule 26(b)(3), states the it is "subject to Rule 26(b)(4)." Therefore, discovery about experts is recognized as work product but discoverable nonetheless.

SPIRIT MASTER FUNDING, LLC v. PIKE NURSERIES ACQUISITION, LLC
287 F.R.D. 680 (N.D.Ga. 2012)

AMY TOTENBERG, DISTRICT JUDGE.

[The first portion of the court's opinion was set out in the foregoing section relating to work product.]

C. Exceptional Circumstances

Pike asserts that exceptional circumstances exist to justify disclosure of Spirit's communications with and documents prepared by its non-testifying consulting experts retained in anticipation of litigation because the information goes directly to proving its counterclaims against Spirit. According to Pike, Messrs. Ramos and Hercules' knowledge and assessments and communications with Spirit go directly to the issue of Spirit's knowledge and whether Spirit breached its obligations under the lease agreements and acted in bad faith.

Rule 26(b) places a twofold burden on the party seeking to overcome the work product privilege and discover protected materials; the requesting party must show both substantial need and undue hardship. Additionally, those parties seeking discovery of facts known or opinions held by consulting experts who are not expected to be called as trial witnesses have the heavy burden of demonstrating the existence of exceptional circumstances. The exceptional circumstances requirement has been interpreted by the courts to mean an inability to obtain equivalent information from other sources.

Pike is correct that it may discover facts that support its counterclaims or defenses. Here, Pike seeks fact work product protected under Rule 26(b) to the extent that Pike requests documents generated in the course of Spirit's investigation into the condition of the property by its consulting experts Ramos and Hercules that summarize or otherwise purport to relate factual information obtained during the investigation. Such information differs from mere facts, which are not protected by the work-product doctrine.

While underlying facts do not enjoy the protection of the work product doctrine, that does not necessarily mean that Pike is entitled to obtain work product documents and materials that contain facts. When the facts are so intertwined with the mental impressions of the attorney or other work product protected materials, other methods exist for obtaining the factual information without disturbing the work-product protection.... The work product doctrine does not protect factual information from disclosure. Rather, it protects a party only from disclosing particular documents containing the information. To accommodate these principles, a party may propound interrogatories and take depositions to obtain the sought-after factual information. Accordingly, because Pike may discover the facts forming the basis of Spirit's decision to reject Pike's attempted termination of the lease on the basis that the building was condemned by other means, i.e., through interrogatories and depositions of Spirit's representatives who took part in those decisions, Pike has failed to satisfy its heavy burden of establishing substantial burden, undue hardship, and exceptional circumstances warranting disclosure of documents subject to the work product privilege.

III. CONCLUSION

For the reasons set forth herein, the Court finds that the facts and opinions of Messrs. Ramos and Hercules are protected by the work product privilege and are therefore not subject to discovery. Pike may discover facts from Spirit's representatives regarding its knowledge of the condition of the property and the basis for its conduct regarding the termination of the lease agreements with Pike, either by interrogatories, depositions, or other requests for production not directed toward work product materials.

NOTES AND QUESTIONS

1. Testifying experts' depositions may be taken before trial but after the expert's report has been provided to opposing counsel. While the 1993 Advisory Committee's Notes suggested that detailed expert reports may eliminate the need for depositions or reduce their length, it is unlikely that a litigator should be satisfied with the report's information which is likely to have been prepared in close consultation with the counsel hiring the expert and which may contain less than satisfactory explanations of the expert's qualifications, experience, conclusions, or reasons in support of the conclusions.

2. Can you obtain discovery about an opponent's experts who will not be testifying at trial? The rules deal with non-testifying experts differently and categorically, explicitly and implicitly. If a non-testifying expert is retained or specially employed, by Rule 26(b)(4)(D), information about her identity or opinion is treated as though it constitutes work product; it is subject to discovery only "showing exceptional circumstances under which it is impracticable for the party to obtain facts or opinions on the same subject by other means." The meaning of "retained or specially employed" matters, because of another implicit category of experts. For an expert who is merely informally consulted (as opposed to retained or specially employed), nothing about her identity or opinion is subject to discovery, no matter how badly the adversary party needs the information.

3. Is the information about non-testifying experts qualified work product or opinion work product? Do "decisions by lawyers about which people to use for confidential pretrial consultation fall into that almost sacrosanct category recognized in the last sentence of the first paragraph of Rule 26(b)(3), namely 'the mental impressions, conclusions, opinions or legal theories of a party's attorney' "?

4. *Work product protection for draft reports.* When a lawyer employs a testifying expert, the expert often will send the lawyer a draft of the report that will ultimately be disclosed to opposing counsel. For years, the discoverability of draft reports was contentious, because the opposing counsel wanted to create the impression that any differences between the draft and the final report were the lawyer's idea.

Draft reports prepared by the expert have protection as Rule 26(b)(3) work product, per Rules 26(b)(4)(B)–(C), as do other disclosures that are otherwise mandated by Rule 26(a)(2). The Rule also provides work product protection for any other communications between any expert required to file a report under Rule 26(a)(2)(B) and the party's lawyer. Exceptions to that general rule relate to communications about the expert's compensation, as well as facts, data, or assumptions provided by the lawyer and considered or relied upon by the expert in forming the opinions to be expressed.

5. *The expert who wears "two hats."* Recall that Rule 26(a)(2)(B) requires disclosure of all materials reviewed, considered, or generated by a designated expert in forming an opinion, unless they were reviewed, considered, or generated uniquely or solely in the capacity as a consultant. When a consulting expert is later designated as a testifying expert, what is the extent of the required disclosure for material the expert has reviewed, considered, or generated?

In 1999, Eastman Kodak Company retained a statistician to determine whether there was statistical evidence of disparities in compensation/job promotions among protected groups of Kodak employees. His results were favorable to Kodak. In a later class action employment discrimination lawsuit, Kodak identified him as a fact witness to testify about his study. At his deposition, when he was asked about similar statistical analyses he did for Kodak in 2003 and 2004, Kodak's lawyer invoked the attorney-client privilege and he declined to answer any analyses-related questions. Kodak later designated him as a testifying expert for purposes of the class action lawsuit. He claimed that in conducting his analysis he did not review any of the unrelated work he did for Kodak in 2003 and 2004.

In *Employees Committed for Justice v. Eastman Kodak,* 251 F.R.D. 101 (W.D.N.Y. 2008), the trial court used an objective standard which required disclosure of "anything received, reviewed, read, or authored by the expert before or in connection with" forming an opinion, as long as the subject matter relates to the opinion. Because the expert was the person responsible for the 2003 and 2004 analyses, he could not claim that he was unaware of the results of his prior work for Kodak. Thus, when he switched roles and became a testifying expert, he was deemed to have "considered" his previous work as a Kodak consultant. Accordingly, he had a duty to disclose the previously "considered" information.

PROBLEMS

1. McCoy is a university expert in evaluating the effect of heat on various metal wiring. He consults for Paulin Electronics occasionally, analyzing the effects of heat on the wire used in Paulin Electronics's product line. Before Vesely's accident, McCoy had performed tests on the wires used in the Paulin Deluxe electric drill. Vesely's attorney sends a notice to Paulin to take McCoy's deposition, but Prizant objects that McCoy's deposition cannot be taken because he is a non-testifying expert. Evaluate the validity of the objection under Rule 26(b)(4)(B).

2. Before suing Paulin Electronics, Vesely's attorney contacts Dr. Friedrich von Dufus, a renowned expert on metallurgy to ask for a preliminary opinion about whether the quality of metals used in the wires for

Paulin Deluxe electric drills was adequate. Von Dufus reviews the information about Vesely's accident and finds that the drill wiring did not malfunction. Vesely's attorney decides not to hire von Dufus and looks elsewhere for an expert with "better" views. In his interrogatories to Vesely, Prizant seeks the names of all experts who have been consulted or retained. Evaluate Vesely's obligation to disclose information about von Dufus.

3. On behalf of Paulin, Prizant learned informally that there are only four other known metal wiring experts—Dr. Dufus, two from the West Coast, and one other person who makes a terrible impression as a trial witness. Prizant hires one of the West Coast experts to testify at trial, and he hires the other only as a non-testifying expert. Meanwhile, as Vesely's attorney begins his preparation of the case he has the same five names as Prizant. Is Vesely's attorney out of luck on locating an expert to consult?

EXERCISE

For the state where a) you intend to practice after graduation, b) your law school is located, and/or c) your professor assigns, go to that state's annotated statutes and research the procedural rules by which discovery is governed. Based on your research, print the rule and bring it to class for discussion. In addition, answer the following questions.

1. Is discovery of certain information mandatory? Is discovery conducted by informal request between counsel or must the trial court approve all discovery?

2. Identify the standards for determining relevancy, privileged information, protective orders, and work product. How are the state standards narrower or broader than the discovery standards in the federal rules?

3. For discovery of expert witnesses, evaluate how the standards of your state are similar or dissimilar from the federal rules.

B. DISCOVERY DEVICES

1. DEPOSITIONS

Federal Rule 30 is one of the few discovery rules that applies equally to parties and non-parties. A party may take any person's deposition, per Rule 30(a). Even a party's attorney's deposition may be taken, but the attorney-client privilege may limit the scope of questioning. Recent amendments to Rule 30 limit the number of depositions to ten by plaintiffs or by defendants as a group, subject to increase by the court or by stipulation. Rule 30(d) provides for a time limit of one day of seven hours for each deposition, which can be extended by stipulation or court order. Similarly, the court's permission is necessary in order to repeat a person's deposition or to take any deposition before the court conducts a discovery conference. Why does the rule impose these limitations?

As the next case shows, the rules enable a party to describe the information sought, while placing the burden on the opposing party to designate a specific person for deposition.

ALEXANDER V. F.B.I.
186 F.R.D. 148 (D.D.C. 1999)

LAMBERTH, DISTRICT JUDGE.

This matter comes before the Court on Plaintiffs' Motion to Compel Re-Designation of Witness on Surveillance Systems Under Fed.R.Civ.P. 30(b)(6) and for Attorneys' Fees and Costs. Upon consideration of plaintiffs' motion, defendant Executive Office of the President's opposition, and plaintiffs' reply thereto, the Court will DENY plaintiffs' motion without prejudice, as discussed and ordered below.

The underlying allegations in this case arise from what has become popularly known as "Filegate." Plaintiffs allege that their privacy interests were violated when the FBI improperly handed over to the White House hundreds of FBI files of former political appointees and government employees under the Reagan and Bush Administrations. The instant dispute revolves around the deposition of John Dankowski, Director of White House Operations.

Dankowski was designated by defendant EOP to testify pursuant to Fed.R.Civ.P. 30(b)(6) Rule 30(b)(6) states, in pertinent part, that:

> A party may in the party's notice and in a subpoena name as the deponent a ... governmental agency and describe with reasonable particularity the matters on which examination is requested. In that event, the organization so named shall designate one or more officers, directors, or managing agents, or other persons who consent to testify on its behalf, and may set forth, for each person designated, the matters on which the person will testify.... This subdivision (b)(6) does not preclude taking a deposition by any other procedure authorized in these rules.

The reasonableness of the testimony sought by plaintiffs is not in dispute. Thus, defendant EOP's duty to designate a suitable witness (or suitable witnesses) was triggered.

Although not disputed, the scope of the testimony sought merits some discussion, as it will bear upon the adequacy of defendant EOP's Rule 30(b)(6) designation. The Court addressed the proper scope of plaintiffs' Rule 30(b)(6) deposition notice in its April 13, 1998 Memorandum and Order denying defendant EOP's motion to quash. In that opinion, the Court described plaintiffs' deposition notice, in pertinent part, as follows:

Deposition request 3 seeks to have a deponent testify regarding "the system of recording devices, whether audio or video, used to record sounds or pictures in any of the office, common, residential, and/or other areas of the White House and the entirety of the [EOP], including the Office of White House Counsel and the Office of the First Lady." . . . Deposition request 8 seeks to have a deponent testify regarding "any recording, transcription, communication, printing, filing, and any and all recordation devices used by Hillary Rodham Clinton and others in the White House in their governmental, official, and/or allegedly private capacities."

. . . Plaintiffs seek to elicit testimony on these audio or visual recordation devices because, in their view, evidence gleaned from such devices could be "highly probative of the partisan misuse of the FBI and government files" at issue in this case. The theory behind this assertion appears to be that "traffic to and from [Craig] Livingstone's office is one of the likely ways to definitively trace what was done with information read and copied out of the physical FBI files."

Defendant EOP designated Dankowski as their Rule 30(b)(6) witness with regard to audio and video recordation systems, also referred to as "surveillance systems." His deposition was taken on June 23, 1998. The dispute currently before the Court involves whether defendant EOP complied with its duties under Fed.R.Civ.P. 30(b)(6) and, if not, what the consequences of that dereliction should be.

. . . [D]efendant EOP does not dispute that plaintiffs have described the matter upon which testimony is sought with reasonable particularity, as required by Rule 30(b)(6). Once it is established that plaintiffs have met this initial burden, a number of duties were triggered that must be met by defendant EOP, as the party named in the notice. At the outset, and most obviously, defendant EOP must designate one or more persons to testify on the subject matter designated by plaintiffs. Defendant EOP met this burden by designating Dankowski. The dispute, however, centers around a number of concomitant duties involved in the preparation and proper designation of the witness.

The Court recently addressed the topic of a party's duties in designating and preparing a witness under Rule 30(b)(6). First, the deponent has a duty of being knowledgeable on the subject matter identified as the area of inquiry. Clearly, a deponent that does not know about the relevant subject matter is useless as a deponent at all. Second, the designating party is under the duty to designate more than one deponent if it would be necessary to do so in order to respond to the relevant areas of inquiry that are specified with reasonable particularity by the plaintiffs. Third, the designating party has a duty to prepare the witness to testify on matters not only known by the deponent, but those that should be reasonably known by the designating party. Obviously, the purpose of a Rule 30(b)(6) deposition is to get answers on the subject matter described with reasonable particularity by the noticing party, not to simply get answers limited to what the deponent happens to know. Fourth, the designating party has a duty to substitute an appropriate deponent when it becomes apparent that the previous deponent is unable to respond to certain relevant areas of inquiry. All of these duties correspond to the ultimate underlying purposes of Rule 30(b)(6)—namely, preventing serial depositions of various witnesses without knowledge within an organization and eliminating "bandying," which is the name given to the practice in which people are deposed in turn but each disclaims knowledge of facts that are clearly known to persons in the organization and thereby to the organization itself.

Plaintiffs assert four arguments on why Dankowski was an inappropriate or non-exhaustive Rule 30(b)(6) witness with regard to the relevant non-Secret Service operated surveillance systems. First, plaintiffs contend that Dankowski is not qualified to testify on the relevant subject matter because he has no expertise in surveillance systems. Second, plaintiffs argue that Dankowski did not adequately prepare for his deposition because, for example, he did not inspect certain premises for surveillance equipment. Third, plaintiffs assert that Dankowski is not knowledgeable about surveillance systems because he doesn't "know whether or not there's a department of the White House . . . that's kept secret from other personnel that's in charge of surveillance." Dankowski Depo. at 47. Fourth, plaintiffs claim that defendant EOP must designate another Rule 30(b)(6) witness on the topic of voice mail recordation because, in their view, Dankowski could not answer adequately the questions posed to him in that regard at the deposition. Upon review of the parties' memoranda and the deposition transcript, the Court rejects plaintiffs' first three arguments in full and plaintiffs' fourth argument in part.

First, Dankowski appears to be the appropriate person for defendant EOP to have designated on the topic of surveillance systems. Dankowski is the Director of White House Operations and is responsible for the purchases of all goods and services for the White House Office. If any non-Secret Service surveillance system was maintained in the White House Office, money, equipment, and services would be required for its use and upkeep. Plaintiffs adduce no evidence that any other person would be more qualified than Dankowski on the relevant subject matter. Therefore, plaintiffs' first argument must be rejected.

Second, the Court finds that Dankowski did adequately prepare for his deposition. In short, he had twelve years of experience in the White House Office, reviewed all of the spending obligation records for the White House Office dating back to 1992, and consulted with three separate individuals to obtain even more information with regard to matters such as staffing for potential surveillance systems. Although some of his preparations involved conversations with political appointees, a point that plaintiffs are fond of making, this fact does not belie Dankowski's proper designation. Dankowski appears to have asked questions of the proper people in order to receive answers; their political affiliation cannot be construed as making his testimony inherently incredible simply because some of these people are, of course, the same political affiliation as the President. Plaintiffs point to no other evidence that would cast doubt upon Dankowski's preparation or testimony. Therefore, plaintiffs' contention that Dankowski was inadequately prepared fails.

Third, the Court expressly rejects plaintiffs' conjecture that a "secret department" may exist within the White House Office independently of the Secret Service that monitors employee activity. Plaintiffs point to absolutely no evidence to support such a claim, aside from the Nixon Presidential tapes incident. When this assertion is combined with plaintiffs' claim that they "are entitled to obtain testimony under oath . . . stating categorically that there is no audio or visual surveillance system at the White House other than what may be operated by the Secret Service," defendant EOP's burden becomes insurmountable. Defendant EOP cannot be expected or required to prove the non-existence of surveillance equipment to an absolute certainty. Dankowski testified repeatedly that he has no personal knowledge of any such systems, has never seen anything that would indicate the existence of such systems, and has never heard anything to indicate that such systems exist. Defendant EOP has met its Rule 30(b)(6) burden in this regard by designating Dankowski to testify about matters known or reasonably known to defendant EOP. Fed.R.Civ.P. 30(b)(6).

The plaintiffs' fourth argument—that Dankowski could not testify fully as to the voice mail system—merits closer attention. Although plaintiffs attempt to dismiss Dankowski's testimony with regard to voice mail in full, they clearly overstate their case in this regard. Dankowski testified competently that the White House Office has a voice mail system. He stated that no other telephone recording devices existed. The voice mail comes into individual mailboxes and accumulates up to a certain limit. Once that limit is reached, the mailbox will not accept further messages. Unopened mail is erased from the system in ten days and opened mail is erased after fifteen. That voice mail system was set up in 1994. Thus, Dankowski has a good understanding of the current voice mail system in the White House Office, and he testified fully in that regard.

The one area, however, to which Dankowski could not testify was pre-1994 voice mail. In this context, the following exchange occurred:

[Plaintiffs' counsel:] When were you first cognizant of the fact that there was a voice mail system at the White House?

[Dankowski:] I believe it came in '94, if I recall correctly.

[Plaintiffs' counsel:] Was there a voice mail system in the White House before that?

[Dankowski:] Not that I recall.

[Plaintiffs' counsel:] You don't know one way or the other?

[Dankowski:] I do not.

. . .

[Plaintiffs' counsel:] So, consequently, you don't really know whether or not a prior system had a permanent voice mail retention system?

[Dankowski:] I do not know that.

As stated above, the relevancy on this area of discovery is limited to the time period beginning in 1992. Thus, Dankowski could not testify as to the status of a certain type of audio recording system from the time period 1992–1994 (although he did state at one point that he does not believe one existed). This information, however unlikely to be helpful to plaintiffs, would be within the realm of discoverable evidence in this case. Thus, plaintiffs are entitled to answers to this limited subject matter.

As was the case with plaintiffs' motion to compel the re-designation of a witness on the White House Office Database (WhoDB), however, plaintiffs' need for answers to these questions does not warrant a new oral deposition at this juncture. Instead, as set out in the Court's Order below, plaintiffs shall be allowed to pose specific interrogatories and requests for production to defendant EOP on the limited subject matter of voice mail systems during the period 1992–1994. If, after they have received written discovery responses on this issue, a new Rule 30(b)(6) oral deposition is warranted, plaintiffs may again move to compel such a deposition at that time. Until then, however, plaintiffs' motion to compel defendant EOP to re-designate a Rule 30(b)(6) witness on the topic of White House Office audio and video recordation devices must be denied without prejudice.

Because the Court will deny plaintiffs' requested relief in all respects except to the extent they are allowed to pose certain limited discovery requests, the only plausible ground for sanctions appears to be Dankowski's inability to testify as to the voice mail systems before 1994. As is clear from the discussion above, Dankowski was thoroughly prepared and testified fully on nearly all of plaintiffs' inquiries. He did have a duty to find out about the existence of voice mail from the period 1992–1994, since this would fall within the plain meaning of an audio recording device and be within the other limits imposed by the Court. But Dankowski's failure to be prepared in this limited aspect cannot be said to be a result of bad faith conduct. Dankowski did consult with the Deputy Assistant for Management and Administration on the general topic of voice mail and the more specific topic of potential voice mail backup systems. Based upon this preparation, the Court does not believe that Dankowski's inability to testify on one narrow issue rises to the level of being sanctionable. Therefore, plaintiffs' request for sanctions will be denied. . . .

NOTES AND QUESTIONS

1. *Notice about the deposition.* A party must give reasonable written notice about the deposition to the deponent and to all other parties. Unless otherwise agreed by all parties and the deponent, a notice of less than one week is likely to be deemed unreasonable. When the parties cannot agree on a date and location for a deposition, the notice is subject to challenge by a motion for a protective order under Rule 26(c). A notice to take a deposition may look like the following:

UNITED STATES DISTRICT COURT WESTERN DISTRICT OF KENTUCKY AT LOUISVILLE

GEORGE W. KERRY   Plaintiff

v.   Case No. 11–007

FLY-BY-NIGHT INSURANCE CO.   Defendant

NOTICE TO TAKE DEPOSITION

To: Ash Johncroft
Smith and Johncroft
200 North Water Street
River City, Kentucky 40001

Please take notice that the defendant in the above-styled action will take the oral deposition by stenographic means of George W. Kerry at the office of the undersigned on February 28, 2016.

The deposition will be taken pursuant to and for all purposes allowed by the Federal Rules of Civil Procedure.

Respectfully submitted,

_____

Howdy Doody
Bar Wars, P.S.C.
6000 Seventh National Tower
Passivity, KY 44444

COUNSEL FOR DEFENDANT

CERTIFICATE OF SERVICE

I certify that on the 12th day of February, 2016, a copy of the foregoing Notice was mailed to Ash Johncroft, Smith and Johncroft, 200 North Water Street, River City, Kentucky 40001, Counsel for Plaintiff.

_____

Counsel for Defendant

_____

A non-party witness is not required to travel more than 100 miles from where she works, lives or regularly transacts business to be deposed, per Rule 45(c)(3)(A)(ii). However, the parties may agree with the deponent to compensate the non-party witness to travel a longer distance. If a party fails to serve a non-party witness with a subpoena for a deposition and that non-party witness fails to show up, the party noticing the deposition may have to pay the expenses of other parties in preparing for and appearing at the deposition. Rule 30(g)(2)

2. *Methods for recording the deposition.* Under Rule 30(b)(3)(A), the notice also specifies the method for recording the deposition testimony, e.g., audio or audiovisual, stenographic means, and the party noticing the deposition is responsible for the costs of the recording method. Rule 30(b)(4) permits the parties to stipulate to a deposition "by telephone or other remote means," or to seek a court order for such a deposition, with a court reporter in the presence of the deponent. The other parties, at their expense, may also arrange to record the deposition by additional means with prior notice. If the party taking the deposition wants the deponent to bring documents to a deposition, the rules permit the party either to describe the documents in the notice of deposition for a party-witness or issue a subpoena under Rule 45 for a non-party witness.

3. *"Deposing" an organization.* As *Alexander* indicates, per Rule 30(b)(6), when a party sues an organization, she may not know who within the entity has knowledge relating to the claim for relief. The notice to take the deposition of a private corporation or a public agency is sufficient if it merely specifies the areas of inquiry with particularity, without naming a specific person to be deposed. The organization then is responsible for designating one or more representatives to appear and answer questions about the areas of inquiry. Assuming that the entity has acted in good faith to identify person(s) who can testify about the areas specified in the deposition notice, the entity is bound by the designee's deposition testimony. If the entity's witness cannot answer questions reflecting those areas, the entity is subject to sanctions. See, e.g., *In re Vitamins Antitrust Litigation,* 216 F.R.D. 168 (D.D.C. 2003).

4. *What happens at the deposition?* At the beginning of a deposition, the person recording the deposition must put on the record a statement about

her name and address, the time, place and date of the deposition, the deponent's name, the administration of an oath, and the identity of all persons present. Rule 30(c)(1) indicates that the deposition questioning is similar to a trial, although most objections (e.g., relevancy) are reserved until the deposition testimony is offered in evidence at trial. An attorney can instruct a witness not to answer a question only to 1) claim a privilege such as the attorney client privilege, 2) enforce a court order limiting the scope of questioning, or 3) stop the deposition for the purpose of making a motion relating to improper harassing conduct.

5. *After the deposition.* On a timely request per Rule 30(e)(1), a deponent has the opportunity to review and correct a deposition transcript in a timely manner, i.e., failure to submit changes within the allowable period waives the right to correct the transcript. If a deponent changes the substance of her answers, the transcript must reflect the reason for the change and later the deponent is subject to impeachment with her earlier answers.

6. *Pre-filing discovery.* When it is important to perpetuate testimony *before* a lawsuit is filed, Federal Rule 27(a)(1) provides an opportunity for conducting discovery by taking a deposition to avoid losing the deponent's information, e.g., a person's memory may be fading. Why is a putative plaintiff unable to conduct discovery for other reasons, e.g., in order to ensure that the complaint she plans to file is accurate and complete? Why is the rule restricted to taking depositions, without the chance to obtain documents?

Under Rule 27, the putative party must file a verified petition for permission to take the deposition. The contents of the petition must include a statement about 1) the petitioner's expectation of being a party in a federal lawsuit but she cannot yet file the suit or cause it to be filed, 2) the petitioner's role in that lawsuit as well as a description of the case, 3) the deponent's identity and the information to be gained from the deposition, and 4) the petitioner's need for perpetuating that information. If the petitioner satisfies the court that justice requires the perpetuation of the information, it will order the deposition.

2. INTERROGATORIES

O'CONNOR v. BOEING NORTH AMERICAN, INC.
185 F.R.D. 272 (C.D. Cal. 1999)

CHAPMAN, UNITED STATES MAGISTRATE JUDGE.

... [P]laintiffs allege that, beginning in approximately 1946, the defendants researched, developed, manufactured and tested various missile and rocket engines, as well as propellants, lasers and nuclear reactors at four facilities located in the greater Simi Valley and San Fernando Valley. . . .

The plaintiffs allege that the activities of the defendants at the Rocketdyne Facilities involved the use and release of certain chemicals, including, among others, trichloroethene (TCE) and hexavalent chromium, as well as the use, storage, generation and disposal of certain radioactive materials. The plaintiffs allege that they were personally exposed to and/or that their properties were contaminated by certain radioactive and/or chemical substances which were released from one or more of the Rocketdyne Facilities [also known as the Hughes, Canoga or DeSoto facilities] and which were dispersed through the contamination area by means of air currents, surface water runoff and/or subsurface ground water.

The plaintiffs further allege that their exposure to these substances has placed them at an increased risk of developing cancer or some other serious illness or disease. As a result, plaintiffs seek the implementation of a court-supervised program of medical monitoring designed to detect early signs of such illness or disease.

The plaintiffs also allege that the defendants' release of these substances has resulted in the contamination of their properties and has diminished the value of their properties, and they have incurred certain necessary expenses in response to the contamination of their properties for which they seek reimbursement under federal law.

The defendants maintain that plaintiffs have not been exposed to any substances released from the Rocketdyne Facilities that place them at an increased risk of illness or disease. The defendants also maintain that plaintiffs' properties are not contaminated by any releases from the Rocketdyne Facilities and that, consequently, plaintiffs are not entitled to recover damages for any harm caused to their properties.

[The court had already certified three classes, and in addition 71 plaintiffs sued for personal injury and wrongful death.]

Plaintiffs' Motion to Compel

I

The plaintiffs served interrogatory nos. 1 through 20 on defendants on November 11, 1997.[3] The defendants filed multiple objections, including relevancy and definitional objections to the interrogatories; however, without waiving their objections, defendants generally responded to the interrogatories under Rule 33(d), stating that the answers to these interrogatories may be derived or ascertained from defendants' business records previously produced to plaintiffs. The

---

[3] These interrogatories generally seek information regarding the identities, quantities, and time periods of hazardous substances used and released at each of defendants' facilities, as well as the locations, dates and results of offsite testing of hazardous substances. Additionally, plaintiffs seek information identifying the locations, nature of, and results from tests on substances in the surrounding area, groundwater, surface water, air, and soil.

plaintiffs argue that defendants' responses are improper in that defendants have not complied with Rule 33(d), and, when answering narratively, have not completely and responsively answered.

... The Court, prior to addressing plaintiffs' motion and its several issues, notes that due to the complex nature of the pending class action, written interrogatories to the defendants are not likely to be particularly helpful or useful to plaintiffs and, more likely than not, will only lead to unnecessary discovery disputes. Rather, the depositions of knowledgeable corporate witnesses under Rule 30(b)(6), or the individually noticed depositions of defendants' employees, will ultimately be more productive.

The nature of the inquiries made by plaintiffs in their interrogatories was sufficiently broad for defendants to answer under Rule 33(d). However, Rule 33(d) is not satisfied by the wholesale dumping of documents. Rather, under Rule 33(d), the responding party chooses to produce business records in answer to the interrogatories—not to avoid answering them. To answer an interrogatory, "a responding party has the duty to specify, by category and location, the records from which answers to interrogatories can be derived." *Rainbow Pioneer No. 44–18–04A v. Hawaii-Nevada Investment Corp.*, 711 F.2d 902, 906 (9th Cir.1983).[7] Thus, when voluminous documents are produced under Rule 33(d), they must be accompanied by indices designed to guide the searcher to the documents responsive to the interrogatories.

Interrogatory no. 18 asks defendants to: IDENTIFY the date and location of your first discovery of CONTAMINATION in the SURROUNDING AREA. The defendants, in their Supplemental Further Responses to interrogatory no. 18, state that:

> BNA first became aware that releases from its SSFL [Santa Susana Field Laboratory] operations in concentrations above normal background had migrated offsite in August or September 1991. Water from a monitoring well approximately one hundred feet north of SSFL on property then owned by the Brandeis-Bardin Institute measured above background for tritium, but below the drinking water standard.

The plaintiffs object that this response is inadequate under Rule 33(d) and that defendants have provided no information with regard to the Hughes, Canoga or DeSoto facilities. However, defendants have narratively answered the interrogatory, rather than rely on Rule 33(d). Additionally, interrogatory no. 18 only requests information regarding defendants' first discovery of contamination, not the first discovery of

---

[7] The defendants, in response to interrogatory nos. 1 through 5, responded that, because the volume of responsive documents is "huge, and listing all the responsive documents would be an overly burdensome endeavor," defendants have identified only a "representative sampling" of some of the documents containing responsive information. Such a response clearly shows lack of compliance with Rule 33(d).

contamination in the surrounding areas of each of the Rocketdyne Facilities; thus, defendants answered the interrogatory.

Interrogatory no. 20 asks defendants to: IDENTIFY all allegations, reports, or claims of OFFSITE CONTAMINATION YOU have received. In their Supplemental Further Responses to interrogatory no. 20, defendants list sixteen lawsuits, including the instant action, and further responded that they "are not aware of specific complaints of contamination of offsite property other than these lawsuits."

The plaintiffs object that this response is inadequate under Rule 33(d), that defendants have provided no information regarding the Hughes, Canoga or DeSoto facilities, and that the response should also list informal complaints. Here again, defendants have narratively answered the interrogatory, rather than rely on Rule 33(d), and defendants have answered the interrogatory, albeit not to plaintiffs' satisfaction.

II

The Court would like to take this opportunity to provide guidance to the parties regarding the use of Rule 33(d), so that, when properly used, both sides will be able to easily find for trial the documents produced during discovery. For trial purposes, it is best to have all documents placed on CD-ROM, which affords a method by which the storage of voluminous documents is less burdensome to the parties. This is not possible, however, without two things: One, a general index describing by topic and subtopic the information in the documents and, two, a locator index identifying the location of each document on CD-ROM. Since the Fourth Amended Complaint spans five decades, the descriptive index should also provide the decade (date) in which the document was created. Because both the descriptive and locator indices must meet the needs of both sides, the Court believes the parties should jointly create these indices. Thus, the parties must meet and confer regarding the indices, and such meeting or meetings shall take place no later than fourteen (14) days from the date of this Order.

Under Rule 33(d), certain documents which would otherwise be responsive may be withheld based on privilege, provided the exercise of the privilege does not prevent the interrogating party from ascertaining or deriving complete answers to the interrogatories and the withheld documents are listed on a privilege log. *Ampex Corp. v. Mitsubishi Elec. Corp.*, 937 F.Supp. 352, 355 (D.Del.1996). For purposes of this action, when defendants choose to answer an interrogatory under Rule 33(d), they may claim only the attorney-client privilege and work product doctrine and they must set forth the purportedly privileged documents on a privilege log. Other privileges, such as the patient-physician privilege and third party privacy rights, are not to be claimed on the privilege log; rather, the protective order, coupled with the redaction of selected information (when necessary), is sufficient to safeguard the interests protected by such privileges and rights. By these limitations, defendants' claims of privilege should not prevent the plaintiffs from ascertaining the complete answers to the interrogatories that are the subject of the pending motion, thereby permitting defendants to answer the interrogatories under Rule 33(d).

As to documents subject to the attorney-client privilege or work product doctrine, the plaintiffs are correct in contending that not all attachments to, or enclosures with, such documents are necessarily protected by the privilege. Rather, to claim the attorney-client privilege or work product doctrine for an attachment to, or enclosure with, another privileged document, the attachment or enclosure must be listed as a separate document on the privilege log; otherwise, such attachment or enclosure must be disclosed. . . .

Defendants' Motion to Compel

IV

Rule 33(c) of the Federal Rules of Civil Procedure provides, in part, for the serving of an interrogatory the answer to which involves "an opinion or contention that relates to fact or the application of law to fact. . . ." Fed.R.Civ.P. 33(c). Here, defendants seek to compel responses to several interrogatories that are essentially contention interrogatories. Such interrogatories are permissible and acceptable under Rule 33(c). . . .

The defendants served the following interrogatory (which the Court will call interrogatory no. 1) on Class I representatives, the Samuels, Class II representatives, the O'Connors, Rueger, and Vroman, and Class III representative, Grandinetti:

> DESCRIBE FULLY EACH ALLEGED EXPOSURE TO YOU TO ALLEGED TOXIC SUBSTANCES WHICH YOU CONTEND WAS CAUSED BY DEFENDANTS' CONDUCT.

Class I representatives initially objected to the interrogatory as being compound, and then answered that they "may have been exposed" through ingestion of airborne releases, soil and surface water contamination. Finally, the Samuels stated that "the amount of toxic substances to which [plaintiff] has been exposed is unknown." The response was supplemented by the Samuels stating, upon information and belief, that additional information regarding their exposure may be determined from documents produced by defendants and these documents show, among other things, that toxic substances have traveled through the air, water or soil in patterns causing them to come in contact with plaintiffs.

The defendants argue that these responses are "evasive or incomplete" and should, thus, be treated as a failure to respond. There is no merit to defendants' argument. The plaintiffs' response to interrogatory no. 1 is sufficient since the clear inference from the response is that plaintiffs do not yet know exactly how they were exposed to contaminants, but exposure occurred. When additional information is known to plaintiffs, they must supplement their response under Rule 26(e). Thus, defendants' motion regarding interrogatory no. 1 is DENIED as to the Class I representatives. . . .

The defendants served the following interrogatory (which the Court will call interrogatory no. 2) on Class I representatives, the Samuels, Class II representatives, the O'Connors, Rueger, and Vroman, and Class III representative Grandinetti:

> For each of YOUR properties allegedly contaminated by DEFENDANTS' conduct, DESCRIBE FULLY THE NATURE AND SCOPE OF THE ALLEGED CONTAMINATION BY TOXIC SUBSTANCES caused by DEFENDANTS' conduct.

All class representatives initially objected to the form of the interrogatory and then answered, stating that their residency is within proximity of one of defendants' facilities and providing general information regarding the use of certain chemicals at the facility. The class representatives also filed a supplemental response identifying specific chemicals and noting that documents produced by defendants show the release of these chemicals into the environment. Finally, plaintiffs argue that they were in the process of further supplementing their responses based upon the documentary evidence provided to them, and defendants knew that these responses would be available by March 15, 1999.

The defendants complain that plaintiffs' responses are inadequate in that they do not identify the substances that could actually be found on plaintiffs' properties, and, further, complain that since some plaintiffs want reimbursement for cleaning up their property they surely must know of the contamination to it. There is no merit to defendants' argument since interrogatory no. 2 does not specifically ask the plaintiffs to identify the toxic substances found on the plaintiffs' properties, nor does the defendants' definition of the phrase "DESCRIBE FULLY THE NATURE AND SCOPE OF THE ALLEGED CONTAMINATION BY TOXIC SUBSTANCES" ask the plaintiffs to identify such substances. Thus, defendants' motion to compel further responses to interrogatory no. 2 is DENIED. . . .

The Court would like to take this opportunity to address the parties and their counsel, to stress that

> [t]he discovery system depends absolutely on good faith and common sense from counsel. The courts, sorely pressed by demands to try cases promptly and to rule thoughtfully on potentially case dispositive motions, simply do not have the

resources to police closely the operation of the discovery process. The whole system of [c]ivil adjudication would be ground to a virtual halt if the courts were forced to intervene in even a modest percentage of discovery transactions. That fact should impose on counsel an acute sense of responsibility about how they handle discovery matters. They should strive to be cooperative, practical and sensible, and should turn to the courts (or take positions that force others to turn to the courts) only in extraordinary situations that implicate truly significant interests.

In re Convergent Technologies Securities Litigation, 108 F.R.D [328, 331 (N.D.Cal.1985)]. . . .

NOTES AND QUESTIONS

1. *Asking.* Parties may send interrogatories to other parties, under Rule 33(b)(2), who must respond in writing within thirty days. Only parties are required to answer interrogatories. How soon can interrogatories be sent? Generally, a party sends interrogatories after the Rule 26(f) discovery conference, but the trial court may permit them earlier. How late can they be sent? While the rules prescribe no deadline for sending them, most trial courts use case management orders to set discovery schedules which establish the deadline for sending interrogatories.

Is there a limit to the number of interrogatories a party can send? Rule 33(a)(1) sets a limit of twenty-five questions, unless the trial court orders otherwise or the parties agree on another number. Court permission to add interrogatories must be consistent with Rules 26(b)(1)-(2). When trial courts apply the limits, the limit often is twenty-five *per interrogatory set*, rather than a total of twenty-five interrogatories. Why? Even after mandatory disclosures under Rule 26(a), many fact patterns underlying claims for relief suggest a need for a variety of types of information.

2. *Opinions or contentions.* Despite the fact that work product may be involved, Rule 33(a)(2) states that an interrogatory may seek "an opinion or contention that relates to fact or the application of law to fact." For example, even though it may reveal something about the answering attorney's mental impressions, an interrogatory is proper if it asks, "In Paragraph 10 of the Complaint, you state that the Defendant drove his vehicle negligently. State the facts supporting your contention that the Defendant drove his vehicle negligently."

3. *Types of interrogatories.*

a. *Factual request:* "Mr. Horner, did you pull a plum from a Christmas pie on December 25, 2015?"

b. *Factual opinion or conclusion:* "Did the person who first advised you to put your thumb in a Christmas pie on December 25, 2015, appear to be laughing?"

c. *Application of law to fact:* "What acts of negligence were committed by defendant?" OR "Upon what factual grounds does plaintiff base the claim asserted in Paragraph 3 of the Complaint that defendant was negligent?"

d. *Legal opinion or conclusion (an objectionable interrogatory, because it constitutes opinion work product):* "What is the constitutional, statutory, common law, or intergalactic basis for your claim?"

4. *Answering.* When a party answers, Rule 33(b)(2) requires that each interrogatory be answered separately and fully in writing, within thirty days of service, unless there is an objection. The scope of information attributable to a party includes information within the control of the party as well as the party's agents. It also includes facts known by the party's attorney as well as factual information provided to the party by other persons. An individual party must sign the answers, verifying their accuracy. For a party-entity, a representative of the entity verifies the answers.

As discussed previously, a party can object to discovery on a variety of grounds. For interrogatories, typical objections are that an interrogatory or a portion of an interrogatory is overly broad, vague, or ambiguous. For example, the interrogatory may be overbroad—asking for information covering a time period that is not included within the events described in the complaint of answer. One method for avoiding objections based on vagueness or ambiguity is to include a clearly expressed glossary of terms used repeatedly in the interrogatories at the beginning of the interrogatories. Other common objections were discussed previously—asking for A) privileged or work product information, B) non-discoverable expert information, C) irrelevant information not calculated to lead to the discovery of admissible evidence, or D) information the production of which is burdensome and oppressive. An objecting party may file a motion for a protective order under Rule 26(c); the party sending the interrogatories may respond to an objection by filing a motion to compel under Rule 37(a). Regardless, the trial court has broad discretion in ruling on objections to interrogatories. As a result, the parties may first try to resolve their interrogatory disagreement in order to avoid judicial intervention in the discovery process.

5. *Rule 33(d)'s option to produce business records.* Suppose the responding party does not feel like expending the resources necessary to find the information sought by the requesting party. Instead of answering an interrogatory, Rule 33(d) allows a party to produce business records, including electronically stored information [ESI]. Unlike a Rule 34 request for production of the documents themselves, the purpose of Rule 33(d) is for the requesting party to discover requested information which happens to be located in the responding party's business records. The rule contains several limitations on a broad application.

- The rule is restricted to business records, rather than personal records or litigation documents such as transcripts.

SEC. B DISCOVERY DEVICES 537

- The responding party must be able to state that the documents contain the requested information. The party also must provide adequate detail so that the requesting party can identify *which* documents contain the requested information.

- The burden of locating the answer must be "substantially the same" for the requesting and the responding party, who has the burden of proof. If the requesting party believes that the burdens are not "substantially the same," she can file a Rule 37(a) motion to compel an answer to the interrogatory from the responding party.

Does the use of Rule 33(d) pose any risks for the responding party? Would you want an adversary party rummaging for information in your client's business files? Before using the Rule 33(d) technique, what questions would you ask your client about the contents of his business files?

EXERCISE

For one of the Introductory Problems from earlier in the Chapter, draft at least ten interrogatories which you as plaintiff's counsel or defense counsel would want to send the opposing party to discover factual information about the case.

3. REQUEST FOR PRODUCTION OF DOCUMENTS

Computers have affected litigation in many ways. In discovery, the availability of "electronically stored information"—ESI—has influenced important changes in the Federal Rules, including the following.

- Rule 16(b)(3)(B) requires pretrial scheduling orders to "provide for the disclosure of" ESI.

- Rule 26(a)(1)(A) states that mandatory discovery includes ESI that the producing party "may use" at trial.

- Rule 26(b)(2)(B) states that a party does not have to produce ESI "from sources that the party identifies as not reasonably accessible. . . ."

- Rule 26(f)(3) defines a discovery plan to include ESI, "including the form or forms in which it should be produced."

- Rule 37(e) permits sanctions for deleting or otherwise losing ESI that should have been preserved in the anticipation or conduct of litigation and which cannot be restored or replaced through more discovery.

Under Rule 34, requests for the production of ESI may "specify the form or forms" in which it has to be produced. The party producing ESI "must produce it in a form or forms in which it is ordinarily maintained or in a reasonably usable form or forms," and "need not produce the same ESI in more than one form." Rule 45, which allows for subpoenas to obtain information in the hands of non-parties, contains similar language.

In *Alexander v. FBI*, 541 F.Supp.2d 274 (D.D.C. 2008), the Plaintiffs alleged that the White House lost two million emails before 1996 as the result of defects in its archiving system. Plaintiffs alleged that a White House technician knew or should have known that problems had occurred which prevented the automated records management system from capturing a significant number of White House e-mails. After fifty days of hearings, the trial judge concluded that no deliberate misconduct had occurred in the filing of affidavits or in representations made to the court.

> The Court has concluded that the essential errors made by the White House Counsel's Office were caused by a lack of familiarity with computer terminology and language and workings by the lawyers involved. Mr. Barry, the computer expert, simply talked a different language, and the lawyers he dealt with did not fully appreciate the significance of some of the information that he gave them, and the information he didn't give them. All of this occurred long before development of current sophisticated ways that lawyers have had to learn to deal with computer experts. It calls to the Court's mind its own experience in dealing with intelligence officials, i.e., if you don't use the right words in your question, you won't get the right answer. You have to learn to ask the question in a number of ways, and probe and examine and get into the nitty-gritty to understand what the truth is. None of the White House lawyers involved in this matter did that. But plaintiffs produced no evidence whatsoever that any of those lawyers deliberately obstructed justice, or deliberately provided what turned out to be false information to the Court. Not only is the evidence not "clear and convincing," as would be required for this Court to rule for plaintiffs on their contempt motion, but there is simply no evidence of any deliberate effort to conceal the truth. Plaintiffs would have the Court infer that some grand conspiracy existed to deprive them of necessary information. Plaintiffs simply have no such evidence.

If the allegations had surfaced more than a decade later, the court would not have been as tolerant about the lawyer's lack of familiarity with computer technology.

When one or more parties seek ESI, the trial court issues a Case Management Order (CMO), described in *Race Tires America v. Hoosier Racing Tire Corp.*, 674 F.3d 158 (3d Cir. 2012). The CMO in that case:

directed the parties to attempt to agree upon a list of keyword search terms, with a party's use of such terms carrying a presumption that it had fulfilled its "obligation to conduct a reasonable search." The CMO further provided that, unless native file format was "reasonably necessary to enable the other parties to review those files," ESI was to "be produced in 'Tagged Image File Format,'" accompanied by "[a] cross reference or unitization file, in standard format (e.g. Opticon, Summation DII, or the like) showing the Bates number of each page and the appropriate unitization of the documents."[2] The CMO further identified specific metadata fields that had to be produced if reasonably available.[3] Finally, the CMO directed the parties to produce "[a]n extracted text file or searchable version . . . for each electronic document in a document level text file (except for any file produced in native format)."[4]

[The parties] each retained separate vendors to assist with the production of ESI. . . . Based upon the vendors' invoices, RTA categorized the activities conducted by the vendors as follows: (1) preservation and collection of ESI; (2) processing the collected ESI; (3) keyword searching; (4) culling privileged material; (5) scanning and TIFF conversion; (6) optical character recognition ("OCR") conversion; and (7) conversion of racing videos from VHS format to DVD format.[6]

In total, [one defendant] produced 430,733 pages of ESI, and [the other defendant] produced 178,413 documents in electronic format. In addition, ten DVDs of racing videos were produced. [The parties paid the ESI vendors more than $365,000.] . . . .

---

[2] The native file format is the "file structure defined by the original creating application," such as a document created and opened in a word processing application. The Sedona Conference, *The Sedona Conference Glossary: E-Discovery & Digital Information Management* 35 (Sherry B. Harris et al. eds., 3rd ed. 2010). Tagged Image File Format ("TIFF") is "[a] widely used and supported graphic file format[ ] for storing bit-mapped images, with many different compression formats and resolutions." *Id.* at 50. TIFF "[i]mages are stored in tagged fields, and programs use the tags to accept or ignore fields, depending on the application." *Id.* Unitization is "[t]he assembly of individually scanned pages into documents." *Id.* at 52.

[3] Metadata is "[d]ata typically stored electronically that describes characteristics of ESI, found in different places in different forms." The Sedona Conference, *supra* note 2, at 34. While "[s]ome metadata, such as file dates and sizes, can easily be seen by users [,] other metadata can be hidden or embedded and unavailable to computer users who are not technically adept." *Id.* For example, in this case, the District Court ordered the parties to produce "metadata fields associated with each electronic document . . . where reasonably available," including, in part, the fields of "BegDoc," "EndDoc," "BegAttach," "EndAttach," "Author," "BCC," "CC," "Company," "Custodian Name," "Date Created," "Date Last Modified," and "Edit Time." Allowing discovery of these metadata fields permitted the parties to seek information that may not have been available in the documents' text.

[4] An extracted text file is a file containing text taken from an original electronic document. *See* The Sedona Conference, *supra* note 2, at 12 (defining "[d]ata [e]xtraction").

[6] OCR is "[a] technology process that translates and converts printed matter on an image into a format that a computer can manipulate . . . and, therefore, renders that matter text searchable." The Sedona Conference, *supra* note 2, at 37.

NOTES AND QUESTIONS

1. *Asking.* Parties can request inspection of documents, electronically stored information, and things only from other parties under Rule 34(a), who also must respond in writing within thirty days. However, requests can be served on non-parties by the issuance of a subpoena *duces tecum* under Rule 45.

How soon can a request for production be made? The rules prescribe a minimum of three weeks after the earlier of when the defendant is served or the Rule 26(f) discovery conference before a party may send requests. Trial courts often use CMOs like the one previously described in *Race Tires America* to set discovery schedules which establish the deadline for responding to discovery requests. Unlike Rule 33, though, there is no limit on the number of requests for production that may be submitted.

2. *What is a document?* An important aspect of a request for production is for the requesting party to define the term "document," for the scope of that definition is determinative of how much effort the answering party must exert to satisfy the request. With newer forms of technology constantly emerging, the Rule 34(a)(1)(A) reference to designated documents is subject to nitpicking as far too narrow. Instead, given the diverse methods of data compilation, the following definition may be used as a starting point but even it is not necessarily exhaustive.

> The term "documents" means all writings of any kind, including the originals and all non-identical copies, whether different from the originals by reason of any notation made on such copies or otherwise, including without limitation, correspondence, memoranda, notes, e-mail messages, diaries, statistics, letters, telegrams, minutes, contracts, reports, studies, checks, statements, receipts, returns, summaries, pamphlets, books, interoffice and intra-office communications, internet communications, notations of any sort of conversations, telephone calls, meetings or other communications, bulletins, printed matter, computer print-outs, teletypes, telefax, invoices, worksheets, all drafts, alterations, modifications, changes, and amendments of any of the foregoing, graphic or oral records or representations of any kind (including, without limitation, photographs, charts, graphs, microfiche, microfilm, videotapes, recordings, motion pictures), and any electronic, mechanical, or electric records or representations of any kind (including, without limitation, tapes, cassettes, discs, recordings, CDs, and computer memories).

By contrast, a request to enter another party's land for "inspection and measuring, surveying, photographing, testing, or sampling" is comparatively simple to make because the address and/or location of the property is relatively fixed.

The requesting party must seek the documents or ESI individually or categorically and describe them "with reasonable particularity." As you might expect, the particularity requirement is often a disputed issue. The requesting party wants the request to be construed as broadly as possible so that maximum disclosure is made, while the responding party wants the request rendered narrowly so that a limited number of documents must be turned over. Why does that matter? Often the requesting party is uncertain about exactly what the other party has in the way of documents. By the permitted breadth of its request, the requesting party is trying to "guess" what documents the other side has in its possession, custody or control. The requesting party also must "specify a reasonable time, place, and manner" of complying with the request.

3. *Answering.* Rule 34(a)(1) also requires the responding party to produce all documents or ESI within its "possession, custody or control." The case law has interpreted the term "control" so that the responder must turn over documents or ESI she has the legal right to demand from others (e.g., her attorney or accountant) as well as those of which she has actual possession (even if they belong to another person).

Besides the objections already mentioned for interrogatories, a responding party may refuse compliance by claiming that the documents or ESI can be procured by the adversary party from another source, e.g., a public record. See, e.g., *Bleecker v. Standard Fire Ins. Co.*, 130 F.Supp.2d 726 (E.D.N.C. 2000). As you might have suspected, the basis for the objection is that it is an undue burden to produce the documents or ESI due to the accessibility of an alternative source.

The responding party must produce the documents or ESI "as they are kept in the usual course of business or must organize and label them to correspond to the categories in the request." A party may respond to a request for ESI "in a form or forms in which it is ordinarily maintained or in a reasonably usable form or forms." Why does Rule 34(b)(2)(E)(i) state those principles? An attorney may not use a system of record-keeping that effectively conceals relevant documents or ESI instead of disclosing them. It is also impermissible for a responding attorney to react to a request by handing over the requested documents or ESI as part of a much larger (and unresponsive) production, i.e., response by avalanche.

Does a responding party comply with Rule 34 if it produces hundreds of e-mails and attachments, but they are produced in a form whereby the requesting party cannot determine which attachments went with which e-mails? See *PSEG Power New York, Inc. v. Alberici Inc.*, 2007 WL 2687670 (N.D.N.Y. 2007) (the court ordered re-production because, as produced, the ESI was not produced "in the usual course of business" or in a "reasonably usable format." What does "reasonably usable format" mean?

4. Does a litigant have a duty to preserve ESI that may be the subject of discovery? In *Zubulake v. UBS Warburg LLC*, 220 F.R.D. 212 (S.D.N.Y. 2003), (often referred to as *Zubulake IV*—the fourth of the seminal e-discovery cases) Judge Scheindlin stated:

> Once a party reasonably anticipates litigation, it must suspend its routine document retention/destruction policy and put in place a "litigation hold" to ensure the preservation of relevant documents. As a general rule, that litigation hold does not apply to inaccessible backup tapes (e.g., those typically maintained for the purpose of disaster recovery) . . . [I]f backup tapes are accessible (i.e., actively used for information retrieval), then such tapes would likely be subject to the litigation hold.

In *Zubulake V*, the court focused on counsel's duty to monitor compliance.

> . . . . Counsel must oversee compliance with the litigation hold, monitoring a party's efforts to retain and produce the relevant documents. Proper communication between a party and her lawyer will ensure (1) that all relevant information (or at least all sources of relevant information) is discovered, (2) that relevant information is retained on a continuing basis, and (3) that relevant non-privileged material is produced to the opposing party.

229 F.R.D. 422, 432 (S.D.N.Y. 2004).

5. Should expert witnesses be used to explain to the fact-finder how search protocols were constructed? In *United States v. O'Keefe*, 537 F.Supp.2d 14 (D.D.C. 2008), Defendant claimed that the federal government had failed to have its employees search their own ESI and had not indicated what software was used to conduct the search. The court held that Defendant's claims of governmental insufficiency must be based on evidence that meets the expert witness requirements of Federal Rule of Evidence 702.

6. ESI may be produced in different forms: (1) paper image files (.pdf and .tiff), (2) image files with text files containing specified metadata, i.e., a "load file," and (3) native. Different types of information may call for different forms of production. Rule 34(b)(2)(E)(ii) provides the procedural mechanism for determining which form is used. The requesting party may specify a form in the request, but if the requesting party fails to specify the form or if the responding party objects (and the court has not ordered a form), the responding party must produce the information in the form in which it is "ordinarily maintained" or in a "reasonably usable form or forms." Rule 34(b)(2)(E)(iii) states that ESI need only be produced in one form one time; it is important to identify the form of production before information is collected because of later potential evidentiary issues.

7. ESI production from a corporate party may involve a multitude of electronic records. How might a court's resolution of an electronic discovery dispute affect a party's decision to consider settlement?

EXERCISE

For one of the Introductory Problems from earlier in the Chapter, draft at least ten requests for production of documents or ESI which you as

4. REQUEST FOR ADMISSIONS

Asea, Inc. v. Southern Pac. Transp. Co.
669 F.2d 1242 (9th Cir. 1981)

WALLACE, CIRCUIT JUDGE.

Southern Pacific Transportation Co. and Harbor Belt Line (the railroads) appeal from a judgment entered in favor of Asea, Inc. (Asea) and from the denial of their motion for a new trial. The railroads' principal contention in this appeal is that the district court erred in ordering admitted certain matters the railroads failed to admit or deny in response to requests for admissions served by Asea. We affirm in part and vacate and remand in part.

Asea, a New York corporation, is the sole United States distributor of electrical transformers manufactured in Sweden by Asea A/B, a Swedish corporation. Asea sold a transformer to the Los Angeles Department of Water & Power. The transformer was transported by merchant vessel from Sweden to the Los Angeles harbor. Pursuant to their contract with Asea, the railroads then took custody of the transformer and shipped it to North Hollywood, California. Upon its arrival, the transformer was inspected by representatives of the railroads and Asea. It was found that the transformer had shifted on the railroad car during transit despite being shored and braced. An electrical check revealed the transformer had shorted. Asea had installed an "impact recorder" on the transformer to measure any impact that might occur during rail carriage. Inspection of the impact recorder tape indicated that, while the transformer was in the custody of the railroads, it had suffered an impact measured at 1.8 on the recorder scale, equivalent to an impact at a speed in excess of 5 miles per hour. Internal inspection of the transformer revealed that it had sustained substantial damage during transit.

On July 10, 1978, Asea filed an action for damages in the district court, invoking its diversity jurisdiction pursuant to 28 U.S.C. § 1332(a), relying on theories of negligence, breach of implied warranty, and violation of California Civil Code § 2194 (inland carrier's liability for loss). The parties engaged in extensive discovery for over one year. On January 22, 1979, Asea served a series of requests for admissions pursuant to Fed.R.Civ.P. 36(a). Those of primary importance in this appeal related essentially to the condition of the transformer at the time the railroads took custody of it, the impact revealed on the impact recorder tape, the location of the transformer at the time the impact occurred, the short discovered in the transformer after its arrival and the reasonable cost of repairing the transformer and returning it to the Los Angeles

Department of Water & Power. The district court allowed additional time to reply. To eighteen of these requests, the railroads responded on May 24, 1979:

> Answering party cannot admit or deny. Said party has made reasonable inquiry. Information known or readily obtainable to this date is not complete. Investigation continues.

Each of the requests for admissions was accompanied by an interrogatory which asked that if the railroads' response was anything other than an unqualified admission, they should state the facts, documents and witnesses upon which the response was based. The railroads answered these interrogatories by insisting they were "(n)ot applicable."

Discovery continued following a pretrial conference held in June, 1979. As a result of further depositions of certain railroad employees, Asea became convinced that the railroads had known the actual cause of the impact on the transformer for many months, and therefore could have admitted or denied the requests for admissions. On December 3, 1979, five weeks prior to trial, Asea moved to have the requests ordered admitted. At the hearing on the motion, the railroads claimed that their responses were proper by authority of Rule 36(a) because they did not have any firsthand information. The district court inquired whether the railroads had "subsequently come into more information that (would) enable (them) to supply more appropriate answers?" Counsel for the railroads responded, "We may possibly, Your Honor," but insisted that "the answers still stand." The railroads claimed the information relevant to the requests for admissions was "wholly within the hands of (Asea)." The court replied:

> (T)hat's what I hear all the time. . . . (T)his case has been here so many times, and you are a constant complainer about the inadequacy of the other side. Now it appears that you're standing behind that same shield yourself saying that you just don't have the information to provide.

The district court took the matter under submission and subsequently granted Asea's motion to order the matters admitted. The railroads' later motion to have these admissions withdrawn was denied.

The railroads contend their responses to the requests for admissions satisfied the requirements of Fed.R.Civ.P. 36(a). In the alternative, they argue that the sanction for failure of a party to make reasonable inquiry prior to answering a request for admission lies in an award of the expenses incurred in proving the fact at trial, pursuant to Fed.R.Civ.P. 37(c), and not in deeming the matter admitted. We have considered this issue carefully because it apparently is a question of first impression. We conclude, however, that a district court may, under proper circumstances and in its discretion, order admitted matters which an answering party has failed to admit or deny, where the information known or readily obtainable after reasonable inquiry was sufficient to enable the answering party to admit or deny.

... The Rule provides that a party may not give lack of information as a reason for failure to admit or deny "unless he states that he has made reasonable inquiry and that the information known or readily obtainable by him is insufficient to enable him to admit or deny." The railroads cite in support of this construction *Adley Express Co. v. Highway Truck Drivers & Helpers, Local No. 107*, 349 F.Supp. 436 (E.D.Pa.1972), where the district court observed that "it would appear that a mere statement in the answer that the answering party has made reasonable inquiry and that the information solicited was insufficient to enable him to admit or deny the requested matter will suffice." *Id.* at 451–52. Their position is further supported by the Advisory Committee's Note, which states:

> The revised rule requires only that the answering party make reasonable inquiry and secure such knowledge and information as are readily obtainable by him. In most instances, the investigation will be necessary either to his own case or to preparation for rebuttal. Even when it is not, the information may be close enough at hand to be "readily obtainable." Rule 36 requires only that the party state that he has taken these steps. The sanction for failure of a party to inform himself before he answers lies in the award of costs after trial, as provided in Rule 37(c).

... We are not persuaded that an answer to a request for admission necessarily complies with Rule 36(a) merely because it includes a statement that the party has made reasonable inquiry and that the information necessary to admit or deny the matter is not readily obtainable by him. The discovery process is subject to the overriding limitation of good faith. Callous disregard of discovery responsibilities cannot be condoned. The abuses of the current discovery rules are well documented. In our view, permitting a party to avoid admitting or denying a proper request for admission simply by tracking the language of Rule 36(a) would encourage additional abuse of the discovery process. Instead of making an evasive or meritless denial, which clearly would result in the matter being deemed admitted, a party could comply with the Rule merely by having his attorney submit the language of the Rule in response to the request. . . .

We hold, therefore, that a response which fails to admit or deny a proper request for admission does not comply with the requirements of Rule 36(a) if the answering party has not, in fact, made "reasonable inquiry," or if information "readily obtainable" is sufficient to enable him to admit or deny the matter. A party requesting an admission may, if he feels these requirements have not been met, move to determine the sufficiency of the answer, to compel a proper response, or to have the matter ordered admitted. Although the district court should ordinarily first order an amended answer, and deem the matter admitted only if a sufficient answer is not timely filed, this determination, like most involved in the oversight of discovery, is left to the sound discretion of the district judge. The general power of the district court to control the discovery process allows for the severe sanction of ordering a matter admitted when it has been demonstrated that a party has intentionally disregarded the obligations imposed by Rule 36(a).

Here, the district judge decided not to require an amended response. Although counsel for the railroads asserted that they would stand pat on the prior responses, she did state that additional answers would be filed if the court required it. But this was not the first discovery problem presented to the court. Far from it. A year of volatile and acrimonious fighting, during which many discovery disputes were placed before the judge as referee, had preceded it. Thus, we cannot say the district judge abused his wide discretion in not requiring amended responses. . . .

The more difficult question is whether that discretion was abused when he imposed the severe sanction of deeming admitted certain key matters described in the requests. This is answered by determining whether the district judge properly found that the railroads did not make reasonable inquiry or that the information readily obtainable was sufficient to allow them to admit or deny the particular requests. The order of the district judge, however, does not state the basis upon which he concluded that the matters should be ordered admitted. There is evidence in the record suggesting that the railroads in fact had sufficient information to admit or deny the requested admissions at the time they submitted their answers to Asea, or that they subsequently discovered sufficient information to require them to amend their answers. It is less clear whether a finding could be made that the railroads failed to make reasonable inquiry. With a sanction as severe as the one imposed, we conclude that a finding by the district court is necessary for proper appellate review. We therefore vacate the judgment and remand for the limited purpose of reconsideration of the order deeming the requests admitted and the filing of appropriate findings of fact. What that reconsideration entails shall be determined by the district court, but we do not exclude an evidentiary hearing if one is determined to be necessary. . . .

NOTES AND QUESTIONS

1. *Asking.* Under Rule 36, each party can require other parties to admit relevant facts and/or authenticate documents that are not in controversy. The procedure can eliminate the necessity of producing

witnesses and evidence to support those facts. As with interrogatories and requests for production, a party usually sends such requests after the Rule 26(f) discovery conference, or sooner with the trial court's permission. The Federal Rules do not limit the number of requests for admission, although local rules may limit the number. To simplify this process, the requesting party should follow Rule 36(a) and set forth each fact or document for which admission or authenticity is requested in a separate paragraph.

2. *Opinions or contentions.* Rule 36(a)(1) states that a request for admission may seek "fact, the application of law to fact, or opinions about either." On the other hand, the rule does not authorize a request that requires a purely legal conclusion, without also applying the law to the facts. For example, in *Tulip Computers Intern., B.V. v. Dell Computer Corp.,* 210 F.R.D. 100 (D. Del. 2002), the court ruled that a request for an admission that a patent was valid is an inappropriate use of Rule 36: "whether a patent is valid would call for a legal conclusion although dependent on factual inquiries." *Id.* at 107.

3. *Answering.* The responding party has an obligation to investigate the requests, and in good faith partially or fully admit, partially or fully deny, state the reasons for the inability to admit or deny, or object to each requested admission, within thirty days of receiving the requests. As the *Asea* court stated, a party cannot avoid the request by being evasive, and the requesting party can move to have the court determine the sufficiency of a denial. When a party believes that part of a request is true and part is untrue, the proper response is to admit the correct portion and deny the incorrect part. If a responding party cannot admit or deny the requested information after a reasonable inquiry, she needs to describe her inability in detail. Why? She risks the court treating her response as insufficient and instead treating the answer as an admission. The objections previously discussed for interrogatories and requests for production also apply to requests for admission.

Rule 36(b) states that an admission is conclusively established unless the trial court permits the admission's withdrawal or amendment. Unlike work product, which applies to cases beyond which it is first raised, the effect of the admission is for the instant case only. At trial, the requesting party can introduce the admission, although it is subject to evidentiary objections.

EXERCISE

For one of the Introductory Problems from earlier in the Chapter, draft at least ten requests for admission which you as plaintiff's counsel or defense counsel would want to send the opposing party to discover factual information about the case.

5. PHYSICAL AND MENTAL EXAMINATIONS

ALI v. WANG LABORATORIES, INC.
162 F.R.D. 165 (M.D. Fla. 1995)

STEELE, UNITED STATES MAGISTRATE JUDGE.

This cause is before the Court on Defendant's Motion To Compel Physical and Mental Examinations of Plaintiff, filed March 22, 1995. Plaintiff's Response and Memorandum in Opposition to Motion To Compel Physical and Mental Examinations of Plaintiff was filed April 3, 1995. On April 18, 1995 the Court heard oral argument on the motion.

Plaintiff's Complaint alleges he was employed by defendant Wang Laboratories, Inc. (Wang) from 1978 until terminated in May, 1993. Plaintiff alleges that during his employment he suffered a work-related injury which caused medical problems involving sclerosis of the cervical joints and bone-spurring, which in turn resulted in his becoming an individual with a "disability" under the American with Disabilities Act (ADA). Plaintiff asserts his termination violated various federal and state statutes because it was caused by unlawful consideration of his age (over 40), an alleged disability, and his national origin. Plaintiff further alleges that he could have and can perform the essential functions of his employment with defendant. Plaintiff claims defendant's actions caused "severe emotional and mental distress", and his requested relief includes compensatory damages "for emotional pain and suffering" and reinstatement to his previous employment position. Defendant denies plaintiff is an individual with a "disability" and denies plaintiff could have performed and can still perform the essential functions of his employment....

Both parties agree that defendant's motion is governed by Fed.R.Civ.P. 35(a). The general principles under Rule 35(a) have been articulated in *Schlagenhauf v. Holder*, 379 U.S. 104 (1964). Defendant must establish that plaintiff's mental condition or physical condition is "in controversy" and must show "good cause" for the mental or physical examination(s). This requires an affirmative showing that the mental or physical condition is "really and genuinely" in controversy and that good cause exists for each particular examination. The Court must decide, by making a "discriminating application", whether the "in controversy" and "good cause" requirements have been adequately demonstrated by the production of sufficient information which allows the Court to perform its function under Rule 35(a). *Schlagenhauf v. Holder*, 379 U.S. at 118–122. This requires a greater showing than for other types of discovery under Rule 26, Fed.R.Civ.P.

The Court need not resolve defendant's assertion that its burden has been satisfied by the pleadings alone. The Court has considered the pleadings and other documents in the court file, the documents submitted at the hearing, and the information from and argument of counsel. The Court finds that this combination provides sufficient information by which the Court can fulfill its function under Rule 35(a). *Schlagenhauf v. Holder*, 379 U.S. at 119.

Defendant claims that plaintiff's mental condition has been placed in controversy because plaintiff claims he suffers continuing emotional and mental distress for which he seeks substantial damages. Defendant seeks the mental examination to determine the existence and extent of plaintiff's mental distress.

The Court agrees with those cases which hold that plaintiff's "mental condition" within the meaning of Rule 35 is not necessarily placed in controversy merely because plaintiff seeks recovery for "emotional distress". A person with no "mental condition" may still suffer emotional distress which is compensable. Plaintiff, however, has gone beyond a mere claim for emotional distress. In answers to interrogatories, plaintiff stated his "personal character and performance were severely and permanently damaged"; he "lost his self esteem and was embarrassed to call on his former customers" and others; he and his wife and son suffered "severe and permanent psychological damage"; his "humiliation and embarrassment" "created a great deal of anger and hatred within him" as well as family problems; he "suffered extreme emotional distress"; he "has been very depressed and remains depressed", and he has had an outbreak of skin and scalp rash attributed to the "ordeal" of his termination. This is clearly sufficient to place plaintiff's mental condition in controversy.

The Court also finds that good cause has been shown for a mental examination. Plaintiff is seeking substantial damages for his alleged emotional injuries. While plaintiff may be content to offer only his own testimony to a jury, defendant is not compelled to limit its case to mere cross examination. Since plaintiff's mental condition is in controversy and substantial damages are asserted, it is essential for defendant to have the reasonable opportunity to challenge plaintiff's claim and testimony. The testimony of an expert is a well recognized and reasonable way of doing so, and an examination of plaintiff by that expert is necessary for the expert to form a meaningful opinion.

The Court finds that plaintiff's physical condition has been placed in controversy. In answers to interrogatories, plaintiff stated he suffered whiplash in a 1979 automobile accident which caused spurs on vertebrae C5, C6, and C7 which indent the thecal sac in his spine. This is asserted to have resulted in chronic cervical pain syndrome, chronic severe neck pains and headaches, chest pains, and muscular pains and spasms in his neck and shoulder area. Plaintiff asserted that his injuries caused permanent restrictions to his lifting, range of motion and ability to work overhead.

Plaintiff also asserted that a physician anticipates his condition will continue to deteriorate and will require surgery in the future. Plaintiff alleges he was and is disabled under the Americans with Disabilities Act, seeks damages under the Act, and seeks reinstatement to his employment. Both plaintiff's current physical condition and his past physical condition have therefore been placed in controversy.

Good cause exists for a physical examination. The expert must conduct such an examination to form a meaningful opinion. In the social security disability context, *Spencer ex rel. Spencer v. Heckler*, 765 F.2d 1090, 1094 (11th Cir.1985) quoted an Eighth Circuit case noting that evaluation in absentia was "medical sophistry at its best." Additionally, a physician is able to provide a retrospective opinion of plaintiff's condition even though he did not examine plaintiff until after the relevant date. . . .

Plaintiff requests that if either or both examinations are permitted, the Court set certain conditions. These include the presence of a court reporter, the presence of plaintiff's wife, or the recording of the examinations. The Court is satisfied that it has the discretionary authority to impose a variety of conditions which, balancing the factors in each individual case, ensure that the interests of justice are obtained. After considering all the circumstances of this case, the Court can find no special need which requires the presence of a court reporter, plaintiff's wife, or other recording equipment. The conditions set forth below are adequate under the circumstances of this case. Accordingly, it is now ORDERED:

1. Defendant's Motion To Compel Physical and Mental Examinations of Plaintiff is GRANTED to the extent set forth below.

2. Plaintiff shall submit to a mental examination by Dr. Ernest C. Miller and a physical examination by Dr. Michael B. Scharf. Each examination will be conducted at the respective business office of Dr. Miller and Dr. Scharf in Jacksonville, Florida during normal business hours.

3. The examinations will be conducted within 20 days after the completion of plaintiff's deposition, unless the parties otherwise mutually agree.

4. The mental examination will focus upon the matters alleged by plaintiff in his Complaint and/or deposition and the mental and emotional injury and damages resulting from the misconduct alleged of defendant. Defendant shall provide Dr. Miller with the appropriate portion of plaintiff's answers to interrogatories, deposition, and such other documents as it deems appropriate.

The examination will include the routine procedures for such an examination. Plaintiff has requested that it also include the Minnesota Multiphasic Personality Inventory examination. Dr. Miller may administer this test, but the Court will not require it. A copy of any resulting report will be provided to plaintiff's counsel.

5. The physical examination will focus upon the injuries alleged by plaintiff in his Complaint and/or deposition and the existence and severity of the injuries and plaintiff's physical capabilities. Defendant shall provide Dr. Scharf with the appropriate portion of plaintiff's answers to interrogatories, deposition, and such other documents as it deems appropriate. The examination will include the routine procedures for such an examination. A copy of any resulting report will be provided to plaintiff's counsel. . . .

NOTES AND QUESTIONS

1. Unless the parties agree, Rule 35 requires a court order before a party must submit to a physical or mental examination. Before a court will order the examination, the moving party must show that 1) there is "good cause" for the testing, and 2) another party's physical or mental condition is "in controversy." Courts are split as to whether a plaintiff's claim for damages due to emotional harm puts her mental condition "in controversy." Compare *Bowen v. Parking Authority of City of Camden*, 214 F.R.D. 188 (D.N.J. 2003) (plaintiff's mental condition not at issue) with *Cauley v. Ingram Micro, Inc.*, 216 F.R.D. 241 (W.D.N.Y. 2003) (mental examination justified).

2. Only a party may be ordered to submit to an exam. Sometimes a person is named as a party in order to effectively put the person's condition "in controversy." For example, in *Schlagenhauf v. Holder*, 379 U.S. 104, 85 S.Ct. 234, 13 L.Ed.2d 152 (1964), the plaintiff class named not only the defendant corporation (with the "deep pocket") as a defendant, but also named as a defendant the corporate employee whose negligence damaged members of the class. Why? To justify an order for his eyesight to be examined.

Schlagenhauf also held the issue of whether "good cause" exists requires a balancing of the need for the information with the party's right to privacy and safety. The "easy" cases for good cause are tort claims in which the plaintiff seeks damages for her personal injuries. On the other hand, as *Ali* indicated, good cause is not as obvious when the person has not placed her mental or physical condition in dispute.

3. The court order for the examination must "specify the time, place, manner, conditions, and scope of the examination," as well as the person conducting the exam. Testing may be for blood, x-rays, EKG, or any other medically accepted test that is both indicated by the condition "in controversy" and is safe for the party. The examiner must be licensed or certified and is often selected by the moving party unless there is an objection. Mental tests are conducted by a psychologist or psychiatrist. The judicial decisions are split about 1) who may be present or observe the testing, and 2) whether observers include attorneys of record.

4. Rule 35(b)(1) provides that by request of the party examined, the moving party must provide a detailed written report by the examiner. In return, the examined party must provide reports of other examinations for the same condition, regardless of when they were conducted. At trial, the examiner may testify as an expert witness.

C. DISCOVERY SANCTIONS

LEE V. WALTERS
172 F.R.D. 421 (D.Or. 1997)

STEWART, UNITED STATES MAGISTRATE JUDGE.

On June 18, 1996, plaintiff Vickie Lee filed a Motion for Sanctions based upon defendants' failure to cooperate in scheduling depositions, to timely file an Answer, and to timely and completely respond to plaintiffs' request for production of documents. On June 24, 1996, when defendants failed to appear for duly noticed depositions, both plaintiffs filed Motions to Compel and for Sanctions. On June 25, 1996, this court granted the Motion to Compel in part and set both motions for sanctions for decision on July 15, 1996, after the close of discovery.

... For the reasons set forth below, this court recommends that plaintiffs' motions for sanctions be granted.

Plaintiffs seeks monetary sanctions against defendants in the sum of $10,000.00 pursuant to FRCP 37(a)(4)(A), (b), and (d), FRCP 26(g), and the court's inherent authority. Because each of the subsections of FRCP 37 and FRCP 26(g) targets a particular form of misconduct for which sanctions may be awarded, each must be analyzed separately.

I. FRCP 37(d)

A. Standard

FRCP 37(d) authorizes the court to impose sanctions against a party who fails: (1) to attend a duly noticed deposition, (2) to serve answers or objections to interrogatories properly submitted under FRCP 33, or (3) to serve a written response to a request for inspection properly submitted under FRCP 34. Sanctions are mandatory for failure to attend a noticed deposition or to respond to a request for production of documents unless the court finds that the failure was "substantially justified or that other circumstances make an award of expenses unjust." FRCP 37(d).

"The burden of establishing substantial justification is on the party being sanctioned." *Telluride Mgmt. Solutions, Inc. v. Telluride Inv. Group*, 55 F.3d 463, 466 (9th Cir.1995). The phrase "substantially justified" does not mean " 'justified to a high degree,' but rather has been said to be satisfied if there is a 'genuine dispute,' or 'if reasonable people could differ as to [the appropriateness of the contested action.]' " *Pierce v.*

Underwood, 487 U.S. 552, 565 (1988) (brackets in original; citations deleted). However, FRCP 37(d) explicitly eliminates the excuse that "the discovery sought is objectionable unless the party failing to act has a pending motion for a protective order as provided by Rule 26(c)." ...

B. Violations

... [D]efendants have committed two violations of FRCP 37(d). It is undisputed that defendants failed to attend depositions duly noticed by plaintiffs on June 24 and 25, 1996. In addition, despite repeated requests, defendants still have not submitted a written response to Plaintiffs' First Request for Production of Documents ("First Request") dated April 19, 1996.

The record reveals that plaintiffs have satisfied the prerequisite to an award of sanctions under FRCP 37(d) in that they attempted to first resolve the issues without judicial intervention.

C. Defendants' Excuses

1. Belated Compliance

Defendants argue that sanctions are inappropriate because they belatedly appeared for depositions and produced most (though not all) of the requested documents, blaming plaintiffs' motion for sanctions on "obvious impatience." This excuse has repeatedly been rejected by the Ninth Circuit. "Belated compliance with discovery orders does not preclude the imposition of sanctions." *North Am. Watch Corp. v. Princess Ermine Jewels*, 786 F.2d 1447, 1451 (9th Cir.1986).

2. Substantial Justification

(a) Document Production

Mr. Barnes does not dispute any of the material facts regarding his failure to timely produce documents. Instead, he states only that he provided all documents "with one minor exception" for "copies of all documents generated around March of 1993 now in the possession of any of the defendants, even if they are duplicates of documents plaintiffs have already seen in the Racing Commission files."

This explanation is deficient for several reasons. First, it entirely fails to address the fact that he has not yet served a written response to the First Request, despite the pendency of these sanction motions. Second, even if a written response to the First Request is unnecessary, given that most of the responsive documents have now been produced, defendants' explanation does not substantially justify the belated production of responsive documents.

Mr. Barnes may have initially believed that producing the Oregon Racing Commission's files would provide plaintiffs with all of the documents requested in the First Request. However, this does not explain why he did not produce any documents until after plaintiffs were forced to seek the assistance of the court at the June 6, 1996 scheduling conference. . . .

(b) Depositions

Mr. Barnes now claims that Mr. Sanders should have understood that he would not be appearing for depositions on June 24, 1996, even though he did not clearly say so. This explanation directly contradicts Mr. Sanders' recollection that just before terminating their last telephone conversation on June 21, 1996, Mr. Barnes said he would seek a protective order. That statement of Mr. Barnes' intention, which Mr. Barnes has not specifically denied, would lead Mr. Sanders to reasonably conclude that Mr. Barnes would not simply ignore the deposition notices. . . .

In sum, Mr. Barnes's failure to appear for the noticed depositions was not substantially justified in the absence of a protective order or, at the very least, a clear and unambiguous agreement by Mr. Sanders to postpone the depositions. As a result, FRCP 37(d) requires the court to order defendants, Mr. Barnes, or both, to pay the reasonable expenses, including attorney's fees, caused by that failure.

II. FRCP 37(a)(4)(A)

A. Standards

In contrast to FRCP 37(d), FRCP 37(a)(4)(A) targets motions to compel discovery. It awards reasonable expenses incurred, including attorney fees, not only when the court grants a motion to compel, but also if the opposing party provides the requested discovery after the motion to compel is filed. FRCP 37(a)(4)(A). An award of expenses is mandated unless the motion to compel was filed without "first making a good faith effort to obtain the disclosure of discovery without court action," the "nondisclosure, response, or objection was substantially justified," or "other circumstances make an award of expenses unjust." FRCP 37(a)(4)(A).

B. Violations

As set forth above, plaintiffs were obliged to file three motions to compel as a result of Mr. Barnes' conduct. . . .

The record reveals that plaintiffs have satisfied the prerequisite to an award of sanctions under FRCP 37(a)(4) because they first attempted to resolve the issues without judicial intervention.

C. Defendants' Excuses

Defendants offer virtually no excuse for forcing plaintiffs to file the motions to compel, other than Mr. Barnes' busy schedule. He proffers several reasons that made it difficult for him to schedule depositions in this case. First, in the Torts and Employment Group of the Trial Division, the area of the Department of Justice in which he works, two of the eight attorneys left during the first part of 1996. Because Mr. Barnes handles between 40 and 50 active litigation files and must travel extensively throughout the Pacific Northwest, he "was required to spend a minimum of twenty-nine days in deposition and attend hearings or trial on 15 different days." This court does not doubt that Mr. Barnes has been very busy and perhaps more so than usual during the first five months of 1996. Nevertheless, the fact remains that he never advised the court that his schedule prevented him from complying with the court's orders. The problem is not when depositions were set, but that Mr. Barnes repeatedly ignored inquiries from opposing counsel, which required plaintiffs to file motions to compel. Mr. Barnes may have been able to avoid these motions had he (or someone else in his office) simply returned Mr. Sanders' telephone calls or responded to Mr. Sanders' letters.

Second, Mr. Barnes notes that scheduling depositions of defendants, who are retired or are employed in the private sector, was more difficult than scheduling depositions of state employees. . . .

This court finds no substantial justification or other circumstances for avoiding the mandatory award under FRCP 37(a)(4)(A) to plaintiffs of their reasonable expenses, including attorney fees, for filing the three motions to compel.

III. FRCP 37(b)

A. *Standards*

Whereas FRCP 37(d) addresses the failure to attend a deposition and FRCP 37(a)(4)(A) addresses motions to compel, FRCP 37(b) targets a party's failure to obey an order to provide or permit discovery. It allows the court to make such orders "as are just," and in lieu or in addition, requires the offending party, its attorney or both "to pay the reasonable expenses, including attorney's fees, caused by the failure" unless it "was substantially justified" or "other circumstances make an award of expenses unjust." *Id.*

A prerequisite for imposing sanctions under FRCP 37(b) is the existence of an "order." However, the term "order" is broadly construed for purposes of imposing sanctions. The "order" need not be in writing. It is a violation of an "order" for purposes of FRCP 37(b) when a party fails to deliver documents it had promised by a certain date. It is not even necessary for the opposing party to move for this order, only that it be issued and disobeyed. . . .

B. *Violations*

The record reveals that defendants disobeyed four orders that fall within the scope of FRCP 37(b). . . .

C. Defendants' Excuses

Defendants offer the same excuses for repeated violations of this court's orders as for their other violations of FRCP 37. As discussed above, this court finds that defendants' failure to comply with the court's orders was not substantially justified. Therefore, the court finds that sanctions are appropriate.

IV. FRCP 26(g)

A. Standards

FRCP 26(g) mandates the imposition of sanctions for conducting discovery irresponsibly. It adopts the certification requirements of FRCP 11 and applies them to "[e]very discovery request, response or objection." FRCP 26(g)(2). Like FRCP 11, its requirements are strict; the standard of care is objective; and the sanctions are mandatory. Due to the similarity, courts have applied the case law applicable to the 1983 version of FRCP 11 to the sanctions language in FRCP 26(g). In fact, sanctions inappropriately imposed under FRCP 11 or 37 have been converted to FRCP 26(g) sanctions.

B. Violation

Although noting that Mr. Barnes has repeatedly failed to comply with the discovery rules, plaintiffs concede that he has managed to avoid sanctions under FRCP 26(g) by filing no discovery responses at all. The imposition of sanctions under FRCP 26(g) rests upon the signing of a discovery document that violates the rule. If the wrongdoing does not involve a violative signature on a discovery request, response or objection, then FRCP 26(g) does not apply. Until defendants file an improper discovery response or objection, plaintiffs must seek sanctions under other rules.

V. Amount of Sanctions . . .

C. Appropriate Sanctions

The decision to impose sanctions under FRCP 37 is left to the court's discretion. *National Hockey League v. Metropolitan Hockey Club, Inc.*, 427 U.S. 639 (1976). . . .

This court may impose even the "most severe" sanction to fulfill the purpose "not merely to penalize those whose conduct may be deemed to warrant such a sanction, but to deter those who might be tempted to such conduct in the absence of such a deterrent." *National Hockey League*, 427 U.S. at 643 (affirming extreme sanction of dismissal for violation of FRCP 37).

In fixing the amount of the sanction, the court may consider a party's entire course of conduct during the proceedings.

For at least the past six months defendants' attorney, Mr. Barnes, has repeatedly failed to cooperate with plaintiffs in good faith in the discovery process, employed dilatory tactics, and repeatedly ignored the rules and this court's orders. He offers no satisfactory explanation for his complete indifference to his professional obligations both to the court and opposing counsel. His egregious dilatory conduct not only has unnecessarily delayed the completion of discovery and the filing of dispositive motions, but also has increased the time and expense of this litigation to plaintiffs and unnecessarily and repeatedly involved the court in resolving ongoing discovery problems.

Mr. Barnes is not a novice attorney, but is a veteran trial lawyer who is or should be aware of the conduct expected of him by this court. Unacceptable conduct by him [has occurred in other cases.] . . . Unless remedial action is taken by this court, Mr. Barnes' pattern of conduct may continue unabated.

. . . At an hourly rate of $120.00, which defendants have not contested, the total award of attorney's fees based on recorded hours is $7,026.00. Although plaintiffs seek an award for additional unrecorded hours and costs, this court is reluctant to do so without supporting documentation.

. . . In addition to an award of expenses, FRCP 37 authorizes the court to make orders "as are just." Federal courts have a number of weapons in their armory of non-monetary sanctions. For example, courts may remove attorneys from cases, order the attorney to attend ethics seminars at the attorney's own expense, dispatch the attorney to the employer's internal disciplinary office, or issue a public reprimand. FRCP 37(b)(2) also authorizes a variety of non-monetary sanctions against the party who fails to obey a court order. . . .

Although not specifically requested by plaintiffs, this court has carefully considered these other types of sanctions in lieu of, or in addition to, an award of expenses. This court is concerned by the fact that other judges and opposing counsel have experienced difficulties with Mr. Barnes in other cases at other times. Furthermore, any sanction that adversely impacts the defendants' ability to present a defense is aimed in the wrong direction: it is Mr. Barnes, and not his clients, who is the offender. Thus, in order to ensure that Mr. Barnes takes appropriate remedial action, this court recommends the issuance of a public reprimand in addition to the award of expenses. A public reprimand will serve the purpose of notifying other attorneys and judges of conduct that this court finds unacceptable, and of ensuring that any such future conduct by Mr. Barnes will be brought to the court's attention and, if appropriate, will subject Mr. Barnes to the imposition of more severe sanctions.

For the foregoing reasons, this court recommends that plaintiffs' motions for sanctions be granted as follows: (1) defendant's attorney, Assistant Attorney General Kendall M. Barnes, be ordered to pay to plaintiffs their expenses in the sum of $7,026.00, and (2) this court publicly reprimand Mr. Barnes by publishing its order.

NOTES AND QUESTIONS

1. *Sources of sanctions.* Rule 37 serves as the primary source for imposing discovery sanctions. In *Societe Internationale Pour Participations Industrielles Et Commerciales, S.A. v. Rogers, Attorney General*, 357 U.S. 197, 78 S.Ct. 1087, 2 L.Ed.2d 1255 (1958), the Court stated:

> In our opinion, whether a court has power to dismiss a complaint because of noncompliance with a production order depends exclusively upon Rule 37, which addresses itself with particularity to the consequences of a failure to make discovery by listing a variety of remedies which a court may employ as well as by authorizing any order which is "just." There is no need to resort to Rule 41(b) [regarding involuntary dismissals], which appears in that part of the Rules concerned with trials and which lacks such specific references to discovery.... Reliance upon Rule 41, which cannot easily be interpreted to afford a court more expansive powers than does Rule 37, or upon "inherent power," can only obscure analysis of the problem before us.

Despite the Court's statement that it is ordinarily inappropriate to go beyond Rule 37 for discovery sanctions, other sources may be necessary. For example, Rule 45(e) authorizes contempt proceedings for a witness failing to obey a subpoena to appear for the taking of her deposition. Rule 26(g) prescribes sanctions similar to Rule 11 against a party, an attorney, or both, if the certification that accompanies a discovery request or response violates that rule.

2. *Sanctions rules.* Rule 37 describes the consequences for failing to cooperate in discovery. Usually, sanctions are applied for failing to comply with a court order. For example, when Rule 35(a)(1) requires a court order or when the court issues a protective order under Rule 26(c), failure to obey the order is punishable immediately using the sanctions listed in Rule 37(b)(2)(A). By contrast, when the parties conduct discovery *without* a court order, the party seeking discovery first must obtain a court order under Rule 37(a)(3). The effect of the order is to require the opposing party to make the discovery sought. A violation of that order is punishable under Rule 37(b)(2)(A). Both a motion to compel (Rule 37(a)(1)) and most motions for sanctions for complete failure to disclose, answer or respond (Rule 37(d)) must include a certification by the aggrieved party that she has attempted to confer with the unresponsive party in an effort to obtain the desired material without court action.

In addition to the federal rules, the Constitution is relevant to whether a sanction is "just." For example, *Societe Internationale* involved the dismissal with prejudice of a complaint in a civil action when the plaintiff had failed to comply with a pretrial production order. The Court held that it would be a denial of due process for a court to dismiss a complaint because of petitioner's noncompliance with a discovery order when it has been established that failure to comply was due to inability and not to willfulness, bad faith, or any fault of the party.

3. *Judicial discretion to impose sanctions.* The appropriateness of imposing sanctions against a party for noncompliance with the discovery rules, if a sanction is to be imposed at all, is within the trial judge's discretion. Rule 37(b)(2)(A) limits a court's discretion to sanctions which are "just." Although the list of sanctions in Rule 37(b)(2)(A) is not exclusive, the listed penalties are the sanctions usually imposed. A court may deem facts established, prohibit evidence from being introduced, strike pleadings, issue a stay of the proceedings until the order is obeyed, dismiss all or a part of the claims, and generally hold a disobedient party in contempt. In addition, the court may impose payment of all expenses including attorneys' fees incurred by the moving party as a result of the failure to comply.

How should a court decide whether sanctions should be imposed? When any noncompliance occurs? When the noncompliance with the discovery order is unreasonable? According to the Supreme Court, the conduct of the offending party should be characterized by a deliberate and pronounced disregard for the order. In *National Hockey League v. Metropolitan Hockey Club, Inc.*, 427 U.S. 639, 96 S.Ct. 2778, 49 L.Ed.2d 747 (1976), the Court reinstated a trial court dismissal for failure to comply with a discovery order, reasoning that

> here, as in other areas of the law, the most severe in the spectrum of sanctions provided by statute or rule must be available to the district court in appropriate cases, not merely to penalize those whose conduct may be deemed to warrant such a sanction, but to deter those who might be tempted to such conduct in the absence of such a deterrent.

Sanctions, then, may be imposed for their deterrent effect in other cases in addition to being a remedy for the wrong committed in the instant case.

Most appellate courts have developed criteria for the imposition of sanctions. For example, in *Wanderer v. Johnston*, 910 F.2d 652, 656 (9th Cir. 1990) the court identified five factors to be applied in considering whether a dismissal or default is appropriate as a Rule 37 sanction: (1) the public's interest in expeditious resolution of litigation; (2) the court's need to manage its dockets; (3) the risk of prejudice to the party seeking sanctions; (4) the public policy favoring disposition of cases on their merits; and (5) the availability of less drastic sanctions. *Mutual Federal Savings & Loan Ass'n v. Richards & Assoc.*, 872 F.2d 88, 92 (4th Cir. 1989) applied a four-factor test: (1) whether the noncomplying party acted in good faith; (2) the amount of prejudice its noncompliance caused its adversary; (3) the need for deterrence of the particular sort of noncompliance; and (4) the effectiveness of less drastic sanctions.

Chapter 11

Taking the Case from the Jury

■ ■ ■

Most cases cannot be resolved on the pleadings alone. If defendant denies any of the essential facts alleged by plaintiff, for example, the case cannot be resolved by a Federal Rule 12(b)(6) or 12(c) motion. The parties will then engage in discovery to try to determine what really happened. In many cases, the task of determining what happened falls to the jury.

However, not all disputed cases must be decided by a jury. Two devices—summary judgment and judgment as a matter of law—allow the judge to review the evidence obtained in discovery and determine whether there is actually any real dispute as to the facts. If the facts are undisputed, the court can decide the case based on the governing law.

Summary judgment and judgment as a matter of law occur at different stages in the trial process. Summary judgment is a *pre-trial* motion. Under Federal Rule 56, a party ordinarily must move for summary judgment within 30 days of the end of discovery. Judgment as a matter of law, by contrast, occurs *during* the trial. The judge has heard all relevant testimony in the courtroom, and in the case of live witness testimony has seen how those witnesses fare under cross-examination.

Notwithstanding these differences, summary judgment and judgment as a matter of law are conceptually quite similar. The judge's task in both situations is not to weigh the evidence or determine which witnesses are credible. Instead, her task is to evaluate all the evidence to see if there really are two irreconcilable sides to the story. If the evidence supports only one side, that side may be able to prevail before trial by moving for summary judgment, or during trial by a motion for judgment as a matter of law.

There is also a third motion a party can bring in a case involving one-sided facts: the motion for a new trial. One of the reasons for a new trial is that the jury verdict is "against the great weight of the evidence." Unlike summary judgment and judgment as a matter of law, however, a new trial does not involve the judge actually deciding the case herself. Rather, as the name suggests, it merely means the case must be tried again. Because of this difference, new trials are covered in Chapter 12.

A. SUMMARY JUDGMENT

Rule 56 governs the summary judgment motion. Take a moment to review the rule. The basic standard has two parts. First, the court must determine there is "no genuine dispute as to any material fact." Notice the use of the words "genuine" and "material"—they suggest minor disputes concerning the facts are not sufficient to send the case to the jury. Second, based on the uncontested facts, the court must determine the movant is entitled to judgment as a matter of law. Rule 56 also dictates the procedure to be followed in summary judgment motions, including how the parties demonstrate the lack of any genuine dispute.

1. THE RULE 56 STANDARD

INTRODUCTORY PROBLEM

Arriving home after a grueling day at work, Forrest Green is shocked to discover that several trees have been removed from his yard. After some investigation, Green sues Lon's Lawn Service. Green claims Lon's employees removed the trees without Green's permission. Lon denies liability.

Green has several witnesses who say they saw a crew of men wearing identical light blue shirts removing trees from Green's yard on the date in question. Although the shirts had writing on them, none of the witnesses could make out the writing. In his answers to interrogatories, Lon admits his employees wear shirts of that color. Green also obtained affidavits from the owners of all the lawn and tree service companies listed in the yellow pages. All these owners swear that their employees do not wear shirts of that color. Finally, one of Green's neighbors testified in her deposition that she had arranged with Lon's to have several trees removed from *her* yard that day, but that Lon's employees never showed up to do the work.

Lon has comparatively little testimony to back up his story. Turnover in the lawn service industry is high, and all of the workers who worked for Lon on the date in question have moved on to other positions. Neither Lon nor Green has been able to track down any of the employees who worked for him at that time. Lon nevertheless sticks by his original story: although he does not deny that the trees were removed, he claims that neither he nor anyone who worked for him is responsible.

Both Green and Lon are confident they will prevail at trial. Green feels that not only is his evidence overwhelming, but Lon has nothing that contradicts it. Lon, by contrast, feels that Green has no direct evidence that it was Lon's employees who removed the trees.

Is either party entitled to summary judgment? How will that party demonstrate the lack of any genuine dispute?

Governing Rule: Rule 56.

CELOTEX CORP. V. CATRETT
477 U.S. 317, 106 S.Ct. 2548, 91 L.Ed.2d 265 (1986)

JUSTICE REHNQUIST delivered the opinion of the Court.

... Respondent commenced this lawsuit in September 1980, alleging that the death in 1979 of her husband, Louis H. Catrett, resulted from his exposure to products containing asbestos manufactured or distributed by 15 named corporations. Respondent's complaint sounded in negligence, breach of warranty, and strict liability. Two of the defendants filed motions challenging the District Court's *in personam* jurisdiction, and the remaining 13, including petitioner, filed motions for summary judgment. Petitioner's motion, which was first filed in September 1981, argued that summary judgment was proper because respondent had "failed to produce evidence that any [Celotex] product ... was the proximate cause of the injuries alleged...." In particular, petitioner noted that respondent had failed to identify, in answering interrogatories specifically requesting such information, any witnesses who could testify about the decedent's exposure to petitioner's asbestos products. In response to petitioner's summary judgment motion, respondent then produced three documents which she claimed "demonstrate that there is a genuine material factual dispute" as to whether the decedent had ever been exposed to petitioner's asbestos products. The three documents included a transcript of a deposition of the decedent, a letter from an official of one of the decedent's former employers whom petitioner planned to call as a trial witness, and a letter from an insurance company to respondent's attorney, all tending to establish that the decedent had been exposed to petitioner's asbestos products in Chicago during 1970–1971. Petitioner, in turn, argued that the three documents were inadmissible hearsay and thus could not be considered in opposition to the summary judgment motion.

In July 1982, almost two years after the commencement of the lawsuit, the District Court granted all of the motions filed by the various defendants. The court explained that it was granting petitioner's summary judgment motion because "there [was] no showing that the plaintiff was exposed to the defendant Celotex's product in the District of Columbia or elsewhere within the statutory period." Respondent appealed only the grant of summary judgment in favor of petitioner, and a divided panel of the District of Columbia Circuit reversed. The majority of the Court of Appeals held that petitioner's summary judgment motion was rendered "fatally defective" by the fact that petitioner "made no effort to adduce *any* evidence, in the form of affidavits or otherwise, to support its motion." ...

We think that the position taken by the majority of the Court of Appeals is inconsistent with the standard for summary judgment set forth in Rule 56(c) of the Federal Rules of Civil Procedure.... In our view, the plain language of Rule 56(c) mandates the entry of summary judgment, after adequate time for discovery and upon motion, against a party who fails to make a showing sufficient to establish the existence of an element essential to that party's case, and on which that party will bear the burden of proof at trial. In such a situation, there can be "no genuine issue as to any material fact,"* since a complete failure of proof concerning an essential element of the nonmoving party's case necessarily renders all other facts immaterial. The moving party is "entitled to a judgment as a matter of law" because the nonmoving party has failed to make a sufficient showing on an essential element of her case with respect to which she has the burden of proof....

Of course, a party seeking summary judgment always bears the initial responsibility of informing the district court of the basis for its motion, and identifying those portions of "the pleadings, depositions, answers to interrogatories, and admissions on file, together with the affidavits, if any," which it believes demonstrate the absence of a genuine issue of material fact. But unlike the Court of Appeals, we find no express or implied requirement in Rule 56 that the moving party support its motion with affidavits or other similar materials *negating* the opponent's claim....

Respondent argues, however, that Rule 56(e), by its terms, places on the nonmoving party the burden of coming forward with rebuttal affidavits, or other specified kinds of materials, only in response to a motion for summary judgment "made and supported as provided in this rule."** According to respondent's argument, since petitioner did not "support" its motion with affidavits, summary judgment was improper in this case. But as we have already explained, a motion for summary judgment may be made pursuant to Rule 56 "with or without supporting affidavits." In cases like the instant one, where the nonmoving party will bear the burden of proof at trial on a dispositive issue, a summary judgment motion may properly be made in reliance solely on the "pleadings, depositions, answers to interrogatories, and admissions on file." Such a motion, whether or not accompanied by affidavits, will be "made and supported as provided in this rule," and Rule 56(e) therefore requires the nonmoving party to go beyond the pleadings and by her own affidavits, or by the "depositions, answers to interrogatories, and admissions on file," designate "specific facts showing that there is a genuine issue for trial."

We do not mean that the nonmoving party must produce evidence in a form that would be admissible at trial in order to avoid summary judgment. Obviously, Rule 56 does not require the nonmoving party to

---

* Rule 56 was amended after this case. The new Rule refers to a genuine "dispute" rather than a genuine "issue." The change in wording would not affect the Court's analysis. [Eds.]

** As indicated in the notes following the case, Rule 56 was later amended to incorporate the approach set out by the Supreme Court. After this amendment, the language quoted by the court no longer appears in the Rule. [Eds.]

depose her own witnesses. Rule 56(e) permits a proper summary judgment motion to be opposed by any of the kinds of evidentiary materials listed in Rule 56(c), except the mere pleadings themselves, and it is from this list that one would normally expect the nonmoving party to make the showing to which we have referred. . . .

Respondent commenced this action in September 1980, and petitioner's motion was filed in September 1981. The parties had conducted discovery, and no serious claim can be made that respondent was in any sense "railroaded" by a premature motion for summary judgment. Any potential problem with such premature motions can be adequately dealt with under Rule [56(d)], which allows a summary judgment motion to be denied, or the hearing on the motion to be continued, if the nonmoving party has not had an opportunity to make full discovery.

In this Court, respondent's brief and oral argument have been devoted as much to the proposition that an adequate showing of exposure to petitioner's asbestos products was made as to the proposition that no such showing should have been required. But the Court of Appeals declined to address either the adequacy of the showing made by respondent in opposition to petitioner's motion for summary judgment, or the question whether such a showing, if reduced to admissible evidence, would be sufficient to carry respondent's burden of proof at trial. We think the Court of Appeals with its superior knowledge of local law is better suited than we are to make these determinations in the first instance.

The Federal Rules of Civil Procedure have for almost 50 years authorized motions for summary judgment upon proper showings of the lack of a genuine, triable issue of material fact. Summary judgment procedure is properly regarded not as a disfavored procedural shortcut, but rather as an integral part of the Federal Rules as a whole, which are designed "to secure the just, speedy and inexpensive determination of every action." Fed. Rule Civ. Proc. 1. Before the shift to "notice pleading" accomplished by the Federal Rules, motions to dismiss a complaint or to strike a defense were the principal tools by which factually insufficient claims or defenses could be isolated and prevented from going to trial with the attendant unwarranted consumption of public and private resources. But with the advent of "notice pleading," the motion to dismiss seldom fulfills this function any more, and its place has been taken by the motion for summary judgment. Rule 56 must be construed with due regard not only for the rights of persons asserting claims and defenses that are adequately based in fact to have those claims and defenses tried to a jury, but also for the rights of persons opposing such claims and defenses to demonstrate in the manner provided by the Rule, prior to trial, that the claims and defenses have no factual basis.

The judgment of the Court of Appeals is accordingly reversed, and the case is remanded for further proceedings consistent with this opinion.

[JUSTICE WHITE'S concurrence is omitted.]

JUSTICE BRENNAN, with whom THE CHIEF JUSTICE and JUSTICE BLACKMUN join, dissenting.

This case requires the Court to determine whether Celotex satisfied its initial burden of production in moving for summary judgment on the ground that the plaintiff lacked evidence to establish an essential element of her case at trial. I do not disagree with the Court's legal analysis. The Court clearly rejects the ruling of the Court of Appeals that the defendant must provide affirmative evidence disproving the plaintiff's case. Beyond this, however, the Court has not clearly explained what is required of a moving party seeking summary judgment on the ground that the nonmoving party cannot prove its case. This lack of clarity is unfortunate: district courts must routinely decide summary judgment motions, and the Court's opinion will very likely create confusion. For this reason, even if I agreed with the Court's result, I would have written separately to explain more clearly the law in this area. However, because I believe that Celotex did not meet its burden of production under Federal Rule of Civil Procedure 56, I respectfully dissent from the Court's judgment.

Summary judgment is appropriate where the court is satisfied "that there is no genuine issue as to any material fact and that the moving party is entitled to a judgment as a matter of law." Fed. Rule Civ. Proc. 56(c). The burden of establishing the nonexistence of a "genuine issue" is on the party moving for summary judgment. This burden has two distinct components: an initial burden of production, which shifts to the nonmoving party if satisfied by the moving party; and an ultimate burden of persuasion, which always remains on the moving party. The court need not decide whether the moving party has satisfied its ultimate burden of persuasion unless and until the court finds that the moving party has discharged its initial burden of production.

The burden of production imposed by Rule 56 requires the moving party to make a prima facie showing that it is entitled to summary judgment. The manner in which this showing can be made depends upon which party will bear the burden of persuasion on the challenged claim at trial. If the *moving* party will bear the burden of persuasion at trial, that party must support its motion with credible evidence—using any of the materials specified in Rule 56(c)—that would entitle it to a directed verdict if not controverted at trial. Such an affirmative showing shifts the burden of production to the party opposing the motion and requires that party either to produce evidentiary materials that demonstrate the existence of a "genuine issue" for trial or to submit an affidavit requesting additional time for discovery.

If the burden of persuasion at trial would be on the *nonmoving* party, the party moving for summary judgment may satisfy Rule 56's burden of production in either of two ways. First, the moving party may submit affirmative evidence that negates an essential element of the nonmoving party's claim. Second, the moving party may demonstrate to the court that the nonmoving party's evidence is insufficient to establish an essential element of the nonmoving party's claim. If the nonmoving party cannot muster sufficient evidence to make out its claim, a trial would be useless and the moving party is entitled to summary judgment as a matter of law.

Where the moving party adopts this second option and seeks summary judgment on the ground that the nonmoving party ... has no evidence, the mechanics of discharging Rule 56's burden of production are somewhat trickier. Plainly, a conclusory assertion that the nonmoving party has no evidence is insufficient. Such a "burden" of production is no burden at all and would simply permit summary judgment procedure to be converted into a tool for harassment. Rather, as the Court confirms, a party who moves for summary judgment on the ground that the nonmoving party has no evidence must affirmatively show the absence of evidence in the record. This may require the moving party to depose the nonmoving party's witnesses or to establish the inadequacy of documentary evidence. If there is literally no evidence in the record, the moving party may demonstrate this by reviewing for the court the admissions, interrogatories, and other exchanges between the parties that are in the record. Either way, however, the moving party must affirmatively demonstrate that there is no evidence in the record to support a judgment for the nonmoving party.

... [T]he nonmoving party may defeat a motion for summary judgment that asserts that the nonmoving party has no evidence by calling the court's attention to supporting evidence already in the record that was overlooked or ignored by the moving party. In that event, the moving party must respond by making an attempt to demonstrate the inadequacy of this evidence, for it is only by attacking all the record evidence allegedly supporting the nonmoving party that a party seeking summary judgment satisfies Rule 56's burden of production. Thus, if the record disclosed that the moving party had overlooked a witness who would provide relevant testimony for the nonmoving party at trial, the court could not find that the moving party had discharged its initial burden of production unless the moving party sought to demonstrate the inadequacy of this witness' testimony. Absent such a demonstration, summary judgment would have to be denied on the ground that the moving party had failed to meet its burden of production under Rule 56. ...

I do not read the Court's opinion to say anything inconsistent with or different than the preceding discussion. My disagreement with the Court concerns the application of these principles to the facts of this case.

Defendant Celotex sought summary judgment on the ground that plaintiff had "failed to produce" any evidence that her decedent had ever been exposed to Celotex asbestos. Celotex supported this motion with a two-page "Statement of Material Facts as to Which There is No Genuine Issue" and a three-page "Memorandum of Points and Authorities" which asserted that the plaintiff had failed to identify any evidence in responding to two sets of interrogatories propounded by Celotex and that therefore the record was "totally devoid" of evidence to support plaintiff's claim.

Approximately three months earlier, Celotex had filed an essentially identical motion. Plaintiff responded to this earlier motion by producing three pieces of evidence which she claimed "[at] the very least . . . demonstrate that there is a genuine factual dispute for trial," (1) a letter from an insurance representative of another defendant describing asbestos products to which plaintiff's decedent had been exposed, (2) a letter from T. R. Hoff, a former supervisor of decedent, describing asbestos products to which decedent had been exposed, and (3) a copy of decedent's deposition from earlier workmen's compensation proceedings. Plaintiff also apparently indicated at that time that she intended to call Mr. Hoff as a witness at trial.

Celotex subsequently withdrew its first motion for summary judgment. However, as a result of this motion, when Celotex filed its second summary judgment motion, the record *did* contain evidence—including at least one witness—supporting plaintiff's claim. Indeed, counsel for Celotex admitted to this Court at oral argument that Celotex was aware of this evidence and of plaintiff's intention to call Mr. Hoff as a witness at trial when the second summary judgment motion was filed. Moreover, plaintiff's response to Celotex' second motion pointed to this evidence—noting that it had already been provided to counsel for Celotex in connection with the first motion—and argued that Celotex had failed to "meet its burden of proving that there is no genuine factual dispute for trial."

On these facts, there is simply no question that Celotex failed to discharge its initial burden of production. Having chosen to base its motion on the argument that there was no evidence in the record to support plaintiff's claim, Celotex was not free to ignore supporting evidence that the record clearly contained. Rather, Celotex was required, as an initial matter, to attack the adequacy of this evidence. Celotex' failure to fulfill this simple requirement constituted a failure to discharge its initial burden of production under Rule 56, and thereby rendered summary judgment improper. . . .

[JUSTICE STEVENS's dissent is omitted.]

NOTES AND QUESTIONS

1. In your own words, explain what the *Celotex* majority requires a party moving for summary judgment to demonstrate. Do the dissenters disagree as to the rule, or as to how the rule is being applied to the facts of the case? Now review Rule 56(c), which has been amended to codify the process described in *Celotex*. Does the Rule comport with your understanding?

2. The Court in *Celotex* holds that the party moving for summary judgment has the initial burden of establishing that there is no genuine issue of material fact. But what happens if the other side does not contest the motion? May the court enter a sort of "default" summary judgment, sparing the moving party the trouble of proving the absence of an issue? See *Vermont Teddy Bear Co., Inc. v. 1-800 BEARGRAM Co.*, 373 F.3d 241 (2d Cir. 2004).

3. In *Celotex*, the party moving for summary judgment was the defendant. Would a court analyze the evidence in the same way if the *plaintiff* had moved for summary judgment?

4. *Burdens*. The reason why the standard differs for plaintiffs and defendants is because of the *burden of production*. Justice Brennan's dissent discusses how the burden affects what a party must show in order to obtain a summary judgment. But what *is* a burden of production, and why are the Justices all assuming it falls on the plaintiff?

The term burden of production may be new to you. On the other hand, you have probably heard of the "burden of proof." The burden of proof in a case is actually made up of three separate burdens: the burdens of *pleading, production* and *persuasion*. Although summary judgment is primarily concerned with the burden of production, an explanation of all three burdens may be helpful.

    a. *Pleading*. You studied the burden of pleading in Chapters 6 and 7. That burden determines who is responsible for bringing up an issue in her pleadings. If neither party includes the issue in the pleadings, the party with the burden may not offer evidence on that issue at trial (although the liberal amendment policy in the federal courts will often allow the party with the burden to correct her oversight when she tries to introduce evidence). A claimant—that is, a plaintiff on its claim, and a defendant on a counterclaim—has the burden of informing the court and the opposing party of the claims she wants to bring. A party defending against a claim has the burden of pleading any affirmative defenses. Thus, for example, in the *Red Deer* case in Chapter 7, the court refused to hear evidence on the affirmative defense of after-acquired evidence because the defendant failed to plead that defense in its answer.

b. *Production.* The burden of production—which is sometimes called the burden of "going forth with the evidence"—applies after the pleading stage. This burden controls who bears the onus of offering evidence on a particular issue. The party with the burden must offer enough evidence that a reasonable jury could find for that party. If the party with the burden offers no evidence on that issue, or so little evidence that no reasonable jury could find for the party, that party *loses* on that issue. In *Celotex*, plaintiff had the burden of production on the issue of causation. To meet that burden, she had to offer evidence showing that her husband had been exposed to defendant's asbestos. Defendant—who did not have the burden—was not required to offer any evidence on that point. The Supreme Court remanded the case to let the lower courts determine whether plaintiff had any evidence to show exposure.

Note that some states would require less of the plaintiff in *Celotex*. Rather than requiring plaintiff to offer enough evidence to allow a reasonable jury to decide in her favor, these states would deny summary judgment as long as plaintiff had a "mere scintilla" of supporting evidence. Although some older federal cases also applied the mere scintilla standard, the Supreme Court has made it clear in cases like *Celotex* that more is required to defeat summary judgment in federal court.

The burden of production usually (but not always) follows the burden of pleading. Consider, for example, a defendant defending a breach of contract claim by arguing the defense of insanity. Defendant would have the burden of pleading insanity, as well as the burden of offering evidence on her mental state to the court.

It is also possible for the burden of production to *switch* to the other side. In *Celotex*, suppose plaintiff had the testimony of ten disinterested OSHA inspectors, all of whom testified that on separate occasions they saw decedent working with asbestos bearing a Celotex label. At that point, plaintiff has offered evidence so compelling that the burden of production would switch to defendant. Although Celotex would not otherwise be required to offer evidence on whether plaintiff's husband had been exposed to its asbestos, if it fails to offset plaintiff's evidence with its own evidence disproving exposure to its asbestos, it would have failed to satisfy the shifted burden of production, and summary judgment for plaintiff would be appropriate.

c. *Persuasion.* The burden of persuasion applies only once the case reaches trial. Basically, it is the standard the jury considers when deciding the case. In a normal civil case, the standard is "a preponderance of the evidence." Under this standard, if neither party offers evidence, or if both parties offer evidence that is equally persuasive, the jury must find for the party who does not have the burden.

In some cases, courts apply a burden of persuasion that is more demanding than the preponderance standard. In criminal cases, for example, the prosecution must prove every element of the crime "beyond a reasonable doubt." The defense, by contrast, must only prove its defenses by a preponderance of the evidence. In civil fraud cases, the party alleging fraud must prove the fraud by "clear and convincing evidence," a standard that is also considerably more rigorous than the preponderance standard.

The burden of persuasion usually falls upon the party with the burden of production, but again there are exceptions. The burden is fixed by law (or in rare cases by agreement of the parties). Unlike the burden of production, the burden of persuasion remains the same throughout the case, and does not "shift" in response to evidence offered by the parties.

5. Does the burden of persuasion affect the burden of production? Suppose P sues D for negligent misrepresentation based on an advertisement. If P has one witness who testifies unequivocally that the advertisement is false, most courts would hold that P has met his burden of production. Now suppose P sues D for fraud (a claim governed by the stricter "clear and convincing evidence" burden of persuasion) based on the same advertisement. Will one witness still be enough to meet P's burden of production, or is something more required?

In *Anderson v. Liberty Lobby, Inc.*, 477 U.S. 242, 106 S.Ct. 2505, 91 L.Ed.2d 202 (1986), the Court held that the burden of production did change along with the ultimate burden of persuasion. But does that make sense? Consider the example set out immediately above. If one person testifies unequivocally that an advertisement is false, and that witness is neither impeached nor rebutted by other witnesses, won't that evidence meet both the preponderance and clear and convincing standards?

6. *Presumptions*. Presumptions can change the burden of production. In certain circumstances, the law provides that proof of some fact creates a presumption that some other fact is true. As just one example, a party who has registered his trademark with the United States Patent and Trademark Office is entitled to a presumption that the mark is valid, and that he is the owner. 15 U.S.C. § 1115(a). A presumption in effect *switches the burden of production* to the other side. Therefore, if our registered trademark owner sues someone for trademark infringement, the owner would merely offer the certificate of registration. If defendant wants to challenge the validity of the mark or claim that plaintiff is not the owner, defendant would have the burden of offering evidence tending to show invalidity or lack of ownership.

7. *Celotex* and amended Rule 56 make it clear that a motion for summary judgment introduces what is in essence a second "burden of production." The party moving for summary judgment has an initial burden of showing to the court that the "no genuine dispute as to any material fact" standard of Rule 56 is satisfied. How the movant goes about meeting that

burden depends in turn on the burden of production for the substantive claims and defenses.

To make sure you understand how these different burdens of production play out, consider the following situations. In each case, who has the burden of showing there is no genuine dispute? How can that party satisfy that burden?

a. P sues D for breach of contract. D denies there was a contract. D moves for summary judgment.

b. Same as (a), except P moves for summary judgment.

c. P sues D for breach of contract. D admits that there was a contract and that D did not perform as stipulated, but argues that a flood made D's performance impossible. P moves for summary judgment, asserting that no flood occurred.

8. In *Celotex*, the Court indicates that a party seeking to avoid summary judgment need not offer admissible evidence, but may use whatever information may be at his disposal, including inadmissible evidence such as hearsay. That statement at first glance seems at least partially at odds with Rule 56(c)(4), which requires that *affidavits* offered to support or oppose a summary judgment motion "set out facts that would be admissible in evidence." However, there is no contradiction. Rule 56(c)(4) does not require that the affidavit itself be admissible evidence. It merely requires that the facts set out in the affidavit be of a type that *could* be admissible.

To illustrate, suppose plaintiff in *Celotex* opposed the summary judgment with an affidavit of witness W. W states in her affidavit, "I saw plaintiff's husband working with Celotex-brand asbestos." If W is available to testify, W's affidavit is inadmissible because it is hearsay evidence. Nevertheless, because the underlying information (what W saw) would be admissible if offered in the proper way (by W testifying in person), the affidavit may be used for the limited purpose of opposing the summary judgment motion.

9. *Timing*. According to Rule 56, what is the *earliest* point at which a party may move for summary judgment? Can a plaintiff move for summary judgment before a defendant even answers? Conversely, is there a point in the proceedings *after* which a party may no longer move for summary judgment? Could a party move for summary judgment in the middle of the trial?

10. Given that a motion for summary judgment may be filed very early in the case, it is entirely possible—and probably common—for one side to lack evidence on one or more crucial issues in the case. Why, then, would a defendant served with a complaint not always file immediately for summary judgment? Given that plaintiff typically has the burden of production on every element of its claim, wouldn't such a motion often catch the plaintiff without evidence to back up one or more elements of its claim—especially when the claim requires proof of defendant's state of mind or other facts

available only to defendant? If the defendant does file a motion immediately, must the court resolve it expeditiously? See Rule 56(d).

11. In Chapter 7, you studied the Rule 12(b) motion to dismiss for failure to state a claim and the Rule 12(c) motion for judgment on the pleadings. Like the motion for summary judgment, these motions can be brought very early in the case. Moreover, although a motion for judgment on the pleadings must be brought "early enough not to delay trial," Rule 12(c), a motion to dismiss for failure to state a claim may be brought at the trial itself. Rule 12(h)(2). Finally, in the federal courts, a dismissal for failure to state a claim and a judgment on the pleadings operate as a final judgment on the issues presented.

What is the difference between a summary judgment motion and these other motions? Review Rule 12(b)(6) and 12(c), and determine which motion is *best* suited to the following situations:

    a.   P sues D for trespass. D's answer admits he entered P's land, but claims that P's property was an attractive nuisance. P feels he should prevail because attractive nuisance is not a defense to a trespass claim.

    b.   P sues D for trespass. P's complaint specifically states the trespass occurred on August 9, 2015. P files his complaint on August 31, 2016, and that date is stamped on the pleading. The statute of limitations for trespass claims is one year. Under governing law, the statute of limitations is tolled at the point the complaint is filed. D wants to get rid of the case based on the statute of limitations.

    c.   Same as b, except that (i) P filed his complaint on August 1, 2016, and (ii) under governing law, the statute of limitation is tolled only when the complaint is *served*. D was not served until August 31, 2016. P has not yet made proof of service. D wants to get rid of the case based on the statute of limitations.

12. In part (c) of the prior problem, there are actually *two* procedural options. If you concluded that D should move for summary judgment, you are correct; for D cannot prevail without proving a fact that is not asserted in the pleadings. But suppose D files a 12(b)(6) motion, and attaches to it an affidavit stating that he was not served until August 31. In these situations, Rule 12(d) states that the 12(b)(6) motion will be converted into a motion for summary judgment. Similarly, a Rule 12(c) motion is converted into a motion for summary judgment if supporting materials are attached.

13. P sues D for a civil rights violation, seeking $1,000,000 in damages. D denies she violated any of P's rights, and in the alternative argues that even if P's rights were violated, P suffered no damages. During discovery, P acquires incontrovertible evidence (including D's admission in a deposition) that D violated civil rights laws. D has no evidence to the contrary. However, the evidence concerning P's damages is less persuasive, with each side having some evidence to support its claims. In this situation, it may be possible for P to obtain a *partial* summary judgment, limited to the question of liability. As

a practical matter, a partial summary judgment operates like an amendment of the pleadings. If the court grants summary judgment to P on the question of liability, the trial will be limited to damages, just as if D had admitted liability in his answer.

Can you conceive of a situation where it would be inappropriate to grant partial summary judgment on fewer than all the issues? Could a court grant summary judgment on damages without determining liability? What if the case involves a request for punitive damages?

2. USING INFERENCES

The battle over summary judgment turns on whether a party has introduced sufficient evidence to satisfy its burden of production. In some cases, that issue will be clear-cut. Take a case in which X and Y are involved in a two-car accident at an intersection with a stoplight. Both X and Y die in the accident. P, the executor of X's estate, sues D, the executor of Y's estate, for wrongful death. P would have the burden of production of showing that the light facing Y was red. However, dead men can't talk. Unless P has some other witnesses who can testify as to the color of the light, a court would grant D's motion for summary judgment.

Many cases, however, are not so straightforward. Suppose P can muster thirty witnesses who will testify in his favor. All thirty testify that the light facing X was green. D moves for summary judgment. Has P met his burden of production? Although he has thirty witnesses, none of them testify directly that the light facing Y was red. Instead, their testimony calls for an *inference*, namely, that the light in question was working properly on the date in question.

The problem of inferences arises quite frequently not only in summary judgment motions, but also in motions for judgments as a matter of law (and motions for a new trial, covered in Chapter 12 pt. F). What does a court do when faced with evidence that calls for an inference? The following case explores the issue.

JORGENSEN V. EPIC/SONY RECORDS
351 F.3d 46 (2d Cir. 2003)

STRAUB, CIRCUIT JUDGE.

... Jorgensen, a musician and songwriter, wrote and copyrighted a song entitled "Long Lost Lover" ("Lover") that he claims has been infringed upon by the songs "My Heart Will Go On" ("Heart") and "Amazed." Written by James Horner and Will Jennings, and sung by Celine Dion, "Heart" was the Academy Award-winning theme song for the 1997 blockbuster movie *Titanic*. Defendants Famous Music Corporation, Fox Film Music Corp. and Blue Sky Rider Songs are the three co-publishers of "Heart," and Defendant Sony Music Entertainment Inc.

("Sony") manufactured and distributed the *Titanic* soundtrack. These defendants are collectively referred to as 'the "Heart" defendants' in this opinion.

"Amazed," a song written by Chris Lindsey, Aimee Mayo and Marv Green, was recorded by the country music group Lonestar and released on their multi-platinum album "Lonely Grill." Defendants Careers BMG Music Publishing ("BMG"), Songs of Nashville Dreamworks, and Warner-Tamerlane Publishing Corp. (collectively 'the "Amazed" defendants') are music publishing companies that administer the publishing rights to "Amazed."

Jorgensen asserts two primary theories by which he hypothesizes that the writers of "Heart" and "Amazed" had access to, and copied his song, "Lover": (i) through his unsolicited mass mailings of "Lover" to a multitude of entertainment companies listed in industry songwriter market books, including the defendants; and (ii) through actual receipt of his mailings by two executives at two of the defendant companies, BMG and Sony. Jorgensen has not named the writers of either song as defendants in this suit.

After discovery, the defendants moved for summary judgment on the ground that Jorgensen had failed to adduce any evidence to support these theories of access. In particular, the defendants argued that, with the two exceptions noted below, Jorgensen had made no showing that any of the defendants ever actually received his submission. Even where Jorgensen established actual receipt, the defendants asserted that there was no evidence that Jorgensen's song had been forwarded to the writers of "Amazed" or "Heart," or to any other third party. In addition, the defendants argued that Jorgensen never had any contact with the writers of either "Amazed" or "Heart," and that Jorgensen had no evidence that the writers of either song would ever have received any tapes of unsolicited material from any of the companies to which Jorgensen sent copies of "Lover."

Bruce Pollock, a managing producer at a BMG division that has no connection with the music publishing company, submitted a sworn declaration in which he admitted having received a compact disc copy of "Lover" from Jorgensen. Pollock stated, however, that he did not give the CD to anyone at any time, including the writers of "Amazed" whom he did not know and had never met.

Harvey Leeds, a Vice President at Sony responsible for reviewing touring budgets for Sony artists, also admitted during his deposition that he had received a few tapes from Jorgensen but stated that he did not listen to them, and had assumed they were thrown away. Leeds also testified that he did not know the "Heart" songwriters.

Based on this evidence from Pollock and Leeds and because Jorgensen did not produce any cover letters or other correspondence to the defendants indicating to whom (or when) he sent his other mailings of "Lover," the District Court held that Jorgensen could not establish that the authors of either "Amazed" or "Heart" had a reasonable opportunity to hear his unpublished work. The court held that "bare corporate receipt" of Jorgensen's work by those defendants who may have received Jorgensen's mass mailings did "not create a prima facie case of access sufficient to defeat summary judgment." And, according to the District Court, with respect to BMG and Sony, the fact that Pollock and Leeds, respectively, admitted receiving Jorgensen's songs, without further evidence that they had forwarded the tapes to the songwriters or anyone else, was similarly inadequate to show access.

The District Court's summary of the evidence regarding Jorgensen's interactions with Leeds and Sony, however, was incomplete. During his deposition, Jorgensen testified at length about multiple conversations that he'd had with both Leeds and Leeds's assistants over the course of three or more years regarding several tapes that Jorgensen sent to Leeds, including at least one tape that contained a recording of "Lover." According to Jorgensen, during every one of these conversations, Leeds or his assistants confirmed that Leeds had received Jorgensen's tapes (including, in particular, the "Lover" tape) and told Jorgensen that his tapes had been forwarded to Sony's Artist and Repertoire ("A & R") Department, the department responsible for helping the company "find, sign and guide new talent." In addition, in response to Jorgensen's Requests for Admissions, Sony indicated that "on limited occasions, writers, producers or musicians affiliated with Sony may have been shown some material solicited by the A & R Dept. at some point during 1995, 1996 and 1997...." This evidence—which the District Court does not appear to have considered—undercuts the defendants' claim that "Jorgensen failed to adduce even a scintilla of evidence" that Leeds "provided [Jorgensen's] song to anyone else...."

DISCUSSION

We review the District Court's grant of summary judgment *de novo*, construing the evidence in the light most favorable to Jorgensen, the non-moving party. Moreover, because Jorgensen is proceeding *pro se*, we read his pleadings "liberally and interpret them to raise the strongest arguments that they suggest." *McPherson v. Coombe*, 174 F.3d 276, 280 (2d Cir. 1999). As the District Court observed, however, our "application of this different standard does not relieve plaintiff of his duty to meet the requirements necessary to defeat a motion for summary judgment."

To prevail on a motion for summary judgment, the defendants must demonstrate the absence of material evidence supporting an essential element of Jorgensen's copyright infringement claim. Jorgensen, to avoid summary judgment, "may not rely simply on conclusory allegations or speculation . . . , but instead must offer evidence to show that [his] version of the events is not wholly fanciful." *Morris v. Lindau*, 196 F.3d 102, 109 (2d Cir. 1999).

In a copyright infringement case, the plaintiff must show: (i) ownership of a valid copyright; and (ii) unauthorized copying of the copyrighted work. A certificate of registration from the United States Register of Copyrights constitutes *prima facie* evidence of the valid ownership of a copyright. Jorgensen secured such registration for "Lover," and the defendants do not dispute the validity of that copyright. Thus, Jorgensen has met the first element of an infringement claim.

To satisfy the second element of an infringement claim—the "unauthorized copying" element—a plaintiff must show both that his work was "actually copied" and that the portion copied amounts to an "improper or unlawful appropriation." "Actual copying may be established by direct or indirect evidence." *Boisson v. Banian, Ltd.*, 273 F.3d 262, 267 (2d Cir. 2001). Because direct evidence of copying is seldom available, a plaintiff may establish copying circumstantially "by demonstrating that the person who composed the defendant's work had access to the copyrighted material," *Herzog v. Castle Rock Entm't*, 193 F.3d 1241, 1249 (11th Cir. 1999), and that there are similarities between the two works that are "probative of copying," *Repp* [*v. Webber*, 132 F.3d 882 (2d Cir. 1997), *cert. denied*, 525 U.S. 815 (1998)] at 889.

Access means that an alleged infringer had a "reasonable possibility"—not simply a "bare possibility"—of hearing the prior work; access cannot be based on mere "speculation or conjecture." *Gaste v. Kaiserman*, 863 F.2d 1061, 1066 (2d Cir. 1988). In order to support a claim of access, a plaintiff must offer "significant, affirmative and probative evidence." *Scott v. Paramount Pictures Corp.*, 449 F. Supp. 518, 520 (D.D.C. 1978), *aff'd*, 607 F.2d 494 (D.C. Cir. 1979) (table), *cert. denied*, 449 U.S. 849, 101 S.Ct. 137 (1980).

1. *The mass mailings of "Lover"*

Jorgensen argues, first, that his act of mailing unsolicited tapes of "Lover" to scores of record and music publishing companies, including the corporate defendants, constituted access because the corporate employees who allegedly received the mailing could have provided the "Heart" and "Amazed" songwriters with a copy of "Lover." With two exceptions reviewed below, however, Jorgensen has not provided *any* reasonable documentation that he actually mailed such tapes (or when or to whom these tapes were purportedly sent). Jorgensen's mass-mailing allegation was, thus, properly rejected by the District Court as legally insufficient proof of access. 2002 WL 31119377, at *5 (noting that Jorgensen "did not maintain a log of where and when he sent his work, or keep receipts from certified mailings to establish a chain of access"); *see also Dimmie v.*

Carey, 88 F. Supp. 2d 142, 146 (S.D.N.Y. 2000) (rejecting plaintiff's claim that the mailing of tapes to a corporation could "be equated with access" where there was no evidence that the tapes were ever received or forwarded to the alleged infringers); *Jorgensen v. Careers BMG Music Publ'g*, No. 01 Civ. 0357, 2002 WL 1492123, at *4–5 (S.D.N.Y. July 11, 2002) (Preska, J.) ("*Jorgensen I*").[4]

2. The submissions to Pollock and Leeds

Jorgensen's second and more narrow theory of access, predicated on Pollock's and Leeds's admissions that they received Jorgensen's submissions, was also rejected by the District Court. . . .

a. *Pollock and the "Amazed" defendants*

In his sworn declaration, Pollock stated that his job as a managing producer in BMG's Special Products division "has nothing to do with the publishing company, Careers BMG Music Publishing, Inc., or working creatively with songwriters at all." Although he conceded that he had received a CD recording of "Lover," Pollock denied that he had ever listened to the song and asserted that he never conveyed the CD "to anyone at any time," much less anyone who "contributed creative ideas or material" to "Amazed" or "Heart." In fact, Jorgensen conceded at his deposition that he had no knowledge that Pollock did anything with the CD that Jorgensen sent to him. Pollock stated that he did not have *any* relationship with the writers of "Amazed," and Jorgensen has submitted no evidence to the contrary. *Cf. Towler v. Sayles*, 76 F.3d 579, 583 (4th Cir. 1996) ("A court may infer that the alleged infringer had a reasonable possibility of access if the author sent the copyrighted work to a third party intermediary who has a *close relationship* with the infringer. An intermediary will fall within this category, for example, if she supervises or works in the same department as the infringer or contributes creative ideas to him.").

Jorgensen's claim against the "Amazed" defendants was properly dismissed because he has not offered any evidence to rebut Pollock's assertions. The most that Jorgensen offers to show a nexus between Pollock and the "Amazed" songwriters is his global assertion that "anything and everything can very well happen." Such speculation does not give rise to a triable issue of access. Jorgensen has not adduced proof of a reasonable possibility that "the paths of [the "Amazed" songwriters] and the infringed work crossed." *Towler*, 76 F.3d at 582. Bare corporate receipt of Jorgensen's work, without any allegation of a nexus between

---

[4] In *Jorgensen I*, a separate action filed the same day as this action, Jorgensen alleged copyright infringement of another of his songs by Eric Clapton's Grammy Award-winning song, "Change the World." The district court granted summary judgment for defendants, finding that Jorgensen's "evidence of access was speculative and/or legally insufficient [such that] no rational fact finder could find in favor of [him]." Jorgensen has not appealed in *Jorgensen I*.

the recipients and the alleged infringers, is insufficient to raise a triable issue of access.

b. Leeds and the "Heart" defendants

At his deposition, Leeds admitted that he had received tapes from Jorgensen but stated that he did not listen to them and he believed that they had been discarded. Leeds testified that his job as a Sony vice president involved reviewing promotional touring budgets and that he was "not involved in the A & R process." Leeds also stated that he did not know the "Heart" songwriters.

Citing this evidence (and echoing their arguments with respect to Pollock), the defendants assert that the mere fact that Leeds had received a copy of Jorgensen's song does not mean that the "Heart" songwriters had a reasonable opportunity to hear it. Defendants argue that it is "undisputed" that Leeds did not forward Jorgensen's tape to the "Heart" songwriters, but they do not address the evidence introduced by Jorgensen that Leeds and his assistants repeatedly told Jorgensen that his tapes—including, in particular, one containing the song "Lover"—were being sent to Sony's A & R department. Leeds, at his deposition, disputed Jorgensen's version of events, testifying that he did not recall ever making such a promise to Jorgensen and that he likely threw Jorgensen's tapes away. Leeds also conceded, though, that it was possible that if there was a tape that he received that he found interesting he might "pass it on" to one of his "friends in the A & R department."

To draw a connection between Sony's A & R department and Horner and Jennings, the creators of "Heart," Jorgensen relied on Sony's admission, in its response to his Request for Admissions, that during the relevant time period, "on limited occasions, writers, producers or musicians affiliated with Sony may have been shown some material solicited by the A & R Dept . . ." In concluding that Leeds "did not forward Jorgensen's package," the District Court made no mention of (i) Jorgensen's deposition testimony to the contrary or (ii) Sony's admission regarding the practices of its A & R Department.

Although the defendants accurately note that Jorgensen has put forth no evidence that the "Heart" songwriters *actually* heard his song, that argument misapprehends Jorgensen's burden. Jorgensen must show a "reasonable possibility of access" by the alleged infringer. He is not required to establish *actual* access.

. . . What is not clear from the record before us is whether Horner and Jennings were songwriters "affiliated" with Sony in the period between when Jorgensen sent his tapes to Sony and when "Heart" was published. Absent some evidence on this issue, a jury could not reasonably infer simply from Sony's access to Jorgensen's work that Horner and Jennings also had such access.

As already noted, it is the defendant seeking summary judgment who must demonstrate a lack of evidence supporting an essential element of plaintiff's claim. The "Heart" defendants, who undoubtedly possess information about the time frame of Sony's affiliation with Horner and Jennings, failed to support their summary judgment motion with any evidence showing the lack of a relationship during the relevant period.[8] Because Jorgensen, appearing *pro se*, may not have appreciated the need to develop this particular evidence in discovery, summary judgment should not have been granted to defendants until the timing of any affiliation was clarified. Viewing the evidence adduced thus far in the light most favorable to Jorgensen and drawing all justifiable inferences in his favor, as we must at the summary judgment stage, we find that the District Court erred in granting summary judgment to the "Heart" defendants. Of course, it would be well within the District Court's discretion to permit limited discovery into the question of the timing of the songwriters' affiliation with Sony and to entertain a renewed motion for summary judgment, as may be appropriate. . . .

CONCLUSION

We have reviewed the record and considered all of Jorgensen's remaining contentions and find them to be without merit. We therefore AFFIRM the District Court's grant of summary judgment in favor of Defendants Careers BMG Music Publishing, Songs of Nashville Dreamworks, and Warner-Tamerlane Publishing Corporation. With respect to Defendants Famous Music Corporation, Fox Film Music Corporation, Blue Sky Rider Songs, and Sony Music Entertainment Inc., however, we VACATE the District Court's grant of summary judgment and remand the case for further proceedings not inconsistent with this opinion. . . .

NOTES AND QUESTIONS

1. *Jorgenson* involves both a presumption and an inference. Presumptions are discussed in note 6 following *Celotex*. Presumptions are especially important in copyright. It can be difficult for a copyright owner suing for infringement to prove defendant actually copied his work. To get around this practical problem, courts will allow plaintiff a presumption: they will presume defendant copied if plaintiff can show that defendant had access to the work, and that defendant's work was substantially similar to plaintiff's. Had Jorgenson been able to show access and substantial

---

[8] The most that the "Heart" defendants offer to challenge the connection between Sony's A & R Department and the alleged infringers is defense counsel's claim in his affidavit that "*upon information and belief,* neither Horner nor Jennings are associated as songwriters with Sony." (emphasis added). That supposition, however, is too tentative to qualify as evidence warranting summary judgment. *See* Fed. R. Civ. P. 56(e) ("Supporting . . . affidavits shall be made on personal knowledge, shall set forth such facts as would be admissible in evidence, and shall show affirmatively that the affiant is competent to testify to the matters stated therein.")

similarity, the burden would switch to defendants to prove that they had *not* copied the work in question.

In the case itself, however, Jorgenson had no evidence that defendants had access to his work. He was instead asking the court to *infer* access based on the fact he had sent copies of his work to some of the defendants.

2. Is the *Jorgenson* court saying that inferences are never allowed? Can a plaintiff ever prevail if it has only circumstantial evidence? If circumstantial evidence is allowed, what test does the court use to determine what inferences are possible?

3. There is an important difference between a presumption and an inference. As noted above, a presumption switches the burden of production. If the court agrees to allow an inference, by contrast, there is no change in the burden. Instead, the party uses the presumption to help it satisfy its burden of producing facts. Allowing the inference only means the issue goes to the jury. In most cases, the jury can determine for itself whether the inference is the most likely version of the story.

4. Conversely, in some situations an inference can be so likely that the jury *must* believe it. Be prepared to offer a hypothetical example of an inference meeting this standard.

5. Consider the following statement: "Negligence cases by their very nature do not usually lend themselves to summary judgment, since often, even if all parties are in agreement as to the underlying facts, the very question of negligence is itself a question for jury determination." *Ugarriza v. Schmieder*, 46 N.Y.2d 471, 474, 386 N.E.2d 1324, 1325, 414 N.Y.S.2d 304, 305 (1979). Do you understand what the court is saying? Is a finding of negligence a finding of fact, or an inference to be drawn from the facts? See *Borden v. CSX Transportation, Inc.*, 843 F.Supp. 1410 (M.D. Ala. 1993) (even when facts are undisputed, whether a particular act constitutes negligence is a jury question); *Roy v. Inhabitants of City of Lewiston*, 42 F.3d 691 (1st Cir. 1994) (judgments about whether a party acted reasonably are made by the jury).

Nevertheless, do not conclude that courts will not grant summary judgment in negligence cases. A quick search will reveal many cases in which summary judgment was granted. For one instructive example, see *Sharpe v. United States*, 936 F.2d 1178 (11th Cir. 1991) (summary judgment for plaintiff). Some of these cases involve proof that defendant was negligent *per se* because he violated a statutory standard. In others, the facts were such that the court concluded that no reasonable jury could conclude defendant's acts were reasonable.

Are there any other issues exclusively within the province of the jury? How about the question of whether two parties have a contract? What about the issue of whether a written contract was ambiguous? On this latter issue, see *ESI, Inc. v. Coastal Power Prod. Co.*, 13 F.Supp.2d 495 (S.D.N.Y. 1998).

6. A summary judgment is a final judgment. If one party is held liable to the other, the winner can collect on the judgment. Similarly, the loser can appeal the judgment to a higher court. However, neither the *denial* of a summary judgment nor the grant of a *partial* summary judgment on fewer than all the issues relevant to a party's claim are considered final judgments. The parties must ordinarily wait until the remainder of the case is resolved before they can collect and/or appeal.

A denial of summary judgment or grant of partial summary judgment can, however, motivate serious settlement discussions. Why do you think this is so? How might one of these decisions affect the parties' perspectives on the potential outcome of the case?

PROBLEMS

1. P sues D for trespass. D's answer admits that she intentionally was on P's property on the date in question. However, D also claims in her answer that at the time she had a good-faith belief that *she* owned the property instead of P. Although D now admits the property belongs to P, she claims her good faith belief shields her from liability for trespass. P disagrees. As P understands the law, a person is liable for trespass whenever he is intentionally on property that belongs to another, even if the person was mistaken as to who owned the property. What motion—12(b)(6), 12(c), or summary judgment—will allow P to test whether his knowledge of the law is correct, and if so, avoid a trial?

2. P sues D for trespass. D's answer admits she was on the land, but asserts that she, not P, owns the land. P has incontrovertible proof that the land belongs to him. D has no proof other than her conclusory statement in her answer. What motion—12(b)(6), 12(c), or summary judgment—will allow P to avoid a trial?

3. Same as Problem 2, except D's answer specifies that she owns the land "pursuant to an oral conveyance from X, which occurred before the date on which D is alleged to have trespassed." Under governing law, a conveyance of real property is not valid unless it is in writing. What motion—12(b)(6), 12(c), or summary judgment—will allow P to avoid a trial?

4. P sues D for fraud in connection with the sale of corporate stock, based on D's glowing representations concerning the future prospects of the corporation. Before filing his answer, D moves for summary judgment. D's motion claims P has no evidence whatsoever tending to show that D knew that his statements were false. Under governing law, a claim for fraud requires proof that the defendant knew the statements were false. Is D's motion timely? Assuming D is correct that P has no evidence that D knew the statements were false, is a court likely to grant summary judgment for D at this juncture?

5. Same as Problem 4, except that D makes its motion after discovery is complete. D's motion simply states, "After extensive discovery, it is clear P has no evidence of a crucial element of a fraud claim; namely, D's knowledge

Sec. B   Judgment as a Matter of Law

that the statements concerning the corporation were false." Is D's motion sufficient?

6. Same as Problem 4, except that D makes its motion after discovery is complete. P's evidence of D's knowledge consists of a statement D made to one of his colleagues. This statement makes it clear D knew the corporation did not have a rosy future. However, this statement was made two weeks *after* D made the representations to P. Will the court grant D's motion?

7. P and D sell very similar products. P sues D for false advertising, based on D's advertising campaign. After discovery, both P and D move for summary judgment. P has evidence that the claims in the advertisement were false, and that D intended to deceive consumers. However, a false advertising claim requires proof that consumers were deceived to their detriment. Because P has been unable to track down any of the people who bought D's product, P has no evidence whatsoever that anyone actually relied on the advertisement. On the other hand, governing law also creates a presumption: if a plaintiff can show that its competitor intended to deceive consumers, courts will presume consumers were in fact deceived. Are either P or D entitled to summary judgment? Does it depend on what evidence D has on the question of reliance?

8. P sues D for defamation, claiming that D is falsely accusing P of infringing D's patented process for preparing lutefisk (cod cured in lye, which is definitely an acquired taste). D counterclaims for patent infringement. In order to prevail on the patent infringement claim, the patent holder must show that the infringing party "made, used, or sold" a product using the patented process. After discovery, P learns that D has no evidence that P made, used, or sold lutefisk using D's process. Can P move for summary judgment? If the motion succeeds, will the court also throw out P's claim?

B. JUDGMENT AS A MATTER OF LAW

INTRODUCTORY PROBLEM 1

Same basic scenario as the Introductory Problem to Part A of this Chapter, except assume summary judgment was denied.

The parties conduct some additional discovery, and the case goes to trial before a jury. At trial, Green calls Driver to the stand. Driver is one of Lon's employees. Driver testifies that on the date in question, Lon asked him to take certain equipment out to a crew working at a certain address. Driver could not find a crew at that address. However, he saw a crew working at Green's house. When Driver informed the crew boss that he had a delivery, the crew boss said, "Thanks, we were expecting Lon to send that stuff." (Assume this testimony is not barred by the hearsay evidence rule.)

Later in the case, Lon himself takes the stand. Lon cannot remember whether he sent Driver anywhere on the date in question. However, Lon then claims that he also had a contract with Green, under which Lon was to remove Green's trees. Lon introduces a written contract with a signature that looks like Green's on it.

Green, however, anticipated this ploy. After Lon steps down, Green calls several witnesses to impeach Lon's testimony. First, these witnesses testify that Lon has three convictions for forgery, all arising out of situations where Lon forged customers' signatures on contracts. Second, Green calls Lon's secretary to the stand. The secretary testifies that, soon after Green filed suit against Lon, she saw Lon writing Green's name on a piece of paper. On this same paper, Lon also wrote a date that was two weeks prior to the date on which Green's trees were removed—the exact same date as the contract that Lon is now using to prove his case at trial. However, because of the lighting and the angle, the secretary cannot say whether the paper that Lon was writing on was the same as the contract that he is now introducing.

At the close of all the evidence, Green moves for judgment as a matter of law. Lon protests, arguing that the jury should decide the case.

Governing Rule: Federal Rule 50.

INTRODUCTORY PROBLEM 2

Same as Introductory Problem One, except that the court denies the motion. The case goes to the jury, which renders a verdict for Lon. Green asks the judge to ignore the jury verdict, and enter judgment for him instead. May the judge enter judgment for Green?

Governing Rule: Federal Rule 50(b).

Summary judgment prevents a trial from occurring. If a case survives summary judgment and makes it to trial, each party is entitled to present its evidence to the factfinder. However, what if the evidence presented at trial makes it clear that one side will prevail? In this situation, a party may move for "judgment as a matter of law" under Rule 50. Under that Rule, a court will grant a party's motion for judgment as a matter of law if "a reasonable jury would not have a legally sufficient evidentiary basis to find for" the opposing side.

For all practical purposes, judgment as a matter of law keeps the case from the jury. However, a court can grant judgment as a matter of law either before the case is submitted to the jury under Rule 50(a), or after the jury returns with a verdict under Rule 50(b). If judgment is granted pre-verdict, the case is truly "kept from" the jury, as the jury does not get to deliberate and decide the matter. If judgment is granted post-verdict, the jury does deliberate and render a verdict, but the judge disregards the verdict and enters a judgment for the verdict loser. Either way, the judge, not the jury, decides the issue.

SEC. B   JUDGMENT AS A MATTER OF LAW   585

The phrase "judgment as a matter of law" is of relatively recent vintage. Historically, courts used the term "directed verdict" to refer to the situation where the judge rendered judgment before the case was submitted to the jury.[1] After the jury returned with a verdict, the court could set aside the jury's findings and enter a "judgment notwithstanding the verdict"—often referred to by the Latin equivalent "judgment *non obstante veredicto*," or simply "JNOV." Although the Rule was amended in 1991 to adopt a uniform terminology, many still prefer the old terminology, as opposed to the somewhat more cumbersome "pre-verdict judgment as a matter of law" and "post-verdict judgment as a matter of law."

When is it appropriate for a court to render judgment as a matter of law? How does the Rule 50 standard compare with the standard for rendering summary judgment? The following case discusses how the Rule 50 standard apples.

KINSERLOW V. CMI CORP., BID-WELL DIV.
217 F.3d 1021 (8th Cir. 2000)

BATAILLON, DISTRICT JUDGE . . .

I. BACKGROUND

Kinserlow, a cement mason working for Fred Weber, Inc. (FWI), brought this action for personal injuries against CMI Corporation, Bid-Well Division (Bid-Well), after he fell from a bridge over a highway in St. Louis County, Missouri. At the time he fell, Kinserlow was operating a bull float, walking backwards and forward on a mini workbridge behind a Bid-Well paving machine, smoothing out concrete. The workbridge had tapered end sections, but no written or painted warnings or guard rails to alert workers that they were coming to the end of the workbridge. Kinserlow, walking backwards, fell from the end of the workbridge to the ground 18' below. He was severely hurt, and his injuries still cause him debilitating pain. His suit against Bid-Well alleged strict liability and negligence.

The primary issue in the suit was the identity of the company that had manufactured the workbridge and then sold or supplied it to FWI. According to the testimony of Kinserlow's witnesses, Bid-Well and another company, Gomaco, both manufacture steel workbridges similar to the one from which Kinserlow fell. Kinserlow's workbridge had lost any identifying markings or labels it might have once had, having apparently been in FWI's inventory since before 1977. The primary evidentiary hurdle for Kinserlow was to establish that Bid-Well manufactured and

---

[1] The phrase "directed verdict" stems from the historic practice of having the judge submit the case to the jury with strict instructions to decide the case in favor of one party. Today, courts have dispensed with that formality, and simply render judgment for the prevailing party.

then sold or supplied the workbridge to FWI. An FWI employee testified that at the time of Kinserlow's accident, FWI had two types of workbridges in inventory, one with filled-in metal triangles placed in the frame and another without filled-in metal triangles but with tapered end sections. Kinserlow's workbridge was one of the latter, and he alleged that Bid-Well had manufactured and sold or supplied it to FWI.

Two FWI employees testified that in their experience, once a concrete company purchased a workbridge and a paving machine, from whatever source, the two pieces of equipment are generally kept together as a set. Kinserlow himself testified that when he worked with a Bid-Well paving machine, he always used a workbridge identical to the one from which he fell. He also testified that when he worked for a different concrete company, he saw Bid-Well paving machines used with workbridges with tapered end sections like the one from which he fell. On the day of his accident, his workbridge was paired with a Bid-Well paving machine. The two pieces of equipment had been in FWI's inventory since at least 1977.

Kinserlow's witnesses offered no direct documentary evidence that Bid-Well had ever sold or supplied a workbridge to FWI prior to the date of the accident, and the FWI employee who would have been responsible for buying the workbridge is deceased. Kinserlow therefore attempted to establish through inference that Bid-Well had sold FWI the workbridge in question. For example, Thomas Held, the president of Allied Construction Company, Bid-Well's primary competitor in the steel workbridge market, testified during Kinserlow's case in chief that Allied Construction was the exclusive distributor of Gomaco paving machines and workbridges in the St. Louis area. Held testified that he could find but one invoice recording a sale of a Gomaco workbridge to FWI; that sale occurred in 1980 and did not involve the sale of a paving machine. He also testified that the Gomaco workbridges he was familiar with—those manufactured and sold after 1984, the year he began working for Allied Construction—all had metal triangles inserted in their frames, unlike the workbridge from which Kinserlow fell.

On cross-examination, however, Held testified that he could not say whether Gomaco workbridges manufactured and sold before 1984 had such triangles. He also did not know what types of workbridges FWI had in inventory on the day of the accident, whether FWI had purchased a Gomaco workbridge from a source other than Allied Construction, or whether Bid-Well had ever sold workbridges with tapered end sections. Kinserlow and his other witnesses made similar admissions on cross-examination: they did not know whether Bid-Well had ever manufactured or sold a workbridge with tapered end sections, or whether Bid-Well had ever sold or supplied a workbridge to FWI prior to the accident.

In contrast, Bid-Well's witness Daniel Napierala, a long-time Gomaco employee, testified that since 1968 when it began building workbridges,

Gomaco alone had been making workbridges with tapered end sections. Napierala said that he had never seen a tapered end section built by Bid-Well or by any other competitor in his seventeen years in the industry. He also testified that beginning in 1984, Gomaco began to put metal triangles on the frame of its workbridges so that warning labels could be attached to the workbridge. He further testified that as an exclusive Gomaco distributor, Allied Construction would have sold only new Gomaco equipment. FWI nevertheless could have acquired its inventory of Gomaco workbridges from a source other than Allied. Bid-Well's only other witness, Jack Lease, has been a Bid-Well employee since 1970. He was originally hired as a design draftsman, and is now Bid-Well's vice president and sales manager. He testified that Bid-Well began manufacturing and selling workbridges in 1975, but had never manufactured or sold workbridges with tapered end sections.

Kinserlow appeals the decision of the trial court to grant Bid-Well's motion, renewed at the close of evidence, for judgment as a matter of law under Federal Rule of Civil Procedure 50(a). The trial court found that Kinserlow failed to establish by a preponderance that Bid-Well—rather than some other manufacturer—had manufactured, sold, or distributed the tapered end section of the workbridge from which Kinserlow fell. Kinserlow argues that the trial court's decision to grant judgment as a matter of law was incorrect because the court improperly weighed the facts presented by the plaintiff against the facts presented by the defendant. Kinserlow contends that the court should have given him the benefit of all beneficial inferences and not considered any of Bid-Well's evidence except as it might have helped his case.

II. DISCUSSION

In both Rule 56 motions for summary judgment and Rule 50 motions for judgment as a matter of law, the inquiry is the same: "Whether the evidence presents a sufficient disagreement to require submission to a jury or whether it is so one-sided that one party must prevail as a matter of law." *Anderson v. Liberty Lobby, Inc.*, 477 U.S. 242, 251–52 (1986). Rule 50(a) allows the judge in a jury trial to enter judgment against a party with respect to a claim or defense "that cannot under the controlling law be maintained or defeated without a favorable finding on that issue," when the party has been fully heard on the issue and "there is no legally sufficient evidentiary basis for a reasonable jury to find for that party on the issue." Fed. R. Civ. P. 50(a).

Our review of the district court's decision is de novo, using the same standards as the district court. The court views the evidence "in the light most favorable to the [nonmoving] party and must not engage in a weighing or evaluation of the evidence or consider questions of credibility." *Smith v. World Ins. Co.*, 38 F.3d 1456, 1460 (8th Cir. 1994). The court should grant judgment as a matter of law "only when all of the evidence points one way and is 'susceptible of no reasonable inference sustaining the position of the nonmoving party.'" *Id.* . . .

The Court [in *Reeves v. Sanderson Plumbing Prods., Inc.*, 530 U.S. 133, 150 (2000)] stated that when entertaining a motion for judgment as a matter of law, a trial court "should review all of the evidence in the record."

> In doing so, however, the court must draw all reasonable inferences in favor of the nonmoving party, and it may not make credibility determinations or weigh the evidence. 'Credibility determinations, the weighing of evidence, and the drawing of legitimate inferences from the facts are jury functions, not those of a judge. Thus, although the court should review the records as a whole, it must disregard all evidence favorable to the moving party that the jury is not required to believe. That is, the court should give credence to the evidence favoring the nonmovant as well as that 'evidence supporting the moving party that is uncontradicted and unimpeached, at least to the extent that that evidence comes from disinterested witnesses.'

Id. at 150–51 (citations omitted).

Kinserlow argues that the evidence he presented at trial, if taken in the light most favorable to him, established by a preponderance that Bid-Well supplied the tapered-end workbridge to FWI. He contends that had the trial court properly drawn all inferences in his favor and avoided weighing his evidence against Bid-Well's, the court would have submitted his case to the jury. Kinserlow argues that he was entitled to the inference that he was on a Bid-Well workbridge when he fell because Gomaco workbridges have metal triangles inserted in their frames; his did not. Moreover, he contends that a Bid-Well sales brochure that showed a Bid-Well paving machine paired with a Gomaco workbridge created an inference that Bid-Well would not have advertised an item in its brochure so substantially similar to the workbridge from which Kinserlow fell unless Bid-Well itself also manufactured or sold such a workbridge.

In a motion for judgment as a matter of law, the nonmoving party is only entitled to the benefit of reasonable inferences. *Fought v. Hayes Wheels Int'l, Inc.*, 101 F.3d 1275, 1277 (8th Cir. 1996). A "reasonable inference is one 'which may be drawn from the evidence without resort to speculation. When the record contains no proof beyond speculation to support the verdict, judgment as a matter of law is appropriate.'" *Id.* (citations omitted). The record is not clear whether the district court rejected as unreasonable the inferences urged on it by Kinserlow or allowed them as reasonable but found them unpersuasive on the issue of product identification. What is clear, however, is that the court evaluated all the evidence in the record in reaching its decision to grant Bid-Well's motion for judgment as a matter of law. The court stated that

> the burden is on the Plaintiff to prove by a preponderance of the evidence that—its case, and I have reached the conclusion in this case that he has not done so and that I will not submit the case to the Jury. I don't believe that there is a legally sufficient evidentiary basis for a reasonable jury to find for the party on the issue of product identification. And in a preponderance of the evidence case, it's—if it's equally divided between the parties, then the party that has the burden—in this case, the Plaintiff—I must rule against them. There's just not enough evidence, in the Court's view, to show that the Defendant CMI, the Bid-Well Division, manufactured, sold, distributed, or placed in the stream of commerce the workbridge tapered end section.

Although the trial court mentions "equally divided" proof, suggesting a weighing of evidence, the court also indicates that Kinserlow failed to meet his burden of production. The evidence as outlined above does not support a reasonable inference that the only Gomaco workbridge in FWI's inventory was acquired in the single sale evidenced by the 1980 Allied Construction invoice. The evidence does not support an inference that Bid-Well paving machines are always paired with Bid-Well workbridges, or that FWI acquired the workbridge from which Kinserlow fell at the same time it acquired the Bid-Well paving machine with which it was paired. Nor does the evidence support an inference that because the workbridge from which Kinserlow fell lacked metal triangle inserts, it was therefore manufactured by Bid-Well. Kinserlow's witnesses could not establish that he fell from a Bid-Well workbridge because they could not testify that Bid-Well had ever manufactured or sold a workbridge with tapered end sections, or that Bid-Well had ever sold or supplied a workbridge to FWI prior to the accident. The trial court did not weigh Kinserlow's evidence against Bid-Well's or make credibility determinations. The trial court simply found that Kinserlow had not offered enough evidence to tie Bid-Well to the workbridge from which Kinserlow fell.

In reaching this conclusion, the court was entitled to give credence to any of Bid-Well's evidence that was "'uncontradicted and unimpeached, at least to the extent that that evidence [came] from disinterested witnesses.'" *Reeves v. Sanderson Plumbing Prods., Inc.*, at 150–51. Kinserlow does not appear to have contradicted or impeached the testimony of Bid-Well's disinterested witness, Gomaco employee Daniel Napierala, that 1) only Gomaco had ever made workbridges with tapered end sections, and 2) Gomaco did not insert metal triangles into the frames of its workbridges until 1984. A strong inference to be drawn from this testimony is that the workbridge from which Kinserlow fell was in fact not manufactured by Bid-Well but by Gomaco prior to 1984. This inference is consistent with the testimony of Kinserlow's own disinterested witness, Thomas Held of Allied Construction, that the Gomaco workbridges with which he was familiar—only those manufactured and sold after 1984, the year he began working for Allied Construction—all had metal triangle inserts. Finally, the inference is consistent with the testimony of Bid-Well's interested witness, Jack Lease, that Bid-Well had never sold or manufactured a tapered end workbridge during his nearly thirty year tenure with the company. . . .

III. CONCLUSION

For the foregoing reasons, the decision of the district court is affirmed.

NOTES AND QUESTIONS

1. The plaintiff in *Kinserlow* claimed that judgment as a matter of law was improper because the judge had "weighed the evidence" in the case. Does that argument correctly reflect the standard set out in Rule 50? Is a court considering a motion for judgment as a matter of law supposed to determine which side has presented a stronger case?

2. The court indicates that plaintiff has no direct evidence showing that the workbridge on which he was injured was manufactured by defendant. Therefore, this case involves an *inference*, much like the *Jorgenson* case in the prior section. But does the defendant in *Kinserlow* really have any direct evidence showing that it did *not* manufacture the workbridge? Indeed, isn't the defendant also asking the court to make an inference in its favor?

Does defendant need any evidence as to who manufactured the workbridge? Would the court have issued judgment as a matter of law if defendant had not introduced the testimony of the Gomaco employee?

3. *Burden of production*. Like summary judgment, judgment as a matter of law turns on the burden of production. If the party without the burden moves for judgment as a matter of law (*e.g.*, a defendant moving for judgment on plaintiff's claim), it can prevail merely by showing that no reasonable jury could find for the other party on one or more elements of the claim or defense. Given the importance of the burden of production, can a court ever grant judgment as a matter of law *for* the party with the burden of production on an issue?

To illustrate, suppose plaintiff sues defendant for breach of an oral contract. Defendant denies there is a contract. At trial, plaintiff offers 20 witnesses who testify that they heard defendant agree to the terms of the contract. Defendant offers no testimony whatsoever. Plaintiff then moves for judgment as a matter of law. Even though plaintiff is the only party who has offered evidence, isn't the jury entitled to disbelieve all that evidence? Re-read carefully the quote from the Supreme Court's *Reeves* case set out in

Kinserlow. Are plaintiff's 20 witnesses interested or disinterested? What if the witnesses are plaintiff's employees? Plaintiff's neighbors?

Although it is fairly uncommon, courts do grant judgment as a matter of law for plaintiffs. See, e.g., *Hurd v. American Hoist and Derrick Co.*, 734 F.2d 495 (10th Cir. 1984) (judgment as matter of law for plaintiff in products liability case); *United States v. Kwoczak*, 210 F.Supp.2d 638 (E.D. Pa. 2002) (judgment as a matter of law for United States in deportation proceeding was appropriate even though the government has the burden of showing grounds for deportation by "clear, unequivocal, and convincing evidence"—a higher burden than that which applies in most civil cases).

4. *Bench trials.* Rule 50 applies only in cases tried before a jury. However, Rule 52(c) provides for a similar mechanism in bench trials. Is the standard under the two rules the same? When determining whether to grant judgment as a matter of law in a bench trial, may the judge weigh conflicting evidence? Does the judge have to draw all reasonable inferences in favor of the nonmoving party?

5. *Summary judgment and judgment as a matter of law compared.* Rule 50 provides that judgment as a matter of law is appropriate when "a reasonable jury would not have a legally sufficient evidentiary basis to find for" the non-moving party. How does that standard compare to the "no genuine dispute as to any material fact" standard for summary judgment set out in Rule 56? After comparing the standards, are you surprised by the statement in *Kinserlow* that the standard for granting judgment as a matter of law is the same as the standard for summary judgment? In fact, you can find hundreds of other decisions containing similar statements. See, e.g., *Schnabel v. Abramson*, 232 F.3d 83 (2d Cir. 2000); *Appelbaum v. Milwaukee Metro. Sewerage Dist.*, 340 F.3d 573 (7th Cir. 2003); *Computer Access Tech. Corp. v. Catalyst Enters., Inc.*, 273 F.Supp.2d 1063 (N.D. Cal. 2003); *Mohr v. Chicago Sch. Reform Bd. of Trs. of the Bd. of Educ.*, 155 F.Supp.2d 923 (N.D. Ill. 2001).

In actual practice, however, there is a small, but real, difference between how willing courts are to keep cases from the jury under the two rules. Generally speaking, it is slightly easier for a party to win a judgment as a matter of law than it is a summary judgment. Why might this be so? Is it attributable to the different wording of the two rules? Or is the difference caused by more practical factors? To what extent could the difference be due to the fact that a judge hearing a motion for summary judgment usually considers only documentary evidence such as affidavits and deposition transcripts, while the judge hearing a Rule 50 motion has heard live witnesses who have been cross-examined in the courtroom? On the other hand, if the judge is not to determine credibility under either Rule, should this difference matter?

6. Some have also suggested there is a difference in the way judges evaluate pre-verdict and post-verdict motions for judgment as a matter of law. *See, e.g., EEOC v. Kohler Co.*, 335 F.3d 766 (8th Cir. 2003). Can you

think of any practical reasons why this might be so? The standard for granting judgment as a matter of law is that "no reasonable jury" could find for the nonmoving party. Put yourself in the shoes of a judge who is considering a post-verdict motion for judgment as a matter of law. If you grant the motion, what are you saying?

7. Read Rule 50 carefully and answer the following questions:

a. D is confident that P has failed to prove her case. D is accordingly surprised when the jury returns a verdict for P. D therefore first files for judgment as a matter of law following the jury verdict. May the court grant the motion?

b. D moves for judgment as a matter of law at the close of P's case. The court denies the motion. D then presents his evidence and the case is submitted to the jury. When the jury returns a verdict for P, D again files a motion for judgment as a matter of law. May the court grant the motion?

Why does Rule 50 require a pre-verdict motion for judgment as a matter of law as a precondition to filing a post-verdict motion? Somewhat surprisingly, the answer has to do with the constitutional right to a jury trial. As you will see in Chapter 12, the seventh amendment merely "preserves" the right to a jury trial as it existed in the late 1700s. It also explicitly provides that "no fact tried by a jury, shall be otherwise reexamined in any Court of the United States, than according to the rules of the common law." In 1792, the common-law courts allowed a court to render judgment as a matter of law before the case was submitted to the jury. However, there was no way the court could overturn the jury once it had rendered its verdict (although the judge could grant a new trial). This historical practice would seem to prevent federal courts from granting a post-verdict judgment as a matter of law.

To get around this constitutional problem, Rule 50 engages in some definitional sleight of hand. Rule 50(a)(2) states that a motion for judgment as a matter of law can only be made before the case is submitted the jury (in other words, the party must move for a pre-verdict judgment as a matter of law). If the judge denies the pre-verdict motion, Rule 50(b) states that that denial "is considered" to be a decision to *delay* ruling. If the moving party files a "renewed" motion after the jury verdict (that is, moves for a post-verdict judgment), the judge can then make a delayed ruling. Of course, the rule is merely a legal fiction. If the party who moved pre-verdict does not move again after the verdict, the judge will not issue a delayed ruling.

Note that prior to December 1, 2006, the result in question (b) above would have been different. The previous version of the Rule specifically required that the pre-verdict motion be made "at the close of all the evidence." The Rule was amended in 2006 to allow any pre-verdict motion to suffice.

8. There are many cases in which a judge has denied a pre-verdict motion for judgment as a matter of law at the close of all the evidence, only to grant the "renewed" motion after the jury has returned with the verdict.

Given that no additional evidence has been offered, what could possibly cause the judge to change her mind? Again, the explanation for this phenomenon is practical. First, if the judge truly feels no reasonable jury could find for the nonmoving side, she may think the odds are quite high that the jury will agree with her and rule for the moving side. Courts of appeal will overturn a judgment as a matter of law if there was a reasonable chance the nonmoving side could have won. A jury verdict, by comparison, is virtually unassailable on appeal. Therefore, the judge would rather have the jury render the decision.

Second, consider what happens if the judge is *wrong* in granting judgment as a matter of law. If the judge grants a pre-verdict motion for judgment as a matter of law, and the court of appeals reverses, what happens? What happens if the judge overturns the jury verdict by rendering a post-verdict judgment as a matter of law and the court of appeals reverses?

9. Suppose the court submits the case to the jury, and the jury deadlocks. Can the court nevertheless grant a timely motion for judgment as a matter of law? Does the fact that this jury could not agree on a verdict mean that reasonable minds could differ? *See Headwaters Forest Defense v. County of Humboldt*, 240 F.3d 1185 (9th Cir. 2000), *judgment vacated on other grounds* 534 U.S. 801, 122 S.Ct. 24, 151 L.Ed.2d 1 (2001).

10. Rule 50 requires a party to file a pre-verdict motion for judgment as a matter of law before it may file a post-verdict motion. By "renewing" the pre-verdict motion after the jury has returned, the party has a chance to ask the judge to reconsider her earlier decision. But can a party forego the post-verdict motion, and simply ask the appellate court to review the trial court's ruling on the pre-verdict motion? The Supreme Court addressed this issue in *Unitherm Food Systems, Inc. v. Swift-Eckrich, Inc.*, 546 U.S. 394, 126 S.Ct. 980, 163 L.Ed.2d 974 (2006), holding that a party must file the post-verdict motion in order to preserve the right to appeal the denial of pre-verdict motion. The Court held that the language of Rule 50 dictated the result.

PROBLEMS

1. P owns a beachfront lot. P's lot is 300 feet deep (measured from the water's edge to the back end of the lot), and 75 feet wide. The beach itself, however, extends inland for only 25 feet. Under state law, a party owns the beach, and can prevent others from using it. P sues D for trespassing on his beachfront lot. D denies that she trespassed. At trial, P's evidence consists of the testimony of two witnesses, W1 and W2. Neither W1 nor W2 actually saw D on P's land. W1 saw D at 8:00 p.m. on the beach of the lot immediately south of P's land. W1 testifies that D was walking north. W2 saw D at 8:15 p.m., standing on the beach of the lot immediately to the *north* of P's lot. D was completely dry when W2 saw her. Because no one saw D actually *on* P's lot, D moves for judgment as a matter of law at the close of P's case. Will the court grant the motion?

2. Same as Problem 1, except that *P* moves for judgment as a matter of law at the close of his case. Will P prevail?

3. Same as Problem 1, except that D does not move for judgment as a matter of law. D instead presents her evidence. D herself does not testify, and none of D's other evidence touches upon the issue of whether D was on P's land. P moves for judgment as a matter of law at the close of all the evidence. Will the court grant P's motion?

4. Same as Problem 1, where D moves for judgment as a matter of law. The court denies D's motion. Is D precluded from raising the same challenge again at a later point in the trial, or after the jury returns with a verdict?

5. Same as Problem 1, except that P does not call W1 and W2. Instead, P calls a different witness, X. X testifies that he saw D walking across P's beach at 8:10 p.m. X states that he was standing east of the eastern edge of P's lot, five hundred feet inland from the beach. On cross-examination, X admits that the sun was setting directly to the west at the moment that he observed D. Nevertheless, X insists that the person he saw was D. At the close of P's case, D moves for judgment as a matter of law. Will the court grant D's motion?

6. Same basic facts as Problem 1, except that P has considerably more evidence. A group of a dozen bishops was vacationing on the beach. All twelve of these bishops state that they saw D walking across P's beach. P also has a photograph of D, taken while D was on P's beach. Finally, D left behind footprints in the sand on P's beach. P had the folks from CSI make plaster casts of these footprints, noting the location and date. The casts match D's feet perfectly.

After P rests, D offers her testimony. D has only one witness—herself. While on the stand, D flatly denies that she walked across P's land. However, on cross-examination, D admits that she has a prior perjury conviction.

P moves for judgment as a matter of law at the close of the evidence. Will the court grant P's motion?

CHAPTER 12

JURY TRIAL

■ ■ ■

> When our civilization wants a library catalogued or the solar system discovered, or any trifle of that kind, it uses up its specialists. But when our civilization wishes anything done which is really serious, it collects 12 ordinary people standing around.
>
> —G.K. Chesterton, *Alarms and Discussions* 212–13 (1911)

Many view trial by lay jury as one of the defining characteristics of the Anglo-American legal system. This is not to say that no other system uses juries. Many nations use some form of jury in criminal cases. A few non Anglo-American nations even allow juries in certain civil cases. But while juries are not unique to the Anglo-American system, it is probably fair to say that in no other system has the jury played so significant a role in defining the nature of an institution. The jury originated in England prior to the Magna Carta. It has served over the centuries as a populist check on government, offsetting the power of the wealthier and often more elitist judges. In this fashion, the jury gave "12 ordinary people standing around" a limited role in government.

Given the crucial role that juries have played in Anglo-American legal history, you may be surprised to learn that the use of juries in civil cases has been steadily decreasing in most Anglo-American nations. The lone exception is the United States. While jury trials in civil cases in the United Kingdom and Canada, for example, are increasingly rare, they remain common in the United States.[1] Both state and federal courts regularly use juries in a wide array of civil cases. Indeed, in the federal courts and most state systems, a party has a constitutional right to have certain cases heard by a jury. That the framers thought the right to a jury trial in a civil case was important enough to enshrine in the United States Constitution speaks volumes about the historic view of the jury in American legal history.

In the United States, then, it seems that juries are here to stay, at least for the foreseeable future. However, a jury trial presents a number of unique issues that do not arise in cases tried before a judge. This Chapter explores these unique questions. Part A discusses the

---

[1] The United Kingdom allows for juries only in certain types of civil cases. In Canada, use of the jury varies from province to province. Throughout Canada, however, juries are used far less frequently than in the United States.

constitutional right to a jury in federal civil litigation. Part B discusses how a party demands a jury. Parts C, D, and E deal with the rules governing jury selection and deliberation. Parts F and G discuss how a court may reject a jury verdict and afford the litigants a new trial.

A. THE CONSTITUTIONAL RIGHT TO A JURY TRIAL IN FEDERAL CIVIL CASES

> The materials for this section are at www.crosscivilprocedure.com.

B. DEMANDING A JURY TRIAL

How does a party make known its desire to have a jury decide the case? Can a party waive its right to have a case tried by a jury?

MARSEILLES HYDRO POWER, LLC v. MARSEILLES LAND AND WATER COMPANY
299 F.3d 643 (7th Cir. 2002)

POSNER, CIRCUIT JUDGE.

[Plaintiff power company sued defendant canal company for breach of a contract to maintain a canal that supplied water to a power plant. Plaintiff's complaint also sought a declaratory judgment that it owed no payments under the contract because of defendant's failure to maintain Defendant demanded a jury in the case. (The detailed facts of the case are set out in Part A of this Chapter, but are not relevant to the issue of demand for a jury.)]

[T]he canal company's principal argument, and the only one we strictly need to consider, is that it was entitled to a jury trial. Rule 38(b) of the civil rules gives a party only ten days* "after the service of the last pleading directed to the issue" (that is, "any issue triable of right by a jury," *id.*) to demand a jury trial on that issue. The canal company filed its demand within ten days after serving on the power company its counterclaim demanding payment of the rent specified in the contract for the use of the canal, which the power company had decided to withhold until the canal was repaired. The district judge thought the demand had come too late, because the rent issue was clearly flagged in the power company's complaint; part of the declaratory judgment sought was a declaration that the power company owed no rent until the canal was back in working order.

[The court then held there was a right to a jury on the counterclaim, but not on plaintiff's claims. This discussion is set out in Part A of this Chapter.]

---

* The Rule was amended after this case to extend this period to 14 days. [Eds.]

... The canal company's demand for a jury, filed within ten days after the counterclaim, was the earliest either party could have demanded a jury trial. At that point the fact that there was a common issue underlying both the equitable and the legal claims, namely the duty if any of the power company to pay rent, and under that issue perhaps the deeper issue of which party had actually broken the contract, became significant. Common issues, if triable at all in the sense that their resolution requires resolving a material dispute of fact, as was the case here, must be tried to a jury in order to prevent a judge's determination from foreclosing a party's right to have the issues in a common law suit tried by a jury. So the demand for a jury trial was timely and its rejection error; and until the jury trial to which the canal company is entitled is completed issuance of an injunction is premature. . . .

NOTES AND QUESTIONS

1. As *Marseilles Hydro* demonstrates, a party can lose its right to a jury trial by failing to demand a jury in timely fashion. If you studied Part A of this Chapter, you saw that in federal court there may be a constitutional right to a jury. Should constitutional rights be waived merely because a party delays in insisting that government honor them? In this context, think back to the question of personal jurisdiction in Chapter 3. The due process clause of the Constitution protects a person from being sued in a state that lacks minimum contacts with that person. Can a party waive this due process protection by failing to assert it in a timely fashion? Review Federal Rule 12(h)(1).

2. Rule 38(c) allows a party to demand a jury trial for specific issues. Of course, as the prior section showed, in cases involving a mix of legal and equitable claims the right to a jury trial may not apply to all of the issues. However, a party may also limit its demand for a jury to fewer than all of the claims that qualify for a jury. If the demand is limited, any other party who desires a jury trial of other issues triable by a jury must also file a timely demand for those issues or waive its rights.

3. If a demand for jury is made without specifying any issues, it is deemed to be a demand for a jury trial on all issues in the case. What if the demand includes issues on which there is no right to a jury trial? The court will limit the jury trial to those issues that qualify for a jury trial.

4. Rule 38(b) requires that a demand for a jury trial of any issue be served within fourteen days after service of the "last pleading directed to the [legal] issue." When the legal issue first appears in a counterclaim, as in *Marseilles Hydro*, this period begins to run when the plaintiff serves its answer to that counterclaim. Of course, a party need not wait until the other side responds. If either party's own pleading includes a legal claim, that party may request a jury along with the claim. Thus, plaintiffs often demand a jury trial in the complaint itself. However, if a party includes a demand for a jury in a pleading, the demand must be set off from the main body of the pleading.

5. In dealing with the issue of timeliness, the court in *Marseilles Hydro* is attempting to determine whether the complaint or the answer was the first pleading raising a legal issue. Why? Does it matter when the issue was *first* raised?

6. In cases filed in state court, the rules governing availability of and demand for a jury may differ significantly. What happens when a case is removed from state to federal court? Rule 81(c)(3)(B) gives a party at least fourteen days following removal to demand a jury.

7. Rule 38(d) provides that once a party files a demand for a jury, she cannot withdraw it without the consent of all parties. Why should the consent of the other parties be required?

8. *Challenging the trial judge's ruling on the jury request.* Suppose a party disagrees with how the judge rules on a demand for a jury. May the party seek immediate appeal by an appellate court, or must she wait until after the trial is complete? As a general rule, 28 U.S.C. § 1291 only allows appeals from "final judgments" of the district court. A ruling on whether to use a jury is clearly not a final judgment under § 1291 because it does not resolve any of the substantive issues in the case.

As discussed in Chapter 14, pt. B, however, there are certain exceptions to the final judgment rule of § 1291. One of these exceptions is the writ of *mandamus*, in which the aggrieved party files what is technically a new action against the trial judge in the Court of Appeals. In most situations, *mandamus* is an extraordinary writ, available only when the party presents a compelling case as to why he needs immediate relief. However, because the right to a jury is enshrined in the Constitution, a party need not present a compelling case to file for *mandamus* based on a trial judge's denial of a jury. Note that this special rule applies only to a *denial* of a jury. Because there is no constitutional right to a bench trial, a party must ordinarily wait until after final judgment to challenge a judge's decision to *grant* a jury trial.

9. Even if no party demands a jury, Rule 39(b) allows the court, in its discretion, to order a jury trial for any or all issues that could have been tried as of right to a jury. That rule gives the court a limited ability to relieve a party of the strict timing rules of Federal Rule 38. The main factors the court considers are whether the demand was made within a reasonable time after the time for demanding a jury expired, whether the failure to make a timely demand was the result of inadvertence, mistake, or excusable neglect, and whether a late motion for a jury trial will prejudice the other parties.

10. How might the availability of a jury trial affect settlement? Whereas the outcome is clear when a party accepts a settlement agreement, there is a risk of loss attached to submitting a dispute to adjudication for resolution. Do you think risks are greater for a jury trial than a bench trial? Is the outcome less predictable? The perception of risk associated with jury trials is said to be one reason companies are increasingly requiring consumers and employees to resolve disputes using binding arbitration.

PROBLEMS

1. P is about to sue D for damages for trespass. What is the earliest point at which P may request a jury? May P include a request along with her complaint?

2. P and D are embroiled in a dispute concerning a contract. On February 1, P serves D with a complaint seeking specific performance of the contract. On February 8, D files an answer, denying that it breached the contract and counterclaiming against P for damages, alleging that P breached the contract. D serves that answer on February 11. On February 23rd, P files and serves its answer to defendant's counterclaim, denying liability on the counterclaim. Can P and/or D still file a timely request for a jury trial? What is the latest date on which P or D may file and serve this request?

C. SELECTING A GROUP OF PROSPECTIVE JURORS

The Jury Selection and Service Act of 1968 (28 U.S.C. § 1861 et seq.) provides a uniform method for selecting jurors in federal civil cases. Each district court has a plan for jury selection consistent with the statute's general requirements: (1) random selection of jurors from voter lists; and (2) determination of juror disqualifications, excuses, exemptions, and exclusions on the basis of objective criteria. The statute also provides that no citizen shall be excluded from jury service "on account of race, color, religion, sex, national origin, or economic status."

Jurors do not have to be drawn from an entire federal district. The local plan must prescribe a method for putting into the master jury wheel at least 1,000 names chosen at random from voter registration lists or lists of actual voters within the district or division. Each county, parish, or similar political subdivision must be substantially proportionally represented in the master jury wheel. Periodically, names are drawn at random from the master jury wheel, and each person whose name is drawn is sent a juror qualification form to complete and return. A judge then determines on the basis of the information provided on the juror qualification form and other competent evidence whether a person is unqualified for, exempt from, or excused from jury service. The remaining names are then put into the qualified jury wheel, from which names are drawn at random as needed for assignment to jury panels.

Any United States citizen who is 18 or over, who has resided for one year within the judicial district, and is able to read, write, speak, and understand the English language is qualified to serve as a juror unless she is incapable, by reason of mental or physical infirmity, to render satisfactory jury service, or has been convicted of or charged with a felony in federal or state court and her civil rights have not been restored. The local plan specifies groups of persons or occupational classes whose members are barred from jury service on the ground that they are exempt. The plan must provide exemption for persons on active service in the armed forces, firemen and policemen, and federal or state public officials actively engaged in the performance of official duties. The plan may also specify groups of persons or occupational classes whose members shall, on individual request, be excused from jury service.

A person chosen for a jury panel from the qualified jury wheel and summoned for service may be excused by the court upon a showing 1) of undue hardship or extreme inconvenience, for a period the court deems necessary; 2) of an inability to render impartial jury service; 3) that her service as a juror would be likely to disrupt the proceedings; or 4) that her service as a juror would be likely to threaten the secrecy of the proceedings or otherwise adversely affect the integrity of jury deliberations.

A party must challenge compliance with the jury selection procedures within seven days after the moving party discovered or, in the exercise of diligence, could have discovered the grounds for challenge, and in any event before the voir dire examination begins. A party also has an unqualified right to inspect jury lists in order to determine whether there is a basis for challenge. The challenge succeeds only if there has been "a substantial failure to comply with the provisions" of the federal statute.

Any party may challenge underrepresentation of particular groups in his jury pool as a violation of the "fair cross-section" requirement. The qualifications of jurors and the selection of jury panels as prescribed in the Jury Selection and Service Act of 1968, are intended to ensure that litigants have their disputes decided by juries chosen from a fair cross section of the community and that all citizens have the opportunity to be considered for service on juries. This requirement applies only to the jury *panel* from which the petit jury is selected. The petit jury, the jury which actually decides the case does not have to reflect a cross-section of the community. *Holland v. Illinois*, 493 U.S. 474, 110 S.Ct. 803, 107 L.Ed.2d 905 (1990). Imagine the difficulties in applying a cross-section requirement to the petit jury, as well as its impact on the voir dire process.

Relief requires a showing that the group alleged to have been excluded is a "distinctive" group in the community, that the representation of this group in the venire from which the jury is selected was not fair and reasonable in relation to the number of such persons in the community, and that this underrepresentation was due to systematic exclusion of the group in the jury selection process. The party claiming discrimination by the systematic exclusion of a particular group has the burden of establishing the exclusion. A sufficiently large disparity between the representation of a group in the population and its representation on jury panels is sufficient to show a prima facie case. The opposing party may rebut a prima facie case by showing that "a significant state interest [is] manifestly and primarily advanced by those aspects of the jury-selection process . . . that result in the disproportionate exclusion of a distinctive group."

FLOYD V. GARRISON
996 F.2d 947 (8th Cir. 1993)

FAGG, CIRCUIT JUDGE.

Mattie Ruth Floyd, a black, brought this civil rights action alleging officer Marty Garrison, a white, used unreasonable and unlawful deadly force by shooting and killing Jason L.C. Floyd. Floyd moved to dissolve the jury pool before trial, and moved for a new trial after the jury returned a verdict for Garrison, because only one of the forty prospective jurors was black. The district court denied the motions. Floyd appeals contending the use of voter registration lists as the sole source for selecting jury pools violates the fair-cross-section requirement of the Jury Selection and Service Act of 1968 (Act) and the Fifth Amendment guarantee of equal protection. We affirm.

The Act requires that jury pools be chosen at random from a fair cross section of the community. 28 U.S.C. § 1861 (1988). To establish a prima facie violation of the fair-cross-section requirement, Floyd must show: (1) blacks are a distinctive group in the community; (2) the representation of blacks in jury pools is not "fair and reasonable in relation to the number of [blacks] in the community;" and (3) "this underrepresentation is due to systematic exclusion of [blacks] in the jury-selection process." *Duren v. Missouri*, 439 U.S. 357, 364 (1979) (Sixth Amendment fair-cross-section requirement); see *United States v. Clifford*, 640 F.2d 150, 154–55 (8th Cir.1981) (*Duren* elements apply to § 1861).

Floyd has failed to establish the third prong of the fair-cross-section test by showing underrepresentation of blacks in jury pools is inherent in the jury-selection process. Floyd merely asserts the use of voter registration lists as the sole source for selecting jury pools does not provide a fair cross section of the community because blacks do not register to vote in the same proportion as other persons. We have consistently approved the use of voter registration lists to select jury pools. The use of voter registration lists is required by the Act and was designed to give qualified citizens an equal chance to be selected for jury pools. Even if proportionally fewer blacks register to vote, "[t]he mere fact that one identifiable group of individuals votes in a lower proportion than the rest of the population does not make a jury selection system illegal or unconstitutional." Absent proof that obstacles are placed in the path of blacks attempting to register to vote, voter registration lists may be used as the sole source for selecting jury pools. *United States v. Freeman*, 514 F.2d 171, 173 (8th Cir.1975).

The Fifth Amendment guarantee of equal protection requires that the procedures used to select jury pools be racially nondiscriminatory. To establish a prima facie equal protection violation, Floyd must show (1) blacks are "a recognizable, distinct class, singled out for different treatment;" (2) blacks were substantially underrepresented in jury pools over a significant period of time; and (3) the jury-selection process is "susceptible of abuse or is not racially neutral." *Castaneda v. Partida*, 430 U.S. 482, 494 (1977).

Floyd has failed to establish the third prong of the equal protection test by showing a discriminatory purpose in the jury-selection process. Floyd concedes there was no intentional discrimination in the random selection of jurors from the voter registration lists, but again contends proportionately fewer blacks register to vote. The use of voter registration lists was intended to eliminate discriminatory and arbitrary selection practices, and Floyd has not shown that blacks are prevented from registering to vote. Thus, the sole use of voter registration lists to select jury pools does not violate equal protection.

Even if Floyd had established the third prongs of the fair-cross-section and equal protection tests, Floyd failed to show blacks were substantially underrepresented on jury pools. Over a thirteen month period, 10.335% of the jurors called for service in the Western Division of the Eastern District of Arkansas were blacks, and 13.8% of the general population in that Division were blacks. The absolute disparity between blacks on jury pools and blacks in the general population was less than 4% (13.8%–10.335%). This underrepresentation is not substantial and does not constitute evidence of a fair-cross-section violation. *Clifford*, 640 F.2d at 155 (absolute disparity of 7.2% is not substantial underrepresentation). The disparity also is not significant enough to prove purposeful discrimination against blacks. Although Floyd contends we should apply a comparative disparity analysis, we decline to adopt that concept as a better means of calculating underrepresentation. We affirm the district court's rulings.

NOTES AND QUESTIONS

1. *Floyd* refers to *Duren v. Missouri*, 439 U.S. 357, 99 S.Ct. 664, 58 L.Ed.2d 579 (1979), in which Missouri "provided an automatic exemption from jury service for any women requesting not to serve." The Supreme Court found the automatic exemption to be a violation of the federal *constitutional* cross-section requirement. Note that *Floyd* involved a violation of the *statutory* cross-section requirement which applies to civil as well as criminal cases. In *Duren*, the Court held that "systematic exclusion of women that results in jury venires averaging less than 15% female violates the Constitution's fair-cross-section requirement."

If the percentage of women appearing on jury pools in Jackson County had precisely mirrored the percentage of women in the population, more than one of every two prospective jurors would have been female. In fact, less than one of every six prospective jurors was female; 85% of the average jury was male. Such a gross discrepancy between the percentage of women in jury venires and the percentage of women in the community requires the conclusion that women were not fairly represented in the source from which petit juries were drawn in Jackson County.

Finally, in order to establish a prima facie case, it was necessary for petitioner to show that the underrepresentation of women, generally and on his venire, was due to their systematic exclusion in the jury-selection process. Petitioner's proof met this requirement. His undisputed demonstration that a large discrepancy occurred not just occasionally but in every weekly venire for a period of nearly a year manifestly indicates that the cause of the underrepresentation was systematic—that is, inherent in the particular jury-selection process utilized. . . .

The resulting disproportionate and consistent exclusion of women from the jury wheel and at the venire stage was quite obviously due to the system by which juries were selected. Petitioner demonstrated that the underrepresentation of women in the final pool of prospective jurors was due to the operation of Missouri's exemption criteria—whether the automatic exemption for women or other statutory exemptions—as implemented in Jackson County. Women were therefore systematically underrepresented . . .

We recognize that a State may have an important interest in assuring that those members of the family responsible for the care of children are available to do so. An exemption appropriately tailored to this interest would, we think, survive a fair-cross-section challenge. We stress, however, that the constitutional guarantee to a jury drawn from a fair cross section of the community requires that States exercise proper caution in exempting broad categories of persons from jury service.

The Court noted that "reasonable exemptions, such as those based on special hardship, incapacity, or community needs," could produce a pool of jurors that was representative of the community.

2. What other groups are "distinctive" for purposes of a cross-section requirement? Young adults and college students are not a distinctive group. Likewise, the exclusion of young people which results from the intermittent recompiling of the jury lists has been justified in the interest of judicial economy. *See Hamling v. United States*, 418 U.S. 87, 94 S.Ct. 2887, 41 L.Ed.2d 590 (1974), rehearing denied 419 U.S. 885, 95 S.Ct. 157, 42 L.Ed.2d 129 (1974). What about other groups? Social Security recipients? Military

veterans? Members of large religious groups within a community? Are there more specific ways to decide whether a group is "distinctive"?

3. *Jury size.* Federal Rule 48 prescribes a jury of no fewer than six and no more than twelve members. In *Colgrove v. Battin*, 413 U.S. 149, 93 S.Ct. 2448, 37 L.Ed.2d 522 (1973), the Supreme Court upheld the propriety of a local rule prescribing a six-person jury. The Court distinguished the constitutional right of trial by jury in civil actions from the "various incidents of trial by jury," reasoning that effective jury performance is not a function of jury size. Do you agree?

Federal district local rules vary from district to district in the number of jurors prescribed. Individual districts' rules set the jury size at six, eight, or twelve. Some local rules follow Rule 48 and provide a range between six and twelve from which the district court can choose. Many local rules also provide the court with discretion to seat a number of jurors different from the rule.

EXERCISE

For the state where a) you intend to practice after graduation, b) your law school is located, and/or c) your professor assigns, go to that state's annotated statutes and research the statutes and procedural rules governing the jury selection process. Based on your research, print the statute or rule and bring it to class for discussion. In addition, answer the following questions.

1. How many persons must sit on a jury in a civil case?

2. What is the method for selecting an array or a panel of jurors? Drivers' licenses? Personal property tax rolls? Another method?

D. CHALLENGING INDIVIDUAL PROSPECTIVE JURORS

INTRODUCTORY PROBLEM

Garner sued the Swell Computer Corp. in local federal court for a product defect. She is seeking more than $10 million in compensatory and punitive damages suffered when her computer's hard drive "crashed," causing Garner to lose her Ph.D. dissertation that she had been writing for two years. At the time of jury selection, forty-eight prospective jurors completed jury questionnaires which included information about the panel member's address, occupation, group affiliations, and prior litigation. The questionnaires disclosed that two jurors worked for the defendant, two worked at the university where Garner is seeking her doctorate, three live in her neighborhood, four belong to a local "Bloggers" club, and one has sued Swell in the past for employment discrimination. In addition, the questionnaires sought information about the prospective juror's spouses. One spouse works for the state consumer protection agency, another works in telephone sales for one of Swell's competitors, and two other spouses are computer science majors at Garner's university.

Assuming that the prospective jurors confirm their questionnaire answers during voir dire, is any juror subject to a successful challenge for cause by either party? If such a challenge is denied by the trial judge, would you advise either counsel to use a peremptory challenge to exclude any of the jurors based on the questionnaire?

Governing Law: 28 U.S.C. §§ 1866(c)(4); 1870.

Under Federal Rule 47(a) the trial court has broad discretion to conduct the examination of prospective jurors or to permit the parties to ask questions. If the court conducts the voir dire examination exclusively, the parties may submit proposed questions, which the court may ask if it deems the questions to be proper. Sufficient questioning is necessary to ensure that the selection process is meaningful.

Usually, voir dire occurs by the court or counsel questioning all prospective jurors simultaneously. However, the court has the authority to conduct individual voir dire, which consumes a lot more time, if there is a concern about answers given by one juror "poisoning" the views of other jurors, e.g., knowledge about the case.

The purpose of voir dire examination is to determine any possible basis for challenging jurors for cause (when the challenging party must establish the prospective juror's explicit or implicit bias) and to develop background information to be considered in the intelligent exercise of peremptory challenges (when the challenging party generally need not offer a reason for the challenge).

Because of its central role in the selection of a fair and impartial jury, the voir dire examination is one of the most important parts of the trial. It is the first opportunity afforded to counsel to address the jury in connection with the case. The impressions the jurors have about the case and about counsel at the conclusion of the examination may last throughout the trial.

If there are reasonable grounds to believe that a juror cannot render a fair and impartial verdict, the juror should be excused for cause. However, disqualification is not required merely because a juror does not understand or immediately accept every legal concept presented during voir dire. The test is not whether a juror agrees with the law when it is presented; it is whether, after having heard all of the evidence, the prospective juror can adjust his views to the requirements of the law and render a fair and impartial verdict.

The court may exercise considerable discretion in deciding whether to excuse an individual juror for cause. Even if the parties fail to make a challenge for cause, the court has an affirmative duty to explore undisclosed information of which it is aware affecting the qualification of an individual juror.

THOMPSON V. ALTHEIMER & GRAY
248 F.3d 621 (7th Cir. 2001)

POSNER, CIRCUIT JUDGE.

The plaintiff brought suit against her employer under Title VII of the Civil Rights Act of 1964, charging racial discrimination. The case was tried, the jury returned a verdict for the defendant, and the plaintiff appeals, arguing that a juror named Leiter should have been struck for cause. If the plaintiff is right, she is entitled to a new trial without having to show that Leiter's presence on the jury caused the jury to side with the defendant. Denial of the right to an unbiased tribunal is one of those trial errors that is not excused by being shown to have been harmless.

But what of the plaintiff's failure to use any of her three peremptory challenges to strike Leiter? She says that she used up her peremptory challenges on jurors whom she considered even less likely to favor her cause than Leiter was. This acknowledgment might seem to imply—since the plaintiff is not contending that any of those jurors had to be stricken for cause—that she can't really think that Leiter was biased; for if Leiter was biased and those other three were not, surely the plaintiff would have used a peremptory challenge to get rid of Leiter first. That doesn't follow. Bias is only one factor in deciding whether to challenge a juror. A lawyer might be utterly convinced that a member of the jury venire would vote against his client no matter what the evidence showed, and yet his belief might be based on a hunch that he could not articulate as a ground for a challenge for cause. He might be more eager to strike that juror than one who had an evident bias (though the judge hadn't been convinced of this), for he might think he could overcome the hurdle posed by that bias more readily than he could persuade the stubborn but not demonstrably biased juror.

. . . [C]ould a defendant preserve the issue of bias simply by failing to use his peremptory challenge to remove the biased juror? Since the use of a peremptory challenge to remove that juror would cure the judge's error, the defendant's failure to use a peremptory challenge to do this might well be thought to make the error a self-inflicted wound, as argued in a concurring opinion in [*United States v.*] *Martinez-Salazar*, 528 U.S. 304, 318–19 (2000). The majority opinion, however, suggests a different view— that the litigant can let the biased juror be seated and seek to reverse the adverse judgment (if one results) on appeal on grounds of bias. The suggestion is dictum, and can be questioned as putting the litigant in a heads-I-win-tails-you-lose position: if he wins a jury verdict, he can pocket his victory, and if he loses, he can get a new trial.

... The important question is whether the plaintiff's constitutional right to an impartial tribunal was infringed. Let us see.

During the voir dire of the jury, the judge asked the members of the venire whether "there is something about this kind of lawsuit for money damages that would start any of you leaning for or against a particular party?" Leiter raised her hand and explained that she has "been an owner of a couple of businesses and am currently an owner of a business, and I feel that as an employer and owner of a business that will definitely sway my judgment in this case." The judge asked her whether "if I instructed you as to what the law is that you would be able to apply the law recognizing that you are a business owner?" To which she replied, "I think my experience will cloud my judgment, but I can do my best." The judge permitted the lawyers also to ask questions of the prospective jurors and Thompson's lawyer asked Leiter, "And you said earlier that you were concerned that your position as a business owner may cloud your judgment. Can you tell me how?" And she replied, "I am constantly faced with people that want various benefits or different positions in the company [what Thompson was seeking from her employer, the defendant, Altheimer & Gray] or better contacts or, you know, a myriad of issues that employers face on a regular basis, and I have to decide whether or not that person should get them." The lawyer then asked Leiter whether she was concerned "that if somebody doesn't get them [benefits sought from their employer] they're going to sue you," and she answered, "Of course." Asked then whether "you believe that people file lawsuits just because they don't get something they want?", she answered, "I believe there are some people that do." In answer to the next and last question, "Are you concerned that that might cloud your judgment in this case?" she said, "I think I bring a lot of background to this case, and I can't say that it's not going to cloud my judgment. I can try to be as fair as I can, as I do every day."

That was the end of the voir dire of Leiter. After refusing to strike her for cause (though urged to do so by the plaintiff's lawyer), and releasing the jurors who had not been selected for the jury (the defendant had also exercised its three peremptory challenges, none overlapping with the plaintiff's), the judge asked the eight remaining jurors, that is, the jurors selected to hear the case, whether they would follow his instructions on the law even if they didn't agree with them and whether they would be able to suspend judgment until they had heard all the evidence. The question was asked to the jurors at large and all either nodded their heads or said yes. The defendant, again perhaps dropping the ball, makes nothing of Leiter's failure at this stage to reiterate her doubts about her ability to exercise an unclouded judgment. The defendant is content to argue that the answers that Leiter gave to the earlier questions by the judge, and the questions by Thompson's lawyer, did not require that Leiter be struck for cause.

Our review of the trial judge's ruling with respect to a challenge for cause is deferential, but not completely supine, and it is pertinent to note that no issue of credibility is presented. There is no argument that Leiter was not telling the truth. The issue is interpretive: did what she say manifest a degree of bias such that the judge abused his discretion in failing to strike her for cause?

. . . When Leiter said that she believed that some people sue their employer just because they haven't gotten a promotion or a raise or some other benefit, she was not manifesting bias. She was expressing a prior belief (prior, that is, to hearing any evidence in this case) that was not only not irrational, but was undoubtedly true—there are indeed some people who will sue their employer just because of disappointment over the failure of the employer to give them something they want. In other words, there are spurious suits, in the employment domain as elsewhere. Leiter could not be thought biased for holding a true belief, or even for holding it unshakably if it is indubitably true. The belief that some employees make bogus claims against employers is so obviously true that it could not be shaken; but inability to set aside a clearly sound belief does not make for a biased juror. It makes for a realistic one. . . .

The question in this case was not whether Leiter's belief that some claims against employers are spurious was true or false (it was, as we have noted, true), but whether this belief would somehow impede her in giving due weight to the evidence and following the judge's instructions. That question was not adequately explored. The last thing Leiter said before the judge refused to strike her for cause was that she couldn't say the "background" she brought to this case wasn't going to "cloud" her judgment. She said she would try to be fair, but she expressed no confidence in being able to succeed in the attempt. She may have realized that because of bad experiences in the past, she might have difficulty separating the logically distinct propositions that some claims against employers are bogus and that this claim must be bogus because it is a claim against an employer.

Had she said she could not be fair, the judge would of course have had to strike her for cause. She did not say that, and so the judge (the defendant . . . does not argue that the plaintiff's lawyer was at fault in failing to follow up his question whether Leiter's background would cloud her judgment) should have followed up by asking her, as he later asked the jury en masse, whether she would follow his instructions on the law and suspend judgment until she had heard all the evidence.

Instead the matter was left dangling, just as it had been in *Martinez-Salazar*. That juror whom the defendant in that case used a peremptory challenge to excuse after the judge refused to excuse him for cause, when asked "whether, if he were a defendant facing jurors with backgrounds and opinions similar to his own, he thought he would get a fair trial," answered: "I think that's a difficult question. I don't think I know the answer to that." 528 U.S. at 308. And when asked whether he "would feel more comfortable erring on the side of the prosecution or the defense," he said he "would probably be more favorable to the prosecution." *Id.* When the judge then scolded him for reversing the presumption of innocence, the juror said, "I understand that in theory." *Id.* The judge nevertheless refused to excuse the juror for cause because "he said . . . he could follow the instructions, and he said . . . 'I don't think I know what I would do,' et cetera." *Id.* at 309. The Supreme Court held that in these circumstances the judge had erred in not allowing the challenge for cause. It is just like our case. The judge didn't push hard enough to determine whether Leiter could relinquish her prior beliefs for purposes of deciding the case.

Had the judge pushed Leiter and had she finally given unequivocal assurances that he deemed credible, his ruling could not be disturbed. But he failed to do that. The venire contained 20 prospective jurors, and more than enough were left to make up a full jury of 8 when he refused to excuse her. A candid and thoughtful person, if one may judge from the transcript, Leiter would probably have made an excellent juror—in another case.

When a prospective juror manifests a prior belief that is both material and contestable (for, to repeat an earlier point, it is not bias to cling to a belief that no rational person would question), it is the judge's duty to determine whether the juror is capable of suspending that belief for the duration of the trial. When as in this case the record contains no assurances that the belief is "shakable," that the prospective juror can exercise a judgment unclouded by that belief, the verdict cannot stand. "When a juror is unable to state that she will serve fairly and impartially despite being asked repeatedly for such assurances, we can have no confidence that the juror will 'lay aside' her biases or her prejudicial personal experiences and render a fair and impartial verdict." *United States v. Gonzalez*, 214 F.3d 1109, 1114 (9th Cir. 2000). That's this case. Missing are those "unwavering affirmations of impartiality" that permitted the district judge in *United States v. Garcia*, 936 F.2d 648, 653 (2d Cir.1991), to find the challenged juror unbiased. Reversed and remanded.

NOTES AND QUESTIONS

1. *Thompson* states that the judge has the "duty to determine whether the juror is capable of suspending that belief for the duration of the trial." How does the court become aware of any information relating to bias, i.e., who has the duty of raising bias issues?

Did Leiter indicate an automatic or absolute viewpoint, regardless of what the evidence might later show? What is the problem with seating someone with Leiter's views on the jury? Aren't those views part of the perspective of a cross-section of the community where the trial is held? What else should the judge have asked Leiter to resolve any confusion about Leiter's views?

2. The term "challenge for cause" is used to include both a juror who fails to meet one or more of the statutory qualifications for jury duty as well as a juror who is biased as between the parties or as to the substance of the dispute. Challenges for cause are determined by the trial judge who exercises considerable discretion in ruling on such challenges. The challenger has the burden of persuading the judge that the prospective juror is not impartial, and the standard of review on appeal is abuse of discretion. There is no limit to the number of jurors who may be struck for cause.

3. As a former law professor, Judge Posner posed another hypothetical in *Thompson*.

> Suppose a member of the venire in a case involving alleged sex discrimination by a fire department stated his belief that men on average have greater upper-body strength than women. Suppose he added that this belief was unshakable in the sense that if some social scientist testified otherwise, he would conclude that he was being fed junk science. Should this juror be disqualified? Not automatically, surely. The relevant questions would be whether he could distinguish averages from individuals, and thus recognize the possibility that a given woman might have greater upper-body strength than a given man, and whether he was so fixated on the average sex difference in upper-body strength that he was not open to the possibility that a woman whose upper-body strength was indeed less than that of the least strong firefighter in the fire department could nevertheless be as good a firefighter, or even a better one.

Thompson v. Altheimer & Gray, 248 F.3d 621, 625 (7th Cir. 2001).

4. As Judge Posner stated in *Thompson*, appellate courts are highly deferential to the trial judge's exercise of discretion in ruling on challenges for cause. For example, two jurors were challenged for cause in a medical malpractice case. One was a patient of the doctor-defendant in the case, and the other worked in a physician's office and had been named as a defendant in a malpractice case. After each prospective juror stated that she could be impartial in hearing the case, the trial judge denied the challenges for cause which were upheld on appeal. *Poynter v. Ratcliff*, 874 F.2d 219 (4th Cir. 1989). Does the case suggest the possibility of *excessive* deference?

5. What happens if a juror gives false information during voir dire, or simply remains silent and does not answer a question which applied to him? As to the issue of false information, a trial court has the discretion to decide whether a post-verdict hearing is necessary to determine juror bias or in exceptional circumstances whether such bias is to be inferred. It must be proved both that the juror failed to answer honestly a material question on voir dire, and that a correct answer would have provided a valid basis for a

challenge for cause. *McDonough Power Equip., Inc. v. Greenwood*, 464 U.S. 548, 104 S.Ct. 845, 78 L.Ed.2d 663 (1984). As for a failure to answer at all, the concern is that the information the juror should have revealed may have justified a challenge for cause or at least would have enabled a party to exercise a peremptory challenge intelligently. Does a prospective juror's failure to answer an applicable question carry as much potential for deception as an affirmative statement of false information?

EXERCISE

As you read the following examples of voir dire questions, consider the propriety and the strategic purpose for each category of questions as well as for individual inquiries being asked of prospective jurors. The question for voir dire is in italics; queries and case law follow the question.

1. *Knowledge and Opinions*. Ordinarily, the court will ask prospective jurors whether they have any prior knowledge or opinions about the case. However, the questions may be too general to elicit accurate responses. If the court rules permit counsel to address prospective jurors directly, counsel may wish to give a capsule summary of the facts to stimulate the memory of the jurors and then to ask the jurors questions about their knowledge about the case or the parties. Consider the following illustrative comments and voir dire examination. What answers to these questions may form the basis for a successful challenge for cause? If a trial judge denies the challenge for cause, will an appellate court deem the denial to be an abuse of discretion? The judge might make introductory remarks to the jurors preceding the questioning.

> JUDGE: This case involves an argument at the intersection of Third Street and Eastern Parkway last August between Jane Doe and Officer Ron Roe. Because liability and monetary damages must be judged solely on the basis of the evidence from the witness stand, there are several questions which must be asked to find out whether you already have knowledge or opinions about this case:
>
> a. *Have you seen or heard anything about this accident in the news media?* Should exposure to pretrial publicity alone result in the disqualification of jurors for cause? *See Murphy v. Florida*, 421 U.S. 794, 95 S.Ct. 2031, 44 L.Ed.2d 589 (1975); *Irvin v. Dowd*, 366 U.S. 717, 81 S.Ct. 1639, 6 L.Ed.2d 751 (1961). The interrogation of jurors about pretrial publicity is obviously necessary to determine this basis for disqualification.
>
> b. *Do you have any knowledge or information about the case from any other source?* Is it relevant that one or more of the jurors served on previous juries involving the same party? Is hearsay information obtained from discussions with persons interested in the case also relevant? For example, is it a valid basis for a challenge for cause if a prospective juror drove to the scene of the event on the evening it occurred and talked to bystanders?

c. *Have you ever formed or expressed an opinion of any kind about this incident?* Does the formation of an opinion prior to trial create an inference that the juror cannot be fair and impartial?

2. *Relationships and Associations.* Normally, the court will identify the parties and will ask the prospective jurors whether they are related by blood or marriage to either of them. The court ordinarily identifies counsel for the parties at the same time and inquires whether the jurors have had any prior associations with counsel. The court may also ask the jurors whether they are acquainted with the persons identified or know anything about them. A related line of inquiry is identification of potential witnesses and the relationships and associations between the jurors and these witnesses. Consider the propriety of the following questions. Is the connection between a juror and any of the following a proper subject for inquiry?

JUDGE: The law recognizes that previous relationships and associations with various people may naturally influence your judgment about the case. For this reason, all of the people who are connected with the trial will now be identified so that these relationships and associations may be explored:

1. The plaintiff in this case is Jane Doe.

2. The defendants are the City of Metroville and Officer Ron Roe.

3. The witnesses who may testify in this case include Detective Paul Poe, Donna Doe, Charlie Coe and Nina Noe.

4. The attorneys involved in the case are Peter Plaintiff and Donald Defense.

5. The trial judge is James Justice.

a. *Are you related to any of these people by blood or marriage?* Once a close relationship is established, without regard to protestations of lack of bias, should the court sustain a challenge for cause and excuse the juror? How would you respond as the judge if the challenge was based upon a relationship when the prospective juror was:

1. The third cousin of the plaintiff?

2. The first cousin of the defense counsel?

3. The first cousin by marriage of a plaintiff's witness?

4. The spouse of the plaintiff's second cousin who knew the plaintiff for a long time?

b. *Do you know any of these people personally?* Does acquaintance alone constitute grounds for a challenge for cause? Does information about any of them based upon rumor or gossip?

c. *Have you had any business or social dealings with any of them?* Should a prospective juror be excused if a key witness is employed by the same organization? Is the number of persons employed by the organization relevant? See, e.g., *Getter v. Wal-Mart Stores, Inc.*, 66 F.3d 1119 (10th Cir. 1995) (juror owned stock in defendant corporation and juror's spouse was employed by defendant; juror's "financial well-being was to some extent dependent upon defendant's"; juror's assertions of impartiality must be discounted; bias is presumed; reversible error).

d. *Have any of you ever sat on a trial jury involving any of these people before?* Should jurors who have served in previous trials of the same party or co-party arising out of the same transaction be excused for cause? What about jurors who have previously served in cases involving similar testimony from the same witness?

e. *As a result of any prior information or dealings of any kind, are you inclined to give more or less weight to what any of these people say or do than you would if you knew nothing about them?* This question goes to the heart of implied bias.

f. *Do you or any of your close friends or relatives belong to any organization or group which has any interest in the outcome of this case?*

3. *Attitudes and Prejudices.* Jurors who know nothing about the case or the persons involved in it may nevertheless have fixed attitudes or strong prejudices which would seriously affect their ability to render a fair and impartial verdict. Courts generally permit the exploration of attitudes and prejudices which bear some reasonable relationship to the issues to be decided by the jury. Since the parties are in a better position to determine what attitudes and prejudices may prove to be crucial as the issues are joined during the trial, the voir dire examination in this area is best left to them. See e.g., *Art Press, Ltd. v. Western Printing Mach. Co.*, 791 F.2d 616 (7th Cir. 1986) (trial judge's questioning restrictions "undermined voir dire's purpose of eliciting information that shows the biases of a venireperson or provides counsel with a basis for exercising peremptory challenges").

To be effective, an examination in this area must expose the jurors to the issues which they will be asked to decide and to the law and facts upon which the issues will be decided. Because questions in this area tend to preview critical aspects of the trial, they are extremely sensitive and must be drawn with great care. Moreover, the jurors have a limited capacity to absorb lengthy voir dire examination. Therefore, a few selective questions which go directly to the theory of the case are much more effective than a laundry list of factors affecting the trial of cases in general. Consider the propriety of the following questions.

JUDGE: The plaintiff will attempt to prove that Ron Roe, who is African-American, wrongfully caused the death of a white man, John Doe. On the other hand, the defendant may show that the death resulted from a racial incident started by John Doe.

Therefore, there are several questions which must be asked about your attitudes in racial matters:

a. *Do any of you have any conscious prejudice for or against African-Americans?*

b. *Have you or your close friends or relatives had any experiences with African-Americans which might influence your judgment one way or the other in deciding this case?*

c. *Do any of you feel that African-Americans are more likely to commit crime than other people?*

d. *Do any of you feel that African-American persons are more prone to violence than other people and are thus more likely to be at fault in a violent incident such as the one involved in this case?*

e. *Would the fact that the case for the plaintiff will depend largely on the testimony of a white law enforcement official affect your decision one way or the other?*

f. *Can you follow the law and judge the decision which Ron Roe made based on what he believed instead of what you feel that you or some other person might have done in that situation?* How is this question relevant to jury selection?

JUDGE: There will be evidence that Ron Roe was drinking at the time of the accident. Because these matters relate to the issues before you, there are several questions which must be asked about your attitudes in this regard.

g. *Do any of you believe that the consumption of alcohol, even in moderate quantities, is wrong?*

h. *Do any of you belong to any group or organization which has taken a position on the consumption of alcohol?*

4. *The Juror's Background.* In addition to matters specifically related to the case to be tried, the prospective jurors may have various items in their backgrounds which could have some bearing on their decision in the case. Although some inquiry into these general matters is undoubtedly proper, the questions frequently appear to the jurors to be prying into their personal lives. Moreover, extensive general questions soon reach the point of diminishing returns, particularly in the area of courtroom procedure.

JUDGE: Unfortunately, some of you may have had some previous exposure to this type of civil case in some fashion or another. There are several questions which must be asked about your experiences and attitudes in this regard.

a. *Have you or any of your close friends or relatives ever been a victim of a traffic accident?*

b. *Have you or any of your close friends or relatives ever been a party or a witness to a traffic accident?*

Sec. D Challenging Individual Prospective Jurors   615

   c. *Have you ever testified in court?*

   d. *Would any experiences which you may have had or may have heard about the courts influence your decision in this case?*

   e. *In light of any experiences which you or your close friends or relatives may have had, would you rather not serve on a jury in this case?*

It is relevant to establish whether a person had sat as a juror in a similar case. However, should the juror's deliberative processes be explored? Even an inquiry into the verdict in an earlier case may be misleading. A juror who held out for a verdict in a previous case may have been waiting for years for a second chance to correct that error. By the same token, a juror who found someone liable may have had second thoughts about the verdict, resulting in reluctance to return another plaintiff's verdict. Consider the following questions.

   JUDGE: Some of you may have previous experience as jurors which might affect your decision in this case. There are several questions which must be asked in this regard.

   f. *Have any of you ever served on a jury panel in any court?*

   g. *Have any of you ever actually served on a jury which tried a civil or a criminal case?*

   h. *Do you feel that any experience which you may have had as a juror would influence you in any way in deciding the issues in this case?*

   i. *Do you understand the difference between the burden of proof in a civil case and a criminal case? In other words, in a civil case, you may decide in favor of either party if you believe that the evidence is even slightly stronger or better or more believable than the evidence on the other side. In a criminal case, it is your duty to find the defendant not guilty unless the prosecution proves guilt beyond a reasonable doubt. Do you understand and agree with those principles?*

   j. *Do you believe that a blameless person is not likely to be sued and accused of causing the wrongful death of another person?*

   k. *Do you understand that the lawsuit which brings the claim to trial is not evidence at all?*

   l. *Do you realize that a trial is the only opportunity which the law gives the parties to present the full facts of this case?*

   m. *If you were asked to render a verdict right now, how would you vote?*

   n. *Would any of you require the defendant to prove that she is blameless to you in some way?*

o. *Do you agree that witnesses belong to no one, and will you consider everything the witnesses say, regardless of who calls them or who is asking questions at the time?*

p. *Will you withhold your judgment until you have heard all of the evidence and the case has been submitted to you for a decision?*

q. *Do you understand that the law limits the evidence which you may hear, and that it is my duty to object whenever I believe that evidence is being introduced in violation of the law?*

r. *Do you promise not to draw any conclusions from my objections and not to hold anything I may do in performing my duty against my client?*

In addition to challenges for cause, each party in federal court has a statutory right to three peremptory challenges. The use of peremptory challenges protects each party's interest in a fair and impartial jury. Generally, no reason is necessary for the use of a peremptory challenge. However, a party in a civil case cannot use peremptory challenges to exclude jurors on account of their race or gender. Several defendants or several plaintiffs may be regarded as a single party for making challenges. Alternatively, the trial court may grant additional peremptory challenges, to be exercised separately or jointly. The procedure by which the parties are required to use their peremptory challenges varies widely from district to district and is regulated by local rule or local custom.

ALVERIO V. SAM'S WAREHOUSE CLUB, INC.
253 F.3d 933 (7th Cir. 2001)

TERENCE T. EVANS, CIRCUIT JUDGE.

Carmen Alverio worked as a food demonstrator at Sam's Warehouse Club. There, she encountered assistant manager Terrence Lloyd who, she claimed, had the disconcerting habit of laterally adjusting his groin while wandering the aisles of the store. Lloyd allegedly began harassing Alverio, and eventually, after matters worsened, she filed suit and went to trial. Sam's Club argued that Lloyd's behavior was not harassing. Alternatively, it asserted the *Ellerth/Faragher* affirmative defense alleging that Alverio failed to take advantage of the store's harassment policy by not telling management of the situation. A jury found in favor of Sam's Club. Alverio then filed a post-trial motion for judgment notwithstanding the verdict or in the alternative for a new trial. The motions were denied. On appeal, Alverio renews her prior objections, asserting that peremptory challenges were used by Sam's Club to exclude females from the jury panel and that admissible testimony was improperly kept from the jury. . . .

SEC. D   CHALLENGING INDIVIDUAL PROSPECTIVE JURORS

Alverio bases her request for a new trial on two arguments—improper jury selection and the exclusion of evidence. We begin with jury selection. The venire consisted of 3 women and 11 men. Judge Cleland conducted voir dire and asked each attorney to exercise three peremptory challenges. Alverio struck three men and Sam's Club struck all three women. Alverio raised a *Batson* challenge, requiring Sam's Club to explain each strike. After reviewing these justifications, Judge Cleland determined that the strikes were not motivated by invidious discrimination.

The rule in *Batson v. Kentucky*, 476 U.S. 79 (1986), that prohibited the use of peremptory challenges based on race has been extended to the exercise of peremptory challenges that are the result of intentional gender discrimination, see *J.E.B. v. Alabama ex rel. T.B.*, 511 U.S. 127 (1994). The right to have jury members selected based on nondiscriminatory criteria also applies in the civil context. See *Edmonson v. Leesville Concrete Co.*, 500 U.S. 614 (1991).

Under *Batson*, allegations of discriminatory peremptory challenges are evaluated via a three-part mini-hearing: (1) the opponent of the strike must make a prima facie showing that the striking party exercised the challenge because of a discriminatory reason; (2) the striking party must next proceed to articulate a gender-neutral reason for the challenge; and then (3) the court must determine whether the opponent of the strike has carried his burden of proving purposeful discrimination. "[T]he ultimate burden of persuasion regarding racial (or gender-based) motivation rests with and never shifts from, the opponent of the strike." *Purkett v. Elem*, 514 U.S. 765, 768 (1995) (per curiam).

The parties do not contest the first step. So, we focus on Sam's Club's proffered reasons and the judge's acceptance of these justifications. However, we keep in mind that "[t]he trial court's determination about the ultimate question of discriminatory intent is a finding of fact, which will be overturned only if clearly erroneous." *United States v. Evans*, 192 F.3d 698, 700 (7th Cir.1999). "Once the trial judge has been persuaded of the neutrality of the . . . reason for striking a juror, we have 'no basis for reversal on appeal unless the reason given is completely outlandish or there is other evidence which demonstrated its falsity.'" *United States v. Griffin*, 194 F.3d 808, 826 (7th Cir.1999) (quoting *Morse v. Hanks*, 172 F.3d 983, 985 (7th Cir.1999)).

Alverio argues that Sam's Club used its peremptory challenges to systematically remove women from the jury pool. She contends that the justification for its strikes—the lack of business experience and knowledge—was pretextual and invalid and argues that this is evidenced by the fact that the challenged female jurors had educational backgrounds that were greater than or equal to that of several of the empaneled male jurors. Finally, she asserts that an all-male jury was particularly unjust, given that the case involved sexual harassment claims which are "women's issues."

Sam's Club, as we said, struck the three females: (1) Nancy Kiec, a 38-year-old, married, unemployed woman with no children; (2) Robin Braxton, a 38-year-old mother of three who had worked as a hospital housekeeper for 3 years; and (3) Patricia Knorps, a secretary for an insurance agent, who had completed some college.[1] The attorney for Sam's Club, William Holloway, explained that he struck Kiec because she was unemployed. He challenged Braxton because she was the only prospective juror who had been a plaintiff in a lawsuit and she was reluctant to discuss the outcome of that case. As for Knorps, Holloway said he was concerned that her job put her in contact with insurance companies and their lawyers. Since Holloway's firm was active in insurance litigation, he was concerned that she might be familiar with his law firm, although she did not claim to have heard of it. In addition, he thought Knorps had given equivocal answers about her level of education, stating only that she completed "some college."

In addition to these particular objections, Holloway stated that his overall objection to all three prospective jurors was their limited work experience. He stated that he was looking for jurors with a level of "sophistication about business and how it is conducted in the work-a-day world." While he considered each juror's education level, his primary concern was work-force participation.

As to the second step of the *Batson* analysis, lawyers are given considerable leeway in formulating a gender-neutral rationale for jury strikes. *United States v. Evans*, 192 F.3d at 701 ("Any neutral reason, no matter how 'implausible or fantastic,' even if it is 'silly or superstitious,' is sufficient to rebut a prima facie case of discrimination.") (quoting *Purkett v. Elem*, 514 U.S. at 768). Here, in addition to identifying unique factors that only affected the three struck jurors—unemployment, participation as a plaintiff in a lawsuit, and employment in an insurance company—Holloway also identified an overarching concern, extensive work-force participation, which he applied consistently to the entire array. All remaining empaneled jurors were employed, and many had considerable work experience.

We have approved the exclusion of potential jurors because of their professions, see *Griffin*, 194 F.3d at 826, and their lack of a profession. *United States v. Jones*, 224 F.3d 621, 624 (7th Cir.2000) (affirming peremptory strike, where prospective juror was unemployed, watched

---

[1] Although at oral argument Alverio bemoaned the rough and tumble nature of the remaining male jurors, she struck the three most educated potential jurors, all of whom held managerial positions. One, Hetrick, was college-educated and served as a business director for a food supplier. Another, Chana, was a public school assistant principal who held a master's degree, and the last, Vaseloff, who had an MBA, served as an electronic engineering manager.

soap operas, and was inactive in her community). We have also held that inadequate education and business experience are nondiscriminatory justifications for excluding prospective jurors. Moreover, where a party gives multiple reasons for striking a juror, it is not enough for the other side to assert that the empaneled juror shares one attribute with the struck juror. Several of the empaneled jurors may have had less formal education than the three female jurors, but Holloway's decision to strike was not based on this factor alone.

Because all the women were removed from the panel, Alverio contends that Sam's Club's proffered reason was pretextual and rested on a stereotype that women have less business experience. First, the exclusion of all members of a specific minority group does not, on its own, establish that the peremptory strikes were discriminatory. Second, we doubt that at this point in time, women can be said to have less work experience than their male counterparts; thus, it is unlikely that "having business experience" can serve as a proxy for "male juror." Even were this true, and Mr. Holloway's stated reason had a disparate impact on female jurors, this would still be irrelevant. The question here is whether Mr. Holloway had a gender-neutral reason for striking these jurors. According to Judge Cleland, he did, and we give great deference to the judge's determination of discriminatory intent. The third step of the Batson jig requires the judge to make a factual determination based on Mr. Holloway's demeanor and credibility. This is a judgment call which the trial judge is in a much better position to make than we are. Even were we to find his decision to be dubious, we would not reverse unless we were left with a "definite and firm conviction that a mistake had been made." Here, we find that Judge Cleland did not err in allowing Sam's Club to strike the three female jurors from the pool.

Finally, we decline Alverio's invitation to find that sexual harassment trials must necessarily include female jurors. The idea that one gender is better suited to hear a class of cases than another, is itself a sexist concept. Alverio contends that this trial involved "women's issues." We disagree. This trial concerned an allegedly hostile work environment created by sexually explicit comments and gestures. Productive work environments, free of harassment, are not merely a woman's worry, they are a national concern. Alverio's assumption that women, by virtue of their gender, are better suited to adjudicate these cases falls prey to the very stereotypical generalizations that the Court sought to eradicate in *J.E.B. v. Alabama ex rel. T.B.*, 511 U.S. at 132–33 (documenting "romantic paternalism" that justified exclusion of women from polluted atmosphere of courtrooms). Moreover, protection from gender-based discriminatory strikes is not a one-way street. It is a right that extends to both genders. . . .

For all these reasons, the judgment of the district court is Affirmed.

NOTES AND QUESTIONS

1. As the Seventh Circuit noted, *Batson*'s analytical structure is in three parts. First, a party may show a prima facie case of purposeful racial or gender discrimination by showing that the facts and any other relevant circumstances raise an inference that the party using the peremptory challenges excluded the veniremen from the petit jury on account of their race or gender. For example, a "pattern" of strikes (e.g., 60% of African-Americans were excluded using the challenges but only 30% of panels undergoing voir dire are African-American) or the questions and statements during voir dire examination and in exercising his challenges may support or refute an inference of discriminatory purpose. If the first step is satisfied, the second step shifts the burden to the opposing party to show a neutral explanation for challenging the jurors, although the explanation need not satisfy the proof justifying exercise of a challenge for cause. Finally, the trial court then will have the duty to determine if the challenging party has established purposeful discrimination.

2. Intentional discrimination in jury selection is prohibited on the basis of both race and gender. For example, in *Hernandez v. New York*, 500 U.S. 352, 111 S.Ct. 1859, 114 L.Ed.2d 395 (1991), the Court found that Hispanics have a right to be free from discrimination in jury selection. Then, in *J.E.B. v. Alabama ex rel. T.B.*, 511 U.S. 127, 114 S.Ct. 1419, 128 L.Ed.2d 89 (1994), the Court extended *Batson* and held that the Equal Protection Clause forbids the exercise of a peremptory challenge based upon the gender of a prospective juror. "Striking individuals on the assumption that they hold particular views simply because of their gender is practically a brand upon them, affixed by law, an assertion of their inferiority."

Does the Batson analysis apply to other "groups"? Ethnic groups? Religious groups? Is the immutability concept the same for *Batson* as it is for a challenge to the array, discussed *supra*?

3. If the chosen race-neutral reasons for the strikes "are so far at odds with the evidence that pretext is the fair conclusion," those explanations may indicate "the very discrimination the explanations were meant to deny." In *Miller-El v. Dretke*, 545 U.S. 231, 125 S.Ct. 2317, 162 L.Ed.2d 196 (2005), the Court found reversible error when the trial court accepted race-neutral explanations which were pretextual. Peremptory challenges were used to strike ten of eleven qualified black venire panel members, when at last two of them were "ostensibly acceptable" to a prosecutor seeking the death penalty, and there were strong similarities between struck black venire members and retained white venire members.

Does *Batson* require the neutral explanation for peremptorily striking a potential juror to be derived from voir dire? Most decisions have answered in the negative. A party may use her own personal knowledge concerning a juror and information supplied from outside sources. The test is not whether the information is true or false; it is whether she has a good-faith belief in the information and whether she can articulate the reason to the trial court in a race-neutral or gender-neutral way which does not violate the defendant's constitutional rights. The trial court then decides whether the party has acted with a prohibited intent.

PROBLEMS

1. Evaluate the "reasonableness" of the explanation offered for the following peremptory challenges in a breach of contract case involving the sale of a home.

   a. African-American female struck because the mortgage on her son's home was recently foreclosed.

   b. African-American male struck because he never owned a home.

   c. White female struck because her stepfather is a real estate broker.

   d. White female struck because her mother is a loan officer at a bank.

2. What result when the only African-American on the venire is struck by the plaintiff with a peremptory challenge "because he absolutely failed to establish eye contact with the plaintiff during questioning, and in plaintiff counsel's amateur psychological opinion, seemed not to be possessed of a certain degree of assertiveness which the plaintiff prefers to have in jurors."

3. In *Davey v. Lockheed Martin Corp.*, 301 F.3d 1204 (10th Cir.2002), a gender-based employment discrimination case, the court found that a prima facie case of discrimination in the exercise of peremptory challenges had occurred after three women were removed from the jury. The court then asked the party exercising the challenges for a neutral explanation.

> Counsel for defendant: There's a common basis for striking actually all three of those people. And that is none of them work in a workplace setting. This is a case of discrimination, alleged discrimination in the workplace. They need to understand concepts such as performance evaluations, rankings, what supervisors are confronted with on a day-to-day basis is something that would be useful to the jurors' understanding of the case. [Ms. Elder] is not working outside of the home. Miss Whitely is not working outside of the home, and Miss Murley is not working for an employer but works for herself selling Mary Kay cosmetics. So frankly, the major basis for striking each one of them is that they do not have current employers and so they would not have that perspective to bring to their deliberations.

> Counsel for plaintiff responded: Your Honor, that's clearly pretexual. Let's take Ms. Elder. Ms. Elder worked for ten years as a nurse. She was a head nurse. Had responsibilities for other individuals whom she was supervising as a nurse. She clearly was someone who was aware of policies and procedures. Nurses have to

follow those policies, and clearly she knew about personnel policies because that was her job.

As judge, how would you respond to the proffer of a neutral explanation for the exercise of a peremptory challenge? Does *Alverio* help you reach a conclusion?

4. On April 13, the Ku Klux Klan held a rally on the steps of the local courthouse. Although the rally itself occurred without incidents leading to arrests, a member of the Klan, Karl Kody, a 25-year-old unemployed Caucasian, swung his uniform at a crowd of people who were protesting the Klan's presence. Several persons in the crowd sued Kody for common law battery. At trial, Karl's attorney, Kalvin Cline, used all three of the defense's available peremptory challenges to remove the following African-Americans from the jury. (Cline's reasons for striking each of the three jurors, though undisclosed to anyone other than Kody at this time, are listed.)

    a. Juror A is Gerald Jones, a 72-year-old retired accountant. Cline felt that Mr. Jones would be antagonistic toward Kody because Kody is unemployed.

    b. Juror B is Victoria Chandler, a 35-year-old garment worker. Cline believed that Ms. Chandler would be hostile toward Kody because of the way he dresses.

    c. Juror C is Stokely Jackson, a 41-year-old salesman who is the President of the local chapter of the NAACP. Cline believed that Jackson would be hostile to Kody because of his political views.

After the defense used its peremptory challenges, no African-American jurors remained on the jury. Prior to swearing in the jurors, is there any motion that you as plaintiff's counsel can present to the judge to question Cline's actions?

EXERCISE

For the state where a) you intend to practice after graduation, b) your law school is located, and/or c) your professor assigns, go to that state's annotated statutes and research the statutes and procedural rules by which the jury selection process is governed. Based on your research, print the statute or rule and bring it to class for discussion. In addition, answer the following questions.

1. What are the rules governing the conduct of voir dire? Must the judge permit counsel for the parties to address the jurors personally?

2. Are any jurors in excess of the statutory number permitted to be selected during jury selection, in case another juror must be excused? If so, how many others may be selected? What is their role, i.e., are they regarded as alternate jurors from the beginning or is the actual jury which will decide the case selected from the remaining jurors as of the time the jurors retire to deliberate? How late may jurors be substituted, at the time the jurors retire to deliberate or later?

SEC. E JURY INSTRUCTIONS AND JURY VERDICTS 623

3. How many peremptory challenges do the rules permit? Can the number be expanded? If so, by what standard?

4. Must a jury verdict be unanimous or may it be a simple or supermajority?

5. After the judge announces the jury's verdict, may the jury be polled so that each juror may be asked whether she agrees with the jury verdict in open court?

E. JURY INSTRUCTIONS AND JURY VERDICTS

1. REQUESTING AND OBJECTING TO JURY INSTRUCTIONS

Before a jury leaves the courtroom to deliberate, the judge must instruct them about the applicable law. Prior to the jury instructions, the parties can request that the judge instruct the jury about certain topics, as well as certain versions of topical instructions. (Even if no party submits requested instructions, the judge still must instruct the jury.) By Federal Rule 51(a), the parties submit proposed jury instructions to the court, no later than the close of the evidence and at an earlier time if the court chooses. Local rules for that trial court also may set time limits for making jury instruction requests. The court may consider late submissions, especially for issues that were unanticipated when the parties submitted their requests.

Before instructing the jury and before the parties' closing arguments to the jury, the trial court informs the parties about the instructions it intends to use. A party may object to a proposed instruction, regardless of whether it was requested by the party. Besides enabling the parties to object to the instructions the trial court intends to give, informing them also permits them to adjust their closing arguments to "fit" the instructions. For example, if the defendant requested an instruction on the defense of assumption of risk but the court declined to instruct the jury about that defense, in the closing argument to the jury the defendant is better off concentrating on arguing the facts to the jury that parallel the actual jury instructions rather than emphasizing the plaintiff's assumption of a risk.

What should the jury instructions include? They should cover every important issue in the case and communicate the applicable principles of law. What follows is a sample jury instruction for the defense of assumption of risk in a tort case.

> The defendant has raised the affirmative defense that the plaintiff assumed the risk of injury from the danger which the plaintiff claims caused his injury. To prove this defense, the

defendant has the burden of proving each of the following propositions:

First, that the defendant and the plaintiff had [an agreement] [a contract] under which the plaintiff was to participate in activities which exposed him to the danger that resulted in the injury of which he complains, namely, _____.

Second, that the danger was one that ordinarily accompanies the activities contemplated in the [agreement] [contract].

Third, that the plaintiff had actual knowledge of this danger and understood and appreciated the nature and extent of the risk;

Fourth, that the plaintiff voluntarily subjected himself to this danger; and

Fifth, that this danger was the cause of the plaintiff's [alleged] [injuries] [damages].

If you decide that each of these propositions has been proved, then your verdict should be for the defendant [as to Count ___]. If, on the other hand, you decide that any of these propositions has not been proved, then the defendant has not proved the affirmative defense of assumption of the risk.

Ill. Pattern Jury Instr. Civ. § 13.01 (2009).

Merely tendering proposed jury instructions to a court does not preserve an objection to those instructions. Rule 51(c)(1) requires a party to object in a timely manner to the instructions on the record, stating "distinctly" both the instruction objected to and the grounds for the objection. An objection to the failure to instruct on an issue or to a particular instruction is not preserved simply by tendering a proposed instruction to the trial court.

JARVIS V. FORD MOTOR CO.
283 F.3d 33 (2d Cir. 2002)

SOTOMAYOR, CIRCUIT JUDGE.

[Plaintiff-driver sued Ford Motor for negligence and strict liability, claiming that a Ford Aerostar minivan's design defect caused sudden acceleration. A jury returned a verdict for the plaintiff on the negligence claim but not on the strict products liability claim, and awarded damages to the plaintiff.]

Immediately after the jury returned its verdict but before the jury was excused, Ford moved for relief on the basis of an inconsistent verdict. The district court agreed with Ford that the jury verdict was "irreconcilable," but did not reach the issue of what relief would be appropriate because, as discussed above, it found the evidence insufficient to sustain a verdict for Jarvis and granted Ford's motion for judgment as a matter of law.

We find that any potential error related to the jury instructions and verdict sheet, and not to the jury's general verdicts and that, therefore, Ford's objection needed to conform to the strictures of Fed.R.Civ.P. 51. We hold that the district court, in finding that Ford had not waived its objection, erred, as a matter of law, in not applying the Fed.R.Civ.P. 51 requirements that any objection must "stat[e] distinctly the matter objected to and the grounds of the objection." Applying this legal standard, we find that Ford's pre-trial statement that the court should charge either negligence or strict liability, but not both, failed to alert the court to the precise nature of Ford's objection and its legal grounding. Finding no "fundamental error" in the instructions, we order the district court to reinstate the jury verdict. . . .

[The jury instructions make it] abundantly clear that the jury was instructed that it could find Ford liable under theories of either negligence or strict liability or both. The verdict sheet given to the jury accurately reflected this by indicating, after question 1(a) concerning strict liability, "IF YOUR ANSWER TO QUESTION 1(a) IS 'NO', THEN PROCEED TO QUESTION 2(a)." Question 2(a), concerning negligence, asked, "Do you find by a preponderance of the evidence that the defendant Ford Motor Company was negligent in the design of the cruise control system in the 1991 Ford Aerostar? (Plaintiff's Burden of Proof)," followed by blanks to check either "yes" or "no." The jury checked the "no" blank in response to question 1(a), and "yes" in answer to question 2(a).

. . . In reviewing de novo the district court's choice of legal standard, we hold that it did not apply the correct standard in ruling that Ford was relieved from the obligation of presenting a more explicit, precise, and reasoned objection before the jury deliberated. Applying the correct standard, we find that Ford did not satisfy the requirements of Fed.R.Civ.P. 51. . . .

Ford claims that once the district court, knowing Ford's preference for charging one but not both theories of liability, decided to send the case to the jury under theories of both negligence and strict liability, Ford was not required to object to the jury instructions or the verdict sheet because it was reasonable to conclude that further objection would be unavailing, echoing the district court's finding that no further objection was necessary. We disagree. At no point in its ruling on Ford's preservation of its objection did the district court consider whether Ford had satisfied the appropriate legal standard that Ford "stat[e] distinctly the matter objected to and the grounds of the objection." Fed.R.Civ.P. 51. We find that Ford did not, and note that the district court's own comments lead to the same conclusion.

In their proposed jury instructions submitted prior to trial, both Ford and Jarvis requested that the court charge the jury on both negligence and strict products liability. After receiving the parties' proposed requests to charge, the judge wrote to the parties asking them to "clarify their positions with respect to the appropriate causes of action in this case." The court inquired, *inter alia*, whether "it would be sensible" to follow the approach taken in *Pahuta v. Massey-Ferguson, Inc.*, 170 F.3d 125, 134–35 (2d Cir.1999), "in which the plaintiff withdrew his negligence cause of action as duplicative of his strict liability claim," stating that the court's research "indicates a substantial overlap in the elements of negligence and strict liability claims for defective design."

Counsel for Jarvis responded that "we do not regard the negligence claim and the strict liability claim as duplicative but, rather, we regard them as distinct, unlike the apparent factual situation referenced in Pahuta v. Massey-Ferguson, Inc." The letter explained that "[t]his claim raises the question whether the defendant Ford acted reasonably in selecting the design for the Aerostar cruise control system, whereas the strict liability claim focuses upon the question whether the Aerostar cruise control system itself was unreasonably dangerous."

Counsel for Ford, in its letter to the district court, responded only that "[w]e have read the *Pahuta* case and agree with the Court that the Court should charge either negligence or strict products liability, but not both." The letter offered no legal argument or citation to any other authority as to why both theories could not be charged. The *Pahuta* case itself does not state that the two causes of action are necessarily duplicative. There, we mentioned in a footnote merely that "[a]t the charging conference, *Pahuta* abandoned a negligence cause of action as duplicative of his strict liability claim." *Pahuta*, 170 F.3d at 134 n. 7. The parties appear to agree, with good reason, that our footnote in *Pahuta* did not decide the issue of the potential overlap of the two theories of liability for all future design defect claims brought under New York law. Tellingly, in arguing on appeal that the causes of action are duplicative as a matter of law, Ford makes no mention of *Pahuta*. . . .

After the charge to the jury, Ford did not object to instructing the jury on both theories of liability or to the instruction in the jury charge and on the verdict sheet that the jury could find Ford negligent but not strictly liable. . . .

We review de novo the district court's interpretation of the legal standard for waiver under Fed.R.Civ.P. 51. We hold that the district court failed to apply the correct legal standard in ruling that the expression of Ford's "fundamental position" sufficed to preserve its objection to the jury instruction and verdict sheet. The district court neither mentioned Fed.R.Civ.P. 51 or its requirements nor applied them in substance.

Applying the requirements of Fed.R.Civ.P. 51 de novo, we find that Ford waived any objection.

Under Rule 51, an objection must "stat[e] distinctly the matter objected to and the grounds of the objection." Fed.R.Civ.P. 51. "The purpose of the Rule is to allow the trial court an opportunity to cure any defects in the instructions before sending the jury to deliberate." *Fogarty v. Near N. Ins. Brokerage, Inc.*, 162 F.3d 74, 79 (2d Cir.1998). The "objections to a charge must be sufficiently specific to bring into focus the precise nature of the alleged error." *Palmer v. Hoffman*, 318 U.S. 109, 119 (1943). . . .

The statement by Ford that "[w]e have read the *Pahuta* case and agree with the Court that the Court should charge either negligence or strict products liability, but not both," failed to state distinctly either "the matter objected to" or "the grounds of the objection." Fed.R.Civ.P. 51. The specific objection that Ford asks this Court to read into its pre-trial correspondence is that the jury's finding that the cruise control system of the 1991 Ford Aerostar was not designed in a defective manner presumes that Ford was not negligent in the design of the cruise control system. Ford's statement that either negligence or strict liability, but not both, should be charged, does not distinctly state this objection. Ford's current contention is not that it was error to charge two theories of liability but rather that, after determining that Ford was not strictly liable, the jury should not have considered whether Ford was negligent. Ford's conduct at the pre-trial conference, if anything, obscured any objection it might have made in its correspondence with the court. At the conference, the speaker identified by Jarvis as "counsel for Ford" explained that "it seems that the claim of the plaintiff here is one of negligence and certain product liability." After the court later asked, "[s]o you don't want me to charge negligence?" the speaker, identified again by Jarvis as a counsel for Ford, responded, "Well, we're going to reserve on that. We want you to leave negligence in for now." Accordingly, Ford did not distinctly state "the matter objected to." In fact, it appears to have asked the court to leave both causes of action in the jury charge.

Neither did Ford state distinctly "the grounds of its objection." In the pre-trial correspondence and conference, Ford made no legal argument for charging only one cause of action outside of the passing reference to our footnote in the *Pahuta* case. In that footnote, we mentioned merely that the plaintiff had voluntarily withdrawn a negligence charge. *Pahuta*, 170 F.3d at 134 n. 7. Ford cited no authority to show why the district court should find the negligence cause of action duplicative of the strict liability claim in this case. In recalling how it came to charge the jury under both theories, the district court remarked simply that the plaintiff had asked for the charge and that in one case, presumably *Pahuta*, "the plaintiff[ ] had agreed to drop one of the claims." After the verdict, in ruling on

Ford's motions, the district court rebuked counsel for not calling its attention earlier to the relevant legal authority in New York regarding the similarities between negligence and strict liability for product defects, indicating its suspicion that it appeared that this failure was "a tactical decision" made "for strategic reasons to refrain from informing us of the overlap and potential for inconsistent verdicts." *Jarvis*, 69 F.Supp.2d at 587 n. 8. In this regard, it appears that the district court agreed that Ford did not distinctly state "the grounds of its objection." Fed.R.Civ.P. 51.

. . . For the reasons stated, under the principles of Rule 51 Ford has waived its objection to verdict inconsistency. . . . In this ten-year litigation, the issue of the jury charge was litigated extensively. Ford asked for this jury charge, presumably for strategic reasons, and was well apprised of the law of waiver. To excuse Ford from the well-established rules of waiver would permit precisely the sort of "sandbagging" that the rules are designed to prevent, while undermining the ideal of judicial economy that the rules are meant to serve.

Although Ford has not requested that we do so, this Court may review jury instructions and verdict sheets for "fundamental" error even when a litigant has not complied with the Fed.R.Civ.P. 51 objection requirements. . . . We have found relief from fundamental error to be warranted when the jury charge "deprived the jury of adequate legal guidance to reach a rational decision." *Werbungs v. Collectors' Guild, Ltd.*, 930 F.2d 1021, 1026 (2d Cir.1991). Because the degree of overlap between negligence and strict liability for design defects is unsettled under New York law, the integrity of the trial was not endangered by the jury instructions and verdict sheet in this case. . . .

NOTES AND QUESTIONS

1. Does the court's opinion exalt form over substance? What is the court's point about the rule's purpose being the avoidance of "sandbagging"?

2. The instructions must include direction to the jurors about the number of jurors required for a verdict. In criminal cases, unanimity is required for a conviction or an acquittal under the federal constitution and most state constitutions. In federal civil cases, Federal Rule 48 states that a verdict must be unanimous. By contrast, in many states the minimum number of jurors who must agree to a verdict is less than unanimity, e.g., 9 of 12 jurors must agree, or 5 of 6 jurors must agree. What is the effect of the distinction? Is a jury more likely to reach a verdict sooner when a supermajority is required rather than unanimity? What is the likely effect of the distinction on jury deliberations?

2. JURY VERDICTS

Trial courts in most civil jury cases instruct the jury to return what is known as a "general verdict," which in a single statement reflects the jury's conclusion about which party wins the case. The essence of a general verdict is "We find in favor of the plaintiff" or "We find in favor of the defendant." Federal Rule 49 describes two alternate methods to a general verdict: a special verdict and a general verdict with interrogatories.

LAVOIE V. PACIFIC PRESS & SHEAR CO.
975 F.2d 48 (2d Cir. 1992)

CARDAMONE, CIRCUIT JUDGE.

This appeal presents a question of waiver. After a young industrial worker suffered a severe injury caused by the equipment she was operating, she sued and obtained a substantial verdict at the hands of a jury. The equipment maker asserts for the first time on appeal that written questions and a verdict form submitted by the trial judge and responded to by the jury resulted in an inconsistency that entitles it to a new trial. Because defendant had ample opportunity—as well as notice of the possible inconsistency to which it presently objects—throughout the entire trial proceedings from pre-trial conference to judgment, yet failed to speak, it must now be ruled that it should hold its peace. . . .

Plaintiff filed suit in the District of Vermont in February 1989 alleging defendants were liable in strict liability for selling a product that was unreasonably dangerous, for breach of implied warranty of merchantability and breach of implied warranty of fitness for a particular purpose, and for negligence. A trial on the merits was held from May 14–25, 1991. At the conclusion of the trial, following a precharge conference, the jury was instructed on the law pertaining to these four alternative theories of liability. The trial court instructed the jury specifically on the theory of negligence as separate and independent from the strict liability and the two warranty theories. No objection was made by defendant at the charging conference or during the charge itself regarding any inconsistency between the different theories of liability, nor did defendant interpose an objection respecting the submission of separate interrogatories and separate general verdict forms to the jury pertaining to each theory.

Although the jury found Pacific not liable for breach of either warranty or on grounds of strict liability, it found both plaintiff and defendant negligent and assigned 85 percent of the liability, or $412,250 in damages, against defendant. Subsequent to the verdict, the jurors were individually polled, and a bench conference was held with counsel. Again, inconsistency of the verdicts was not raised on any of these occasions.

After the jury was discharged and before the judgment was entered, defendant moved on May 30, 1991 for judgment notwithstanding the verdict or, in the alternative, for a new trial. Pacific declared that insufficient evidence supported the jury's finding of negligence on defendant's part, the evidence plainly showed the conduct of GE's employees was an efficient intervening proximate cause, and the verdict was the product of jury sympathy. Once again, no objection on the ground of inconsistency was noted. The trial court denied these motions.

On defendant's appeal from the $422,536.35 judgment, it challenges for the first time the verdicts the jury handed down as irreconcilably inconsistent. It contends, therefore, negligence is entirely subsumed by breach of warranty and strict liability. Findings of no liability under either of those theories require, as a matter of law, a finding of no negligence on its part as the seller. Defendant alternatively contends the evidence adduced at trial is insufficient as a matter of law to support a finding of negligence.

The parties disagree whether the forms submitted to the jury called for special verdicts, as contemplated by Fed.R.Civ.P. 49(a), or a general verdict accompanied by written answers to interrogatories, as contemplated by Fed.R.Civ.P. 49(b). The trial court submitted two sets of forms to the jurors for their use in reporting their decisions. First, on a form with "Special Verdict" printed across the top, the jury was asked whether defendant breached either of the two implied warranties, whether it was strictly liable, whether it or plaintiff was negligent, whether any of these findings were a proximate cause of plaintiff's injuries, and what percentage of contribution and amount of damages was attributable to each cause of the injuries. The trial court also requested the jury to complete a second form labeled "Verdicts" that asked whether defendant was liable to plaintiff under each of the four alternative theories and for what amount.

Rule 49 of the Federal Rule of Civil Procedure states that a trial court may request from a jury a special verdict or a general verdict accompanied by answers to interrogatories. Under Rule 49(a) special verdicts are described as "a special written finding upon each issue of fact." A general verdict accompanied by answers to interrogatories, provided for in Rule 49(b), permits a jury to make written findings of fact and to enter a general verdict. The distinction between the two provisions is that under Rule 49(a) the jury answers primarily factual questions for the benefit of the trial court which then applies the law to those answers. Under Rule 49(b), the jury after being fully instructed answers the interrogatories, renders a general verdict and the trial court enters judgment on the jury's verdict.

In this case, the trial court's first set of forms called for answers to specific questions that would have served as either special verdicts, as contemplated by Rule 49(a), or answers to interrogatories, as contemplated by Rule 49(b). But the second set of forms was a hybrid; it did not offer the jurors only the ultimate choice normally called for by a general verdict—the defendant is liable to the plaintiff for a specified amount of damages, or the defendant is not liable to the plaintiff. Instead, it purported to ask for general verdicts on different theories of liability. Since the jury's fact-finding with respect to the different theories of liability was already properly elicited by the first set of detailed questions, the jurors should have been asked on the general verdict form only whether the defendant was liable to the plaintiff, and, if so, what damages are awarded. Despite the somewhat unusual nature of the general verdict forms submitted to the jury, it is apparent that the trial judge was endeavoring to use the provisions of Rule 49(b) and was seeking a general verdict accompanied by answers to interrogatories.

Although Rule 49(a) provides no instructions to the trial court for resolving jury inconsistencies in its special verdicts, we have held that judgment may not be entered pursuant to inconsistent special verdicts. Rule 49(b) instructs the trial court how to proceed when there are inconsistencies between the answers to the interrogatories and the general verdict. "When the answers are inconsistent with each other and one or more is likewise inconsistent with the general verdict, judgment shall not be entered, but the court shall return the jury for further consideration of its answers and verdict or shall order a new trial." Fed.R.Civ.P. 49(b).

Where there are seeming inconsistencies between interrogatory responses and a general verdict, a trial court should normally attempt to reconcile them. When the verdicts are not capable of reconciliation and resubmission of the determinations for reconsideration or clarification is not possible because the jury has been discharged, a new trial may be—but is not always—required.

The charge to the present jury required that it consider the necessary legal principles given to it by the trial court and make determinations of ultimate liability. In such case, the answers to the questions submitted to the jury are not special verdicts, despite the use of those words in the title appended to the form, and Rule 49(a) therefore does not apply. Further, the alleged inconsistency to which defendant points is between two general verdicts on different legal theories and not between a general verdict and responses to interrogatories. Hence, the instruction given to trial courts under Rule 49(b) has no application.

In any event, we think defendant waived its challenge to the jury verdict as inconsistent. It had ample opportunity to raise its objection to the alleged inconsistency and the course of the trial proceedings put it on notice that an inconsistency might arise. At a bench conference before the parties made their opening statements, Judge Coffrin noted the potential for inconsistencies between the four theories of recovery plaintiff alleged. He commented on the overlapping nature of the alternative theories again on the last day of trial. The instructions he gave the jury were discussed in detail with counsel at a precharge conference and at the bench just prior to the actual charge. Counsel were well aware of the content of the verdict forms submitted to the jury, including the separate questions relating to the four alternative theories.

After the jury returned its verdict, the district court polled the jurors individually and held a brief conference at the bench prior to the jury's discharge during which aspects of the verdict were discussed with counsel. Post trial motions were filed on May 30, 1991 and a hearing held on them on July 15, 1991. At no time throughout all these proceedings did defendant's counsel suggest the possibility that the verdicts rendered were inconsistent. . . .

Judgment affirmed.

NOTES AND QUESTIONS

1. Rule 49(b) describes a process by which the trial court may ask the jury to return a general verdict, but to accompany that general verdict with answers to certain interrogatories about particular issues in the case. A general verdict with interrogatories under Rule 49(b) requires the jury to give close attention to the more important fact issues and the jury's answers serve to check the propriety of the general verdict. One benefit of using this type of verdict is that if some legal error requires setting aside the general verdict and the answer to some of the interrogatories, it may be unnecessary to relitigate other issues already decided under properly submitted questions. For example, with no error on the issue of liability and causation, a new trial may be confined to damage issues.

The disadvantage of a general verdict with interrogatories is that the interrogatory answers may be inconsistent with each other *and* with the general verdict. The last part of Rule 49(b) addresses these issues. If the general verdict and the answers to specific questions are compatible, the court enters a judgment on the verdict and the answers. If the answers are consistent with each other but one or more of them is inconsistent with the general verdict, the trial court has three options: order the jury to deliberate further, order a new trial, or disregard the general verdict and order a judgment on the basis of the interrogatory answers (on the theory that special findings prevail over a general verdict). Finally, if the answers are inconsistent with each other and one or more of them is also inconsistent with the general verdict, the court must either order further deliberations or order a new trial.

2. Under Rule 49(a), the trial court has the authority to dispense with a general verdict altogether, and instead to submit various fact issues in the case to the jury in the form of individual fact questions, on each of which the jury is to return a special verdict. From the special verdict answers, the judge constructs the equivalent of a general verdict. A special verdict asks the jury to decide specific factual questions such as "At the time of the accident, was the plaintiff wearing her seat belt?" Because Rule 49(a) does not address the

issue of inconsistency between answers, courts have had to improvise rules on inconsistency. Answers should be consistent with each other, and it is the duty of the trial court to harmonize them if possible. When the answers are inconsistent, a new trial is likely unless the judge asks the jury to reconsider its verdict in an attempt to remove the inconsistency.

3. In *Bills v. Aseltine*, 52 F.3d 596 (6th Cir. 1995), plaintiff brought a civil rights action against police officers for allowing a private security agent to participate in a search of her residence. After the court submitted special verdict interrogatories to a jury, it entered judgment for the officer who invited private security agent into plaintiff's home during execution of search warrant. The plaintiff appealed.

> [Plaintiff] Bills argues that a special interrogatory on the verdict form did not state all the issues, was inaccurate, and consequently misled the jury. The verdict form provided to the jury stated: "Was it unreasonable under the circumstances for the defendant to invite [private security guard] William Meisling to enter plaintiff's home on August 20, 1987?" The court submitted questions asking if [police officer] Aseltine had a "reasonable and good faith belief" that he was not violating Bills's rights, and if his conduct proximately caused injury to Bills. The court also asked the jury to assess damages if appropriate. Bills contends that the court should have submitted her proposed special interrogatory: "Did Sgt. Aseltine unreasonably exceed the scope of the search warrant for the generator by permitting William Meisling, the Chief of Security at the Milford Proving Grounds, to enter the plaintiff's premises and conduct a general inspection for the suspected stolen GM property?"
>
> Whether a court uses a special or general verdict rests in its discretion, as does the content and form of any interrogatories it chooses to submit. *Portage II v. Bryant Petroleum Corp.*, 899 F.2d 1514, 1520 (6th Cir.1990). Therefore, an appellate court reviews for an abuse of discretion. Federal Rule of Civil Procedure 49 governs the use of special verdicts and general verdicts with interrogatories. A special verdict is used where the jury finds only issues of fact and the court applies the law, as opposed to a general verdict with interrogatories, which is used to give close attention to certain factual matters.
>
> The court below clearly used the latter. "Where special verdicts are involved, the jury's sole function is to determine the facts; therefore, neither an instruction on the law nor a summary concerning their role in relation to the law was necessary." *Id.* at 1521. The court's twenty-four jury instructions discussed legal matters in detail, and also required the jury to apply the law to the facts. The verdict form served only to direct the jury's attention to the most important issues: reasonableness, good faith, proximate cause, and damages.

Bills's proposed interrogatory is admittedly more detailed, but asks a question that is only slightly different. The plaintiff emphasizes whether Aseltine unreasonably exceeded the scope of the search warrant, while the court focuses on whether Aseltine's invitation was unreasonable. Undoubtedly, Bills would have preferred to remind the jury through the interrogatory that Meisling's presence was beyond the scope of the search warrant for the generator. However, that is the job of Bills's attorney at closing argument.

Bills cites several cases for the obvious proposition that special interrogatories must fairly present the relevant issues to the jury. Yet reasonableness, good faith, proximate cause and damage are the relevant issues. Further, the interrogatories must be considered in the context of the entire jury charge. In light of the court's detailed jury instructions, the interrogatories were neither inaccurate, misleading nor confusing.

4. Why do trial courts not favor special verdicts or general verdicts with interrogatories under Rule 49? First, as with discovery requests, it may be difficult for a judge to frame precise and accurate questions, leading to a corresponding increase in the chance for error. Second, jurors may misunderstand the relationship between the questions and give inconsistent answers. It is not surprising, then, that trial courts generally exercise their discretion not to use these "different" types of verdicts.

PROBLEMS

1. In a products liability case, the trial court submits a general verdict with interrogatories. The interrogatories address such fundamental issues as negligence, proximate cause, and the complete defense of assumption of risk. The jury returns with a general verdict for the plaintiff, and answers to the following interrogatories:

Was the defendant negligent?	Answer: Yes
Did the plaintiff assume the risk of injury?	Answer: Yes

Is there a problem with this verdict? If not, what should the court do? If so, what remedy is available to fix any problem?

2. Same as #1, except that the jury returns with a general verdict for the plaintiff, and answers to the following interrogatories:

Was there a defect in the product?	Answer: No
Was the defect the proximate cause of the plaintiff's injury?	Answer: Yes

Is there a problem with this verdict? If not, what should the court do? If so, what remedy is available to fix any problem?

3. Same as #1, except that the jury returns with a general verdict for the plaintiff, and answers to the following interrogatories:

Was there a defect in the product?   Answer: Yes

Was the defect the proximate cause of the plaintiff's   Answer: Yes
injury?

Is there a problem with this verdict? If not, what should the court do? If so, what remedy is available to fix any problem?

4. Same as #1, except that the jury reports to the court that it has agreed on a general verdict but cannot agree on the answer to one or more of the interrogatories. Can the trial judge withdraw all of the interrogatories and enter a general verdict?

EXERCISE

For the state where a) you intend to practice after graduation, b) your law school is located, and/or c) your professor assigns, go to that state's annotated statutes and research the procedural rules by which jury instructions and jury verdicts are governed. Based on your research, print the rule and bring it to class for discussion. In addition, answer the following questions.

1. As for jury instructions,

a. Are standard jury instructions used?

b. Must proposed instructions be in writing?

c. Are there any circumstances, e.g., plain error, when an instruction will be reviewed on appeal, without the need for an objection having been made?

d. Is the jury instructed before or after counsel's closing arguments?

2. As for jury verdicts,

a. Do the rules provide alternatives to a general verdict? If so, what types of alternative verdicts are used?

b. If the answer to the first part of 2.A is yes, what remedies are available when alternative verdict answers are inconsistent with each other and/or with the general verdict?

F. NEW TRIAL

INTRODUCTORY PROBLEM

Lincoln sued Kennedy Railroad Corp. for damages incurred from a train derailment that spilled toxic substances on Lincoln's farm causing damage to his soil and animals. At the conclusion of the four-day trial, the jury returned a verdict in favor of the defendant. After the verdict, Lincoln's counsel decided to file a motion for a new trial, in which Lincoln alleged several trial errors. After the second day of trial, without asking the trial judge's permission, two jurors visited the site of the derailment and reported their observations to the other jurors. During the jury's deliberations, the deputy bailiff told the jurors that they needed to find in favor of the railroad; otherwise the railroad company could relocate its headquarters to another community. In addition to the allegations of jury tampering and misconduct, Lincoln's counsel renewed objections she had made during trial to three of the court's rulings on the admissibility of evidence and to one of the trial court's instructions to the jury. Each of the court's decisions on evidentiary issues and on the jury instruction appeared to help Kennedy Railroad defend against Lincoln's allegations of negligence.

Are the allegations raised by Lincoln in the motion for new trial proper grounds for seeking a new trial?

Governing Rule: Rule 59(a).

The governing principle for Federal Rule 59(a) is that a court has the authority and the duty to order a new trial whenever it is necessary to prevent injustice. The federal standard is stated in broad terms, due to the impracticality of listing all the possible grounds for a new trial. (Some states in their rules do enumerate specific grounds for a new trial.) The appellate standard of review is for abuse of the trial judge's discretion.

New trials may be granted in bench trials and jury trials. Rule 59(a)(1)(B) allows a new trial to be granted in a bench trial "for any reason for which a rehearing has heretofore been granted" in federal courts. The trial court may take "additional testimony, amend findings of fact and conclusions of law or make new ones, and direct the entry of a new judgment."

In effect, the Federal Rule prescribes any ground for a new trial that has already been the basis for granting a new trial in another jury trial. The typical grounds for a new trial are that procedural errors at trial tainted the jury's decision-making process, e.g., improper admission or exclusion of evidence or improper jury instructions. The rationale for these grounds is that the errors led the jury to consider inappropriate information in reaching its verdict or to use the wrong rules of law in assessing liability or damages.

A trial court also can grant a new trial on the ground that the verdict was against the great weight of the evidence. A new trial on this basis is somewhat similar to a judgment as a matter of law, covered in the prior Chapter. However, there is a fundamental difference: rather than decide the case himself, the judge orders another trial, often with a different jury.

What does it mean for a judgment to be against the great weight of the evidence? The trial judge believes that there was sufficient evidence for the case to be submitted to the jury, and that a rational jury could decide in favor of the verdict-winner. Therefore, the case is not as one-sided as one warranting the grant of summary judgment or judgment as a matter of law. Nevertheless, the great weight of the evidence favors the verdict-loser. The judge is not required to view the evidence in the light most favorable to the verdict-winner, i.e., she is free to weigh the evidence for herself including an assessment of credibility. In other words, the judge can sit as a "13th juror." If the judge believes that the jury made a serious and clear mistake in its verdict, she can grant a new trial.

PIESCO V. KOCH
12 F.3d 332 (2d Cir. 1993)

KEARSE, CIRCUIT JUDGE.

This case, previously before this Court on appeal from the granting of summary judgment in favor of defendants, returns to us following the entry of judgment in favor of plaintiff after trial. Defendants City of New York (the "City"), its Department of Personnel (DOP), Juan Ortiz, and Nicholas LaPorte, Jr., appeal from a judgment entered in the United States District Court for the Southern District of New York after a jury trial before John S. Martin, Jr., Judge, awarding plaintiff Dr. Judith Piesco $1,800,000 in compensatory damages against all defendants, $50,000 in punitive damages against Ortiz, and $50,000 in punitive damages against LaPorte, on her claim under 42 U.S.C. § 1983 (1988) for termination of her employment in retaliation for the exercise of her speech rights under the First Amendment to the Constitution. . . . For the reasons below, we . . . vacate the denial of a new trial and remand for consideration of the new-trial motion under the proper legal standard.

[Piesco was hired to develop and administer employment examinations for various City jobs.] By all accounts, Piesco's tenure at DOP began well. For the period September 20, 1982, to June 30, 1983, both [of Piesco's supervisors] Ortiz and LaPorte rated her work "outstanding," concluding that Piesco had "proven to be a valuable asset to this agency." [H]owever, there is substantial dispute as to the quality of her performance thereafter.

In December 1984, DOP administered Examination Number 4061 ("No. 4061"), a test for whose development Piesco's bureau had responsibility, for the position of entry-level police officer. The test was modeled after the previous test for that position, Examination Number 1175 ("No. 1175"), but apparently was simplified by the removal of several complex questions. In February 1985, representatives from DOP and the Police Department met to set the "pass mark" for No. 4061, i.e., the score deemed to be the minimum passing grade. The pass mark for No. 1175 had been 82 (115 correct answers out of 140), but Piesco, arguing that No. 4061 should have a higher pass mark to compensate for its reduced complexity, pressed for a pass mark of 89 (125 correct out of 140). She argued that anything less would pass unqualified candidates. Eventually, the matter was compromised, and the pass mark was set at 85. Piesco testified that she had viewed that mark as inappropriate but had essentially thrown up her hands, stating, "You do what you want to do." In contrast, one participant at the meeting testified that Piesco did not express any disagreement with setting the mark at 85 when that compromise was reached. Ortiz testified that Piesco told him that though a pass mark of 89 was preferable, 85 was acceptable, and "she could live with an 85."

In early 1985, the New York State Senate Committee on Investigation, Taxation, and Government Operations, chaired by Senator Roy M. Goodman, established a committee to review the City's Police Department ("Goodman Committee"). Representatives of the Goodman Committee met with Piesco, Ortiz, and LaPorte at the DOP offices in June 1985. At that meeting, Piesco told them that, in her view, given the pass mark of 85, any moron could pass No. 4061.

Ortiz testified that he was surprised to hear this view because he had met with Piesco at least once every two weeks and she had never complained to him that the pass mark was too low. He also testified that after that initial meeting with the Goodman Committee representatives, Piesco recanted and agreed with him that 85 was an acceptable pass mark. In the wake of that meeting, Laporte suggested to Piesco that she needed to "learn to tell the truth more creatively," in light of the potential for negative publicity from use of terms such as "moron." During the following month, Piesco twice went to meet with representatives of the committee but did not disclose those meetings to Ortiz or Laporte.

On July 11, 1985, Piesco testified at a hearing of the Goodman Committee. At that hearing, Senator Goodman asked Piesco, "Would a functional illiterate pass the entrance examination to the Police Academy?" Piesco answered, "At the pass mark set, I would say that it is possible." There was apparently no attempt during the hearing to define either "functional illiterate" or "possible" with any specificity. At trial, in response to questioning from the court, Piesco clarified that by "functional illiterate" she meant "people who may not be able to appropriately read and write and understand," or "who could read words but could not draw enough inference from what they were reading to apply the concepts, particularly within the context of a given function, such as to be a police officer you have to understand concepts such as illegal search and seizure"; by saying that it was "possible" that such persons could pass if the pass mark were 85, she meant "likely."

Ortiz sent a letter to the Mayor on the day after Piesco's committee testimony, calling that testimony "irresponsible." He testified at trial that his first opportunity to try to discuss in detail with Piesco why she felt the

85 pass mark was unacceptable was a meeting on July 31, 1985. He began by asking her whether she had read the exam, but she stood up and said, "You don't know a f* * * * * * thing about testing. I am fed up with your bull* * * * and ineptitude." When Ortiz asked Piesco to calm down, she responded, "I don't have to do a f* * * * * * thing, why don't you fire me?" Ortiz promptly terminated the meeting and placed a letter of reprimand in Piesco's personnel file.

As indicated above, Piesco's performance for the first nine months of her tenure was rated "outstanding." For the following year, 1983–84, her performance was rated "very good," and in March 1983, July 1983, and May 1984 she received the maximum permissible merit raises in salary. For the year ending June 30, 1985, however, Ortiz and Laporte rated Piesco's performance "marginal." Both testified that the ratings were indicative solely of the continual decline they had observed in Piesco's performance, and that they had scrupulously avoided considering Piesco's remarks to the Goodman Committee because those remarks occurred after June 30, the end of the evaluation period. LaPorte informed Piesco of the 1984–85 evaluations personally on August 13, 1985. . . .

On December 27, 1985, Ortiz terminated Piesco's employment.

In the meantime, on December 19, 1985, Piesco commenced the present action under 42 U.S.C. § 1983, alleging principally that defendants' unfavorable personnel actions had been taken in retaliation for her testimony to the Goodman Committee, in violation of her First Amendment rights. The complaint was amended shortly thereafter to allege that the dismissal of Piesco on December 27 was a further act of retaliation. The amended complaint sought more than $8 million in compensatory and punitive damages.

[After trial,] [t]he jury, with appropriate instructions as to the burdens of proof, was asked to return a special verdict determining, as to liability, (1) whether Piesco's statements before the Goodman Committee were constitutionally protected, (2) whether the fact that she made those statements was a substantial or motivating factor in defendants' decision to terminate her employment, and (3) whether defendants would have dismissed her even if she had not made those statements. As to the first question, the jury was instructed that it must find that Piesco's statements were protected if it found that her testimony before the committee was truthful and responsive to the questions asked.

The jury answered the first two liability questions in the affirmative, finding that Piesco had established by a preponderance of the evidence that her statements to the Goodman Committee were constitutionally protected and that the fact that she made those statements was a substantial or motivating factor in defendants' decision to discharge her. The jury found that defendants had not established by a preponderance that they would have dismissed Piesco regardless of her statements. In response to questions addressed to damages, the jury found that Piesco should receive $1,800,000 as compensatory damages, and that she should receive $50,000 each from Ortiz and Laporte as punitive damages. [The trial court denied defendants' post-trial motions for judgment as a matter of law and for a new trial. After ruling that the trial court properly denied the post-trial motion for a judgment as a matter of law, the court turned its attention to the motion for a new trial.]

Defendants' alternative motion for a new trial was based on their contention that the jury's findings were against the weight of the evidence. In ruling on this motion, the district judge stated that if he had been the factfinder he "clearly would have reached a different result," however, he viewed this Court's then-recent decision in *Dunlap-McCuller v. Riese Organization*, 980 F.2d 153, 158 (2d Cir.1992) ("*Dunlap-McCuller*"), as holding that such a motion could not be granted unless the jury's verdict could be characterized as "egregious," a standard that he felt was not met here:

> If I were the factfinder, I clearly would have reached a different result. The uncontradicted facts on the record indicate that plaintiff was a difficult employee who went out of her way to antagonize those with whom she worked. It is hard to believe that any employee could reasonably expect to remain in her position for any substantial time after telling her immediate supervisor "I am fed up with your bull* * * *. . . . I don't have to do a f* * * * * * thing. Why don't you fire me?" . . .

> In addition, the evidence that plaintiff met secretly with the staff of the State Senate committee and lied about these meetings when she was subsequently questioned also suggests that she would not have remained in her position long even if her superiors fully respected her right to exercise her First Amendment freedoms. In addition, Judith Levitt testified that she would not have retained plaintiff in her position after Ms. Levitt succeeded Ortiz as personnel director in February 1986.

> Yet all of these facts were before the jury which apparently found that, but for her exercise of her First Amendment rights, plaintiff would have continued in the City's employ until her retirement and would have received regular pay increases during her remaining years as a City employee. Clearly, I believe this conclusion is wrong and appears to ignore the uncontradicted testimony of Judith Levitt that she would have fired Dr. Piesco for reasons unrelated to her State Senate testimony. Thus, I would be prepared to find that the jury's result was seriously erroneous which, according to the Second Circuit's decision in *Smith v. Lightning Bolt Productions*, 861 F.2d 363, 370 (2d Cir.1988), could justify the grant of a new trial.

SEC. F NEW TRIAL 641

More recently, however, the Second Circuit has cautioned that "the grant of a new trial on weight of the evidence should be reserve[d] for those occasions where the jury's verdict was *egregious.*" *Dunlap-McCuller v. The Riese Organization,* [980 F.2d at 158] (emphasis added). Because I do not believe the jury's verdict can be characterized as egregious, the motion for a new trial is denied.

Defendants contend that the court erred in applying an "egregious" standard, rather than the "seriously erroneous" standard, in ruling on their motion. Piesco contends that a district court's denial of a motion for a new trial is not reviewable. Though there is support for the proposition that the denial of a new trial is unreviewable in some circumstances, such a decision is plainly reviewable to the extent that the challenge is that the district court applied the wrong legal standard. We agree with defendants that the court did not apply the proper standard.

In numerous cases prior to *Dunlap-McCuller,* this Court had described the power of the district court to grant a new trial based on the weight of the evidence as one that could properly be exercised only if the court viewed the jury's verdict as "seriously erroneous." This formulation was adopted in *Bevevino v. Saydjari,* 574 F.2d 676, 684 (2d Cir.1978), to standardize the conceptual framework within which such motions should be decided. In the ensuing years, the "seriously erroneous" formulation was used in at least a dozen cases, including several in the same year in which *Dunlap-McCuller* was decided. In *Dunlap-McCuller,* a majority of the panel stated that "the grant of a new trial on weight of the evidence grounds should be reserved for those occasions where the jury's verdict was egregious." 980 F.2d at 158. For several reasons, we do not view this statement as having changed the legal landscape.

First, the *Dunlap-McCuller* statement was dictum. The panel had ruled that as to the contention that the district court erred in assessing the weight of the evidence, the panel had no authority to review the grant of a new trial. Second, a panel of the Court lacks the authority to overrule the prevailing law of the Circuit. Third, there is no suggestion in either of the *Dunlap-McCuller* opinions that the panel believed a new standard was being established. The concurring opinion, for example, described the majority as "not[ing]" that a new trial should not be granted unless the verdict was egregious, a description that treats the majority as recognizing an existing standard rather than adopting a new standard. Further, the majority opinion itself took explicit pains to follow the procedural law of this Circuit, stating, for example, "we are constrained by prior precedent in this Circuit, and consequently must hold that the district court's grant of a new trial is not reviewable," 980 F.2d at 157, and "[t]his panel is ... not empowered to overturn a longstanding precedent in this Circuit that has recently been reaffirmed by another panel," *id.* at 158. Given these statements, we think it inconceivable that the *Dunlap-McCuller* panel meant, sub silentio, to change the substantive standard that had been reaffirmed in four of our cases just months earlier.

In sum, the *Dunlap-McCuller* majority's obiter use of the word "egregious" was not meant to represent a change in circuit law. We construe its use of that term as an intended equivalent of "seriously erroneous," and we conclude that "seriously erroneous" remains the general standard that the district court should apply in ruling on a motion for a new trial on the ground that the jury's verdict is against the weight of the evidence, bearing in mind, as always, that [w]here the resolution of the issues depended on assessment of the credibility of the witnesses, it is proper for the court to refrain from setting aside the verdict and granting a new trial.

Accordingly, we reverse the order denying a new trial and remand for consideration under the proper standard.

NOTES AND QUESTIONS

1. Most new trial motions seek a retrial on all fact and law issues. However, Rule 59(a) enables a party to obtain a trial on "some" of the issues. If an error at trial requires a new trial on one issue that is separate from other issues in the case, and the error did not affect the determination of other issues, the scope of the new trial may be limited to the single issue. For example, a court can grant a new trial motion for damages only when the liability issues were properly determined. A new trial on damages only is improper, though, if there is a reason to think that an alleged error about damages may also have affected the liability issue. (A court will not grant a partial new trial on an issue that was not litigated at the first trial.)

2. *Erroneous evidentiary rulings.* A common ground for seeking a new trial is that the trial court committed reversible error in its evidentiary rulings. For example, in *Ruvalcaba v. City of Los Angeles*, 64 F.3d 1323 (9th Cir. 1995), a vehicle passenger brought a civil rights claim for excessive force during a traffic stop. After a jury verdict for the city and the officers, plaintiff moved for a new trial on the ground that the court had permitted the defendant officers "to testify about their knowledge of Ruvalcaba's criminal history." Citing the trial court's broad discretion, the Ninth Circuit affirmed the denial of plaintiff's new trial motion.

> The district court permitted the police officers to testify in a limited manner about their prior contacts with Ruvalcaba. This testimony was relevant to establish the facts and circumstances known to the officers during their confrontation with Ruvalcaba. In addressing an excessive force case under the Fourth Amendment, "the question is whether the officers' actions are 'objectively reasonable' in light of the facts and circumstances confronting them, without regard to

their underlying intent or motivation." *Graham v. Connor*, 490 U.S. 386, 397 (1989).

Keeping in mind that this trial involved the officers' alleged use of excessive force during the entire confrontation with Ruvalcaba, we conclude that the district court properly allowed the officers to testify about the facts known to them regarding Enrique Ruvalcaba's criminal past. The district court also properly admonished the jury to consider Ruvalcaba's prior bad conduct only in determining whether the officers' actions were reasonable under the circumstances. There was no abuse of discretion in admitting this evidence.

3. *Remittitur*. When a trial court determines that a jury award is excessive, it may offer the verdict-winner a reduction, known as remittitur, in exchange for the court's denial of a motion for a new trial. The verdict-winner's acceptance of the court's offer is a waiver of the right to appeal and the jury's verdict will be reduced to the maximum amount the jury could have awarded without being excessive. In *Eiland v. Westinghouse Elec. Corp.*, 58 F.3d 176 (5th Cir. 1995), the jury responded to plaintiff's product liability claim by awarding $5,000,000.

Of the $5 million in compensatory damages awarded to Eiland, approximately $3.6 is noneconomic loss, including pain and suffering, disfigurement, and impairment not accounted for in lost wages. Westinghouse made a post-trial motion for new trial or for remittitur, which the district court denied.

Mississippi law provides that a court may grant a remittitur if it finds that the damages are excessive "for the reason that the jury or trier of the facts was influenced by bias, prejudice, or passion, or that the damages awarded were contrary to the overwhelming weight of credible evidence. If such . . . remittitur be not accepted then the court may direct a new trial on damages only." Miss.Code Ann. § 11–1–55 (1972). Likewise, this circuit's case law provides for remittitur if the award is excessive, and new trial on damages alone if the plaintiff declines the remitted award.

There is a strong presumption in favor of affirming a jury award of damages. The damage award may be overturned only upon a clear showing of excessiveness or upon a showing that the jury was influenced by passion or prejudice. The decision to grant or deny a motion for new trial or remittitur rests in the sound discretion of the trial judge; that exercise of discretion can be set aside only upon a clear showing of abuse. *Id.* However, when this court is left with the perception that the verdict is clearly excessive, deference must be abandoned.

A verdict is excessive if it is "contrary to right reason" or "entirely disproportionate to the injury sustained." *Caldarera v. Eastern Airlines, Inc.*, 705 F.2d 778 (5th Cir.1983). While pain and suffering is not easily susceptible to monetary quantification, and the jury has broad leeway, "the sky is simply not the limit for jury verdicts, even those that have been once reviewed." *Simeon v. T. Smith & Son, Inc.*, 852 F.2d 1421 (5th Cir.1988). Eiland no doubt experienced intense pain during his initial treatment, and was left with a lifetime of disfigurement and some degree of disability. However, he was able to return to work part time within a few months, and full time by the end of two years. After a review of the record, we have concluded that the $5 million verdict was excessive and the district court abused its discretion in denying Westinghouse's motion for remittitur.

Our power to grant a remittitur is the same as the district court's. We determine the size of the remittitur in accordance with this circuit's "maximum recovery rule" by reducing the verdict to the maximum amount the jury could properly have awarded. Of course, our reassessment of damages cannot be supported entirely by rational analysis, but involves an inherently subjective component. *Id.* In our view, $3 million is the maximum the jury could properly have awarded in this case.

4. *Additur.* When a federal court finds that a jury award is inadequate, it cannot offer the verdict-winner an increase in the size of the verdict, known as additur, in exchange for the court's denial of a motion for new trial. The court's only option is to order a new trial. In *Dimick v. Schiedt*, 293 U.S. 474, 55 S.Ct. 296, 79 L.Ed. 603 (1935), Supreme Court held that additur violates the Seventh Amendment right to a jury verdict. It invades the province of the jury by granting an amount in excess of the jury's award. By contrast, remittitur results in an amount that is within the amount that the jury awarded. State courts, by contrast, are not bound by the Seventh Amendment, and may be free to use additur.

5. *Judge's own initiative.* Rule 59(d) permits a court to grant a new trial on its own initiative, without the need for a party to file a motion. The court's *sua sponte* order may be for any of the reasons that a party could request a new trial by motion. See, e.g., *Pryer v. C.O. 3 Slavic*, 251 F.3d 448 (3d Cir. 2001) (new trial granted when the verdict was against the great weight of the evidence). In *Pryer*, the jury awarded nominal damages of $1.00. Because of the additur principle, the trial court lacked the authority to increase the damage amount. Thus, the trial court's only way to express its displeasure with the jury's verdict for the plaintiff was to grant a new trial.

6. *Newly discovered evidence.* Courts have the authority to grant a new trial based on newly discovered evidence. However, few new trials are sought on this basis because a party must file a motion for new trial within twenty-eight days after the entry of judgment. Rule 59(d). Because that time frame is usually too short for newly discovered evidence to have been "discovered," newly discovered evidence is relied on as a remedy under Rule 60(b)(2) for vacating the judgment with a longer time to make that motion. See Part G of this Chapter.

7. *Altering or amending the judgment.* Rule 59(e) permits a party to file a motion asking the court to alter or amend its judgment, instead of granting a new trial. As with a motion for new trial, the appellate standard of review is abuse of discretion. The common grounds for a motion to alter or amend include an intervening change in the law, newly discovered evidence, correction of a clear error, and prevention of manifest injustice.

8. *Motions for judgment as a matter of law joined with motions for new trial.* The grant of a new trial based on the great weight of the evidence helps to deal with the same sort of problem addressed by judgment as a matter of law; namely, jury verdicts that are not supported by the evidence. Verdict losers accordingly will often want to file both motions, hoping for a judgment in their favor, but willing to accept a new trial as a second-best option. Because both Rule 50 and Rule 59 require the respective motions to be filed within 28 following entry of judgment (time periods that, unlike most periods in the rules, cannot be extended because of Rule 6(b)(2)), a party must file both the judgment as a matter of law and new trial motions within the same time frame. The judge must also rule on both motions, even though if the judge *grants* judgment as a matter of law, the new trial motion may seem moot. In such a case, Rule 50(c)(1) specifies that the judge's ruling on the new trial motion is "conditional."

9. When only a motion for a new trial is filed, an order granting a new trial is generally not immediately appealable because there is no final judgment from which to appeal. That ruling can be appealed, but not until *after* the new trial. (An order denying a new trial is appealable immediately, because the trial court already has or soon will enter a judgment on the verdict.)

When the verdict-loser files *both* a motion for a judgment as a matter of law and a motion for a new trial, the appealability issue depends on the court's disposition of the motions. Rules 50(c) and (d) govern.

- Trial court grants the JML motion and conditionally rules on the new trial motion. Rule 50(c)(1) permits the immediate appeal of the JML grant, regardless of the ruling on the new trial motion. Why? If the appellate court reverses the grant of the JML motion, it already knows the trial court's attitude toward a new trial and can evaluate that conditional ruling as well.

- Trial court denies the JML motion and grants the new trial motion. That ruling is not immediately appealable because there is no final judgment. The trial court holds the second trial.

- Trial court denies both the JML motion and the new trial motion. The trial court's ruling is immediately appealable, because the trial court has entered a judgment on the verdict.

PROBLEMS

1. Abbott sues Costello. After a bench trial, the judge finds for Abbott and enters judgment for Abbott. Costello believes that the judge improperly excluded important evidence. What post-trial motion should Costello make to the trial court?

2. In Problem #1, if the judge grants the motion, what relief can she provide to Costello?

3. Abbott sues Costello, who moves for a judgment as a matter of law after all the proof is presented but prior to the jury instructions. The court denies Costello's motion, and the jury finds for Abbott. Costello moves for a judgment as a matter of law within three days after the judgment. The judge denies the motion five weeks later. Costello then moves for a new trial, on the ground that the judge improperly excluded important evidence. What should the judge do?

4. Abbott sues Costello, who moves for a judgment as a matter of law after all the proof is presented. The court denies Costello's motion, and the jury finds for Abbott. Costello believes that the judge should have granted the judgment as a matter of law motion. What motion(s) should Costello file?

5. In Problem #4, Abbott is satisfied with the verdict but is also convinced that his case would have been stronger if the judge had not excluded important evidence that he offered at trial. What should Abbott do about his objection to the exclusion of evidence?

6. After a jury verdict for Abbott, Costello moves for a new trial on the ground of improper jury instructions. The judge grants the motion. Can Abbott appeal?

7. Same facts as Problem #6, except that Costello's motion for new trial is denied. Can Costello appeal?

8. Same facts as Problem #6, except that in addition to a new trial motion Costello moves for judgment as a matter of law. The judge grants that motion and conditionally grants the new trial motion as well. Can Abbott appeal?

9. Same facts as Problem #6, except that the judge denies the judgment as a matter of law motion but grants the new trial motion. Can Abbott appeal?

EXERCISE

For the state where a) you intend to practice after graduation, b) your law school is located, and/or c) your professor assigns, go to that state's annotated statutes and research the procedural rules by which new trial motions are evaluated. Based on your research, print the rule and bring it to class for discussion. In addition, answer the following questions.

1. Is the state rule for new trial motions a "laundry list" of grounds for granting a new trial, or is it similar to the federal rule which simply incorporates case law by reference?

2. Describe whether the state rule establishes standards for the appealability of new trial grants.

G. RELIEF FROM JUDGMENT

Federal Rule 59 requires that motions for a new trial be filed within 28 days following entry of judgment. This 28-day period cannot be extended. In many cases, however, a party will not discover grounds for a new trial until after the Rule 59 period has expired. In these situations Rule 60 provides a limited safety valve. The Rule authorizes a court to give a party relief from a judgment, which depending on the circumstance may be a new trial, or even an order setting aside the judgment without another trial.

Federal Rule 60(a) allows a trial court, on its own or by motion, to correct clerical errors in judgments, orders or other parts of the record. What is meant by a "clerical mistake"? The classic example is the "slip of the pen," where a judge erroneously added three zeros to a $1,000 judgment, converting it to a $1,000,000. That clerical error can be corrected at any time.

Federal Rule 60(b) covers mistakes made by the parties, as well as a number of other justifications for relief from a judgment. Review Rule 60(b). As you can see, relief is not available under the Rule merely because the judgment was against the great weight of the evidence. Instead, the Rule focuses on procedural problems, misconduct by an opposing party, or other events the party may not have known about within the 28 days following entry of judgment. Subsection c(1) requires parties to bring all Rule 60(b) motions within a "reasonable time," and further sets a maximum period of one year for motions under subparts b(1), (2), and (3). Because of Rule 6(b), that one-year period cannot be extended, unlike most other time limits in the Rules.

A motion for relief from a judgment under Federal Rule 60(b) requires a court to balance two important considerations: the finality of a judgment versus the justice of the outcome signified by the judgment. Usually, finality prevails, with the rationale being that in order to encourage parties to prepare fully for trial, a judgment-winner ought to rely on a resulting judgment. If a party believes that a trial court made a judicial error, the proper remedy is to file a timely motion for a new trial and/or appeal the judgment. Given the policy importance of final judgments, Rule 60 relief is seldom granted. There is, however, one exception: Rule 60 is often used successfully as a device for setting aside default judgments under Rule 55(c), as the following case illustrates.

TATE v. RIVERBOAT SERVICES, INC.
305 F.Supp.2d 916 (N.D. Ind. 2004)

MOODY, DISTRICT JUDGE.

[Plaintiffs filed a claim for overtime wages under federal maritime laws. After being served with the complaint, defendant failed to file an answer or respond to the complaint in a timely manner. After the plaintiffs demanded judgment for over $1,000,000 on the clerk of the court, the clerk entered a default and a default judgment was entered for the plaintiffs. Six weeks later, the defendant filed a motion to vacate the entry of default and the default judgment under Rule 60(b).]

III. DEFENDANT'S MOTION TO VACATE

Defendant seeks to set aside the default and judgment entered against it on September 11, 2003, pursuant to Fed.R.Civ.P. 60(b). Relief under Fed.R.Civ.P. 60(b) is an "extraordinary remedy and is granted only in exceptional circumstances." *McCormick v. City of Chicago*, 230 F.3d 319, 327 (7th Cir.2000) (internal quotation marks and citation omitted). However, because "the philosophy of modern federal procedure favors trials on the merits," *A.F. Dormeyer Co. v. M.J. Sales & Distrib. Co.*, 461 F.2d 40, 43 (7th Cir.1972) (internal quotation marks and citation omitted), Rule 60(b) relief is granted more liberally in those cases where the relief is sought to vacate a default judgment.

It is in the context of a default judgment that defendant seeks relief under Rule 60(b). In particular, defendant seeks relief pursuant to Rule 60(b)(1) which authorizes courts to free a party from the constraints of a final judgment against it for reasons of "mistake, inadvertence, surprise, or excusable neglect." Fed.R.Civ.P. 60(b)(1). To prevail on its Rule 60(b)(1) motion to vacate the default judgment against it, defendant must show: (1) good cause for the default; (2) quick action to correct the default; and, (3) the existence of a meritorious defense to the original action.

A. Good Cause

Federal Rule of Civil Procedure 60(b)(1) provides that good cause can consist of "mistake, inadvertence, surprise, or excusable neglect." It is the latter [sic]—"excusable neglect"—which defendant asserts was the cause of its failure to respond to plaintiffs' complaint in a timely manner, and thus, the cause of the default judgment entered against it.

The Supreme Court has adopted a "flexible understanding" of "excusable neglect," *Pioneer Inv. Services Co. v. Brunswick Associates Ltd. P'ship*, 507 U.S. 380 (1993), which "encompass[es] situations in which the failure to comply with a filing deadline is attributable to negligence." *Id.* at 394. Defendant admits that it was negligent in responding to plaintiffs' complaint, and plaintiffs seem to agree that ordinary negligence caused defendant to miss the deadline for filing an answer to their claims for seamen's wages.... [T]he fact that defendant's failure to respond to plaintiffs' complaint was caused by ordinary negligence, rather than some extraordinary circumstance over which the defendant did not have control, does not preclude this court from finding that defendant's actions constitute excusable neglect and therefore warrant relief under Rule 60(b)(1).

Ultimately, the important question here is whether or not defendant's "neglect" is "excusable." In determining whether defendant's neglect is excusable, this court must take account of "all relevant circumstances" surrounding defendant's failure to timely respond to plaintiffs' complaint, including: (1) defendant's reason for failing to comply with its filing deadline; (2) the potential impact of defendant's neglect upon judicial proceedings; (3) the danger of prejudice to plaintiffs should defendant's neglect be deemed excusable; and, (4) whether defendant acted in good faith. *Id.* at 395. Accordingly, this court shall now review the "relevant circumstances" of this case in order to determine whether defendant's failure to timely respond to plaintiffs' complaint is, in fact, "excusable."

First, defendant argues that the delay in responding to plaintiffs' complaint was the result of confusion over several lawsuits pending, or recently dismissed against defendant, all involving the same overtime wage claims presented by the same groups of plaintiffs who are, (or were), all represented by the same attorney. In particular, defendant points to confusion caused by the nearly identical-styled captions of the instant action and the Illinois Tate case, and the nearly identical list of plaintiffs involved in both lawsuits. Accordingly, defendant argues that confusion over "which claims were proceeding, which claims were resolved and whether there were, in fact, new lawsuits being filed" against defendant, caused defendant's attorney to neglect her obligation to respond to plaintiff's complaint, and this negligence resulted in the default judgment against defendant.

Plaintiffs admit that there were, and are a number of cases pending against defendant involving the same issues, the same or similar plaintiffs, and the same plaintiffs' attorney. Nevertheless, plaintiffs argue that these other cases are "of no moment," as any confusion caused by them cannot excuse defendant's default. (" 'Confusion' has never been a reason under Rule 60(b)(1) FRCP for relief from a judgment or default order."). However, plaintiffs do not cite to any law to support this argument, nor can this court find any cases stating that confusion over multiple cases involving the same plaintiffs and claims is not a factor that courts may consider when determining whether a party's neglect in complying with filing deadlines is excusable. Perhaps confusion alone cannot excuse a party's default, but the court must review "all [the] relevant circumstances" surrounding a default. See *Pioneer*, 507 U.S. at

395. Therefore, this court fails to see why a genuine confusion over multiple similar cases involving the same plaintiffs and defendant may not, in combination with all of the other relevant circumstances this court must look at, aid in excusing a defaulting party's neglect of deadlines. And, it seems to this court, that defendant's confusion was in fact genuine as, after all, even this court was, at first, a bit confused over "which claims were proceeding [and] which claims were resolved" against defendant. Moreover, this court's general experience confirms that multiple lawsuits in multiple venues involving the same claims by the same parties can cause a certain amount of confusion which sometimes (unfortunately) results in missed filing deadlines.

Second, defendant argues that because it acted promptly in seeking to vacate the default judgment against it, neither plaintiffs nor any proceedings have been prejudiced by defendant's neglect, and neither plaintiffs nor any proceeding would be prejudiced should this court vacate the default judgment in this case. The court agrees. First, as this matter did not progress past the complaint, vacating the judgment in this case would not prejudice any judicial proceedings. Second, as this case is relatively young, (it was instituted in this court less than a year ago), it is improbable that any necessary and/or important information concerning this case would have been lost or would be prejudicially difficult to retrieve. In addition, plaintiffs' attorney is engaged in at least two other currently-active cases in the Northern District of Indiana involving the same overtime wage claims thus making it likely that little additional work would be needed to pursue this lawsuit should the default judgment be vacated.

Ultimately, should this court vacate the default and judgment against defendant, plaintiffs would merely be required to pursue their case on the merits of their claims, or rather, do what they were (presumably) prepared and capable of doing before default judgment was entered. Certainly, assuming plaintiffs are indeed entitled to overtime wages from defendant, vacating the default judgment against defendant may delay the receipt of those wages from sometime in the near-future to sometime in the less-near-future, but such a delay seems relatively minor in comparison to the cost suffered by defendant—a judgment against it of over one million dollars—should the default judgment be allowed to stand. Moreover, any prejudice suffered by a minor delay in receiving their overtime wages—should plaintiffs even be entitled to those wages—waxes thin against the Seventh Circuit's "well-established policy favoring a trial on the merits over a default judgment," *C.K.S. Engineers*, 726 F.2d at 1205; a policy which helps to promote a fair system of justice by ensuring that decisions made by the administrators of that system are generally based upon a full presentation of the evidence. Therefore, were this court to vacate the default judgment against defendant, it would be very unlikely that plaintiffs or any proceedings would suffer prejudice.

SEC. G RELIEF FROM JUDGMENT

Finally, there is not any evidence to suggest that defendant acted in any other manner than in good faith while dealing with (or neglecting to deal with) this lawsuit; even plaintiffs do not argue that defendant acted in bad faith. Ultimately, since 1999, defendant's attorney, Ms. Mannix, has been actively involved in defending RSI in other related actions. Indeed, the day after plaintiffs' attorney moved for entry of default in this case, Ms. Mannix was engaged in defending RSI in the Harkins matter. The fact that defendant and Ms. Mannix have been actively involved in litigating other similar suits involving different combinations of the same plaintiffs and the same overtime wage claims strongly suggests, at least to this court, that neither defendant nor its attorney have acted willfully in neglecting to timely respond to plaintiffs' complaint in this case.

Therefore, as neither the plaintiffs nor any judicial proceeding would be appreciably prejudiced by this court's decision to vacate the default judgment against defendant, and as the default judgment rendered against defendant is attributable to a genuine confusion and was not caused willfully, this court believes the circumstances of this case excuse defendant's negligence in failing to respond to plaintiffs' complaint in a timely manner. Accordingly, this court finds that the circumstances of this case constitute "excusable neglect" within the meaning of Rule 60(b)(1). Defendant has therefore demonstrated "good cause" for its default.

B. Quick Action to Correct the Default

Rule 60(b) provides that a motion for relief from a judgment by reason of mistake, inadvertence, excusable neglect, etc., "shall be made within a reasonable time," but "not more than one year after the judgment, order, or proceeding was entered or taken." The defendant filed its motion for relief under Rule 60(b)(1) on October 29, 2003, approximately one-and-a-half months after learning of the entry of a default judgment against it. Thus, defendant was well within the one-year period prescribed by Fed.R.Civ.P. 60(b). However, in some cases, even a Rule 60(b)(1) motion filed within one year may be rejected as untimely if not made within a reasonable time. "What constitutes a 'reasonable time' ultimately depends on the facts of each case including the reason for delay, the practical ability of the litigant to have learned about the grounds of the judgment earlier, and the degree of prejudice to the other parties." *Kagan v. Caterpillar Tractor Co.*, 795 F.2d 601, 610 (7th Cir.1986).

The delay between the filing of defendant's motion and the entry of default judgment was approximately fifty (50) days. Defendant claims that this delay was ultimately due to "scheduling difficulties." Generally, "scheduling difficulties" alone, (without further explanation), would not be enough to convince this court to excuse such a delay. However, considering such scheduling difficulties in combination with the Seventh

Circuit's preference for litigating claims on the merits rather than letting harsh sanctions, like a default judgment, stand, see *C.K.S. Engineers*, 726 F.2d at 1205, and considering the other relevant circumstance of this case, such as the fact that the delay is unlikely to prejudice plaintiffs' position or claims, it seems that fifty days is not so tardy as to compel denial of defendant's motion. More importantly, neither defendant nor its attorney have shown any disrespect for, or have a history of demonstrating disrespect for the court or its processes, and, where such is the case, "courts have been inclined towards leniency," *Palmer v. City of Decatur*, 814 F.2d 426, 430 n. 6 (7th Cir.1987); this is especially true in the context of vacating a default judgment. Accordingly, this court finds that defendant has filed its Rule 60(b)(1) motion within a reasonable time after default judgment was entered against it.

C. Meritorious Defenses

Not only must defendant show that it had good cause for the default and that it acted quickly in attempt to cure the default in order to prevail on its Rule 60(b)(1) motion, but, defendant must also demonstrate that it has a "meritorious defense" to plaintiffs' claims. This does not mean that defendant needs to prove that its defense would, beyond a doubt, succeed in defeating the default judgment against it. Rather, defendant need only present a defense "which at least raises a serious question regarding the propriety of [the] default judgment and which is supported by a developed legal and factual basis."

In its motion to vacate the default judgment against it, defendant asserts that the claims of several of the plaintiffs in this action are barred by res judicata. . . . Plaintiffs readily admit that at least one of them—plaintiff Ringbauer—has filed more than one suit against defendant in which he voluntarily dismissed his claims pursuant to Fed.R.Civ.P. 41(a)(1); and, therefore, plaintiffs allow that Ringbauer may be dismissed, if need be, from the instant action. This admission alone certainly "raises a serious question regarding the propriety of [the] default judgment" against defendant. See *Phipps*, 39 F.3d at 165. Indeed, if Ringbauer is barred from bringing his claim against defendant, then the default judgment against defendant is wholly inappropriate as it includes plaintiff Ringbauer's claim.

Even without plaintiffs' admission however, defendant nevertheless still has a meritorious defense based upon res judicata. The docket reports for both the Ringbauer and Harkins cases, (provided to this court by defendant), and plaintiffs' Notice of Dismissal in the Illinois Tate case, (of which this court has taken judicial notice), demonstrate that many of the plaintiffs involved in this case have indeed dismissed their claims twice (and even three times in some instances) against defendant pursuant to Fed.R.Civ.P. 41(a)(1). . . .

SEC. G RELIEF FROM JUDGMENT 653

Accordingly, as defendant has demonstrated good cause for the default, has shown quick action, (given the circumstances of this case), to correct the default, and has clearly presented a meritorious defense to this action, this court hereby grants defendant's Motion to Vacate Entry of Default and Entry of Default Judgment.

NOTES AND QUESTIONS

1. Was *Tate*'s analysis consistent with *Pioneer*? Is the *Tate* court too flexible in its interpretation of what constitutes "excusable neglect"? How is the presence of prejudice, quick action, or a meritorious defense relevant to the justification for the neglect? Should any of those elements discussed in *Tate* be limited to Rule 55(c) motions to set aside default judgments using Rule 60(b) grounds, or are they applicable to all Rule 60 motions?

2. *Newly discovered evidence.* Rule 60(b)(2) allows for a new trial when the judgment loser obtains new evidence "that, with reasonable diligence, could not have been discovered in time to move for a new trial." While this may sound like a common ground for courts to grant relief, new trials under this provision are rare. The court in *Jones v. Lincoln Elec. Co.*, 188 F.3d 709 (7th Cir. 1999), required the party to prove five elements in order to obtain relief:

   a. That the evidence was discovered following trial;

   b. That due diligence on the part of the movant to discover the new evidence is shown or may be inferred;

   c. That the evidence is not merely cumulative or impeaching;

   d. That the evidence is material; and

   e. That the evidence would probably have changed the result in the original case.

The court denied relief, finding both that much of what the party offered was not "new," and that any new material was not likely to have affected the outcome.

Why are courts so reluctant to grant relief for newly discovered evidence? Are courts attempting to encourage more complete trial preparation?

3. *Fraud, misrepresentation, and other misconduct of an adversary.* Through the case law, a distinction has developed between Rule 60(b)(3) fraud and fraud on the court, which is said to be governed by Rule 60(b)(6). Not every fraud connected with presentation of a case is regarded as a fraud on the court. An example of fraud involves a nondisclosure by a party or attorney. Any wrong was between the parties only, rather than a fraud on the court, which involve a direct assault on the integrity of the judicial process, i.e., far more than an injury to a single litigant. *Hazel-Atlas Glass Co. v. Hartford-Empire Co.*, 322 U.S. 238, 64 S.Ct. 997, 88 L.Ed. 1250 (1944). Examples of fraud on the court include misrepresentations, bribery of a

judge, perjury where the attorney is involved, or employment of a particular lawyer in order to improperly influence the court. If you think these examples draw blurred lines, you are not alone, as some courts also experience difficulty making the distinction. However, the distinction may be important given the absence of a time limit for Rule 60(b)(6) fraud on the court. If you are in doubt about which provision is applicable, argue that both parts of the rule apply and let the court pick the applicable provision.

4. *Void judgment.* Rule 60(b)(4) simply states that relief from a judgment is available because the judgment is void. A judgment is void if the court lacked jurisdiction 1) over the subject matter; or 2) over the parties, when the motion is made to vacate a default judgment. Unlike most decisions under Rule 60(b), the issue of void judgments is a matter of law, rather than being discretionary with the court.

5. *Change of circumstances.* Rule 60(b)(5) provides relief from a judgment when the judgment is satisfied, released or discharged, when a prior judgment on which the current judgment is based has been reversed or vacated, or any other time when continued enforcement of the judgment would be unfair. The first clause, dealing with satisfied judgments, is rarely grounds for relief. Once a judgment has been paid, there is ordinarily no compelling reason for a court to cancel it.

The second basis is limited to cases where the current judgment is based on a prior judgment, e.g., a judgment in a suit to enforce a prior judgment which has been reversed. This basis is inapplicable merely because a case relied on as precedent by a court in rendering the current judgment has been reversed, because otherwise so-called final judgments would lose much of their "finality." It applies instead where the court felt compelled to treat a prior decision as controlling under claim or issue preclusion, doctrines discussed in Chapter 13.

The third application of Rule 60(b)(5) occurs when it is no longer equitable that the current judgment should have prospective application, i.e., the trial court can modify a decree with prospective effects in light of changed circumstances. The "prospective effect" aspect means that the main impact of Rule 60(b)(5) will be in cases involving injunctive or declaratory relief, rather than judgments for damages. The operative rationale is that it is no longer fair to enforce a judgment as a result of legislation or a change in the operative facts. In *Frew v. Hawkins*, 540 U.S. 431, 124 S.Ct. 899, 157 L.Ed.2d 855 (2004) noted this purpose of Rule 60(b)(5) as applied to consent decrees.

> The Rule encompasses the traditional power of a court of equity to modify its decree in light of changed circumstances. In *Rufo v. Inmates of Suffolk County Jail*, 502 U.S. 367, 112 S.Ct. 748, 116 L.Ed.2d 867 (1992), the Court explored the application of the Rule to consent decrees involving institutional reform. The Court noted that district courts should apply a "flexible standard" to the modification of consent decrees when a significant change in facts or law warrants their amendment.

Rufo rejected the idea that the institutional concerns of government officials were "only marginally relevant" when officials moved to amend a consent decree, and noted that "principles of federalism and simple common sense require the [district] court to give significant weight" to the views of government officials.

The federal court must exercise its equitable powers to ensure that when the objects of the decree have been attained, responsibility for discharging the State's obligations is returned promptly to the State and its officials.

The Supreme Court revisited Rule 60(b)(5) in *Horne v. Flores*, 557 U.S. 443, 129 S.Ct. 2579, 174 L.Ed.2d 406 (2009), another decision dealing with institutional reform. In this case, the State of Arizona sought relief from a District Court order requiring it to fund English-Language Learner students in a particular way. The state argued it was satisfying its obligations to these students in a different manner. The Court found several changed circumstances that might justify relief (including passage of the federal "No Child Left Behind" law), and remanded to the Court of Appeals to consider these factors. It also indicated that federalism concerns—namely, that a federal court was issuing orders involving state budgets—should have made the lower courts especially sensitive to a "changed circumstances" argument.

6. *"Any other reason."* The catchall provision is Rule 60(b)(6), which permits motion to be filed relieving a judgment-loser from the judgment for "any other reason justifying relief." *Pioneer Inv. Services Co. v. Brunswick Associates Ltd. P'ship*, 507 U.S. 380, 394–95, 113 S.Ct. 1489, 123 L.Ed.2d 74 (1993), relied on by *Tate*, also discussed the scope of Rule 60(b)(6) relative to Rule 60(b)(1).

> Rule 60(b)(6) ... empowers the court to reopen a judgment even after one year has passed for "any other reason justifying relief from the operation of the judgment." These provisions [Rule 60(b)(1) and 60(b)(6)] are mutually exclusive, and thus a party who failed to take timely action due to "excusable neglect" may not seek relief more than a year after the judgment by resorting to subsection (6). To justify relief under subsection (6), a party must show "extraordinary circumstances" suggesting that the party is faultless in the delay. If a party is partly to blame for the delay, relief must be sought within one year under subsection (1) and the party's neglect must be excusable.

On a broader scale, the policy of Rule 60(b)(6) was stated in *Liljeberg v. Health Services Acquisition Corp.*, 486 U.S. 847, 108 S.Ct. 2194, 100 L.Ed.2d 855 (1988). The rule gives federal courts broad authority to grant relief from a final judgment "upon such terms as are just," provided that the motion is made within a reasonable time. Rule 60(c)(1). It is appropriate to consider the risk of injustice to the particular parties, the risk that the denial of relief will produce injustice in other cases, and the risk of undermining the public's confidence in the judicial process.

7. *Meritorious defenses.* As *Tate* indicates, generally a federal court will grant a motion to set aside a default judgment under Rule 55(c) only after the party in default demonstrates a meritorious defense to the action. On the other hand, when the judgment is void, no other defense is necessary. In *Peralta v. Heights Medical Center, Inc.*, 485 U.S. 80, 108 S.Ct. 896, 99 L.Ed.2d 75 (1988), the Court held that "under our cases, a judgment entered without notice or service is constitutionally infirm." The defendant was entitled to set aside a default judgment, although he did not have a meritorious defense. Why? He had not been properly served with process which could have provided him notice about the case so that he could have avoided the adverse consequences of a judicial sale.

8. *Independent actions to seek relief from judgments.* Rule 60(d)(1) also permits litigants to file an "independent action" to prevent miscarriages of justice. The time limits of Rule 60(c)(1) are inapplicable to these separate lawsuits. An example of an appropriate independent action occurs when the judgment was obtained through a fraud on the court, which provides a court with the inherent authority to set aside a judgment. See Note 3.

EXERCISE

For the state where a) you intend to practice after graduation, b) your law school is located, and/or c) your professor assigns, go to that state's annotated statutes and research the procedural rules by which motions for relief from a judgment are evaluated. Based on your research, print the rule and bring it to class for discussion. Is the state rule for granting relief from judgments a "laundry list" of grounds for granting relief? Are the grounds narrower or broader than the Federal Rule 60?

CHAPTER 13

THE EFFECT OF A JUDGMENT

■ ■ ■

A. ENFORCING A JUDGMENT

> The materials for this section are at www.crosscivilprocedure.com.

B. PRECLUSIVE EFFECT OF A JUDGMENT: AN OVERVIEW

A judgment resolves a given dispute. However, that same judgment may also affect how *other* legal disputes are resolved. After all, judges do not like to reinvent the wheel. If a question decided in one case is presented again in a later case, the court hearing the second case will naturally give some deference to the earlier decision. There are two compelling reasons for this deference. The first is *efficiency*. Resolving a dispute is expensive and time-consuming. To the extent a court can avoid some of this cost by relying on the results in an earlier case, it helps reduce the cost of operating a court system.

The second concern is *consistency*. If two judges are both called upon to decide the same question in two separate cases, they might decide the question differently. Such inconsistency not only diminishes people's perceptions of the legal system, but also can leave parties not knowing how they should act in the future.

The desire for efficiency and consistency has spawned a number of separate but related, doctrines that give the results in one case some controlling effect in later litigation. The first, *stare decisis*, is a doctrine with which you should already be quite familiar. Once a question has been decided in one case, later courts faced with that same legal question will consider the earlier ruling in their own determination. The strength of a case as precedent depends on several factors, including its age and whether it was issued by the same court system.

The remainder of this Chapter does not deal with *stare decisis*. Instead, it deals with several other doctrines under which a judgment can have an effect on later litigation. The main focus will be the doctrines of *claim preclusion* and *issue preclusion*. Under the doctrine of claim preclusion, the subject of Section C, a party may be barred from presenting claims or defenses that were, or should have been, litigated by that party in an earlier case. Section D deals with the related doctrine of *issue preclusion*, which prevents the relitigation not of entire claims, but instead of particular issues that were actually decided by the court in the prior case. Sections E and F (in the electronic Appendix) deal with other issues affecting both claim and issue preclusion, namely, which parties are bound by preclusion, and how claim and issue preclusion apply when the first and second courts are located in different states. Finally, Section G (also in the Appendix) explores two other doctrines—law of the case and judicial estoppel—that are of the same basic *genre* as claim and issue preclusion, but have their own unique considerations.

Although you may detect some basic similarities between *stare decisis* and claim and issue preclusion, it is important to realize that there are fundamental differences. First, *stare decisis* applies to all prior cases, even if the litigants are completely different. In the doctrines discussed in this Chapter, by contrast, the parties in the first and second cases will either be the same or closely related. Second, unlike *stare decisis*, claim and issue preclusion do not apply to pure questions of law. To illustrate, imagine a case in which plaintiff, a trespasser, sues defendant for injuries plaintiff sustained when he ran into defendant's electric fence. The court will use *stare decisis* to determine the purely legal questions of whether a landowner owes a trespasser a duty, and if so what the standard of care is. However, if there is another case in which a court found that that same landowner was negligent for maintaining that same electric fence, it may apply the doctrine of issue preclusion to preclude the landowner from arguing that he was not negligent.

The third difference between *stare decisis* and claim and issue preclusion is the degree to which the first judgment binds the second court. In *stare decisis*, the court may refuse to follow any decision except that of a higher court. A court is especially likely to ignore precedent rendered by courts in other states or nations. Under claim and issue preclusion, by contrast, the prior decision is binding on the second court. If preclusion applies, the second court must prevent relitigation of the claim or issue even if the court disagrees with the result or the analysis in the earlier case. Moreover, claim and issue preclusion apply even if the first decision is rendered by a trial court—and, in most cases, even if that court is situated in another state.

One *caveat* before embarking on our tour of preclusion: the terminology in this area can be quite confusing. Many cases (including some in this Chapter) use the older terms *res judicata* to refer to claim preclusion, and *collateral estoppel* to refer to issue preclusion. To make matters even more ambiguous, many courts also use the term *res judicata* as a collective term to refer to both forms of preclusion. Still others use the phrase *estoppel by bar* to refer to one type of claim preclusion. Although we have attempted to use the modern and more descriptive

C. CLAIM PRECLUSION

INTRODUCTORY PROBLEM

While riding the Tilt-A-Whirl at a county fair, plaintiff hits her head on a protruding metal bar. Plaintiff sues the fair operator. After discovery is complete, the court enters a summary judgment for plaintiff for $5,000. Defendant pays the judgment in full.

Five years later, plaintiff suffers a *grand mal* epileptic seizure. Plaintiff's physician determines the earlier accident was the proximate cause of this condition. Plaintiff accordingly sues the fair operator again, this time seeking $200,000 in damages.

Defendant moves to dismiss the case, arguing that plaintiff has already litigated this claim. Is plaintiff's claim barred? *See Faulkner v. Caledonia County Fair Ass'n*, 869 A.2d 103 (Vt. 2004).

Variation 1: What if defendant had not paid the prior judgment?

Variation 2: What if defendant had evidence in the first case—perhaps the result of a Rule 35 physical examination—that made it clear to defendant that plaintiff would develop epilepsy? What if defendant not only had such evidence, but wrongly refused to disclose it in discovery?

1. THE BASICS OF CLAIM PRECLUSION

Claim preclusion prevents a party from litigating a claim that was or should have been litigated in a prior case. It stems from the sensible notion that a party should have only "one bite at the apple." Once the party has litigated a particular legal wrong, she should not be able to litigate that same wrong again in a different case. The issue, however, is determining what we mean by a single legal wrong. Courts have adopted different approaches to the problem. The next case discusses the two leading approaches.

RODGERS V. ST. MARY'S HOSPITAL
149 Ill.2d 302, 597 N.E.2d 616 (1992)

CHIEF JUSTICE MILLER delivered the opinion of the court . . .

Facts

Rodgers filed a medical malpractice action in the circuit court of Macon County on May 27, 1986, alleging the wrongful death of his wife, Brenda, who died at the hospital two days after giving birth to their son. Named as defendants in the medical malpractice action were Brenda's obstetricians, her radiologists, and the hospital. The circuit court entered summary judgment in favor of the hospital on May 13, 1988. Rodgers did not appeal the summary judgment in favor of the hospital.

Rodgers proceeded to trial against the obstetricians and radiologists. On June 10, 1988, the jury found in favor of Rodgers on his claims against the obstetricians and assessed damages at $1.2 million. The jury found the radiologists not liable and Rodgers did not appeal that finding. The obstetricians appealed, but the appeal was dismissed by stipulation of the parties on May 24, 1989, when Rodgers and the obstetricians agreed to settle the medical malpractice claim for $800,000.

In the meantime, on September 25, 1987, Rodgers had filed a separate complaint for damages against the hospital alleging that the hospital breached its statutory duty to preserve for five years all of the X rays taken of Brenda (see Ill. Rev. Stat. 1987, ch. 111 1/2, par. 157–11 (X-Ray Retention Act)). He claimed that the X rays were crucial to proving his case against the obstetricians and radiologists. On April 12, 1988, on motion of the hospital, the circuit court dismissed that complaint without prejudice.

Rodgers amended his complaint and brought the present action against the hospital on May 25, 1989, the day after he reached the $800,000 settlement with the obstetricians. In his complaint, Rodgers alleged that Brenda's death was caused by a sigmoid colonic volvulus, and that the condition appeared on an X ray that the hospital had a duty to preserve. Rodgers alleged that the hospital's failure to preserve the X ray was a breach of its duty arising from the X-Ray Retention Act and from the hospital's internal regulations. Rodgers asserted that because the hospital failed to preserve the X ray, Rodgers was unable to prove his case against the radiologists. He further alleged that had he recovered against the radiologists and the obstetricians jointly and severally, the verdict would have been paid in full and would not have been appealed. He thus sought $400,000 in damages from the hospital, the difference between the $1.2 million verdict and the $800,000 settlement. The trial court dismissed the amended complaint on the grounds that Rodgers' settlement with the obstetricians and failure to appeal the judgment in favor of the radiologists barred his loss-of-evidence claim against the hospital. Rodgers appealed.

The appellate court reversed the judgment of the circuit court. The appellate court held that Rodgers' amended complaint stated a statutory cause of action that was not barred by *res judicata* or waived by Rodgers' post-judgment settlement with the obstetricians. We granted the hospital's petition for leave to appeal. The issues presented are whether there is a statutory cause of action under the X-Ray Retention Act and whether Rodgers' suit is barred by his earlier settlement with the obstetricians or by res judicata.

Discussion

We first address whether the statute grants Rodgers a private cause of action by implication. [The court held that the statute created a cause of action.] . . .

The hospital next contends that Rodgers' settlement with the obstetricians operated as a waiver of any subsequent claims against the parties in the original malpractice case and that Rodgers' claimed damages of $400,000 were self-imposed when Rodgers voluntarily settled for less than the amount of the judgment. We find nothing to support the hospital's waiver argument.

As the appellate court pointed out, a rule that a post-judgment settlement bars an action for loss of evidence in this situation would be contrary to well-established principles of joint liability. When a plaintiff settles with one party, the remaining tortfeasors remain jointly and severally liable for the full amount of the judgment, minus the amount of the settlement. Additionally, such a rule would discourage settlement of disputed claims. Accordingly, we believe that the present claim against the hospital must remain intact, despite Rodgers' settlement with the obstetricians. . . .

Finally, the hospital argues that even if Rodgers' amended complaint states a cause of action, the action is barred by the summary judgment rendered on May 13, 1988, in favor of the hospital in the malpractice case. The doctrine of res judicata provides that a final judgment on the merits is conclusive as to the rights of the parties, constituting an absolute bar to a subsequent action involving the same claim, demand, or cause of action.

To determine whether causes of action are the same for *res judicata* purposes, Illinois courts have adopted two tests. The first is called the "same evidence" test. Under that test, *res judicata* bars a second suit if the evidence needed to sustain the second suit would have sustained the first, or if the same facts were essential to maintain both actions. The second test is the "transactional" approach, which considers whether both suits arise from the same transaction, incident, or factual situation. The transactional approach provides that " 'the assertion of different kinds or theories of relief still constitutes a single cause of action if a single group of operative facts give rise to the assertion of relief.' " *Pfeiffer* [*v. William Wrigley Jr. Co.*, 139 Ill. App. 3d 320], 323, 484 N.E.2d 1187 (1985), quoting *Baird & Warner Inc. v. Addison Industrial Park, Inc.* (1979), 70 Ill. App. 3d 59, 64, 387 N.E.2d 831.

We conclude that under either test, res judicata does not bar the present action. Here, Rodgers' amended complaint against the hospital is based on a different cause of action than that underlying his prior claim against the hospital, obstetricians, and radiologists. The present action is for loss of evidence; the first was for medical malpractice. The same evidence would not sustain both verdicts, and the facts essential to each suit did not arise from the same transactions or incidents.

To obtain a favorable verdict on the present cause of action, Rodgers must show that but for the hospital's failure to preserve all X rays of Brenda, he would have prevailed against the radiologists and that in so doing he would have recovered more than $800,000 of the damages awarded by the jury in the medical malpractice suit. These facts would not have sustained a verdict in the medical malpractice action. There the issue was whether the doctors or hospital negligently caused Brenda's death. The X ray was lost after Brenda died and could therefore not have affected the defendants' exercise of care in treating Brenda. Furthermore the existence of the duty to preserve the X ray, the incidents causing the X ray to be missing at trial, and the facts surrounding the potential evidentiary value of the missing X ray are circumstances unrelated to determining medical malpractice liability in the first cause of action. Thus, under either test for identical causes of action, res judicata does not bar the present action. . . .

In sum, Rodgers' amended complaint states a cause of action implied by statute. It is for the trier of fact to determine whether the hospital's failure to preserve the X ray proximately caused Rodgers to lose his malpractice case against the radiologists, and if so, to what damages Rodgers is entitled. The present action is not barred by Rodgers' settlement with the obstetricians in the earlier medical malpractice suit, or by res judicata.

Accordingly, we affirm the judgment of the appellate court.

NOTES AND QUESTIONS

1. Unlike many of the doctrines discussed in Civil Procedure, preclusion began as—and to this date largely remains—a court-created doctrine. Therefore, our discussion will focus more heavily on case law and the *Restatement* than the discussion in the other Chapters.

2. Illinois is somewhat unique in that it purports to follow *both* of the leading tests for determining whether a particular claim is barred by claim preclusion. *See also Whitaker v. Ameritech Corp.*, 129 F.3d 952 (7th Cir. 1997). Most states follow only the "same transaction" approach. That approach is also favored by the authors of the *Restatement of Judgments*, as evidenced by sections 24 and 25:

RESTATEMENT OF THE LAW (SECOND): JUDGMENTS*

§ 24. Dimensions of "Claim" for Purposes of Merger or Bar—General Rule Concerning "Splitting"

(1) When a valid and final judgment rendered in an action extinguishes the plaintiff's claim pursuant to the rules of merger or bar (see §§ 18, 19), the claim extinguished includes all rights of the plaintiff to remedies against the defendant with respect to all or any part of the transaction, or series of connected transactions, out of which the claim arose.

(2) What factual grouping constitutes a "transaction", and what groupings constitute a "series", are to be determined pragmatically, giving weight to such considerations as whether the facts are related in time, space, origin, or motivation, whether they form a convenient trial unit, and whether their treatment as a unit conforms to the parties' expectations or business understanding or usage.

§ 25. Exemplifications of General Rule Concerning Splitting

The rule of § 24 applies to extinguish a claim by the plaintiff against the defendant even though the plaintiff is prepared in the second action

(1) To present evidence or grounds or theories of the case not presented in the first action, or

(2) To seek remedies or forms of relief not demanded in the first action.

3. In a state like Illinois that has adopted both tests, does the "same evidence" approach have any real practical significance? Can you ever think of a case where two claims would be supported by much of the same evidence, and yet do not arise from the same transaction or related series of transactions?

4. California follows a different approach to claim preclusion called the "primary rights" test. Under that approach, two claims comprise the same cause of action if they involve "1) a primary right possessed by the plaintiff, 2) a corresponding primary duty devolving upon the defendant, and 3) a delict or wrong done by the defendant which consists in a breach of such primary right and duty." *Citizens for Open Access to Sand and Tide, Inc. v. Seadrift Ass'n*, 60 Cal.App.4th 1053, 1067, 71 Cal.Rptr.2d 77, 86 (1998) (citations omitted). What is a "primary right?" Suppose that P was involved in an automobile accident with D, in which P suffered both personal injury and damage to his automobile. Could P sue for personal injury and property

---

* Copyright 1982 by the American Law Institute. Reprinted with permission. All rights reserved.

damage in separate actions, under the theory that two different "primary rights" (bodily integrity and property rights) were involved?

5. *Splitting.* The main goal of claim preclusion is to prevent a plaintiff from "splitting" a single dispute into multiple claims and litigating those claims in two or more cases. Plaintiff may try to split a single transaction in several different ways, including (a) splitting the injury (for example, suing for medical expenses and pain and suffering in separate cases), (b) using separate legal theories (for example, products liability and breach of warranty) and (c) splitting the relief (for example, suing separately for damages for past harm and for an injunction to prevent threatened future harm).

6. The different approaches discussed in the main case and these notes are really nothing more than different views as to how broadly we should define a dispute. As noted in Section B of this Chapter, all forms of preclusion are concerned with efficiency and consistency. Given that all of the tests for preclusion require some connection between the claims in the first and second cases, all will help prevent inefficient duplicative litigation. But do all of the tests really further consistency? If two claims arise out of the same transaction, but do not involve the same evidence, is there a risk of inconsistent judgments?

7. When the first case is litigated in federal court, the claim preclusive effect of the judgment is measured by a *federal* standard, at least in cases involving federal and constitutional claims. The federal standard is the "same transaction" approach of the Restatement (Second). *Massachusetts School of Law at Andover, Inc. v. American Bar Ass'n*, 142 F.3d 26, 38 (1st Cir. 1998).

8. *Series of transactions.* What does the Restatement mean by a "series of connected transactions?" Suppose that Andre Preneur, an aspiring businessman, wants to open a dozen Moondoe Coffee Shops. Andre enters into twelve franchise agreements with Moondoe Corp. The parties signed all of the agreements at the same time, and at the same closing. All twelve agreements are identical except for the information about location of the coffee shop. When Andre's business acumen proves to be less acute than he thought, he is unable to make the minimum payments under all twelve agreements. Must Moondoe attempt to enforce all twelve agreements in the same suit? Most courts would hold no: the different contracts are different transactions, notwithstanding their similarity.

What about installment payments under a single contract? Suppose Andre fails to make both the January and February payments under the agreement relating to his Main Street coffee shop. Under the so-called "Rule of Accumulated Breaches," if Moondoe sued Andre in March for only the January installment, claim preclusion would prevent it from bringing a separate action for the February installment. However, Moondoe could sue separately for any additional installments that came due after it filed its case on the January installment. For example, suppose Moondoe sued for the January installment on February 28. Although it would need to join the overdue February installment in that action, it could bring a separate action for the March and any later installments that came due after the case was filed. Of course, Moondoe might also be able to use Federal Rule 15(d) to supplement its complaint in the original case to add the later-occurring installments.

The Rule of Accumulated Breaches is subject to a limited, but important exception. If the installments are paid using separate instruments—such as a note, check, or coupon on a bond—the Rule of Accumulated Breaches does not apply. Suppose that Andre paid the rent on his Main Street store in advance, delivering separate post-dated checks for each month's rent. After the January, February, and March checks bounce, Landlord sues, but only for the January check. Landlord could bring separate suits for the other two checks. The rationale for this seemingly odd rule lies in the policy of ensuring that these sorts of instruments remain freely assignable. If someone buying a note or coupons from a bond had to worry that her right to recover might be barred by claim preclusion, she might give far less than full value for the instrument.

9. How should a defendant raise claim preclusion? Can the defendant move to dismiss for failure to state a claim? Or is summary judgment the proper way to raise the issue?

10. Generally speaking, claim preclusion only applies to a single plaintiff and defendant. Suppose that while crossing a street, Walker and Jogger are both struck and injured by a car driven by Driver. Driver swears the crossing light was malfunctioning. Walker sues Driver, but loses at trial. Walker now wants to sue City for failing properly to maintain the crossing light. Because Walker's claim against City is considered legally distinct, claim preclusion will not bar Walker's suit against City. Similarly, Jogger's rights are legally distinct, and so claim preclusion will have no effect on Jogger's suit(s) against either Driver or City.

This general principle is subject to some qualifications. First, as you will see in Part E of this Chapter, in some cases (although not in this example) two people with a legal relationship will be treated as one person for preclusion purposes under the doctrine of *privity*. Second, as Part D of this Chapter demonstrates, although claim preclusion may not bar Walker's suit against City, *issue preclusion* may prevent Walker from relitigating certain key questions in the case.

11. Even though a single plaintiff may ordinarily sue two defendants for the same injury, that plaintiff can collect only once. If P obtains separate $10,000 judgments against D1 and D2 for the same injury, and collects $10,000 from D1, he cannot recover anything from D2. D2's defense in this situation is not claim preclusion, but instead the substantive defense that the judgment has been satisfied.

2. PRECLUDING COUNTERCLAIMS, CROSS-CLAIMS, AND DEFENSES

The prior section dealt with how a plaintiff is forced to litigate in a single case all transactionally-related claims she has against a single defendant. But what about other claims that parties have against each other? Does claim preclusion also apply to claims other than those by a plaintiff against a defendant? The answer turns both on judge-made rules of claim preclusion and the applicable rules of procedure.

RESTATEMENT OF THE LAW (SECOND): JUDGMENTS*

§ 22. Effect of Failure to Interpose Counterclaim

(1) Where the defendant may interpose a claim as a counterclaim but he fails to do so, he is not thereby precluded from subsequently maintaining an action on that claim, except as stated in Subsection (2).

(2) A defendant who may interpose a claim as a counterclaim in an action but fails to do so is precluded, after the rendition of judgment in that action, from maintaining an action on the claim if:

(a) The counterclaim is required to be interposed by a compulsory counterclaim statute or rule of court, or

(b) The relationship between the counterclaim and the plaintiff's claim is such that successful prosecution of the second action would nullify the initial judgment or would impair rights established in the initial action.

Counterclaims. As you learned in Chapter 2, the Federal Rules and most state procedural rules contain a compulsory counterclaim provision. Federal Rule 13(a), for example, requires a defendant to file all counterclaims that he has against the plaintiff arising from the same transaction or occurrence as the plaintiff's claim against the defendant, unless one of the narrow exceptions applies. *Restatement* § 22(2)(a) explicitly acknowledges these compulsory counterclaim rules. In the vast majority of cases, then, you need look no further than Rule 13(a) or its state-court counterpart to determine if a claim is barred by the party's failure to raise it as a counterclaim in the prior case.

If Rule 13(a) does not apply, or one of the exceptions applies, most courts follow an approach similar to that set out in § 22(2)(b). Under this rule, it is not enough that the counterclaim arises from the same transaction or occurrence as the claim. Instead, the counterclaim is barred only if allowing it might "nullify the initial judgment" or "impair

---

* Copyright 1982 by the American Law Institute. Reprinted with permission. All rights reserved.

Sec. C Claim Preclusion 667

rights established in the initial action." Some of the Illustrations set out in the comments to § 22 help elucidate this principle:

> 1. A brings an action against B for the negligent driving of an automobile by B resulting in a collision with an automobile driven by A. B fails to plead and judgment by default is given against him. B is not precluded from subsequently maintaining an action against A for his own injuries on the ground that those injuries were the result of A's negligence.
>
> 3. A brings an action against B for the purchase price of a boiler sold by A to B. B defends on the sole ground that the price has been paid, and judgment is given for A. B is not precluded from subsequently maintaining an action against A, in which he alleges that A was guilty of breach of warranty and that the boiler was defective and exploded, causing damage to B. (B is precluded, however, from seeking restitution of any amount paid pursuant to the judgment. . . .)
>
> 9. A brings an action against B for failure to pay the contract price for goods sold and delivered and recovers judgment by default. After entry of final judgment and payment of the price, B brings an action against A to rescind the contract for mutual mistake, seeking restitution of the contract price and offering to return the goods. The action is precluded.*

In Illustration 9, do you see how the second case threatens to "nullify the judgment" in the first? Why does that same reasoning not apply in the other two Illustrations? In Illustration 1, for example, B's counterclaim asserts that A was negligent. But if A was negligent, then B should have prevailed because of contributory negligence (or at least reduced A's recovery under comparative fault). Would allowing B to recover against A nullify the judgment in Case One? Would it impair A's rights?

Why is the "common-law compulsory counterclaim rule" so narrow? After all, isn't one of the justifications for claim preclusion that we want to avoid inconsistent results? In both Illustrations 1 and 3, isn't it inconsistent to allow A to recover in Case One—an outcome that presupposes that A was not negligent (Illustration 1) or that A's goods conformed to the contract requirements (Illustration 3)—and then to turn around and allow B to recover for that same negligence or defect? Does it matter that P has chosen the forum for Case One? *See* Restatement of the Law (Second): Judgments § 22, comment a. Note, however, that the rule applies even if B sues in the same court that heard the first case.

Three additional points are worth stressing. First, unlike Rule 13(a), the common-law compulsory counterclaim rule applies only if the plaintiff

---

* Copyright 1982 by the American Law Institute. Reprinted with permission. All rights reserved.

prevails in the first case. If the defendant prevails, he is free to assert his claim in the second case. If plaintiff lost Case One, there is no risk of inconsistency by allowing the defendant to bring Case Two. Second, the common-law rule applies only if defendant did not assert the issue in question as a defense in Case One. If defendant litigated the issue and lost, it will be barred by *issue* preclusion from relitigating that same issue as part of a claim in Case Two. Issue preclusion is discussed in Part D of this Chapter.

Third, do not forget the point made at the outset of this discussion: If the claim is barred by a compulsory counterclaim rule like Federal Rule 13, that rule takes precedence over the common-law rule. Federal Rule 13(a) is grounded in efficiency, not consistency. Under Federal Rule 13(a) it is irrelevant whether allowing the counterclaim would nullify the first suit, or even if there is a risk of logical inconsistency.

Cross-claims. Neither Federal Rule 13(a) nor *Restatement* § 22 apply to cross-claims. Generally speaking, cross-claims are always optional. A party is free to assert a claim in Case Two even if she could have asserted it as a cross-claim in Case One. This general rule even applies when the party was a plaintiff in Case One. Thus, if P1 and P2 sue D in Case One, P1 is free to sue P2 in a separate case, even though the case arises from the same transaction or occurrence as Case One.

Remember, however, that once one co-party files a claim against the other, Federal Rule 13(a) comes into play. In the prior example, if P2 had filed a cross-claim against P1, P1's claim could be a compulsory counterclaim, and therefore barred by Federal Rule 13(a) if not filed in Case One. See the *Rainbow Management* case in Chapter 2, pt. C.

Pure Defenses. A defense is not a claim. Pure defenses are never barred by claim preclusion. Suppose L sues T for failing to pay rent in January. T defends by arguing that he paid the rent. L prevails. L now sues for failure to pay the February rent. T now defends by arguing the lease is invalid because L lied about the premises. Even though allowing T to prevail on that defense creates a risk of logical inconsistency (do you see how?), T is free to assert the defense in Case Two.

Note, however, that if T *does* litigate the defense in Case One and loses, he will be barred by *issue* preclusion from asserting the defense again in Case Two.

3. FINAL JUDGMENT ON THE MERITS

A court ruling is not entitled to claim preclusion effect unless it constitutes a final judgment on the merits. This phrase is unfortunately not as clear as it may seem. Basically, a judgment is considered "final" with respect to a given claim if the trial judge is finished dealing with the claim, other than ordering entry of final judgment. A judgment after a full trial clearly meets this test. Similarly, a summary judgment—even a summary judgment on fewer than all the claims—is considered final on the claims involved. Default and consent judgments likewise are entitled to claim preclusion effect.

What does it mean for a judgment to be "on the merits?" A judgment is on the merits if it is based on the substance of plaintiff's claim and any defenses, rather than on a procedural ground. Therefore, a dismissal for lack of subject matter jurisdiction, personal jurisdiction, or venue is not a judgment on the merits. What about a 12(b)(6) dismissal for failure to state a claim? In the federal courts, a dismissal for failure to state a claim (and by implication a 12(c) judgment on the pleadings) is "on the merits" unless the judge explicitly states otherwise in the order of dismissal. *Federated Department Stores v. Moitie*, 452 U.S. 394, 399 n.3, 101 S.Ct. 2424, 69 L.Ed.2d 103 (1981). Many states disagree, even if their rules are based on the Federal Rules. In diversity cases, the federal court will look to state law for the effect of dismissals. See the discussion of the *Semtek* case in Chapter 5 pt. B.

Dismissals and judgments based on the statute of limitations are a special case. In most situations, a forum will apply its own statute of limitations, even when the claim arises under the law of another state. RESTATEMENT OF THE LAW (SECOND): CONFLICT OF LAWS § 142. Therefore, while a dismissal based on the statute of limitations in the courts of State A will prevent the plaintiff from suing again in State A, it will generally not bar a suit on that claim in State B, as long as the limitations period in State B is longer.

Note that finality turns on whether the *trial* court is finished with the claim. That a judgment may have been appealed does not affect its finality. If an appellate court overturns Case One while Case Two is pending, the court in Case Two will base its rulings on the appellate decision. If the court in Case Two enters judgment before the appeal of Case One is complete, however, the plaintiff faces a potential quandary. In that situation, plaintiff's only recourse is to reopen Case Two pursuant to a rule like Federal Rule 60(b)(5) (allowing a judgment to be reopened when "it is based on an earlier judgment that has been reversed or vacated."). See Chapter 12 pt. G.

4. EXCEPTIONS TO CLAIM PRECLUSION

Claim preclusion is a strict doctrine. Nevertheless, certain exceptions lessen its sting. These exceptions allow a party to allege a claim in Case Two even if it arises from the same transaction as the claim in Case One.

Some of the exceptions are relatively obvious. For example, if the parties agree or the court in Case One expressly states that plaintiff may sue again, claim preclusion does not apply. Other exceptions are more technical in nature. If the first action is *in rem* rather than *in personam*, counterclaims by the defendant are never compulsory. *See also* Federal Rule 13(a), which incorporates the same exception. Because we still maintain the myth that an *in rem* action is a suit against the property rather than the owner, as a technical matter only the property is bound.

Finally, there are exceptions to claim preclusion based on substantive policy. The negotiable instruments exception to the Rule of Accumulated Breaches is one example. Beyond this situation, courts split concerning what sorts of substantive policies are significant enough to warrant relieving the parties of the effects of claim preclusion.

PROBLEMS

1. After P and D are involved in an automobile accident, P sues D for the injuries that P suffered. The court enters judgment for D. P then sues D for the damage to P's automobile. How should D raise the defense of claim preclusion? Assuming D raises the issue in the proper fashion, will D prevail?

2. Same facts as Problem 1, except assume P prevails in the first trial. Does this change in facts affect D's chances of prevailing on claim preclusion?

3. P recently purchased an office suite software package from D. When D demonstrated the software prior to the sale, P thought it looked highly similar to another office suite sold by the software giant Gil Bates. Accordingly, at P's insistence, the contract between P and D contained a clause in which D warranted that the software does not infringe any copyright or violate any other rights of third parties.

Shortly after the sale, Gil Bates sued P for one million dollars for copyright infringement. Bates obtained a $600,000 judgment in this case. One week after P paid the judgment to Bates, a design defect in the office suite program causes the computers in P's headquarters to malfunction. P loses all of his data, including irreplaceable customer lists and tax records.

P sues D for breach of the contractual warranty, seeking reimbursement for the money it paid Bates. After a long and acrimonious trial, the court enters judgment for P for $600,000. P then brings a products liability action against D, seeking to recover the value of the lost data. D argues that this action is barred by claim preclusion. Is D correct?

4. Same facts as Problem 3, except that the court in the first case (the case involving the contractual warranty) enters a default judgment for P.

5. Same facts as Problem 3, except that D did not pay the first judgment. P accordingly brings an action on the judgment in a different court, hoping to obtain a new judgment that he can use to execute on property owned by D in that area. D argues the second action is barred by claim preclusion. Assuming the majority "same transaction" test applies, is D correct?

6. Because of soaring tuition costs, P Law School implements a program that allows students to pay tuition in monthly installments. Law

Student D takes advantage of the program. D pays the January 1 installment, but cannot pay the February 1 and March 1 installments. On March 5th, P sues D for the February installment. D's answer admits she did not pay. Therefore, on April 7th, the court enters judgment on the pleadings for P.

P now sues D for the March 1 and April 1 installments. D argues that the claims for both months are barred by claim preclusion. Is D correct?

7. Same facts as Problem 6, except assume that claim preclusion bars neither claim. D files an answer in the second case in which she admits not making the payments, but argues that the tuition contract is invalid under state usury law. Under state law, a borrower such as D who enters into a usurious contract is relieved of the obligation to pay all amounts owed under the contract. Thus, if D is correct, she could attend school without paying tuition. P counters by arguing that because D's usury argument would also have applied to the *January* installment, D is barred by claim preclusion from making the argument in this later case. Is P correct?

8. P sues D for a tort in State Alpha. The court grants summary judgment to D based on the one-year Alpha statute of limitations. P then brings the exact same claim before a court in State Beta, where the statute of limitations has not yet expired. D argues the claim is barred by claim preclusion. Is D correct?

D. ISSUE PRECLUSION

In some ways, issue preclusion can be thought of as a "backup" to claim preclusion. Claim preclusion is a sword that cuts with a broad swath, barring one or more complete claims from a case. When claim preclusion does not apply, however, a party still may be barred from litigating one of more *issues* involved in a case by the doctrine of issue preclusion. Compared to claim preclusion, issue preclusion is more like a surgical scalpel, with a narrower and more precise cut. Nevertheless, both swords and scalpels can be fatal weapons. To the extent a barred issue is a crucial element in a claim or defense presented in Case Two, issue preclusion can control the outcome of an entire claim.

INTRODUCTORY PROBLEM

Tenant leases space from Landlord in a "strip" shopping center (a center where each store has its own entrance, but shares parking). The lease gives Tenant the right to "make such use of the common areas, including the parking lot, as reasonably necessary."

In early August, Tenant holds a two-day "Dog Days" sale. Because the air conditioning unit in the center is not cooling his store sufficiently, Tenant decides to hold the sale outdoors. Tenant accordingly moves much of its inventory into the parking lot, placing it under large tents.

When Landlord learns of this, he sues Tenant for damages for breaching the lease. Tenant admits holding the sale, but denies liability based on two arguments. First, Tenant argues that holding a two-day sale in the parking lot is not an unreasonable use of the lot. Second, Tenant argues that even if such a sale is unreasonable, Landlord failed to provide Tenant the notice of breach called for by the lease. The case is submitted to the jury, which returns a general verdict for Tenant.

In late October, Tenant advertises its one-day "Columbus Day Sale," which, given the lovely weather, Tenant wants to hold in the parking lot. This time, however, Landlord is prepared. Landlord gives Tenant notice that holding a sale in the parking lot would breach the lease. Tenant ignores the notice, and holds the sale anyway. Landlord therefore sues Tenant a second time for damages for breach of lease.

Tenant realizes that claim preclusion does not bar this new action. Tenant nevertheless argues that the earlier case established that holding a one-day or two-day sale in the parking lot is a "reasonable use" within the meaning of the lease. Is Tenant correct in arguing that Landlord is precluded from relitigating this issue?

Variation: Suppose the jury in the first case had rendered a special verdict finding both that the August sale was not unreasonable, and that Landlord had failed to provide the required notice.

The test for claim preclusion asks if the same basic event or transaction is involved in two cases. Similarly, issue preclusion focuses on whether the same issue is before the court in the two cases. Aside from this parallel, however, there is a fundamental difference in the way the two doctrines operate. In claim preclusion, it is irrelevant whether the claim in question was actually presented in Case One. In issue preclusion, by contrast, it is crucial not only that the issue have been presented to the court in Case One, but that it was fully litigated and decided by the court in a way that could have affected the outcome of that case. This difference makes the analysis of issue preclusion more technical in several ways.

Issue preclusion has four basic "elements." First, the two cases must involve the same issue. Second, that issue must have been actually litigated in Case One. Third, the court in that case must actually decide that question. Finally, the ruling on the question must have been necessary to the judgment rendered by the court in Case One. Each of these elements presents its own special difficulties, and will be discussed in turn.

The more complicated analysis in issue preclusion gives you a strong incentive to treat issue preclusion as a backup to claim preclusion. If the entire claim is barred, it is largely irrelevant whether particular issues relevant to that claim are barred. Therefore, to save yourself time and

1. SAME ISSUE

WILLIAMS V. CITY OF JACKSONVILLE POLICE DEPT.
599 S.E.2d 422 (N.C. App. 2004)

TYSON, JUDGE.

The City of Jacksonville Police Department ("Jacksonville Police Department"), Officer Billy J. Houston ("Officer Houston"), and Officer Earl K. Burkhart ("Officer Burkhart") (collectively, "defendants") appeal from an order denying their Motion for Summary Judgment. We reverse.

I. Background

Plaintiff originally filed this action on 2 March 2000 in Onslow County Superior Court from incidents that arose during a traffic stop of plaintiff by defendants. Plaintiff asserted claims for: (1) "personal injuries, pain and suffering, humiliation, loss of liberty and emotional distress" that he suffered as a result of defendants' "negligence, malicious and wanton conduct;" (2) "the action of Defendants violated the 4th and/or the 14th Amendments to the U.S. Constitution, protecting against unlawful seizures;" (3) "the acts and conduct of the Defendants ... constitutes [sic] false arrest and negligence under the laws of the State of North Carolina;" and (4) "The City of Jacksonville intentionally or negligently failed to properly train its officers...."

Defendants removed the action to the United States District Court for the Eastern District of North Carolina ("the U.S. District Court") pursuant to plaintiff's assertion of a violation of the Civil Rights Act, Title 42 U.S.C. § 1983 and moved for summary judgment. By Order entered 29 May 2001, the Honorable James C. Fox, Senior U.S. District Court Judge, granted defendants' motion. Judge Fox found, as a matter of law: (1) defendants had probable cause to stop and detain plaintiff; (2) defendants acted reasonably in conducting a pat-down search and in using "threat of force;" and (3) defendants did not use excessive force. Judge Fox also concluded, "Because the officers [Houston and Burkhart] did not commit any constitutional violation, summary judgment is also appropriate as to the plaintiff's claims against the City of Jacksonville." Judge Fox's Order stated, "To the extent that the plaintiff's complaint alleges state law causes of action, the court, pursuant to 28 U.S.C. § 1367(c)(3), declines to exercise supplemental jurisdiction over such pendent claims, and ORDERS these claims DISMISSED without prejudice."

Plaintiff timely filed a new complaint on 16 November 2001 asserting the causes of action stated in his earlier complaint, except for deleting his claim for violations of the Fourth and Fourteenth Amendments of the

United States Constitution. Defendants filed an answer and asserted thirty defenses, including governmental immunity, public duty doctrine, and *res judicata*/collateral estoppel. Defendants moved for summary judgment and asserted, "Plaintiff's pendant [*sic*] state tort claims are premised on either the lack of probable cause or the unreasonableness of Defendants' conduct . . . [and] are barred under the doctrines of *res judicata* and collateral estoppel in that the necessary elements of Plaintiff's claims have been previously adjudicated in favor of Defendants." The trial court denied defendants' motion. Defendants appeal.

II. Issues

The issues presented are whether: (1) this appeal is interlocutory; and (2) the trial court erred in denying defendants' Motion for Summary Judgment because the doctrines of *res judicata* and collateral estoppel bar plaintiff's claims.

[The court first held that the appeal was timely.] . . .

V. *Res Judicata* and Collateral Estoppel

The trial court concluded neither *res judicata* nor collateral estoppel precluded plaintiff's claims and denied defendants' Motion for Summary Judgment.

"The companion doctrines of *res judicata* (claim preclusion) and collateral estoppel (issue preclusion) have been developed by the courts for the dual purposes of protecting litigants from the burden of relitigating previously decided matters and promoting judicial economy by preventing needless litigation." *Bockweg* [*v. Anderson*, 333 N.C. 486, 428 S.E.2d 161 (1993)], 333 N.C. at 491, 428 S.E.2d at 161.

> Where the second action between two parties is upon the same claim, the prior judgment serves as a bar to the relitigation of all matters that were or should have been adjudicated in the prior action. Where the second action between the same parties is upon a different claim, the prior judgment serves as a bar only as to issues actually litigated and determined in the original action.

Id. at 492, 428 S.E.2d at 161 (citations omitted). Our Supreme Court has distinguished between these two doctrines:

> Under the doctrine of res judicata or "claim preclusion," a final judgment on the merits in one action precludes a second suit based on the same cause of action between the same parties or their privies. The doctrine prevents the relitigation of all matters . . . that were or should have been adjudicated in the prior action. Under the companion doctrine of collateral estoppel, also known as "estoppel by judgment" or "issue preclusion," the

determination of an issue in a prior judicial or administrative proceeding precludes the relitigation of that issue in a later action, provided the party against whom the estoppel is asserted enjoyed a full and fair opportunity to litigate that issue in the earlier proceeding.

Whitacre P'ship v. Biosignia, Inc., 358 N.C. 1, 15, 591 S.E.2d 870, 880 (2004) (internal citations and quotations omitted). *Res judicata* precludes a party from "bringing a subsequent action based on the 'same claim' . . . litigated in an earlier action. . . ." *Id.* Collateral estoppel bars "the subsequent adjudication of a previously determined issue, even if the subsequent action is based on an entirely different claim." *Id.*

VI. *Res Judicata*

. . . Here, Judge Fox expressly declined to review plaintiff's state claims, and stated in his Order, "To the extent that the plaintiff's complaint alleges state law causes of action, the court, pursuant to 28 U.S.C. § 1367(c)(3), declines to exercise supplemental jurisdiction over such pendent claims, and ORDERS these claims DISMISSED without prejudice." Plaintiff's complaint, filed after the U.S. District Court's ruling, alleged causes of action under state law for negligence, false arrest, and assault. By dismissing these claims without prejudice, plaintiff's "subsequent action" is not "based on the 'same claim' as that litigated in an earlier action." *Whitacre P'ship*, 358 N.C. at 15, 591 S.E.2d at 880.

We hold that plaintiff's claims are not barred by *res judicata* as Judge Fox's Order addressed only plaintiff's claims under federal law and the United States Constitution. Judge Fox expressly declined to rule on plaintiff's causes of action controlled by state law.

VII. Collateral Estoppel

Defendants assert that the doctrine of collateral estoppel precludes plaintiff's suit in state court. "Under the doctrine of collateral estoppel, when an issue has been fully litigated and decided, it cannot be contested again between the same parties, even if the first adjudication is conducted in federal court and the second in state court." *McCallum* [*v. N.C. Coop. Extension Serv.*, 142 N.C.App. 48, 542 S.E.2d 227 (2001)], 142 N.C.App. at 52, 542 S.E.2d at 231 (citation omitted). . . . For collateral estoppel to bar a party's subsequent claim:

> (1) the issues to be concluded must be the same as those involved in the prior action; (2) in the prior action, the issues must have been raised and actually litigated; (3) the issues must have been material and relevant to the disposition of the prior action; and (4) the determination made of those issues in the prior action must have been necessary and essential to the resulting judgment.

Id. at 54, 542 S.E.2d at 233.

Here, the federal court's Order addressed the issue of whether "Defendant Billy Houston and Defendant Earl K. Burkhart violated [plaintiff's] Fourth and Fourteenth Amendment rights during a traffic stop...." In granting summary judgment for defendants on the issues of unlawful seizure and excessive force under the United States Constitution, Judge Fox ruled, among other things, Officer Houston and Officer Burkhart: (1) did not "expand[ ] the permissible scope of the stop;" (2) did not use excessive force because "the threat of force displayed by Houston in order to persuade the driver not to leave the scene was not unreasonable;" (3) "did not violate the plaintiff's Fourth Amendment rights" by asking the plaintiff to step out of his vehicle; and (4) "a pat-down search was not unreasonable under the circumstances...." The U.S. District Court held, "Because the officers did not commit any constitutional violation, summary judgment is also appropriate as to the plaintiff's claims against the City of Jacksonville [Police]."

Following entry of the U.S. District Court's Order, plaintiff filed a new complaint in state court and asserted claims for negligence, false arrest, and assault. Plaintiff also asserted the Jacksonville Police Department negligently trained its officers. While the U.S. District Court's Order did not rule on defendants' ultimate liability for these claims, the Order ruled on several underlying issues and identical elements of these claims. To the extent the U.S. District Court ruled on these issues, plaintiff is barred from relitigating the issues in state court.

A. Negligence

Plaintiff's complaint alleges Officer Houston and Officer Burkhart acted negligently in their official and individual capacity.... A law enforcement officer may be held liable for use of "unreasonable or excessive force" upon another person. N.C. Gen. Stat. § 15A-01(d)(2)(2003).

In the U.S. District Court's Order, Judge Fox held, "Viewed from the perspective of an objectively reasonable police officer, the court concludes that the threat of force displayed by Houston ... was not unreasonable." Additionally, the officers' actions did "not amount to an unreasonable seizure," and the "pat-down search was not unreasonable under the circumstances...." The issues regarding the reasonableness of Officer Houston and Officer Burkhart's actions were litigated in federal court. Plaintiff is precluded from relitigating the issue of whether the officers acted reasonably in performing their official duties. The trial court erred in failing to grant summary judgment for defendants in their official capacity on the issue of negligence.

"To withstand a law enforcement officer's motion for summary judgment on the issue of individual capacity, plaintiff must allege and forecast evidence demonstrating the officers acted maliciously, corruptly, or beyond the scope of duty." *Prior* [*v. Pruett*, 143 N.C.App. 612, 550 S.E.2d 166 (2001), *disc. rev. denied,* 355 N.C. 493, 563 S.E.2d 572 (2002)], 143 N.C.App. at 623, 550 S.E.2d at 173–74. . . .

In support of his claim that defendants acted negligently in their individual capacity, plaintiff asserts that Officer Houston "intentionally," "negligently[,] and maliciously pointed a loaded weapon" at plaintiff. Other than this broad assertion, plaintiff presents no other allegation or forecast of evidence to show that defendants acted "maliciously, corruptly, or beyond the scope of duty." *Prior*, 143 N.C.App. at 623, 550 S.E.2d at 174. The U.S. District Court ruled that Officer Houston acted reasonably in pointing his service weapon at plaintiff. Plaintiff is collaterally estopped from relitigating this issue.

Plaintiff's complaint also alleges that defendants "intentionally destroyed dispatch tapes" and "conspired to unnecessarily call the plaintiff's supervisor to the scene. . . ." Judge Fox's Order recites these allegations and indicates that he considered these actions in ruling on plaintiff's claim under 42 U.S.C. § 1983. The U.S. District Court's Order does not rule on the ultimate issue of defendants' *negligence* in their individual capacity. However, Judge Fox's award of summary judgment to defendants essentially ruled both officers' actions were reasonable; neither officer violated plaintiff's constitutional rights; and their actions did not extend "beyond the scope of duty." *Id.* Collateral estoppel precludes plaintiff's suit on the issue of negligence for Officer Houston and Officer Burkhart in their individual capacity. The trial court erred in denying defendants' Motion for Summary Judgment on the issue of negligence.

B. *False Arrest*

"Under state law, a cause of action in tort will lie for false imprisonment, based upon the 'illegal restraint of one's person against his will.' A false arrest, *i.e.*, one without proper legal authority, is one means of committing a false imprisonment." *Myrick v. Cooley*, 91 N.C.App. 209, 212, 371 S.E.2d 492, 494, *disc. rev. denied*, 323 N.C. 477, 373 S.E.2d 865 (1988). Probable cause is an absolute bar to a claim for false arrest.

In the prior federal court action, Judge Fox ruled that Officer Burkhart had probable cause to detain plaintiff because "plaintiff admittedly drove his vehicle in excess of the speed limit." Further, Judge Fox ruled that defendants did not unreasonably expand the permissible scope of the stop. As probable cause is an absolute bar to plaintiff's claim, he is collaterally estopped from relitigating this issue. Plaintiff's claim for false arrest fails. The trial court erred in failing to grant summary judgment on plaintiff's claim of false arrest.

C. Assault

" '[A] civil action for damages for assault . . . is available at common law against one who, for the accomplishment of a legitimate purpose, such as justifiable arrest, uses force which is excessive under the given circumstances.' " . . .

In the prior federal court action, Judge Fox held that defendants' display of force and the subsequent pat-down search of plaintiff were reasonable under the circumstances. Collateral estoppel bars plaintiff from relitigating these issues and bars plaintiff's assault claim in state court. The trial court erred in failing to grant summary judgment in favor of defendants on plaintiff's assault claim.

D. Jacksonville Police Department

"Without an underlying negligence charge against the [law enforcement officers], a claim of negligence against the [department] can not [sic] be supported." *Prior*, 143 N.C.App. at 622, 550 S.E.2d at 172–73. To the extent collateral estoppel bars plaintiff's claims against defendants' in their official governmental capacity, plaintiff is precluded from asserting a negligence action against the Jacksonville Police Department.

VII. Conclusion

Plaintiff's claims are not barred by *res judicata*. However, the trial court erred in failing to grant summary judgment in favor of defendants based on collateral estoppel. Essential elements of plaintiff's claims for false arrest and assault were raised, litigated, and ruled upon in the U.S. District Court's Order. . . .

Reversed and remanded.

JUDGES BRYANT and STEELMAN concur.

NOTES AND QUESTIONS

1. The court's ruling on *res judicata*, or claim preclusion, is based on one of the exceptions discussed in Part C.4 of this Chapter. Which exception is the court using?

2. What issues are common to the constitutional and state-law claims?

3. Do you agree that these common questions are really the "same issue?" What about the fact that the claims in Case One and Case Two have different origins? Might the question of what is "reasonable" behavior by the officers be determined differently under state tort law as compared to the Constitution? Indeed, isn't the purpose of the fourth and fourteenth amendments to hold state officials to a *higher*—or at least different—standard than they would be held to anyway under state tort law?

4. P sues D for negligence, based on injuries P sustained in an automobile accident. P sues in a court that has no compulsory counterclaim rule. After a full trial, P obtains a judgment for $10,000.

After judgment is entered, D now sues P to recover for the injuries D sustained in the same accident. Because the first court had no compulsory counterclaim rule, claim preclusion does not bar the suit. Will issue preclusion nevertheless apply? If P alleges that D was contributorily negligent, will D be barred from relitigating the issue of D's negligence? Is negligence the same as contributory negligence? While negligence is acting unreasonably toward someone else, isn't contributory negligence acting unreasonably toward *yourself*? What if D's negligence in Case One consisted of carrying a surfboard on top of the car without adequately tying it down?

5. *Burden of persuasion*. Differences in the burden of persuasion can also affect whether two cases involve the same issue. A party who lost on an issue in Case One will not be barred from relitigating that issue if the burden of persuasion facing that party is lower in Case Two, or if the burden has switched from that party to the other side. Apply this basic principle to the following scenarios. In each of the scenarios, assume claim preclusion does not bar Case Two.

a. X and Y are neighbors. A dirt road lies near the border between their properties. X sues Y for trespass, alleging the road lies on X's land, and that Y is using it without permission. The court enters judgment for Y, specifically finding that X failed to prove she owned the road.

Later, Y sues X for trespass, alleging that X has been using the road since entry of judgment in the first case. X denies that Y owns the road. Y argues that issue preclusion applies to the question of ownership. The two cases do not involve the same issue.

b. State prosecutes C for assault, arguing that C assaulted victim V. C is convicted. Later, V brings a tort action against C for assault. Victim claims C cannot relitigate the question of whether he committed the assault. The two cases involve the same issue.

c. Same as b, except that State *lost* the first case. When V sues C, C argues the issue of whether the assault occurred has already been litigated and decided. The two cases do not involve the same issue.[1]

2. ACTUALLY LITIGATED

The requirement that the issue be actually litigated in Case One is one of the most significant differences between claim and issue preclusion. Claim preclusion often applies to claims that were not themselves presented in Case One, but are grounded in the same event as claims that were presented. By contrast, if an issue was not actually

---

[1] In Part E of this Chapter, you will learn that regardless of whether the cases involve the same issue, C cannot use issue preclusion against V because V was not a party to the first case.

litigated, issue preclusion can never apply to that issue. Therefore, a default judgment or involuntary dismissal for failure to prosecute will never have issue preclusion effect, even though both may have claim preclusion effect. Consent judgments likewise do not bar relitigation of the issues relevant to the claims.

Judgments or dismissals based on procedural grounds present a variation on this theme. A dismissal based on lack of subject matter jurisdiction, or a summary judgment based on the statute of limitations, does have issue preclusion effect, but only on the narrow issue of, respectively, whether the first court had subject matter jurisdiction, or whether Case One was filed in timely fashion in the chosen forum. If plaintiff sues again in that court, the action will be dismissed on the same ground. However, if plaintiff files in a *different* jurisdiction, the underlying questions of jurisdiction and statute of limitations may be governed by a different law, and issue preclusion accordingly may not apply.

How do you prove whether an issue was (or was not) actually litigated in an earlier proceeding? If the earlier court issued a written opinion, the discussion in that opinion may make it clear that a particular issue was contested. In the absence of a written opinion, the parties may introduce extrinsic evidence as to what issues were actually litigated in Case One.

Unlike claim preclusion, issue preclusion applies the same way regardless of the status of the party as plaintiff, defendant, or third-party defendant in Cases One and Two. As long as that party actually litigated the issue, and provided the other elements are met, issue preclusion will prevent that party from relitigating the question in Case Two, even if her party status has changed. (Of course, as discussed in the immediately prior section, a change in the party's status from plaintiff to defendant or vice versa may also result in changes in the burden of persuasion, which may render issue preclusion inapposite.)

3. ACTUALLY DECIDED

Suppose P sues D for breach of contract. D counters by invoking the affirmative defense of waiver of the breach. If P wins the case at trial, we are sure what the factfinder decided. In order to prevail, P must demonstrate that there was a contract, and that D breached the contract. Similarly, P would not prevail unless the court found that P did not waive the breach. Should P later sue D for another breach of the same agreement, D will be precluded from arguing that there was no contract. (Do you see why the other issues will *not* be precluded?)

But what if P loses Case One? Can we be sure of *why* P lost the case? The analysis of this question turns in large part on whether the first decision was rendered by a jury using a general verdict on the one hand, or by a judge or jury using a special verdict, on the other. If the case was decided by a judge or by special verdict, the judge or jury must make specific findings on every issue. In this case, we know what the factfinder found. The only issue is whether all of those findings are necessary to the judgment, which is an issue explored in the next section. This section, by contrast, discusses how issue preclusion applies in the case of general jury verdicts, where the basis for the holding may not be clear.

Take the breach of contract case hypothesized above. If P loses a general verdict, we have no way of knowing whether P lost because the jury found there was no contract, or because of issues peculiar to the first case; namely, that there was at that time no breach by D, because P suffered no damages, or because P waived the earlier breach. Because there is no way to be sure of the reason(s) for the holding, courts do not give *any* of the issues issue preclusion effect in later litigation (except in the rare situation where all the issues in Case One and Case Two are exactly the same, in which case claim preclusion is likely to apply anyway).

4. NECESSARY TO THE JUDGMENT

As discussed in the prior section, the question of whether an issue is necessary to the judgment arises primarily in bench trials and cases utilizing a special verdict. In these situations, we know what the factfinder found. Depending on the claims and defenses asserted, however, it may have been logically possible for the factfinder to reach the same result without addressing one or more issues. In that case, do the unnecessary findings have issue preclusion effect?

STEMLER V. FLORENCE
350 F.3d 578 (6th Cir. 2003)

BOGGS, CHIEF JUDGE.

Appellant/cross-appellee William Chipman, administrator of the estate of Conni Black, ... [appeals] the district court's order granting summary judgment for the defendants in this civil action arising out of an encounter between Conni Black and Susan Stemler, on the one hand, and police officers from the City of Florence, Kentucky and Boone County, Kentucky. ...

This case arises out of an incident that occurred on February 19, 1994. We have reviewed this case on a previous appeal. Briefly, Black was killed in a car accident shortly after police officers allegedly removed her from Stemler's car and placed her in the truck of her boyfriend, Steve Kritis. Both Black and Kritis had been drinking heavily, and after an altercation between them at a bar, Black left with Stemler in Stemler's car. Kritis then began to chase the women on the streets of Florence before both the car and the truck were stopped by the police after a concerned citizen alerted them to the situation. Stemler was arrested for driving under the influence. Witnesses say that all the police officers present repeated Kritis's assertion that Stemler was a lesbian to each other and to others present. No police officer ever checked Kritis for intoxication or asked him to leave his truck. Black was either escorted or carried from Stemler's car to the passenger seat of Kritis's truck. Kritis then drove away and turned onto the northbound lanes of I–75. According to Kritis, Black, who had passed out, woke up and began to hit Kritis. He began to hit back and lost control of the truck. The truck swerved and collided with the guardrail. Black was partially ejected from the passenger-side window [and killed]. . . .

I. The Claims

. . . On March 7, 1994, William Chipman, the administrator of the estate of Conni Black, filed a wrongful death action in the Boone County Circuit Court against Florence police officers Dusing, Dolan, and Wince; Boone County police officers Rob Reuthe and Chris Alsip; the City of Florence; and Ron Kenner, the Boone County Sheriff. [The court refers to this state-court litigation as the *Chipman* case.] The Boone County Circuit Court entered summary judgment on behalf of the defendants on Chipman's wrongful death claim. The Kentucky Court of Appeals reversed the Circuit Court. The Kentucky Supreme Court then reversed the Court of Appeals and reinstated the summary judgment ordered by the Boone County Circuit Court. *City of Florence v. Chipman*, 38 S.W.3d 387 (Ky. 2001). [In this ruling, the Kentucky Supreme Court stated, "Black was never in custody or otherwise restrained so as to give rise to a special relationship between the police officers and Black." 38 S.W.3d at 392. Absent this special relationship, the officers owed no duty to Black.]

Chipman also filed a complaint in federal court against the same defendants on March 31, 1994. [The court refers to this case as *Stemler*.] The complaint alleged that the defendants were liable under 42 U.S.C. § 1983 for Black's wrongful death because they had displayed deliberate indifference by forcing her into Kritis's car.

Chipman's federal claims were dismissed by the district court in 1994. The district court granted the individual officers' motions to dismiss under Federal Rule of Civil Procedure 12(b)(6), for failure to state a claim, on the ground of qualified immunity. The district court also granted the motions for summary judgment of Florence and Boone County.

On appeal, we upheld the district court's order granting summary judgment to the municipal defendants, Florence and Boone County. [*Stemler v. Florence*, 126 F.3d 856 (6th Cir. 1997)] at 866. However, we reversed the district court's dismissal of Chipman's claims against the individual officers. We held that Chipman had pled facts sufficient to maintain her substantive due process claim against the individual officers. The only state court decision prior to our decision was the Boone County Circuit Court decision awarding judgment to the defendant officers, holding that Black was not in custody when the pickup struck the guardrail and that none of the state actors were the direct cause of her death on the highway. We stated in *Stemler* that "while these findings are entitled to preclusive effect, they are irrelevant to the merits of her substantive due process claim." *Id.* at 870 n.12. [The earlier decision also discussed the meaning of the term "in custody," and concluded by stating, "Under any definition of the term, Black was in the defendant officers' custody at the time she was forced into Kritis's truck. *Id.* at 868–69.] The case was remanded to the district court for further proceedings consistent with the opinion.

. . . [On remand, the] district court found that the decision of the Kentucky Supreme Court barred their claims under the doctrine of issue preclusion. The issue that the district court found could not be relitigated was whether Black was in "custody" when she got into Kritis's car because, according to the district court, the Kentucky Supreme Court had held that Black was never in custody. . . .

II. Chipman's substantive due process claim

Chipman argues that our resolution of the custody issue in his favor in Stemler should have had preclusive effect on the Kentucky state courts. He argues that our opinion's holdings constituted the "law of the case" and the district court erred in applying the doctrine of issue preclusion based on the state court proceedings. The officers argue that the district court was correct in deciding that issue preclusion barred the relitigation of the issue of custody. . . .

A. *Issue Preclusion*

In order for issue preclusion to apply in Kentucky, (1) the issue in the second case must be the same as the issue in the first case, (2) the issue must have been actually litigated, (3) the issue must have been actually decided, and (4) the decision on the issue in the prior action must have been necessary to the court's judgment. The district court found that all four factors were met when the Kentucky Supreme Court resolved Chipman's state claims.

In order for Chipman to prevail in the Kentucky state courts, the Kentucky Supreme Court stated that he had to show "the existence of a duty and unless a special relationship was present, there is no duty owing from any of the police officers. . . ." *Chipman*, 38 S.W.3d at 392. The court went on, stating that "in order for the special relationship to exist, two conditions are required: 1) the victim must have been in state custody or otherwise restrained by the state at the time the injury producing act occurred, and 2) the violence or other offensive conduct must have been committed by a state actor." *Ibid.* The court held that "there is no evidence from which it can be ascertained that Black was in state custody or otherwise restrained by the police at the time the pickup truck struck the guardrail with the fatal result. In addition, there is no evidence to support a claim that the conduct which caused the pickup truck to leave the roadway and strike the guardrail was the result of the actions of the police officers." *Ibid.*

The Kentucky Supreme Court also stated that Black was *never* in custody. This is precisely the issue that is relevant in a § 1983 action. In order to prevail on the § 1983 claim, Chipman needs to show that the defendant officers "violated substantive due process by placing [Black] at risk of harm from a third party. . . ." *Stemler,* 126 F.3d at 867. The court must first determine whether "the plaintiff and the state actors had a sufficiently direct relationship such that the defendants owed [Black] a duty not to subject her to danger," and then "the court must also conclude that the officers were sufficiently culpable to be liable under a substantive due process theory." *Ibid.* As to the first part, the relevant inquiry is whether Black was in custody at the time the officers allegedly forced her into Kritis's truck.

First, the Kentucky Supreme Court stated that there was no evidence in the record to support a finding that Black was ever in custody, the same issue that is necessary to Chipman's federal claim. Second, the custody issue was actually litigated in the state courts: in the Boone County Circuit Court, the Kentucky Court of Appeals and the Kentucky Supreme Court. The Kentucky Supreme Court found that there was no evidence to support a finding that Black was ever in custody in the context of deciding the appeal of a summary judgment motion. A summary judgment order is a decision on the merits. Third, the issue was actually decided by the Kentucky Supreme Court. The court made an explicit statement that there was insufficient evidence to support a finding that Black was in custody.

However, the Kentucky Supreme Court's statement that she was never in custody was not necessary to its judgment. The Boone County Circuit Court held that there was no genuine issue of material fact regarding whether Black was in custody at the time the pickup struck the guardrail—the point at which the injury-producing act occurred. Specifically, it stated she was not in custody at this point. This was the only holding necessary for the affirmance of the Boone County Circuit Court's judgment. As we noted in discussing this lower court decision in *Stemler,* the holdings of the state court on this issue are entitled to preclusive effect. Nonetheless, this precise issue is irrelevant to the substantive due process claim.

As the Kentucky Court of Appeals (now the Kentucky Supreme Court) stated in *Sedley v. City of West Buechel,* 461 S.W.2d 556, 558 (Ky. 1971):

The general rule is that a judgment in a former action operates as an estoppel only as to matters which were necessarily involved and determined in the former action, and is *not conclusive as to matters* which were immaterial or *unessential to the determination* of the prior action or which were not necessary to uphold the judgment. (Emphasis added).

As the Kentucky Supreme Court correctly stated, our statements in *Stemler* regarding whether Black was in custody were dicta, as the only issue before us at that point was the sufficiency of the allegations in the complaint. Similarly, the statements of the Kentucky Supreme Court regarding whether Black was *ever* in custody are dicta, as they are not necessary to the state courts' disposition of the case. The actual holding of the Kentucky Supreme Court reads:

> In order for a claim to be actionable in negligence, there must be the existence of a duty and unless a special relationship was present, there is no duty owing from any of the police officers to Black to protect her from crime or accident. In order for the special relationship to exist, two conditions are required: 1) the victim must have been in state custody or otherwise restrained by the state at the time the injury producing act occurred, and 2) the violence or other offensive conduct must have been committed by a state actor. Neither of these factors can be found from the undisputed material facts in this case. There is no evidence from which it can be ascertained that Black was in state custody or otherwise restrained by the police at the time the pickup truck struck the guardrail with the fatal result. In addition, there is no evidence to support a claim that the conduct which caused the pickup truck to leave the roadway and strike the guardrail was the result of the actions of the police officers.

City of Florence v. Chipman, 38 S.W.3d 387, 392 (Ky. 2001) (emphasis added and citations omitted).

The Kentucky Supreme Court would have reached the same result if it had found that Black was in custody at the time she entered Kritis's truck, so long as it found she was not in custody at the time the truck hit the guardrail.

The district court erred in finding that issue preclusion barred Chipman's substantive due process claim.

B. Claim Preclusion

The defendant officers also argue that claim preclusion should bar Chipman's claim against them. [The court held, applying Kentucky law, that claim preclusion did not apply.]

[Reversed and remanded on the due process claim.]

NOTES AND QUESTIONS

1. In *Stemler*, the court considers whether two earlier statements—one by the Sixth Circuit, the other by the Kentucky Supreme Court—are entitled to issue preclusion effect. Why does the court refuse to afford issue preclusion effect to either statement? Are the concerns the same for each statement?

2. Why does issue preclusion only apply when a statement in an opinion is necessary to the judgment? As long as the factfinder specifically indicates its finding, why should that finding not be entitled to issue preclusion effect?

3. The Kentucky courts conducted a full and, from all appearances, fair trial in the first case. Isn't it somewhat insulting for the Sixth Circuit to ignore all the Kentucky's court's efforts, and refuse to apply issue preclusion?

4. *Alternate reasons.* Cases in which a court gives two or more alternate reasons for a holding also present questions as to whether an issue is necessary to the judgment. To illustrate, suppose P buys accounting software from D, a computer programmer. The parties negotiate a detailed contract, in which D warrants the software will perform in certain ways. When the software fails to perform, P sues D both for breach of express warranty (the specific provision in the contract) and the implied warranty of fitness for a particular purpose (a warranty imposed by law whenever a party indicates that he is buying goods for a particular purpose). After a bench trial, the judge finds for P. The judge's opinion explicitly states the software violated both the express warranty and the implied warranty of fitness.

Later, X, another purchaser of the software who is engaged in the same line of business as P, sues D. Although the contract between X and D contains no express warranty, X claims a violation of the implied warranty of fitness for a particular purpose. Will the finding in *P v. D* that the software violated the implied warranty have issue preclusion effect in *X v. D*?

Note that this situation differs from that in the main case. Because P won his case against D, we know that *one* of the alternate findings (express or implied warranty) was necessary to the judgment. The other finding could be dictum. But can we be sure which is which? Because of these concerns, the *Restatement* takes the position that *none* of the alternate grounds for a holding are entitled to issue preclusion:

RESTATEMENT OF THE LAW (SECOND): JUDGMENTS*

§ 27. Issue Preclusion—General Rule

. . .

Comment:

i. Alternative determinations by court of first instance. If a judgment of a court of first instance is based on determinations of

---

* Copyright 1982 by the American Law Institute. Reprinted with permission. All rights reserved.

two issues, either of which standing independently would be sufficient to support the result, the judgment is not conclusive with respect to either issue standing alone. . . .

There are . . . persuasive reasons for analogizing the case to that of the nonessential determination. . . . First, a determination in the alternative may not have been as carefully or rigorously considered as it would have if it had been necessary to the result, and in that sense it has some of the characteristics of dicta. Second, and of critical importance, the losing party, although entitled to appeal from both determinations, might be dissuaded from doing so because of the likelihood that at least one of them would be upheld and the other not even reached. . . .

5. Isn't the *Restatement*'s approach to the alternate holdings problem especially insulting to the earlier court? Given that at least one of the alternate holdings is absolutely necessary, should the first court's efforts be overlooked merely because it took the time and trouble to address *all* of the relevant claims? Doesn't the Restatement's approach assume that the first court acted carelessly in all but one of its findings? Is the lack of incentive to appeal really "of critical importance", as the comment suggests?

Because of these concerns, many courts reject the *Restatement* view and find that *both* rulings have issue preclusion effect, unless something in the record suggests that one of the rulings may truly have been dictum.

5. EXCEPTIONS

There are more exceptions to issue preclusion than to claim preclusion. The *Restatement* provides a list of commonly-recognized exceptions:

RESTATEMENT OF THE LAW (SECOND): JUDGMENTS*

§ 28. Exceptions to the General Rule of Issue Preclusion

Although an issue is actually litigated and determined by a valid and final judgment, and the determination is essential to the judgment, relitigation of the issue in a subsequent action between the parties is not precluded in the following circumstances:

(1) The party against whom preclusion is sought could not, as a matter of law, have obtained review of the judgment in the initial action; or

(2) The issue is one of law and (a) the two actions involve claims that are substantially unrelated, or (b) a new determination is warranted in order to take account of an intervening change in

---

* Copyright 1982 by the American Law Institute. Reprinted with permission. All rights reserved.

the applicable legal context or otherwise to avoid inequitable administration of the laws; or

(3) A new determination of the issue is warranted by differences in the quality or extensiveness of the procedures followed in the two courts or by factors relating to the allocation of jurisdiction between them; or

(4) The party against whom preclusion is sought had a significantly heavier burden of persuasion with respect to the issue in the initial action than in the subsequent action; the burden has shifted to his adversary; or the adversary has a significantly heavier burden than he had in the first action; or

(5) There is a clear and convincing need for a new determination of the issue (a) because of the potential adverse impact of the determination on the public interest or the interests of persons not themselves parties in the initial action, (b) because it was not sufficiently foreseeable at the time of the initial action that the issue would arise in the context of a subsequent action, or (c) because the party sought to be precluded, as a result of the conduct of his adversary or other special circumstances, did not have an adequate opportunity or incentive to obtain a full and fair adjudication in the initial action.

Note that some of the situations addressed by § 28 can be viewed either as exceptions or simply as situations in which an element of issue preclusion is not satisfied. For example, the fourth exception, where the burden of persuasion differs, could be resolved by concluding that the cases do not involve the "same issue." See Note 5 following *Williams* above. Similarly, exceptions 5(b) and (c) arguably involve situations where the issue in question was not actually litigated. Whether these cases are treated as exceptions or as part of the basic issue preclusion analysis has no effect on the outcome.

PROBLEMS

1. P sues D for products liability, seeking damages for injuries P suffered when using D's product. D counters with the affirmative defense of assumption of the risk. P prevails in a general verdict. When the product again injures P a few months later, P sues D again. Which of the following issues (if any) will be subject to issue preclusion?

    a. Whether the product was defective

    b. Whether P suffered injury

    c. Whether P assumed the risk

2. Same as Problem 1, except that P lost the case in a general verdict. Which of the issues (if any) will be subject to issue preclusion?

3. D is prosecuted for assaulting P. D is convicted after a full trial. P then brings a civil assault case against D. The elements of civil and criminal assault are identical. P argues that issue preclusion bars D from arguing that he did not assault P. Is P correct?

4. Same as Problem 3, except that D was acquitted in the criminal action. D argues that issue preclusion bars P from arguing that D assaulted P. Is D correct?

5. P sues D for damages for breach of contract. D's answer admits there was a contract, but denies breach. P wins a general verdict at trial.

P now sues D again, arguing another breach of the same contract. This time, D raises the defense of statute of frauds. Will issue preclusion bar D from making this assertion?

6. P and D are competitors. P sues D for defamation in state court based on a statement that D made about P's product. D denies liability using a general denial. At trial, P offers extensive evidence that the statement was false, and of P's damages, none of which was contradicted by D. The parties contest only one issue: whether D knew the statement was false. The jury renders a general verdict for D.

P then sues D in federal court under a new federal false advertising statute. Because federal jurisdiction under this new statute is exclusive, claim preclusion does not apply. Unlike state defamation law, this federal statute makes a competitor liable for a false statement regardless of whether the party knew the statement was false. P therefore moves for summary judgment on the basis of issue preclusion. Will issue preclusion apply?

7. P, a "frequent flyer" with D airlines, suffers from a serious allergy to peanuts. Two years ago, P had a life-threatening allergic reaction to a dish containing ground peanuts that he ate on one of D's flights. P sued D for negligence. In a bench trial, the judge entered judgment for D, specifically finding that D did not act negligently in serving a dish containing peanuts to P. That finding was the sole stated basis for the decision.

Last month, P suffered another peanut reaction on a flight operated by D. P again sues D for negligence. D moves for summary judgment, arguing that issue preclusion controls on the issue of whether it is negligent to serve peanuts on an airline. Is D correct?

8. D, a large fast food corporation, uses P, a shipping company, to deliver supplies to its many locations. P and D enter into separate contracts in each state in which P performs services. The wording of all these contracts is identical. Every contract contains a clause providing that it is "governed by the law of the state where P performs shipping services under this contract."

Rising fuel costs lead P to ask for an increase in its compensation under these contracts. D is sympathetic to P's plight, and agrees to amend all the contracts to increase the price paid to P. P provides no additional consideration for these amendments.

Several months after the amendments, P discovers D has been paying only the old price under the contracts. P therefore sues D in Alabama, under the Alabama contract. D argues the amendment is invalid because D received no additional consideration. P argues that under the provisions of the Uniform Commercial Code, which is in force in Alabama, no additional consideration is needed to amend a contract "between merchants." The court rules that P is not a merchant because it does not sell goods, and accordingly enters judgment for D.

P then brings another suit against D, also in Alabama. This time, however, the claim seeks compensation under all the *other* contracts. All of the states in question have adopted the Uniform Commercial Code provision that applied in the earlier case. D argues issue preclusion controls on the question of whether P is a merchant. Is D correct?

9. P sues D for negligence. D argues both that she was not negligent, and that plaintiff's contributory negligence bars recovery. The case is submitted to the jury using a special verdict. The jury finds both that D was not negligent, and that P was negligent. The court therefore enters judgment for D. Which, if either, of these two rulings—D's negligence, or P's contributory negligence—will have issue preclusion effect in later litigation?

E. PARTIES AFFECTED BY CLAIM AND ISSUE PRECLUSION

The materials for this section are at www.crosscivilprocedure.com.

F. APPLYING PRECLUSION ACROSS STATE LINES

The materials for this section are at www.crosscivilprocedure.com.

G. DOCTRINES SIMILAR TO PRECLUSION

The materials for this section are at www.crosscivilprocedure.com.

CHAPTER 14

APPEALS

■ ■ ■

Much law school reading involves appellate court opinions. And yet, at this point in your law school career you probably have only a vague idea of how the appellate process works. A basic understanding of appeals will help you understand why appellate opinions make such good teaching tools. First, appellate courts usually concentrate their attention on one or a few crucial issues, instead of rehashing all the evidence presented at trial. Second, appeals tend to focus on issues of law. Although an appellate court can overturn a trial court's findings of fact, it will afford considerable deference to the trial court on most factual issues.

This Chapter provides a short, but systematic, study of the appellate process. However, time considerations prevent an in-depth study of all the myriad issues that arise in appeals. This Chapter accordingly only hits the "highlights": issues that arise with some regularity, and for which the law is either non-obvious or subject to stark differences of opinion.

A. WHO MAY APPEAL

INTRODUCTORY PROBLEM

While crossing the street on a sunny day, Pedro Pedestrian was struck and injured by an automobile operated by Diane Driver. Pedro sues Diane in state court for his injuries, asking for $100,000 in damages. Pedro's complaint sets forth two counts of negligence. First, Pedro claims Diane was negligent because she failed to maintain her brakes. Second, Pedro claims Diane was negligent because she was drunk while operating the automobile. The case goes to trial, and both sides submit extensive evidence. The judge directs the jury to deliver a special verdict. The jury returns with a $100,000 verdict for Pedro. In the special verdict, the jury specifically states Diane was not drunk, but that she did fail to maintain the brakes on her vehicle. The court enters judgment in accordance with the verdict.

Although Pedro was awarded the full $100,000, he nevertheless wants to appeal the jury's finding that Diane was not drunk. Pedro has heard a rumor that Diane is about to file for bankruptcy. If she does, she can discharge most of her debts, including any liability for ordinary negligence. However, a debtor in bankruptcy cannot discharge a debt arising from driving while intoxicated. Pedro therefore wants his judgment to state Diane was drunk, so that the $100,000 debt is not dischargeable if Diane files for bankruptcy.

Ignoring the issue of whether he would *win* an appeal, may Pedro even file an appeal in this case?

Only a party who loses at trial has the right to appeal. That rule makes perfect sense. Parties who win everything they wanted at trial have no reason to appeal. But what does it mean to "lose" a case? Suppose that a court in a trespass case enters a $20,000 judgment for plaintiff. Defendant may, of course, appeal. Yet plaintiff can also appeal if, for example, her complaint asked for anything more than $20,000 in damages. In essence, in the context of appeal it is entirely possible—and indeed fairly common—for *all* parties to lose a case.

The next case presents a more subtle variation on this theme. Defendant technically won at trial. However, defendant claims its victory is Pyrrhic, as it has potentially negative consequences for the defendant.

IN RE DES LITIGATION
7 F.3d 20 (2d Cir. 1993)

JON O. NEWMAN, CHIEF JUDGE.

. . .

Background

Some background information concerning DES and the varying approaches to DES liability adopted by different states will assist in understanding Boehringer's motivation in attempting to appeal from the interlocutory rulings. Between 1941 and 1971, approximately 300 pharmaceutical companies marketed DES, a synthetic form of estrogen, for the prevention of miscarriages. In 1971, the FDA banned DES after determining that the drug caused vaginal adenocarcinoma, a form of cancer, and adenosis, a precancerous vaginal or cervical growth, in the daughters of women who took the drug. Although it was made in pills of different shapes and colors, all DES was chemically identical, and druggists generally filled prescriptions from whatever stock they had on hand. Most women ingesting DES did not know the identity of the manufacturer, and by the time their daughters realized they had been injured by DES, it was often impossible to determine the manufacturer.

Faced with this situation, the California Supreme Court adopted a "market share" theory of liability. See *Sindell v. Abbott Laboratories*, 26 Cal.3d 588, 163 Cal.Rptr. 132, 607 P.2d 924, *cert. denied*, 449 U.S. 912 (1980). The Court held that a plaintiff could recover by showing that her injuries had been caused by DES and by joining as defendants "the manufacturers of a substantial share of the DES which her mother might have taken." *Id.* at 612, 163 Cal.Rptr. at 145, 607 P.2d at 937. Each manufacturer would "be held liable for the proportion of the judgment represented by its share of [the] market unless it demonstrates that it could not have made the product which caused plaintiff's injuries." *Id.* In a later case, the California Court clarified that liability was several only, with the consequence that if less than all manufacturers are joined, a plaintiff will recover less than 100 percent of her damages.

The New York Court of Appeals substantially adopted the *Sindell* approach. . . .

On September 30, 1991, a group of plaintiffs, comprising women allegedly injured by DES, along with their husbands, filed the instant suit in the Eastern District of New York against 33 manufacturers, or successors to manufacturers, of DES. The plaintiffs, who are New York or foreign residents, asserted jurisdiction on the basis of diversity of citizenship. The sole appellant, Boehringer, is a Delaware corporation authorized to do business in New York. Boehringer never sold or manufactured DES, but it is the successor to Stayner Corporation, which manufactured limited amounts of DES in Berkeley, California, between 1949 and 1971. Stayner sold products in California, Washington, Oregon, and Montana. It never marketed any products in New York, was not licensed to do business in New York, and had no significant contacts with New York. . . .

On October 25, 1991, Boehringer moved to dismiss for failure to state a claim and for lack of personal jurisdiction. Judge Weinstein denied the motion in his April 13, 1992, opinion. He concluded (1) that the New York long arm statute reached Boehringer; (2) that this exercise of jurisdiction was constitutional; (3) that New York would apply its law to Boehringer; (4) that application of this choice of law rule was constitutional; (5) that the complaint stated a claim against Boehringer under New York substantive law; and (6) that New York substantive DES law was constitutional. . . .

On September 14, 1992, apparently at Boehringer's request, the District Court entered a judgment that provides:

> [T]he case having been fully resolved as to all parties and claims by settlement or adjudication on the merits, It is ORDERED AND ADJUDGED that all of the claims in this action, including specifically cross-claims, are DISMISSED, without costs, subject to the right of any party to re-open the final judgment if any settlement is not consummated.

At oral argument, Boehringer attempted to give a fuller explication of the procedural history behind this judgment. Boehringer stated that all the other defendant DES manufacturers settled with plaintiffs, but that Boehringer refused to do so. Trial then commenced against Boehringer, but the plaintiffs declined to present any evidence. The District Court then orally dismissed the complaint as to Boehringer for want of prosecution.

Discussion

... The only appellant is Boehringer, the defendant in the District Court. The plaintiffs have declined to contest Boehringer's appeal, neither filing a brief nor appearing for argument. Apparently their settlements with other defendants diminished their interest in attempting to establish Boehringer's liability. ...

It is the defendant's lack of standing that impels us to dismiss this appeal. Boehringer prevailed on the merits by successfully moving to have the plaintiffs' complaint dismissed with prejudice for lack of prosecution. Ordinarily, a prevailing party cannot appeal from a district court judgment in its favor. There are, however, two exceptions to this rule. One exception arises when the prevailing party is aggrieved by the collateral estoppel effect of a district court's rulings. Boehringer observes that at least 42 DES cases are pending against it in New York, and states that it fears that the trial courts in these cases will accord preclusive effect to Judge Weinstein's jurisdictional and choice of law rulings. We disagree, however, that the matters resolved in the April 13 order have collateral estoppel effect. Relitigation of an issue in a second action is precluded only if "the judgment in the prior action was dependent upon the determination made of the issue." 1B James W. Moore, et al., *Moore's Federal Practice* ¶ 0.443[1], at 760 (2d ed. 1993). The judgment in this case is not dependent upon the interlocutory rulings in favor of the plaintiff. Upon the failure of the plaintiffs to prosecute their suit, the District Court was free to enter a judgment dismissing the complaint whether or not there was personal jurisdiction over Boehringer and whether or not New York law applied to Boehringer. ...

[O]ur decision to decline appellate review of the District Court's order confirms the lack of any possible collateral estoppel effect arising from the District Court's interlocutory rulings. See *Restatement (Second) of Judgments* § 28(1) (1982) (relitigation of an issue not precluded if "party against whom preclusion is sought could not, as a matter of law, have obtained review of the judgment in the initial action"). Thus, whether or not other trial judges find Judge Weinstein's opinion a persuasive precedent, they are not bound to apply it in any subsequent litigation against Boehringer.

The second exception to the rule prohibiting appeal by a prevailing party arises, in some circumstances, where a prevailing party can show that it is aggrieved by some aspect of the trial court's judgment or decree. In *Electrical Fittings Corp. v. Thomas & Betts Co.*, 307 U.S. 241 (1939), the District Court had entered a judgment for the defendant, finding that the defendant had not infringed the plaintiff's patent but also finding that the patent was valid. We dismissed the defendant's appeal, since the finding of validity did not support the decree and would not have estoppel effect. The Supreme Court reversed and held that we should have "entertain[ed] the appeal, not for the purpose of passing on the merits, but to direct the reformation of the decree." Id. at 242. Judge Learned Hand later explained the Supreme Court's terse decision as follows:

> The Supreme Court did not differ with us in thinking that the finding [of validity] was immaterial, but nevertheless it directed us to strike it from the decree. The rationale of that decision was that the defendant was entitled to have it out because, although it was not an estoppel, it might create some presumptive prejudice against him.

Harries v. Air King Products Co., 183 F.2d 158, 161 (2d Cir.1950) (footnote omitted).

Electrical Fittings is distinguishable in at least two ways. First, Boehringer's appellate brief does not ask us to vacate any portion of the judgment; what Boehringer seeks is a reversal of the interlocutory rulings. . . .

Second, and more importantly, the District Court's rulings on personal jurisdiction and choice of law do not appear on the face of the judgment, as was the case with the finding of validity in *Electrical Fittings*. The judgment in this case says only that the complaint is dismissed. We therefore are confronted with an "appellant" that seeks no modification of the judgment as entered. In these circumstances, appellate jurisdiction is improperly invoked.

Accordingly, the appeal is dismissed. Boehringer's motion for a ruling on the merits is denied.

NOTES AND QUESTIONS

1. Defendant in *DES* claimed that although it was held not liable in the case, the decision might negatively affect it in other cases. Be prepared to explain how defendant claimed the judgment could harm it in the future.

2. If you have studied issue preclusion (Chapter 13, pt. D), try to restate the *DES* court's argument as to why issue preclusion (which the court calls collateral estoppel) would not apply. Is the court's analysis correct?

3. Do you agree that the distinctions the court draws between the case at bar and *Electrical Fittings*, where appeal was allowed, are meaningful? Why should it matter whether the findings appear on the face of the judgment?

4. Why does the law deny a prevailing party the opportunity to appeal? Isn't the simple fact that a party is going to the time and expense of filing an appeal sufficient evidence in itself that there is something about the ruling that is unsatisfactory to that party?

B. THE TIMING OF AN APPEAL—THE "FINAL DECISION" RULE

The materials for this section are at www.crosscivilprocedure.com.

C. SCOPE OF APPELLATE REVIEW

Sections A and B of this Chapter deal with who can appeal a case, and when an appeal may occur. But what does the appellate court do with the case once it gets there? Many of you are aware from your course in legal research that the court of appeals will often have a hearing at which each side may present its arguments. Beyond that, however, you may never have focused specifically on an appellate court's power to review what the trial court has done.

At the risk of oversimplification, there are two main issues that arise in appellate review. First, the appellate court cannot necessarily review all issues that were adjudicated by the trial court. For many issues, appellate review is possible only if the appealing party raised the issue at trial. Second, even when an issue was properly raised below, the court of appeals usually does not try the issue anew. Instead, the appellate court will give a certain degree of deference to the trial court's decision. Each of these issues is addressed in turn.

1. NEED TO RAISE THE ISSUE BELOW

At the risk of sounding trite, the role of an appellate court is to *review* what the trial judge did. Therefore, as a general matter a court of appeals will not hear arguments that did not form part of the trial court's decision. As with every general rule, however, there are exceptions. The first is *subject matter jurisdiction*. As you learned in Chapters 4 and 7, a party can raise subject matter jurisdiction at any time, even for the first time on appeal. Indeed, even if no party raises the issue, the appellate court can consider *sua sponte* whether the trial court had subject matter jurisdiction. The limits on federal subject matter jurisdiction are so fundamental and important that the ordinary rules about waiver of rights by failure to assert them is set aside.

The second main exception to the general rule applies to the party who won at trial. A prevailing party may ask the appellate court to affirm on *any* ground, even if the trial court did not rely on that ground as a basis for its judgment. Although a few courts have suggested that an appellee may raise entirely new theories on appeal in order to sustain a judgment, the weight of the precedent makes it clear that the argument must have been presented at trial in some form:

> (I)t is likewise settled that the appellee may, without taking a cross-appeal, urge in support of a decree any matter appearing in

the record, although his argument may involve an attack upon the reasoning of the lower court or an insistence upon matter overlooked or ignored by it. By the claims now in question, the [appellant] does not attack, in any respect, the decree entered below. It merely asserts additional grounds why the decree should be affirmed.

United States v. American Rwy Express Co., 265 U.S. 425, 435–36, 44 S.Ct. 560, 68 L.Ed. 1087 (1924). *See also Dandridge v. Williams*, 397 U.S. 471, 475–76 n. 6, 90 S.Ct. 1153, 25 L.Ed.2d 491 (1970); *Skipper v. French*, 130 F.3d 603, 610 (4th Cir. 1997); *Boggs v. West*, 188 F.3d 1335 (Fed. Cir. 1999).

As noted in section A of this Chapter, in some circumstances a prevailing party may also appeal. However, a party need not appeal if all it wants to do is offer alternate arguments to affirm the holding. Filing a cross-appeal is necessary only of the party seeks either to increase his own rights or to diminish the rights of his adversary. *Montgomery v. City of Ardmore*, 365 F.3d 926, 944 (10th Cir. 2004).

Contemporaneous Objection Rule. The contemporaneous objection rule is a corollary to the general principle that a party may only argue issues tried below. To preserve the right to appeal based on a supposed error that occurred at trial, the aggrieved party must object to the error in timely fashion. A timely objection is one raised in time to prevent significant harm from occurring. For example, objections to the proposed jury instructions must be raised before those instructions are submitted to the jury, or those objections are lost. Moreover, if the mistake continues to manifest itself later in the trial, the party may be required to restate its objection on one or more additional occasions. For example, if the judge wrongfully allows hearsay evidence over defendant's objection, and plaintiff's attorney refers to that evidence in his closing argument, defendant should object again to preserve the right to appeal.

The contemporaneous objection rule is tempered by certain exceptions and limitations. First, there are limits on the requirement that a recurring objection must be repeated. For example, if a judge rules that a particular witness is an expert, the opposing side should enter an objection into the record at that point. However, the party need not restate its objection every time that witness offers an opinion.

Second, if the trial judge makes a "clear error," the party need not object at all. The clear error exception is exceedingly limited. An error will be deemed clear only if it is so manifestly incorrect that it leads one to believe that the judge has a basic bias against the party.

The rationale for the contemporaneous objection rule is fairly obvious. No trial is free from errors. However, to deal with those errors by way of the appellate process is very inefficient, as each appeal involves considerable "start up" time for the appellate panel. To encourage efficiency, then, the rule requires the parties to give the trial judge at least one chance to correct her own mistake.

2. THE STANDARD OF REVIEW

The role of the appellate court is not to retry the case. Thus, the appellate court will give a certain amount of deference to the rulings of the trial court. However, the appellate court does not give equal deference to all findings. The amount of deference varies depending on the nature of the particular issue being reviewed.

Basically, the standard of review turns on whether the issue is one of fact, law, or something committed to the trial court's discretion. With respect to findings of *fact*, the appellate court gives a great deal of deference. The appellate court assumes the trial court's findings are correct unless it is clearly demonstrated otherwise. Federal Rule 52(a) calls this standard of review "clearly erroneous"; some states use different terminology to express the same basic idea. For questions of *law*, by contrast, the appellate court gives no deference at all. This standard of review is commonly referred to as "*de novo*", and allows the appellate court to reverse merely if it disagrees with the trial court. Because determining the governing rule of law does not depend on an evaluation of the evidence presented at trial, there is no need for the court of appeals to give any deference on pure issues of law. Finally, there are certain issues—for example, the decision whether to grant a new trial—that are left to the *discretion* of the trial judge. For these issues, the appellate court will overturn only if the trial judge's decision was an "abuse of discretion." The abuse of discretion standard is even more deferential than the clearly erroneous standard.

This division between questions of fact, law, and discretionary matters is not nearly as clear as it may seem at first glance. What exactly do we mean by a question of "fact" or "law?" The following materials provide a brief glimpse into this complex issue.

LAVOIE V. PACIFIC PRESS & SHEAR CO., 975 F.2d 48 (2d Cir. 1992). Lavoie, an industrial worker, was hurt by a machine. Lavoie sued the manufacturer of the machine for negligence. The jury found defendant negligent, and defendant appealed. Defendant argued that the jury erred in finding both that defendant was negligent and that its negligence was the proximate cause of plaintiff's injuries. Defendant argued that the acts of plaintiff's employer (GE) were an intervening cause. The court refused to overturn the jury findings:

> Defendant's burden in this regard is a substantial one. In Vermont, only verdicts that are not "justified by 'any reasonable view of the evidence'" will be overturned. See *Claude G. Dern Electric, Inc. v. Bernstein*, 144 Vt. 423, 479 A.2d 136, 138 (1984)

(quoting *Crawford v. State Highway Board*, 130 Vt. 18, 285 A.2d 760, 764 (1971)). A jury finding of negligence will be preserved unless reasonable persons reviewing the record, construed in favor of the prevailing party could not draw different conclusions and would reach a different result. Federal law applies a similar standard. The record reveals an ample basis for the finding of negligence by Pacific, and we therefore need not select between federal and state standards.

Defendant contends further that a finding of negligence against it may not stand because it was not a proximate cause of plaintiff's injuries. Pacific points to testimony that Lavoie would not have been injured if her co-workers had not turned off the non-integrated light curtain which GE had installed to protect operators of the machine. The alleged negligence of plaintiff's co-workers constituted, defendant continues, an efficient intervening cause of the injuries, making any negligence by defendant merely a contribution to but not a cause of the accident. We disagree.

Like the predicate question of negligence, the issue of proximate cause is one for the jury, and nonprevailing parties who seek to challenge such findings face similar substantial burdens. The law in Vermont makes clear that more than one act of negligence, each contributing to produce a harm, may be a concurring proximate cause. . . . If negligent conduct by a third person was a foreseeable consequence that, "in the eye of the law, the person charged was bound to anticipate, the causal connection is not broken." *Beatty v. Dunn*, 103 Vt. 340, 154 A. 770, 772 (1931). . . .

Once again defendant fails to sustain its heavy burden for overturning findings of the jury, this time that defendant's negligence was a proximate cause of plaintiff's injuries. Sufficient evidence is present in the record that supports the finding that Pacific should have anticipated [various negligent acts and omissions by GE and its employees]. Such a failure on GE's part would not work to absolve defendant of liability if Pacific should have anticipated that GE's efforts would not be adequate.

OREGON TRAIL ELEC. CONSUMERS COOP., INC. V. CO-GEN CO., 168 Or.App. 466, 7 P.3d 594 (2000). Oregon Trail, an electric cooperative, bought electricity from Co-Gen under a written contract. Oregon Trail later filed suit for a declaratory judgment that the price should be modified to reflect the public interest. The trial court determined that the contract did not allow Oregon Trail to seek to modify the purchase price, and accordingly entered judgment for Co-Gen. The court of appeals affirmed. However, it reviewed the trial judge's rulings on the meaning of the contract partly under a "clearly erroneous" standard, and partly under a *de novo* standard:

> The pertinent principles we follow in construing a contract are well-settled. In the absence of an ambiguity, the trial court in the first instance, and this court on appeal, determines the meaning of a contract as a matter of law. A contract provision is legally ambiguous if it has no definite significance or if it is capable of more than one reasonable and sensible construction in the context of the agreement as a whole. In deciding whether an ambiguity exists, the court is not limited to mere text and context but may consider parol and other evidence. Likewise, if the contract is ambiguous, the trier of fact may consider other evidence of the parties' intentions and construe the language of the agreement accordingly. Where the trial court's construction of the contract depends on factual inquiries, we review the court's factual findings for "any evidence." Our review otherwise is for legal correctness, which means that we determine, as though in the first instance, how the contract should be construed.

AETNA CASUALTY AND SURETY CO. V. LEAHEY CONSTRUCTION CO., INC., 219 F.3d 519 (6th Cir. 2000). Aetna provided a surety bond to Leahey Construction Company in connection with a construction project. When Aetna was called upon to pay under the bond, it sued Leahey, a bank, and an accounting firm, alleging that Leahey's financial condition had been misrepresented in the negotiations for the surety agreement. The jury entered judgment for Aetna, and the judge denied defendants' motion for judgment as a matter of law. On appeal, one of defendants' claims was that the judge should have entered judgment as a matter of law on two of plaintiff's claims; namely, aiding and abetting fraud and conspiracy to commit fraud. The appellate court upheld the trial judge's ruling on aiding and abetting, but overturned the ruling on conspiracy. In so ruling, the court also had to determine whether the state or federal standard of review applied in a diversity case:

> The standard of review applicable to a district court's determinations pursuant to Rule 50 of the Federal Rules of Civil Procedure in a diversity action has been summarized by this court as follows:
>
> > [A] federal court sitting in diversity reviews *de novo* legal determinations raised by a Rule 50 motion, and must apply the forum state's standard of review "only when a Rule 50 challenge is mounted to the sufficiency of the evidence supporting a jury's findings. No deference is appropriate in

diversity cases to the trial court's resolutions of legal questions."

Palmer v. Fox Software, Inc., 107 F.3d 415, 418 (6th Cir.1997).

An appellate court reviewing a diversity action, however, "need show no deference to the trial court's assessment of the sufficiency of the evidence before a jury, even if state law so requires." *K & T Enters.*, 97 F.3d at 176. As will become apparent, the defendants' challenge to the district court's denial of their Rule 50 motions is "mounted to the sufficiency of the evidence" and, therefore, this court must apply Ohio's standard of review. . . .

In reviewing the evidence presented at trial, the court held that the jury could reasonably have found that defendants aided and abetted fraud. However, on the conspiracy claim, the court held that it was unreasonable on the evidence presented for the jury to infer a conspiracy.

NOTES AND QUESTIONS

1. Can *Lavoie* and *Oregon Trail* be reconciled? How can a finding of negligence involve a question of fact, while a finding of the meaning of a contract—which like negligence deals with the state of mind of the parties—involve a question of law?

2. In *Oregon Trail*, how important is it that the contract was in writing? Would an appellate court apply the *de novo* standard of review to a finding of negligence *per se* based on a violation of a statute?

3. In *Aetna*, do you understand why the court applied the *de novo* standard to a trial judge's ruling on judgment as a matter of law, given that the grant of judgment as a matter of law requires evaluation of the evidence?

4. When an appellate court reviews a finding of fact, does it matter whether that finding was made by a judge or a jury? Most courts hold that when reviewing a jury verdict, the standard applied by the court of appeals is the same as a trial judge would apply when asked to set aside a jury verdict. Is that standard more or less deferential than the clearly erroneous standard?

5. Are there limits to how much deference a court can give to a jury verdict? In *Honda Motor Co., Ltd. v. Oberg*, 512 U.S. 415, 114 S.Ct. 2331, 129 L.Ed.2d 336 (1994), the Court was faced with a provision in the Oregon Constitution which forbade judicial review of the amount of punitive damages awarded by a jury "unless the court can affirmatively say there is no evidence to support the verdict." The Court held that the provision violated the due process clause of the fourteenth amendment to the United States Constitution. Due process, the Court reasoned, requires some meaningful judicial review of a jury's award of punitive damages.

6. *Abuse of discretion*. The abuse of discretion standard is reserved for certain rulings that are subject to the discretion of the trial judge, such as rulings on a new trial, rulings on preliminary injunctions and temporary restraining orders, and the scope of sanctions for discovery and Federal Rule 11 violations. How does the abuse of discretion standard differ from the clearly erroneous standard?

Unfortunately, there is no single accepted definition of "abuse of discretion." As one appellate court noted, "Abuse of discretion is famously slippery—its meaning can vary between contexts, and there has been little consensus over the years as to precisely what the phrase means." *Zervos v. Verizon New York, Inc.*, 252 F.3d 163, 169 note 4 (2d Cir. 2001). Another court surveyed various definitions of the term:

> One view is represented by the statement in *Delno v. Market St. Ry.*, 124 F.2d 965, 967 (9 Cir. 1942):
>
>> Discretion, in this sense, is abused when the judicial action is arbitrary, fanciful or unreasonable, which is another way of saying that discretion is abused only where no reasonable man would take the view adopted by the trial court. If reasonable men could differ as to the propriety of the action taken by the trial court, then it cannot be said that the trial court abused its discretion.
>
> A sharply contrasting view was voiced by Chief Judge Magruder in *In re Josephson*, 218 F.2d 174, 182 (1 Cir. 1954):
>
>> "Abuse of discretion" is a phrase which sounds worse than it really is. All it need mean is that, when judicial action is taken in a discretionary matter, such action cannot be set aside by a reviewing court unless it has a definite and firm conviction that the court below committed a clear error of judgment in the conclusion it reached upon a weighing of the relevant factors.
>
> The Ninth Circuit, without citation of *Delno*, has since followed or even gone beyond the *Josephson* formulation, see *Pearson v. Dennison*, 353 F.2d 24, 28 n. 6 (9 Cir. 1965) (Duniway, J.):
>
>> We do not much like the term "abuse" in this context. It has pejorative connotations not here appropriate. But it has become the customary word. Perhaps "misuse" is milder. What we mean, when we say that a court abused its discretion, is merely that we think that it made a mistake. There are, however, cases in which the term abuse is appropriate.

Buffalo Courier-Express, Inc. v. Buffalo Evening News, Inc., 601 F.2d 48, 59 note 18 (2d Cir. 1979).

7. *Appeal of rulings on motion for judgment as a matter of law*. As discussed in Chapter 11, a party may not file a post-verdict motion for judgment as a matter of law unless he has filed a pre-verdict motion. In *Unitherm Food Systems, Inc. v. Swift-Eckrich, Inc.*, 546 U.S. 394, 126 S.Ct.

980, 163 L.Ed.2d 974 (2006), the Supreme Court held that in some cases the post-verdict motion may also be necessary. The verdict loser in that case had filed a pre-verdict motion, but had not renewed the motion after the verdict. Instead, the party challenged the judgment itself on appeal, arguing that it was not supported by the evidence. The Court held that the party's failure to file a post-verdict motion for judgment as a matter of law precluded the party from challenging the judgment based on the sufficiency of the evidence. In some ways, then, Rule 50 treats the post-verdict motion as a necessary means of preserving any objections to the ruling on the pre-verdict motion.

D. UNITED STATES SUPREME COURT REVIEW

The materials for this section are at www.crosscivilprocedure.com.

INDEX

References are to Pages
"E-Chap." refers to electronic supplement

ALTERNATIVE DISPUTE RESOLUTION, E-Chap. 9
Arbitration, E-Chap. 9.B.1
Mediation, E-Chap. 9.B.2

APPEALS, 691
Final judgment rule, E-Chap. 14.B
Interlocutory appeals, E-Chap. 14.B
Scope of review, 696
Supreme Court review, E-Chap. 14.D
Timing, E-Chap 14.B
Who may appeal, 691

APPLICABLE LAW, 263
Choice of law, 264
Erie doctrine, 272

CASE MANAGEMENT, 495, E-Chap. 9
Court-annexed ADR, E.Chap. 9.C
Discovery conference, 495, 521
Judicial settlement conference, E-Chap. 9.C
Pre-trial conference, E-Chap. 9.C

COLLATERAL ESTOPPEL, 671

DEFAULT JUDGMENTS, 477

DISCOVERY, 493
Depositions, 521
Experts, 516
Inspection of documents, 537
Interrogatories, 529
Mandatory disclosure, 494
Physical and mental examinations, 548
Privileged matter, 501
Production of documents, 537
Relevant matter, 496
Request for admission, 543
Sanctions, 552
Scope of discovery, 496
Work product, 504

DISMISSALS, 431
Involuntary dismissal, 440
Voluntary dismissal, 432

DISPOSITIVE MOTIONS, 454, 486, 495, 561
Default judgment, 495
Failure to state a claim, 454
Judgment as a matter of law, 583
Judgment on the pleadings, 486
Summary judgment, 562

DISPUTES, 8

JOINDER OF CLAIMS AND PARTIES, 27, E-Chap. 8
Class actions, E-Chap. 8.E
Counterclaims, 28
Cross-claims, 42
Defendants, joinder by, E-Chap. 8.A
Defendants, joinder of, 35
Impleader, E-Chap. 8.A
Interpleader, E-Chap. 8.D
Intervention, E-Chap. 8.B
Multiple claims, 46
Multiple parties, 35
Necessary parties, E-Chap. 8.C
Plaintiffs, joinder of, 35

JURY TRIAL, 595
Challenge for cause, 604
Constitutional right, E-Chap. 12.A
Demanding a jury trial, 596
Jury instructions, 623
Peremptory challenge, 616
Selecting group of prospective jurors, 599
Verdicts, 628
Voir dire of prospective jurors, 604

LITIGATION TIMELINE, 19

PERSONAL JURISDICTION, 53
Change of venue, 151
Forum non conveniens, 158
Personal jurisdiction, 53
Rule 12(b) challenges, 449
Service of process, 373
Venue, 144

PLEADING, 323, 431
Affirmative defenses, 467
Answer, 459
Amending pleadings, 415
Complaint, form of, 333
Federal rules, 333
Heightened pleading standards, 362
Objecting to statement of a claim, 454
Philosophy and history of pleading, 323
Pleading standards, 339
Prayer for relief, 371
Responding to the answer, 473

Responding to the complaint, 448, 459
Supplemental pleadings, 427
Veracity standards for filed documents, 396

POST-TRIAL MOTIONS, 583, 635
Judgment as a matter of law, 583
New trial, 635
Relief from judgment, 647

PRE-ANSWER MOTION, 448

PRECLUSION, 657
Applying preclusion across state lines, E-Chap. 13.F
Claim preclusion, 659
Doctrines similar to preclusion, E-Chap. 13.G
Issue preclusion, 671
Judicial estoppel, E-Chap. 13.G
Law of the case, E-Chap. 13.G
Merger and bar, 659
Parties affected by preclusion, E-Chap. 13.E

REMOVAL, 241

RES JUDICATA, 659

SERVICE OF PROCESS, 373

SETTLEMENT, E-Chap. 9.C
Court-annexed ADR, E-Chap. 9.C.2
Judicial settlement conferences, E-Chap. 9.C.1
Offer of judgment, E-Chap. 9.D

SUBJECT MATTER JURISDICTION, 173
Amount in controversy, 206
Challenging subject matter jurisdiction, 452
Diversity of citizenship, 186
Federal question, 176
Removal, 241
Supplemental jurisdiction, 218

VENUE, 144
Change of venue, 151
Federal statutory standards, 145
Forum non conveniens, 158
Transfer, 151